The SAGE
Handbook of

Qualitative Geography

Quantitative Geography

The SAGE
Handbook of

Qualitative Geography

Edited by

Dydia DeLyser, Steve Herbert,
Stuart Aitken, Mike Crang and
Linda McDowell

⑤SAGE

Los Angeles | London | New Delhi
Singapore | Washington DC

Contents

Notes on Contributors

Stuart C. Aitken is Professor of Geography at San Diego State University. His books include *The Awkward Spaces of Fathering* (2009), *Approaches to Human Geography* (with Gill Valentine, 2004), *Geographies of Young People* (2001), *Family Fantasies and Community Space* (1998), *Place, Space, Situation and Spectacle: A Geography of Film* (with Leo Zonn, 1994) and *Putting Children in Their Place* (1994). He publishes widely in edited book collections and academic journals including the *Annals of the AAG, Antipode, Transactions of the IBG, CaGIS, Society and Space,* and *Environment and Planning A*. His interests include film, critical social theory, qualitative methods, GIS, children, families and communities. Stuart is past co-editor of *The Professional Geographer* and current North American editor of *Children's Geographies*.

Fernando J. Bosco is Associate Professor of Geography at San Diego State University. His main research interest is critical analysis of space–society relations, with specific foci on networks, relational thinking and social change. He has written about the spatialities of social movement networks, the globalization of NGO's networks dealing with children's poverty, and the geographic dimensions of the US war on terrorism. More recently he has been working on issues of community and citizenship, focusing on the Hispanic and Latino population in San Diego. Fernando takes a broad perspective when it comes to research: he enjoys being outside conducting fieldwork, but he also likes working with qualitative analysis software packages, and conducting archival research.

David Butz is Professor and Graduate Program Director in the Department of Geography at Brock University, and a member of the editorial collective for *ACME: An International E-Journal for Critical Geographies*. He has been conducting community level research in northern Pakistan since 1985, on such topics as irrigation agriculture, portering labour, community development, modernization and social change, and has published several articles on this work. He is currently working with Nancy Cook on an ethnographic study of a road building project in Shimshal, a small farming community in Pakistan's Karakoram Range.

Meghan Cope is Associate Professor and Chair of Geography at the University of Vermont, in Burlington, Vermont, USA. An urban social geographer motivated by the intersections of place, power, identity, and knowledge, her most recent work involves working with children and youth. Her research is primarily qualitative, using participatory ethnographic research approaches to learn about the geographic meanings and processes that matter to marginalized groups, and that construct cities as spaces of oppression and empowerment. Over the past 10 years, Cope has also developed an associated interest in critical perspectives on Geographic Information Systems (GIS) and, with her former graduate students, has explored methods of combining qualitative research with GIS.

Mike Crang is a Reader in Geography at Durham University. He has written and edited seven books, including *Thinking Space* with Nigel Thrift (Routledge, 2000), *Tourism: Between Place and Performance* with Simon Coleman (Berghahn, 2002), and *Doing Ethnographies* with Ian Cook (Sage, 2007), and has published more than 50 other papers and essays. He has worked on issues of heritage, memory, tourism, and mediated geographies. More recently he has followed these interests to look at digital media geographies and the uneven digital terrains of the contemporary city. He is currently working on a project on wastescapes and cultural economies of waste.

Dydia DeLyser is Associate Professor of Geography at Louisiana State University where she teaches cultural geography, qualitative research, and writing at the graduate and undergraduate levels. Her qualitative research – largely on tourism, landscape, and social memory in the American West – has been both ethnographic and archival. Dydia has published on these topics in book chapters and in journals such as the *Annals of the Association of American Geographer*, *Journal of Geography in Higher Education*, *Journal of Historical Geography*, *Cultural Geographies*, and *Social and Cultural Geography*, as well as in her book, *Ramona Memories: Tourism and the Shaping of Southern California* (University of Minnesota Press, 2005). She serves as North American editor of *Cultural Geographies* and as Louisiana State University's Faculty Athletics Representative to the NCAA.

J.D. Dewsbury is Senior Lecturer of Human Geography at Bristol University. His research centers on bodies, performativity, and the concept of the event in continental philosophy, as well on the performing arts. His recent publications have been on the work of Alain Badiou and post-phenomenological theories as he works towards a book, *Performative Spaces: Politics, Subjectivity, and the Event*.

Jason Dittmer is Lecturer in Human Geography at University College London. He received his PhD at Florida State University and specializes in the intersection of geopolitics and popular culture in audience imaginations. He is the author of *Popular Culture, Geopolitics, and Identity* (Rowman and Littlefield, forthcoming) and co-editor of *Mapping the End Times: American Evangelical Geopolitics and Apocalyptic Visions* (Ashgate, forthcoming).

James Duncan teaches cultural geography at the University of Cambridge and is a Fellow of Emmanuel College. His publications include *The City as Text: The Politics of Landscape Interpretation in the Kandyan Kingdom* (Cambridge University Press, 2005), *Landscapes of Privilege: The Politics of the Aesthetic in Suburban New York* (Routledge, 2003), and *In The Shadows of the Tropics: Climate, Race and Biopower in Colonial Ceylon* (Ashgate, 2007).

Nancy Duncan teaches cultural geography at the University of Cambridge and is a Senior Member of Robinson College. Her publications include *BodySpace: Destabilizing Geographies of Gender and Sexuality* (Routledge, 1996) and *Landscapes of Privilege: The Politics of the Aesthetic in Suburban New York* (Routledge, 2003).

Sarah Elwood is Associate Professor in the Department of Geography at the University of Washington. Her research interests intersect critical GIS, urban political geography, qualitative methods, and participatory action research. She has recently completed a long-term participatory project examining the use and impacts of geographic information systems and GIS-based spatial knowledge in neighborhood revitalization, urban planning and problem solving. She is currently beginning research on the use and impacts of user-generated spatial data and mapping web services.

Amy K. Glasmeier is Department Head of Urban Studies and Planning at the Massachusetts Institute of Technology, and Professor of Geography and Regional Planning there. She serves as an adviser and researcher for the Appalachian Regional Commission, and from 2005 to 2007 she was reappointed as the John Whisman Scholar of the Commission. She has worked with numerous federal agencies, and international development organizations, in constructing development policies to alleviate poverty and promote economic opportunity. She is currently developing a series of reports for the Ford Foundation on the utilization of energy as a catalyst for community economic, business, and workforce development in low-wealth communities. The project examines the potential to rapidly deploy energy efficiency and renewable-energy investments to achieve economic security for families and business.

Steve Herbert is Professor of Geography and Law, Societies, and Justice at the University of Washington. He is interested in the regulation of space, primarily through law. He has conducted ethnographic research in both Los Angeles and Seattle, work that produced two books – *Policing Space: Territoriality and the Los Angeles Police Department* (University of Minnesota Press, 1997) and *Citizens, Cops, and Power: Recognizing the Limits of Community* (University of Chicago Press, 2006). An additional book – *Banished: Social Control in Contemporary Urban America*, co-authored with Katherine Beckett – is forthcoming from Oxford University Press.

Thomas Herman is the Project Director at the Center for Interdisciplinary Studies of Youth and Space at San Diego State University. Tom conducts research on children's and families' relationships with urban neighborhood environments and has written about the practical and ethical considerations related to conducting qualitative research with children. Tom also consults with community-based organizations and local governments in the San Diego area to provide support to projects that benefit children and families.

Peter Jackson is Professor of Human Geography at the University of Sheffield (UK). He is the author of *Maps of Meaning: An Introduction to Cultural Geography* (Routledge, 1989) and co-author of *Shopping, Place and Identity* (Routledge, 1998). He was Director of the recently completed research program on 'Changing Families, Changing Food' (funded by The Leverhulme Trust) and is currently embarking on a new project, 'Consumer Culture in an Age of Anxiety' (funded by the European Research Council).

Kari B. Jensen, originally from Norway, is Assistant Professor of Global Studies and Geography at Hofstra University, New York. She has previously taught at the Pennsylvania State University, and at the University of Oslo. Her research interests include childhood in different cultural contexts, child labor and education, and cultural challenges resulting from international migration. Her doctoral research focused on child domestic workers in Dhaka, Bangladesh – their perceptions of life, identity, work conditions, use of private and public space, opportunities for education, and relationship to employers. Jensen is now doing research on young people's experiences growing up in multi-cultural families in the US.

Mei-Po Kwan is Distinguished Professor of Social and Behavioral Sciences and Dr. Martha L. Corry Faculty Fellow in the Department of Geography at the Ohio State University. She is currently Editor of the *Annals of the Association of American Geographers* and Associate Editor of *Geographical Analysis*. She received the UCGIS Research Award from the University Consortium for Geographic Information Science (UCGIS) and the Edward L. Ullman Award from the Transportation Geography Specialty Group of the Association of American Geographers. Her research interests include research methods; geographies of gender, race, and religion; information and communication technologies; geographic information science and systems; and feminist perspectives on geospatial technologies.

Hayden Lorimer is Senior Lecturer in Human Geography, Department of Geographical and Earth Sciences, University of Glasgow. His research interests are in historical and cultural geography, specifically in the social history of geographical ideas and topographic cultures. Most often, his studies hover somewhere between the not-so-distant past and the almost-present. They allow critical engagement with a series of themes: landscape, memory, biography, fieldwork, science, nature, and mobility. Sometimes, they invite a creative engagement with narrative.

Sara MacKian, is Senior Lecturer in Health and Social Care at the Open University (UK), having trained and performed as a geographer for the best part of her academic career. With a particular interest in qualitative methods she uses the geographical imagination to explore experiences of health, disease and well-being. This has led to studies on ME, maternal health, gay men's health and civil society's relationship with public health; and resulted in over twenty publications including papers in a range of journals such as *Social and Cultural Geography*, *Health and Place*, *Critical Social Policy*, *Policy and Politics* and *Health Policy and Planning*. More recently Sara has been researching the use of alternative spiritualities to enhance well-being, from which she is writing a single-authored book with Palgrave Macmillan: *The Spirituality of Everyday Life: Spaces of Experience and Practice*.

Deborah G. Martin is Associate Professor in the Graduate School of Geography at Clark University. She is an urban geographer with interests in place identity, local politics, social movements (particularly neighborhood activism), and qualitative methodologies. Her current research project examines legal dynamics of land use conflicts, especially the role of legal professionals in neighborhood mediation and contestation. She teaches an undergraduate research-design course and graduate qualitative-research seminar.

Linda McDowell is Professor of Human Geography at the University of Oxford. Her main research interests are in economic change, service-sector growth, gender divisions of labor, organizational cultures, migration, global cities, and feminist theory. She is author of many books, most recently including *Redundant Masculinities? Employment Change and White Working Class Youth* (Blackwell, 2003) and *Hard Labour: The Forgotten Voices of Latvian Migrant 'Volunteer' Workers* (UCL Press, 2005). *Working Bodies: Interactive Service Employment and Workplace Identities* will be published by Wiley-Blackwell in 2009. She has contributed chapters on feminist analysis, methodology, economic change, and the culture of work and organizations to many collections, as well as published papers in a wide range of geographical journals. She was elected as a fellow of the British Academy in 2008.

Garth Myers is Director of the Kansas African Studies Center and Professor of Geography and African/African-American Studies at the University of Kansas. He is the author of two books and co-editor of a third book, all on African urban geography topics. He has published more than three dozen articles and book chapters on issues in African human geography, focusing on cultural-historical concerns as well as political geography and urban development.

Paul Routledge is a Reader in Human Geography at the Department of Geographical and Earth Sciences at the University of Glasgow. His research interests include global-justice networks, resistance movements, activism, and geopolitics. He is co-editor of *The Geopolitics Reader* (Routledge, 2006), and co-author with Andrew Cumbers of *Global Justice Networks: Geographies of Transnational Solidarity* (MUP, 2009).

Polly Russell's research focusses on contemporary food production and consumption. Through collaborations with the British Library National Life Stories, Polly has collected and archived over 100 oral-history recordings with food producers. Most recently Polly worked on 'Manufacturing Meaning Along the Food Commodity Chain,' an ESRC/AHRC study focused on the social, cultural, and economic significance of food in Britain. Polly works as a Content

Specialist at the British Library looking after collections relating to Human Geography and Anthropology. She has published articles in *Transactions of the Institute of British Geographers*, the *Journal of Rural Studies*, *Sociologica Ruralis*, and *Oral History*. Polly is also a cookery writer and co-author of *Kitchen Revolution* published by Ebury press.

Mona Seymour is a doctoral candidate in the Department of Geography at the University of Southern California. Her dissertation examines shared urban spaces and their human and nonhuman inhabitants, focusing on socio-cultural and institutional influences on human-avian geographies in US cities. Other research pertains to environmental and social sustainability in urban regions, including the greening and revitalization of urban alleyways, critical perspectives on new 'sustainable' communities, and park- and open-space quality in greater Los Angeles.

Karen E. Till is Associate Professor at the School of Public and International Affairs, Virginia Tech University. Her geo-ethnographic work explores place-making, personal and social memory, and creative and collaborative research practices in urban settings. Her publications include: *The New Berlin: Memory, Politics, Place* (University of Minnesota Press, 2005), the co-edited volume *Textures of Place: Rethinking Humanist Geographies* (University of Minnesota Press, 2001), numerous articles and book chapters, including 'Artistic and Activist Memory-Work: Approaching Place-Based Practice' in the launch issue of *Memory Studies* (2008), and essays in art exhibition catalogues. She is currently working on three book-length projects, *Interim Space*, *Wall Remnants* and *Wounded Cities*.

Annette Watson is Assistant Professor in the Political Science Department at the College of Charleston. Her research examines the politics of knowledge in the context of environmental sustainability and social justice: she questions what constitutes legitimated scientific discourse and what knowledge becomes subjugated in environmental management. Her work engages critical geographic approaches to decolonize disciplinary narrative conventions, and she experiments with alternative narrative forms to open spaces that would recognize non-academic expertise.

Jennifer Wolch is Dean of the College of Environmental Design at the University of California, Berkeley and the William W. Wurster Chair of City and Regional Planning. Her research focuses on metropolitan sprawl, physical activity and urban design, urban environmental justice and political ecology, and society–animals relations. She has also investigated problems of urban poverty, homelessness, human-service delivery, and the evolution of state–civil society relations. With Jody Emel, she edited *Animal Geographies: Place, Politics and Identity in the Nature/Culture Borderlands* (Verso, 1998), and has published articles and book chapters on population diversity and attitudes toward animals, racialization and animal practices, and the place of animals in the city.

Introduction: Engaging Qualitative Geography

Dydia DeLyser, Steve Herbert, Stuart C. Aitken,
Mike Crang and Linda McDowell

In this chapter we welcome you to the *SAGE Handbook of Qualitative Geography*, and describe what we believe to be the significant issues and challenges for qualitative human geography in the twenty-first century. Our goal for this volume is to introduce scholars, both veteran and novice, to the world of qualitative geography, and to engage them in the collective and collaborative process of forwarding qualitative geography in the twenty-first century. This, we recognize, is a challenge in itself, for this handbook, like the handbooks in other fields that came before, seeks to reach and engage multiple audiences. We aim, in partnership with the chapter authors, to engage advanced and graduate students preparing to undertake their first major qualitative projects, established scholars already richly experienced in diverse approaches to qualitative research, those scholars who wish to broaden their horizons into new areas of qualitative research, and we also welcome those who are considering qualitative research for the first time. Often, these audiences may come together, as in a graduate seminar where instructors and students collaboratively launch productive

discussions about the issues and ideas raised by the chapters. Our hope is to engage geographers in a thought-provoking, ongoing, and ever-developing discussion of how to *do* qualitative geography, and to persuade others, from other fields, of the value of our spatial perspectives.

The early twenty-first century marks a marvelous time for qualitative geography. In concert with what some have called a 'quiet methodological revolution' across the social and policy sciences as well as the humanities (Denzin and Lincoln, 2005a: ix), geography is fostering an efflorescence in the prevalence and sophistication of qualitative research. The abundance of high-quality qualitative research reveals itself in academic journals and conferences, in dissertation research by newly-minted PhDs and in book-length works by more seasoned scholars. It is evident, as well, in the diverse range of qualitative methods productively and insightfully employed by contemporary geographers, many of which are engaged in this volume. Meanwhile, there has been a 'spatial turn' as well, across a range of disciplines as many researchers look to the spatialities and geographies of the social world, and, as we shall suggest, attend to the spatialities of research itself.

Significantly, the proliferation of qualitative geography marks not just an increase in output, but also an increase in methodological acuity and sophistication among geographers. The 'just do it' approach to qualitative research of past decades – where geographers entered the field with little preparation or training – has largely been shelved in favor of an active engagement in the complexities of 'explicitly qualitative research' in geography that we now see addressed by an array of books and articles *about* qualitative research, as well as an increasing number of specialized courses in PhD-granting geography programs (DeLyser, 2008: 235; Martin, this volume).

Looking back over the past decades, it is clear that qualitative methods have ceased to be on the fringe of our discipline, and that they are today vital to our current practice of human geography. That transformation emerged not without challenge – the rise of qualitative geography has been (and in some places continues to be) the subject of resistance and controversy, anger and acrimony, as other methods seemed to some to be challenged, and qualitative methods appeared, according to the norms of physical science, anecdotal, not replicable, and not generalizable (see, for example, Openshaw, 1998; Martin, 2001; Crang, 2002; 2003; Fotheringham, 2006). We regard those attacks as now largely historic, and in this volume we stand ready not just to argue for the importance and relevance of qualitative work, but also to broaden and refine both the scope of the methods used and their practice in human geography. And since these methods are no longer novel imports from other disciplines, this seems a good time to also ask what a geographic sensibility might have to offer to their practice.

In this handbook we seek to contribute to the discussions of what a geographical approach to qualitative methods looks like and what it offers, in a text that aims to treat the issues and topics of qualitative human geography at a peer-to-peer level. We seek, in this volume, not just to review what has been done, but to offer an agenda of what can be done. Thus, at a vibrant time for qualitative research in human geography, the authors and editors of this volume seek to engage our peers, and our future peers, in spirited debates about the future of qualitative geography.

In so doing, we seek to address four pressures that confront contemporary qualitative geographers in different ways: our interactions with other methods and processes of research; our approaches to issues of relevance in a world where political issues and policy concerns may at times strike a delicate balance with poststructural academic engagements; our understandings of the difference that a geographical perspective itself makes to qualitative research; and finally our own theoretical innovations and movements that may push away from the humanist and social-constructivist foundations of qualitative geography. While each chapter addresses these pressures in different ways, in this introduction we assess them explicitly, in the context of a broader discussion that situates qualitative research within human geography. First, though, we briefly introduce the book's structure and chapters.

ORGANIZATION OF THE BOOK

Since the purpose of this book is to engage readers in conversations about how to conceive of, carry out, and carry forward qualitative research in the twenty-first century, we have organized the text into three sections designed to mirror the ways that the qualitative-research process is often, though by no means always, experienced. The three sections of the book move from conceptualizing research (and the researcher's place within it) and situating that in broader academic, political, and social currents, through multiple and intersecting means of carrying out research, to issues and processes of broader engagement and circulation. Each chapter author draws from qualitative research in various fields, and also draws upon their own research experiences, linking those to the themes of the chapters to show, through the experiences of these individuals, how the ground-up empirical details of qualitative research can be linked to the broader social, theoretical, political, and policy concerns of qualitative geographers. While the introductions to each of the sections outlines their content in more detail, here we offer a brief sketch of the contents of the book, drawing on examples from just a few of the chapters to provide a flavor of the vivid and varied world of discovery we believe readers will find in qualitative geography, and in this handbook.

Part I, 'Openings' features chapters that introduce the history of qualitative research, and examine the multifaceted positioning of the researcher in social, political, and theoretical contexts. These chapters each engage in different ways the complex epistemological, ontological, and philosophical backbones of qualitative geography. They situate the researcher within the disciplinary (and transdisciplinary) historical formations that shape qualitative inquiry, and frame the explorations of individual methods in the next section. So, for example, Meghan Cope situates her own work within the history of qualitative research in geography, while Sarah Elwood links her participatory-GIS research to the broader issues of ontology and epistemology that arise when qualitative and quantitative methods are mixed.

Part II, 'Encounters and Collaborations' includes chapters that each engage, in detail, with a particular strategy of inquiry, a particular qualitative method. Here, the tools and techniques used by qualitative geographers are described, challenged, and urged forward. Some chapters address established methods widely used in geography. In Hayden Lorimer's case, qualitative geographers have long undertaken archival research, but few have discussed it from a methodological standpoint. Here Lorimer uses dust

as both object and metaphor to think through what he terms the 'make-do-methods' of archival practices, mustering his work with elderly reindeer herders in Scotland to show how archival research can transcend the archive. Nancy and James Duncan traverse the well-traveled terrain of landscape interpretation, before moving to explore the implications of post-structuralist understandings of landscape for their own work in Sri Lanka and New York, and pointing out the methodological implications of such an approach to conceptualizing landscape.

Other chapters in this section engage methods with which geographers are likely less familiar. David Butz uses his research with villagers in rural Pakistan to show how autoethnography can be moved from a study of the self within the research to embrace also the complex constructions of selves that his ethnographic participants seek to convey to him and others. Peter Jackson and Polly Russell mobilize their life-history interviews with poultry farmers in Britain to show how such rich sources can reveal the narrative structures within which people situate their lives, and, in so doing (and like Butz's work), shed light on how people seek to convey themselves to themselves, and others.

The chapters in Part III, 'Making Sense' embrace and critique the ways that qualitative research is analyzed, interpreted, and communicated – and show how those processes might be moved into the future. Ideas addressed in the first section, and methods addressed in the second, are now directly related to the communication of research – to a broader geographical praxis. Here, for example, Garth Myers draws connections between his fieldwork in Tanzania, his academic position at a US university, and postcolonial theory, to examine the negotiations between the personal and the political that qualitative researchers must engage. And Paul Routledge details his participation with the Clandestine Insurgent Rebel Clown Army in the UK to explore power relations in the constructions of activist geographies that are themselves designed to empower resisting others to take control of their own lives in the face of oppressive power relations.

However undertaken and with whatever aims, qualitative research is a *process* that begins with the biographically situated, physically embodied researcher – the researcher who her- or himself is shaped and influenced in ongoing ways by issues of class, 'race,' ethnicity, gender, age, ability, sexuality, and community (Denzin and Lincoln, 2005b). To sum up, in the most straightforward sense, each qualitative geographer begins with her- or himself, and moves both outward and inward to research questions that may originate in the researcher's training and theoretical background, but must be embedded in the community and/or environment the researcher studies. The researcher uses her- or himself as a 'research instrument' – collecting data, but also filtering, feeling, experiencing, and analyzing field experiences and challenging personal understandings. Qualitative researchers recognize our own involvement in creating, not just describing the worlds we study. And we work *with* (not 'on') the communities we study. We seek to give voice to those with whom we work, but most often it is we who write the reports, we who author the articles – the qualitative researcher, as a trained analyst, uses her or his own skills and her or his own voice to focus the experiences of others, and to help the voices of others speak more loudly, or more clearly, (most often) in an academic arena (see chapters by DeLyser, MacKian, Myers, and Routledge in this volume).

Thus, the qualitative-research process engages the socially and biographically situated researcher and her or his training, experience, and background; it entangles those in ongoing ways with the communities studied; and it links the situated researcher to theoretical ideas current in academic discourse, as well as to political and policy concerns, in order to further those issues.

In short, the organization of the book is designed to take researchers through the process of conceptualizing and carrying out qualitative research, where theory is linked to methods or strategies of inquiry, where the multiply situated researcher engages the empirical world, and where what we once thought of as 'research results' are sensitively communicated both to the communities engaged and the community of scholars of which the researcher is part.

Because our goal has been to create a benchmark volume, one that pushes issues and debates in qualitative geography to the edges of the envelope, we realize too that not all readers will necessarily agree with the arguments in each chapter. Indeed, each chapter is an individual social construction by its author(s), working with the editors, to convey a dialog we believe is important to put forward. Different authors and different editors would have created very different chapters. And that is as it should be. Thus, we see this volume not only as one summation of state-of-the-art qualitative geography, but also as a launching point for new discussions and new engagements, new issues and new ideas. We welcome your feedback – in correspondence, at conferences, in publications – as we together embrace and create the futures of qualitative geography. In what follows here, we highlight the four arenas of debate and development.

THE RESISTED RISE OF QUALITATIVE GEOGRAPHY

Qualitative research, as Meghan Cope's chapter in this volume illustrates, has always been part of the practice of human geography. But the broad acceptance of contemporary, methodologically articulate qualitative research has been, in many places and many cases, hard won. It was, after all, just about a half-century ago, that the long-enduring efforts of the 'quantitative revolution' sought to transform the discipline. The goals of that broad movement are understandable in the context of the post-WWII Anglo/American academy: to transform geography from an ideographic discipline concerned only with the specific, to one nomothetic, one engaged in the pursuit of general principles or 'laws' of science, and, in so doing, achieve recognition for the discipline among the natural sciences. Aligned, for the most part, with a putatively positivist science, quantitative geography forged forward, carried on waves of technological advances (in statistical methods and computational capability), constructing and employing large data sets in the pursuit of generalizable knowledge until, for a time in the mid-twentieth century, a quantitative-inspired paradigm became dominant in the discipline (for narratives see Cloke *et al.*, 1991; Livingstone, 1993; Johnstone and Sidaway, 2004).

Amid this fervor for numerical sophistication and explanation, qualitative human geographers, traditionally mute on the subject of methods and methodology, initially offered little response. By the 1970s, however, humanist, feminist, and some radical geographers argued for a qualitative *human* geography that recognized and validated human experience, and they led campaigns for the recognition of qualitative work as valid and valuable (Cloke *et al.*, 1991; Livingstone, 1993; Johnstone and Sidaway, 2004; Crang, 2005; DeLyser, 2008; Cope, this volume). For some committed positivists (though these have always been a minority among quantitative researchers) and quantitative modelers, these efforts to gain acceptance of qualitative work were received as a battle for primacy and/or a threat to claims to be a scientific discipline – the rise of qualitative work that was theoretically and methodologically sophisticated came to be seen as a challenge to the supremacy of the quantitative episteme. In some quarters of the discipline a qualitative–quantitative divide emerged that appeared to pitch practitioners against one another, and advocates of a narrowly scientized discipline continued for decades to argue against the 'squelchy soft approaches' of qualitative geography (Cloke *et al.*, 1991; Livingstone, 1993; the quote is from Openshaw, 1998: 317; see also Martin, 2001; Johnstone and Sidaway, 2004).

The absence, in qualitative research, of large-N data sets, and the widespread avoidance, by qualitative researchers, of statistical analyses, led many (both inside and outside of qualitative research) to mistakenly equate qualitative research with research without numbers (Bogdan and Ksander, 1980). This superficial understanding of qualitative research as 'ungeneralizable,' or idiographic, led to a ready classification of such work as not 'scientific' according to the models of physical science (see Openshaw, 1998; Martin, 2001 for vitriolic assessments). True enough: qualitative researchers do not engage in hypothesis testing and laboratory experiments. Indeed, as Norman Denzin and Yvonna Lincoln remind us in their *Handbook of Qualitative Research*, the very word qualitative implies 'an emphasis on the qualities of entities and on processes and meanings that are not experimentally examined or measured (if measured at all) in terms of quantity, amount, intensity, or frequency' (2005b: 10). Sympathetic studies have attempted to reconcile this profound ontological and epistemological difference through, for instance, the widely held realist formulation that qualitative research uses intensive rather than extensive methods (Sayer and Morgan, 1986). Thus statistical analysis looks at the (extensive) regularities and patterns of outcomes while qualitative methods examine the mechanisms, processes and practices in intensive detail. This elegant squaring of the circle often then suggested some harmonious 'triangulation' of methods, offering complementary perspectives. While appealing, this synthesis has come under strain for attending to neither of the truth claims and constructions of the methods which tend to proceed from incommensurable understandings of the social world – and indeed the notion of a depth ontology relating processes to structural patterns has itself been subjected to consistent critique (but see Elwood in this volume on the ontological and epistemological challenges and rewards of mixed-methods research).

Qualitative researchers work explicitly to explore the world in its found form (in work that is termed, for that reason, naturalistic). We recognize and validate the complexity of everyday life, the nuances of meaning-making in an ever-changing world, and the multitude of influences that shape human lived experience (pluralities from which quantitative summaries must abstract). We work to acknowledge the researcher's whole person as a research instrument in our inter-actions with the people with whom we work, and with whom we both collect and construct our empirical materials (our data). Qualitative researchers, as Denzin and Lincoln point out, 'stress the socially constructed nature of reality, the intimate relationship between the researcher and what is being studied, and the situational constraints that shape inquiry. They seek to answer questions that stress *how* social experience is given meaning' (2005b: 10). Indeed, qualitative research places the researcher in and amongst the findings, rather than deploying the scientized rhetoric of the disembodied, neutral, and detached observer.

Methodologically, the discipline of geog-raphy has a long and troubling history of using the figure of the detached observer, untrammeled by the social relations of the field and the academy, in ways that hid colonial, gendered, and racialized forms of knowledge (Bondi and Domosh, 1992). Substantively, in geography in particular, given our discipline's long-standing commit-ments to understanding the roles of place in providing the ongoing sustenance (both material and symbolic) that enables any social group to perpetuate itself, the role of people, in turn, in shaping those places, and our understanding of space as more than a neutral surface upon which human and non-human phenomena are inscribed, qualitative methods rose to meet the challenges of immersing ourselves deeply in particular places that we might better understand how places themselves influence ways of life and understandings of the world, as well as how ways of life and understandings of the world

influence particular places (Ley, 1988; Herbert, 2000). However, this is rather more than simply suggesting the triumph of 'areal differentiation' after all these years, even if such a perspective does sensitize us to the situatedness and competing nature of world views. It is rather that the immersed and situ-ated view points from the thick of things are now seen as better vantage points than some imagined Archimedean overlook.

Still, it has been only after decades of struggle for recognition, and at times it sometimes seems after both sides have fought each other to exhaustion, that we have arrived at the point where today, in most geography programs, scholars are able to move beyond the qualitative–quantitative divide that in the last half-century caused such animosity, acri-mony, and anxiety. Today, most geographers recognize that qualitative and quantitative methods are not opposed to one another, but instead represent different ontological and epistemological approaches to knowledge and data – they may be used to answer differ-ent questions, and they do so in very different ways, from very different groundings. Though positivist/quantitative approaches once sought dominance in human geography, geographers of the twenty-first century (along with scholars across the humanities and social- and policy-sciences) now broadly recognize the importance of issues of mean-ing, perception, values, intentions, motiva-tions, and understandings – issues that demand methods of inquiry that can access the subjectively experienced, ever-changing world 'live,' and in the places where those meanings and interpretations emerge. We recognize the complexity of everyday reality, the multitude of influences that shape lived experience, and the importance of the spatial contexts of human interaction. That is to say, we recognize the importance of qualitative approaches in human geography. We have also come to recognize the importance of geography to understanding the situated nature of feelings, meaning, values, practices, and knowledge. Indeed, we have come to acknowledge the importance of geographies of knowledge in situating our accounts of these – relating field, audience, and academy along with the relational positions of informants, researchers, and readers.

So too, it was not long ago that researchers both quantitative and qualitative aspired to achieve objectivity in their research with human subjects, and aimed to conduct that research from a distanced standpoint to acquire the gloss of scientific authority and respectability. Today, in most geography programs, scholars have been able to move beyond the simplistic subjective–objective dichotomy once imposed upon research, to understand instead a social world where pure objectivity is impossible because each researcher finds her- or himself enmeshed in the social world he or she studies, and where the understanding of lived experience (of both research participants and the researcher) calls for an empirically grounded and necessarily subjective approach that acknowledges the situatedness of all knowledge (Harraway, 1991; Dwyer and Limb, 2001; Harding, 2001; Denzin and Lincoln, 2005b). Indeed, qualitative geographers have come to understand that it is through prolonged and empathetic interactions with members of a social group that researchers can develop insights into the patterned regularities and meaning structures that shape group, individual, and place identities (Ley, 1988; Herbert, 2000).

Close to the action in these ways, qualitative geographers explore the rich tissue of social life in all its myriad and intricate forms, most often beginning from the ground up, working toward broader, contextualized understandings (Herbert, this volume; see Harding, 2001). And because qualitative researchers must generally become deeply enmeshed with the people and places we study, we are invariably affected through our full array of senses, and are forced to reckon with the wide array of emotions we feel as humans – making it impossible to pretend we are either purely objective or detached from our 'data.' In fact, as later chapters will show in detail, these sensual and emotional engagements are best seen not

as impediments to understanding but rather as vehicles for it (in addition to the chapters in this volume, see also McCormack, 2003; Bondi and Davidson, 2004; Davidson and Milligan, 2004; Thrift, 2004; Bondi, 2005; Davidson *et al.*, 2005).

Where laboratory-based researchers, building on the research of others, seek confirmation (or more rarely, strict positivists seek refutation) of an hypothesis they themselves generate through controlled experiments that they (and their assistants) conduct, contemporary qualitative geographers engage a 'naturalistic' approach to research – we leave the laboratory and the computer to study people, places, and phenomena as much as possible *in situ*, and seek to validate not only our own perspectives (because we all hold ideas about how the world works), but especially also the meanings that the people we work with bring to the topic of study, a topic that itself often emerges and always develops through the research process. Grounding theory in observation, interaction, analysis, and interpretation – or, as Claire Dwyer and Melanie Limb (2001: 11) put it, making theory 'accountable to fieldwork' – requires of qualitative geographers a commitment to actively engaging, through diverse means, the empirical worlds we study.

These commitments, in turn, require a creative and often open-minded, or open-ended, approach to what was once called 'data gathering.' Techniques described in this book separately (of necessity, in order to engage them in detail) – techniques including participant observation and ethnography, interviewing, life history, focus groups, auto-ethnography, visual analysis, landscape interpretation, archival research, textual and discourse analysis, GIS, animal geographies, and non-representational approaches – are in practice often used in combinations, combinations that will be unique to each field site and each field experience; combinations that may even emerge in the moment once the research is already underway. Thus, although qualitative geographers plan our research in advance, the complex and ever-changing intersubjective nature of research with human subjects calls for creative approaches to circumstances, the adaptation of old techniques, and the invention of new combinations – both in the planning and during the research. Qualitative research, as Denzin and Lincoln (2005b: 5) put it, is 'inherently multi-method in focus.' Today, with a strong tradition of methodologically sophisticated qualitative geography and with the battles of the qualitative–quantitative divide now mostly behind us, qualitative geographers pursue work not only from our own methodological groundings, but reach out also to incorporate quantitative work in mixed-methods research (see Elwood, this volume) as we strive to conduct research that is relevant and appropriate from methodological, political, academic, and policy standpoints.

BALANCING CONCERNS

If in the mid-twentieth century, the largest challenge to qualitative research in geography was posed by the quantitative revolution, by century's end the social sciences and humanities were shaken by an entirely different challenge, that of the 'crisis of representation' emerging in the main from anthropology (Marcus and Fischer, 1986; Turner and Bruner, 1986; Clifford and Marcus, 1986; Geertz, 1988; Clifford, 1988, see Aitken in this volume). And in the new century, new ideas about research as performative and as a more-than-representable act urged qualitative geography in yet other directions (see, for example, McCormack, 2003; Lorimer, 2005; Thien, 2005; Thrift, 2007). Through all these challenges, qualitative geographers have sought also to remain genuinely engaged with the communities where we place our work, and often to continue to produce work that is politically progressive and/or actively policy oriented. Importantly, in the midst of this, qualitative work has walked the delicate lines between sympathy for and engagement with those we

study while avoiding uncritical cheerleading, even as we work through the awkward positions and issues of engaging with those – often but not always – in positions of power whose practices we might wish to critique. Viewing these challenges together, we can see issues of performance, relevance, and praxis in a complex light.

It was the crisis of representation in the 1980s that challenged notions of reporting from a 'real world' out there and a correspondence theory of truth, and urged scholars across the social sciences and humanities to question the complex interconnections between our observations, our interpretations, and the realities we both perceive and represent in our work. Qualitative researchers in numerous fields, often led by feminist or postcolonial scholars, responded with written work that questioned the authority of the author, and sought new understandings of truth (McDowell, 1995; Jones *et al.*, 1997; Rosaldo, 1989). Distanced objectivity was discarded and situated positionality embraced through an understanding of the biographically situated researcher who yields influence in the outcomes of his or her own research. This new embrace led also to what Denzin and Lincoln (2005: 19) describe as the current 'triple crisis of representation, legitimation, and praxis' and the ongoing rethinking of the role of qualitative research in the academy and the world at large.

In response to the 'sordid legacies' of social-science-research practices linked to exploitative colonialist endeavors around the world as well as to cultures of deprivation and cycles of poverty within industrialized nations, qualitative research in the twenty-first century has become increasingly action-, policy-, and community-oriented (Denzin and Lincoln, 2005b: 1; see also Smith, 1999). As Denzin and Lincoln point out (2005b: 2), though there were colonialists before there were ethnographers, 'there would be no colonial, and now no neocolonial, history were it not for this investigative mentality that turned the dark-skinned Other into the object of the ethnographer's gaze. From the very beginning, qualitative research was impli-cated in a racist project.' Today, aware of those legacies, involved in decolonization, and committed to 'creating spaces where those who are studied (the Other) can speak' (Denzin and Lincoln, 2005b: 26), qualitative researchers across academic disciplines strive to engage in equitable and emancipatory research practices.

In geography, as Gail Davies and Claire Dwyer point out (2008: 399), an 'emphasis on the political and public intersections of research practice is now both commonplace and contested.' Critical geographic praxis, action research, and policy-oriented research seek social relevance and community engage-ment, at times from different standpoints. Some uphold a distinction between 'applied' forms of geographic engagement that serve the interests of the state or business, and a critical geographical praxis (Fuller and Kitchin, 2004). But even research that proves useful to the government (perhaps for its policy applications) need not slavishly serve the state. Much qualitative work follows the tradition that seeks to both give voice to those unheard or silenced by the powerful, and also to speak truth, or at least their truths, back to power (perhaps the apogee of this work is partisan participation; see Routledge this volume). As Rachel Pain (2006: 251) carefully points out, policy-oriented, applied geographers often engage in 'counter-policy research' that resists and offers critiques of the state's policies. Further, distinguishing between 'applied geographers ... as uncritical servants of the state, while critical geographers actively challenge the status quo' (Pain, 2006: 253) does little to further anyone's emancipatory agenda, and, as Fuller and Kitchin (2004: 3) remind us, until relatively recently, few geographers (of any stripe) 'had married their empirical research, activism, and writing' agendas. Participatory, emancipatory, and policy-oriented research can, as the chapters in this volume illustrate, be richly engaged, on the ground, from multiple academic orientations (see chapters by Aitken, Herbert,

Jensen and Glasmeier, Elwood, Watson and Till, Butz, Myers, Routledge, and Martin). The point, as feminist geographers have made clear, is that we seek 'an academic praxis that is emancipatory and empowering for the participants in the research' (Jones et al., 1997; Fuller and Kitchin, 2004: 3). There are many ways such a valuable com-mitment can be made manifest, but it is also revealing in itself as a statement, since it reflects how much qualitative work has focused on representing silenced or invis-ible knowledges, rather than unpacking the hegemonic.

This understanding of engaged knowledge production has not been easily achieved nor is it uncontested, but, as each of the chapters in this volume reveals, such questions have been richly addressed by qualitative geogra-phers leading to different answers, different engagements, and different kinds of qualita-tive geography. What is perhaps most impor-tant, as Stuart Aitken urges in his chapter in this volume, is the ethic of care with which contemporary qualitative research is conducted.

Geographies of qualitative research

The chapters in this book each demonstrate explicitly, in their own ways, what difference place and space make to qualitative research, and what a geographic sensibility brings to qualitative research. Some of the broader points deserve attention here as well, for sometimes geographers are too quickly drawn into simplistic and mechanistic defini-tions of place and space that can become a way of too rigidly framing the world. Because, of course, all activities take place somewhere, space is everywhere, and connected in perhaps banal-seeming ways to everything we do – so much so that it may at times seem not worth mentioning. Nevertheless, space is uneven and differenti-ated, and so 'places' differ. It is for precisely these reasons that it is crucial to take account of spatial difference and inequalities *methodologically* – the intensive methods of qualitative research are geared specifically to illuminate the taken-for-granted and to establish the significance of being 'here,' rather than 'there.' But one of the challenges posed in research on place is that, as humans, we are profoundly attached to particular places, and that may at times overwhelm our abilities to say something articulate about them. Here too, the intensive methods of qualitative research can help shed light on beneath-the-surface meanings.

Careful qualitative research also helps us transcend the binary space and place that were once relegated to in geography, where space was seen as an abstraction (perhaps akin to a flat Euclidean surface awaiting the mapping of people's activities), while places were infused with the senses of identity and belonging from which meaning is derived (Cresswell, 2004). Such a binary – easy to slip into – at times continues to hold sway among geographers, and all too easily leads to aligning qualitative work with lived place and quantitative work with abstract space. But the restrictions imposed by such binary views can be revealed by attempting to nest other concepts like community, neighborhood, landscape, and care-scape into either of the two categories. As the chapters in this book reveal (see, for example, Aitken, Watson and Till, Lorimer, and Dewsbury), contemporary qualitative geographers work beyond such simplified conceptualizations. Indeed, these efforts to understand, in complex and ongoing ways, not just space and place, but also the mutual constitution of spaces, places, and human behavior at all scales are crucial for qualitative researchers – be they geographers, anthropologists, sociologists, psychologists, urban planners, or economists. At the very least, not doing so risks the possibility of losing important contexts and relations. At worst, we lose important social, cultural, economic, and political insights.

Qualitative research in many fields has at times been seen as exclusively concerned with the local (and the ideographic). But recent geographic work has shown that even small places are not isolated, not defined

only by the local, but are interconnected, unbounded in space and time, and that places may more appropriately be seen as relationally 'articulated moments in networks of social relations and understandings' (Massey, 1993: 66). Places, in other words, are constituted by processes that transect multiple scales, and are constituted out of the spatial and temporal relations between differently scaled and embedded processes. Certainly the sense of a localizable, containable field site – where one might find one culture occupying one bounded place – comes under pressure as material, political, social, economic, and cultural relations are stretched through space and time to work interactively with any given space, place, and environment, creating social relations of empowerment and disempowerment, connection and disconnection (Marston, 2000). This raises the issue of how to conduct ethnography and qualitative research in general at an 'awkward scale,' bridging worlds of power, knowledge, and material flows (Comaroff and Comaroff, 2003). The task for contemporary qualitative geographers (that the chapters in this volume, particularly those by Aitken, Herbert, Jensen and Glasmeier, Elwood, Watson and Till, Butz, and Duncan and Duncan, Lorimer, Myers, Routledge, and Martin, address) is to engage the people we work with, and the places where we work, across diverse social sites, challenging and revealing the complexity of a locally globalized world, to 'recover the local as a site of significant practices' that upset the overarching discourse of globalization, engaging relations of production and social reproduction alike to gain 'theoretical and practical purchase on the very places where ideas are formed, actions are produced, and relationships are created and maintained' (Marston *et al.*, 2005: 427) – and with this to factor the different localities, scales and relations between them in the production of academic knowledge itself.

However, even the awareness or recognition of a sense of place in fieldwork is something oddly and unfortunately attenuated in much geographical scholarship, especially

work based around interviews. So, for example, geographers grounding their research in
semi-structured interviews often have little to
say about the place of the fieldwork, except-
ing some commentary focused at the macro
scale (the city or region, though in multi-
sited work that too often disappears), with
virtually no discussion of the micro-locales
of the research (the offices, meeting rooms,
etc.). At the level of methodological practice,
simply paying heed to where we conduct our
interviews and focus groups is hugely influential to the kinds of knowledge we create,
even if printing those insights may lead to
challenges at the level of ethical practice,
since identifying specific places (a factory,
an office) in published work may breach confidentiality and put individuals at risk.

Recent work by those attuned to (and willing to write about) the differences such
spaces may make in research suggests that
we think through how the spaces of our fieldwork both constrain and enable different
people to say different things. Beyond the
important thoughtfulness that interview locations be accessible, different field settings
also offer affordances to different sorts of
interactions. Some interviewees may be
unable to speak freely in their offices, others
with their partner or parent in the same room,
others still may be put off by a setting's
ambience – too formal, too masculinist, too
public. Conversations, and the power structures that underlie those conversations, are
shaped, in part, by the settings where they
take place (Valentine, 1999; Elwood and
Martin, 2000; McDowell, 2001; Sin, 2003;
see also the chapters by McDowell, Jackson
and Russell, Bosco and Herman, and Butz in
this volume). But attention to a fixed place of
interview is not the only means of further
understanding the micro-geographies of
qualitative research. Indeed, we might look
as well to a more mobile and active use of
locales, where, for instance, a walk in the
neighborhood may help people recall and
talk through events, or organize their thoughts
(Anderson, 2004; Kusenbach, 2003).

Neither has much traditional ethnographic
work in geography work paid more nuanced

heed to place and space. While sensitive, to be
sure, to the role of place in the lives of informants, geographers have had less to say on the
constitution of the field as a site of investigation. Drawing from (traditional work in)
anthropology, ethnographic work in geography long presented the field site as a singular totality to be described in all its aspects in
order to enable readers to grasp the embedded
logics and values of the 'local people.' But in
the contemporary world of global connectivity
and mobility, that spatial sense of a field site as
bounded and locatable may be no longer ten-
able. Contemporary multi-site and trans-local
ethnographies draw our attention to how
studying a culture is no longer about simply
going 'there' and studying 'it,' because 'it' is
'simultaneously supralocal, translocal and
local, simultaneously planetary and, refracted
through the shards of vernacular cultural practices, profoundly parochial' (Comaroff and
Comaroff, 2003: 151; see also Burawoy *et al.*,
2000). Through such research our sense of the
spatiality of the field is being expanded and
refashioned to explore the complex entanglements of scales, venues, milieus, movements,
and mobilities, leading to a rethinking of the
spaces of ethnographic fieldwork and their
connections (see Marcus, 1998; Hyndman,
2001; Hannerz, 2003; Cook, 2004; Katz, 2004;
Watson and Till, and Butz this volume).

Other recent work in the discipline has
pointed to the spatial construction of knowledge itself as an area for geographic investigation – to think of both the academy and the
field as sites of knowledge production, with
different practices often applying within
each. Geographers have begun to consider
the relations between these spaces and how
they structure the production of knowledge
not just 'out there' in the field but back 'in
here,' in the often un- or under-examined
academy (Crang, 2003: 139–40; Crang,
2005) and how that produces what has been
called the 'expanded field' (Crang and
Cook, 2007: 133, 170). Such efforts seek to
deliberately disrupt the division in many
academic practices that keep separate the
various spaces of practice, research, analysis,
interpretation, and presentation (see chapters

by Jensen and Glasmeier, Lorimer, DeLyser, MacKian, Myers, Routledge, and Martin, in this volume).

Historically, a distinction between field science versus home-based research is often traced back to the arguments of Georges Cuvier and Alexander von Humboldt. Cuvier argued it was in the academy that one could make analytic connections prohibited by the particularities of the field, or as he put it 'it is only in one's study that one can roam freely throughout the universe' making the academy a kind of nowhere outside the world (Massey, 2003: 75) – that it was only men who had a study in an academic institution or even a room of their own at home is less often remembered. More recently, the classic work of the Chicago School of Sociology with their oft-cited but now all-too-rarely-read ethnographies provides other ready examples of the binary between fieldwork and office work, empirically grounded and abstract concepts. Their detailed books on different districts of the city, where each district was seen as particular and localized, can be seen in contrast to their abstract diagram of concentric circles now free-floating and universal, detached from the field (Gieryn, 2006, see Aitken in this volume). Indeed through all their work there is, Thomas Gieryn argues, an oscillation between spatialities of 'here' and 'anywhere' – moving from specific, grounded findings to generalized, abstract statement; from field to laboratory; from a discourse celebrating immersion to one privileging detachment. It is this notion of a detached, placeless, 'God-trick' (Haraway, 1991) that a spatiality of an expanded field seeks to overcome by connecting and embedding the spaces of fieldwork and analysis.

But we may go farther as well, because the field encounter and its particularities sanction so much qualitative work with not just the authority, but also the responsibility, of being there, of being a witness (Marcus, 2005). As Davies and Dwyer note, qualitative geography is 'increasingly expected to be mobile' in multiple ways: whether through transnational research, knowledge transfer, or transdisciplinarity, the value of our research may be increasingly seen to stem from 'its ability to move from the contexts of production to those of application and collaboration, from the university to policy' (2008: 400). Such movements, in turn, demand

> increasing sophistication in conceptualizing the links between spaces of public engagement and the spaces and relations of everyday life, to trace how political subjectivities may be further transformed or sustained as they move across space ..., and to chart the time-spaces through which personal and political trajectories may unfold over time... (Davies and Dwyer, 2008: 403–4).

They point to thinking about the processes of translation, mobilization, and connection entailed in devising work in the academy in order to make claims relevant to others (Davies and Dwyer, 2008). In this sense, then, we may be refashioning a sense of academics as translators and interpreters rather than legislators or 'scientists' establishing truth claims (Bauman, 1987). And this is translation not as a background process, but translation staged as the enactment of producing qualitative research, where the very staging of making sense is seen as part of the research process, part of the research, and part of the research result (see DeLyser, and MacKian, this volume). Even so, we must remain aware of the ever-present constraints on who may 'be there' based on class, income, gender, age, ethnicity, ability, and personal responsibilities to multiple others. The old pattern of categorical inequalities continues to structure research access. Nevertheless, if we understand processes rather than objects of knowledge, that offers some beginnings to think through new theoretical challenges for qualitative research.

ONWARD, WITH OUR OWN TRADITIONS

Some recent work in qualitative geography has begun to push in broadly affective and 'more-than-representational' directions (Lorimer, 2005; Davies and Dwyer, 2007). This takes many forms, from one building on Actor Network Theory to a post-phenomenology, from geographies of practice to emotional geographies, but key tenets across this work include a skepticism about knowledge, self-knowledge, and representations – about explaining a part of the world in terms of something else, as these contemporary qualitative geographers often express a wariness of using theory to explain events, or society to explain technology, or representations to explain practices. Together, such work encompasses very different efforts by qualitative geographers to move beyond the ways social analysis can (inadvertently) solidify, stabilize, and embalm social life in order to make it an object of study and representation. And that rejection of stability proffers instead a world of multiplicities and uncertainties where clarity may not be achievable, or desirable (Law, 2004; Laurier and Philo, 2006; Davies and Dwyer, 2007). As Sarah Whatmore has put it (2003: 89–90), the spoken and written word have constituted, for qualitative geographers, the primary forms of 'data,' but the world holds many voices, speaking through many different types of things that may 'refuse to be reinvented as univocal witnesses.' Thus, recent work often shares a sense of multiple worlds in motion, worlds concerned with doings, makings, happenings, and feelings, rather than strictly images, texts, or results; and of worlds of uncertainty, '[i]mpasses, silences and aporias' rather than observable/reportable certainties (Laurier and Philo, 2006: 353).

Such efforts draw attention to a methodological conundrum: much qualitative geography has embraced an unquestioned balance between ontological constructivism and epistemological realism (Crang, 2001). In other words, we have looked carefully and critically at how people make diverse truths, but much of that work has taken a fairly straightforward (and uncritical) approach to how we, in turn, represent those truths. And that may

be especially true in making claims for our research, and indeed in following an imperative to speak truth to power.

If we have above (and, collectively, before) addressed debates on the value of and issues with epistemological realism in human geography, these new works ask us to continue pursuing that, and now also to rethink the construction of the world to include not just the agency of those we study along with that of the researcher in shaping that world, but also the agency of the material and biological worlds in our work and our world (see chapters by Wolch and Seymour, and Dewsbury in this volume). This is not to reinforce a dichotomy between the material and immaterial, but rather to encourage attention to the ephemeral, the fleeting, the immanence of things and places (Davies and Dwyer, 2007).

These works urge us to rethink, from different (and divergent) theoretical perspectives, the assumptions of humanistic geography in qualitative research – assumptions about meaning making, about knowledges, about agency, and about forms of representing the world. They further urge us to move onward in our longstanding engagements with the emotional and the embodied natures of our research encounters and again rethink 'what it means to "know" something, and thus … open social science research to different kinds of knowing evidenced through embodiment or emotionality' in ways of knowing that 'shift from comprehension to apprehension' (Davies and Dwyer, 2007: 258).

Meanwhile, some who accept the critiques and insights this new theoretical work offers ask too about its customarily formidable level of abstraction, where empirical research with others (the perhaps more traditional qualitative methods of interviewing or participant observation, for example) is most often sublimated in favor of research grounded in the writer's own carefully deconstructed experience. Arguments about solipsism once put forward in response to feminist directives for self-reflexivity in research are raised anew. And further, there is current concern that the 'pure, blank spaces of social encounter offered up as open-ended, experimental arenas for the forging of a revisionist, expressive ethics of affect' (Lorimer, 2008: 3) might erase the very embedded senses of different experiences, lives, circumstances, pressures, and possibilities at the core of so much qualitative work.

Perhaps we are working, in multiple ways, with multiple methods, to find a geographical praxis that may speak to a world always in the making. Eric Laurier and Chris Philo, for example, have offered to view what some see as the 'threat' proffered by non-representational theory to the legacy of the 'cultural turn' in geography as promise instead.

> A promise of beginning inquiries less fixated on solving or explaining problems in theory *with theory;* a promise to return to just what our wordy worlds have to offer in their shatterproof transparency, their abundant detail and their living motion. ... [To] undertake investigations that do not begin by *defining* their phenomenon, but seek instead to learn from the investigation what defining, describing, proving, caring, observing, sharing, encountering or even breakfast...might be. ... [To] re-find (to re-search) the wonder of perfectly everyday events, full of possibilities, representational and not-representational. ... [For] there is so much to learn from continuing to revisit the places that (we assume) we already know (about) (Laurier and Philo, 2006: 353, 355, 356).

Nevertheless, a call to attend to affect and emotion, as well as the spontaneous, may not be enough without guidance on what to look for or what matters – a careful methodological exploration of these new possibilities is in order (and is addressed, in different ways, by the chapters that follow). Embedded in the needs of representation and translation, after all, lie also connection and 'throwntogetherness,' (Massey, 2005) as well as possibilities to channel senses of becomings and the hope to forward emancipatory agendas. What this may suggest is research as a material practice of translation not only between conceptual worlds, but as a practical, embodied, interactive, co-constitutive process. As John Law has argued, our messy world is ordered

through analytical practices that tend to focus only on a narrow range of appropriate objects, practices that make some things apparent because we have distorted them into clarity (2004: 2). He continues:

> So it seems to me that we're balancing on a knife-edge. We want to order. In particular, we hope to tell stories about social ordering. But we don't want to do violence in our own ordering. And in particular we don't want to pretend that our ordering is complete, or conceal the work, the pain, and the blindnesses that went into it. It is an uncomfortable knife-edge. It violates most of the inclinations and dispositions that we have acquired in generations of commitment to 'the scientific method' and its social, political and personal analogues (Law, 1994: 8).

Acknowledging this analytical praxis of translation and transformation is far from the Cartesian geography of the subject, located and fixed at the center of events (who 'thinks' and 'is'). Indeed, as Law points out, 'ethnography is a product, an interactive outcome, and nothing to do with observation by neutral or disembodied intellects' (Law, 1994: 17). Instead of that stable subject there is a 'logic of continuous transfer' that means that the 'vertical, univocally oriented node that bound the subject to the world is dissolved' and thus that the notion of the singular authorial presence becomes unstable (Polizzi, 2000: 251). Perhaps this leads to Michel Serres' reimagining of thinking and authorial presence.

> Who am I then? A node of emission and reception, an open interchange, equipped with the pure possibility of a short circuit, that absorbs and redistributes, by bursts and eclipses, the continual tonality ... a structure of exchange, unthinkable without exchange .... We think then by interception, I think interception and by the random decision of intersubjectivity. Who else am I? A discontinuous virtuality of sorting, of selection in intersubjective thought (Serres in Polizzi, 2000: 251).

That sort of spatial imaginary of circulating, translating, transforming knowledge may lead us to a new methodological acknowledgment of the complex links binding an entangled local and global, near and far, present and absent, material and immaterial, I and not I in our work. Perhaps qualitative geographers, with Laurier and Philo (quoting

Michael Joyce), may 'wish to inhabit … "aporetic space,"… something grounded in encounters great and small, as "the space of doubt, scepticism, and consideration which eventually yields *possibility* …, valorisation, persistence, and meaning'" (Laurier and Philo, 2006: 360). Perhaps we might follow the film work of Trinh Minh-ha where she suggests that

> The story never stops beginning or ending. … Its (in)finitude subverts every notion of completeness and its frame remains a non-totalizable one. The differences it brings about are differences not only in structure, in the play of structures and of surfaces, but also in timbre and in silence … in the choice and mixing of utterances, the ethos, the tones, the paces, the cuts, the pauses. The story circulates like a gift; an empty gift which anybody can lay claim to by filling it to taste, yet can never truly possess. A gift built on multiplicity. One that stays inexhaustible within its own limits. Its departures and arrivals. Its quietness. (1989: 1–2).

Such a focus upon placing stories not just in context, but setting the relations of contexts in motion, may 'transform the topographical places into topological spaces that trace the ensemble of [people's] spatializing practices,' embracing 'narrative trajectories … marked by mobile, folding, and interpenetrating relations among people, nature, and the cultural matrix of which they are a part' that do not so much 'map spaces but create shifting storylines of linkages that do not crystallize into fixed form' (Odin, 1997: 602). Perhaps all of that can help too to form an enlivening spatiality with which to think through, and to forward, qualitative geographies in the twenty-first century.

ACKNOWLEDGMENTS

We wish to thank Robert Rojek at Sage for encouraging and supporting this project over its lengthy gestation period, all of the chapter authors for their insights as well as their patience, and Bethany Rogers for editorial assistance.

REFERENCES

Anderson, J. (2004) 'Talking whilst walking: a geographical archaeology of knowledge,' *Area* 36 (3): 254–61.

Bauman, Z. (1987) *Legislators and interpreters: on modernity, post-modernity, and intellectuals.* Ithaca, NY: Cornell University Press.

Bogdan, R. and Ksander, M. (1980) 'Policy data as a social process: a qualitative approach to quantitative data,' *Human Organization* 39 (4): 302–9.

Bondi, E. (2005) 'Making connections and thinking through emotions: between geography and psychotherapy,' *Transactions of the Institute of British Geographers* NS 30: 433–48.

Bondi, E. and Davidson, J. (2004) 'Spatializing affect; affecting space: an introduction,' *Gender, Place and Culture* 11 (3): 373–5.

Bondi, E. and Domosh, M. (1992) 'Other figures in other places: on feminism, postmodernism and geography,' *Environment and Planning D: Society and Space* 10 (2): 199–213.

Burawoy, M., Blum, J. A., Sheba, G., Zsuzsa, G., Thayer, M., Gowan, T., Haney, L., Klawiter, M., Lopez, S.H., Riain, S. and Thayer, M. (2000) *Global ethnography: forces, connections, and imaginations in a postmodern world.* Berkeley: University of California Press.

Cloke, P., Philo, C. and Sadler, D. (1991) *Approaching human geography: contemporary theoretical debates.* London: Guilford.

Clifford, J. (1988) *The predicament of culture: twentieth-century ethnography, literature, and art.* Cambridge, MA: Harvard University Press.

Clifford, J. and Marcus, G.E. (eds) (1986) *Writing culture: the poetics and politics of ethnography.* Berkeley: University of California Press.

Comaroff, J. and Comaroff, J. (2003) 'Ethnography on an awkward scale: postcolonial anthropology and the violence of abstraction,' *Ethnography* 4 (2): 147–80.

Cook, I. (2004) 'Follow the thing: Papaya,' *Antipode* 36 (4): 642–64.

Crang, M. (2001) 'Filed work: making sense of group interviews,' in M. Limb and C. Dwyer (eds) *Qualitative Methods for Geographers: Issues and Debates.* London: Arnold. pp. 215–33.

Crang, M. (2002) 'Qualitative methods: the new orthodoxy?,' *Progress in Human Geography* 26 (5): 647–55.

Crang, M. (2003) 'Qualitative methods: touchy, feely, look-see?,' *Progress in Human Geography* 27 (4): 494–504.

Crang, M. (2005) 'Qualitative methods: there is nothing outside the text?' *Progress in Human Geography* 29 (2): 225–33.

Crang, M. and Cook, I. (2007) *Doing ethnographies.* London: Sage.

Cresswell, T. (2004) *Place: a short introduction.* New York: Wiley Blackwell.

Davidson, J. and Milligan, C. (2004) 'Embodying emotion, sensing space: introducing emotional geographies,' *Social and Cultural Geography* 5 (4): 523–32.

Davidson, J., Bondi, E. and Smith, M. (2005) *Emotional geographies.* Aldershot: Ashgate.

Davies, G. and Dwyer, C. (2007) 'Qualitative methods: are you enchanted or are you alienated?' *Progress in Human Geography* 31 (2): 257–66.

Davies, G. and Dwyer, C. (2008) 'Qualitative methods II: minding the gap,' *Progress in Human Geography* 32 (3): 399–406.

DeLyser, D. (2008) 'Teaching qualitative geography,' *Journal of Geography in Higher Education* 32 (2): 233–44.

Denzin, N. and Lincoln, Y. (eds) (2005a) 'Preface,' in *The handbook of qualitative research.* London: Sage. pp. ix–xix.

Denzin, N. and Lincoln, Y. (eds) (2005b) 'Introduction: the discipline and practice of qualitative research' in *The handbook of qualitative research.* London: Sage. pp. 1–33.

Dwyer, C. and Limb, M. (2001) 'Introduction: doing qualitative research in geography,' in M. Limb and C. Dwyer (eds), *Qualitative methodologies for geographers: issues and debates.* London: Arnold. pp. 1–20.

Elwood, S. and Martin, D. (2000) '"Placing" Interviews: location and scales of power in qualitative research,' *Professional Geographer* 52 (4): 649–57.

Fotheringham, S.A. (2006) 'Quantification, evidence and positivism,' in S. Aitken and G. Valentine (eds) *Approaches in human geography: philosophies, people and practices.* London and Thousand Oaks: Sage Publications. pp. 237–50.

Fuller, D. and Kitchin, R. (2004) 'Radical theory/critical praxis: academic geography beyond the academy?,' in D. Fuller and R. Kitchin (eds) *Radical theory and critical praxis: making a difference beyond the academy?* Vernon and Victoria, BC: Praxis (e)Press. pp. 1–20.

Geertz, C. (1988) *Works and Lives: the anthropologist as author.* Stanford, CA: Stanford University Press.

Gieryn, T.F. (2006) 'City as truth-spot: laboratories and field-sites in urban studies,' *Social Studies of Science* 36 (1): 5–38.

Hannerz, U. (2003) 'Being there ... and there ... and there! Reflections on multi-site ethnography,' *Ethnography* 4 (2): 201–16.

Harding, S. (2001) 'Comments on Walby's "Against epistemological chasms": the science question in science revisited,' *Signs* 26 (2): 541–5.

Haraway, D.J. (1991) 'The science question in feminism and the privilege of partial perspectives,' in D.J. Haraway (ed.) *Simians, cyborgs and women: the reinvention of nature.* London: Free Association Books. pp. 183–201.

Herbert, S. (2000) 'For ethnography,' *Progress in Human Geography* 24 (4): 550–68.

Hyndman, J. (2001) 'The field as here and now, not there and then,' *Geographical Review* 91 (1 and 2): 262–72.

Johnston, R.J. and Sidaway, J.D. (2004) *Geography and Geographers: Anglo-American human geography since 1945.* 6th edition. London: Hodder Arnold.

Jones, J.P. III, Nast, H. and Roberts, S. (eds) (1997) *Thresholds in feminist geography: difference, methodology, representation.* Lanham, MD: Rowman and Littlefield.

Katz, C. (2004) *Growing up global: economic restructuring and children's everyday lives.* Minneapolis: University of Minnesota Press.

Kusenbach, M. (2003) 'Street phenomenology: the go-along as ethnographic research tool,' *Ethnography* 4 (3): 455–85.

Laurier, E. and Philo, C. (2006) 'Possible geographies: a passing encounter in a café,' *Area* 38 (4): 353–63.

Law, J. (1994) *Organizing modernity.* Oxford: Blackwell.

Law, J. (2004) *After method: mess in social science research.* London: Routledge.

Ley, D. (1988) 'Interpretive social research in the inner city,' in J. Eyles (ed.), *Research in human geography.* Oxford: Blackwell. pp. 121–38.

Lorimer, H. (2005) 'Cultural geography: the busyness of being "more-than-representational",' *Progress in Human Geography* 29 (1): 83–94.

Lorimer, H. (2008) 'Cultural geography: nonrepresentational conditions and concerns,' *Progress in Human Geography* 32 (4): 551–9.

Livingstone, D. (1993) *The geographical tradition: episodes in the history of a contested enterprise.* London: Wiley Blackwell.

Marcus, G. (2005) 'The anthropologist as witness in contemporary regimes of intervention,' *Cultural politics: An International Journal* 1 (1): 31–50.

Marcus, G. (1998) *Ethnography through thick and thin.* Princeton, NJ: Princeton University Press.

Marcus, G. and Fischer, M. (1986) *Anthropology as cultural critique.* Chicago: University of Chicago Press.

Marston, S. (2000) 'The social construction of scale,' *Progress in Human Geography* 24 (2): 219–42.

Marston, S., Jones, J. P. III and Woodward, K. (2005) 'Human geography without scale,' *Transactions of the Institute of British Geographers* 30 (4): 416–23.

Martin, R. (2001) 'Geography and public policy: the case of the missing agenda,' *Progress in Human Geography* 25 (2): 189–210.

Massey, D. (1993) 'Power geometry and a progressive sense of place,' in J. Bird, B. Curtis, T. Putnam, G. Robertson and L. Tickner (eds) *Mapping the futures: local cultures, global change.* London and New York: Routledge. pp. 59–69.

Massey, D. (2003) 'Imagining the field,' in M. Pryke, G. Rose and S. Whatmore (eds) *Using social theory: thinking through research.* London: Sage. pp. 71–88.

Massey, D. (2005) *For space.* London: Sage Publications.

McCormack, D. (2003) 'An event of geographical ethics in spaces of affect,' *Transactions of the Institute of British Geographers* 28 (4): 488–507.

McDowell, L. (1995) 'Understanding diversity: the problem of/for theory,' in R. Johnston, P. Taylor and M. Watts (eds) *Geographies of global change.* London: Blackwell. pp. 280–94.

McDowell, L. (2001) 'Working with young men,' *Geographical review* 91 (1 and 2): 201–14.

Odin, J.K. (1997) 'The edge of difference: negotiations between the hypertextual and the postcolonial,' *Modern Fiction Studies* 43 (3): 598–630.

Openshaw, S. (1998) 'Towards a more computationally minded scientific human geography,' *Environment and Planning A: Environment and Planning* 30 (2): 317–32.

Pain, R. (2006) 'Social geography: seven deadly myths in policy research,' *Progress in Human Geography* 30 (2): 250–9.

Polizzi, G. (2000) 'Hermeticism, messages, and angels,' *Configurations* 8 (2): 245–69.

Rosaldo, R. (1989) *Culture and truth: the remaking of social analysis.* Boston: Beacon.

Sayer, A. and Morgan, K. (1986) 'A modern industry in a declining region: links between method, theory and policy,' in D. Massey and R. Meegan (eds), *Politics and method: contrasting studies in industrial geography.* London: Routledge, Keegan and Paul. pp. 147–68.

Sin, C.H. (2003) 'Interviewing in "place": the socio-spatial construction of interview data,' *Area* 35 (3): 305–12.

Smith, L.T. (1999) *Decolonizing methodologies: research and indigenous peoples.* Dunedin, New Zealand: University of Otago Press.

Thien, D. (2005) 'After or beyond feeling?: a consideration of affect and emotion in geography,' *Area* 37 (4): 450–56.

Thrift, N. (2004) 'Intensities of feeling: towards a spatial politics of affect,' *Geographiska Annaler Series B* 86: 57–78.

Thrift, N. (2007) *Non-Representational theory: space, politics, affect.* London: Sage.

Trinh, T.M. (1989) *Woman, native, other: writing postcoloniality and feminism.* Bloomington: Indiana University Press.

Turner, V. and Bruner, E. (eds) (1988) *The anthropology of experience.* Urbana, IL: University of Illinois Press.

Valentine, G. (1999) 'Doing household research: interviewing couples together and apart,' *Area* 31 (1): 67–74.

Whatmore, S. (2003) 'Generating materials,' in M. Pryke, G. Rose and S. Whatmore (eds), *Using social theory.* London: Sage. pp. 89–104.

PART I
Openings

Openings: Introduction

Dydia DeLyser

Nobody, of course, is born knowing how to conceptualize research and plan for its eventualities. Still, too often when we do begin to plan our own research, a focus on a research 'topic' overrides attention to methods and methodology. But the methodologically articulate qualitative research of the twenty-first century demands care, caution, and attention to issues of why and how we carry out our research the way we do, not just what we do it 'on.' My own case in undertaking PhD research was one of methodological kismet, for when I began my career as a graduate student in the early 1990s I still had no idea that there was such a thing as 'research design,' and I couldn't distinguish between methods and methodologies. The Chair of my department advised me to take a qualitative-research course in another department (the geography department did not offer one in those days) – it was a course I didn't know I 'needed' at the time. When, later that semester, a research topic emerged, I drafted a proposal – based on participant observation, interviewing, and archival research – with what felt like great certainty. In fact though, I had scant idea of how to prepare myself for the project, or what conducting the research would entail. That would take more courses in qualitative research, more reading, more thinking, and more practice.

I followed up on all of those, and, over the course of several seasons of participant observation, interviewing, and archival research I engaged in a study of a popular California ghost town, a place where I also lived and worked each summer. And, though I was already very familiar with the place and its history as well as with the tourists and the staff before I began doing 'research' there, my training in qualitative methods and methodologies prepared me, not just for how to study that place, but also for some of the very different challenges that becoming 'the ethnographer' of that place demanded. I learned (among other things) to scrutinize my own role in the community – to understand how my own subjectivity played a role in interpreting the town's past for the thousands of tourists I spoke to each year. I learned to take seriously (as part of my research as well as part of my life) the changing-but-ongoing relationships I had with other staff members, people who were co-workers but also 'informants.' I learned to be thoughtful about how to ask questions, and careful about how to understand answers. I learned to link empirical observations to theoretical insights, to draw broader conclusions from what I was observing and of course much more besides (DeLyser, 1998; DeLyser, 2001). In short, I learned to take research design, to take methods and methodology, seriously. For it is research design that can first link theory with methods (or strategies of inquiry), and it is careful research design that helps situate the researcher within her or his field as well as in the empirical world (Denzin and Lincoln, 2005a). These are the engagements of the chapters in this section.

For scholars both seasoned and novice, starting out on research can be an exciting, challenging, and even daunting task. One involving planning and conceptualizing the research itself, expanding one's theoretical and methodological horizons, situating the research within the researched community as well as the broader world, and attempting to come to terms with, and to carefully craft, one's own place within the research. The aim of this section of the handbook is to introduce the concepts and ideas that must ground such beginnings for qualitative geographers. Before moving on to a consideration of different qualitative methods in the next section, these five chapters address issues foundational to any study. Each chapter is concerned in its own way with the historical, socio-spatial, personal, and political groundings of qualitative research in human geography – with the way that our work is conceptualized and then situated in the world.

Together the authors of these chapters detail the ways that qualitative researchers address the foundations and the soundness of our research. Unlike the tests of rigor and validity familiar from quantitative approaches, because qualitative geographers often interact directly and significantly with the people they study, qualitative research is done through the embodied qualitative researcher who must come to terms with her or his own situatedness, as well as the partiality of the research itself. Indeed, the authors in this section all reach beyond the once-vaunted notions of objectivity and impartiality to genuine engagements with people and communities as well as the self.

Today, most qualitative researchers understand that the world we study is, to a large degree, socially constructed. Grounded, nevertheless, in the very real realities of – and

between – liberation and oppression, inclusion and exclusion, embrace and loss, along with everything else that makes up the world we share, qualitative researchers understand that different people experience those realities and our world differently, and, as Steve Herbert's chapter points out, aim our research at gaining in-depth understandings of those experiences. We seek, Herbert makes clear, to shed light, in different ways, on how people make sense of the world as they perceive it, even while we acknowledge our own immersion in that world. These ontological and epistemological understandings ground qualitative geography, and indeed qualitative research in a wide array of different fields (see Denzin and Lincoln, 2005b). The authors of the chapters in this section raise, explain, and complicate those understandings.

As Sarah Elwood makes clear, such an understanding is critical: if we are to do research well, we cannot merely mix-and-match methods, methodologies, epistemologies, and ontologies. We must instead proceed from a grounding in the linkages between methodology, ontology, and epistemology, to recognize the extent to which particular ontologies and epistemologies may favor particular methods, even though they do not completely determine one another. As Elwood points out, most often quantitative-based work proceeds from an ontological understanding that reality can be accurately measured, represented, and modeled by research, whereas qualitative researchers believe that research – and the researcher – in part shape the world we study, and thus that our representations are fundamentally partial. In other words, while for quantitative geographers research represents reality, for qualitative geographers research (in part) constitutes that reality, and must be constructed to acknowledge and work from that understanding.

In geography, as Meghan Cope's chapter details, our awareness of these issues and the kind of methodological acuity that their attention demands is a relatively new development, even though doing qualitative research is not. Indeed, though some may think of qualitative research in geography as a recent endeavor (a response, perhaps, to the quantitative revolution that began in the 1950s), Cope demonstrates not only the oldness of qualitative research in human geography, but also its long-standing foundational importance to geographic inquiry. Qualitative methods, she points out, have *always* been a part of human geography – ancient Romans, colonial-era explorers, and traditional twentieth century human geographers all relied on qualitative methods. And since their legacy – our history – includes the darkness of exploitation along with the glimmer of new, even liberatory, research, those who today undertake qualitative research in human geography will be well served to understand that history.

And further, though many have viewed the quantitative revolution as an assault on qualitative research in human geography, Cope instead details how such a challenge energized qualitative researchers, leading to the methodologically articulate 'explicitly qualitative' research of today (DeLyser, 2008: 235). Cope thus reads the quantitative revolution not as a deterrent, but rather as a stimulus to today's explicitly qualitative geography, one that compelled a rigorous attention to methods, reflexive understanding of how those methods were implemented, and self-critical understanding of the roles of the researcher in the research. The perspectives of feminist scholars and feminist geographers across different subfields, Cope argues, led this charge forward from the quantitative revolution, with many practitioners waging hard-fought personal battles to remake 'theory and practice in part by paying attention to methods.'

Of course research in most quarters of contemporary human geography is no longer about battling for or against the quantitative revolution, but rather about constructing research that is methodologically appropriate for the circumstances, the communities involved, and the research questions. Indeed, Elwood, in her chapter, suggests we move

beyond the qualitative–quantitative divide and advocates for 'local epistemologies' that recognize that any research question can (and should) potentially be approached from different conceptual frameworks and yet yield (different though) robust, valid, and appropriate insights. With this in mind, she advocates for methods based on their potential to foster socially and politically progressive outcomes.

Also looking to foster progressive outcomes, Kari Jensen and Amy Glasmeier describe and advocate for policy-centric research that is socially situated, and action-oriented. Their work, like Elwood's, methodologically diverse and tailored to each research circumstance and research question, proceeds as a means of insightful research engagement geared to inform audiences both public and academic, in work that is problem-driven, action-oriented, and applied.

To Jensen and Glasmeier, it is their situatedness that distinguishes them as action-oriented academics – a situatedness that has led them beyond the once-lauded positivist goals of objectivity and impartiality, to a rich engagement with the communities they work with. As Stuart Aitken in his chapter makes clear, this situatedness must be linked to a personal politics of research encounters, and can be understood through the productive spatialities such encounters can engender. The researcher, he points out, must cross multiple axes of difference in order to *learn with* others. Understanding those not only as axes of difference but also vectors of connectedness, Aitken's chapter seeks to shed light on the politics of difference and cultural distinctiveness and move beyond the politics of representation. If past attempts, Aitken argues, have often been about taming space, qualitative geographers now must go beyond that. We must, he rallies, embrace our encounters of diversity in the context of places, expand our horizons to the myriad forms of dislocation and surprise that our 'thrown-togetherness' (Massey, 2005) creates, and open our research to an affective politics of difference.

That is important, Cope and Aitken make clear, because qualitative research in geography has long been wrapped up in our problematic encounters with the Other as well as often flawed understandings of ourselves. Just as Cope details a history of qualitative geography, Aitken presents a history of scholarly encounters with the Other, from the 'exotic other' as research 'object' of colonialism and imperialism, to the traditional cross-cultural research that produced empirical 'results' amid an apparent vacuum of interpersonal relations between researcher and researched, through the crisis of representation with its focus on reflexivity and the politics of representation, to contemporary engagements in activist, post-colonial, and border methodologies where research concerns do not emanate solely from the researcher, and non-representational methodologies that draw in affect and emotions.

Clearly, much of qualitative research is grounded in relationships – relationships that take time and, as Aitken argues, responsibility and care to nurture. Since qualitative researchers must vest so much of their time and energy in building connections in the field, and since qualitative-research methods like participant observation and interviewing are in themselves highly time consuming, qualitative researchers, as Herbert's chapter points out, often select but one case study on which to found their research. This kind of richly engaged, solidly grounded qualitative research has the potential to yield significant insights into the peoples, places, interactions, and meanings that are constructed in and through the site of the case study. But, Herbert points out, empirical richness (and care in building and maintaining relationships) is only part of good qualitative research. Qualitative geographers, in seeking to contribute to scholarship in our field, must also reach beyond our particular case studies to engage theoretical ideas that enable our empirical research to speak to scholars working in other settings. Researchers who are simultaneously drawn to deep immersion in a local context *and* to a more abstracted analysis face significant challenges as we strive for a grounded and locally relevant yet also more theoretically engaged view that can move beyond the strict specifics of locality. Herbert urges qualitative geographers to embrace both the difficulty of this challenge and the advantages of working with it in our efforts to link fine-grained case studies to broader theoretical and policy concerns as we pursue and forward engaged qualitative geography.

Thus, though starting out qualitative research, and carrying it through in a caring and responsible manner will never be easy, the authors of the chapters in this section seek to (together and apart) situate geographers within our history of qualitative research and encounters with the other and ourselves; to acknowledge our methodological, philosophical, and theoretical groundings; and to heed our policy- and community-oriented obligations. Together they signal the broad recognition of explicitly qualitative research in human geography, and the responsibility that engaged qualitative research demands.

REFERENCES

DeLyser, D. (1998) '"Good, by God, we're going to Bodie!": landscape and social memory in a California ghost town,' Unpublished PhD Dissertation, Department of Geography, Syracuse University.

DeLyser, D. (2001) '"Do you really live here?" thoughts on insider research,' *Geographical Review* 91 (1 and 2): 441–53.

DeLyser, D. (2008) 'Teaching qualitative geography,' *Journal of Geography in Higher Education* 32 (2): 233–44.

Denzin, N. and Lincoln, Y.S. (2005a) 'Introduction: the discipline and practice of qualitative research,' in N. Denzin and Y.S. Lincoln (eds) *Handbook of qualitative research.* London: Sage. pp. 1–32.

Denzin, N. and Lincoln, Y.S. (eds) (2005b) *Handbook of qualitative research.* London: Sage.

Massey, D. (2005) *For space.* London: Sage.

2

A History of Qualitative Research in Geography[1]

Meghan Cope

In one sense the documented history of qualitative research in geography starts in 1988, with the publication of John Eyles' and David M. Smith's *Qualitative Methods in Human Geography*, the first book to *explicitly* focus solely on this topic. Indeed, the past twenty years (and especially the past ten) have been remarkably productive, with geographers generating more qualitative work and more discussion of qualitative methods than ever before and doing so in increasingly critical, reflexive ways. The rich variety of qualitative geography produced in the past two decades both inspired this volume and is represented here; however, it does not sufficiently constitute a broader history of qualitative research in geography. In fact, qualitative research cannot be separated from the history of geography at any point: as long as there have been attempts to 'write the world' (*geo-graphy*), there have been qualitative methods of observation, synthesis, analysis, and representation.

There are two key differences between the contemporary era of qualitative geography and that which came before it. First, geographers of the past did not *call* their research

'qualitative' (or 'quantitative' for that matter) – it was constituted by more or less systematic observations and theories of places and people with certain techniques used, but little reflection on methodology. What we have seen in the contemporary period is a transformation toward being more explicit about methods, a shift that has been largely sparked by reactions against the quantitative revolution of the 1950s and 1960s. Second, prior to the 1980s, even in those instances where geographers did explicitly discuss their methods, they usually did so in quite uncritical ways. This is not to say that researchers did not ever acknowledge weaknesses of their models or explain why they chose one technique over another – many did – but justifying the use of one set of region-defining criteria over another is fundamentally different from rigorously critiquing the influence of one's own presence on the flow of conversation in a focus group. This second transformation can be traced to emerging understandings of the power of epistemology, critical feminist perspectives on the research process and products, and the 'cultural turn' in geography, which turned a newly critical eye toward all stages of research from formulating the questions to data production,[2] from one's own position along social axes of difference to the problematic representation of other's views.

These two shifts – toward being explicit and being critically reflexive about qualitative research – form a backdrop for this chapter. I begin by reviewing ways of reading past geographies as qualitative, engaging with two historical periods: exploration and the 'old' regional geography. I then shift gears and identify four common characteristics of contemporary qualitative geography that have deep roots: the triangulation of data and methods; the collaborative production of knowledge through engagement with the 'other'; accounting for both context and human agency in the production of place; and reflexive consideration of power, the personal, and the political. I use these four characteristics as a way to excavate a small selection of past geographic practices and pull out their links to current work.

In some ways, constructing a history of qualitative research in geography is not much different from other qualitative research projects: begin with a general research question ('How have geographers engaged in qualitative research?'), observe the field (read lots of texts), consider my own interests and existing knowledge of the issue (acknowledge my own positioning, such as an interest in urban social geography and training in Anglo-American doctrine, while simultaneously trying to keep a broader perspective), produce data (identify trends and themes, in this case shamelessly cherry-picking the juicier quotes), pay attention to the process (reflect on how different materials have entered – or been left out of – the scope of what I am representing here), attempt to synthesize the material into something grounded but compelling that allows us greater understanding of the world. Thus, this chapter itself simultaneously represents a qualitative research endeavor through its methodology and shares an interpretation of the results.

HISTORICAL CONTEXT: FORCES OF PRODUCTION OF GEOGRAPHIC KNOWLEDGE

Two strong themes run through the history of geography that deserve special attention here for their influence on both the content and the methods of geography: exploration and a concern for regions. I call these the forces of production of geographic knowledge because they both formed the basis of much of the discipline's canon and from the beginning posed unique methodological problems that needed to be solved by practitioners. The other reason I call out these themes is that their legacies have been revisited many times in various ways, such that they are always still informing our understanding of geography and the world. For example, there have been many new examinations of old texts and personalities that use contemporary critical lenses to view the past and that re-shape our current understandings of geographic disciplinary history (see for example, Livingstone, 1993; Godlewska and Smith, 1994; Godlewska, 1999a, b; Livingstone and Withers, 1999, 2005; Driver, 2001; Martin, 2005). These works are perhaps most helpful in reminding us that we should not be surprised that geography has meant different things in different contexts (times, places, intellectual climates); nor should we be surprised that geography has always employed both qualitative and quantitative methods of research, looked at both the particular and the general, and engaged with multiple scales of social and natural processes. Finally, reviews of exploration and accounts of regions remind us that in various ways there have long been tensions between, on one hand, the search for an objective 'truth' (or fundamental ordering processes of various sorts) and, on the other hand, the quest to understand subjective experiences of the world.

We are currently, of course, still grappling with these very issues.

Early geographies: Exploration and human–environment relations

The history of 'writing the world' necessitates a critical look at the two 'Cs' that underlie geography in its infancy: colonialism and capitalism. The two went hand-in-hand as powerful European states of the fifteenth century and beyond began to systematize their methods of production, consumption, and exploitation, creating new demands for goods and labor and simultaneously meeting these demands by developing new supplies (furs, sugar, cotton, human slaves, etc.) from around the globe. While the growth of geography depended on these two dubious parents (not to mention the extended family of patriarchy, racism, and so on), this background is important for understanding our present disciplinary knowledge, methodology, and practice.

In their review of historical practices of sociology and anthropology, Norman Denzin and Yvonna Lincoln (2005: 2) note:

> The agenda was clear-cut: The observer went to a foreign setting to study the culture, customs, and habits of another human group. Often this was a group that stood in the way of white settlers. Ethnographic reports of these groups were incorporated into colonizing strategies, ways of controlling the foreign, deviant, or troublesome Other.

Not to be outdone by those disciplines, geography's collusion with colonialism is vetted by David Livingstone (1993: 170) 'There is something to be said for the claim that geography was the science of imperialism *par excellence*. Exploration, topographic and social survey, cartographic representation, and regional inventory – the craft practices of the emerging geographical professional – were entirely suited to the colonial project.'

Indeed, there was nothing like mercantile capitalism to stimulate the production of geographic knowledge (and vice versa). After all, investors and merchants held enormous stakes in a core principle of geography: areal differentiation. They had to know where certain things existed in natural abundance (such as beaver pelts) or could be produced in large quantities (such as tea leaves) in order to transform them into commodities and bring them to European markets. Early explorers might have caught the travel bug independently, but they had to find sponsors for their excursions and who better than kings, queens, wealthy landowners, and the up-and-coming bourgeoisie? So while Europe explored the world for profit and domination, geographic knowledge was produced through Europeans' eyes. That which caught the attention of Alexander von Humboldt or other geographic explorers was that which was different from Europe, and hence began a fascination with 'the other'. At the same time, the emergence of the age of reason and the core values of the Enlightenment, such as the notion that educated people (not just clerics or mystics) could understand the world rationally through scientific discovery, fostered a supportive underlying epistemology. Of course, we now recognize that the 'other' could only be constructed vis-à-vis the 'self' (and the reverse is true too); that is, people, places, and practices that are strange and different titillate the senses because of their departure from our own familiar surroundings, cultures, and interactions, but encounters with them simultaneously construct our selves in particular ways.

This is an important insight – that which was familiar and normal to European explorers became the standard against which everything else on the globe was compared, judged, and evaluated. And how did the explorer-conquerors do research? They observed; they asked questions; they tasted, smelled, heard, and felt different places; they took notes and wrote diaries and drew maps and brought 'specimens' back to the folks at home. In sum, they produced qualitative and quantitative data about what they experienced, synthesized these data with their existing knowledge, and produced representations that were heavily and unabashedly skewed by their own perspectives. In a sense, they laid the groundwork for geographic study of a sort that would shape the production of geographic knowledge for centuries and go largely unchallenged until the late twentieth century, when the 'cultural turn', critical perspectives such as Marxism and humanism, and – perhaps most significantly – feminism, tackled the process and products of imperialist, capitalist, and masculinist geography (a project that is by no means complete). These recent shifts have greatly enhanced the rigor, diversity, and critical reflexivity of the discipline and the way it is practiced, as evidenced in this volume.

In the late nineteenth century the temporal overlap of the still-powerful British Empire and rapidly-rising American industrial hegemony fostered great leaps in innovation and scientific understanding, both through sponsorship of research and demand for new technologies and science. In geography, lively intellectual communities in Britain, France, Germany, and increasingly in the US, meant that the discipline was not only integral to the explorations and categorizations of regions, but also was central to theorizing and debating over what phenomena were being discovered and what knowledge was being produced. The word 'methods' frequently appears in contemporary geographic work, such as Halford Mackinder's *On the Scope and Methods of Geography* (1887 [1996]), but its meaning tended toward broad statements of what one should pay attention to, such as political boundaries or which landscape morphologies were conducive to agricultural production. The specific techniques of investigation were limited by available data, tools of the times, direct observations, and social and cultural lenses colored by imperial forces.

Late nineteenth and early twentieth centuries attractions of scientific reasoning and logical explanations created a climate in which all aspects of humanity and nature were held up for scrutiny and scholarly

debates raged over issues whose currency still resonates: the boundaries between nature and society, causal processes of areal differentiation, and the mutual conditioning of culture and environment. Overall, then, the age of exploration and scientific discovery facilitated and enabled the production of geographic knowledge, and some of that production of knowledge would be deemed 'qualitative' in today's terms.

Early geographies: Regional approaches

The concept of 'the region' has a long-standing position in emerging geographies over the centuries, but in the late nineteenth and early twentieth centuries, the task of regional descriptions became the distinct purview of geography, with various players focusing on different strategies. For example, in the 1930s Richard Hartshorne (quoted in Johnston, 1987: 39) defined geography as:

> a science that interprets the realities of areal differentiation of the world as they are found, not only in terms of the differences in certain things from place to place, but also in terms of the total combination of phenomena in each place, different from those at every other place.

Some scholars worked to identify the core commonalities that would allow a region to be classified as a region (such as Mackinder), while others took a more systematic approach to define categories of regions across the globe (e.g. A. J. Herbertson's attempt to use climate categories to define the earth's regions), the two approaches often intersecting (for a review, see Cloke *et al.*, 1991). Theoretical frameworks underlying regional geographies attempted to identify more thoroughly the interaction of humans and the environment, whether through the environmental determinism of Ellen Churchill Semple and Ellsworth Huntington, the search for commonalities defining a region, or the anti-determinist work of Paul Vidal de la Blache and Carl Sauer, who explicitly sought to document the active roles of human agents in the formation of regions and landscapes (see Livingstone, 1993, for a lively review of various characters, debates, and disagreements that shaped the different trajectories of 'regional' geography).

But what of methods? The primary methodology of 'old' regional geography could perhaps be summed up by the term 'cataloguing'. Counting and qualifying the instances of phenomena, whether they were characteristics of slope and elevation or agricultural practices, and linking them to the locations in which they were found was followed by descriptive narratives to elaborate on the uniqueness and similarities of different locations; overall this constituted the process of constructing a 'scientifically' discerned region. The differing philosophical underpinnings between (say) Huntington and Vidal de la Blache – specifically in terms of the direction of cause and effect – shifted the cataloguing method somewhat, depending on whether the conceptual goal was to document the (putative) impact of climate on residents' industriousness (à la Huntington) or to illustrate the intersection of human action and *genres de vie* (ways of life) with the environment to create unique *pays* (the Vidalian approach). Overall, however, through our current lens of the early twenty-first century, cataloguing and description seemed to employ a mixed bag of what we would now call qualitative and quantitative methods, using field observations of people and places, historical climate records, population censuses, production records (e.g. farm outputs), and talking with residents directly. While in many ways 'old regional geography' and its tendency toward uncritical, atheoretical description are derisively held up as a dark chapter in our past, methodologically these scholars often used mixed methods in ways that we are more recently re-discovering (see, for example, Godlewska's (1999a) account of Humboldt's integrative methods and visual representations).

HISTORICAL GEOGRAPHIES AS A SOURCE FOR 'A HISTORY OF QUALITATIVE RESEARCH'

The above section identified two primary forces in the production of geographic knowledge – exploration and the concept of the region – which serve to frame this chapter. However, rather than trudging through the timeline of geography evaluating each period on its methodological character, revealed by exhaustive references to geographers of the past, I instead develop a set of common themes and practices of contemporary qualitative geography and use them to explore earlier geographies, providing pointers to further resources for those who are interested in the details. In this way, instead of a sequential narrative, I am aiming to produce more of a historical unfolding based on thematic examination of the roots of qualitative geography using particular examples as illustrations of historical practices. I start, however, by considering one of the risks of such an undertaking.

Risks and caveats

Robert Mayhew (2001) notes that in the mid- and late-twentieth century it became popular to revisit past geographic work through more contemporary philosophical or theoretical lenses, searching for some ancient bases of the theory *du jour*, while simultaneously critiquing past geographers for their short-sightedness (except for those few whose ideas are similar to the preferred theory and are consequently held up with great regard). So, for example, those searching for a rigorous 'scientific' basis for geography in its deep past would valorize those historical icons who attempted to create systematic analyses for the purpose of identifying universal laws, and then use these analyses as proof that a strong 'scientific' core of geography is long-standing and thus central to the discipline. They might even call this geography's 'essence'. However, Mayhew puts forth a considerable critique when he suggests that these exercises commit a serious error – an error that critical scholars might recognize as essentialism. Mayhew suggests:

> Essentialist histories of geography, then, have too simplistic a conception of historical identity, wherein what is presently definitive of geography is seen as always having held that role ... By their refusal to recognize that the scope and purpose of geography change over time rather than residing in an essence, historians of geography were forced to look for geographers who would fit an anachronistic conception of geography as an independent discipline, and were therefore obliged to look to writers who did not adhere to the dominant contemporary definition and generic conventions of geography. (2001: 394)

More recently, Mayhew says, historians of geography during the 1990s and into the new millennium have shifted toward re-visioning past geographies through critical social-science lenses such as Marxism, feminism, post-colonialism, etc. in the effort to reveal past world-views as symptomatic of the partiality of knowledge and the influence of power. Along the way, such re-visions sometimes skewer the discipline or its founding figures for the myriad ways they served capitalism, patriarchy, colonialism, and other processes of modernity, rationalism, or 'science', but often, singular personages have stood out as exceptions and are thus worthy of acclaim. Thus, Mayhew concludes, 'just as an earlier generation constructed histories of geography to prove the scientific respectability of the discipline, so contemporary historians of geography seek to prove the discipline's social-scientific respectability' (2001: 398).

Mayhew's critique is a concern for this chapter. I am looking through a particular lens – qualitative research – at historical performances and products of geography that were constructed in different times and places, and thus run the risk of imposing contemporary standards on former practices. Further, I could also be guilty of creating a

teleological position for qualitative research. That is, by attempting to call out the methods of earlier geographic practices, I risk over-reading qualitative elements in these geographies in my search for strong roots, thereby setting up a false sense of methodological inevitability. Taking Mayhew's cautions to heart, I endeavor here to illustrate the diversity of methods of data production, analysis, and representation used in past geographies, not to judge them by current standards but rather to identify some of the paths that have led to our present realm of qualitative geographic practices.

This strategy will also, I hope, avoid some of the problems that arise from taking a broad-brush 'paradigm shift' approach to disciplinary methodological histories (cp. Winchester, 2005). Geographic knowledge production has not proceeded along neat, sequential, distinct, or uniform paths, either conceptually or methodologically. We certainly see a wide variety of methodological and conceptual practices in geography today, so to inscribe any era with a singular characteristic serves to mask the diverse realities. For instance, in the late nineteenth and early twentieth centuries while some geographers were busy 'proving' that certain climate conditions resulted in 'inferior' human races, others were highly critical of such endeavors (e.g. Franz Boas); while some geographers were elevating regional description to the highest pedestal, others were engaged in what we might now call participatory research and critical pedagogy for social empowerment, such as Patrick Geddes' drive to teach people about their cities for the purpose of 'social awakening and betterment' (quoted in Livingstone, 1993: 279). That is, given the scholarly discord and disagreement of *any* given period (see Driver, 2001; Livingstone, 1993 for detailed reviews), the notion of paradigms as emerging, dominating, and then being challenged within a given field is perhaps too simplistic for the actual messiness, the 'co-existing heterogeneity' (Massey, 2005), of real-life scholarship and knowledge production.

Keeping Mayhew's cautions in mind, then, and staying away from rigidly linear 'paradigm' accounts, I consider a series of common principles and practices of qualitative research in geography for which we can see some traces in early geography. In the following explorations I attempt to base my reasoning on fairly broad interpretations of research practices, which form the groundwork for examining the differences and continuities between 'then' and 'now'.

Broadly speaking, there are many characteristics of contemporary qualitative geographic research that have long-standing relevance in the discipline. Here, I identify and elaborate upon four of these characteristics as examples, which then serve as entry points to a targeted survey of past qualitative geographic practices. The first of these involves the *triangulation of data and methods*; that is, the purposeful and integrated use of diverse sources of data that are produced through a variety of available research techniques and equipment. The principle of triangulation suggests that errors will be minimized by drawing from diverse sources and types of data, though in practice they may also produce divergent results or contradictions that can be equally interesting to pursue. Ideally, producing data through multiple sources is followed by employing analytical methods that integrate diverse data into a comprehensible narrative with some explanatory power toward a well-grounded production of knowledge (for examples, see Kesby *et al.*, 2005; Elwood, 2006).

The second common characteristic of qualitative work is the social production of knowledge through engagement with the 'Other'. The rules of engagement have clearly shifted toward critical reflexivity in recent years; for instance, there is an increased understanding that even the very process of research serves to (re)construct the Other vis-à-vis the Self, and concerns for how (or even whether) to represent Others' viewpoints are frequently raised in the disclosures section of methodology statements (for examples, see Mohammad, 2001; Nairn, 2005). Using

current terminology, then, we can say that paying attention to and respecting diverse subjectivities and multiple truths in the form of local knowledges also has a long tradition in geographic research, however non-reflexive that attention may have been.

The third characteristic I explore here is that of *integrating context and causality*. 'Context' is taken to mean the powerful forces of the broader economic, political, cultural, social, and physical processes that influence places and people. 'Causality' here refers to a way of seeing the world through the effects of human agency, relations, connections, networks, and experiences. The distinctive intersections (in time and space) of these processes require the recognition of people as knowledgeable social agents in shaping their own identities, power, meanings, and places. Today these concerns are connected to questions of the uniqueness of places while simultaneously attending to, on one hand, the diverse experiences of that place, and, on the other hand, the multitude of connections and commonalities between places (Dyck, 2005; Massey, 2005).

The fourth, and final, characteristic I engage with in some ways saturates all the others; it is the understanding that power relations shape not only every aspect of doing our research, but also everything we study, from 'the personal' to 'the political'. The influence of feminist perspectives on geographic practice and methods in the past 20 years thus serves as a way to bring this history of qualitative research into the present.

This is by no means a comprehensive list of the central principles of contemporary qualitative geography (for alternate approaches see Crang, 2002, 2003; Davies and Dwyer, 2007), but it is enough to serve as a small opening through which to examine historical practices. I employ these four characteristics here to provide examples of how this thematic approach can shed new light on older geographies, specifically four key 'moments' in geographic history: the ancient geographies, the age of exploration and colonialism, the cultural geographies of the

Berkeley School, and the influence of feminist (and other critical) approaches.

The triangulation of data and methods

As I have suggested, geographers today are increasingly *explicit* in their use of multiple-methods (qualitative, quantitative, cartographic) as a way to weave together data from multiple sources and engage in rigorous, integrative, context-sensitive analysis (Clifford and Valentine, 2003). However, it is clear that there is nothing particularly new about this approach, except perhaps the naming and explicit reflexivity of multi-methods research in this regard. That is, using multiple methods to collect and interpret data has a long tradition in geography, but the 'methods wars' of the late twentieth century had perhaps clouded our rear-view mirror and rigidly placed us on opposing sides of a qualitative/quantitative divide. In the past two decades we have reached the point where quantitative methods have been reclaimed from an assumption of underlying positivism (Lawson and Staeheli, 1990), and qualitative methods have been reclaimed from accusations of wishy-washy anecdotes (Baxter and Eyles, 1997), and we are now poised to put into practice the potential of not only multiple methods, but mixed-methods, whereby the blending of research practices becomes iterative, reflexive, and integrated (Knigge and Cope, 2006).

How far back does the tendency toward integrating multiple data sources and methods go? Clues gleaned from an 1881 English translation from German of Heinrich Kiepert's *A Manual of Ancient Geography* suggest that this tendency has shaped geography from the beginning. From Kiepert's late-nineteenth century viewpoint, these geographers – Greeks such as Strabo, Ptolemy, Herodotus, Eratosthenes, as well as Romans such as Pliny – were thoroughly steeped in the 'two sides of the Science' (the Science being geography). The two sides Kiepert

identified were *drawing* and *description*. The first connotes mapping, which in ancient times was characterized by incremental improvements in mathematical and astronomical discoveries and the invention of better measuring instrumentation and representation practices, such as stereographical projection (Kiepert, 1881). The second side Kiepert calls 'ethnographical survey' in which the power of description was invoked. The following excerpt is telling in both its representation of the 'ethnography' of antiquity and Kiepert's nineteenth century perspective on it:

> Besides the purely mechanical formation of the earth's surface and its local distinctions according to quality of soil and climate, the organic nature which fills this surface is also matter of geographical observation. And in this department the human race takes a pre-eminent place, on account of the almost unlimited freedom with which they move from place to place, and their power of inuring themselves even to the most extreme conditions of climate. The human race moreover has to be considered in its particular divisions, known as nations, and these not regarded, as in antiquity, as children of the soil which from time to time they have chanced to inhabit, but rather quite apart from it and in connection with their mutual resemblances or specific distinctions. (1881: 6)

By engaging with the dual practices of drawing (map-making with all its attendant illustrative and categorizing methods) and ethnographic descriptions (primarily based on identifying commonalities and differences in language, body types, and skin coloring), the Greeks and Romans set the stage for the integrative tendencies of geography that we revisit today. Particularly when we consider the Romans and their compulsion to measure, catalogue, and order their Empire with new levels of precision (all the better to dominate vast expanses and populations), we see early traces of the use of multiple *forms* of data, *sources* of data, and *methods* of producing and analyzing data. Indeed, Kiepert located the integration of multiple methods at the very foundations of geography:

> Among [these] must be mentioned in the first rank the first systematic work which deals with geography *at once from a mathematical, physical, and*

historic standpoint, whose author, Eratosthenes of Cyrene, Director of the Library of the Museum at Alexandria (230–195 BC), is properly speaking the founder of this science. (1881: 4, emphasis added)

We know little about the Greek and Roman geographers' methods of data production *per se*, but scholars such as Margarita Bowen (1981) have traced the roots of scientific empiricism back to them, including such practices as observing and recording facts about the world with the goal of understanding the broader patterns. The resulting drawings and descriptions suggest a variety of spatial measurement techniques and equipment, social and economic surveys, interviews, personal empirical observations, and interpretation of archival data. This raises the question of the social production of knowledge, especially as it is intertwined with the social construction of *places*, and on this count geography has a long (and thoroughly oppressive) history.

For example, the Romans did not just *map* existing features they encountered in their empire-building forays, they also built new pathways, centers, and landscapes using their new engineering techniques and units of measurement; they took censuses of people (enslaving some of them along the way), thereby cataloguing and constructing various 'Others'; they counted and calculated production, materials, and labor; and they integrated these data for purposes of continued dominion and wealth-building to maintain control and productivity. Indeed, the construction of empires seems to necessitate the integration of multiple methods and sources of data, particularly about interactions between people and land, creating a seductive opportunity for geographers in a range of capacities. What Brian Hudson noted for *fin-de-siècle* geography was, therefore, not unique to that time or place:

the study and teaching of the new geography at that time largely, if not mainly, to serve the interests of imperialism in its various aspects including territorial acquisition, economic exploitation, militarism, and the practice of class and race

domination. (1977; quoted in Smith and Godlewska, 1994: 4)

This thread of empire brings us to another illustrative example drawn from the imperialism of European powers during the 'Enlightenment'. How did the explorers of the sixteenth to nineteenth centuries participate in the social production of knowledge (and thus the construction of place), particularly with regard to engaging with Others?

The social production of knowledge: Encountering, constructing, and representing the 'Other'

Despite the common practice of invoking individual names (of Greek and Roman philosophers or of key European enlightenment explorers) for their pivotal roles in early geographic thought, the production of knowledge has never been a solitary achievement. Critically reflexive readings of the accounts of travel, exploration, and fieldwork can reveal the ways that geographic knowledge has always been collectively (though not necessarily cooperatively) produced, is always influenced by political and economic goals of various parties, and involves multiple sources of tension, power, silencing, and (mis)representation. Of course, critical reflection is a fairly recent development in field-based scholarship (though see Driver's (2001) account of the angst felt by Joseph Conrad and Claude Lévi-Strauss). So while past geographers cannot be retrospectively judged by current standards of rigor (and indeed, today's standards are by no means static, universal, or definitive), past geographies can be examined for the processes of the production of knowledge as practiced in the day.

The production of knowledge involves diverse material, social, and textual resources brought together in a specific context, by specifically located actors, and for various spoken and unspoken purposes. Contemporary qualitative research in geography has been strengthened by such understandings. Take, for example, the issue of field work.

Felix Driver demonstrates the constant 'becoming' of the field through active production, as well as its connections to bodies and discourses:

> If we think of geographical knowledge as constituted through a range of embodied practices – traveling, seeing, collecting, recording, mapping, and narrating – the subject of fieldwork becomes difficult to escape. The field in this sense is not just 'there'; it is always in the process of being constructed, through both physical movement – passage through a country – and other sorts of cultural work in other places. It is produced locally by the spatial practices of fieldwork, and discursively through texts and images. (2001: 12–13)

Further, David Ley and Allison Mountz (2001) raise vital questions of the ethics of field work, first asking 'to what extent is interpretation of the "other" an act of social and cultural privilege?' They press on: 'This anxiety has raised the question for some researchers whether interpretation of the "Other" is *ethically defensible*' (235, emphasis added). Ley and Mountz then wonder if representation of the Other is even possible at all 'when researchers are so thoroughly saturated with the ideological baggage of their own cultures?' (235). Of course, most of Western/Northern geographical knowledge of the past two thousand years has been based on processes of identifying and defining *difference* through place comparisons, categorizing peoples, and actively constructing 'Others' in part to define 'Self', in favorable terms to the latter. The point, then, is not merely that knowledge production depends on collective contributions (which may or may not be voluntary), but also that the primary processes of qualitative geographic research involve multiple material, physical, and ideological tensions.

The story of French explorer Jean-François de Galaup, Comte de Lapérouse is instructive here. Michael Bravo (1999) provides a theoretically ambitious account of Lapérouse's 1787 exploration of Sakhalin and the explorer's determination that this landform was indeed an island. One interesting piece of this for my purposes here is that Lapérouse came to this insular conclusion through encounters with several different groups of local residents and without actually circumnavigating the isle himself. Bravo's excavation of this process illuminates several relevant themes:

> The apparent autonomy and authority of *Navigation* [a figure in a painting depicting Lapérouse's journey] and his geographical preeminence were derived from the institutional power of the King and Navy, the knowledge of the savants of the Academy of Sciences, and especially, the fine-precision surveying and astronomical instruments the navigators possessed as they voyaged around the world. In this sense, the navigators operated their ships and instruments like the rugged, reliable machinery that they in fact were. However, during various landfall episodes on these voyages, the officers turned away from their instruments to consult the local people and to solicit geographical information from them in the form of hand-drawn sketches or maps. (Bravo, 1999: 199–200)

> The reciprocal obligation of the explorer is to register wonder or astonishment and to offer tribute to his own patrons and savants by naming and returning with evidence of some kind, such as a description or specimen. (1999: 203)

First, Lapérouse's mandate was framed within the political-economic imperial goals of the eighteenth-century French government, which not only provided the material necessities for global voyages, but also shaped his construction of otherness in people and place. Second, the social production of knowledge involved the collaboration of locals – in this case, an indigenous man drawing in the sand to show Lapérouse that Sakhalin was an island, as well as corroboration of the fact by different indigenous groups who had little contact with each other. Third, we need to consider the field experience of the scientists in the party, which depended heavily on their conceptual notions of what was worthy of notice, how the different and exotic were represented, what made it into the record of their encounters, and what was left out. Finally, to continue the theme from above, and draw these together, Lapérouse used multiple methods of data production, including the material tools of the ships and the instruments of navigation, and the techniques of cartography; they used established protocols for non-violent encounters with unknown (to him) Others; and, finally, Lapérouse had in his party expert translators to ease communication and to categorize the peoples encountered, artists to capture visual representations, and naturalists to catalogue the ephemera of landscape. He also – crucially, as we see – depended on the place knowledge of local residents. However, these sources of knowledge were not considered equal: in keeping with the values of the age of reason, the instrumentation and direct observation by Lapérouse and his party were considered by the scientific community back in France as the only *reliable* methods and, indeed, his account was derided for the fact that Lapérouse himself did not circumnavigate Sakhalin. In this case, local knowledge was 'supplemental, contingent, and unessential to geographical truth' (Bravo, 1999: 200) in the view of the patrons of the voyage, despite the fact that Lapérouse himself found them convincing.

These points in combination call attention to various tensions geographers are still confronting, such as what to do when 'scientific' instrumentation and local knowledge contradict each other (Nightingale, 2003); anxieties about field work's effects in rigidifying 'otherness' through researchers' ignorance of their own roles (Nairn, 2005); the instability of perceived and reified categories (Cahill, 2007); and the influence of personal backgrounds, experience, and 'scientific' credentials in researching and representing 'others' (Ley and Mountz, 2001). Thus, our current ability to be critically reflexive on the relations between Self and Other in the production of geographic knowledge is shaped in part by the long-standing practices of exploration and observation, talking with people about their places, and the quest for contextual knowledge.

Integrating context and causality

Geographers through the ages (and today) have frequently prided themselves on being integrative, pulling together the many strings of the physical and human world to understand places, processes, and peoples. On a practical level this is related to the specific research techniques of triangulation and using multiple methods, but on a more theoretical and epistemological level, this integration is about a way of seeing the world through its relationships, networks, causalities, and connections. This is not the sole domain of qualitative research by any means, but qualitative research can be a particularly helpful route to achieving such integration, even within a mostly quantitative project, by contextualizing large-scale findings, providing nuanced understandings of complex processes, identifying connections between places, and eliciting the meanings of phenomena through people's lived experiences.

Consider the comments of Douglas Freshfield in 1887 regarding 26-year-old Halford Mackinder, when he said that Mackinder was correct in seeing that 'geography was not a science of description nor of distribution, but of causality' (quoted in Livingstone, 1993: 191). Despite what followed in much of the twentieth century, during the early twentieth century heyday of regional geography and the 'spatial science' approaches of the mid-century, the quest for integrating context and causality was always present somewhere in the discipline, and qualitative research was there to help (see Martin, 2005 for a thorough review of the diversity of geographical practices and methods in the twentieth century in Britain, the US, and a host of other countries). In what follows I trace lightly some of the key moments and perspectives of twentieth-century British and American geography, identifying some of the steps and mis-steps toward synthesis and integration, and focusing in particular on the epistemological and methodological interventions geographers enacted through their research, debate, and scholarship.

Partly in reaction against the weaknesses of the environmental determinism of the turn of the twentieth century, many geographers turned back to areal differentiation and toward developing integrated understandings of unique places, making the region the primary object of study. As mentioned earlier in this chapter, descriptive narratives accounting for all the characteristics of a distinct region were raised to a supposed art form to the extent that geography as a discipline charged itself with the task of identifying all the regions of the world, describing them, and constructing categories of them based on similarities and differences. The region became the object and purpose of many (though not all) geographers' work but, despite elaborate categorical systems designed to identify commonalities and differences between regions, the descriptive narrative was losing favor by the mid-twentieth century for its superficiality, questionable 'relevance' in an increasingly 'scientific' age, and the tedium of place names, features ('capes and bays'), and trading products. The two World Wars generated a broader societal drive toward the 'hard' sciences and engineering, which, along with various technological developments allowing faster computational operations, produced a seductive solution to the problems of regional geography in the form of 'spatial science', also known as the 'quantitative revolution' (for reviews, see Johnston, 1987; Cloke et al., 1991; Livingstone, 1993; Martin, 2005).

While a full accounting of the quantitative revolution is not feasible here, I will point to two basic issues that emerged at mid-century in the discipline, which are intrinsically related to each other and highly relevant here. The first is epistemological, that is, related to ways of knowing. Regional geographers typically represented an approach based on *ideographic* epistemologies; that is, they primarily studied unique instances of things (e.g. regions, landscapes) as a way of understanding the world. The emergence of spatial science was based primarily on the *nomothetic* epistemologies of positivism and empiricism; that is, they believed that there were underlying systems of order in human society that mirror the laws of the natural

world, and they sought to reveal these universal laws through their research based on empirical observations. Indeed, some of the most trenchant debates in geography, such as that between Schaefer and Hartshorne in the early 1950s (see Johnston, 1987 for a full account), were based on whether geography should focus on 'special knowledge' (understanding the particular, such as knowing regions in depth) or 'general knowledge' (seeking universal principles and laws). The second issue is methodological. While it was never entirely true that early twentieth century regional geographers *only* used qualitative methods or spatial scientists *only* used quantitative methods, that assumption became hardened as epistemological disagreements extended outwards to include methods. These disagreements also made the association between positivism and quantification more rigid, and further fostered the notion that *rigorous* research should follow the principles of spatial science.

However, several scholars have pointed out more recently that the quantitative revolution of the 1950s and 1960s was really more a 'blip' on the time-line of methodological and epistemological developments in the discipline (e.g. Winchester, 2005). Even at the time, in the early- to mid-twentieth century, not everyone was convinced by the dynamic duo of quantification and positivism. One early critic (and one also critical of the lack of human agency in environmental determinism and the tedium of regional geographies), Carl Sauer, wrote the following observation about the beginnings of spatial science in the 1930s and the manic drive to quantify and discern the order of seemingly everything:

[Geographers] gathered statistical data, drew topical maps, and constructed graphs, all under continuing revision to be kept up to date. Things, people, places were quantitative aggregates to be related. Numbers in their spatial distribution were the common concern, which in the course of time became sophisticated to theories of spatial order, *independent of real place or time*. The new breed had little experience or need of the traditional interests of geography in the physical, biotic, and cultural diversity of the earth. It was not interested in the past beyond the short run of statistical series, but was concerned with projecting the future. The applied geographer attached to the world of business learned the use of statistics to chart the flow of trade. A few were beginning to construe an abstract world of hypothetical space and time. (Sauer, [1974] 1981: 283–4, emphasis added)

Indeed, Sauer's work and, more broadly, that of the Berkeley School's 'cultural landscape' team that Sauer led, offers an instructive counter-narrative to the typical 'paradigm shift' view of geographic methods and philosophy that trots from environmental determinism to regional description to spatial science and so forth. The key to this lies in the methodological and conceptual basis of cultural landscapes as integrating context and causality, as synthesizing multiple processes (physical and human) over space and time. Crucially, for our purposes here, the Berkeley School also engaged its scholars in both inductive field work *and* the identification of broader, more theoretical processes. Of course, many flaws in the cultural landscape field have been noted, such as overstating the boundaries between 'nature' and 'culture', ethnic and racial generalizations (e.g. 'German settlers as a group were most preoccupied with becoming permanently established as farmers wherever they settled' (Sauer, [1941] 1981: 13), and unquestioned assumptions about gender roles across time and place. However, the integrative practices of Sauer *et al.* had an important role in influencing geographic practice and thought, particularly in the US.

Another critique is that details on the methods of Sauer and the Berkeley School are unfortunately slim. Sauer himself made wide use of existing geological field surveys, known anthropological findings, and field-based descriptions of a range of natural and physical characteristics to weave his landscapes textually. One of his few statements of method refers to his own regional geography training in the 1910s and 1920s:

We went out to learn what we could with a fair background of landforms and a liking of the

landscape. We were expected to gain understanding by observing the relations of man [*sic*] to physical environment ... [We] stopped whenever we found something to engage our attention as significant by being there. By such reconnaissance we tried to describe the geographic pattern of human activity and interpret its meaningful assemblage, and began to ask how the things seen came to be together. A first exercise in learning that geography is spatial differentiation of nature and culture. (Sauer, [1974] 1981: 282)

Later exposure to anthropologists influenced Sauer's development of cultural themes through the study of archaeology, history, and cultural systems. In some ways, however, the field methods used in the cultural landscape work of Sauer and others are seen merely as hints seeping through the resulting narratives that are again the result of synthesis and integration:

Our first expedition was to Baja California ... we returned for a number of field seasons, ranging to the southern end of the long and sparsely inhabited peninsula. It was our field school of physical and human geography, out of which came a variety of studies. Former missions, in part ruins, were guides to reconstruction of past conditions and thus to include aboriginal life, here and there still existing. Also we began to go south along the Pacific mainland of Mexico, there learning about Indian crops and agriculture. (Sauer, [1974] 1981: 285)

And, of course, speculative hypotheses were everywhere:

It is incredible that early humans, whatever the disputed quality of their brains, should have sat about the fire generation after generation without experimenting with it, especially in relation to food. (Sauer, [1970] 1981: 297)

For all its methodological silences and conceptual leaps of faith, however, Sauer and the Berkeley School acted as one of several camps of geographers who remained critical of and resistant to the enticements of spatial science, partly on the basis of epistemology but also on the basis of integrating context and causality. Returning once more to Sauer, consider this eloquently summary:

As the social sciences have substituted symbols for individuals and communities we now have a contemporary school of 'mathematical geographers' which would disregard the age-old interest in making sense of the diversity of land and its life. A generalized humankind is to be subsumed by mathematical symbols and functions of spatial relation. I do not think that such sophistication is valid in concept, nor that it gives grace and truth to the geographical imagination. Geographers stray from their course when they turn from phenomenon and location to abstraction of numbers. (Sauer, [1967] 1981: 241)

So, in some ways the 1960s were dark days for those cultural geographers, as well as humanists, phenomenologists, behavioralists, and other non-positivist or anti-positivist geographers, as they were considered to be less 'scientific' than the spatial scientists in a time when science was seen as the solution to the problems of a world torn by recent wars and when academic departments had to justify their legitimacy. By the early to mid-1970s, however, cracks in the spatial science foundation were being actively pried wider by these critics, setting the stage for both the 'cultural turn' in geography and the explosion of qualitative research done explicitly and reflexively.

Part of this prying open was again based on the conviction that geographers needed to achieve the integration of context (economic, political, cultural, environmental) with causality (human agency, experiences, thoughts, emotions, relations, networks); this might be aided by quantitative *methods*, but positivism as an epistemology, with its law-seeking goals, got in the way. As two critics put it at the time 'The [spatial scientists] insisted on ... logical and internally consistent theories and models. Yet, none of their theoretical constructs were ever complex enough to describe the real world accurately. They had achieved internal consistency while losing their grip on reality' (Guelke, 1971; quoted in Johnston, 1987: 153). And:

[T]he idea of synthesis itself becomes more important as it becomes obvious that our larger problems transcend narrow subject-matter fields ... integration ... in a larger understanding is still achieved, however aided by statistical methods and computers, by the judgment of wise men [sic] who have cultivated the habit of seeing things together. (R.C. Harris, 1977; quoted in Johnston, 1987: 152)

Interestingly, it was increasingly the wise *women* in geography who used emerging feminist perspectives to bring context and causality together in fresh ways (see Women and Geography Study Group, 1984 for early examples); to push for critiques and analysis of masculinist assumptions about geography, 'science', and society; and to reshape both qualitative and quantitative research in the discipline. Indeed, it is perhaps feminism that should be primarily acknowledged for the shift toward being explicit and reflexive about methods.

Despite critiques and cracks such as R.C. Harris' and Leonard Guelke's, however, the overly-assumed legitimacy, accuracy, and rigor of quantitative research saturated the discipline and put non-spatial-scientists on the defensive for several decades. Through the 1980s and 1990s increasing numbers of geographers – both young and not-so-young – were exploring the possibilities and strengths of qualitative research but, importantly, they had to defend their choices, document and legitimize their methods, and explain to (often positivist) committee members or journal editors why their research techniques were appropriate and their findings not merely anecdotal. The shorthand of how one statistical operation was chosen over another that served as justification for quantitative methods did not work in qualitative research, so these geographers had no choice but to be highly explicit about their methods, carefully build a case for the methods' legitimacy and worth, and reflect on their own biases (not believing in the 'value-free' myth of objectivity) and how their work was influenced by these perspectives.

Thus, in many ways – methodologically, epistemologically, and theoretically – the quantitative revolution was actually the best stimulus imaginable for a newly rigorous approach to qualitative geography because it required a new level of explicit attention to methods, to thinking reflexively about how methods were employed, and to becoming more self-critical about the position and values of the researcher in the context of data production, analysis, and representation. At this moment, some key shifts in the broader social sciences were instrumental in facilitating the qualitative reactions in geography, namely the rise and expansion in critical theory (feminism, anti-racism, post-colonialism, queer theory, etc.) and the 'cultural turn' (particularly characterized by post-modernism and post-structuralism). These theoretical developments formed the conceptual framework for newly invigorated qualitative research in geography, while the re-discovery of field work practices, which were freshened up by feminist and other critical perspectives, was spurred on by the rejection of spatial science and its dehumanizing effects.

Power, 'the personal', and 'the political'

Taking off in the 1980s, feminism provided geographers with a different way of looking at the world, a critical lens that shone new light on taken-for-granted social and spatial processes. Feminism was the gateway for many young geography scholars in the 1980s and 1990s who were looking for new critical ways to do research, write, and teach. The 'second wave' of feminism may have hit popular culture and some other academic disciplines in the early 1970s, but geography was a difficult landscape to penetrate (to twist around a masculinist, colonialist metaphor!) and significant gains only started to appear in the 1980s (e.g. WGSG, 1984), after substantial personal and professional struggles. Within geography, some sub-disciplines were earlier to accept and adopt feminist perspectives, while others are still relatively resistant. The superficially obvious unevenness of women's opportunities in everyday life (such as literacy and access to education, as well as health care and other services), as well as the perennial gender divisions of labor at every scale, from household to national government, meant that urban and economic geography were some of the earlier feminist grounds. But – and this is

crucial – this is also due to some key people who happened to be in these sub-fields, like Jan Monk, Susan Hanson, Doreen Massey, Linda McDowell, Gerry Pratt, and many others who pushed for women to be included in standard analyses, for gender to be recognized as a significant element of difference, and ultimately, for the engagement with 'gender' as not only a set of power relations that intersects and conditions other power relations, but also as a discourse that helps support oppression in other forms such as colonialism, heteronormativity, and racism. Other subfields – strong feminist practitioners notwithstanding – have been slower to adapt to critical perspectives. Consider Mona Domosh's (1997) comments on historical geography. I quote her at length because she so beautifully draws together the struggles involved, the epistemological epiphany needed for feminist work, and the links between theory and methods:

> [T]he past twenty years have witnessed the intellectual deconstruction of notions of 'truth' that inhere in the world, and with it the unraveling of a belief in 'objective' knowledge. Instead, we envision knowledge as the creation of the hearts and minds of real people existing within their own social and cultural parameters. But historical geography has positioned itself outside these discussions, moribund ... in an antiquarian world aloof from the problematics of recent social and cultural theory. As a result, both the epistemological and methodological assumptions of historical geography have not been seriously challenged. Those of us who have tried to reckon with these challenges and to formulate a historical geography of difference have found the task forbidding, at least in part, I will argue, because we have accepted traditional historical methodology ... What I want to suggest in this chapter is that a formulation of a feminist historical geography must begin with an examination of its methodological stances, because by accepting the assumptions of the more-traditional historical geography, even one that includes women, we only reinscribe the very categories we may want to dismantle. In other words, what I am calling for is not necessarily a shift in the object of study (women's spaces instead of men's spaces), but a shift in how we conceive of those spaces to begin with, and with this, a reformulation of methodology sensitive to the gendered construction of all landscapes. (Domosh, 1997: 226)

Here Domosh sums up so much of what feminists were up against in the 1980s and 1990s – a male-dominated discipline that might allow parallel studies of 'women's spaces' to complement traditional studies of 'men's spaces' but did not want to overhaul its deeply entrenched beliefs in categories, methods, and knowledge itself. And it certainly was not open to having a bunch of 'uppity' women (and a few men) shift the bedrock of the discipline by critiquing everything from who makes the department coffee to who gets first authorship to who gets to define 'truth'. Domosh, following (as we all were to some degree) Nancy Fraser (1989), Linda Nicholson (1986), and Joan Scott (1988) argues for a re-making of theory and practice in part by paying attention to methods.

Feminism, then, helped create a strong backbone for a revival of qualitative methods (and, of course, has contributed to more rigorous quantitative methods too), as well as the exploration and development of new sorts of geographic inquiry, in part because it inherently valued listening to real people explain what was going on in their lives. The catchphrase of the 1970s social movement, 'the personal is political' was genuinely useful in justifying paying attention to everyday life, even if the events recounted were judged 'minutiae' by others. We had the sense that small, mundane things were important and worthy of scholarly inquiry and feminism not only backed this up, it also forced us to consider new questions critically, such as multiple forms of oppression and the complicity of patriarchy with racism, classism, ageism, colonialism, heteronormativity, ablism, and a host of others. The catchphrase also led feminist geographers to turn a critical eye on our own methods and practice to consider issues of researcher positionality, the exploitation of research subjects and their knowledges, how to 'write' and with whose voice, and what to do with the privileges of academia (to the extent that we had them). Thus, feminism has not only given us strength, but also demanded much in return.

More recently, feminism has continued to drive a critical engagement with methods, including facilitating new forms of engaging with quantitative research, such as through the medium of GIS and in the increased use of 'mixed-methods' research (see for example: Kwan, 2002; Elwood, 2006; Kwan and Knigge, 2006; Pavlovskaya, 2006; Cope and Elwood, 2009). Again, qualitative researchers have feminism to thank for making inroads into traditionally masculinist methodologies. Since 2000, the body and scope of feminist critical GIS has grown enormously, due in part to many of the same phenomena: strong initiators, a solid critical perspective, and young scholars (men and women) who have already so strongly internalized themes of anti-essentialism, multiple subjectivities, power, discourse, and identity that their practice of geography is already knit together in ways that previous generations (including their advisors!) could only dream of.

CONCLUSION: BECOMING AND BEING EXPLICIT AND REFLEXIVE

To bring this to the present, I engage in a bit of personal reflexivity by considering the influences and contexts of my education in geography and early career. Good examples like Trevor Barnes's (2001) and Pamela Moss's (2001) tracings of key professional connections and collisions demonstrate the value of such efforts. However, I undertake this with some caution, recognizing Mike Crang's (2003: 497) concern that 'exhortations to reflexivity and disclosure tend to depend upon and reproduce problematic notions of a stable, tightly defined, unchanging research project conducted by a singular researcher.' As can be seen in the following account, my own progression in qualitative methods was anything but stable or tightly defined!

My formative moments as a qualitative researcher came as a master's student at the

University of Colorado at Boulder in the early 1990s. I had always been fascinated by people's everyday lives, especially historically, and my background in sociology suggested that 'life in the city' was a perfectly acceptable topic for scholarly inquiry. As I completed coursework in urban geography I began weaving these interests together through a geographic lens. My advisor, Lynn Staeheli, loaned me Laurel Thatcher Ulrich's *A Midwife's Tale: The Life of Martha Ballard, Based on Her Diary, 1785–1812* (1991), which had just come out. I loved the way the author recreated Ballard's life and the way she used the midwife's spare diary entries to pull out insights on the roles of women, violence, sex, health, and the quirks of small-town Maine at the turn of the nineteenth century. After hearing my enthusiasm for the book, though, I think Lynn had a bit of a panic, worrying that I might take the diaries by early Colorado women that I had discovered too far, and she teased me about doing geographies of frontier washer-women. At that time, and in that place, using women's diaries as 'data' in geographic research – especially when I only had access to five of them (so much for an 'n' of 30!) – was really pushing the bounds of legitimacy. My MA thesis research encapsulated all that was 'soft' and weak in the eyes of the discipline; studying *women*, examining their mundane, *everyday* activities, and using *qualitative* methods at a time when we were all reading the grandiose works of David Harvey 1989 and Edward Soja 1989, and doing so under an advisor who was only in her second year as an assistant professor who had to 'prove' herself to the male establishment. Indeed, all this must have cost Lynn some lost sleep.

Lynn had good reason for concern on my behalf. There was little published in the way of methodological guidelines for qualitative research by 1990 (the notable exception of John Eyles and David Smith (1988) was based on health geographies and I had a hard time leaping from their material to historical diaries), so any discussion of my 'methods' was going to rest on anthropologists and sociologists. Further, Lynn and my other committee members had been at least partly schooled in the supremacy of quantitative methods, so she was understandably worried about me getting into difficulties with the committee, yet she was also unfailingly supportive of my ideas and approach. One day she came upstairs to my shared attic office and gently suggested that I create some summary statistics from census data that could serve as both a contextual backdrop and a quantitative stamp of legitimacy. Although I bristled at this at first, I soon discovered the wonders of the manuscript census, with its scratchy handwritten entries and microfilm headaches, as well as oddities of how people's ethnicities and occupations were categorized. In the end, Lynn was right (of course): I got a lot more out of spending a few days in the bowels of the Denver library compiling census data on women in Colorado in the early twentieth century than I would have from using only the diaries, and it also served me well in justifying my research practice as 'rigorous' and systematic, intrinsically valid, though not necessarily generalizable.

This story seems pretty laughable now compared to the amazing range of methods we now routinely read about (symbolized by this volume). In fact, white women's frontier diaries seem very tame and relatively uncomplicated as both a population and a data source compared to working with homeless children, illegal immigrants, white supremacists, or people in the mental health system, using methods ranging from street theater to *bricolage* to participatory activism, as geographers have done since that time. I was fairly unaware of my positionality, was unreflexive on details of the 'body' or the project of white settlement, and never considered the question of whether my 'field work' was a discursive process. Of course, my subjects were also dead, but even that does not seem to be an excuse for ignoring discourse in our hyper-vigilant post-millennial geographies. But how did we get from my 1990s experience to where we are now?

Fast-forward through my PhD research at Boulder, which involved more archival work; even though I had an 'n' of more than 50 oral histories, I still used mostly qualitative methods. I then spent a decade at one of the premiere GIS-related geography departments in the United States (SUNY-Buffalo), where I felt like a valued but fundamentally peculiar species. This experience made me realize that having a diversity of methods, theories, applications, and epistemologies is a strength for a discipline, not a call to battle. While I had moments of frustration justifying my work, my approach, and occasionally even my presence in the department, I had already started honing my defense of qualitative research and critical social theory while in graduate school. As an assistant professor at Buffalo, the need to articulate and explain exactly how I was contributing to geographic knowledge was another pivotal experience. Indeed, I only started thinking explicitly and reflexively about methods in this departmental context and without it I probably would not have started the Qualitative Research Specialty Group of the Association of American Geographers in 2000, nor would I have written the various pieces on qualitative work and feminist epistemology that now appear on my CV, nor – most likely – would I have received NSF funding for a grant involving lots of methods I had never tried (artwork; participatory mapping; child-led photo tours; quilting) with a social group with whom I had limited experience (children).

The late 1980s and early 1990s were in many ways a turning point, not just for me, but many practitioners of qualitative geographical research. Reflecting on qualitative research in anthropology, Denzin and Lincoln (2005: 3) identify nine 'moments' in qualitative research, ranging from the 'traditional' (1900–1950) to the 'fractured future' (2005 onwards). I have tried, in this chapter, to avoid creating such periods, preferring to trace tendencies and perspectives as they manifested in different moments in order to build a more thematic understanding of some historical and present practices.

My reluctance to make a timeline comes from two realizations that are informed by looking back at the *doing* of geography and by my own experiences. First, I have been studiously considering Mayhew's cautions against 'essentialist histories of geography', and indeed, in the course of reading for this chapter, I have seen very little uniformity of method practices at any given time. Boas, Conrad, Geddes, Sauer, and countless feminists went against prevailing trends and so did many others in less-celebrated forms. So while the trends are significant in themselves, they hardly seem worthy of having a period named for them and time brackets put around their edges. And, as I have argued here, many of the central themes of qualitative research have older roots; for example, humanists were plugging away in the 1970s and 1980s at drawing attention to experience and emotion, while the recently emerging interest in affect, actants, and ANT has made good use of both humanism and the alchemy of the recent cultural turn and qualitative renaissance.

My second source of reluctance comes from having observed a great deal of continuity in the use of various methods. While some people throw off their graduate school methods training (or never listened in the first place) and whole-heartedly embrace, indeed, *create* new methods in a discipline, others find new and better ways to use the same methods that their early training was based upon. As a graduate student and then an assistant professor I came to understand that not everyone was going to wave a critical theory flag or push the boundaries of edgy qualitative research, and, while I often disagreed with the positivist epistemologies of some colleagues' work, it did not mean their research was worthless – and here's where that separation of epistemology and methods is so crucial. Indeed, there are insights to be gained from better large-scale quantitative analysis, there is value in developing new forms of mapping in GIS, and who am I to critique a spatial statistics model that helps fire fighters get to the fire more quickly? Just because I did not believe in the sanctity of positivism, or even the possibility of 'value-free research', did not mean the methods needed tossing out. Being in this context also clarified my thinking about doing rigorous research across the quantitative-qualitative spectrum (for example, moving from 'generalizing' to larger populations toward 'abstracting' commonalities based on process-oriented research (Baxter and Eyles, 1997)), and about separating one's epistemology from the methods (e.g. not all quantitative research is based on positivist assumptions (Lawson, 1995)).

Into the new millennium we have seen the expansion of the scope and practice of methods, new forms of working with and learning about people and places, and new texts have emerged to reflect and educate, some of which are now going into second and third editions (in addition to this volume, see Limb and Dwyer, 2001; Clifford and Valentine, 2003; Flowerdew and Martin, 2005; Hay, 2005). Taken together, these convergences of critical theories, stimulated by the broader context of disciplinary history and practice and enacted through the convictions of many individuals, have set the scene for the current era of qualitative geography in which we see the expanded commitment to explicit discussion of methods' strengths and weaknesses and reflexive consideration of the processes and positionalities. And in keeping with those old forces of production of geographic knowledge, we are using these new positions to explore new worlds and think critically about the constructions of many unique places of all sorts.

NOTES

1.   The first word of this chapter's title is important to note: 'A'. One can almost imagine a continuum of first words here. I could have called this 'The History of Qualitative Research in Geography' without much trouble, but as I typed it the word 'The' seemed overly definitive, singular, reeking of pretend objectivity, as if there was only one history

to be revealed and unfurled without complication or dispute. At the other end of the spectrum, I could have called this chapter 'My History of Qualitative Research in Geography'; this is in some ways the most honest title because I have chosen the path, threads, themes, and inclusions/exclusions of the chapter (in consultation with the editors, of course), but it's also on the narcissistic side. Ultimately, I settled on 'A History …' as a way both to acknowledge the inevitable partiality of any endeavor such as this and attempt to build on common ground sufficiently so that the chapter 'speaks' to all readers.

2.   Throughout this chapter I refer to 'data production' rather than data 'acquisition', 'gathering', or 'collection' as a way to highlight the fact that data are not pre-existing bits of information to be shepherded into a database, but, rather, are socially produced, contingent, and contextually constructed by and through the process of research. I submit that this is just as true for quantitative research as it is for qualitative.

REFERENCES

Barnes, T. (2001) 'Retheorizing economic geography: from the quantitative revolution to the "cultural turn"', *Annals of the Association of American Geographers* 91 (3): 546–65.

Baxter, J. and Eyles, J. (1997) 'Evaluating qualitative research in social geography establishing "rigour" in interview analysis', *Transactions of the Institute of British Geographers* 22 (4): 505–25.

Bowen, M. (1981) *Empiricism and geographical thought: from Francis Bacon to Alexander von Humboldt.* Cambridge: Cambridge University Press.

Bravo, M. (1999) 'Ethnographic navigation and the geographical gift', in D.N. Livingstone, and C.W.J. Withers (eds) *Geography and Enlightenment.* Chicago: University of Chicago Press. pp. 199–235.

Cahill, C. (2007) 'The personal is political: developing new subjectivities through participatory action research', *Gender, Place, and Culture* 14 (3): 267–92.

Clifford, N. and Valentine, G. (2003) *Key methods in Geography.* London: Sage.

Cloke, P., Philo, C. and Sadler, D. (1991) *Approaching human geography: an introduction to contemporary Theoretical Debates.* New York: Guilford Press.

Cope, M. and Elwood, S. (2009) *Qualitative GIS: mixed-methods approach.* London: Sage.

Crang, M. (2002) 'Qualitative methods: the new orthodoxy?', *Progress in Human Geography* 26 (5): 647–55.

Crang, M. (2003) 'Qualitative methods: touchy, feely, look-see?', *Progress in Human Geography* 27 (4): 494–504.

Davies, G. and Dwyer, C. (2007) 'Qualitative methods: are you enchanted or are you alienated?', *Progress in Human Geography* 31 (2): 257–66.

Denzin, N. and Lincoln, Y. (2005) 'Introduction: the discipline and practice of qualitative research', in N. Denzin and Y. Lincoln (eds) *The Sage handbook of qualitative research* (3rd Edition) Thousand Oaks, CA: Sage Publications. pp. 1–32.

Domosh, M. (1997) 'With "stout boots and a stout heart": historical methodology and feminist geography', in J.P. Jones, H. Nast and S. Roberts (eds) *Thresholds in feminist geography: difference, methodology, representation*. Lanham, MD: Rowman and Littlefield. pp. 225–37.

Driver, F. (2001) *Geography militant: cultures of exploration and empire*. Malden, MA: Blackwell.

Dyck, I. (2005) 'Feminist geography, the "everyday", and local-global relations: hidden spaces of place-making', *The Canadian Geographer* 49 (3): 233–43.

Elwood, S. (2006) 'Negotiating knowledge production: the everyday inclusions, exclusions, and contradictions of participatory GIS research', *The Professional Geographer* 58 (2): 197–208.

Eyles, J. and Smith, D. (1988) *Qualitative methods in human geography*. Cambridge. Polity Press.

Flowerdew, R. and Martin, D. (2005) *Methods in human geography: a guide for students doing research projects* (2nd Edition) Harlow: Longman.

Fraser, N. (1989) *Unruly practices: power, discourse, and gender in contemporary social theory*. Minneapolis: University of Minnesota Press.

Godlewska, A.M.C. (1999a) 'From enlightenment vision to modern science? Humboldt's visual thinking', in D.N. Livingstone, and C.W.J. Withers (eds) *Geography and enlightenment*. Chicago: University of Chicago Press. pp. 236–75.

Godlewska, A.M.C. (1999b) *Geography unbound: French geographic science from Cassini to Humboldt*. Chicago: University of Chicago Press.

Godlewska, A. and Smith, N. (1994) *Geography and empire*. Oxford: Blackwell.

Harvey, D. (1989) *The urban experience*. Baltimore, MD: The Johns Hopkins University Press.

Hay, I. (2005) *Qualitative research methods in human geography* (2nd Edition) South Melbourne: Oxford University Press.

Johnston, R.J. (1987) *Geography and geographers: Anglo-American human geography since 1945* (3rd Edition) London: Edward Arnold.

Kesby, M., Kindon, S. and Pain, R. (2005) 'Participatory approaches', in R. Flowerdew, and D. Martin (eds) *Methods in human geography: a guide for students doing research projects* (2nd Edition) Harlow: Longman. pp. 144–66.

Kiepert, H. (1881) *A Manual of ancient geography*. London: Macmillan.

Knigge, L. and Cope, M. (2006) 'Grounded visualization: integrating the analysis of qualitative and quantitative data through grounded theory and geo-visualization', *Environment and Planning A* 38 (11): 2021–37.

Kwan, M-P. (2002) 'Feminist visualisation: re-envisioning GIS as a method in feminist geographic research', *Annals of the Association of American Geographers* 92 (4): 645–61.

Kwan, M-P. and Knigge, L. (2006) 'Doing qualitative research using GIS: an oxymoronic endeavor?', *Environment and Planning A* 38 (11): 1999–2002.

Lawson, V. (1995) 'The politics of difference: examining the quantitative/qualitative dualism in post-structuralist feminist research', *The Professional Geographer* 47 (4): 449–57.

Lawson, V. and Staeheli, L. (1990) 'Realism and the practice of geography', *The Professional Geographer* 42 (1): 13–20.

Ley, D. and Mountz, A. (2001) 'Interpretation, representation, positionality: issues in field research in human geography', in M. Limb and C. Dwyer (eds) *Qualitative methodologies for geographers: issues and debates*. New York: Oxford University Press. pp. 234–47.

Limb, M. and Dwyer, C. (2001) *Qualitative methodologies for geographers: issues and debates*. New York: Oxford University Press.

Livingstone, D.N. (1993) *The geographical tradition: episodes in the history of a contested enterprise*. Cambridge, MA: Blackwell.

Livingstone, D.N. and Withers, C.W.J. (1999) *Geography and enlightenment*. Chicago: University of Chicago Press.

Livingstone, D.N. and Withers, C.W.J. (2005) *Geography and revolution*. Chicago: University of Chicago Press.

Mackinder, H. (1887 [1996]) 'On the Scope and Methods of geography', reprinted in J. Agnew, D.N. Livingstone and A. Roger (eds) *Human geography: an essential anthology*. Cambridge, MA: Blackwell. pp. 155–72.

Martin, G. (2005) *All possible worlds: a history of geographical ideas* (4th Edition) New York: Oxford University Press.

Massey, D. (2005) *For space*. London: Sage.

Mayhew, R.J. (2001) 'The effacement of early modern geography (c. 1600–1850): a historiographical essay', *Progress in Human Geography* 25 (3): 383–401.

Mohammad, R. (2001) '"Insiders" and/or "outsiders": positionality, theory, and praxis', in M. Limb and C. Dwyer (eds) *Qualitative methodologies for geographers: issues and debates*. New York: Oxford University Press. pp. 101–20.

Moss, P. (2001) *Placing autobiography in geography*. Syracuse, NY: Syracuse University Press.

Nairn, K. (2005) 'The problems of utilizing "direct experience" in geography education', *Journal of Geography in Higher Education* 29 (2): 293–309.

Nicholson, L. (1986) *Gender and history: the limits of social theory in the age of the family*. New York: Columbia University Press.

Nightingale, A. (2003) 'A feminist in the forest: situated knowledges and mixing methods in natural resource management', *ACME: An international E-journal for Critical Geographies* 2 (1): 77–90.

Pavlovskaya, M. (2006) 'Theorizing with GIS: a tool for critical geographies?', *Environment and Planning A* 38 (11): 2003–20.

Sauer, C.O. ([1941] 1981) 'Settlement of the humid east', in *Selected essays*. Berkeley, CA: Turtle Island Foundation. pp. 3–15.

Sauer, C.O. ([1967] 1981) 'On the background of geography in the United States', in *Selected Essays*. Berkeley, CA: Turtle Island Foundation. pp. 241–59.

Sauer, C.O. ([1970] 1981) 'Plants, animals, and man', in *Selected Essays*. Berkeley, CA: Turtle Island Foundation. pp. 289–318.

Sauer, C.O. ([1974] 1981) 'The fourth dimension of geography', in *Selected essays*. Berkeley, CA: Turtle Island Foundation. pp. 279–86.

Scott, J. (1988) *Gender and the politics of history*. New York: Columbia University Press.

Smith, N. and Godlewska, A. (1994) 'Introduction: critical histories of geography', in A. Godlewska and N. Smith (eds) *Geography and empire*. Oxford, UK: Blackwell. pp. 1–12.

Soja, E. (1989) *Postmodern geographies: the reassertion of space in critical social theory*. New York: Verso Press.

Ulrich, L.T. (1991) *A midwife's tale: the life of Martha Ballard, based on her diary, 1785–1812*. New York: Vintage Press.

Winchester, H.P.M. (2005) 'Qualitative research and its place in human geography', in I. Hay (ed.) *Qualitative research methods in human geography* (2nd Edition) South Melbourne: Oxford University Press. pp. 3–18.

Women and Geography Study Group (1984) *Geography and gender*. London: Heinemann.

3

'Throwntogetherness': Encounters with Difference and Diversity

Stuart C. Aitken

[O]ne of the truly productive characteristics of material spatiality ... [is] its potential for the happenstance juxtaposition of previously unrelated trajectories, the business of walking around a corner and bumping into alterity, of having (somehow, and well or badly) to get on with neighbours who have got 'here' ... by different routes from you; your being here together is, in that sense, quite uncoordinated. This is an aspect of the productiveness of spatiality which may enable 'something new' to happen.

(Massey, 2005: 94)

I remember sitting in Fernanda's spotless living room surrounded by her four children, Lucy, Lilia, Marcia and Nemo.[1] Fernanda is flitting in and out, offering Joel, Adriana, Janet and I *café con leche*. She has worked full-time in a local maquiladora since her husband died. The household is supported by her $65 a week and the tips that two of the older children bring back from their labor at a local supermarket. Collectively, these two young people earn more than their mother and, on a good week, the older boy (who helps supervise other child packers at the supermarket) can earn $80. Lucy, at 15 years of age, is now too old to 'volunteer' in the government-sponsored supermarket

program.[2] There are concerns about what she can do that would be as lucrative as the supermarket job. The four older children sit politely, attentively listening to Janet's translation of my questions. My other translator, Adriana, a native of Tijuana, often breaks in with a more parochial revision of the translation that is met with nods of understanding, thoughtful contemplation and, more often than not, a barrage of responses. The barrage shifts into a cacophony of laughter and more eager responses. Adriana laughs also and, posing more questions, gradually takes over the interview. I am not sure how much of this Janet is getting. I know how little I am getting; a Spanish class taken years previously and a few stunted conversations in restaurants does not begin to prepare me for this kind of banter. Embarrassed by my inability to pick up anything but a few words from the conversation, I think about enrolling in more Spanish classes – perhaps an *'intensivo'* – and busy myself by playing with Fernanda's youngest daughter who is bringing out some of her toys for my approval. Later, I am taken on a tour of the property, which stands on a steep slope in one of Tijuana's poorest and most crime-ridden *colonias*. Here I get to engage more fully with the children as a group as we point, gesticulate and generally have fun trying to understand each other. One of the daughters is particularly proud of her responsibilities with the chickens. I meet Uncle Raul, who is building a house next door. Like Fernanda's older structure, his new house is primarily comprised of cinder-blocks and, when done, it will become his principle residence. He is also responsible for building a smaller wooden home down the side of the canyon, which is rented out to Fernanda's cousin from Mixteca, a poor rural region in SW Mexico. Most of Fernanda's family are now moved to Tijuana. She and her husband were the first to come, eight years ago. I want to know how her husband died and what that loss has meant to her but know not how to broach the issue through my translator. My concerns about intruding on a sensitive area overshadow my curiosity. As we get ready to leave I find I cannot engage the old departmental field vehicle in four-wheel-drive to back up on the treacherously steep dirt road. My rear wheels spin in loose sand. One of Uncle Raul's friends comes out and moves his vehicle so we don't have to back up: Sympathetic looks at the American professor who does not know how to negotiate a Tijuana street.

I've lived in this border region for over 20 years and am currently working on projects involving a diverse array of young people spanning the geographies of relatively new Latino immigrant communities in San Diego to old fish camps on the Sea of Cortez where the children trace their ancestry back six generations to when the Jesuit Missionaries arrived in Baja California. I struggle with my lack of Spanish, my whiteness, my adultness, my status, my relative affluence and my ability to escape to the mesa upon which I work and live comfortably, but most of all I struggle with my research agenda and the ways it relates to the lives of these young people and their families.

Through a variety of qualitative methods, is it sufficient to simply rework other people's experiences through my experiences and my writing? In this, all I offer is my perspective on being in their worlds. What violence do I permeate with this perspective? I like making friends with these young people. I enjoy their laughter at my attempts to communicate in Spanish. I like hanging out with them and learning about their worlds. A huge issue with my arrogance here, I think, is that even if I accept that I cannot write for so-called 'others,' my suggestion that writing about 'my perspective on being in their worlds' calls in to question the *a priori* existence of many different, distinct 'cultures' and an unproblematic distinction between my perspective (or, as Akhil Gupta and James Ferguson (1992) call it, 'our own society') and that of another.

What I want to get to in this chapter is the notion that out of connectedness arises a politics of difference, of cultural distinctiveness if you will, that is simply not reducible to a politics of representation because it is also about the emotions that encounters with difference and diversity entail. What I mean, in a nutshell, is that political acumen often foments from emotionally connections. Ruth Behar (1996) points out that emotive drives arise from the potential vulnerability embedded in qualitative methods that can 'break hearts.' I have no doubts today that qualitative research is heart work, but it also has a powerfully political potential.

A few weeks ago I sat with the son of a Mexican migrant laborer and listened to him talk of his life with his father as they traveled around the US following seasonal employment. When he got to the part where he sat at his fathers' death bed and they got to reconcile some of their differences, there were tears in both our eyes. At that moment, the research was not as important as the shared heartache. I connected through my friend to the reconciliation that never happened for my father and I, and in our emotions we found common ground. No words can articulate that connectedness. The experience comprises a politics of difference that is unrepresentable. The practice of qualitative research is not 'academic' in the sense that it is objective or devoid of feelings. It is very much about feelings that are, as Nigel Thrift (2004: 64) points out, 'a push in the world.' I am now pushed to think about the important geographies of family reconciliations and I am beginning to work with some communities at the border on substance abuse intervention programs involving fathers and their families.

The push of heart work, I aver, is where a power over the politics of otherness finds a form that is material and geographic. Doreen Massey (2005: 149–52) calls this material and geographic connection *throwntogetherness,* which she describes as 'the politics of the event of place ... [P]laces pose in particular form the question of our living together' and the problem with so-called spatial politics is that they are concerned with how the 'irreducibility' and 'instability' of space can be ordered and coded, 'how the terms of connectivity might be negotiated ... Just as so many of our accustomed ways of imagining space have been attempts to tame it.' In sum, this chapter is about recognizing that taming and suggesting, in a halting and uneven way, an avenue to get beyond it by recognizing the power of affect.

This chapter, then, is about encountering diversity in the context of places, identities, and an affective politics of difference. It is about the problematic geographies of ethnography, oral histories, archival research, interviews and all other qualitative methods that attempt to order the beauty and chaos of diversity by tying it to some known, coded and tamed space. To clarify my reading of how this came about, I begin with perhaps the most ordered theories of encounter that distanced the so-called exotic 'other' through colonialism and imperialism. I note the common aspects of oppression through, amongst other things, spectacles that tie 'others' in distant places to 'others' nearer at hand, down the road, across the tracks. This is followed by a discussion of spaces of identity that tackle newer wisdoms on encounter, which begins with what has come to be

called the 'crisis of representation' and leads to post-colonial and border methodologies. In the final section, I point to new geographies of care that suggest hope for renewed and responsible modes of encounter with difference.

THEORIES OF ENCOUNTER

I surprise myself with a compulsion to note at the outset that encountering diversity is not about going to the other side of the planet (or the other side of the tracks) to find and engage people who are not like me. I say this because, as a qualitative researcher who embraces fieldwork as a geographic strategy, I do not think I am as yet methodologically beyond this kind of colonial way of knowing difference through ordered space. The past two decades witnessed a protracted discussion about the ways we, as academics, encounter difference and qualitative research publications are now awash with stories of how much we think about where we position ourselves in relation to those we study. I am troubled with the spatial orders suggested by this positioning and my lack of progress methodologically in embracing the chaos and complexities of encounter. There is much going on rhetorically *and* I still *do* ethnographies, mappings, oral histories and so forth, perhaps complicating these field contexts with adjectives such as critical, participatory, embedded or situated. How well do these adjectives move me beyond my arrogance, my fears and the safety of my 'tried and true methodologies,' the safety of my white, male, stoic suite whose spikes protect me from any kind of long-term commitment to responsibility and care (Figure 3.1)?

A suit of spikes

A few months ago I was part of an interview team focusing on substance abuse amongst high-school kids. Sean Crotty and

Figure 3.1 'Wildman' costume, 18th or 19th century, Germany or Switzerland.
Two-piece leather suite with wood spikes and iron chain, and metal helmet with metal spikes.
Source: **Exhibit in "Witness to a Surrealist Vision," The Menil Collection, Houston, 2005.**

I interviewed Mike, a young man who has been in and out of juvenile hall and who struggles with methamphetamine and marijuana addiction (Crotty *et al.*, 2008). The interview was conducted in one of our conference rooms at the university. I pushed this location because I was busy and did not want to take the time to visit Mike's home. I persuaded Sean that this was a quieter location and that Mike might enjoy the experience of campus. Throughout the interview I felt disconnected, like I was wearing academic robes bristling with spikes. I was the professor and this was my space. I owned it.

Mike worked really hard to tell his story; he was nervous and I think that he found the whole context overwhelming if not intimidating. I judge that I was the problem, and yet the interview went well despite my spikes. At that particular moment I was too busy to care about Mike in ways that I wanted to care. We wrote our essay on Mike's daily life and it is a good representation in large part because Sean is emotionally connected to this young man and continues working with him as a friend and mentor. I learned that sometimes my commitment to a book editor is more important than my commitment to those who give up their time and energy to be part of my research. And when I perform this particular kind of connection – when I create a you–me distinction where my work is more important than this moment with you – I perform the kind of inhumanity that is represented in Figure 3.1.

Difference is complicated, comprising multifarious axes that are about, amongst other things, performed ethnicities, sexualities, politics, ages, abilities, class relations, education and knowledge bases, and cultures. It is also about global connections, and yet the moral and ethical considerations of communicating across axes of difference may well be the same everywhere.[3] For the most part, at least in principle, I accept that difference needs to be more than an us–them proposition and yet the history of qualitative methods suggests a calculated distancing that positions me as a researcher behind the safety of a spiked suit.

Different people in distant places

From the vantage point of the colonized – the subalterns, the subjects of investigation, the so-called participants and co-creators of our work – the term 'research' is inextricably linked with European colonialism. The ways in which scientific research is implicated in the worst excesses of imperialism remains a powerfully remembered history for many of the world's colonized peoples to the extent that Linda Tuhiwai Smith (1999: 1) exclaims that 'the word itself, *research* is probably one of the dirtiest words in the indigenous world's vocabulary.' Writing from the vantage point of the colonized, she suggests that research 'offends the deepest sense of our humanity.' Part of that offence is methodological because '… it is difficult to discuss *research methodology* and *indigenous peoples* together, in the same breath, without having an analysis of imperialism' (Smith, 1999: 2).

Jane M. Jacobs (1996) argues that imperialism and colonialism are terms that may be differentiated by their positioning within the power geographies of empire itself. Imperialism belongs to the metropolitan core and expands to the colonial periphery. Colonialism, by this definition, is a specific articulation of imperialism associated with territorial, cultural, and economic invasions. At its base, it is about the expansion of capitalism through the conquest of other people's lands and labor in the service of the metropolitan core. Our contradictory present moment, then, is as much about now as then, as much about imperial global as classist local, as much about place as a fractured semblance of political identities. In short, imperialism and colonialism along with classism, racism, ageism, ableism, sexism and so forth are about spatial ordering that puts 'others' in their place and protects my sensibilities behind an impenetrable suit of spikes.

My discussion of imperialism and colonialism begins with a journey through early encounters with difference with the caveat (from my encounter with Mike) that this form of colonial research still occurs, even amongst those of us with the best intentions. Indeed, the belief that our research is benefiting the world in some way is, in and of itself, an arrogance of Western ideology and scientific training that points to problematic political innocence in an as-yet-to-be-unwoven imperialist world (cf. Jacobs, 1996). Also, it is worth noting that past colonial research into the lifeworlds of 'others' was not always exploitative and maliciously tied to centers of capital. Nonetheless, there are many clear connections (then and today) between the discipline of geography and imperialism.

Empirical documentation

In prior so-called conventional cross-cultural research the relations between researcher and researched were left unexamined in favor of purely empirical speculations. What is now known as colonial research has a long history in qualitative fieldwork and is derived in part from this blind empiricism that left domination and exploitation unexamined. Difference was accepted as a natural, pre-given context of lived experience and the task of the qualitative researcher was to document the wild, dissonant ways of different people in distant places. Early on, there was nothing better than letting the so-called facts speak volumes, highlighting the spectacle of others. Geographic work such as that of Carl Sauer and the Berkeley school of cultural geography was heavily influenced by the empiricism of British and US anthropologists from the nineteenth century. These 'modern' geographers traced their roots to the fieldwork of Alexander von Humbolt who, in 1845 and after several decades of self-financed travel, began writing down 'everything that is known about the earth' in his popular *Kosmos*, which included a later volume on all the ways that 'humans' efforts describe the earth' (quoted in Martin and James, 1993: 131). This empiricism was powered by questionnaire and interview as the main methods of colonial administrators, missionaries, traders, and the odd scientifically inclined aristocrat such as von Humbolt. The data were sent back from the colonial periphery to the metropolitan heartland where experts evaluated their worth.

A noted ethnographic example of the time is Sir James George Frazer's *The Golden Bough* (1900), which described in detail regional folklore and legends that relate to magic and religion. The cultural imperialism of this celebrated work finds its most explicit form in Frazer's suggestion that the truly civilized races are the ones whose minds evolve beyond magical and religious belief to embrace the rational structures of scientific thought. Frazer's conjectures were based on observation, measurement and assessment. Indigenous peoples were measured from their heads to their toes and, for the most part, assessed as infantile and mentally inferior. In a volume on Maori culture that was based in part on measurement of cranium size, for example, the totality of a people and their history were judged as comprising 'generations of mental indolence' from the 'comparative smallness of the brain' (Thompson, 1859: 81, quoted in Smith, 1999: 1).[4]

Visualizing 'others'

Given the penchant of empiricism for documenting the observable, it is no accident that by the mid-nineteenth century the medium of photography illustrated ethnographic field-notes, suggesting truth through visual evidence. These encounters lead to the development of theories concerning the separate ethnic origins and the biology of racial difference proffered by US anthropologists such as Louis Agassiz and Samuel Morton (Mitchell, 2002). Toward the end of the nineteenth century, photography and the politics of race were pushed further by popular figures such as Edward Curtis and John Wesley Powell (Figure 3.2) (Fowler *et al.*, 1981; Jackson, 1992). Using John Berger's (1972) 'ways of seeing' as a radical approach to representation, Peter Jackson (1992) notes that visual politics became increasingly important in the compilation of scientific 'evidence' of racial difference.

That Curtis and Powell often 'doctored' their photographs of Native Americans to remove problematic 'modern' artifacts and to create a romantic sense of a lost, but also inferior, civilization seemed of little concern: 'The Victorian penchant for scientific measurement and classification was soon brought to bear on the question of "racial" origins and human evolution, providing scientific legitimation for imperial expansion overseas'

Figure 3.2   John Wesley Powell with Ute woman, probably in Uinta basin.
Source: **Photograph by J.K. Hillers (1874), from the Smithsonian Institution, Bureau of American Ethnology Collection.**

(Jackson, 1992: 91). And the spectacle of the visual provided not only an anchor for scientific empiricism, it also highlighted ethnographic methods as appropriate for political commentary and social reform.

As ethnographic methods and the advent of small hand-held cameras toward the end of the nineteenth century aided imperial expansion overseas, construction of the 'other' returned, with an empirical gaze, to the metropolitan core. Jacob Riis' *How the Other Half Lives* (1890) is a classic example of the early use of visual representations and ethnographies at the heart of the metropolitan core to highlight the spectacular as a political commentary. The book was replete with visual imagery of grimy alleys, dank buildings and the gaunt, seemingly depraved, looks of poor immigrant children (Figure 3.3). Riis promoted the book and the need for social reform with anthropological lectures illustrated by lantern slides, bringing visual evidence of the exotic other on the streets of American cities. The outrage of middle-class viewers was tempered by a sanitized voyeurism – a prototype for virtual tourism – where the slum could be viewed safely and without accompanying dirt, odious smells and seeming human vulgarity. Importantly for the possibility of social reform, paired lantern slides enabled a simultaneous inspection of immigrant children before and after rehabilitation (Gagen, 2000). The clarion call here was to control these despicable slums as breeding grounds for crime and depravity through spatial means by removing the children to institutions and foster homes. In addition, space was appropriated in American and European cities for playgrounds that could accommodate these young people and help transform them into a pliant citizenry. In a study of the Playground Association of America (PAA), Elizabeth Gagen (2000) notes how playing fields for older boys were constructed solely for sports such as baseball or football where rambunctious individuals learnt how to perform heroically, to obey authority and be loyal on a team to the point of personal sacrifice. Consequently, they were prepared for civil life and war. Girls as part of these urban playgrounds, in contrast, were taught quiet non-competitive activities such as sewing and knitting in preparation for patriotism and domestic life. In the UK, Margaret McMillan similarly was able to put poor children on the political agenda of the British Labor Party. Like Riis, McMillan described striking vignettes that allowed her readers to 'see' the need for cleaning up notoriously 'poor and derelict' parts of southeast London (Steedman, 1995: 2).

The positioning of the urban poor as a separate class in this way was important for three reasons. First, seemingly unruly children were placed under a controlling public eye. Second, their disciplined bodies were put on display in public parks to attest to the social and spatial changes underway. Third, a larger colonial project is instilled whereby the metropolitan core produces and defines all peripheral spaces. With foster care, playgrounds, surveillance, spectacle and discipline,

Figure 3.3   Mullen's Alley, c. 1888. Museum of the City of New York, The Jacob A. Riis Collection.

the control of space, the control of bodies and the control of social reproduction are interwoven in the same project, which by the nineteenth century was quite definitely global. American schooling and playground projects were extended to other countries through an imperial doctrine couched in the new discipline of developmental psychology that pointed to primitivism and infantilization of children at home in direct association with the colonial other abroad (Gagen, 2008).

Measurement and control of bodies in space proceeded through the imperial, colonial, classist, racist and sexist moments of the late nineteenth and early twentieth centuries. Louis Sullivan's (1923) 'anthropometric' text, for example, provided detailed instructions about posing subjects against a regular grid in order to ensure accurate measurements of body shape and size. Clearly, posing and capturing images, and then later doctoring negatives, suggests an inherent inequality in the relationship between the researcher and the researched, our society and their tribes (as well as us as adults against our children). Riis' and Curtis' work contains evidence of manipulation and deliberate deception and, as Jackson (1992: 97) rightly points out, this 'merely highlights the extent to which all representations of other cultures are an ideo-logical fiction – cultural constructions which reveal in their making the interests that they serve.' Curtis' ways of seeing, and Riis' con-trivances of the depraved were common amongst lay and academic contemporaries, establishing a legitimacy for an imperialist, colonial and class-based supremacy.

The sales of the von Humbolt's *Kosmos* and, a little later, Frazer's *The Golden Bough* and Riis' *How the Other Half Lives*, suggest the immense popularity of texts that docu-mented, represented, exoticized and spectac-ularized the 'other' from elsewhere and the 'other' on our own doorstep.

A reification of 'man's role in the changing the face of the Earth[5]

Von Humboldt's penchant for describing *all* the ways mankind's efforts describe the earth continued apace through the mid-twentieth century. Within academic geography a set of theoretical structures underpinned by science reified the conjoining of qualitative methods (used to document facts about people and places) with conventional wisdom on spaces and environments as containers for human endeavors. The Vienna Circle championed logical positivism in the 1930s with the purpose of redirecting the scientific method to the study of human behavior and the out-come of that behavior in changed environ-ments (Kitchin, 2006). Geographers embraced some of the central analytical and deductive tenets of positivism to the extent they sug-gested that behaviors (and cultures) could be explained, or at least elaborated, through very specific understandings of environments as stages upon which human activities evolved while at the same time transforming those environments (space as a Euclidean co-determinant of human activities was a logical extension of these ideas). The quantitative/qualitative divide has been discussed *ad nau-seum* in geography, and to a large extent there is a demonizing of positivism and quantification (see Fotheringham, 2006)

while at the same time few contemporary qualitative geographers acknowledge early complicities with logical positivism and cur-rent complicities with neo-colonialism.

Positivism is based on the premise that empiricism must reach the goal of positive knowledge. At its best, positivism prioritizes the actual, the certain, the exact, the useful, the organic and the relative. The facts derived from fieldwork – data contained within field-logs, diaries, carefully crafted maps, inter-views and discussions – are rigorously analyzed, triangulated with other facts, and placed within the semblance of systematic models for further analysis and interpreta-tion. And this is the huge legacy of scientific empiricism: that data are testable, verifiable, and generalizable to some domesticated understanding of the way things are without the messiness of subjectivity, ideology and emotion. It is, to a large degree, about the taming of peoples and spaces.[6]

What many cultural geographers did not recognize through a large swathe of the twentieth century was that their stalwart clar-ity, their science – their phenomenology as Sauer (1925) called it – was already always tainted by subjectivity, by value-laden clas-sifications and meanings that emanated from a prior colonial and imperialist worldview and was unquestioningly superimposed upon people who were different and spaces that were thoroughly tamed. Under traditional banners of science and academic research, cultures and peoples were reinvented and redefined to fit inside the worldview of the research, which was predicated for the most part by imperialist classifications and philo-sophical systems.

The irony of expedition

Bill Bunge turned some of these notions on their head with his formulation of 'geograph-ical expeditions' in Detroit and Toronto in the 1970s (Bunge, 1973; Bunge and Bordessa, 1975). Cutting his academic teeth as an apocalyptic messenger of science and spatial modeling, Bunge was the first to move away from a perspective that, he felt, capitulated to empire and capitalism (Merryfield, 1995). Bunge set out to do two things that are of import to this discussion. First, using settings in North American cities ironically, he highlighted the cultural arrogance of exotic ethnographic work elsewhere. For example, his famous map of Detroit with infant mortality rates from the global south superimposed was one of the first suggestions of the nearness of seemingly distant issues. Second, by focusing on immediacy, he wrecked known positivist wisdom about people and space. His 'fly cover baby regions' map, for example, was created from field observations of whether houses had screens on windows and doors (Figure 3.4).

Another irony of Bunge's work is that, throughout, he is a staunch supporter of the merits of quantification and the search for scientific theory. As such, his studies are peppered with quantitative data (such as census based infant mortality records) and aggregate spatial models that contrive a study of spatial structure and interaction. For example, he uses the Chicago School's famed concentric ring model of urban ecological structure to argue that the changes we need to focus on are not based on classic economic theory but on theories of exploitation (Figure 3.5). His central theme of spatial (particularly children's) oppression, however, is built from his use of poignant qualitative and participatory methods. His quixotic search for a truly spatial understanding – what he called spatial primitives – notwithstanding, Bunge embraces lessons from the field. For example, he describes encounters with African-American women who 'hated my concern about the three dimensionality of the species ... filled with hatred against me because I did not notice the children being murdered by automobiles in front of their homes or children starving in front of abundant food. "Immediacy" was their cry, "To Hell with the World!"' (Bunge, 1971: 170).

The spatial models of the time, as those of today, are to a large extent privileged knowledge claims because for the most part they do not speak directly to people's needs. As a search for what we know of today as situated knowledge, Andrew Merryfield (1995: 50) argues that Bunge's expeditions were ahead of their time, providing 'a conceptual platform from which to call into question all privileged knowledge.' Bunge began with models, and ended with mapable data that emerged from extensive fieldwork, producing knowledge that enabled the creation of new kinds of maps. Donna Haraway (1991: 191) calls these 'maps of consciousness' for people, who by virtue of their class, ethnicity, sex or age are marginalized through masculinist, racist and colonialist domination.

Situated knowledge is embedded in local areas, conditioned through time and embodied in people and their actions. It was not until the 1990s that geographers in qualitative methods realized fully the importance of this form of encounter. For Bunge, in the 1970s, there were no social theories of situatedness. Nonetheless, he saw the ways that economic models of the time masked important social and economic contexts, because they missed sites of reproduction where marginalized groups – children, injured workers, retired workers, unemployed workers and sexually, racially, ethnically and religiously discriminated-against workers – constitute the majority of the working class even during periods of full employment (Bunge, 1971). To offset this problem he reworked standard models such as those of the Chicago School of Urban Ecology to emphasis oppression (Figure 3.5).

Bunge's practice – his fieldwork – was to live with those who were marginalized, to bring them into his home, to muddy up the contexts of his and their lives by bringing them on campus and to colleagues' homes (often unannounced and to the annoyance of his colleagues). The irony of his fieldwork is that it was not at all like an 'expedition' in the contrived colonial sense but rather it strove for exploration that went both ways, and attempted to transcend the contrived classes of capitalism to get at the humanity below.

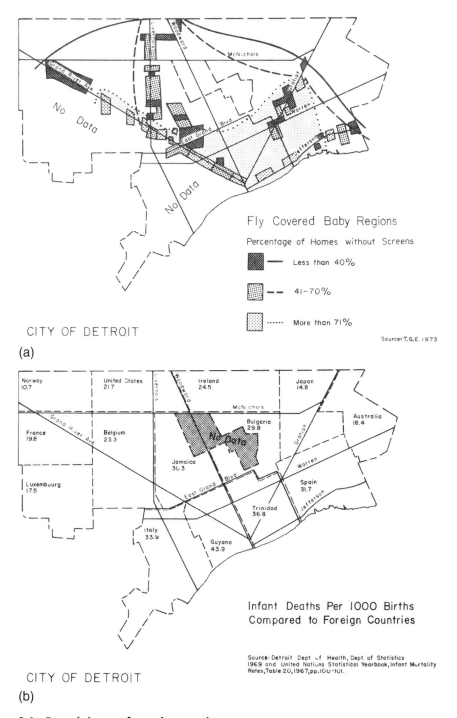

Figure 3.4   Bunge's 'maps of consciousness.'

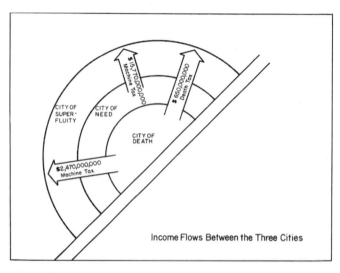

Income Flows Between the Three Cities

Figure 3.5   Bunge's ironic use of Burgess' spatial model of Urban Ecology.

Bunge's 'positionality' was Marxist and his intent was to stir a revolution that was as obviously the next step to him as if it were part of Darwin's theories of evolution (cf. Bunge, 1973). This kind of biological and political teleology is clearly problematic because it suggests a very specific form of encounter. As researchers grappled with these problematic and overarching ways of knowing other people and how they crept into aspects of their work, they also began to feel that perhaps there were even more foundational problems that related not to overarching theories but to modes of encounter, representation and legitimation.

QUESTIONING REPRESENTATION AND LEGITIMATION

An academic crisis began brewing in the 1970s, stemming in part from uncertainty about how to approach so-called subjects and how to write about them. The context that Bunge was so comfortable with did not resonate elsewhere in the discipline where, for perhaps the first time, researchers working with people were very unclear about how to situate themselves in relation to whom and

what they studied. New work began questioning how the relations 'between researched and researcher inform our agendas and knowledge claims, how our work is affected by the communities and places we study, and how immersion in particular cultural (including economic and political) frameworks and academic and theoretical traditions informs research goals and methods' (Nast, 1994: 54). Quantitative surveys and questionnaires were easily discounted as distanced from the participants and not reflecting anything but a problematic average person. And yet, as we have seen, qualitative methods were also a large part of the methodological agendas of imperialism and colonialism.

Ethnography and participant observation were also questioned for their penchant for distancing researcher from researched and serving personal academic agendas (e.g. promotion and tenure) rather than the agendas of the researched. Ethnography, in its traditional usage, was seen as problematic if it was simply about the creation of data and 'writing about culture' was its literal definition. In their introduction to *Writing Culture* – a book that became emblematic of the crisis of representation – James Clifford and George Marcus (1986: 2) note that when our writing about culture is not problematized it 'reflects the persistence of an ideology claiming transparency of representation and immediacy of experience. Writing reduced to method: keeping good field notes, making accurate maps, writing up results.' Mike Crang (2005) points out two problems with this. First, traditional empirically-based ethnography risks missing points if informants disavow, hide or lie about their interests. To call ethnographies fictions may raise empiricist hackles. But a fiction does not connote a falsehood; it suggests rather an inherently partial – committed and incomplete – truth (Clifford and Marcus, 1986). Second, and perhaps more critically, as a tautological process, a traditional ethnography that suggests a truth, like most basic empiricism, cannot by definition bring new understandings to bear on issues. This of course, is not to suggest that all traditional ethnography was (or is) tautological.

Through the 1980s, a slue of writing in anthropology, geography, sociology, education and elsewhere suggested an interpretative turning point (Price, 1983; Marcus and Fisher, 1986; Clifford, 1988; Rosaldo, 1989). Pablo Vila (2003) sums up this changed way of knowing in terms of several agendas coming together simultaneously: (i) a noting of the complicity of Western ethnography with colonialist and imperialist projects; (ii) a recognition that any representation is fundamentally the product of asymmetrical power relations; and (iii) an acknowledgment that ethnographic writing is part of institutionally, historically and politically situated forces. This was not just a representational crisis that pointed out the problems of qualitative attempts to capture lived experience, it was also a legitimation crisis whereby several axioms of science – validity, generalizability, reliability – were called into question.

The end of empirical legitimation

The work of James Clifford (1988), and George Marcus and Martin Fischer (1986) along with Clifford Geertz (1988) on 'the

crisis of representation' suggested that not only did teleological thinking rest on unsteady premises about how the world developed, but almost all aspects of academic field accounting rested on teetering foundations. The implication is that it was no longer possible to assume a mantle of scientific objectivity that Victorian anthropologists and cultural geographers adopted in their descriptions of other cultures. Marcus and Fischer (1986) looked back at the classic anthropological texts of Bronislaw Malinowski and Franz Boas to argue that their representation of 'the other' was hugely problematic and clearly said more about them as researchers than any suggested truth about the peoples they studied. Here, for example, is Malinkowski (1967) discussing an encounter with a village in the Trobriand Islands in 1917: 'On the whole the village struck me rather unfavorably … disorganization … rowdiness. At moments I was furious with [the inhabitants], particularly because after I gave them their portions of tobacco they all went away' (quoted in Geertz, 1988: 73–74).

At this time, anthropologists were still likened to explorers discovering the exotic other and presenting objective scientific clarity, but Malinkowski's remarks suggest a much messier process that indicates clear affective dimensions. His field account is about space that is chaotic and disorganized and people who are rowdy. His reaction at this display of life 'as is' was, at moments, fury! The crisis of representation questioned the possibility of representing others in a value-free way after visceral encounters of this kind. It challenged contemporary research and writing to be more reflexive and emotive, and – like Bunge a decade earlier – it called into question all the fury of sex, class and ethnicity. The seeming innocence that may have once informed somewhat distanced methods and theories was now lost in the move towards a more critical sense of cultural politics. This critical sense rejected scientific objectivism, value-free writing, naturalism, positivism, complicity with colonialism and theories that structure ways of life inflexibly. Feminist, queer, post-colonial and post-structural theories now gain legitimacy, while at the same time I am pushed to question my political position vis-à-vis those with whom I work.

My writing may call attention to a politics of representation, and it is also always a representation in and of itself. But this begs questions about how it can be something more, and in what ways this 'more' is about the productiveness of spatiality? In this way complicity with imperialism continues. My crisis (of representation? of affect?) asks if it is possible to effect change. But perhaps before that question is engaged it is important to understand more cleanly what is meant by the *spaces of fieldwork* because fieldwork is perhaps the (emotional) 'heart of geography … the most magical, essential, and challenging part of being a geographer' (Stevens, 2001: 66). One answer to the question of crisis, I aver, is a fundamental and emotive acknowledgment of diverse spaces of encounter in a chaotic throwntogetherness.

CHAOTIC SPACES OF ENCOUNTER

If I acknowledge the tamed spaces of colonialism, imperialism and positivism, then what kind of space do I produce and occupy in the field? Of late, there has been a lot of discussion about what is meant by the field and fieldwork, and about related multiple versions of embeddedness, positionality, situatedness, out-there-ness and in-here-ness (Howitt and Stevens, 2005). Cindi Katz (1994) elaborates a space-of-betweenness, which is not quite out there with others and not quite in here, safely ensconced in an office. She points out that 'under conditions of globalization and post-positivist thought in the social sciences we are always already in the field – multiply positioned actors, aware of the partiality of all our stories and the artifice of the boundaries drawn in order to tell them' (Katz, 1994: 66). I'll have more to say about this kind of produced space in a moment, for it begs questions that relate to

how difference is encountered. But first, it is clear that more needs to be said about the discursive moment and spatial practices to which Katz alludes.

Discursive spatial practice

Ruth Fincher and Jane Jacobs (1998) note that taking difference seriously does not at all imply the practice of joyous indulgence in diversity, nor does it cast research into a form of depoliticized relativism. Power, inequality and politics all come in to play when taking difference seriously: oppression, injustice and exclusion all work through regimes of difference. And the importance of re-theorizing spaces of difference is the importance of a real, relevant and *located* politics of difference:

> Emphasizing difference does not simply mean charting new, more nuanced uneven geographies … [i]t also means attending to the various ways that specificity – both social and spatial – can transform structures of power and privilege; the ways that oppressed groups can, through a politics of identity and a politics of place, reclaim rights, resist and subvert. (Fincher and Jacobs, 1998: 2)

Over the last two decades, sensitivity to difference in part responds to the convincing insights of the subaltern, those 'others' who are the so-called empirical evidence of past scientific enquiry, and who have known well the structuring of difference and the importance of identity politics (Anzaldúa, 1987; Spivak, 1988, 1990; Bhabha, 1994; Smith, 1999). Their voices challenge single authoritative narratives and help open up a space in which difference is theorized in new ways. This space is a new post-colonial space and is informed by a body of writing I'll have more to say about in a moment. A second, related focus on difference and, in particular, identity politics comes from a feminist perspective on the ways that identities are embedded in frameworks of power. The work of Judith Butler (1990, 1993) stimulated a feminist focus on structures of difference and the ways authority is encoded through processes of regulation and repetition whereby uneven empowerment gains legitimacy.

Butler (1990: 24) argues that specific forms of power are differentially constituted through repeated performances: '… *gender* is not a noun, but neither is it a set of free-floating attributes, … gender is performatively produced and compelled by the regulatory practices of gender coherence.'

When difference is talked about methodologically there is clear resonance with the idea that there are important distinctions between people and groups. These distinctions may be marked along axes of age, gender, ethnicity, sexuality, culture or any other referent. Most often, difference is articulated through a complex combination of defining characteristics, and so any one person or group may by understood as multiply and variably positioned. We are all racialized, classed *and* gendered to some degree or another, and there is no certainty in how these three axes of difference (for there are many more) coalesce to provide opportunities or to structure constraints. Moreover, these are not stable or pre-given categories of existence and so their mapping in the traditional sense is hugely problematic. This is why Bunge's ironic mappings of difference are so effective (Figure 3.5).

The methodological problem is not just to map patterns but to chart the varied processes through which difference is constituted and to elaborate how these processes are embedded in power relations. Some of these relations are embedded and/or repeated to the extent that they may appear natural or, at least, legitimate. Iris Marion Young (1990) helps us considerably in this regard by suggesting how we might approach a politics of difference. For Young, it is not about mapping and thus reifying categories of difference. She points out that this is already done as standard practice in politics and planning. Although contemporary society is discursively committed to equality, at the ideological level injustices to those categorized as 'other' are veiled in everyday habits and cultural meanings (Young, 1990). Side-stepping patterns, Young focuses on variable vectors of power and the oppressions they produce. She takes explicit axes of oppression such as racism, sexism, ageism and homophobia, and reformulates them into five broader modalities of power that involve issues of justice beyond distribution; these she labels exploitation, marginalization, powerlessness, cultural imperialism and violence (Young, 1990). By so doing, Young is attempting to move beyond neat categories of difference and singular alignments between oppressed and oppressor. By pluralizing the category of oppression in this way, Young opens methodological possibilities that avoid the exclusive and oversimplifying effects of denying difference within groups or leaving out important ways that groups are oppressed. By adding the complexities of multiple axes of oppression without diluting the force of oppressive practices she provides a methodology for highlighting the myriad ways difference is articulated as a form of disenfranchisement. It addresses the problem, for example, that feminists and anti-racist theorists have with Marxism's reduction of all oppressions to class oppression that leaves out the very specific oppressions of Blacks and women. Methodologically, each of Young's five criteria of oppression can be operationalized; 'each can be applied through the assessment of observable behavior, status relationships, distributions, texts and other cultural artifacts' (1990: 64). The criteria serve as a qualitative assessment of claims that a group is oppressed, or an adjudication of whether or how a group is oppressed. In short, they provide a unifying benchmark from which researchers may assess powerful oppressions. This is different from a problematic mapping of difference through census categories and yet it does not offset the political power of ironic mapping such as those provided by Bunge. And, importantly, it is very different from a celebration of difference through which categories of existence are gaily represented *ad nauseam*. Such as position reifies a one-dimensional form of exotic otherness that situates the researcher as an impotent tourist, representing badly the lives of oppressed peoples. Further, beyond a mapping of patterns, this methodology acknowledges throwntogetherness and the powerful spaces of interdependency that are elaborated through this kind of connection. Throwntogetherness is complicated, and political cooperation 'requires first that people whose lives and actions affect one another in a web of institutions, interactions, and unintended consequences acknowledge that they are together in ... a space of mutual effect' (Young, 2000).

Expansive spaces and border methodologies

Recognizing the vital role of highlighting my own positionality in spaces of mutual effect, the question arises of how to dialogue with other people in different contexts. Clearly, I cannot say anything I like and pass it off as coherently derived and trustworthy. Vague judgments may be as damaging as lies and contrived contexts. It is problematic, as Jim Thomas (1993) suggests, to leap to conclusions that fit our sensibilities without demonstrable and cogent theoretical and empirical linkages. And yet, as we have seen, theory and empiricism are problematically contrived in and of themselves without a full accounting of intuition, affect and moral sensibilities. In this regard, understanding the nuances of connection is important. One of the most difficult aspects of field encounters is to resist our conception of the familiar and the domestic. Madison (2005: 6) argues that domestication diminishes 'the capacity to envision alternative life possibilities; domestication will prohibit new forms of addressing conflict, and it will dishonor the foreign and the different.' To avoid the boundedness of domestication, self-reflexivity is vital because it forces me to acknowledge the way power is expressed through me, and it leads to an examination of my privilege and my bias at the same moment as I denounce the power structures that surround those I encounter. By so doing, I expand space and diminish the bounding power of my conception of the familiar and the domestic.

For me, some of the most fruitful encounters with diversity complicate the whole notion of identity and difference. My earlier recounting of an interview with the son of a Mexican migrant laborer fomented a shared experience that related to the ways he connected with his father and I did not. It was an emotive expansion of space and time that took him to the deathbed of his father in Illinois and to my last meeting with my father in Scotland. The interview took our Saturday afternoon, placing us on his deck overlooking a sun-drenched valley in East San Diego; it embraced our different experiences of fathering and connected the ways we were fathered in a space that expanded to encompass two continents. The nuances, complexities and contradictions that are found in recent border literature suggests precisely this kind of expansive space (Vila, 2003). It is, in a very real sense, about identity politics in spaces-of-betweenness that expand beyond national boundaries to the frontiers of sun-drenched Californian valleys and urban neighborhoods; that expand beyond the norms of academic research; that expand beyond the known of science and art (Anzaldúa, 1987; Cisneros, 1989; Price, 2000). It is the work of a generation of qualitative researchers who are influenced by the 'crossing borders' metaphor (Vila, 2003); a metaphor that embraces all aspects of my work. My border research is as much about crossing the street to talk to my neighbor as is about crossing into Tijuana to talk to child laborers; it is about crossing campus to talk to computer scientists while at the same time experimenting with communicating ideas through music rather than words. Borders are real and imagined.

For border researchers, the material conditions of lived reality cannot be divorced from social, economic and cultural boundaries that involve contradictions, conflicts and shifts in political identities. And, like all the contemporary qualitative methodologies discussed in this book, border methodologies are engaged theoretically. Unlike the nineteenth and twentieth centuries empiricism discussed earlier, border methodologies recognize that there are no pure facts, just facts framed in multiple ways of knowing. Similarly, there are no pure observations, but rather observations embedded in a theory-laden vocabulary (Vila, 2003). Border crossing, then, is about literal borders and it is also about crossing genres, crossing methodologies and getting beyond the borders of empiricism and science into and out of literature, art and lived experience.

Border methodologies also open up new spaces of fieldwork where involvements are multiple, conflicting and ambiguous. And this is where Katz's spaces-of-betweeness is called into question: I am not the presumed outsider that I was constructed as by traditional research, nor am I an insider. Importantly, I do not leave behind my desires, expectations and longings for myself and for those with whom I learn. And, I am defined by alliances and separations that are sometimes hugely problematic.

I have no authority to speak for Fernanda and her children, and there is always danger that what I say may 'render the practices of the oppressed visible to those who dominate' (Katz, 1994: 71). Shortly after I spent the day with Fernanda and her family I am in Silvia's office at COLEF, Tijuana's research university. My Mexican colleague, friend and collaborator asks me, 'What about the children, Stuart? What are we doing for them?' We talk about the problem of suggesting that the children get involved with organized labor. A similar move in Mexico City resulted in the supermarkets pulling their support from the child packers' program. We talk about getting involved to help the children get more health care benefits. We talk about how sensitive Mexican officials are to foreign academics making policy recommendations. Is it better, perhaps, that I am not part of these young people's lives, even for a short time?

Decolonizing research and critical encounters

The question of activism highlights a normative stance that opposes colonialism and imperialism. Postcolonial research, informed by feminism and post-structuralism, is not only a reaction to an older problematic form of qualitative research, it is also intended to contribute to issues of justice, equality, self-determination and welfare through methodologies that explicitly value rights, concerns, desires, knowledge, well-being, and it acknowledges the relations between the researched and the researcher. Richie Howitt and Stan Stevens (2005) aver that decolonizing research goes further still in its attempt to use the research process to break down problematic cross-cultural discourses and asymmetrical power relations. Smith (1999) argues that postcolonial research needs to foster self determination and cultural affirmation. Howitt and Stevens (2005: 35) point out that this:

> Requires acknowledging and repudiating the dynamics of power that shape colonial research interactions with subordinated and marginalized peoples and groups, attempting to overcome whatever ethnocentrisms and paternalism we bring to the research and whatever suspicion we are greeted with, persuading people that we a worthy of being taught and capable of learning, and being willing to put aside preconceptions (and academic and activist preoccupations), to listen and to be of service to local concerns and projects.

In participatory, collaborative research an effort is made 'to create a space for more involvement by "others" as an integral part of the research process' so that locally relevant issues are addressed and self-determination and human rights supported (Howitt and Stevens, 2005: 43). The problem, of course, is to be clear on who is being given the opportunity to participate in whose project, and whose agendas dominate the research.

I like the idea of critical encounters, which forefront self-reflexivity and ethical responsibilities to address processes of unfairness and injustice within a particular lived locale. In this regard, I follow Madison's (2005: 5) definition of ethical responsibility as a 'compelling sense of duty and commitment based on moral principles of human freedom and well-being, and hence a compassion for the suffering of lived beings.' In many ways, this is a normative stance whereby I commit to focusing on lived conditions with an eye toward seeing ways to change them into something that they could be, perhaps toward greater freedom and equity. Critical encounters in the field are also always attempts to get below the surface. This may not happen in the field where immediacy contravenes in important ways. And yet, oftentimes it is the immediacy of connection that highlights critical reflection (Aitken, 2001). There is less of an inclination to discipline and domesticate knowledge and more of a drive to accommodate possibilities. From lived experiences in the field I find evidence that challenges institutions, disciplines and regimes of knowledge – including my own. If I am practicing qualitative methods that engage difference with approaches that push toward de-colonizing and de-domesticating peoples' lives then I must also be open to the de-colonization and de-domestication of myself, my society and my discipline.

If critical encounters are about uncovering unfairness and injustice, they are also about using the considerable resources within my grasp to effect change. This may include communicative skills and writing as well as abilities to dig up and uncover evidence of injustice. However, in the case of the Tijuana child supermarket workers any suggestion that the children should formally organize their labor might result in the supermarkets pulling support for the welfare program that they currently help fund, as happened in Mexico City. And yet, ultimately, I want to work through moral dilemmas and make a stand. Rather than involve organized labor, Silvia and I talk about suggesting modest health care benefits for the Tijuana child workers. And, this is something that I, as an American professor, cannot spearhead. My hope is that critical encounters of this kind move toward contributing to emancipatory knowledge and opening up avenues for social and spatial justice to creep in like a panther.

Beyond the discursive: Post-critical and experimental encounters

I am perplexed as I try to unravel the ways the young supermarket workers in Tijuana are burdened heavily and also liberated by the chimera of capitalism (Aitken, 2008). In a halting, naive and experimental way, I try to get at the ways that the machinations of borderspaces and so-called economic development are tied up with what I call children's *integral* (from the Spanish, meaning whole and essential) development in complex, irreducible and affective ways. I combine issues of child labor and globalization with a theoretical focus on transformative and affective political identities that foment from representations and actions that take place in particular material spaces. I make use of Deleuzian post-structural perspectives on affect to argue that young people and their labor are a remedy and an exacerbation to the fantastic promises of economic development. I am aided by Nigel Thrift's (2004: 64) overview of nonrepresentational theory, which provides something that is both concrete and relational with his suggestion that affect is 'a sense of push in the world.' The push may be a tug/movement/thrust to outrage, anger and action with witness to the exploitation of child laborers or it may be a push to spiritual enlightenment and stillness through the beauty of child laughter in the workplace. These are pushes toward emotions that inspire the world, and are part of what I call post-critical qualitative methods.

Experimental theorists like Gilles Deleuze are engaged in different 'modes of encounter' that elaborate meanings of 'difference' and 'multiplicities' that are, for me, a huge aid in de-colonization and de-domestication, in letting go of my presumptions over the classes and categories of being that seem to fit. The early writing of Deleuze (1986) inspires my speculations, with particular emphasis on what he says about affect and difference. His work suggests to me that what is presented through qualitative methods is not something that can be analyzed through texts, linguistic methods or representations. The focus turns, rather, toward how qualitative encounters with difference make me feel; the non-representable that churns my stomach or makes me smile. In short, Deleuze provides me with a theoretical acknowledgment that methods that break my heart provide an appropriate way of knowing.

Affect has some currency in geography today with calls for a more coherent understanding of emotions (Davidson *et al.*, 2006). Kay Anderson and Sue Smith (2001: 7) claim that the neglect of emotions in academic research suppresses 'a key set of relations through which lives are lived and societies made.' Emotions are all about encounters – they are highly political, racial and sexual – but they are rarely accommodated by academics as an important component of public action, care and responsibility. To paraphrase Anderson and Smith (2001), there are times and places where lives are explicitly lived through pain, love, shame, passion, anger and so forth to the extent that it is hard to discount the ways emotional relations dictate social practices.

Deleuze's concerns with emotion are spatialized in his work on geo-philosophy with Félix Guattari (1983, 1987). The corpus of Deleuze and Guattari's work suggests a non-representational and non-discursive way of knowing that relates difference to ways that ordered spaces are disrupted in quirky and relational ways. This way of knowing elaborates the possibility of affective disruptions and how those play out in qualitative encounters. Affective disruptions are difficult to represent and yet they point to ways that I connect in chaotic spaces of throwntogetherness. Deleuze's focus on the non-representable points to the possibility of understanding difference from a place that is ill-formed, undomesticated and indeterminate but nonetheless gets at the heart of current debates on the importance of emotional geographies (cf. Anderson and Smith, 2001; Thrift, 2004; Aitken, 2006; Davidson *et al.*, 2006). It is impossible for me to write a complete narrative about affective connections.

My connection with the son of the migrant laborer is ours alone and no documentation through writing or video can bring you thoroughly into that experience in the same way that I can never know my friend's connection with his father, and yet I may be able to bring you into connection with that part of you that understands the possibility of reconciliation. Ultimately, my writing is a form of representation and a form of domestication, and yet it may be possible to move you through clear, open and lively text. This may seem a banal and obvious point, but it is important because it moves me closer to an articulation of geographies of care.

Caring encounters: Openness, heterogeneity and liveliness

For Carrier (1998: 189), the act of representation in and of itself is really about the 'domestication of difference' and so, I argue, in that I want to get beyond domestication, I also want to go beyond representations to a more emotive form of responsibility and care. By fixing identity, representations domesticate and placate difference because they do violence to the possibility of Deleuze's multiple modes of encounter. And here is an important geography. Massey (2005) points out that spatiality and representation are often equated with each other and this is a problematic form of enframing that relates to the kinds of closure with which Clifford, Marcus, James and Fisher struggled. Any kind of spatial framing – out-there-ness, spaces-of-betweenness, in-here-ness – like representation is a containment (if just for a moment) of movement, of surprise, of freedom. By so doing, I hold the world still and, in that moment, I analyze its structure and conjecture on the processes that formed that structure. To get beyond that moment is to get beyond spatial frames.

An important moment for geography was when Henri Lefebvre (1991), in his opening arguments about *The Production of Space*, pointed out that the use of the concept 'space,' in popular and academic discourse, is hugely problematic. To use the term space, or to corrupt it with a qualifier such as spaces-of-betweenness, argues Massey (2005: 17), pushes an imagination 'with the implacable force of the patently obvious' and 'that is the trouble' with space. Massey (2005: 19) suggest that space in this form of usage can come to be associated with inanity and disassociated from 'its full insertion into the political.' Rather, Massey embraces Ernesto Laclau's insistence on the intimate connection between dislocation and the possibility of politics. Spaces-of-betweenness, for example, suggest a particular representation, an ideology of closure, a too neat tripartite structure between participants in a larger project that – when it comes to writing – is more often than not hugely and problematically mine. For Laclau, relatedly, spatialization is equivalent to hegemonization. Spatial framings are the product of ideological closure, a picture of the dislocated world as somehow coherent (Massey, 2005: 25). Massey goes on to point out with Michel de Certeau that there is an important connection between the modern scientific method that emerged with writing (letters and journals) from nineteenth century empiricism and the creation of a blank space (de Certeau's *espace propre*) not only for the objects of knowledge but also for the act of writing and representing. For de Certeau (1984), the importance of spatial stories with all the nuances of narratives through movement and surprise is lost to science as 'the writing of the world' (see also Curry, 1996). In order to disrupt this spatial coherency and rekindle the dynamism of real life, Massey (2005: 26) argues that we need to get beyond Laclau's and de Certeau's 'equation of representation and spatialization' because the spatial is not stable; it cannot flatten the life out of movement and time. What is required for the opening up of the political, argues Massey (2005), is simultaneously a space of freedom (from Bergson), dislocation (from Laclau) and surprise (from de Certeau). The spaces of my fieldwork and my encounters require similar

characteristics to derive a respect that removes them from the vestiges of containment and order, from the oppressions of privilege and entitlement, from the circumscription of denouement. It is a field of opening and experimentation, of playfulness and feeling.

CARING MORE

Part of the taming of space arises from preconceived notions I have of comfort through familiarity. Material places are important to the extent that I am contextualized by where I live. I live in a literal border region today by choice and yet it is not by any grand planning on my part. A job offer brought me here. This 'chance of space,' to quote Massey (2005: 151), 'set me down next to' Fernanda and her family. For a short period of time we are throwntogether. I go to her home and move through that experience to feel difference and similarity that offsets what is theoretically suggested and what is rendered materially. The distilling of my awkwardness through Fernanda's graciousness surprises me and it is from this acuity – which is personal, self-reflexive and political – that I begin writing this chapter. I am surprised by the tears I shed with the migrant laborer's son. The surprise is not from the tears but that they flowed from shared grief, experienced differently. And there is more writing to come from that experience (cf. Aitken, 2009). Ultimately, then, my writing is about the ways throwntogetherness results in forms of 'dislocation' and 'surprise' that enable the opening up of the political. If I preconceive my place through familiarity (or, worse, through ownership) I foreclose upon the possibility of surprise and dislocation. I foreclose upon the opening of the political.

With this chapter I've tried to trace some of the beginnings of encounters with difference through space and throwntogetherness. I articulate a number of spatial frames – beginning with colonialism and imperialism – that are hugely and dramatically problematic.

I finish up with experimental methodologies that are not foreclosed upon by neat spatial forms of engagement. I argue that these encounters must be known and felt as affective because affect is a sense of push in the world, and it is the most important component of public action, care and responsibility. Fernando Bosco (2008) points out that an ethics of care highlights questions about how responsibility is enacted, and how caring about others is negotiated and mediated across space. Bosco articulates a critical ethics of care that sees people as interdependent and where the *affective* plays a primary role in any encounter. A recognition of emotion and an affective push foments sincerity, compassion and integrity as an important heart of qualitative research.

What might strategies of care entail for qualitative researchers who want to move beyond spaces-of-betweenness? At its most hopeful, a new space is produced for fieldwork that enables the surprise and incoherence from which an affective, open and lively politics of difference is possible. It is recognition of the power of this space of *throwntogetherness* that enables a divesting of spatial frames that heretofore have limited our ability to know one another. Encountering difference, then, is about us knowing simultaneously that there are no rules of space and place that are not of our own contrivance and that, inevitably and always, we as researcher and researched make spaces and places. It is knowing that our encounters are always temporary, provisional and partial, and, as spatial acts, they connect with our need to communicate and identify; that is, hopefully, with our need to care.

NOTES

1.   The visit was part of a collaborative US-Mexican research project on child labor in Tijuana from which we published a number of papers. The project involved ethnographic interviews with children, parents, school teachers and non-governmental organization (NGO) workers. We hung out with the children

and observed them at work surreptitiously (their employers did not endorse our project). See Aitken *et al.* (2006) and Jennings et al. (2006) for discussion of some of the qualitative research involved in the study and Aitken (2008) for a theoretical discussion of the study as it relates to the politics of representation There is also a large quantitative survery, which is as yet unpublished. Names of people (except co-authors) and local places are changes as part of SDSU's Institutional Review Board requirements.

2.   They are called 'volunteers' because children under 15 years of age are not legally allowed to work in Mexico unless they are part of a family member's business. The supermarket child packers are not paid, but can earn over twice Tijuana's minimum wage in tips.

3.   When I show up at someone's door for an interview, what do I bring with me other than a degree in higher education and a letter of introduction from an Institutional Review Board describing the legal complexities of being a research subject? Although the trappings of officialdom (degrees and IRB approvals) are important at one level, they add to the spikes of my costume. On the one hand I am asking to be part of someone's life for a while and, on the other, I am imposing on them the legal and contractual nuances of that connection. Surely sincerity, compassion and integrity are more important to initial encounters than are attributes that suggest elitism and distance.

4.   By the early twentieth century, popular hunger for more detail, more exotic facts and spectacular images required less superficiality and led to prolonged engagements in peripheral locations. To this end, some of the empirical evidence that powered Frazer's work was later discredited on the basis of more rigorous documentation. Detailed participant observation fieldwork spawned the work of Bronislaw Malinowski (1926) and Franz Boas (1931) in UK and US anthropology respectively along with Carl Sauer (1925) in US geography and the beginnings of the Chicago School's sociological laboratories in poor immigrant communities.

5.   This sub-title comes from a historic text from the 1950s that brought together much of the writing of the Sauerian school (Thomas, 1956).

6.   Following the example of the University of Chicago, many universities established 'settlement houses' in the slums from which 'dozens of researchers … scoured the area for information, much of it highlighting the mostly awful aspects of local life' (Jablonsky, 1993: xiii). The settlement houses of the Chicago sociologists were urban laboratories that took researchers into 'back of the yards' and poor immigrant neighborhoods elsewhere so that they could collect data and document living conditions. A form of 'domesticating' data was prevalent whereby empirical evidence was contorted and contrived to fit into parsimonious models of reality. I am

amazed, when I encounter the famous Chicago models of urban ecology in contemporary textbooks, that rarely is there any mention of the ethnographies derived from the settlement houses. It seems that the spatial urban models of concentric rings, sectors and multiple-nuclei exist beyond the lives of those from whom they were derived.

REFERENCES

Aitken, S. (2001) 'Playing with children: immediacy was their cry', *Geographic Review* 91 (1–2): 496–508.

Aitken, S. (2006) 'Leading men to violence and creating spaces for their emotions', *Gender, Place and Culture* 13 (5): 491–507.

Aitken, S. (2008) 'Desarrollo integral y fronteras/ integral development & borderspaces', in S. Aitken, A.T. Kjørholt and R. Lund (eds) *Global childhoods: globalization, development, young people*. London: Routledge. pp. 113–30.

Aitken, S. (2009) The awkward spaces of fathering. Farnham, Surrey. Ashgate Press.

Aitken, S., Estrada, S.L., Jennings, J. and Aguirre, L. (2006) 'Reproducing life and labor: global processes and working children in Tijuana', *Childhood* 13 (3): 365–87.

Anderson, K. and Smith, S. (2001) 'Emotional geographies', *Transactions of the Institute of British Geographers* 26 (1): 63–88.

Anzaldúa, G. (1987) *Borderlands/la frontera: the New Mestiza*. San Francisco: Aunt Lute Books.

Bahba, H.K. (1994) *The location of culture*. New York: Routledge.

Behar, R. (1996) *The vulnerable observer: anthropology that breaks your heart*. Boston: Beacon Press.

Berger, J. (1972) *Ways of seeing*. Harmondsworth: Penguin.

Boas, F. (1931) *The mind of primitive man*. New York: Macmillan.

Bosco, F. (2008) 'Global aid networks and hungry children in Argentina: thinking about geographies of responsibility and care', in S. Aitken, A.T. Kjørholt and R. Lund (eds) *Global childhoods: globalization, development, young people*. London: Routledge. pp. 55–76.

Bunge, W.W. (1971) *Fitzgerald: geography of a revolution*. Cambridge, MA: Schenkman.

Bunge, W.W. (1973) 'The geography', *The Professional Geographer* 25 (4): 331–37.

Bunge, W.W. and Bordessa, R. (1975) *The Canadian alternative: survival, expeditions and urban change*. Geographical monographs 2, Toronto: York University.

Butler, J. (1990) *Gender trouble: feminism and the subversion of identity*. New York: Routledge.

Butler, J. (1993) *Bodies that matter: on the discursive limits of 'sex'*. New York: Routledge.

Carrier, R.M. (1989) 'The ontological significance of Deleuze and Guattari's concept of the body without organs', *Journal of the British Society for Phenomenology* 29 (2): 189–206.

Cisneros, S. (1989) *The house on Mango Street*. New York: Vintage Books.

Clifford, J. (1988) *The predicament of culture: twentieth century ethnography, literature and art*. Cambridge, MA: Harvard University Press.

Clifford, J. and Marcus, G.E. (1986) *Writing culture: the poetics and politics of ethnography*. Berkeley, CA: University of California Press.

Crang, M. (2005) 'Analysing qualitative data', in R. Flowerdew and D. Martin (eds) *Methods in human geography*. London: Prentice Hall. pp. 218–32.

Crotty, S., Moreno, C. and Aitken, S.C. (2008) '"Each and every single story about me ... there's like a huge twist to it": growing up at risk in the United States', in C. Jeffreys and J. Dyson (eds) *Telling young lives*. Philadelphia: Temple University Press. pp. 97–112.

Curry, M.R. (1996) *The work in the world: geographical practice and the written word*. Minneapolis: University of Minnesota Press.

de Certeau, M. (1984) *The practice of everyday llife*. Berkeley, CA: University of California Press.

Davidson, J., Bondi, L. and Smith, M. (2006) *Emotional geographies*. Aldershot: Ashgate Press.

Deleuze, G. (1986) *Cinema 1: the movement-image*. trans. Hugh Tomlinson and Barbara Habberjam. London: The Athlone Press.

Deleuze, G. and Guattari, F. (1983) *Anti-Oedipus: capitalism and schizophrenia*. Minneapolis: University of Minnesota Press.

Deleuze, G. and Guattari, F. (1987) *A thousand plateaus: capitalism and schizophrenia*. London: The Athlone Press.

Fincher, R. and Jacobs, J. (1998) *Cities of difference*. New York: Guilford Press.

Fotheringham, S.A. (2006) 'Quantification, evidence and positivism', in S. Aitken and G. Valentine (eds) *Approaches in human geography*. London: Sage Publications. pp. 237–50.

Fowler, D., Euler, R. and Fowler, C. (1981) 'John Wesley Powell and the anthropology of the Canyon country', *Geological Survey Professional*

Paper 670. Washington DC: US Government Print Office.

Frazer, J.G. (1900) *The golden bough: a study of magic and religion*, 2nd edition. London: Macmillan.

Gagen, E. (2000) 'An example to us all: child development and identity construction in early 20th century playgrounds', *Environment and Planning A* 32 (4): 599–616.

Gagen, E. (2008) 'Reflections of primitivism: development, progress and civilization in imperial America, 1898–1914', in S. Aitken, A.T. Kjørholt, and R. Lund (eds) *Global childhoods: globalization, development, young people*. London: Routledge. pp. 15–28.

Geertz, C. (1988) *Words and lives*. Stanford, CA: Stanford University Press.

Gupta, A. and Ferguson, J. (1992) 'Beyond "culture": space, identity and the politics of difference', *Cultural Anthropology* 7 (1): 6–23.

Haraway, D. (1991) *Simians, cyborgs and women: the reinvention of nature*. London: Routledge.

Howitt, R. and Stevens, S. (2005) 'Cross-cultural research: ethics, methods and relationships', in I. Hay (ed.) *Qualitative research methods in human geography*. Oxford: Oxford University Press. pp. 30–50.

Jablonsky, T. (1993) *Pride in the jungle: community and everyday life in back of the yards Chicago*. Baltimore: The Johns Hopkins University Press.

Jacobs, J.M. (1996) *Edge of empire: postcolonialism and the city*. London: Routledge.

Jackson, P. (1992) 'Constructions of culture, representations of race: Edward Curtis's "way of seeing."', in K. Anderson and F. Gale (eds) *Inventing places*. Melbourne: Halsted Press. pp. 89–105.

Jennings, J., Lopez Estrada, S. and Aitken, S. (2006) 'Learning and earning: relational scales of children's work', *Area* 38 (3): 231–40.

Katz, C. (1994) 'Playing the field: questions of fieldwork in geography', *The Professional Geographer* 46 (1): 67–72.

Kitchin, R. (2006) 'Positivist geographies and spatial science', in S. Aitken and G. Valentine (eds) *Approaches in human geography*. London: Sage Publications. pp. 20–9.

LeFebvre, H. (1991) *The production of space*. Oxford: Blackwell Press.

Madison, D.S. (2005) *Critical ethnography: method, ethics, and performance*. Newbury Park, CA: Sage.

Malinowski, B. (1926) *Crime and custom in savage society*. New York: Harcourt Brace.

Malinowski, B. (1967) *A diary in the strict sense of the term*. New York: Harcourt Brace.

Marcus, G.E. and Fisher, M. (1986) *Anthropology as cultural critique*. Chicago: University of Chicago Press.

Martin, G.J. and Preston, J.E. (1993) *All possible worlds: a history of geographical ideas*, 3rd edition. Oxford: Oxford University Press.

Massey, D. (2005) *For space*. London: Sage Publications.

Merryfield, A. (1995) 'Situated knowledge through exploration: Reflections on Bunge's "geographical expeditions"', *Antipode* 27 (1): 49–70.

Mitchell, M.N. (2002) '"Rosebloom and pure white," or so it seemed', *American Quarterly* 54 (3): 369–410.

Nast, H. (1994) 'Women in the field: critical feminist methodologies and theoretical perspectives', *The Professional Geographer* 46 (1): 54–66.

Price, P. (2000) 'Inscribing the border: Schizophrenia and the aesthetics of Atztlán', *Social and Cultural Geography* 1 (1): 101–16.

Price, R. (1983) *First time: the historical vision of an Afro-American people*. Baltimore: Johns Hopkins University Press.

Riis, J. (1890) *How the other half lives*. New York: Charles Scribner's Sons.

Rosaldo, R. (1989) *Culture and truth*. Boston: Beacon Press.

Sauer, C. (1925) 'The morphology of landscape', *University of California Publications in Geography* 2 (2): 19–54.

Smith, L.T. (1999) *Decolonizing methodologies: research and indigenous peoples*. London and New York: Zed Books, University of Otago Press.

Spivak, G.C. (1988) 'Can the subaltern speak?', in C. Nelson and L. Grossberg (eds) *Marxism and the interpretation of culture*. Urbana: University of Illinois Press. pp. 271–313.

Spivak, G.C. (1990) 'Poststructuralism, marginality, postcoloniality and value', in P. Collier and H. Geyer-Ryan (eds) *Literary theory today*. Ithaca, NY: Cornell University Press. pp. 219–44.

Steedman, C. (1995) *Strange dislocations: childhood and the idea of human interiority, 1790–1930*. Cambridge, MA: Harvard University Press.

Stevens, S. (2001) 'Fieldwork as commitment', *Geographical Review* 91 (1): 66–73.

Sullivan, L.R. (1923) *Essentials of anthropometry: a handbook for explorers and museum collectors*. New York: American Museum of Natural History.

Thomas, J. (1993) *Doing critical ethnography*. Newbury Park, CA: Sage.

Thomas, W.L. (1956) *Man's role in changing the face of the earth.* Chicago: University of Chicago Press.

Thompson, A.S. (1859) *The story of New Zealand: past and present – savage and civilized.* London: John Murray.

Thrift, N. (2004) 'Intensities of feeling: towards a spatial politics of affect', *Geografiska Annaler* 86 (1): 57–78.

Vila, P. (2003) *Ethnography at the border.* Minneapolis: University of Minnesota Press.

Young, I.M. (1990) *Justice and the politics of difference.* Princeton, NJ: Princeton University Press.

Young, I.M. (2000) *Inclusion and democracy.* Oxford: Oxford University Press.

4

A Taut Rubber Band: Theory and Empirics in Qualitative Geographic Research

Steve Herbert

INTRODUCTION

A mother of a 'disappeared' young man marches in a Buenos Aires plaza. A student activist confronts a tank in a Beijing public square. A group of citizens mobilizes to rename a city street for an iconic figure. A parishoner makes the sign of the cross upon entering church. A police officer increases his potential mobility by releasing his seat belt as his patrol car enters a neighborhood he considers violent.

Each of these incidents illustrates a core assumption of the discipline of human geography: that spatial context matters to the conduct of social action. In each of these scenarios, location shapes how individuals behave. In these and other instances, people's actions are conditioned by the setting where they occur. Indeed, social action is *always* significantly embedded in place. Many geographers seek to understand this significance, to explicate the context dependence of human activity.

This is especially true for many qualitative researchers in human geography. Absent the rich detail that qualitative research affords, we are unable to appreciate fully the formative role of place. For this reason, qualitative research in human geography often focuses on a single case, the better to uncover the everyday processes through which groups build their worlds in and through place. The impulse is toward depth, toward ever-more comprehensive understandings of what a place means to those who inhabit it.

But no matter how encyclopedic a qualitative geographer might wish to be, he or she is simultaneously a social analyst. That implies a need to draw more general, theoretical conclusions about the case(s) under study. Thus, just as there is a drive toward greater depth, there is simultaneously a need to make broader assessments. Like a taut rubber band, the qualitative researcher is stretched in two directions. To be sure, all researchers, regardless of methodological bent, experience this tension between the general and the particular. But qualitative researchers experience it with especial acuteness, because they typically explore spatial contexts in considerable detail.

To be so stretched can be psychically discomforting and intellectually challenging.

Yet the challenge can be managed success-fully; in-depth examinations of a single case, or small number of cases, can yield significant theoretical pay-offs. The goals of this chapter are to explain why and how this is true.

I move toward these goals through four sections. In the first, I review some key background assumptions that underlie the use of qualitative methods in human geography. One of these concerns the formative role of place in structuring social activity. From this assumption, it is a short step to a recognition of the need to explore the deep tissue of everyday life, and the various means by which social groups attach themselves to a locale. This drive toward intensive examination, however, must be countered with the concomitant obligation to make more general, theoretical assertions about the data that emerges.

In the second section, I explore the entrance of theory into our qualitative examinations. For some, theory must be foregrounded at the beginning of our explorations; for others, theory is left to emerge from the data. I review these arguments, and suggest that neither approach is possible or desirable. Better to recognize that a good social analyst is perpetually tacking back and forth between theory and data. It thus makes little sense to quibble about starting and stopping points, but rather to focus upon the nature of the conversation between general assertions and empirical realities.

The caliber of that conversation depends on the researcher shrewdly choosing the right case to examine. In the third section, I explore different strategies for making this choice. Sometimes, researchers choose a case that is considered representative of others. This bolsters confidence in generalizations from the specific instance at hand. Other times, researchers might investigate more than one case. If two situations are similar in some respects and different in others, the researcher can learn much from comparing them. A third strategy is to choose a case that seems anomalous. To explain an

outlier can enable the expansion of existing theory. Each of these three strategies is meritorious; none possesses an inherent superiority. Indeed, each has been used to great theoretical benefit. What is important is choosing an option consciously and thoughtfully. The fourth section is a brief conclusion.

BACKGROUND ASSUMPTIONS

As noted above, qualitative researchers in human geography take as a basal assumption that place importantly shapes social action. Much human behavior is incomprehensible absent an understanding of the locale in which it transpires. What is considered socially appropriate varies significantly from place to place; the bedroom, the boardroom, and the barroom each enable different sorts of activities. Given the influence that place exerts on human action, it follows that the capacity to define space is an important source of social power. It is a significant capacity indeed to be able to label a space, to decide who can inhabit it, and to shape what can occur there (Sack, 1986).

The role of space in shaping social action is often so taken for granted that its importance is neglected. Much qualitative research in human geography seeks to disinter this taken-for-grantedness. Some such research, for example, reveals the historical legacies of places, how the echoes of the past reverberate in the contemporary construction and use of particular landscapes (Basso, 1984; Delyser, 1999; Forest and Johnson, 2002; Till, 2005). Such places have meanings associated with a perhaps imagined past, yet these meanings shape the experience of the present. These spaces speak to those who inhabit and visit them, and reinforce particular sets of cultural meanings.

Because places can exert such power, the politics of their control and meaning are often charged. Debates over place names, for example, can be contentious (Alderman,

2000; Nagar, 1997). More combatively, when different groups demand hegemony over the same place, violence can ensue. From the West Bank (Yiftachel, 2000) to the streets of Belfast (Dowler, 1998), battles over the meaning and control of space can be intense and bloody.

Given its importance to social action, space becomes an important focus for anyone seeking to understand a particular group's way of life. But the constitutive role of place cannot be read from the results of a broad survey. It must, instead, be examined through direct experience with the group in question, through close contact and ongoing interaction. One must, in the words of Clifford Geertz (1973: 21) acquire 'exceedingly extended acquaintances with extremely small matters.' This occurs over long stretches of time in repeated engagements, through extended interviews or observations, or some combination of the two. For this reason, the qualitative researcher is forced, by constraints of time and resources, to concentrate attention on a single case, or small number of cases. This is the only way to acquire data of sufficient depth and breadth to make confident claims about the role that space plays in constituting a social group. Indeed, it is hard to imagine the discipline of geography without at least some of its practitioners so acquainting themselves with space's constitutive role. Large-n studies may provide the seeming assurance of generalizability, but they necessarily rely on a fairly thin understanding of space. As David Ley (1988: 126) puts it,

> The geographer's charge to interpret the complex relations of people and place requires a methodology of engagement not detachment, of informal dialogue as well as formal documentation. There is both an ontological and epistemological requirement that place as a human construction be granted more respect and complexity than the profile it displays from the pages of the census.

Yet appreciating and understanding space's constitutive role is no simple matter. Besides engaging in long acquaintance with those who build, inhabit, and control a space, the qualitative researcher must translate everyday events into some larger understanding of social and spatial relations. This necessarily involves interpretation. The cultural significance of a given social act is often not obvious. With extended exposure and ongoing reflection, the qualitative researcher can make confident inferences about what a particular social behavior means to the members under study. Daily experience is interpreted against some broader understanding, and this understanding is used to evaluate experience, in an ongoing, recurring process. The researcher becomes a research instrument, and uses his or her developing cultural consciousness to better understand the group in question.

Qualitative research's acceptance of the necessity of interpretation often leaves it susceptible to the charge that it is not properly scientific. For some, interpretation means a lack of the objectivity often alleged to be central to scientific practice. Qualitative researchers can thus be rendered as mere methodological field hands; they simply unearth descriptive nuggets that more rigorous scientific methods render explainable. Take, for instance, the critique of ethnography by George Rengert (1997: 469):

> Ethnographic research is the least scientific of the research approaches since, by definition, it involves a small sample size, is difficult to replicate, and contains a great deal of subjectivity and interpretation on the part of the researcher. Ethnographic research needs to be supplemented with carefully designed research projects in which the ideas developed are subjected to scientific rigor.

From this perspective, strict adherence to presumably standardized procedures will minimize interpretation and breed confidence in the resultant generalizations.

There are two key responses to this critique. The first is that interpretation is central to all scientific practice, no matter how 'objective' its practitioners claim to be (Gieryn, 1999; Knorr-Cetina, 1981; Latour, 1987; Lynch, 1985). All researchers necessarily must tack back and forth between their readings of data and their theoretical understandings; neither data nor theory are ever naive. Further, all knowledge arises from specific social milieu, and cannot be understood in isolation from those milieu (Flyvbjerg, 2001).

The second point – and this is the central argument of this chapter – is that qualitative data can be as useful for theory building as data collected in any other fashion. Large-n statistical studies, conducted through ostensive standardized procedures, cannot lay hegemonic claim to the project of theory development. Indeed, those who immerse themselves in a particular social group quickly discover just how difficult it is to construct generalizable theory. As Michael Burawoy (1998: 11) notes: 'Living in the time and space of those one studies makes it difficult to fit the world into a predefined template. One begins with one set of questions and ends with very different ones.' Awareness of social context thus makes what he calls 'positive science' largely inoperable. Further, the empirical record gives the lie to attempts at methodological superiority for large-n analyses. Qualitative methods are used in analyses done in an astonishing range of (sometimes overlapping) theoretical traditions, and employed to interrogate and illuminate a dizzying variety of social processes – culture, science, gender, economics, and politics, to name just a few (Walton, 1992).

But to state this truism – that qualitative data can be central to the construction and refinement of theory – is not to gainsay the challenge that confronts those who employ qualitative methods. The simultaneous impulses to achieve empirical depth *and* analytic breadth, to pursue immersion *and* reflection, do stretch the researcher. They require a constant tacking back and forth between one pole and the other. Yet this challenge can be met with great effectiveness, and yield insightful analyses.

Two key issues then emerge. One involves where and how to bring theory into the enterprise. The other concerns the case(s) the researcher chooses. The next two sections

focus on these in turn. Before proceeding to those discussions, however, it is necessary to address the issue of positionality. This issue has roiled the waters in recent years, because it challenges the seeming neutrality and omniscience once accorded the researcher (Marcus and Fisher, 1986; Butler, 2001; Cook, 2005; Myers, in this volume). In asserting that a qualitative researcher can refine theory, I may seem to endorse implicitly a notion of an objective observer, one set strongly apart from the phenomena under study. Such an observer is clearly an impossibility. Even somewhat detached qualitative researchers are not entirely abstracted but deeply involved, not completely aloof but engaged in the situations they observe (Clough, 1992; Gubrium and Holstein, 1997; Kobayashi, 2001). Further, some researchers – particularly those engaged in what has been termed 'participatory action research' (Reason and Bradbury, 2001; Routledge, in this volume) – seek to use their findings to assist the groups under study. In this way, the alleged divide between the researcher and the researched is consciously bridged. The erosion of this divide makes it possible for multiple voices to emerge with greater force in the ensuing analysis.

This reconsideration of the omniscience of the researcher helps, in addition, to remind ourselves of the constraints we face. No matter how broad our analytic scope, each of us is limited – by our histories, our failures to understand others fully, our lack of imagination. These realities force upon us a necessary modesty, an acceptance of the incompleteness of our analyses (Cook, 2005; Herbert, 2000). This modesty should animate the research throughout, and reflect clearly in published work.

Even if one seeks to debunk the objective, detached observer, this does not diminish the power and utility of empirically-deep and theoretically-capacious qualitative analysis. Humans can empathize and reflect thoughtfully upon social experience. However limited our abilities, we can still attempt to understand others and to tell insightful stories about the world as it is built and experienced. To do so well requires that we consider how to incorporate theory and how to choose cases for analysis. I consider each of these issues in the next two sections.

FROM WHENCE THEORY?

If we wish to compose theoretically-informed and theoretically-instructive qualitative work, one question to consider is just where theory enters into the enterprise. In one view, represented most prominently by the 'grounded theory' approach (Glaser and Strauss, 1967), our theory arises inductively. We compose our theoretical categories *from* the data; our conceptual frameworks emerge from analytic interaction with our findings. By contrast, a more deductive approach suggests a need to start with theory and work down. Here, we begin with a theoretically-driven question, then gather and analyze data to answer it. Each of these approaches makes sense, and each has been used to great benefit. However, each presents an ideal model that cannot be followed strictly. A better depiction of common practice is that researchers are constantly tacking back and forth, always mobilizing some theoretical framework yet perpetually troubling that framework with the data at hand. If this is the case, then we must confront two critical questions: (1) Have we brought the right theoretical questions to our data?; and (2) Are we maintaining a high-quality conversation between our theory and our data?

The grounded theory approach is important to the history of qualitative research. It implicitly endorses the importance of rich empirical detail. It also, and importantly, pushes the researcher to suspend his or her theoretical predilections as much as possible, to avoid allowing an overwrought conceptual apparatus to obscure the ability to see the world through the eyes of those one studies. From this perspective, great respect must be given to the realities that one experiences in the field. Immersion in a new culture provides an opportunity to see the world anew; indeed, one could argue that this is a principal point of the enterprise.

Yet it is called grounded *theory* for a reason. The goal is not a descriptive catalog of a group's world view, but a broader story that reveals some aspect of human experience. So, theoretical categorization is critical to the grounded theory approach. The strategy is to build the theory up from the data, rather than vice-versa. Importantly, the strategy is to so build theory through rigorous and replicable methods. As Kathy Charmaz (2003: 253) summarizes it, 'Grounded theory methods consist of systematic inductive guidelines for collecting and analyzing data to build-middle range theoretical frameworks that explain the collected data.' Researchers move through various steps in collating, coding and categorizing the data to arrive at progressively more abstract constructs. These constructs are then brought back into data analysis, to assess their capacity to illuminate the empirical record. This rigorous approach mimics other 'scientific' practices, and thereby presumably accords qualitative research greater legitimacy (Glaser and Strauss, 1967).

There are differences within those who practice grounded theory regarding just how strictly inductive the enterprise needs to be (compare Glaser, 1992 with Strauss and Corbin, 1990). Whatever these differences, there is a shared loyalty to the data, a deep commitment to trying to prevent pre-existing theoretical schemas from obscuring our awareness on the ground. This openness to the data, combined with a willingness to build theoretical constructions through elaborated and replicable strategies, explains grounded theory's popularity.

Yet there is no reason to dismiss a more deductive approach to building theory through qualitative work. Although there is an understandable tradition within qualitative research to remain theoretically uninhibited enough to be open to the data, it is surely incorrect to presume that we can shed our conceptual frames entirely. Indeed, without use of such frames we cannot decide what amongst the manifold flow of experience constitutes data. Surely we are looking for *something* when we listen to our respondents, and likely because of a theoretical interest that sent us into the field in the first place.

Given this, it is more than plausible to follow the lead of analysts like Buroway (1998) and Martin Bulmer (1982), who suggest the need to *start* with theoretically-derived questions and to map a research strategy with those in mind. Better to be self-conscious about our theoretical presuppositions so we can make clear-eyed decisions about what data to seek. This way, we are in a better position to converse between our theory and our empirical observations; we are clear about our theoretical commitments, and can reconsider them with the data we collect.

Still, Buroway's commitment to a deductive approach by no means diminishes his admonitions to listen closely to what his qualitative data tell him. As he colorfully describes it:

> Our stance toward theory is kamikaze. In our field-work we do not look for confirmations but for theory's refutations. We need first the courage of our convictions, then the courage to challenge our convictions, and finally the imagination to sustain our courage with theoretical reconstruction. If these reconstructions come at too great a cost we may have to abandon our theory altogether and start afresh. (Buroway, 1998, 20)

Thus, Buroway's allegiance to a deductive process does not lessen his willingness to shed his theoretical commitments as he learns from the field. He strives to remain open to the data, and to question perpetually his conceptual apparatus.

From here, it becomes possible to reject inductivism or deductivism as an either/or choice. These stances really only specify the starting point of an analysis; they say little, in and of themselves, about the content of our subsequent work. And even so, it is surely inaccurate to say that either we start gathering data with a theory-free mind, or that we pick our cases only because they possess

some explicable theoretical interest. We always bring some questions to the data we gather and collect, and we sometimes pick cases because they are compelling for reasons that cannot be specified in strictly theoretical terms (Stake, 1995).

Because we cannot locate precisely where we start on the continuum between deductivism and inductivism, there is no need to argue about the proper originating point. The critical issue is just how well we conduct the conversation between our theoretical concepts and the data we uncover. What is necessary is not a commitment to a particular starting location, but a religious willingness to remain open to experiences in the field and to reconsider continually our theoretical presuppositions. Only these practices will enable a robust conversation between theory and data.

In this way, good inductive and deductive work does not differ; neither, one might add, does qualitative and quantitative work. A high-quality conversation between theory and data is characteristic of any good social science, regardless of its methodological orientation. Qualitative research is identical to any other work that tells broader stories with and about particularized realities.

That said, qualitative researchers do differ in one fundamental respect from those who engage in statistical analysis or other forms of more positive social science: they examine a single or small number of cases. The fine-grained detail characteristic of qualitative work requires a more restricted empirical domain. This restrictive focus can run seemingly counter to the quest for generalization. How can one make confident theoretical claims from a sample size as small as one? What lessons can one draw that can be transferred to other cases? It is to this sticky issue that I now turn.

ON PICKING A CASE

Qualitative researchers in geography commonly address questions of meaning and process: what it means to a particular group to build a home, how a group understands itself and its world through the active construction of place (Herbert, 2000). To probe the soft tissue of meaning and to reveal central processes requires an intensive examination of a single or small number of cases. As sample sizes increase, so does the difficulty of in-depth understandings of meaning and process. Case studies are thus the bread and butter of qualitative work.

Besides enabling exploration of the deeper workings of socio-spatial life, case studies promote the high caliber discussion between theory and data discussed above. Deep familiarity with a single case makes it easier to move continually between theoretical propositions and empirical findings; one can revise concepts in light of ongoing research, and redirect the research with evolving concepts. As Charles Ragin (1992: 5) summarizes it: 'This feature explains why small-N qualitative research is most often at the forefront of theoretical development. When N's are large, there are few opportunities for revising a case.'

Given the unavoidable importance of case studies for qualitative research, the question then becomes how to pick the case(s) to investigate. For some, cases might merit attention solely because of the inherent interest they possess for a researcher (Stake, 1995). Yet the theoretically-ambitious researcher will likely want a stronger motivation. Only then can one draw lessons that can be applied elsewhere with confidence.

Three strategies for case selection possess a strong track record for inspiring confidence in subsequent theoretical conclusions. One of these is to pick a case that can stand as a representative sample of a larger class. This can enable the development of theory that can apply to other cases. Another strategy is to choose more than one case, and compare them to one another. Such comparative work can expand theoretical understandings by explaining the existence and significance of similarities and differences between the cases. A third strategy is to pick a case that differs from others in the same category.

Such a case would likely lie outside the explanatory capacity of existing theories. To explore, and seek to explain, the anomalous case thus represents an opportunity to enlarge extant theory. I explore each of these strategies in more depth below.

The representative case

The logic of choosing a representative case is straightforward. If the researcher picks a site that possesses significant characteristics in common with other sites, then generalizations about one can plausibly extend to others. Many places and social organizations do possess important similarities. Take urban policing which is my particular research area. There is strong evidence that urban police departments possess analogous organizational and cultural structures, and that they face the same challenges and realities. For instance, tense relations between police departments and many residents of poor, minority-dominated neighborhoods are ubiquitous. Any researcher who engaged in an intensive examination of any one of those neighborhoods, and who illuminated structured interaction patterns, could plausibly draw conclusions that would pertain to other locations.

Examples of this strategy abound, inside and outside of geography. Indeed, this is the approach used most commonly. One can think, for instance, of classic works such as Erving Goffman's *Aslyums* (1961), in which he developed the concept of the 'total institution,' one that encompassed the entirety of the occupants' lived experience. Much as Michel Foucault (1977) mobilized the metaphor of the panopticon to illustrate the operations of discipline, Goffman used the notion of the total institution to characterize many facilities that control their inhabitants. In a more contemporary vein, Clifford Shearing and Philip Stenning (1992) analyze a more quintessentially post-modern landscape, Disney World, to illustrate the embeddedness of social control mechanisms. They tell a story of how one of their daughters was reminded by a person dressed as Mickey Mouse of the need to not walk barefoot. When the young girl complained that her shoes had generated a blister, Mickey quietly insisted that to remain unshod would necessitate expulsion from the park. Shearing and Stenning use Disney World as a representative instance of how, in their view, contemporary social control is so sutured into the fabric of everyday life as to become unnoticed, and hence less open to critique and resistance.

In a similar fashion, I use ethnographic data from observations in both Los Angeles and Seattle to make larger arguments about the nature of the police's territorial power and their social construction of the communities they serve (Herbert, 1997, 2006). Although writing in different contexts, both Nicholas Fyfe (1992) and Ralph Saunders (1999) similarly employ field observations to draw conclusions about the role of the police in regulating urban social life. To isolate one particular state agency such as the police also enables one to make general observations about state power. This is a strategy adopted by Alison Mountz (2004) who mobilizes ethnographic data derived from observations of the Canadian Immigration Service. She demonstrates, among other things, how the contemporary state governs with an eye toward the media. Given the mediated nature of contemporary state power, it is reasonable to conclude that the phenomena Mountz describes and analyzes are found in other state agencies in other geographic contexts (see D'Arcus, 2006).

Similarly, many world cities host large immigrant populations, the members of which often struggle to find a political place for themselves. Anna Secor (2004) uses interviews with women in Istanbul to reveal how migrants come to an understanding of themselves as citizens, how they develop a sense of voice in a political space between their past, present, and future. Melissa Wright (2004) also interviews women, in her case in Ciudad Juarez, host of several low-wage manufacturing plants. Wright seeks to

understand how the work and worth of women are evaluated and resisted in these spaces created by new circuits of globalized capital. Although both Istanbul and Ciudad Juarez are unique places, the phenomena that Secor and Wright study occur in other, similar contexts. Their analytic lessons can illuminate dynamics elsewhere.

Countless other examples could be mobilized here as illustrations of this commonly-adopted approach of selecting a representative case. In adopting this strategy, the analyst bears some burden to explain to the reader why the case was chosen. Once this is accomplished, the single-case strategy can generate theoretical lessons applicable to other situations.

Of course, there is always an open question concerning the extent to which dynamics in one place are replicated elsewhere. Indeed, one way in which an analyst's theoretical schema can be assessed is by employing it in another locale. Through such comparative analysis, the sturdiness of a particular framework can be assayed. Some qualitative researchers build such a comparative component into their analysis from the start. I turn now to a review of the advantages of this case selection strategy.

The comparative strategy

It is understandable why the choice of a single, representative case is the most commonly-used. Qualitative research is incredibly time-intensive, particularly if one is examining a culture distinct from one's own. It is a slow process to develop enough cultural familiarity with the site and enough rapport with its members to be able even to ask the right questions, much less develop faith in one's answers to those questions. It thus not a surprise that explicitly comparative qualitative work is less often used, despite the advantages of this approach.

The obvious strength of comparative work is that it births insights from the cataloguing of similarities and differences across sites

(Ragin, 1987). Typically, the analyst chooses a particular arena of social action to study, and then examines how and why it varies across space. For instance, I was interested in how urban communities interacted with police agencies. I chose to study three Seattle police beats that were contiguous yet demographically variant. Not surprisingly, I found that residents of more affluent communities were less fearful of crime and more satisfied with police service than those in more disadvantaged areas. The wealthier were also more confident in their ability to exercise political voice. For this reason, residents of poorer neighborhoods were more suspicious of efforts to devolve political authority to communities, because they were afraid that richer communities would be better-served (Herbert, 2006). Byron Miller (2000) also investigated three different urban communities, in his case to determine the landscape of political resistance to nuclear weapons. By comparing three contiguous localities – all in the greater Boston area – with three different levels of activism, Miller was able to explain what local factors account for greater or lesser degrees of political action. Rachel Silvey (2003) accomplishes something similar, although in a different national context, that of Indonesia. She contrasts two sites with varying degrees of activism by women workers. She demonstrates how one community's greater level of activism is due to a work force that is dominated by immigrants who are less tied to place. Women in the less active community were enmeshed in local ties that celebrated female quiescence.

A comparative strategy can be used to highlight processes that stretch across locales. This is precisely what Cindi Katz (2004) accomplishes in her analysis of Howa, a Sudanese village. Her particular interest lay in the effects of a large-scale agricultural development there, primarily in terms of its impacts on children. Katz contrasts her stories from Howa with those from her home, New York City, which was reeling from de-industrialization. Katz is able to show how global capitalism compels restructuring in both places, with similar implications for children. As she put it,

> The derailment of New York children's futures, along with the shaky conditions of their present, struck me as startlingly similar to what was happening to children in Howa and elsewhere in Sudan as a result of agricultural 'development.' With obvious differences, children in both settings were being displaced from futures that had been reasonably secure just a generation earlier. (Katz, 2004: 159)

Suzanne Friedberg (2004) also does a comparative global analysis, but she links places through a single commodity, green beans. She follows the beans from production sites (Burkina Faso) to consumption sites (Europe) to show the culture of transnational food chains. She analyzes the discourses that emerge along these chains, particularly those which focus on the safety of imported food. Her analysis thus compares places as it simultaneously coheres them in an assessment of global capitalism. Both her work and Katz's demonstrate the particularly potent advantages of comparative qualitative analysis for understanding the realities of increased globalization. In-depth examinations of place can demonstrate the impact of globalization in local settings. What such localized assessments reveal is not just the top-down imposition of global forces, but the role of local dynamics in transforming and perhaps resisting these forces (see Eade, 1997; Lin, 1998; Marcus, 1998; Buroway, 2000; Gille and Riain, 2002).

In short, the comparative approach can generate broad assessments of the relationships between places and various social forces. As one contrasts multiple places, one can catalogue both the factors that generate difference and those that compel similarity. Far from merely cataloguing the minutia of places, such comparative analysis yields theoretical lessons of trans-local consequence.

The anomalous case

Yet another strategy exists to use qualitative data to expand existing theory. In this approach, one deliberately chooses a site because it belies expectations; it does not bear out what either theory or common sense would expect. If one can gather data that explains the anomaly, one can rewrite existing theory. Once expanded, the theory is more robust, and therefore better able to explain dynamics in other cases. As Burawoy (1998: 16) explains:

> We begin with our favorite theory but seek not confirmations but refutations that inspire us to deepen that theory. Instead of discovering grounded theory we elaborate existing theory. We do not worry about the uniqueness of our case since we are not as interested in its representativeness as its contribution to reconstructing theory.

Take, for instance, the classic ethnography by Herbert Gans (1962) of a disadvantaged neighborhood in Boston. On the exterior, the neighborhood possessed all the characteristics of 'social disorganization,' a classic concept of pioneering Chicago sociologists, who sought to understand the social experiences of poor urbanites. In the neighborhood Gans studied, the buildings were in disrepair, the streets littered, the residents engaged in boisterous public behavior. Yet through a prolonged ethnographic engagement, Gans discovered not disorganization, but a strong social structure and robust cultural values. Contrary to the expectations of urban planners, who sought to redevelop the area, or of conventional sociologists, who would have expected social disarray, Gans found a group with enduring ties to one another. Their social structure was most notable for being distinct from mainstream values, yet this was a conscious choice. The residents wished to retain their Italian culture against pressures to assimilate with American culture. They buttressed their cultural autonomy with social practices that emphasized their interdependence. In much the same way, other ethnographers of poor communities have demonstrated that beneath the veneer of seeming disorganization lies a network of connections that enable individual and collective survival (Gilliom, 2001; Stack, 1974), even if that occurs in the context of criminal activity (Jankowski, 1991; Bourgois, 1995).

Burawoy also seeks instances of social behavior that defies expectations. In one instance, he examined the persistence of the 'color bar' that structured employment opportunities in Zambia. These racial restrictions endured even after overt government attempts to nationalize industry and to eliminate racial discrimination. His ethnographic perspective, gained from working inside the Zambian copper industry, enabled him to understand the various external and internal pressures that preserved the employment status quo (Buroway, 1972). Similarly, he wondered why workers in industrial settings not only tolerated exploitative working conditions, but actively increased their own productivity. He discovered that it was simply more fun to develop games and other forms of competition on the shop floor, even though these had the effect of increasing the workers' rate of exploitation (Buroway, 1979). In this finding, he echoes the classic ethnographic account of Paul Willis (1977), who found that working-class 'lads' in English schools furthered their own marginalization through the various antics they devised to make secondary school more tolerable.

The virtues of the anomalous case strategy are hopefully clear. If a case runs counter to the expectations of existing theory, then a researcher who understands those dynamics can restructure theory to make it more capacious and effective. Just like the representative and the comparative strategies, this option provides an opportunity to make broader assertions about the significance of the case under study. It can provide an effective means by which the researcher travels from theory to data, and back again.

CONCLUSION

This recurring journey between theory and data can be an arduous one, especially for those who employ qualitative methods.

The discovery that comes from these methods emerges only because of deep immersion with a particular social group in a particular place. Qualitative methodologies enable us to understand the richness and complexity of human experience, the central meanings and ongoing processes that structure socio-spatial life. Through probing conversations and ongoing interactions, the qualitative researcher learns how the world is understood and experienced from another perspective. However, at all times there is a simultaneous pull in the other direction, toward more abstracted analysis of the field data. The qualitative researcher is thus stretched tautly, pushed toward deep immersion whilst pulled toward theoretical conclusion.

My aim in this chapter was to highlight both the difficulty of this challenge and the advantages of embracing it. The history of social scientific work, inside and outside the discipline of geography, is littered with examples of insightful work by those skilled practitioners who sought to stretch themselves between the richness of qualitative exploration and the quest for theoretical elaboration. Certainly if our aim is to draw lessons about the centrality of place to the conduct of social action, we must take up this challenge. Fortunately, there is much exemplary work that demonstrates how this challenge can be addressed.

For some practitioners, it is important to start from the data and work up; for others, one must start from theory and work down. I suggested here that, despite whatever merit attends to either approach, this is something of a false debate. Regardless of where we start, the important issue is the caliber of the conversation between our theoretical conclusions and our field data. Whether we succeed in generating insightful analyses depends primarily on whether we are able to connect insightfully our abstract generalizations with our particular observations.

However, it is critically important to choose the right case to examine. I explored three strategies for case selection, each of which can serve the researcher well. Neither is inherently superior to the others; the critical issue is to choose from amongst them wisely. Each of them makes possible what any other social science methodology can generate – theoretical developments that can be applied to other contexts.

Of course, no theory is so complete as to close the conversation. Theory is never fully-formed, never fully capable of explaining a vast number of instances. Regardless of how thoughtfully we arrive at our generalizations, these are always, as Geertz (1973: 29) notes, 'essentially contestable.' Part of the reason for this is that human experience is varied and complex, always open-ended and forever changing. Qualitative methods are best able to capture the processes through which these complexities are expressed. These methods thus best enable us to explore the richness of human efforts to build social worlds in and through place, and to make general observations about how and why these processes occur as they do. This is the central challenge, and the central benefit, of employing qualitative methods in human geography.

REFERENCES

Alderman, D. (2000) 'A street fit for a king: naming places and commemoration in the American South', *The Professional Geographer* 52: 672–83.

Basso, K. (1984) 'Stalking with stories: names, places, and moral narratives among the Western Apache', in S. Platter (ed.) *Text, play and story: the construction and reconstruction of self and society.* Washington DC: American Ethnological Society. pp. 19–55.

Bourgois, P. (1995) *In search of respect: selling crack in El Barrio.* Cambridge: Cambridge University Press.

Bulmer, M. (1982) *The uses of social research: social investigation in public policy-making.* Boston: G. Allen & Unwin.

Buroway, M. (1972) *The colour of class on the Cooper mines: from African advancement to Zambianization.* Manchester: Manchester University Press.

Buroway, M. (1979) *Manufacturing consent.* Chicago: University of Chicago Press.

Buroway, M. (1998) 'The extended case method', *Sociological Theory* 16: 4–33.

Buroway, M. (2000) 'Reaching for the global', in M. Buroway, J. Blum, S. George, Z. Gille, T. Gowan, L. Haney, M. Klawiter, S. Lopez, S. O'Riain, and M. Thayer (eds) *Global ethnography: forces, connections, and imaginations in a postmodern world*. Berkeley and Los Angeles: University of California Press. pp. 1–40.

Butler, R. (2001) 'From where I write: the place of positionality in writing', in M. Limb and C. Dwyer (eds) *Qualitative methods for geographers*. London: Arnold. pp. 264–76.

Charmaz, K. (2003) 'Grounded theory: objectivist and constructivist methods', in N. Denzin and Y. Lincoln (eds) *Strategies of qualitative inquiry*. Thousand Oaks, CA: Sage Publications. pp. 249–91.

Clough, P. (1992) *The end(s) of ethnography: from realism to social criticism*. Newbury Park, CA: Sage Publications.

Cook, I. (2005) 'Positionality/situated knowledge', in D. Atkinson, P. Jackson, D. Sibley and N. Washbourned (eds) *Cultural geography: a critical dictionary of key concepts*. London: Tauris. pp. 16–26.

D'Arcus, B. (2006) *Boundaries of dissent: protest and state power in the media age*. New York: Routledge.

DeLyser, D. (1999) 'Authenticity on the ground: engaging the past in a California ghost town', *Annals of the Association of American Geographers* 89: 602–32.

Dowler, L. (1998) '"And they think I'm just a nice old lady": women and war in Belfast, Northern Island', *Gender, Place and Culture* 5: 159–76.

Eade, J. (1997) *Living the global city: globalization as local process*. New York: Routledge.

Flyvbjerg, B. (2001) *Making social science matter: why social inquiry fails and how it can succeed again*. Cambridge: Cambridge University Press.

Forest, B. and Johnson, J. (2002) 'Unraveling the threads of history: Soviet-era monuments and post-Soviet national identity in Moscow', *Annals of the Association of American Geographers* 92: 524–47.

Foucault, M. (1977) *Discipline and punish: the birth of the prison*. London: Allen Lane.

Friedberg, S. (2004) *French beans and food scares: culture and commerce in an anxious age*. Oxford: Oxford University Press.

Fyfe, N. (1992) 'Space, time and policing: toward a contextual understanding of police work', *Environment and Planning D: society and Space* 10: 469–81.

Gans, H. (1962) *The urban villagers: group and class in the life of Italian-Americans*. New York: Free Press.

Geertz, C. (1973) *The interpretation of cultures*. New York: Basic Books.

Gieryn, T. (1999) *Cultural boundaries of science: credibility on the line*. Chicago: University of Chicago Press.

Gille, Z. and Riain, S. (2002) 'Global ethnography', *Annual Review of Sociology* 28: 271–96.

Gilliom, J. (2001) *Overseers of the poor: surveillance, resistance, and the limits of privacy*. Chicago: University of Chicago Press.

Glaser, B. (1992) *Basics of grounded theory: emerging vs. forcing*. Mill Valley, CA: Sociology Press.

Glaser, B. and Strauss, A. (1967) *The discovery of grounded theory: strategies for qualitative research*. Chicago: Aldine.

Goffman, E. (1961) *Asylums: essays on the social situation of mental patients and other inmates*. Garden City, NY: Anchor Books.

Gubrium, J. and Holstein, J. (1997) *The new language of qualitative method*. New York: Oxford University Press.

Herbert, S. (1997) *Policing space: territoriality and the Los Angeles Police Department*. Minneapolis: University of Minnesota Press.

Herbert, S. (2000) 'For ethnography', *Progress in Human Geography* 24: 550–68.

Herbert, S. (2006) *Citizens, cops and power: recognizing the limits of community*. Chicago: University of Chicago Press.

Jankowski, M. (1991) *Islands in the street: gangs and American society*. Berkeley and Los Angeles: University of California Press.

Katz, C. (2004) *Growing up global: economic restructuring and children's everyday lives*. Minneapolis: University of Minnesota Press.

Knorr-Cetina, K. (1981) *The manufacture of knowledge: an essay on the constructivist and contextual nature of science*. Oxford: Pergamon.

Kobayashi, A. (2001) 'Negotiating the personal and political in critical qualitative research', in M. Limb and C. Dwyer (eds) *Qualitative methods for geographers*. London: Arnold. pp. 264–76.

Latour, B. (1987) *Science in action: how to follow scientists and engineers through society*. Cambridge, MA: Harvard University Press.

Ley, D. (1988) 'Interpretive social research in the inner city', in J. Eyles (ed.) *Research in human geography*. Oxford: Blackwell. pp. 121–38.

Lin, J. (1998) *Reconstructing Chinatown: ethnic enclave, global change*. Minneapolis: University of Minnesota Press.

Lynch, M. (1985) *Art and artifact in laboratory science: a study of shop work and shop talk in a research laboratory*. London: Routledge & Kegan Paul.

Marcus, G. (1998) *Ethnography through thick and thin.* Princeton: Princeton University Press.

Marcus, G. and Fisher, M. (1981) *Anthropology as cultural critique: an experimental moment in the human sciences.* Chicago: University of Chicago Press.

Matthews, S.A., Detwiler, J.E. and Burton, L.M. (2005) 'Geoethnography: Coupling geographic information analysis techniques with ethnography methods in urban research', *Cartographica* 40.

Miller, B. (2000) *Geography and social movements: comparing nuclear activism in the Boston area.* Minneapolis: University of Minnesota Press.

Mountz, A. (2004) 'Embodying the nation-state: Canada's response to human smuggling', *Political Geography* 23: 323–45.

Nagar, R. (1997) 'The making of Hindu communal organizations, places and identities in postcolonial Dar Es Salaam', *Environment and Planning D: Society and Space* 15: 707–30.

Ragin, C. (1987) *The comparative method: moving beyond qualitative and quantitative strategies.* Berkeley and Los Angeles: University of California Press.

Ragin, C. (1992) 'Cases of "what is a case?"', in C. Ragin and H. Becker (eds) *What is a case? Exploring the foundations of social inquiry.* Cambridge: Cambridge University Press. pp. 1–18.

Reason, P. and Bradbury, H. (eds) (2001) *Handbook of action research: participative inquiry and practice.* Thousand Oaks, CA: Sage Publications.

Rengert, G. (1997) 'Review symposium', *Urban Geography* 18: 468–69.

Sack, R. (1986) *Human territoriality: its theory and history.* Cambridge: Cambridge University Press.

Saunders, R. (1999) 'The space community policing makes and the body that makes it', *The Professional Geographer* 51: 135–46.

Secor, A. (2004) '"There is an Istanbul that belongs to me": citizenship, space, and identity in the city', *Annals of the Association of American Geographers* 94: 352–68.

Shearing, C. and Stenning, P. (1992) '"Say cheese": the Disney order that is not so Mickey Mouse', in C. Shearing and P. Stenning (eds) *Private policing.* Newbury Park, CA: Sage Publications. pp. 317–23.

Silvey, R. (2003) 'Spaces of protest: gendered migration, social networks, and labor activism in West Java, Indonesia', *Political Geography* 22: 129–55.

Stack, C. (1974) *All our kin: strategies for survival in a black community.* New York: Harper and Row.

Stake, R. (1995) *The art of case study research.* Thousand Oaks, CA: Sage Publications.

Strauss, A. and Corbin, J. (1990) *Basics of qualitative research: grounded theory procedures and techniques.* Newbury Park, CA: Sage Publications.

Till, K. (2005) *The New Berlin: memory, politics, place.* Minneapolis: University of Minnesota Press.

Walton, J. (1992) 'Making the theoretical case', in H. Becker and C. Ragin (eds) *What is a case? Exploring the foundations of social inquiry.* Cambridge: Cambridge University Press. pp. 121–38.

Willis, P. (1977) *Learning to labour: how working class kids get working class jobs.* Farnborough: Saxon House.

Wright, M. (2004) 'From protests to politics: women's worth, and Ciudad Juarez modernity', *Annals of the Association of American Geographers* 94: 369–86.

Yiftachel, O. (2000) 'Social control, urban planning and ethno-class relations: Mizrahim in Israel's development towns', *International Journal of Urban and Regional Research* 24: 417–34.

5

Policy, Research Design and the Socially Situated Researcher

Kari B. Jensen and Amy K. Glasmeier

During the last decade, geographers have called for more policy-centric geographic research aimed at social change (Peck, 1999; Massey, 2000, 2001, 2002; Martin, 2001a, b; 2002; Dorling and Shaw, 2002; Valentine, 2005; Ward, 2005; See the debate originally aired in *Transactions*, 1999).[1] The same authors ask: Why, given the perspective geographers bring to social issues, are they so rarely engaged in policy discourses (Glasmeier, 2006, 2007)? Some authors argue the lack of engagement by geographers is due to the banality of most policy research, for example, planning activities. Others suggest the academic reward system devalues policy research and, in fact, penalizes faculty who do it. Still others suggest policy research supports the status quo rather than seeking to change it.

In our view, a distinction can be made between policy research about a pre-specified problem, where the goal is to work within existing interpretations, and policy relevant research that seeks to inform the understanding of the underlying problem and redefine and reshape problem understanding. The former diminishes the researcher as an active agent of problem specification while the latter is explicit regarding the role of the

researcher as an active agent in defining and shaping the policy research inquiry. In this chapter, we argue that in order to be able to work toward social change, it is important to be conscious of one's social situatedness. As two researchers we take this term to mean the perspective of the problem by the researcher and the positionality of the investigator relative to the problem. We argue that situatedness is what distinguishes action-oriented academics. Most academics do not subscribe to this perspective and most explicitly avoid engagement, believing that such situatedness entails taking and acting on a position and, hence, retreating from objectivity and impartiality. But as socially situated researchers, we see our being socially situated as providing new insight into the research inquiry which allows us to define and shape it.[2] In this paper, by means of two vignettes, we lay out how we became who we are, and what this means for the research we do.

Our research experiences and practices build on different ontologies, epistemologies and methodologies, and we explore different topics played out in a range of geographical areas. Our *research design* also typically varies according to the problems we explore and our personal experiences with specific research topics. But we share fundamental similarities. We believe in and work from multiple methodologies. We both have experiences with quantitative and qualitative methodologies and believe both have important functions according to our research questions and the messages we wish to convey. And our underlying philosophy is the same: We are concerned about the distributional implications of contemporary capitalism, and we have as a goal to improve or make more humane the lived experience of individuals.

As *socially situated* researchers, we see the demonstration of good citizenship as intrinsically linked to our roles as academicians. Accordingly, we want to inform public discourse as well as inform and engage several kinds of audiences – and not just the academic. We are conscious of the social context of our research and sensitive to the use of our findings and want our research participants to understand our findings. Put simply, our research is problem-driven, action-oriented and applied.

Our understanding of what it means to be a *socially situated researcher* is linked to the existing literature on *situated knowledge*. Donna Haraway developed the concept of *situated knowledges* in 1987 (Haraway, 1996), when she rejected the common epistemological claim of a 'view from nowhere.' She argued for a new kind of objectivity – which she called feminist objectivity – based on making a person's positionality known and realizing that all knowledge stems from a particular combination of researcher and place. Haraway uses this focus on positioning to strongly criticize both relativism and 'totalizing versions of claims to scientific authority' (1996: 117). By inaugurating this new meaning of objectivity, Haraway is '[…] arguing for politics and epistemologies of location, positioning, and situating, where partiality and not universality is the condition of being heard to make rational knowledge claims' (1996: 121). According to Juliana Mansvelt and Lawrence Berg (2005: 253),

Haraway's conception of objectivity requires a different form of writing practice, one in which we should reject the third-person narrative and 'reflect upon and analyse how one's position in relation to the processes, people, and phenomena we are researching actually affects both those phenomena and our understanding of them.' In a review and critique of feminist geographers' encounters with situated knowledges, Gillian Rose writes:

> The imperative to situate the production of knowledge is being formulated by feminist geographers through a rhetoric of both space and vision. Doreen Mattingly and Karen Falconer-Al-Hindi (1995: 428–29) are typical in their statement that, in order to situate ourselves, it is necessary 'to make one's position vis a vis research *known* rather than invisible, and to *limit* one's conclusions rather than making grand claims about their universal applicability.' (1997: 308)

Many geographers, especially feminist geographers, have pointed to the importance of positionality and/or situated knowledge (Katz, 1992; McDowell, 1992; Pratt, 1992; Schoenberger, 1992; Dyck, 1993; England, 1994; Nast, 1994; Radcliffe, 1994; Mattingly and Falconer-Al-Hindi, 1995; Moss, 1995; Rose, 1997; Nightingale, 2003). Situating knowledge means shedding light on the research process but not 'navel-gazing' (Farrow *et al.*, 1995 in Rose, 1997). Reflexivity about the research process becomes a necessary part of the writing. 'This reflexivity looks both "inward" to the identity of the researcher, and "outward" to her relation to her research and what is described as "the wider world"' (Rose, 1997: 309). However, Rose criticizes feminist geographers' attempts to be self-reflective and writes that 'the search for positionality through reflexivity is bound to fail' (1997: 311). One of the reasons for failure is that 'reflexivity may be less a process of self-discovery than of self-construction' (1997: 313). It goes beyond the scope of this article to engage in this debate, and it is only briefly referred to in Jensen's personal research story later in this chapter. Michael Samers summarizes nicely the shift in geography from traditional, scientific knowledge to situated knowledge:

> ... [M]any geographers wanted to dismiss metatheory (that is 'grand' or 'totalizing' theory that attempted to explain everything through a single theoretical lens). Rather, knowledge should be 'situated' (so called 'situated knowledges') in which the researcher's position should be explicit and 'locatable'. As Merrifield puts it, 'Under such circumstances, knowledge is always embedded in a particular time and space; it doesn't see everything from nowhere but *sees something from somewhere*.' (1995: 51; 2006: 274)

Moving forward from this definitional introduction,[3] we each reflect on our own positionality regarding our research as understood through two interventions. First, we discuss how our research fits into community-based discourses that speak to and inform our own approach to research. Second, we use a particular instance of research execution to demonstrate how we actualize 'situatedness' in the context of a research project. Created with policy relevance in mind, our research exemplifies historically and culturally situated research respectively.

PERSONAL RESEARCH EXPERIENCE: AMY GLASMEIER

My approach to research is informed by a group of scholars who vigorously engaged in activist public scholarship dating to the 1970s. Most influential were Bennett Harrison, Barry Bluestone, Ann Markusen, Doreen Massey, and Dick Walker[4] among others, who focused their research efforts on understanding contextual change and the effect of structural factors. As exemplified by their work, concrete problems could not be studied from afar, as a disinterested researcher. In fact, in many instances, the work of Bluestone and Harrison (1982), Markusen and Wheaton (1983), and Massey and Richard Meagan (1982) explicitly engaged communities affected by change. The research projects these scholars engaged in were built upward and forward from an historical understanding.

Thus, my orientation toward research was formed by role models who investigated a problem by building research inquiries from the ground up, rooted in history and emphasizing place. In sum, what I do is start from history and theorize about a situation or problem based on an accumulation of ideas and interpretations of that situation, issue or problem.

As an economic geographer, I am part of a group of scholars who argue economic geography can inform public policy (see Glasmeier, 2006; see also a long discussion that took place in *Transactions*, starting in 1999, among Jamie Peck (2000), Mark Banks and Sarah MacKian (2000), and Jane Pollard *et al.* (2000)). While a number of commentaries have been written about this, in general, these discussions focus on the absence, rather than the presence, of a geographic voice in policy conversations (Peck, 1999; Martin, 2001a, b; Martin *et al.*, 2004 among others). This absence is due in part to institutional constraints – limited rewards for conducting policy research (see Peck, 1999, for example) – but more precisely, to the difficulty of translating between the two worlds (Glasmeier, 2006, 2007). This dilemma is a far greater issue in the US than in Europe, where geographers actively engage in policy research (although even there, engaging in the policy process is more the exception than the rule). Part of this absence is about methodology (Johnston and Plummer, 2005). As I have written elsewhere, while citing others, policy research is evidence-based and usually statistical in method (Glasmeier, 2007). Qualitative research, on the other hand, is first and foremost used to construct context and to build new theory rather than affirm existing theory. While I recognize that it is optimal to use qualitative research methodology for theory building as opposed to theory testing (Yin, 1994), nonetheless, at least in the US, policy research is articulated within a framework of 'normal science' and elaborated using a positivist methodology. Description, in this case, is an afterthought, because a 'multiple perspectives approach,' which is a hallmark of geographic research, is all too often regarded as simply too subjective for policy research. Having said this, there is a growing use of qualitative research in informing policy on welfare reform – a significant step forward (Skinner *et al.*, 2005; Matthews *et al.*, 2005). In this case, qualitative research findings are being used to test 'policy theory,' enabling evaluation of policy theory in terms of a match with policy problem. This reinforces my approach to research which draws upon a mixed-method perspective while recognizing – if not claiming outright – the importance of 'situation' (though less explicitly pointed to than by feminist scholars).

My ontology is a cross between critical realism and critical structuralism. Trained by both neoclassical and Marxist economists and geographers, I work in the area of public policy and part of my scholarly activity includes working with groups, organizations and firms. In this capacity, I do everything from providing public education and analyzing specific problems to summarizing the research of others and testifying on behalf of particular policies and practices.

The public policy link works because ultimately I am a pragmatist, concerned with tangible items of daily concern. Motivated initially more by my heart and less by my head, I have learned that success in a policy context evolves from problem-identification and problem-solving. By observing persons who were successful, I realized that a clear definition and a theory of the policy problem are key. Accordingly, I have adjusted my expectations to reflect what could be done rather than what I personally felt was the 'complete' or right solution. As Ron Johnston said in conversation with his colleague Paul Plummer of Bristol, 'Policy makers don't want problems unless you simultaneously have solutions to them and the solutions are costless or you have figured out how to pay for them.'

I also am a malleable problem-driven researcher. My career to date is stimulated by problems that ultimately lead to scholarly outcomes – not the other way around – a convergence which is not total or always realized and which sometimes has to be planned. Many of my projects do not lead to scholarly output, so one of my challenges is to recognize what is convertible and what is not.

Of late, my approach to research has had another component: including students in my work – especially the policy work – so as to help them see the bigger issues confronting society. Integrating theory with experiential learning, especially at formative points in one's development, makes room for consideration of major social issues (racism, sexism, classism). I have learned that people who learn from what they see and experience can usually contribute more to problem-solving than those who are told what to think about. This is illustrated by a class for grads and undergrads – entitled 'Health, Economics and the Environment for Children of Appalachia' – which I co-led with two very able colleagues (Cindy Brewer and Stephen Matthews). The plan was to use library research, lectures, movies and field visits to revisit some of the early elements of the Appalachian Regional Commission (ARC) program that provided community funding for healthcare infrastructure and other service programs for children in the region. While that evaluation occurred, the course also gave the students an understanding of 'situated knowledge' as they learned about and experienced the lived realities of individuals not well understood and, in some cases, forgotten by the members of the broader society – namely, the poor of Appalachia.

Preconceptions: We all have them

Most of the students had not ventured into Appalachia, and thus, the experience held both mystery and myth. Early in the class, the students were surprisingly frank about their positionality and expressed strong opinions of the region's residents in television-informed language – hillbillies, moonshine, pollutions, hicks. Like many others, the students expected to find poorly dressed, largely inarticulate individuals with little connection to the outside world and antiquated views of life with some students even suggesting that the problems and conditions of Appalachia were the result of individual weakness and regional backwardness. As their professor, I wasn't sure how to explain without being excessively explicit that the students' stereotypes were just that – preconceptions based on inadequate information and external influences (e.g., family and media). The students' firsthand field experiences made a greater impression than anything I could possibly have included or said in the classroom.

From the moment we began our field research in January, students began to recognize the importance of 'context.' The counties the students visited ranked high on the ARC distress index – a measure of low income and high poverty and unemployment – and also did poorly based on our own indicators (level of education, availability of health care, etc.). These were places where teen pregnancy is common, job opportunities are few, health care is scarce, and the loss of school lunch programs during the summer results in children losing 10 per cent of their body weight. When jobs are available, they are low salaried and barely pay the bills. Interviews with healthcare and education professionals, parents and children, church members and local officials further 'situated' the students and provided opportunities to reflect on who they were and their own differences in upbringing. A second round of interviews in March confirmed the significance of their own situatedness and that of the children of Appalachia where life is tenuous and something as simple as lunch or three meals a day was not guaranteed for everyone – much less for children.

What the students pieced together after dozens of interviews was the story of the challenges facing children trying to grow up healthy in Appalachia. The story has chapters with each one tied to age and a cycle of self-awareness and understanding. In short, the students realized that children in Appalachia begin life much as children in other areas but across their life course, the aspirations of children in Appalachia change as they come to understand and confront their economic insecurity, limited mobility, and parental distress. Lacking interventions, these children see few options, and out of these realizations and insights grow differences in teen pregnancy, dropout rates, drug use, and general alienation. According to the children themselves, the lack of opportunity eventually leads to a sense of complacency and reduced valuation of traditional institutions like education.

The students didn't develop that picture easily. While they returned with anecdotes and evidence about supports such as Head Start, lunch programs, and guidance counseling, they also returned with stories about the impact of material goods on a child's calculus of well-being. Such things as long bus rides to and from school, schools with limited physical resources, and expectations of family life that paralleled the suburbs or television shows reinforced the fundamental importance of context. The students came to realize as well that by age 14, children in Appalachia believe that no matter what they do, no matter what happens around them, their situations will not change contextually.

The students' reflection over the life of children in Appalachia changed markedly over the semester. Some took everything they saw in stride while others were haunted by the experience. None were left unaffected.

Their understanding of their own situatedness and the situatedness of the children of Appalachia made a considerable impression on the students in the project. And it made an impression on state policy makers. By sheer coincidence, the students' scheduled presentation of their final report to the ARC occurred at the ARC Washington offices, after a particularly difficult discussion among Commission members about the creation of a Mississippi Delta Commission. Over lunch, the students stood in their suits – in many cases, their best clothing – and proceeded to tell the commissioners the story of the children of Appalachia.

At the close of the presentation, the secretary of state and co-chair of New York came up and congratulated the students, remarking how moved he was to hear what the students had learned. More importantly, he commented that he hadn't thought about the problem in quite the same way as the students' presentations had revealed it, and that he, too, would have to rethink many of his stereotypes in order to make sense of the region's important challenges.

While the students' presentation did not change the future, the Commission did subsequently reinforce the focus of its efforts almost exclusively on distressed counties, those places which had been left behind since 1980 and only marginally cared for. Was the presentation what tipped the balance? No. Did it help? Perhaps.

Shifting to a second experience, in Jensen's explanation of her postitionality and social situatedness that now follows, we will see how some of the discussed aspects play out when research is carried out with people who are not only representative of a different socioeconomic status, but who live in a country far from the researcher's country both in terms of geographical distance and culture.

PERSONAL RESEARCH EXPERIENCE: KARI B. JENSEN[5]

Before discussing how I came to do the research that I do, I briefly present three of the geographers who have inspired me with their socially situated research: Lakshman Yapa, Geraldine Pratt, and Cindi Katz.

Yapa's discourse analytical research springs out of his empathy with poor people and his situatedness historically and culturally both in Sri Lanka and here in the US (see Yapa, 1996, 1998, 2002). He sees a grave problem with how we (i.e., academicians) think about poverty. Yapa argues that agency must be mobilized in all sectors and at all levels of society in order to solve poverty problems. By singling out the poor and placing them in a 'poverty sector' ready for analysis, we keep seeing 'them' as the problem and ourselves as part of the non-problem. This leads to ineffective solutions to poverty. If we don't change the poverty discourse, we will never be able to eradicate poverty. Being situated in the US as a university professor who tries to engage his students in caring about poor people, Yapa has over a period of eleven years been co-designing research projects with his students and people from the local community by bringing the students to his poverty project in Philadelphia where they use a mix of qualitative and quantitative methods, including GIS, to explore local community issues such as community gardens, nutrition projects, local credit unions, and self-employment opportunities through the building of entrepreneurial skills.

Pratt's participatory action research in Canada with domestic workers from the Philippines is another example of socially situated research (see Pratt, 2004). In her role as a white middle-class woman at an age and in a life situation in which many choose to pay domestic workers to handle childcare and household chores, she began to ponder what life is like for the immigrant women who take these jobs. By working closely with the Philippine Women Centre in Vancouver over many years, she has used her cultural situatedness to create knowledge about these women's struggles for increased respect as human beings and skilled workers in Canadian society. Pratt accomplished this by employing poststructuralist feminist theory and a creative mix of methodologies – among them interviews, participant observation, and role-playing. Together with the Philippine Women Centre, she even created 'a small theatre of experimentation in which domestic workers could be outrageous and pursue their own flights of fantasy, in ways that are also instructive about the conditions of domestic workers in Vancouver' (Pratt, 2004: 192).

Katz' longitudinal ethnographic research with children in rural Sudan, coupled with her research with children in Harlem in New York City, demonstrates a unique way of pinpointing local problems stemming from global economic restructuring (see Katz, 2004). The importance of her research is a result of her being a historically and culturally situated researcher. Several fieldtrips to the Sudan over a 15-year period have made her capable of insightful interpretation and reflection on the work and play of the children in the specific locality of their village – herding animals, harvesting wild edible plants, and collecting fuel wood and water. In the Sudan, she analyzes the effects on children of the introduction of an internationally funded governmental agricultural project that forces the villagers to change their way of living from being subsistence farmers to becoming workers in the mechanized cultivation of basic food commodities. In New York, she analyzes the steep decline of manufacturing jobs and the detrimental effects on working-class children, and especially how these effects are visible in schools and public spaces. Katz' research reflects her feminist and Marxism-inspired focus on social reproduction, and her research design is a rigorous mix of small-scale surveys and participant observation, play, conversations, and archival work.

My ontology is postmodern because I refuse to identify with one grand narrative such as Marxism, feminism, or neoliberalism, and because I see the value of different voices. Postmodernists are often misunderstood because of a lack of understanding of the different types of postmodernism. I do not identify with 'skeptical postmodernists' who reject the possibility of finding truth, who talk about the abolition of social science, and who are extremely relativist. I see myself as an 'affirmative postmodernist' because, although I reject the meta-narratives of modernism, I see potential in social movements and take ethical stands (see Yapa, 1996). My epistemology is constructivist because I view language as 'constitutive and constructive rather than reflective and representative' (Phillips and Hardy, 2002: 13).

Language and discourses construct social reality and do not only reflect reality. The concepts we use to describe the world are not neutral; they mediate our understanding of the world. Since discourses produce reality, it is important to analyze the prevailing discourses on the topic I study – childhood and child labor in Bangladesh.

To some extent, I agree with Rose's critique of the difficulties in making one's positionality known to an audience. Working from a constructivist epistemology, I see discourses as mutually constituted between the researcher and the researched, and thus I agree with Rose that 'researcher, researched and research make each other' (1997: 316). According to Rose, this implies that 'the identity to be situated does not exist in isolation but only through mutually constitutive social relations, and it is the implications of this relational understanding of position that make the vision of transparently knowable self and world impossible' (1997: 314). Even the knowledge we have about ourselves is partial. However, if the researcher makes a sincere attempt to describe and explain to the audience what has led her into the topic and her relationship to it and to participants, the research will be more valuable than without such reflections.

I was trained in human geography at the University of Oslo, Norway, and at the Pennsylvania State University. Both my advisers, Jan Hesselberg and Lakshman Yapa, respectively, have inspired me by their focus on social injustice and the conviction that it is possible to work for social change through academia. Since 1989, I have been inspired by my Bangladeshi husband to focus on the many-faceted problems of poor people in Dhaka, Bangladesh. By spending time not only with books and articles about the various obstacles to a fulfilling life that poor people face, but also by spending time in the field in Bangladesh and with Bangladeshi immigrants in Norway and the US, I have situated myself in the cultures that I aim to understand. While in Bangladesh, I consciously spent more time with poor and middle-class people in their places than with poverty experts and others representing academic and public poverty discourse.

One aspect of Bangladeshi life that took getting used to during my first stay with a middle class family was the presence of a servant in the house who was supposed to take orders from everybody. It made me think a lot about the situation of domestic workers[6] in general, and especially of those who start working as children. This brought me into some heated conversations with Bangladeshis about their treatment of domestic workers and about responsibility for their workers' access to education and savings. Having been born and raised in Norway, where we have a strong welfare state and traditionally a strong sense of people's equal rights and access to services, my reactions to the rigid class system in Bangladesh were very negative.

While I had basic knowledge of the social system in Bangladesh before going there, the knowledge I acquired by living there, especially when taking part in the daily life of local people of different social classes, was different and mind-boggling. This inspired me to do research on reasons for poor children's low participation rate in primary schools in Dhaka and gradually led me to explore different forms of child labor in Bangladesh.

By employing a mix of discourse analysis and critical ethnography, I explored different discourses in Bangladesh on childhood and child labor, and how these discourses shape the lives of child domestics. I analyzed three main discourses on childhood and child labor in Bangladesh: the human rights discourse, the employers' discourse, and the working children's own discourse. The human rights discourse was explored by reading policy reports, newspaper articles, academic books and articles, and by interviewing teachers and people working for national and international non-governmental organizations (NGOs) and the government. For exploration of the employers' discourse and the children's discourse, I had to rely heavily on interviews/conversations, because

of the limited written discourse available. When I was in the field, I realized that the most valuable way I could spend my time in Dhaka was to be with the child workers and their employers in their daily life. An example of events that led to this realization was that an employer who had demonstrated her mistrust in the value of education for child domestics, in a formal interview later on expressed the complete opposite. With the tape recorder in front of her, she suddenly evoked the human rights discourse that she had dismissed just a few weeks earlier when we spent some time together one afternoon. This and similar incidents made me realize that ethnography had to become a more prominent methodology than planned if I were to discover what goes on in people's minds.[7] Spending time in situations where research participants' attitudes could be demonstrated became a requisite for doing policy-relevant research. I wanted my research to help improve the recruitment of child domestics to schools, both because domestics I talked with wanted to have access to education and because I found that it is crucial for them to be able to spend some time outside the households in which they live and work so that they can build a social network to rely on in case of abuse and neglect. This required an understanding of the mindsets of the employers and domestics that would not be attainable by just having them answer my questions. If I had not spent time getting to really know some of them I would not have realized the importance of chatting and just being together. The need for being flexible while doing socially situated research means that it is impossible to foresee exactly what kind of research design will be the most relevant or efficient. This has important consequences for the IRB[8] process. Being aware of the need for flexibility and discussing it openly with the IRB before fieldwork can save the researcher frustrations and waste of time in the field.

Were my decisions about research design a result of my social situatedness? To some extent, yes. Being familiar with the power-play between child domestics and their employers helped me make informed decisions about the design of interviews and it also helped me understand when, where, and how it was feasible to conduct interviews and more unstructured research techniques. I could as well have chosen another mix of methodologies and methods, although as a researcher who is culturally situated I do prefer primary data. I started out with some intriguing problems ('Primary education in Bangladesh is free but still school participation among poor people is very low, even in Dhaka where most people live nearby schools' and 'How are the lives and work conditions of child domestic workers in Dhaka constituted by prevailing discourses and what can be done to improve their quality of life?'), and I used feasible methods to discuss those problems. In the first study I conducted research *on* children (i.e., interviewing primarily the children's guardians and teachers, not so much the children themselves), whereas when researching child domestic workers an important component of my research was critical ethnographic research *with* children.

CONCLUSION

In sharing our research stories, we demonstrate that socially situated researchers can work from different ontologies, such as critical realism and postmodernism, and also from a wide variety of epistemologies. We suggest here that historical and cultural situatedness adds significantly to the strength and rigor of research and facilitates policy-relevance. Public policy research is not just about working within existing interpretations, but in many cases, it is about reinterpreting understandings and recasting problems, especially when extant policy practice is ineffective. In the case of poverty research, we fail to address and resolve poverty because we operate in a political context in which alternative interpretations

of underlying causes challenge the dominant discourse and therefore are rejected. This conundrum does not invalidate alternative inquiry; in fact it demands it be undertaken. We further illustrate this by showcasing some geographical research which is predominantly historically situated and other geographical research which is predominantly culturally situated. Socially situated geographical research employs a wide spectrum of interesting and creative methodologies, ranging from case study to discourse analysis. Being socially situated usually entails fieldwork and requires familiarity with the history, culture, and social issues of that specific place. Socially situated researchers are often pragmatic when it comes to applying specific methods such as interviews and theater performances. Being socially situated means that our research springs from real-world problems and a preoccupation with the implications of our findings for real life, but does not tie us to one type of research design. In some cases, the research design evolves gradually while in the field and even during the writing process afterwards (see, for instance, Pratt, 2004: 191–3). This necessitates a flexible approach to the IRB process, and if conveyed properly to the IRB, it can save the researcher time and frustrations while in the field. Both quantitative and qualitative studies may arise from being socially situated, but the research questions will reflect the position of the researcher. By being explicit about our personal, material, institutional, and geopolitical position as researchers and our historical and/or cultural situatedness, we can enhance the quality and policy-relevance of our research.

ACKNOWLEDGMENTS

The authors thank the external reviewers and the editors Steve Herbert and Stuart Aitken for helpful comments, and also Margaret Hopkins, writer and Communications Director, Center on Policy Research on

Energy, Environment, and Community Well-being, Penn State.

NOTES

1. See Rachel Pain (2006) and Kevin Ward (2006, 2007) for an overview of policy research in geography. We recognize that our list of references is not an exhaustive list of all geographical research covering the topics of this article.

2. See Jacquelin Burgess (2005), Noel Castree (2005), Sally Eden (2005), and Susan Owens (2005) for commentaries on the importance of situatedness in policy research.

3. Jennifer Hyndman (2007) and others advertise for a wider understanding of positionality building on Richa Nagar (2002), who criticizes US academicians for focusing their reflexive attempt too much on the individual researcher instead of on 'the ways in which those identities intersect with institutional, geopolitical and material aspects of their positionality' (Nagar, 2002 quoted in Hyndman, 2007: 37).

4. These same scholars were the mentors of many budding economic geographers who were activists in their own right (Michael Storper, Erica Schoenberger, Susanna Hecht, and others. These names are joined by many others).

5. Some of the information in this section is based on Jensen (2007a, b).

6. I prefer the term 'domestic worker' to 'servant' because of all the negative connotations attached to the term 'servant.'

7. This is related to what Berit Vandsemb refers to as 'the importance of establishing a collaborative relationship or friendship with the informants in order to get them to tell their stories' (1995: 421, citing Oakley, 1981). My experience is that collaborative relationships or friendships are best attained by spending as much time as possible with people in their different social settings, such as in their home, their workplace, and in the parties and other meetings they go to. Hence the need for participant observation and ethnography.

8. IRB stands for Institutional Review Board, which is the panel in each University here in the US which approves research projects' ability to protect research participants.

REFERENCES

Banks, M. and MacKian, S. (2000) 'Jump in! The water's warm: a comment on Peck's "grey geography"', *Transactions of the Institute of British Geographers* 25 (2): 249–54.

Bluestone, B. and Harrison, B. (1982) *The deindustrialization of America*. New York: Basic Books.

Burgess, J. (2005) 'Follow the argument where it leads: some personal reflections on "policy-relevant" research', *Transactions of the Institute of British Geographers* 30 (3): 273–81.

Castree, N. (2005) 'Forum: geography and environmental policy', *Transactions of the Institute of British Geographers* 30 (2): 271–2.

Dorling, D. and Shaw, M. (2002) 'Geographies of the agenda: public policy, the discipline and its (re) "turns"', *Progress in Human Geography* 26 (5): 629–46.

Dyck, I. (1993) 'Ethnography: a feminist research method?', *Canadian Geographer* 37 (1): 52–7.

Eden, S. (2005) 'Green, gold and grey geography: legitimating academic and policy expertise', *Transactions of the Institute of British Geographers* 30 (3): 282–6.

England, K. (1994) 'Getting personal: reflexivity, positionality, and feminist research', *Professional Geographer* 46 (1): 80–9.

Glasmeier, A. (2006) 'On the intersection of policy and economic geography: selective engagement, partial acceptance, and missed opportunities', in S. Bagchi-Sen and H.L. Smith (eds) *Economic geography: past, present and future*. London: Routledge. pp. 208–20.

Glasmeier, A. (2007) 'Methodologies, epistemologies, and audiences', in A. Tickell, E. Sheppard, J.A. Peck and T. Barnes (eds) *Politics and Practice in Economic Geography*. London: Sage. pp. 210–20.

Haraway, D. (1996) 'Situated knowledges: the science question in feminism and the privilege of partial perspective', in J. Agnew, D. Livingstone and A. Rogers (eds) *Human geography: an essential anthology*. Malden, MA and Oxford: Blackwell Publishing. pp.108–28. (first published in *Feminist Studies* 14: 575–600, 1988).

Hyndman, J. (2007) 'Feminist geopolitics revisited: body counts in Iraq', *The Professional Geographer* 59 (1): 35–46.

Jensen, K.B. (2007a) 'Child domestic workers in Dhaka: a geographical study of discourses, work, and education'. Unpublished Doctoral Dissertation, Pennsylvania State University.

Jensen, K.B. (2007b) 'Opportunities for agency and social participation among child domestic workers in Bangladesh', *Children, Youth, and Environments*

17 (1): 148–70. Available http://www.colorado.edu/journals/cye/.

Johnston, R.J. and Plummer, P.S. (2005) 'What is policy-oriented research?', *Environment and Planning A* 37 (9): 1521–6.

Katz, C. (1992) 'All the world is staged: intellectuals and the projects of ethnography', *Environment and Planning D: Society and Space* 10 (5): 495–510.

Katz, C. (2004) *Growing up global: economic restructuring and children's everyday lives.* Minneapolis, University of Minnesota Press.

Mansvelt, J. and Berg, L. (2005) 'Writing qualitative geographies, constructing geographical knowledges', in I. Hay (ed.) *Qualitative research methods in human geography.* New York: Oxford University Press. pp. 248–65.

Markusen, A. and Wheaton, L. (1983) 'The Berkeley economy: an update', in D. Minkus and T. Duster (eds) *Economic development in Berkeley.* Berkeley: Institute for the Study of Social Change. pp. 10–23.

Martin, R. (2001a) 'Geography and public policy: the case of the missing agenda', *Progress in Human Geography* 25 (2): 189–209.

Martin, R. (2001b) 'The geographer as social critic: getting indignant about income inequalities', *Transactions of the Institute of British Geographers* NS 26 (3): 267–72.

Martin, R. (2002) 'A geography for policy, or a policy for geography? A response to Dorling and Shaw', *Progress in Human Geography* 26 (5): 642–4.

Martin, R., Gray, M., James, A.l and Plummer, P. (2004) 'Expanding the role of geography in public policy', *Environment and Planning A* 36 (11): 1901–6.

Massey, D. (2000) 'Editorial: practicing political relevance', *Transactions of the Institue of British Geographers* NS 25 (2): 131–3.

Massey, D. (2001) 'Geography on the agenda', *Progress in Human Geography* 25 (1): 5–17.

Massey, D. (2002) 'Geography, policy and politics: a response to Dorling and Shaw', *Progress in Human Geography* 26 (2): 645–6.

Massey, D. and Meegan, R. (1982) *The anatomy of job loss: the how, why and where of employment Decline.* London: Methuen.

Matthews, S.A., Detwiler, J.E. and Burton, L.M. (2005) 'Geoethnography: coupling geographic information analysis techniques with ethnography methods in urban research,' *Cartographica* 40 (4): 75–90.

Mattingly, D.J. and Falconer-Al-Hindi, K. (1995) 'Should women count? A context for the debate', *The Professional Geographer* 47 (4): 27–35.

McDowell, L. (1992) 'Doing gender: feminism, feminists and research methods in human geography', *Transactions of the Institute of British Geographers* 17 (4): 399–416.

Moss, P. (1995) 'Embeddedness in practice, numbers in context: the politics of knowing and doing', *The Professional Geographer* 47 (4): 442–9.

Nagar, R. (2002) 'Footloose researchers, "traveling" theories, and the politics of transnational feminist praxis', *Gender, Place, and Culture* 9 (2): 179–86.

Nast, H.J. (1994) 'Opening remarks on "Women in the field"', *The Professional Geographer* 46 (1): 54–66.

Nightingale, A. (2003) 'A feminist in the forest: situated knowledges and mixing methods in natural resource management', *ACME: An International E-Journal for Critical Geographies* 2 (1): 77–90. Available http://www.acme-journal.org/index.html.

Owens, S. (2005) 'Making a difference? Some perspectives on environmental research and policy', *Transactions of the Institute of British Geographers* 30 (3): 287–92.

Pain, R. (2006) 'Social geography: seven deadly myths in policy research', *Progress in Human Geography* 30 (2): 250–9.

Peck, J. (1999) 'Grey geography?', *Transactions of the Institute of British Geographers* 24 (2): 131–5.

Peck, J. (2000) 'Jumping in, joining up, getting on', *Transactions of the Institute of British Geographers* 25 (2): 255–8.

Phillips, N. and Hardy, C. (2002) *Discourse analysis: investigating processes of social construction.* Thousand Oaks, CA: Sage.

Pollard, J., Henry, N., Bryson, J. and Daniels, P. (2000) 'Shades of grey? Geographers and policy', *Transactions of the Institute of British Geographers* 25 (2): 243–8.

Pratt, G. (1992) 'Spatial metaphors and speaking positions', *Environment and Planning D: Society and Space* 10 (3): 241–3.

Pratt, G. (2004) *Working feminism.* Philadelphia: Temple University Press.

Radcliffe, S.A. (1994) '(Representing) post-colonial women: authority, difference and feminisms', *Area* 26 (1): 25–32.

Rose, G. (1997) 'Situating knowledges: positionality, reflexivities and other tactics', *Progress in Human Geography* 21 (3): 305–20.

Samers, M. (2006) 'Changing the world: geography, political activism, and Marxism', in S. Aitken and G. Valentine (eds) *Approaches to human geography.* Thousand Oaks, CA: Sage. pp. 273–85.

Schoenberger, E. (1992) 'Self-criticism and self-awareness in research: a reply to Linda McDowell', *The Professional Geographer* 44 (2): 215–8.

Skinner, D., Matthews, S.A. and Burton, L.M. (2005) 'Combining ethnography and GIS technology to examine constructions of developmental opportunities in contexts of poverty and disability', in T. Weisner (ed.) *Discovering successful pathways in children's development: mixed methods in the study of childhood and family life.* Chicago: University of Chicago Press. pp. 223–39.

Valentine, G. (2005) 'Geography and ethics: moral geographies? Ethical commitment in research and teaching', *Progress in Human Geography* 29 (4): 483–7.

Vandsemb, B.H. (1995) 'The place of narrative in the study of third world migration: the case of spontaneous rural migration in Sri Lanka', *The Professional Geographer* 47 (4): 411–25.

Ward, K. (2005) 'Geography and public policy: a recent history of "policy relevance"', *Progress in Human Geography* 29 (3): 310–9.

Ward, K. (2006) 'Geography and public policy: towards public geographies', *Progress in Human Geography* 30 (4): 495–503.

Ward, K. (2007) 'Geography and public policy: activist, participatory, and policy geographies', *Progress in Human Geography* 31 (5): 695–705.

Yapa, L. (1996) 'What causes poverty?: a postmodern view', *Annals of the Association of American Geographers* 86 (4): 707–28.

Yapa, L. (1998) 'The poverty discourse and the poor in Sri Lanka', *Transactions of the Institute of British Geographers NS* 23 (1): 95–115.

Yapa, L. (2002) 'How the discipline of geography exacerbates poverty in the third world', *Futures* 34 (1): 33–46.

Yin, R. (1994) *Case study research: design and methods* (2nd Edition). Thousand Oaks, CA: Sage.

6

Mixed Methods: Thinking, Doing, and Asking in Multiple Ways

Sarah Elwood

INTRODUCTION

The notion of mixing methods rests a bit uneasily alongside long-standing debates in geography that have sought to demarcate clear separations between quantitative and qualitative methods, or between positivist, humanist, post-structuralist, and other epistemological perspectives. At some moments, these discussions have questioned whether the discipline's defining forms of inquiry ought to focus upon the particularity or generality of spatial phenomena and patterns (Hartshorne, 1939; Schaefer, 1953). At other moments, geographers have disagreed about the appropriateness of quantitative and qualitative methods for describing or explaining a diversity of human spatial activities, experiences, and perceptions (Chorley and Haggett, 1967; Harvey, 1969; Buttimer, 1976; Tuan, 1976). Sometimes, attention has centered on a particular research method, as in the 'GIS (geographical information systems) wars' of the mid 1990s (Pickles, 1995). While articulated in different terms, these various methodological and epistemological debates share a common tendency to try to separate different research paradigms as purportedly incompatible, and to advocate for the appropriateness of particular data types and modes of analysis over others. With GIS, for instance, critics positioned it as a strictly quantitative method inextricably linked to positivist ways of knowing, while advocates defended the scientific rigor of GIS-based methodologies (Taylor and Overton, 1991; Openshaw, 1991; 1992; Lake, 1993).

Ironically, in tandem with these persistent boundary making and gate keeping efforts in the discipline, geographers have been conducting mixed methods research for decades. Our methodological literature is replete with thoughtful reflections on how different epistemological and methodological approaches might be integrated to bridge many of the conceptual and practical gulfs produced by these disagreements about epistemology and methodology. Researchers using quantitative or geovisual methods in feminist geography have examined the ontological, epistemological, and political challenges of mixing these approaches (Mattingly and Falconer-Al Hindi, 1995; Kwan, 2002a). Political ecologists have sought ways of integrating quantitative analyses of remote sensing imagery with qualitative analysis of oral histories or interviews (Robbins, 2001a, b; Nightingale, 2003). Participatory action research, with a growing presence in geography, also commonly incorporates a mixed methods approach (Pain, 2003, 2004). The methodologies and epistemologies of GIScience are increasingly diverse as well, as researchers consider forms of data, representations, and analyses that might constitute qualitative GIS (Sieber, 2001; Kwan and Knigge, 2006).

This active engagement with mixed methods provides a tremendous opportunity to create ways of doing research that intersect contested epistemological and methodological differences, and to disrupt persistent efforts to frame different paradigms and modes of inquiry as inherently incompatible. In this chapter, I will examine some of the central philosophical, practice, and institutional dilemmas of mixed methods research. I begin by discussing some of the epistemological and ontological challenges of mixed methods research, and several conceptual frameworks that are helpful in accommodating multiplicity at these levels. In the second section, I consider some practical considerations in carrying out mixed methods research, including questions about research design and the ways that we can (or should) produce and represent knowledge in mixed methods research. The third section outlines some of the institutional and disciplinary challenges that shape these theoretical and practical considerations of mixed methods research. Many of the examples I will discuss are drawn from mixed methods research that incorporates GIS. In part this is because it is the area of research with which I am most familiar. But more importantly, I have emphasized GIS because it is an area of geography that has a great deal to gain from mixed methods approaches. While many other research areas in geography have used mixed methods for a very long time, these approaches are significantly more recent in GIS.

One clarification is necessary at the outset. Some discussions of mixed methods research in the social and behavioral sciences devote a great deal of attention to separating 'multimethod' and 'mixed method' research, usually differentiating the two approaches based on how different data types or analysis techniques are used in relationship to one another. Approaches in which qualitative and quantitative data are analyzed in parallel but separate fashion to inform a research question in different ways are usually deemed multimethod, with mixed method referring to some degree of integration of across data types and modes of analysis (Tashakkori and Teddlie, 2003). But this distinction is not clearly articulated across the literature, nor is there widespread agreement about whether it is even possible to integrate at epistemological or ontological levels (Dixon and Jones, 1998). Here, I consider mixed methods approaches to be those that rely upon multiple types of data, modes of analysis, or ways of knowing, but may use these elements in a variety of ways in relationship to one another, for multiple intellectual and analytical purposes.

EPISTEMOLOGIES AND ONTOLOGIES IN MIXED METHODS RESEARCH

For many of us, our engagement with mixed methods begins in practice, at the moment when we formulate research questions that require multiple forms of data or modes of analysis. This initial moment of project formulation and research design requires confronting several of the central conceptual dilemmas of mixed methods research. From the outset, it is necessary to consider the conceptual purpose or intended intellectual goals of mixing methods. Secondly, conceptualizing mixed methods research also necessitates engaging questions about the extent to which different epistemologies and underlying assumptions about knowledge and ways of knowing can or should be integrated within a project.

In the methodological literature on mixed methods, several perspectives are offered with respect to the intellectual purpose or potential contribution of these approaches. Some justifications focus on validation, arguing that qualitative or quantitative data and analysis techniques might be used together to highlight discrepancies in data or interpretation (Eyles and Smith, 1988; Phillip, 1998; Cresswell, 2003). Other justifications tout the complementarity of different methods, arguing that they may be used together to enhance the explanatory power of our research, because different data types and modes of analysis interrogate different processes and interactions. Qualitative analysis of interviews may potentially illuminated meanings, relationships, and interactions not made visible through quantitative analysis of survey data. Alternatively, quantitative analysis of survey data might reveal patterns helpful in examining broader structural relationships (England, 1993; Hanson and Pratt, 1995, 2003).

Susan Hanson and Geraldine Pratt's (1995) study of changing gender roles and household livelihood strategies amidst economic restructuring, for instance, used quantitative data to characterize the changing labor markets and economic geographies of their case study region, but used ethnographic interviews to explore households' economic decision making and men's and women's involvement in paid and unpaid labor. The quantitative portion of this project illustrated how global economic restructuring was operating in specific regional and local contexts. The qualitative portion of the study illustrated how households responded to these shifts, as well as how structures such as gender and class shaped these responses. In this approach to mixed methods, the quantitative and qualitative elements of the methodology are both used to link broad structural processes with their particular or localized manifestations, but each element informs a different set of structures or processes – economic restructuring, gender, and class.

Other researchers take the perspective that mixing methods produces new knowledge, not through the complementarity of different data types and analysis techniques, but through the integration of different methods at analytical, interpretive, or epistemological levels. Hong Jiang (2003) and Andrea Nightingale (2003) for instance, use remote sensing data and ethnographic interviews together, analyzing both as socially and politically constructed texts representing landscape and landscape change. Both authors suggest that neither of these texts provide a complete perspective upon their research questions, but show how they may be used together to create multi-faceted and multi-scalar explanations of landscape change. These and other integrating approaches to mixed methods disrupt traditional groupings of some data and analysis techniques as quantitative and others as qualitative. LaDona Knigge and Meghan Cope's (2006) grounded visualization technique, for instance, applies grounded theory techniques usually associated with qualitative data and analysis to GIS-based spatial data that is both quantitative and qualitative.

These perspectives on the intellectual contributions of mixed methods research rely on different underlying assumptions about data collection and analysis, as well as knowledge and knowing. A validation-oriented approach to mixed methods research treats the objects of inquiry in research as wholly knowable. Data collection and analysis are framed as relatively unproblematic ways of gathering and representing information about the world. In contrast, conceptualizations that focus on the productive complementarity of multiple methods understand knowledge as situated and different ways of knowing as inherently partial. This approach to mixed methods is strongly informed by feminist theory and method, particularly feminist critiques of science and objectivity (Harding, 1986; Haraway, 1991). Integrating approaches to mixed methods research rest on similar assumptions, but conceive of the relationship between different methods or paradigms in a slightly different way. Specifically, approaches to mixed methods like those developed by Knigge and Cope (2006) conceive of mixed methods as rooted in a unique hybrid epistemology, rather than a strategic collision between separate epistemologies.

Thus, mixing multiple data types and modes of analysis may serve a variety of purposes in research, including validating different forms of data, generating insights from complementary approaches, or integrating to create new knowledge. Conceptualizations of mixed methods that focus on either their complementary or integrating potential raise a question about the extent to which a research project can or should draw on multiple epistemologies or ontologies. Is it possible to integrate or simultaneously hold multiple assumptions about the nature of the social world, our knowledge about it, and appropriate means of producing, interpreting, and representing knowledge? In part, answers to this question depend upon how we understand the relationship between epistemology and methodology, namely, the extent to which epistemology prescribes particular methods. In the broader literature on mixed methods in social and behavioral sciences, this relationship is characterized in several ways. Some scholars take the position that different epistemologies or paradigms for knowledge production are incompatible, while others argue that different paradigms may be complementary, building better understanding when deployed together because of these different perspectives. Some researchers contend that mixed methods research is rooted in its own unique epistemology, a sort of pragmatist meta-paradigm that bridges traditional divisions between, for instance, positivist, realist, or constructivist approaches (Greene and Caracelli, 2003; Teddlie and Tashakkori, 2003).

In geography, there is significantly stronger consensus about the relationship between epistemology and methodology than the relationship between epistemology and ontology. These debates have not directly discussed mixed methods, instead focusing more on the relationship between qualitative and quantitative methods. Many critical reflections on methodology over the past decade develop the position that epistemology informs but does not determine appropriate data sources and modes of analysis. For instance, recent re-examinations of the quantitative revolution in geography have attempted to de-couple associations between positivism and quantitative methods, arguing that a great many quantitative research efforts are rooted in other epistemologies (Phillip, 1998; Barnes and Hannah, 2001; Sheppard, 2001). Examining the compatibility of feminist epistemologies with quantitative methods, researchers have argued that the manner and ends to which quantitative data and analysis techniques are used determine their appropriateness to feminist methodologies or epistemologies, similarly suggesting that epistemology and method are not necessarily linked in fixed or singular ways (Lawson, 1995; Mattingly and Falconer-Al Hindi, 1995; McLafferty, 1995; Moss, 1995). Emergent work in feminist and qualitative GIS takes a similar position. A number of researchers have argued that while GIS has traditionally lent itself to representation and analysis of quantitative and cartographic expressions of knowledge, GIS-based research may be informed by realist, pragmatist, positivist, and other paradigms (Pavlovskaya, 2002; Schuurman, 2002a; Kwan, 2002c; Pavlovskaya, 2006).

This notion of an epistemological flexibility or multiplicity in GIS-based research methods is closely linked to recent assertions that visualization and visual methods are not necessarily detached or objectifying ways of knowing (Kwan, 2002b; Crang, 2003). While not directly addressing mixed methods, these re-examinations of GIS, visualization, and quantitative, qualitative, and feminist methods are invaluable in creating conceptual spaces for mixed methods to flourish. They do so by emphasizing that epistemology and methodology do not rigidly determine one another and that the connection between them may be actively engaged and reconstructed by researchers, for a variety of intellectual and political purposes. A researcher might adopt a realist epistemology and quantitative research methods not from the perspective that this approach is complete or most 'accurate', but because its representations might be most informative and useful in a given situation. Alternatively, a researcher might engage the visual methods of geospatial technologies to explore and interpret qualitative expressions of spatial knowledge, experience, and behavior. Kevin St. Martin (2005), for example, uses GIS to represent in visual form fishers' experientially-derived knowledge about productive fishing sites, but uses interviews and activity logs to explore additional mechanisms and sources of information (beyond direct experience) that shape the spatial patterns of their fishing practices. At its conceptual levels, mixed methods research requires this fluidity and multiplicity in relating epistemology and methodology.

Conceptualizing a separation between epistemology and ontology is far more problematic. A common rejoinder in critical discussions of methodology in geography has been that ontological assumptions guide the ways in which it is possible to know or produce knowledge. Victoria Lawson (1995) and Deborah Dixon and John Paul Jones (1998), for instance, note that from a given ontological position, some epistemologies and methods will be more appropriate than others. Assuming a social and physical world that is predictable and coherent, a positivist or realist approach to investigating it would be appropriate, as would quantitative forms of data and analysis. Beginning from an assumption that the world is shifting, contradictory, and not knowable in any fixed way requires a constructivist or post-structuralist approach, and different ways of producing knowledge in research. Ontology and epistemology also inform research practice by shaping our view of whether research serves to represent or constitute reality. If we assume once again a world that is predictable and coherent, our research functions to gather and communicate information about this world. If we assume a shifting contradictory reality that is constructed through our knowing and doing, then as Lynn Staeheli and Victoria Lawson

(1995) have argued, it is impossible to know this world outside of naming it. From this position, research plays a role in constituting that world. Jessie Poon (2004) contends that these different conceptualizations of the ontological role of research align along epistemological and methodological lines, with quantitative human geographers tending to assume that their concepts and data represent or model reality, and qualitative human geographers tending to assume their concepts and data constitute reality. These alignments suggest the difficulty of separating ontology and epistemology.

Conceptual debates about the relationships between epistemology, ontology, and methodology influence mixed methods research in several ways. Efforts by some scholars to disrupt fixed associations between particular epistemologies and methods have fostered creative attempts to integrate data types and analysis techniques previously associated with separate research paradigms, as seen in discussions of quantitative feminist research or qualitative GIS. Viewing epistemology and method as linked in multiple and flexible ways makes room for a mixed methods approach. But many of the researchers cited above point to the difficulty of mixing at the ontological level, suggesting that combining assumptions about the nature of reality is problematic. This uneasiness about how ontology and methodology intersect informs divergent characterizations of particular methods and the world views they are said to promote. For instance, we continue to see disparate accounts of the ontologies that can underlie research conducted with GIS. Some scholars insist that GIS requires assuming a fixed stable world, while others suggest that GIS may be used to represent multiple shifting forms of knowledge, perception, or emotion, rooted in a very different set of assumptions about reality and how it is produced.

A significant challenge of mixed methods research lies in articulating a philosophy of knowledge and accepted practices for developing knowledge that can not only accommodate but also integrate multiple ways of knowing. In the case of geography, many researchers draw on multiple epistemologies in practice, even while disciplinary discourse has at times assumed and constructed a separation between them (thus, the 'quantitative/qualitative divide'). Mixed methods approaches challenge this separation of multiple epistemological commitments because they insist upon the possibility of mixing ways of knowing. A number of critical reflections on theory and method in the discipline have discussed conceptual frameworks that accommodate epistemological complexity or multiplicity. Such conceptualizations have a great deal to offer our continued philosophical and practical discussions of mixed methods research in geography.

Dianne Rocheleau (1995) has noted the utility of Donna Haraway's (1991) strong objectivity in guiding flexible but conceptually coherent combinations of qualitative and quantitative methods. Strong objectivity asserts the partiality of knowledge, without prioritizing one paradigm or technique over another. From this perspective, methodological pluralism is possible if researchers directly address the partiality of their knowledge production practices. Like strong objectivity, Marcus Doel's (2001) soft ontology suggests that it may be possible to produce research practices that are sensitive to what he sees as an irresolvable contradiction between fixed/categorical ways of knowledge and fluid/constructivist ways of knowing. Helga Leitner and Eric Sheppard (2003) suggest Helen Longino's (2002) local epistemologies as a productive philosophy for bridging divisions between critical and other approaches to urban geography. Local epistemologies adopt the perspective that for any research question, there may be multiple conceptual frameworks from which to generate an explanation that is valid, appropriate, and acceptable in a given situation. The appropriateness of particular epistemologies is therefore contingent upon a variety of socio-political and philosophical

considerations, and epistemological consensus is not necessary (Longino, 2002).

Finally, pragmatism has a great deal to offer as a framework for negotiating the relationship between methodologies and philosophies of knowledge in mixed methods research. Pragmatism holds that knowledge is produced through experience, not discovered, that the world is both created and known through social processes, and that the validity of scientific knowledge is best evaluated by its capacity to enable better understanding or social change (Smith, 1984; Maxcy, 2003; Mertens, 2003). Geographers have long recognized the potential of pragmatism as a philosophical basis for developing knowledge through a range of methodologies. Susan Smith (1984), in one of the first encounters with pragmatism in the geography literature, showed how a pragmatist philosophy of knowledge can position ethnography and other participatory methods as legitimate ways of producing knowledge. Pragmatism has also informed feminist and participatory research methods in geography, both of which draw on the notion that the appropriateness of different forms of knowledge is determined by their potential to produce social change in a given situation (Lawson, 1995; Rocheleau, 1995; Schuurman, 2002b; Pain, 2004). From such a perspective, a mixed methods approach is appropriate and methodologies are open to being combined and reworked by researchers in practice.

Two common threads link these efforts to conceptualize more flexible or plural approaches to epistemology and methodology: Insistence on the critical reflexive agency of researchers as agents of knowledge production, and suggestion that multiple methods are valuable in research practice in spite of epistemological difference. Such a perspective enables us to acknowledge gaps and tensions between different forms of knowledge, while also recognizing the different social and political power of particular forms of knowledge and research paradigms. This perspective leaves room for researchers to prioritize methods based upon their capacity to foster socially and politically significant outcomes, as well as their theoretical appropriateness to particular research questions. While not resolving some of the ontological and epistemological dilemmas described above, a pragmatist approach enables us to *do* mixed methods research, tackling important questions that cannot be adequately engaged with a more singular approach.

MIXED METHODS IN PRACTICE: INTERPRETIVE, ANALYTICAL, AND POLITICAL ISSUES

Geographers have long asked research questions that require investigating multiple data sources, intersecting human and physical phenomena, and processes that operate at multiple spatial scales. As a result, the existing literature provides a rich source of insights upon many of the practical issues that arise in doing mixed methods research, even if they are not always articulated as part of mixed methods research practice. These discussions occur in multiple areas of research in the discipline. For political ecologists, efforts to understand the intersection of ecological and human processes frequently require mixed methods. In feminist geography, an understanding of knowledge as partial has motivated some to pursue mixed methods as a way to try to incorporate complementary forms of knowledge and analysis. Critical GIScience has relied heavily on mixed methods in attempting to alter GIS to enable inclusion of qualitative and quantitative forms of spatial knowing, and in efforts to use GIS for research practices that are broadly inclusive of diverse social groups and ways of knowing. Participatory action research, because of its pragmatist orientation toward using research to inform intervention in social and physical environments, has also relied strongly on mixing methods. Of course, mixed methods approaches are used across geography, but these research

areas are particularly illustrative of some of the important practical issues involved in conducting mixed methods research. These include questions about how to incorporate analysis of multiple and divergent types of data; interpret the meanings of multiple data and analyses with respect to contingent factors or broader processes and relationships; and most appropriately engage the intellectual and political authority of different forms of data and analysis.

Using multiple data sources presents a number of challenges for analysis and interpretation. On one level, incorporating multiple data types into a research project may be problematic because these data lend themselves to divergent forms of representation, analysis, and communication. For instance, critical GIS researchers have noted the difficulty of incorporating multiple forms of spatial knowledge into a GIS, and the greater ease of using traditional cartographic representations of quantitative data. As mixed methods approaches to GIS have emerged, researchers have developed multimedia techniques to transcend these limitations. They use text boxes, sound files, photographs, sketches, 3-D representations, and animations to include qualitative data, shifting, or multiple representations of a single space, or spatial perceptions and emotion (Al-Kodmany, 2000; Shiffer, 2002; Harrower, 2004; Kwan and Lee, 2004). But including multiple data has proved far easier than facilitating multiple modes of analysis, because the traditional analytical techniques of GIS tend to rely on exploring or measuring spatial relations between tangible fixed phenomena.

Emerging qualitative GIS techniques offer some existing directions toward more integrated or multiple modes of analysis. Knigge and Cope's (2006) grounded visualization, described previously, is one such technique. Grounded visualization draws on Barney Glaser and Anslem Strauss's (1967) grounded theory as an inductive means of building theory through iterative coding and analysis of qualitative data, but incorporates GIS-based visualization of spatial data as part of this process. With this technique a researcher might use GIS to represent, compare, and contrast multiple forms of geographic knowledge about a neighborhood, such as land use or property condition information from local government, and similar information gathered through walking surveys or interviews with residents. In research on the use and impacts of GIS by community development organizations, I use a kind of grounded visualization to explore how these groups use GIS to produce and negotiate different accounts of local needs, conditions, and priorities. Working with dozens of maps produced by community organizations as part of their neighborhood revitalization activities, I explore these maps as texts that produce representations of people, place, and needs, in pursuit of particular political projects. But in tandem, I also use interviews with community development staff about their production and use of these maps, to expand and refine my analysis of the maps themselves. The maps, cartographic representations of particular agendas and goals, tell one story, but interviews with staff members about these maps allow additional and sometimes different stories to emerge. I review these visual and textual narratives together, working back and forth between them, to try understand similarities, contradictions, and points of difference.

Rachel Pain and colleagues (2006) have used an approach they call 'qualified GIS' to analyze the results of ethnographic interviews about residents' perceptions of safety in tandem with GIS-based analysis of street lighting and incidences of crime. Qualified GIS uses qualitative forms of data and analysis to further explore propositions developed through GIS analysis, not to confirm or refute them, but to refine them or better understand the questions being considered. This project used GIS to explore whether areas with low levels of street lighting were also characterized by higher levels of crime. It also used ethnographic interviews with residents to generate information on places they perceived as unsafe. The GIS analysis did not show a strong association between darker areas and incidence of crime, but the interviews revealed a strong perception among residents that these areas were unsafe. Taken together, the results of this analysis suggest that low lighting in neighborhoods is problematic, but for different reasons than typically articulated by policy makers, offering a far more nuanced interpretation of the associations between street lighting, crime, and perceptions of safety.

In qualitative methods, recent calls to diversify the traditionally text-focused data sources and analysis techniques of qualitative methods by incorporating visual and performative ways of knowing (Crang, 2005) presents similar challenges. Several scholars address the difficulty of using text-based and performative approaches together, noting that many of the modes of analysis typically applied to text-based forms of qualitative data are unsuitable for understanding the meaning of performative practices within a research project (Pratt, 2000; Cahill *et al.*, 2004). Geraldine Pratt (2000) describes her difficulty in determining how to interpret transcripts of role playing performances by her research partners in a collaborative project with Filipina domestic workers. The role playing performances, she notes, initially felt like blunt stereotypes, which she found far more difficult to engage analytically than transcripts of interviews in which participants offered their direct reflections and experiences. As well she questions what meanings and possible interpretations are lost in using a textual transcript of the performance after the fact. As in the case of qualitative GIS, these discussions suggest that co-presentation of different forms of data or ways of knowing is far simpler than integration in analysis.

Another analytical or interpretive challenge in mixed methods research lies in deciding what to do when different data contradict each other. For example, in research on the use and impacts of GIS in community-based planning and neighborhood revitalization, I have found that different forms of data frequently foster divergent meanings or interpretations of neighborhood change. Analysis of maps produced by community organizations to support their work often suggests that 'community development' is primarily understood and accomplished through capital investment in the built environment. But in contrast, participant observation at community meetings may suggest that 'community development' is defined and sought through enriching networks of mutual support, knowledge development, and action among residents. Faced with these (and other) contradictory framings of what seems to constitute community development, there are a variety of ways I might proceed with analysis and interpretation.

One option, rooted in earlier validation-focused approaches to mixed methods research, would be to treat these different meanings as evidence of error or misinterpretation (Eyles and Smith, 1998; Cresswell, 2003). But if we begin from the notion that all ways of knowing are partial, this opens the door to examining and interpreting contradictions between different methods in more theoretically and empirically productive ways. As Kim England (1993) suggests, we can assume that different ways of knowing might be complementary, revealing insights not evident with another method or form of data. With the contradiction described above, we might conclude that community development has multiple meanings in this community, but that participant observation of residents and analysis of GIS-based maps each only illustrate one of these meanings.

Or, as Nightingale (2003), Paul Robbins (2003), and Hanson and Pratt (2003) suggest, we can examine these ambiguities to reach new insights not otherwise evident. In my earlier example of contradictory framings of community development, I also incorporated analysis of semi-structured interviews with community organization staff members. This material supported the notion that multiple definitions of community development are indeed at work in the community. But this material showed additionally how community

organization professionals strategically create, re-work, and combine these meanings to gain support for a range of projects or policy goals, and to make up for the limited meanings that can be communicated through any single form of representation or communication. In this case, their use of GIS lends itself most readily to illustrating community development as capital investment, but they negotiate other meanings and practices of community development in other forums. The strategic and self-aware way in which they do so becomes evident through a mixed methods approach that interrogates contradictions to try to develop new insights.

All of these approaches to dealing with multiple data or methods (whether in the face of contradictions or not) employ a kind of triangulation. Triangulation is a long-standing approach to working with multiple methods or forms of data in the social sciences. It is an interpretive practice in which researchers examine different data or results in relation to one another. But as England (1993) demonstrates, triangulation is not one practice, but several, each of which may be undertaken for different purposes. She used triangulation among different forms of qualitative data and data sources for all of the purposes described above, for crossing-checking or verification, for complementarity, and for generating new insights. These different approaches to triangulation have different ontological roots. Triangulation for validation assumes, for instance, the possibility of a fixed reality that is knowable in unambiguous ways. Triangulation to produce new insights assumes not just that knowledge and ways of knowing are partial, but that ways of knowing themselves are engaged in producing particular realities. This latter understanding of triangulation places a great deal of emphasis upon the responsibility of researchers to thoughtfully interpret contradictions and silences between different data sources and modes of analysis and critically reflect upon a range of possible meanings.

While triangulation is perhaps the most discussed framework for working with multiple forms of knowledge in mixed methods research, there are many other creative practices for representation and analysis. In geography and beyond, some scholars adopt multi-vocal approaches to illustrating research processes and findings. Margery Wolf (1992) offers one such model, presenting her research in three parallel texts, as a piece of fiction, as field notes, and as a social science article. Geraldine Pratt and Elia Kirby (2003), writing on a collaborative political theater project, note that performative techniques are useful in fostering multiple modes of doing and presenting research. Mike Crang's (2005) call for performance-based qualitative approaches suggest similar multi-vocal approaches. New practices in visualization and visual methods, including participatory diagramming, counter-mapping, and feminist or qualitative approaches to GIS, also bridge multiple forms of data and ways of knowing (Kesby, 2000; Pavlovskaya, 2002; Williams and Dunn, 2003; Knigge and Cope, 2006). These approaches do not necessarily elide challenges of interpreting contradictions and silences across multiple methods or offer integrated multi-modal forms of analysis. Nonetheless, they offer creative ways of analyzing and presenting research, and hold great promise for researchers who are seeking to engage these intersections in productive ways.

Mixed methods research also presents a number of questions about how to incorporate multi-scalar forms of data, understand how different elements of a research design speak to the particularity of findings or enable generalization to other situations, and relate situated micro-level processes to those that occur at broader levels. Mixed methods research from political ecologists is particular useful in illustrating these challenges and potential approaches to addressing them, because of the ways in which it examines intersecting human and physical processes and the engagement of individuals, institutions, and social groups with these processes. For instance, Karl Zimmerer's (2003) research on biodiversity conservation in agriculture shows the necessity of examining how regional economies and networks of exchange affect the availability and costs of seeds, as well as how gender roles in farming and the choices of individual households both respond to and influence this broader economy. In this project, mixed methods were used to show the limits of models of seed management that solely reference biophysical processes such as climate and soil zones. Quantitative results of a survey of farmers' planting patterns and sources of seeds revealed a complex pattern of seed management that includes inter- and intra-community exchanges that involve households, local communities, and seed markets or fairs. Ethnographic data from interviews with households provided further explanatory detail, to explore structures and processes not evident in the survey results. The interviews, for instance, showed that gender differentiates the roles of men and women in seed management, and by extension, their roles in agrobiodiversity conservation.

Robbins (2001b) provides another example of mixed methods in political ecology research, in a project investigating the social and ecological consequences of modernist land management practices and their influence upon global landscape change. He uses evidence drawn from satellite imagery, historical documents, household production practices, and state land management policies. This project too is faced with the challenge of integrating evidence from multiple scales and sources. Robbins (2001b) navigates these challenges by using different data sources and analysis techniques to explore and explain different mechanisms that affect global landscape change, through a specific case example in northwestern India. Land use/land cover change analysis using remote sensing techniques provides a broad regional characterization of ecological change. Content analysis of historical documents reveals the role of institutions, such as the British colonial regime, in producing landscape change through specific management practices *and* through discursive constructions of landscapes as 'natural' or 'social'. Ethnographic interviews with state planners and with local residents show both how these discourses and policies endure across time, and how they become enacted at highly localized scales. Together, these methods and analyses weave a robust inter-scalar explanation.

As Zimmerer (2003), Robbins (2001a, b), and others have illustrated, use of multiple data sources and analysis techniques can enable investigation of multiple causal relationships and potential explanations of complex processes. But in such approaches it may be difficult to interpret how these different data sources (and by extension, the processes they investigate) are related. That is, in practical terms, How should a researcher relate material taken from interviews with local farmers about their production and acquisition of seeds and other agricultural inputs to a regional survey of pricing and regulatory structures? In what ways are the farmers' responses locally contingent, and how can we understand which aspects of local conditions are important determinants of their engagement with broader structures that operate the regional level? These analytical challenges occur not so much within single data types or modes of investigation, but when we attempt to intersect these elements to inform research questions together. Mixed methods projects that have been effective in navigating this challenge share some common characteristics, such as carefully conceptualizing and articulating the relationships between structural processes and local contexts, and clearly establishing which methods and data may be best used to get at which aspects of these relationships.

For instance, Thomas Bassett's (2005) analysis of wild game depletion in west Africa uses a detailed conceptualization of game depletion as co-produced by habitat change and hunting pressure. He shows how these two mechanisms result from intersecting social, institutional, and biophysical changes, including structural adjustment policies, competition between farming and herding, rising presence of firearms, the involvement of hunters associations in producing public security, farmland expansion, and declining farming revenues. The research uses longitudinal surveys with rural households to gather both qualitative and quantitative data on rural economies, household livelihood strategies, and wild game markets. What enables this study to effectively link qualitative and quantitative data gathered at local levels with broader macro-economic shifts and national and international policy change is the clear conceptual framework within which these data are incorporated. Locally-gathered data illustrating rising number of hunters can, for instance, be interpreted as both a causal agent in game depletion as well as the result of national policies promoting the role of armed hunters' associations in providing public security.

Marianna Pavlovskaya's (2002) study of household participation in multiple economies (formal, informal, monetary, and non-monetary) in post-Soviet Moscow shows similar attention to building a careful conceptual frameworks, but employs mixed methods in a slightly different manner. She uses GIS and qualitative interviews with households to illustrate the extent to which single-paradigm macro-economic studies of urban restructuring in post-Soviet economies do not fully explain the experiences, strategies, and constraints experiences at the household level. Macro-economic studies posit a diversification of urban services after privatization, which in turn is thought to lessen the domestic labor of women. Pavlovskaya constructs a fine scale spatial database of urban service establishments before and after privatization, and maps these data to show such an expansion of urban services. However, she uses data from ethnographic interviews to illustrate several omissions from the GIS analysis of formally established urban services. The interviews show that households also rely heavily on a range of other strategies for meeting their daily life needs, including informally established businesses, and bartering or in-kind exchange of goods and services. As well, the interviews revealed that many households could not afford to patronize formal businesses, in spite of their expanding presence. This use of GIS-based analysis together with inductive interviews of house-holds highlights critical silences in theoriza-tions of post-Soviet economic transitions that have been developed from broad scale mac-ro-economic approaches.

Finally, doing mixed methods research requires careful consideration of the differen-tial discursive and political authority that may be granted particular methods and forms of data. That is, how should we relate multi-ple forms of knowledge and action in ways that are socially and politically influential in progressive ways, while also accounting for the tendencies of all forms of data, analysis, and representation to silence or exclude in some manner? Geographers have noted that different research paradigms and forms of data support different types of political prac-tice and may hold more or less sway with various audiences. The literature is replete with mixed methods research projects that illustrate the differential power of various data and research practices. Examining the role of quantitative methods in feminist geography, Lawson (1995) and Sara McLafferty (1995), for instance, show that quantitative data and methods are powerful tools for illustrating and combating gendered and other inequalities. Matthew Turner (2003) points to the scientific authority that is granted to GIS and remote sensing in many academic and policy making forums, and by extension, to research that incorporates these methods. Reflecting on a mixed methods participatory research project with Filipina nurses living and working in Canada, Pratt and Hanson (2003) note that these partici-pants used quantitative representations to communicate their experiences with govern-ment authorities, and artistic or performative practices with other audiences.

My participatory GIS research with com-munity development agencies in U.S. cities suggests similar strategic engagement with the differential power and authority of par-ticular forms of data or research techniques. My research partners have found that local knowledge gathered from residents may be discounted as biased when presented as indi-vidual oral or textual accounts of experi-ences, but when incorporated in visual or cartographic form in a GIS, may be granted greater legitimacy in planning and policy making. Conversely, quantitative data or car-tographic representations of community needs may be rejected by local residents as inaccurate or insufficiently nuanced (Elwood, 2002). In response, these activists and orga-nizations have developed flexible strategies for sifting their data, representations, and interpretations to maximize their influence (Elwood, 2006). In a past project, I worked with a community group that 'translated' residents' experiential descriptive accounts of neighborhood conditions into quantitative and cartographic representations of neigh-borhood needs, because they felt these repre-sentations were more likely to influence local level decision makers. But at the same moment that the organizations' use of GIS was garnering demonstrably greater influ-ence in these forums, many residents were obviously being marginalized in an increas-ingly technical and limited discourse of neighborhood change (Elwood, 2002).

Understanding the social and political impacts of this community's use of GIS and interpreting this conflict demanded mixed methods. These impacts were being negoti-ated in multiple arenas, from the data struc-ture and content of their GIS, to terminology and forms of knowledge being used and vali-dated at community meetings, to the ideas and priorities advanced in maps produced and used by the organization. But the dilemma for me has been (and continues to be) how to understand the significance and power of competing narratives produced in different ways. Does the 'translation' of experiential knowledge into GIS-based data structures or maps for greater influence in particular forums necessarily alter the significance of alternative discourses and representations, if these other forms of knowledge are engaged and welcomed in other arenas? Can two or more very different ways of knowing co-exist in mutually productive ways when one is granted greater legitimacy and validity than another? These questions are persistently troubling for me in my own work, for philosophical, methodological and political reasons.

For mixed methods research, the differential scientific and political authority granted to different modes of investigation is both opportunity and challenge. As the examples above illustrate, incorporating quantitative data and analysis in a previously qualitative project may generate greater political influence in some circumstances. But strategic deployment of multiple methods for political influence is never unproblematic. McLafferty (1995) discusses participatory research conducted by a group of breast cancer survivors to study a disease cluster in the Long Island area, noting that while quantitative data from this project were especially effective in gaining the attention and involvement of public health officials, these data were later interpreted by policy makers in ways with which the researchers disagreed. Illustrating another potential problem, participatory GIS research has noted that GIS use in collaborative planning and decision-making is prone to excluding already marginalized individuals and social groups, if these groups are unable to understand GIS-based data or express their own knowledge in those forms (Weiner and Harris, 2003; Elmes *et al.*, 2004). Thus in using mixed methods research to mobilize any sort of political practice, it is imperative to consider the power of particular ways of knowing with different audiences, and to explore ways of addressing the potential silences and exclusion of any method.

In sum, practicing mixed methods requires responding to a range of intellectual and political considerations throughout the process of research, from formulation of question and goals, to interpretation and analysis of data gathered, to critically reflective application of research findings. On one level, we must decide when and how to use multiple forms of data and analysis techniques, to inform one another as well as different aspects of a research question. In analysis and interpretation, questions may arise about how the meaning of ambiguities, silences and contradictions between data sources, or about how to relate data that are rooted in very different ways of perceiving and representing the world. The literature on mixed methods tends not to offer definitive solutions to these dilemmas, instead reasserting the intellectual value of multiple modes of investigation and the necessity for researchers to be critical and reflexive agents in navigating its logistical, interpretive, and political challenges. As researchers, however, we respond not only to these intellectual and practical considerations in research, but also to institutional and disciplinary expectations and norms about data, method, and representation. Thus, in the next section, I turn to institutional challenges of doing mixed methods research within academic contexts that have more commonly engaged in singular modes of inquiry.

INSTITUTIONAL CHALLENGES IN THE ACADEMY AND BEYOND

As Erica Schoenberger (2001) notes, the very definition of academic disciplines involves validating particular epistemological commitments, and by extension, particular approaches to doing research. In geography, debates about epistemology and methodology have tended to divide quantitative and qualitative methods or inductive and deductive approaches, or to promote and defend a particular epistemology while rejecting others. Mixed methods research contests quantitative–qualitative or inductive–deductive divisions, and disrupts efforts to constrain epistemological diversity. But just because mixed methods research has been present in geography for an extended period does not mean that it is necessarily widely accepted. Nor is it necessarily fully understood within the institutional and disciplinary forums of our profession, including funding competitions, publication processes, peer review, and graduate education. In this section, I will examine the practical consequences of the predominance of single-paradigm or single-method approaches in research and methodological training, the need for constructive dialogue about evaluating mixed methods research, and the tangible institutional resources that are needed for its continued growth. In part, this section identifies a number of limitations upon mixed methods research that stem from these institutional and disciplinary contexts. But I would underscore here that mixed methods approaches are nonetheless rewriting institutional and disciplinary norms about appropriate research practices in creative and significant ways, and will continue to do so. Mixed methods in participatory action approaches promote an engaged and active link between knowledge construction and social change. Projects that integrate inductive and deductive approaches to building knowledge challenge the proposition that epistemologies are necessarily separate and singular. Mixed methods are important precisely because they confront and reframe established tenets of our academic institutions and their validated research practices.

In geography and other social sciences, epistemological and methodological disagreements have had the effect of promoting reliance on a single paradigm or suite of methods because they have tended to also reject other approaches. Our methodological training tends to reinforce these allegiances to a single approach, since many of us have significantly greater depth of experience and training in either quantitative or qualitative methods. Charles Teddlie and Abbas Tashakkori (2003) note that graduate education in mixed methods research is relatively underdeveloped, with very few graduate programs in the social and behavioral sciences directly including mixed methods training. In practice, many geographers who use mixed methods approaches seem to have developed

them either in collaboration with mentors who themselves use mixed methods or by independently assembling an amalgam of methods courses.

The predominance of approaches that rely on a single paradigm or suite of methods means that explaining and justifying a mixed methods approach to journals, funders, or peers can present some difficulties. Even if reviewers are supportive of a mixed methods approach, they may not have sufficient methodological background to offer constructive criticism on both qualitative and quantitative components. A reviewer may be prepared to evaluate qualitative and quantitative aspects of a mixed methods project, but still not be sufficiently familiar with mixed methods to evaluate the ways in which a project intersects different types of data or modes of analysis. In practical terms, writing successful proposals and publishing research findings with mixed methods designs may mean bearing the additional burden of explaining intellectual practices of knowledge production and validation in mixed methods research. In presenting and reviewing mixed methods work, it is important to remember that we all play an active role in creating or constraining spaces for mixed methods in the discipline. Part of the responsibility lies with reviewers, not to reject an approach simply because they are unfamiliar with it, and part with authors, to clearly explain mixed methods practices for developing and validating knowledge, as these are used in a particular project. Disciplinary gate-keeping around epistemology and method still occurs, without a doubt, but we have opportunities to disrupt these practices through the ways that we present and evaluate mixed methods research.

Recent revival of conversations about 'policy relevant' research in geography, as well as shifts in the kind of data and research validated by policy makers themselves, reveal a troublingly persistent tendency to prioritize singularity in epistemology and method. Some geographers have suggested that post-structural and hermeneutic epistemologies do not lend themselves to research findings that can readily inform policy, or suggest that an absence of quantitative methods training threatens analytical rigor in the discipline (Wheeler, 2000; Martin, 2001). Others have responded by noting that a broad range of research, both theoretical and applied, can inform policy and decision-making, and that understanding and creating effective policy for a complicated world calls for epistemological and methodological diversity (Imrie, 2004; Wyly, 2004; Lake, 2005). Simultaneously, many policy and decision-making forums have begun to prioritize certain forms of evidence and ways of knowing over others. Research in urban geography has demonstrated, for instance, that policy-makers from national to local levels tend to prioritize quantitative evidence over qualitative evidence, with a strong preference for measurable benchmarks and tangible outcomes (Elwood, 2004; Newman and Lake, 2004; Curran, 2005; McCann, 2008). Regardless of how we define policy relevant research, these trends toward legitimizing quantitative evidence and methods are problematic for mixed methods research for several reasons. They point to the persistence of epistemological and methodological disagreements in geography and promote a methodological simplicity or singularity that has the potential to limit the recognition and validation of more complicated approaches.

These reassertions of singular approaches aside, we are nonetheless seeing growing acceptance of methodological and epistemological diversity in some areas of geography, with parallel emergence of new ways of mixing methods. The past decade or more of methodological critique and emphasis upon the partiality of all ways of knowing has problematized research and method in many important ways. But this period of methodological critique is also linked to what Lake (2005) terms a methodological uncertainty in the discipline, and what Mountz and Prytherch (2005) identify as an epistemological eclecticism. These authors note that these shifts have left us with relatively few accepted

reference points for evaluating the rigor and robustness of research. Rigor and robustness are concepts that have been oft-used in the methodological literature in geography, but rarely for a purpose beyond rejecting another paradigm or suites of methods.

For mixed methods research, this leaves any number of questions about designing good research. How does or should reliable mixed methods research integrate its different approaches? How should we conceptualize the reliability of findings in projects whose methods may prioritize generality and particularity in multiple and divergent ways? What terms and concepts can we use to critique mixed methods research constructively, without perpetuating a tendency to critique method as a way of rejecting the intellectual reasoning behind methodological choices? As Pratt and Schuurman (2002) and Leitner and Sheppard (2003) have noted, debates about the appropriateness of research paradigms and methods are as much about social and political negotiations of power and knowledge in academia as they are about underlying epistemological and ontological differences. This is why I include this discussion as part of the institutional contexts that shape mixed methods research. Questions of validity and rigor in mixed methods research practices are being negotiated in and through the processes of funding, publication, and peer review in which we all participate.

Finally, a few words about the institutional resources necessary to support continued growth in mixed methods research collaborations. Given the conceptual and methodological complexity of mixed methods projects, many are undertaken by collaborative teams that bring together scholars with multiple areas of substantive and methodological expertise. This trend is expanding, as national funding agencies such as the National Science Foundation prioritize support for such collaborative and multidisciplinary projects. As anyone who has undertaken collaborative or interdisciplinary research knows, such intersections are extremely challenging and above all, time consuming. It is far simpler to divide the tasks of a multi-method research endeavor in parallel but separate fashion among members based on substantive or methodological expertise. Far more difficult is the task of building a collaborative intellectual effort that is methodologically, analytically, and interpretively integrated. Yet the latter is precisely what excellent collaborative mixed methods research must seek, especially given the 'single paradigm' training in which many of us were schooled as graduate students and junior scholars. Equally time consuming is the task of preparing oneself to effectively adopt a new methodologically approach, as many of us must do in order to participate in mixed methods research. Ironically, the source of institutional support that is most important to building these collaborative and integrating intellectual engagements – time – is increasingly difficult to secure, even while our institutions tout the value of interdisciplinarity.

Thus, part of the challenge facing the continued development of mixed methods research in geography includes working to create institutional spaces and tangible forms of support that enable researchers to engage new techniques and approaches. For mixed methods research to gain greater intellectual traction as an approach that is not only valued and legitimized, but critically understood and practiced in geography, creating such spaces is essential. For this effort, I would underscore that we encounter the epistemological and methodological diversity of geography in myriad ways in our daily professional lives. Reading groups, seminars, courses, visiting lectures, and other activities present collective opportunities to engage with mixed methods research in geography more directly and constructively than we have thus far done. Even if our own current research practices are rooted in a single paradigm or single method, growing institutional imperatives toward collaborative projects and interdisciplinary work make it ever more likely that we will need some fluency in mixed methods research in the future.

CONCLUSION

The growth of mixed methods research in geography in the past decade has been supported by critical re-examination of methodology in the discipline, underwritten by assumptions that knowledge is socially, politically, and institutionally constructed, as are our research paradigms and methods. This critical engagement with research and knowledge production is reflected in such areas as a recent re-examination of quantitative methods and the emergence of previously unthinkable methodological collisions such as qualitative GIS. In this chapter, I have outlined some conceptual, practical, and institutional considerations inherent in mixed methods research. These include the appropriateness and feasibility of mixing epistemologies and the relationship between epistemology and method, considerations of when and how to integrate multiple forms of data and modes of analysis within a single project, and the roles of institutional and disciplinary structures that constrain or foster mixed methods approaches. My discussion of these aspects of mixed methods research shares with other critical reflections on methodology an emphasis on reflexivity and critical agency, and the difficulty of working between and across entrenched epistemological and methodological divisions (Leitner and Sheppard, 2003; Turner and Taylor, 2003; Wolch, 2003; Barnes, 2004).

The thoughtful and creative development of mixed methods research in geography depends in large part on individual and collective efforts to engage in this critical reflective practice and support the efforts of other scholars who are doing it. Trevor Barnes and Matthew Hannah (2001) have called for the development of a 'third geographer', one who bridges quantitative and qualitative approaches for more integrated 'both/and' epistemologies and methodologies. I would argue that such geographers have been all around us for a very long time, but that growing discussion of mixed methods approaches affords new opportunity to recognize and legitimize their efforts to conceptualize and articulate their work in ways that transcend singularly quantitative or qualitative approaches. In the conceptual, practical, and institutional arenas of research, it is no small challenge to engage multiple paradigms, and communicate effectively to audiences more familiar and comfortable with a single paradigm.

Finally, future discussion and practice of mixed methods research in geography must confront epistemological and methodological questions outside well-worn quantitative-qualitative debates. Growing focus in human geography on emotion, affect, performativity theory, and non-representational theory poses particularly challenging epistemological and methodological questions. Performative ways of knowing, for instance, resist methodological compartmentalization into discrete methodological acts of data collection, analysis, and communication of results. Affect, as a non-cognitive way of knowing, is similarly difficult to engage methodologically. Pointing to these and other new theoretical engagements in human geography, Crang (2003; 2005) has argued for the need to extend qualitative methods beyond traditionally text-focused forms of evidence, modes of analysis, and ways of knowing. Such an effort would challenge many of the fundamental propositions that have traditionally informed both quantitative and qualitative methods, such as the assumption of a clear separation between representation and practice. Mixing methods in creative and intellectually productive ways in geography will involve not only our continued efforts to bridge quantitative–qualitative divisions, but to consider how our research methods can engage some of these newest and most challenging theoretical developments in the discipline.

REFERENCES

Al-Kodmany, K. (2000) 'Extending geographic information systems (GIS) to meet neighborhood planning needs: recent developments in the work of the University of Illinois at Chicago', *The URISA Journal* 12 (3):19–37.

Barnes, T. (2004) 'Placing ideas: genius loci, heterotopia, and geography's quantitative revolution', *Progress in Human Geography* 28 (5): 565–95.

Barnes, T. and Hannah, M. (2001) 'The place of numbers: histories, geographies, and theories of quantification', *Environment and Planning D: Society and Space* 19 (1): 379–83.

Bassett, T. (2005) 'Card-carrying hunters, rural poverty, and wildlife decline in northern Cote d'Ivoire', *The Geographical Journal* 171 (1): 24–35.

Buttimer, A. (1976) 'Grasping the dynamism of the lifeworld', *Annals of the Association of American Geographers* 66 (2): 277–92.

Cahill, C., Arenas, E., Contreras, J., Jiang, N., Rios-Moore, I. and Threatts, T. (2004) 'Speaking back: voices of young urban Womyn of color. Using participatory action research to challenge and complicate representations of young women', in A. Harris (ed.) *All about the girl: culture, power, and Identity.* New York: Routledge. pp. 231–42.

Chorley, R. and Haggett, P. (1967) *Models in geography.* London: Metheun

Crang, M. (2003) 'Qualitative methods: touchy-feely, look-see?', *Progress in Human Geography* 27 (4): 494–504.

Crang, M. (2005) 'Qualitative methods: there is nothing outside the text?', *Progress in Human Geography* 29 (2): 225–33.

Cresswell, T. (2003) *Research design: qualitative, quantitative and mixed methods approaches.* 2nd ed. Thousand Oaks, CA: Sage.

Curran, W. (2005) 'Being and becoming in urban geography', *Urban Geography* 26 (3): 257–60.

Dixon, D. and Jones, J.P. III (1998) 'My dinner with Derrida, or spatial analysis and poststructuralism do lunch', *Environment and Planning A* 30 (2): 247–60.

Doel, M. (2001) 'Qualified quantitative geography', *Environment and Planning D: Society and Space* 19 (2): 555–72.

Elmes, G., Dougherty, M., Callig, H., Karigomba, W., McCusker, B. and Weiner, D. (2004) 'Local knowledge doesn't grow on trees: community-integrated geographic information systems and rural community self definition', in P. Fisher (ed.) *Developments in spatial data handling.* Berlin: Springer-Verlag. pp. 29–40.

Elwood, S. (2002) 'GIS use in community planning: a multi-dimensional analysis of empowerment', *Environment and Planning A* 34 (5): 905–22.

Elwood, S. (2004) 'Partnerships and participation: reconfiguring urban governance in different state contexts', *Urban Geography* 25 (8): 755–70.

Elwood, S. (2006) 'Beyond cooptation or resistance: urban spatial politics, community organizations, and GIS-based spatial narratives', *Annals of the Association of American Geographers* 96 (2): 323–41.

England, K. (1993) 'Suburban pink collar ghettos: the spatial entrapment of women?', *Annals of the Association of American Geographers* 83 (2): 225–42.

Eyles, J. and Smith, D. (eds) (1988) *Qualitative methods in human geography*. Cambridge: Polity.

Glaser, B. and Strauss, A. (1967) *The discovery of grounded theory*. Chicago: Aldine.

Greene, J. and Caracelli, V. (2003) 'Making paradigmatic sense of mixed methods practice', in A. Tashakkori and C. Teddlie (eds) *Handbook of mixed methods in social and behavioral research*. Thousand Oaks, CA: Sage. pp. 91–110.

Hanson, S. and Pratt, G. (1995) *Gender, work, and place*. London: Routledge.

Hanson, S. and Pratt, G. (2003) 'Learning about labour: combining qualitative and quantitative methods', in A. Blunt, P. Gruffield, J. May, M. Ogborn and D. Pinder (eds) *Cultural geography in practice*. New York: Oxford University Press. pp. 106–18.

Haraway, D. (1991) *Simians, cyborgs, and women: the reinvention of nature*. New York: Routledge.

Harding, S. (1986) *The science question in feminism*. Ithaca, NY: Cornell University Press.

Harrower, M. (2004) 'A look at the history and future of animated maps', *Cartographica* 39 (2): 33–42.

Hartshorne, R. (1939) *The nature of geography: a critical survey of current thought in the light of the past*. Lancaster, PA: The Association of American Geographers.

Harvey, D. (1969) *Explanation in geography*. New York: St. Martins.

Imrie, R. (2004) 'Urban geography, relevance, and resistance to the "policy turn"', *Urban Geography* 25 (8): 697–708.

Jiang, H. (2003) 'Stories remote sensing images can tell: integrating remote sensing analysis with ethnographic research in the study of cultural landscapes', *Human Ecology* 31 (2): 215–32.

Kesby, M. (2000) 'Participatory diagramming: deploying qualitative methods through an action research epistemology', *Area* 34 (4): 423–35.

Knigge, L. and Cope, M. (2006) 'Grounded visualization: integrating the analysis of qualitative and quantitative data through grounded theory and visualization', *Environment and Planning A* 38 (11): 2021–37.

Kwan, M. (2002a) 'Introduction: feminist geography and GIS', *Gender, Place and Culture* 9 (3): 261–2.

Kwan, M. (2002b) 'Feminist visualization: re-envisioning GIS as a method in feminist geography research', *Annals of the Association of American Geographers* 92 (4): 645–61.

Kwan, M. (2002c) 'Is GIS for women? Reflections on the critical discourse in the 1990s', *Gender, Place and Culture* 9 (3): 271–9.

Kwan, M. and Knigge, L. (2006) 'Doing qualitative research with GIS: an oxymoronic endeavor?', *Environment and Planning A* 38 (11): 1999–2002.

Kwan, M. and Lee, J. (2004) 'Geovisualization of human activity patterns using 3D GIS: a time-geographic approach', in M. Goodchild and D. Janelle (eds) *Spatially integrated social science*. New York: Oxford University Press. pp. 48–66.

Lake, R. (1993) 'Planning and applied geography: positivism, ethics, and geographic information systems', *Progress in Human Geography* 17 (3): 404–13.

Lake, R. (2005) 'Urban crisis redux', *Urban Geography* 26 (3): 266–70.

Lawson, V. (1995) 'The politics of difference: examining the quantitative/qualitative dualism in poststructural feminist research', *The Professional Geographer* 47 (4): 449–57.

Leitner, H. and Sheppard, E. (2003) 'Unbounding critical geographic research on cities: the 1990s and beyond', *Urban Geography* 24 (6): 510–28.

Longino, H. (2002) *The fate of knowledge*. Oxford: Oxford University Press.

Martin, R. (2001) 'Geography and public policy: the case of the missing agenda', *Progress in Human Geography* 25 (2): 189–210.

Mattingly, D. and Falconer al-Hindi, K. (1995) 'Should women count? A context for the debate', *The Professional Geographer* 47 (4): 427–35.

Maxcy, S. (2003) 'Pragmatic threads in mixed methods research in the social sciences: the search for multiple modes of inquiry and the end of the philosophy of formalism', in A. Tashakkori and C. Teddlie (eds) *Handbook of mixed methods in social and behavioral research*. Thousand Oaks, CA: Sage. pp. 51–90.

McCann, E. (2008) 'Expertise, truth, and urban policy mobilities: global circuits of knowledge in the development of Vancouver, Canada's "four pillar" drug strategy', *Environment and Planning A* 40 (4): 885–904.

McLafferty, S. (1995) 'Counting for women', *The Professional Geographer* 47 (4): 436–42.

McLafferty, S. (2002) 'Mapping women's worlds: knowledge, power, and the bounds of GIS', *Gender, Place and Culture* 9 (3): 263–69.

Mertens, D. (2003) 'Mixed methods and the politics of human research: the transformative-emancipatory perspective', in A. Tashakkori and C. Teddlie (eds) *Handbook of mixed methods in social and behavioral research*. Thousand Oaks, CA: Sage. pp. 135–164.

Moss, P. (1995) 'Embeddedness in practice, numbers in context: the politics of knowing and doing', *The Professional Geographer* 47 (4): 442–9.

Mountz, A. and Prytherch, D. (2005) 'Introduction – digression analysis: a decidedly editorial introduction to the symposium on the state of urban geography; dispatches from the field', *Urban Geography* 26 (3): 243–46.

Newman, K. and Lake, R. (2004) 'Democracy, bureaucracy and difference in community development politics since 1968', in *Annual Meeting of the Association of American Geographers*. Philadelphia, PA.

Nightingale, A. (2003) 'A feminist in the forest: situated knowledges and mixing methods in natural resource management', *ACME: An International E-Journal for Critical Geographies* 2 (1): 77–90.

Openshaw, S. (1991) 'A view on the GIS crisis in geography, or, using GIS to put Humpty-Dumpty back together again', *Environment and Planning A* 23 (5): 621–28.

Openshaw, S. (1992) 'Further thoughts on geography and GIS – a reply', *Environment and Planning A* 24 (4): 463–6.

Pain, R. (2003) 'Social geography: on action orientated research', *Progress in Human Geography* 27 (5): 649–57.

Pain, R. (2004) 'Social geography: participatory research', *Progress in Human Geography* 28 (5): 652–63.

Pain, R., MacFarlane, R., Turner, K. and Gill, S. (2006) 'When, where, if and but: residents qualify the effect of streetlighting on crime and fear in their neighbourhoods', *Environment and Planning A* 38 (11): 2055–74.

Pavlovskaya, M. (2002) 'Mapping urban change and changing GIS: other views of economic restructuring', *Gender, Place and Culture* 9 (3): 281–9.

Pavlovskaya, M. (2006) 'Theorizing with GIS: a tool for critical geographies?', *Environment and Planning A* 38 (11): 2003–20.

Phillip, L. (1998) 'Combining quantitative and qualitative approaches to social research in human geography – an impossible mixture?', *Environment and Planning A* 30 (2): 261–76.

Pickles, J. (ed.) (1995) *Ground truth: the social and political implications of geographical information systems*. New York: Guilford.

Poon, J. (2004) 'Quantitative methods: past and present', *Progress in Human Geography* 28 (6): 807–14.

Pratt, G. (2000) 'Research performances', *Environment and Planning D: Society and Space* 18 (5): 639–51.

Pratt, G. and Kirby, E. (2003) 'Performing nursing: the B.C. Nurses Union Theatre Project', *ACME: An International E-Journal for Critical Geographies* 2 (1): 14–32.

Pratt, G. and Schuurman, N. (2002) 'Care of the subject: feminist and critiques of GIS', *Gender, Place and Culture* 9 (3): 291–9.

Robbins, P. (2001a) 'Fixed categories in a portable landscape: the causes and consequences of land cover categorization', *Environment and Planning A* 33 (1): 161–79.

Robbins, P. (2001b) 'Tracking invasive land covers in India, or why our landscapes have never been modern', *Annals of the Association of American Geographers* 91 (4): 637–59.

Robbins, P. (2003) 'Beyond ground truth: GIS and the environmental knowledge of herders, professional foresters and other traditional communities', *Human Ecology* 31 (2): 233–53.

Rocheleau, D. (1995) 'Maps, numbers, text, and context: mixing methods in feminist political ecology', *The Professional Geographer* 46 (1): 458–66.

Schaefer, F. (1953) 'Exceptionalism in geography: a methodological examination', *Annals of the Association of American Geographers* 43 (3): 226–49.

Schoenberger, E. (2001) 'Interdiscipinarity and social power', *Progress in Human Geography* 25 (3): 365–82.

Schuurman, N. (2002a) 'Reconciling social constructivism and realism in GIS', *ACME: An International E-Journal for Critical Geographies* 1 (1): 75–90.

Schuurman, N. (2002b) 'Women and technology in geography: a cyborg manifesto', *The Canadian Geographer* 46 (3): 258–65.

Sheppard, E. (2001) 'Quantitative geography: representations, practices, and possibilities', *Environment and Planning D: Society and Space* 19 (2): 535–54.

Shiffer, M. (2002) 'Spatial multimedia representations to support community participation', in W. Craig, T. Harris and D. Weiner (eds) *Community participation and geographic information systems*. London: Taylor & Francis. pp. 309–19.

Sieber, R. (2001) 'Rewiring for a GIS/2', *Cartographica* 39 (1): 25–40.

Smith, S. (1984) 'Practicing humanistic geography', *Annals of the Association of American Geographers* 74 (3): 353–74.

St. Martin, K. (2005) 'Mapping economic diversity in the first world: the case of fisheries', *Environment and Planning A* 37 (6): 959–79.

Staeheli, L. and Lawson, V. (1995) 'Feminism, praxis, and human geography', *Geographical Analysis* 27 (4): 321–38.

Tashakkori, A. and Teddlie, C. (2003) 'The past and future of mixed methods research: from triangulation to mixed model design', in A. Tashakkori and C. Teddlie (eds) *Handbook of mixed methods in social and behavioral research*. Thousand Oaks, CA: Sage. pp. 671–702.

Taylor, P. and Overton, M. (1991) 'Further thoughts on geography and GIS – a preemptive strike', *Environment and Planning A* 23 (8): 1087–90.

Teddlie, C. and Tashakkori, A. (2003) 'Major issues and controversies in the use of mixed methods in the social and behavioral sciences', in A. Tashakkori and C. Teddlie (eds) *Handbook of mixed methods in social and behavioral research*. Thousand Oaks, CA: Sage. pp. 3–50.

Tuan, Y. (1976) 'Humanistic geography', *Annals of the Association of American Geographers* 66 (2): 266–76.

Turner, M. (2003) 'Methodological reflections on the use of remote sensing and geographic information science in human ecological research', *Human Ecology* 31 (2): 255–79.

Turner, M. and Taylor, P. (2003) 'Critical reflections on the use of remote sensing and GIS technologies in human ecological research', *Human Ecology* 31 (2): 177–82.

Weiner, D. and Harris, T. (2003) 'Community-integrated GIS for land reform in South Africa', *The URISA Journal* 15 (APAII): 61–73.

Wheeler, J. (2000) 'Have we lost a generation of urban geographers?', *Urban Geography* 21 (5): 377–9.

Williams, C. and Dunn, C. (2003) 'GIS in participatory research: assessing the impacts of landmines on communities in north-west Cambodia', *Transactions in GIS* 7 (3): 393–410.

Wolch, J. (2003) 'Radical openness as method in urban geography', *Urban Geography* 24 (7): 645–6.

Wolf, M. (1992) *A thrice-told tale: feminism, postmodernism, and ethnographic responsibility*. Palo Alto: Stanford University Press.

Wyly, E. (2004) 'The accidental relevance of American urban geography', *Urban Geography* 25 (8): 738–41.

Zimmerer, K. (2003) 'Geographies of seed networks and approaches to agrobiodiversity conservation', *Society & Natural Resources* 16 (7): 583–601.

PART II

Encounters and Collaborations

Encounters and Collaborations: Introduction

Steve Herbert

I still recall with great vividness my introduction to the world of the Los Angeles Police Department (LAPD). After months of waiting and negotiation, I finally gained permission to do extensive fieldwork in one LAPD patrol division. On a warm August evening, I entered the station house of the Wilshire Division, located in the center of the city. I identified myself to the officer working the front desk, and sat to wait on a hard wooden bench. After a few minutes, a burly police sergeant entered the lobby from a side door. He introduced himself, and then escorted me through the back of the station to his awaiting patrol car in the rear parking lot. As we exited the lot to begin my first ride-along, I asked the sergeant if there was anything I needed to know. I presumed I would learn something about how to use the police radio in case of an emergency. Instead, the sergeant asked, 'Have you ever shot a gun before?'

So began eight months of fieldwork with this and other sergeants in the LAPD. Initially quite taken aback by the suggestion I might need to use a gun during fieldwork, I ultimately came to see the sergeant's question in a wider light. Prolonged immersion helped me view it as one instance of a powerful current within the cultural world that officers construct, one that emphasizes masculinist

strength and derring-do. Some of this was expressed through questions like the sergeant's, which was obviously designed to signal to me, as a newcomer, the danger in the world I was about to enter. I eventually understood why this emphasis is so significant – particularly in Los Angeles, police work is often violent. But I also learned that this sergeant, and others like him, oftentimes court danger when less-confrontational courses of action exist. In other words, the sergeant helped construct the realities he faced.

This snippet is told not to relive a war story from the field, but to illustrate both the often-dynamic reality of qualitative research and the range of challenges it presents. As I listened to the sergeant's question, I immediately came to grips with several characteristics of qualitative fieldwork: that I was an active agent in the data I would gather; that I would help create this data through ongoing interactions with people like the sergeant; that I had to decide how to respond to his question, and, in the process, how to define myself in relation to the officers I would observe.

Unable to process these realizations all that quickly, I decided my best response to the sergeant was honesty. No, I admitted to him, I had never before shot a gun. The sergeant looked at me askance, and headed out to his first call.

Luckily, whatever loss of status accompanied my ignorance of gun culture was regained by the end of the night. The sergeant began to enjoy the questions I posed to him, and warmed to the role of guide to the world of policing. This I came to see as another reality of qualitative data collection: if approached by someone who possesses genuine interest in them, most people will open themselves up to a wide range of questions. Because few of us rarely get a chance to outline all of the latent knowledge we possess, most warm to an opportunity to do so. This means that there are nearly infinite opportunities for the qualitative researcher to ascertain how different groups construct their social and spatial worlds.

The chapters included in 'Encounters and Collaborations' make obvious this wide palette of research options. Each chapter reviews a qualitative method that can be used to great benefit by a researcher seeking to explore some aspect of the expansive terrain of human geography. Collectively, these chapters provide unparalleled evidence of the vibrancy of qualitative work in contemporary human geography. As the use of these methods deepens, the range of questions geographers can ask widens. As different of these methods are combined together, broader understandings of socio-spatial dynamics are made possible. As researchers seek new ways of situating themselves vis-à-vis those they study, new modes of conducting research come into focus.

Separately, each chapter in this section provides an introduction to a particular method. The authors provide a sense of the types of questions one can profitably pursue by following these research traditions. Happily, the range of uses of each method is becoming ever wider in the discipline of geography. In this fashion, qualitative geographers perpetually, and provocatively, push research horizons. Yet to push research beyond traditional boundaries is not always a simple matter. Accordingly, each chapter provides a sense of some of the challenges that one necessarily confronts when using the method under discussion.

Together, the chapters provide an exceptional place to explore the opportunities that qualitative research presents for a human geographer. The authors make clear the wide array of research questions we can ask, and the diverse theoretical traditions we can engage. They emphasize the open-ended, ever-evolving nature of qualitative research, how it is that situational dynamics make the research process an ongoing act of thoughtful improvisation. They recognize the value of bringing different research practices together in the same enterprise, the better to see a particular social phenomenon from multiple perspectives. And they explore the often complicated interplay between the researcher and the researched, as well as the various ways that relationship can be developed, to both further the research process and to provide ample voice for those we engage in the field.

The breadth of qualitative methods could hardly be better displayed than through a reading of these chapters. That each of these chapters describes research practices that are now commonplace in the discipline is particularly striking evidence of the centrality of qualitative inquiry to contemporary human geography. Further, each chapter makes plain how each method can be used to pose a range of questions from a range of theoretical perspectives. The chapter by James and Nancy Duncan on landscape interpretation, for example, reviews the history of this method in illustrative detail. They demonstrate how the reading of landscapes was used in both the distant and recent past to ponder geographic questions emanating from multiple theoretical paradigms. Post-structural and feminist theoretical work is particularly important to more contemporary work in qualitative human geography. This is evident in Stuart Aitkens's and Mei-Po Kwan's chapter on Geographic Information Systems (GIS). They argue for a more fluid and open approach to GIS, one that enables a researcher to combine sophisticated mapping techniques with other methodologies. The impress of post-structuralist thinking is also clear in Jason Dittmer's review of discourse analysis. That examining discourse is a serious pursuit by human geographers is largely a consequence of the impact of post-structuralism, and Dittmer does an admirable job of tracing its indelible impact and various cross-currents. Unsurprisingly, the contemporary energy of the field of cultural studies also finds expression in several of these chapters, most notably in Jennifer Wolch's and Mona Seymour's chapter on animal geographies. They underscore the necessity of understanding the place of animals in cultural dynamics, the better to appreciate how non-humans are incorporated into everyday life. If that chapter challenges the focus exclusively on human actors and respondents of much qualitative work, then J.D. Dewsbury's challenges the focus upon the verbal and textual, drawing upon the post-phenomenological theory that has arisen to challenge post-structuralism's linguistic origins with theories of immanence and transcendental empiricism, with performative methods attuned to seizing the moment rather than finding the pattern behind it.

Of course, one need not embrace any particular theoretical approach to do qualitative research – Jennifer Wolch's and Mona Seymour's chapter indeed illustrates how qualitative methods can speak with, about and for animals, and many qualitative pieces already engage the performative, affective and practice based principles hailed in JD Dewsbury's chapter. Indeed, one of the great strengths of qualitative work is its adaptability. In fact, adaptability is itself a characteristic the qualitative researcher would be well-advised to cultivate, as many of these chapters make plain. This is most clear in the chapters that focus on different types of interview technique – Linda McDowell's on traditional interviews, Peter Jackson and Polly Russell's on life histories, and Fernando Bosco and Thomas Herman's on focus groups. Typically, interviewers approach their conversations with research subjects

with some pre-determined questions, yet also leave room for the exploration of unanticipated topics and new directions. Each of these chapters does an admirable job of describing the fluidity that so typically characterizes these conversations, and the resultant need for the researcher to remain open to new information.

This ever-evolving relationship between researcher and researched is another theme that threads through several of these chapters. Bosco and Herman treat this issue with especial consideration, foregrounding it in a thoughtful discussion of how we as researchers can most sensitively and productively structure our relationships in the field. Their discussion closely follows that of Karen Till and Annette Watson, who are similarly interested in structuring new types of collaborations with those populations with whom they conduct ethnographic research. It may seem counter-intuitive, but this theme emerges, as well, in David Butz's chapter on autoethnography. Although autoethnography does acutely focus on the researcher, it differs from autobiography because it situates the narrator in wider social and cultural fields. The autoethnographer therefore deliberately queries just how he/she is located in relationship to particular social groups and spatial locations. Butz's insightful discussion helps us see that the ethnographic researcher is multiply-positioned – sometimes an insider, sometimes an outsider, sometimes at points in between, and always negotiating a position with those in the field.

This concern with positionality is not just pertinent during the data collection process. It also arises during the 'writing up' phase. Here, we must choose how to represent those we studied to others. As Linda McDowell astutely notes, as writers, we are speaking for those with whom we interacted; we become the voice of those we interviewed, observed, or otherwise engaged. And, as Michael Crang makes clear, if we employ visual images in our completed research, we must make conscious choices about just how to represent the realities we analyze. The politics of representation are thereby inescapably present throughout the qualitative research process, and need to be addressed directly in our work. Even if no simple solution emerges from the discussions about representation, many of the authors here address these challenges in a forthright and creative manner.

Just as the authors query how to locate oneself as a researcher and how to represent those under study, they also question what it means to be in the field. The creative application of new methodologies translates, in part, into new imaginings of where one can go to do research. Hayden Lorimer, for instance, reviews how the notion of an 'archive' is now much more expansive than simply a repository of dusty books in the catacombs of a library. In part because of shifts in technology, primarily the transportability of laptop computers, the historical geographer can now more easily collect information in multiple sites, and thus can expand what constitutes qualitative data. Till and Watson also embrace the notion of expansiveness, in part through their discussion of 'multi-site' ethnography, and the means by which it can be employed to trace a process that transcends any particular place.

In evaluating the impress of a macro-scale process on multiple places, the multi-site ethnographer pursues the goal of all good research: to locate and evaluate localized circumstances within the field of wider social forces. Unsurprisingly, this emerges as a theme in many of these chapters. Michael Crang, for instance, urges those who use visual data in their work to query just how visual images are constructed, by whom, and for what purpose. This means situating images within broader political force fields, the better to assess the power they can exert, reinforce, and, possibly, challenge. Jason

Dittmer makes the same point with respect to discourse. Common ways of understanding and representing reality, as expressed through discursive data, help create a collective common sense, the operation of which can work to perpetuate particular social relationships. To capably deconstruct a discursive artifact means to assess its power, both as rhetoric and as political product.

I attempted much the same task in assessing the LAPD sergeant's question about my prowess with a gun (or, in my case, the lack thereof). On the one hand, it was a discursive tactic, a means to acquire information. On the other, it was a performance by a cultural actor, one situated within a significant political institution. The police, after all, are the coercive arm of the state. It was no accident that I was compelled to wonder just how the police socially construct that coercive power, how they represent their capacity to use it to a newcomer to their world such as myself.

This is just one isolated instance of the value and challenge of conducting qualitative research in contemporary human geography. The chapters that follow provide ample other examples of the uses to which a wide array of methods can be put to help us better understand and appreciate the processes and meaning structures that undergird socio-spatial life. Employed separately, or in some combination, each of the approaches explored in these chapters provides the qualitative researcher a chance to wrestle ably with the challenges of apprehending the world from a different perspective, and of evaluating how localized worlds are enmeshed in globalized processes. A close reading of the chapters that follow will help all of us to address those challenges thoughtfully, and to find yet more creative ways of expanding the boundaries of qualitative research.

7

Ethnography and Participant Observation

Annette Watson and Karen E. Till

Alaska, USA, 2003

AW: Until I was seated in the Piper Navajo propeller plane, flying above the roadless boreal forest, I was excited to begin my fieldwork. I had finally secured a community partner for my ethnography of regulatory wildlife management; as I neared the Arctic Circle, however, my growing distance from the road system caused my excitement to cool. After touching down on the gravel airstrip, I was driven along muddy roads that haphazardly connected log cabins and HUD homes. Throughout the Koyukon Athabascan village I noticed the fluttering of ripped, soiled, and frayed tarps that were draped as if meant to shelter the smokehouses beneath them; the windows on the squat, dark cabins seemed small. I thought of the approaching dim December days to come; I could hardly imagine living here through the Arctic winter.

Later that night, sitting alone attending the Memorial Potlatch ceremony, I had problems eating the food that would be rude not to accept. I almost gagged from the slimy quality left in my mouth by the fat used in Indian Ice Cream, but it was the whitefish that made me sick. As I shrugged over the toilet of the City Office, the building where I laid my bedroll for the night, I felt like I had the worst hangover in the world, without ever having had a drop to drink. Sweating, and with the taste of fish in my mouth, I wondered whether it was food poisoning, a parasite, or my own nervousness over this fieldwork and 'doing it right.' I only knew that something felt very wrong.

As demonstrated by this account of beginning a research project, ethnography is an intersubjective form of qualitative research through which the relationships of researcher and researched, insider and outsider, self and other, body and environment, and field and home are negotiated. The insights of ethnography are oftentimes derived through regaining one's bearings after becoming disoriented, whether through bodily discomforts or the political volatility of research settings (e.g., Hays-Mitchell, 2001). Annette's fieldnotes reflect her biases about 'civilization,' about the visibility of poverty, even about what is edible. Yet she recognized that her field site lay within the same United States wherein she grew up: she spoke a shared language of English and even watched many of the same television shows. Nevertheless, as a Caucasian and Westerner, she felt disoriented amongst this Alaska Native community.

Annette's reflections highlight how divisions between 'home' and 'field' are never clear-cut (compare DeLyser, 2001; Gilbert, 1994; Till, 2001). Ethnography is about this process of articulating differences and sameness, an act of bounding 'here' and 'there' (Hyndman, 2001). Within geography, ethnography is a research strategy used to understand how people create and experience their worlds through processes such as place making, inhabiting social spaces, forging local and transnational networks, and representing and decolonizing spatial imaginaries.

In this chapter we describe methods, techniques, and realizations experienced through creating ethnographic knowledges. We first offer a brief overview of existing work in geography, and then provide a more practical section about participant-observation, highlighting both the iterative character of this research approach and the ways that ethnographic practices are constantly punctuated with concerns about representation. Although ethnographies draw upon a myriad of source materials, including formal interviews, material culture, performances, images, and texts, we focus on observation, reflection, and learning – including recording, analyzing, and representing qualitative data – because participant-observation is perhaps the defining method that distinguishes ethnography from other qualitative research designs. We conclude by discussing the implications of the current ethical discussions about 'decolonizing ethnography' that emphasize dialogic research practices that include academic and non-academic experts, rather than knowledges produced from studying 'foreign others.'

GEOGRAPHY AND ETHNOGRAPHY

Ethnography first developed within anthropology, which emphasized the importance of studying the indigenous cultures of individual places (e.g., Malinowski, 1922). Following the 'crisis of representation' in social sciences during the 1980s, anthropologists critically reflected upon the ontological status of the concept of 'culture,' the routes (rather than roots) of cultures, and the histories and ethics of ethnographic practice more generally (Clifford, 1988, 1997; Clifford and Marcus, 1986; Emerson *et al.*, 1995). Ethnographic research is now prominent in such fields as education (Bogdan and Biklin, 1998) and sociology (Burowoy *et al.*, 1991; Latour and Woolgar, 1986), and within

geography in the subfields of cultural ecology, development studies, feminist studies, and social, political, cultural, and nature-society geography (Ley, 1974; Carney and Watts, 1991; Katz, 1992; Moore, 1993; Herbert, 1997; Western, 1997; DeLyser, 1999; Wright, 1999; Del Casino Jr., 2001; Dowler, 2001; Willis, 2002; Elder, 2003; Goldman, 2007). Regardless of the discipline, ethnographers explore topics that are difficult to research and represent using quantitative techniques, and ask research questions that may not be readily accessed through language. Ethnographers use a range of methods and time-intensive techniques to conduct their work, including: participant observation; participant action research; writing field notes and memos; sketching maps; gathering visual, material, and documentary materials; engaging in informal conversations; asking people to document and describe their everyday worlds; and conducting in-depth to semi-structured interviews, focus group interviews, and/or surveys.

Geographers have brought our discipline's theorizations of space, place, scale, landscape, and environment to develop further understandings of spatial processes and concepts in ethnography. We study how everyday social interactions create public and private spaces at multiple scales, including bodies, cities, neighborhoods, and tourism sites. Through studies about everyday geographies, space and politics, and multi-local sites and networks, geographers research the complex power and ethical relations that accompany such practices. Recent works, for example, include studies about children's geographies, transnational citizenship and belonging, activist networks, geographies of surveillance and human–nonhuman relations.

Ethnographic observations of, and interactions with, others highlight how bodies interact, meld, and constitute social spaces, and thereby create inclusions and exclusions. Hester Parr's research about what constitutes 'normal' bodily movements in urban public spaces, including streets, parks, and public squares, developed significant insights about embodied social relationships, including gender, sexuality, and health. Her work also called attention to the role of non-linguistic forms of communication, as well as the theoretical and ethical problems with the researcher's self/body as contained in the research process (Parr, 1998, 2001). Studying leisure and tourism, Arun Saldhana mapped the hierarchical social spaces of beaches and clubs in Goa that created a rave culture scene created through temporality, place, music, drugs, and viscous groupings of racialized bodies (2007). In Phuket, Thailand, and Bali, Indonesia, Rory Gallagher explored the spaces of monetary and non-monetary sexual activity among transgendered individuals living near tourist beaches. A complex ecology of race, skin color, age, bodily shape, language skills, and class became evident in the diaries kept by participants in the study, an ecology that shaped the life chances of a diverse group of people engaged in some way with sex work and tourism (Gallagher, 2007).

Asking people to talk about objects is also a way to understand everyday movements and emotional worlds. Luke Dickens followed the movements of graffiti crew members, artistic institutions, found objects and events throughout London to understand how writers, stencillers, artists and others made and remade the street, art gallery and city (2008). Katie Walsh asked British expatriates in Dubai to discuss mundane objects, such as photographs, postcards, or plastic bowls, that people brought to their new homes to understand feelings of (dis)location and attachment (2006). In a different setting, Mary Thomas used autophotography to learn more about the ways teenage women in Charleston, South Carolina, experienced sexuality, subjectivity, and belonging (2005).

Geographers are particularly sensitive to the different forms of power/knowledge that enable access for some individuals and prevent movement for others. Hannah Weston, for example, examined HIV prevention policies through outreach work to men who have sex with men (MSM) in Delhi and Indian immigrant and Asian-British men in London (2003, 2005). Using a participatory action research framework with an international HIV prevention charity organization, Weston found that the exchange of knowledge between Delhi and London, particularly around issues of cultural sensitivity relating to religion and sexuality, was productive. Yet stigma, argued Weston, operated differently for immigrant men in London, who were able to frequent spaces beyond the constraints of their religion, unlike MSM in Delhi who faced pervasive repression and violence. In a very different urban context, Anna Secor explored questions of citizenship for women in Istanbul, who either challenged or accepted being classified as 'citizen' or 'stranger' through such spatial tactics as anonymity in the city or through participation in schools, neighborhoods, and workplaces (2004). Examining gendered immigrant social relations within Europe, Patricia Ehrkamp asked Turkish women living in Marxloh, Germany, to draw mental maps to ascertain how they defied patriarchal relations in their neighborhoods by avoiding some streets and corners, and being present, and thereby creating, other social spaces (forthcoming).

Geographers are also making significant contributions to the larger field of what anthropologist George Marcus (1986, 1995) calls multi-sited or multi-local ethnography (e.g., Jackson et al., 2004; compare Burowoy et al., 2000; Hannerz, 2003). We are particularly well-suited to conducting multi-sited, transregional and comparative research projects because of our long tradition of theorizing 'local' places as co-constituted within the 'globalized' world system, a perspective that interdisciplinary scholars have only recently explored (Escobar, 2001; Gupta and Ferguson, 1997). Multi-sited ethnographic projects in geography analyze the forms and effects of: globalization through networks and locales; the multiple space-times of consumption and production; tourism and whiteness; nature-society relations; transnational citizenship; and movements of peoples, including refugees and expatriates, across political territories (Hyndman, 2000; Jackson *et al.*, 2004; Voight-Graf, 2004; Yeoh and Willis, 2005; Wright, 2006; Watson, 2007).

At the scale of the region, Andrew Tucker's (2009) research on queer identities in and around Cape Town, South Africa, demonstrates how social groups have positioned themselves in relation to their local heteronormative communities and through the city's socio-economic environments (at multiple scales). He studied numerous sites within three distinct areas in the city – places defined by, and that continue to be affected through, the legacies of state-sponsored racism under apartheid. These include centrally located 'white' urban neighborhoods; outlying 'black' African townships; and 'coloured' locations. Tucker's fieldwork challenged the spatial abstractions used by many scholars to represent sexuality and race, including 'global' flows, 'Western' queer identities, and 'local homosexualities.' He found that any one person's enactments of queer public identity are limited and enabled by his ability to approach and destabilize a heterosexual/homosexual binary through historical discursive formations, present-day social relations within queer communities, differential access and mobility to mainstream and/or queer spaces at a variety of scales, and the day-to-day material constraints resulting from apartheid.

Transnational multi-sited ethnographic projects in geography also provide methodological approaches to understanding and countering the uneven effects of global capitalism. Cindy Katz, for example, developed the concept of 'countertopography' to juxtapose ethnographic insights about abstract global processes in different parts of the world (Katz, 2004). Katz explored the circumstances of children in Howa, Sudan, and in New York City at different moments in time to analyze how children growing up during periods of economic transition are connected to and displaced from global economic systems. Abstract scholarly categories, including economic restructuring, disinvestment in social reproduction, and

the exoticization of places were made concrete through Katz's detailed analysis of children's geographies. More than comparative 'thick description,' countertopography is a way of imagining the spatial that challenges dominant ways of thinking about globalization and thereby may enable new political possibilities.

Finally, geographers now contribute to what Laurel Richardson (2003) calls creative analytical practice in ethnography (compare Crang and Cook, 2007). Rather than using ethnographic data only as evidence to support theoretical claims, representational forms more common to the creative arts are used to communicate insights and ideas, including fiction, poetry, drama, theater, satire, and allegory, and music, video, and photographs (e.g., Richardson, 1998, 2003). Karen, for example, tried to provide an autocritique of her claims to ethnographic authority through performative fragments that interrupted the conventional design and expectations of a scholarly book (Till, 2005). Between formal chapters, personal encounters with everyday spaces of the city offered alternative narratives and topographies of place making and memory. Photographs and maps, sometimes with ethnographic quotations, worked to represent, remind and question textual discussions.

Geographers also use a range of media to communicate their ideas and interactive work beyond academic institutions. Using video-ethnography techniques, Justin Spinney (2006) filmed his and other cyclists' journeys to work through London (using bicycle helmet cameras and portable microphones). Responding to their conversations about these films, Spinney now edits and creates videos with other cyclists that, in addition to his published work, explore how the bicycle is a social place that allows cyclists to enjoy embodied feelings of riding. In another example of the use of new media for a range of publics, Toby Butler worked with local residents and authorities to create *Memoryscape*, a series of audio walking tours about the histories of the River Thames in London that are available on the web (Butler and Miller, 2005; Butler, 2008). One tour, *Driftings*, resulted from allowing a piece of wood to drift along the river; where it hit the bank, Butler researched the area and created 'stops' for the walk. The audio 'data' of the tour invites listeners to experience their environments in new ways through music, interview passages, and commentary. Holly McLaren explored the creative possibilities of transdisciplinary collaboration by commissioning a scattered site exhibition of new art works in Oswestry, near the Welsh-English border (2008). Visitors and artists explored how national borders shape the knowledges and sensuous experiences of place through visiting exhibitions, performance installations, walks, webpage, and exhibition catalogue.

As these examples demonstrate, geographers have developed in-depth studies, conceptual frameworks, and creative practices to advance discussions beyond the discipline about spatial processes (migrations, economic flows, globalization, identity formation) and concepts (place, space, environment). But how do ethnographers 'do' their research? Using examples from our own work, in the following section we discuss participant observation and offer practical suggestions for students of ethnography. As we discuss below, ethnographers do not simply 'collect' forms of visual and material culture or conduct interviews; they participate with others in the creation of knowledge and meaning through social interactions.

ETHNOGRAPHY IN PRACTICE: PARTICIPANT-OBSERVATION

Alaska, USA, Later Reflections on Fieldwork, 2008

AW: I was so thankful for my background in theater because, when I first went to the field in 2003, I found my misadventures could not be so immediately recorded in text. I continued to develop my skill of memorization during every conversation and every camping trip because the 'nature' of these trips did not lend itself to the writing of field notes. Like the day I traveled with a hunter by snow machine along a trap line at −20°F; those days I participated in moose hunts by driving the boat; when I recorded data for the biologists' goose survey; when I worked at an elder's fish camp, without electricity for my laptop. For each of these trips, I waited until I returned to my cabin in the village, whereupon I opened my laptop and would write for hours. While some direct quotes from my companions would be lost, I nevertheless found that my capacity to remember would improve with each day of the practice.

My memories would also be prompted by the digital photos I took; with a large memory card, I could take a hundred high-quality photos before having to download them. I also used digital video to record the landscape, interviews, and subsistence activities, which also helped prompt my memory upon replaying them. My observations of environmental management meetings could be copiously documented *in situ* – with detailed written observations of verbatim debates, individual comings and goings, and even the sounds and smells of particular moments. But when I participated in subsistence and scientific practices, I had to employ my experience as an actor to memorize as much as to play the role required by the situation.

Minneapolis, Memo on fieldnote journals (while moving house), 2008

KT: When packing my office, I enjoyed revisiting my fieldnote journals, each of which is a different size, form, shape and color. They are for me akin to companions, being present during periods of uncertainty, learning and reflecting. Flipping through their pages, I note that some were written from both directions (when I need two different beginnings/sections): jottings and sketches were taken during events (such as at exhibitions, rallies, social gatherings, and/or when taking pictures); reconstructed conversations were scribbled after interviews; and memos and personal reflections were written over meals or at cafes at a more leisurely pace. Most notebooks have papers sticking out (ads, newspaper articles, flyers, maps, business cards, scraps 'borrowed' to scribble down a note or idea), bound by some sort of rubber-band, leather noose or string. These journals represent research encounters marked by an intensity in space and time.

Yet as I am returning to these earlier inscriptions, as well as my research files, photographs, and marked up pages of transcripts, a number of unexpected memories resurface. I remembered people I haven't seen in years, some of whom I met for an afternoon. I remember their gestures, their stories, their dreams. Others I have gotten to know better, and have since developed long-term relationships. I realize how much richer my current research is through the continual unfolding of these past interactions, even though these 'formal' research moments have passed.

Selecting a way to record notes is no small act for an ethnographer: we write and represent our work using a range of registers that enable the iterative nature of our research. Ethnographers interact with others, write, sketch and record (alone or with others) – to remember, document and reflect. We describe, interpret and analyze, and continuously revise and revisit our writings.

Of all the ways we interact with people and non-human natures in our work, participant-observation and its recording and analysis distinguishes ethnography from other qualitative research approaches. In this and the following section we look at how ethnographers document and participate in the everyday worlds, spatial processes, and place-making practices we study. Recorded *observations* of our interactions with others may take the form of fieldnotes, photographs, and sound and/or video clips. When we work through, reflect upon, and analyze our primary recorded and material data, we develop questions and insights about our work, and begin the difficult task of representing our research findings. As we describe below, our embodied and emotional *participation* in various contexts and through our interactions requires more than getting the 'facts' right; it demands 'doing' it *well*, and with humility and empathy.

OBSERVATIONS

The research method of observation entails description of and reflection upon embodied and emotional experiences, intersubjective and material exchanges, and social and non-human interactions. Observing and writing fieldnotes about everyday geographies, emotions, fluid social spaces, and material encounters is more a practice of discovery than an 'objective' form of reporting. Language is never a transparent signifier of witnessed events; furthermore, recording practices (through notes, video, audio, maps) always involve ethical choices.

Writing, photographing, and recording helps us understand how people make worlds, places, and meanings, and how the minutiae of buildings, animals, trees, people, movements, sounds, smells, tastes, and lights constitutes the lived experiences of these environments. When we write to remember and record, we often jot down those details that strike us in some way as telling and mundane about a place and/or situation. We may also take note of our emotional responses and frames of mind when experiencing events, interactions, and movements, and reflect upon how our presence may or may not be accepted in the social situations and settings we study (of which we are part). From notes, sketches, photographs and other forms of mappings, we attempt to create rich descriptive accounts of the everyday settings, routine interactions, and unusual (or not) situations of our work.

Taking photographs also records and represents our research experiences, such as documenting changing environments: a sequence of photos may track either the succession of building sites in a particular neighborhood or the effects erosion has on a village. For Karen, the physicality of writing notes and taking photographs is an important part of her research practice: it slows her down. Photography in particular requires bracketing and framing choices that make her pay attention to the processes of saturation and duration, as well as the particulars of things at a precise moment. It is a way she interacts with the urban environment, as well as a way to communicate with others familiar with a locale. While Karen tends to photograph landscapes, buildings, and objects, in Cape Town she began taking intimate pictures of people at events that were later used in exhibitions, webpages, or for other organizational purposes, including gifts. She was surprised to find that both young and old people liked being photographed (something she herself doesn't enjoy), and she now uses photographs to talk with people about topics and ask for advice or opinions.

Annette also found people to be very responsive to having their pictures taken; most of her images were of subsistence and scientific practices and of the changing boreal landscape, images she envisioned would be used for her academic presentations, teaching, and publications. What surprised her the most, however, was the response to videos: in addition to giving people clips on DVDs or video tapes, she would replay many at people's houses and witness their responses. On many occasions these viewing events yielded some of her best insights – people could respond to the way they performed a task, or use the video to teach their children about practices like hunting (cf. Spinney, 2006). Other times, people would request that certain activities be recorded even when not in her immediate 'research agenda,' like ceremonies or evidence of climate change. They often wanted and expected her to 'document' these practices for them; all videos and photos she shared with the tribal councils and native organizations with whom she works, and has even resulted in collaborative public outreach projects (e.g., Huntington, 2008).

Our examples illustrate how recording systems depend upon our questions and research projects. Karen, for example, uses sets of notebooks to document and reflect upon the places and peoples she studies.

KT: I usually have one small, central notebook that fits in my camera bag, purse or large pocket; I have it with me at all times. It has my contact info, notes about photographs I have taken (where/when/what I was thinking at the time), and is available for reflections at any time. Sometimes I like to reread this notebook when going back home on a bus or train, or on non-research days. Flipping through the pages reminds me of what I need to do and triggers ideas as well. My other notebooks are of various sizes and are dedicated to a particular case study. Systematic entries of observations, questions, translations, and sketches allow me to use the same notebook for multiple research trips. I also have an oversized journal that isn't tied to a particular case study. In it, I make connections to theoretical readings and have the space to draw, brainstorm, and connect impressions, ideas and interpretations.

After writing in her field journal(s), Karen later types her notes on a computer according to descriptive, reflective, and interpretative/analytical notes (cf. Bogdan and Biklin, 1998; Wolcott, 1994). This makes coding easier later (see below), as well as allows her to fill in the details of the jottings in her notebooks. When she conducts interviews or observes key events, there is a more urgent need to 'translate' these immediately to an electronic form, because specific details may be forgotten. After spending a week or so in the same place, Karen tries to set aside a writing day to work through her notebooks and type up notes. On such days, her journals will be spread all over the desk, along with brochures, maps, and collected on-line documents. Beginning with filling in details from the last set of fieldnotes, her writing process 'moves around the table' and through the screen, and results in a number of descriptive texts, reflection pieces (or memos, described below), and many, many questions – about words and phrases, people and places, how the work is going – as well as numerous 'to do' lists.

By contrast, because Annette works in rural and indigenous communities who are suspicious of visitors that have historically oppressed them, she reserves most of her writing for private moments on her laptop. She is sensitive to the ways that writing in public may be construed as treating tribal peoples as objects of knowledge, or as 'problems' to be 'fixed' – only what she most fears to be lost, like crucial dialogue or phrases, she might sketch down upon a small notebook. Except for longer trips, she would return to her private room or cabin and write after every encounter or observation, doing this from one to four times a day:

AW: Once I have my laptop at hand, I usually begin writing any verbatim dialogue I heard or was involved in. When I don't remember the exact words someone uses, I leave off the quotes and just paraphrase, but often while I'm engaged in the re-telling, I'll remember specific words someone used to describe their experiences or philosophy. Then as the dialogue takes shape, I'll begin filling in the circumstances of the events, the details of the landscape, peoples' moods or movement or dress. And then in brackets I'll write my responses to the event(s), or ideas upon which to memo later. In this way my writing practices themselves are non-linear.

Later, Annette loads her documents into a qualitative data analysis software program, *Atlas.ti*, and reads them over again. The program allows her not only to digitally organize and recall the textual and visual materials according to their themes, quotes, and codes, but it also helps Annette analyze this data through the program's simple Boolean operations.

Like Karen, throughout the process Annette continues to write her responses and thoughts in the form of *memos* that reflect upon and interpret her research experiences. Both of us understand our writing as a safe space to explore, think through, and represent knowledges, desires, and fears. In memos, we question our experiences and assumptions, pay attention to processes, respond to our embodied and emotional presences, consider the material and visual cultures that constitute what is being studied, scrutinize various relationships with research fields and partners, and elaborate upon our insights. We also make connections to other studies or previous work in memos, and raise critical questions that inform future theoretical readings.

Alaska, USA, 'Science as Culture,' July 22, 2003

AW: At the Turning Science to the Service of Native Communities conference, I remember talking ('performing') my project to X. I said, 'I want to understand the ways that *my* culture is being affected.' The woman leaned toward me and asked, 'And what is your culture?' I immediately realized that she thought I meant a Native culture, and I responded sheepishly, fumbling with my words after I was so good at eloquently describing my research question, 'I, uhm, Western Science, my culture being the West, my culture's belief in science'.... I seemed to be the only one who labeled 'science' as having its own 'culture.' Many people, at this conference and otherwise, seem to regard science as a tool that you can choose – or

not – to use, but it is its own culture. Yet are there political ramifications to calling it this? Could it jeopardize claims for Indigenous Knowledge?

A more systematic way to analyze fieldnotes, including memos, is through *coding*, wherein we identify general patterns, clarify connections and relations, develop possible insights and refine ideas. Coding also provides us with the opportunity to reframe our research foci, which is particularly valuable early on in the research process, as well as later, when we prepare to conduct more formal interviews. While the origins of coding stem from the sociological tradition of grounded theory (Glaser and Strauss, 1967; Strauss, 1987), ethnographers do not understand this practice as objective. Instead, open coding is a form of brainstorming, whereby the researcher revisits materials to think about possible ideas, themes, and issues at different times during the research project (compare Charmaz, 2006). More focused coding is used to identify and clarify patterns and relationships in the primary data collected. An iterative analytic practice, coding allows the ethnographer to break apart, relate, and recombine the materials generated in the research process. It may be used in combination with, or alongside of, other analytical approaches including: qualitative or quantitative content analyses, narrative analysis, conversation analysis, forms of discourse analysis, semiotic analysis, hermeneutics, psychoanalytical analysis, and phenomenological approaches (Denzin and Lincoln, 2000; Rose, 2001).

Coding as a research practice varies quite considerably for ethnographers; where Annette described earlier using the qualitative data analysis software *Atlas.ti*, Karen proceeds with coding by hand using the following general sequence. First, she goes through all of her descriptive and reflective fieldnotes rather quickly, including her memos, her lists, her comments on documents (advertisements, maps, internet pages), and, later on, conversation and interview transcripts. Either section by section, but most often line by line, she circles words, underlines key phrases, and makes notes to herself. Then, she goes back through the same notes working more slowly. She writes words in the margins of her notes that generalize her understandings of topics and relationships; she also identifies key words or concepts that are used by the peoples she studies/with whom she works. Then she goes through her notes once again, to discern emerging patterns and repetitions, or cross-out topics that seem either too abstract or too narrow. She might then make lists of key words and concepts, and organize them under general topics. Within a list, she tries to identify categories and note (or infer) relationships between types (structured hierarchically, clustered, working horizontally or in other ways). She often writes memos during and following coding, especially about key terms or unexpected relationships that emerge through this process. Annette's process is similar, but all her work is done electronically, highlighting text within the software program.

For Karen, working through (later typed) notes by hand is an important way to visualize and analyze her data in its entirety. At a later phase of this process, she creates piles of (photocopied) notes marked by different colored pens, organizes them on the floor or a large table according to categories, and physically reorganizes into piles at various locations that stand for the relationships she wants to emphasize in her final writings. These piles of notes are then clipped and placed into manila folders for use when writing formal chapters or articles; using post-it notes, she identifies and cross-references other key themes in the folders with the original typed up notes, memos, and transcripts. For Annette, the process of coding is also a process of digitally organizing her data; she uses the Boolean tool in *Atlas.ti* to search for related quotes, memos, and other primary data when writing chapters or articles.

As our discussion of 'observation' suggests, we write to offer audiences rich descriptions and detailed accounts that depict the worlds, environments, peoples, contexts, and meaning-makings we have researched, engaged in, and learned from. What is not so apparent in the published texts of ethnographers is the almost obsessive manner in which we revisit our writings, sketches, codings, and other materials to represent the insights derived from our research. We may also work collaboratively (gaining approval on quotes or passages, asking for advice on form or content, or writing with someone). Regardless of the outcome and products, writing is always a political act; how, what, and for whom we write can lead to further engagements.

PARTICIPATION

What we have already suggested is that every ethnographic project results from a series of encounters, or participations, with 'others' that need to be negotiated in context. Participant-observation requires that ethnographers pay close attention to, and sometimes partake in, everyday geographies so they can become familiar with how social spaces are constituted in various settings. Only by participating with others can ethnographers better understand lived, sensed, experienced, and emotional worlds (Crang and Cook, 2007; Herbert, 2000). Interviews do not alone constitute ethnography, because, in many cases, interviewees cannot report upon what they 'do' – for 'doings' are often unconscious or unarticulated practices.

Participation requires ethical responsibility to the peoples with whom one works. When representing others' lives, we must do so with care, and in ways that do not reinforce the inherently uneven power relations that privilege the researcher rather than the researched. One's 'sense' of what is appropriate comes from reading numerous ethnographies of the communities with whom one wishes to study, and from observing and learning their spoken and unspoken rules. Yet even when we try to understand the implicit rules of cultural norms, we may break still other rules and find that we have acted inappropriately. Kim England, for example, expressed anxiety over her fears 'of academic voyeurism' before she abandoned her research with a lesbian community (England, 1994: 84). She also questioned the role of supplicant that some feminists adopt while learning from their informants, arguing that such a role is disingenuous because of the inherently exploitative nature of written representation. Some researchers have thereby developed projects that 'study up,' meaning that their ethnographies depict the lifeworlds of peer groups, individuals in positions of power, or those people otherwise recognized as 'experts' (e.g., Gilbert, 1994). Jennifer Hyndman (2001) notes that studying up ensures that research is a relational activity and one that does not co-opt the time and intellect of subaltern peoples.

Participation may also unexpectedly result in new possibilities for collaboration, participatory projects, and even political action. Karen, for example, was invited to present her work at international workshops and conferences (for academics, experts, and practitioners), and to advise on public panels about proposed places of memory in Berlin. Through conversations with practitioners and citizens from different countries, she began to develop a larger comparative project (that is ongoing) about 'wounded cities' in different parts of the world, beginning with new research in Cape Town. There she met with many groups and organizations, and began to work collaboratively with some individuals and in association with other institutions and groups, working on grants, documenting events through notes and photographs, and transcribing interviews. Through this research with artists, scholars, citizens, and practitioners, she began working differently in Germany and embarked on new work on similar themes through community service learning projects in the United States. As a result of the generosity of others, Karen has come to understand the creative potential of ethnography as a form of memory-work that

may complement local place-based artistic and activist engagements in countries with difficult pasts (Till, 2008).

For Annette, her research and writing practices led her to develop writing partnerships not only with tribal members, but also with the non-native agency representatives she worked with. For example, while observing wildlife management meetings she heard a need for funding additional meetings, which led to her coordinating a larger grant project to promote more 'holistic' data gathering and management. Her participation also led to her writing a policy document aimed to speak to wildlife managers, rather than academic geographers – and her hope is that it will not only bridge understanding between tribal subsistence users and non-Native agency personnel, but also change the kinds of data privileged in the management regime: arguing for more qualitative studies as a means to understand the ethics of human–nonhuman relations, as well as articulate and assess social-ecological resilience. Our research experiences about memory-work and human–nonhuman natures resonate with Paul Routledge's (2001) insights that collaborative work with activists in their political struggles must include not just writing, but physical action, even taking to the streets if necessary.

Because working ethnographically is always a political act, with political effects, in the final section we turn our critical gaze to the politics of knowledge production within geography. While many authors call attention to their positionality, the focus remains on the researcher her/himself, in terms of individual choices, rather than about how these choices are situated within particular disciplinary histories and debates. Below we discuss projects that 'decolonize' ethnography and call for social change. We argue that participatory and community-based research designs are necessary to develop co-generative inquiry, and that our representational practices must legitimate expert knowledges beyond the limits of academic institutions and settings.

DECOLONIZING ETHNOGRAPHY

Alaska, USA, June 2003

AW: 'Why should we continue to be the private zoos for anthropologists?' (Deloria, 1969: 99). I read that question as I sat on the beach of Nome, Alaska. I awaited a meeting with a Native leader who might agree to facilitate a community partnership with the local Native organization. I alternated between reading Deloria's book and watching a few miners in their wet suits wade in the tide, vacuuming up onto rafts Nome's famed gold-laced sand. Perhaps in part because of *where* I read it, *Custer Died For Your Sins: An Indian Manifesto* remains the most formative volume in my intellectual development – because I was a geographer about to 'do' participant-observation and ethnography. And I needed to confront how as a non-Native researcher I might, even inadvertently, treat this Native community as my own private zoo.

Ethnographers could also be called miners, sometimes writing regardless of their impacts upon the peoples they objectify. While Annette's meeting that day in Nome went well, the collaboration she desired would never get off the ground; there was no answer to her subsequent phone calls and emails, and an uncomfortable cordiality existed the next times she ran into the native leader at other locales. Rather than confront him she instead chose to respect the unclear indication, the mere hint, that she as a researcher was unwelcome.

Vine Deloria questioned why disciplines like anthropology should assert an exclusive 'license' to represent Indian peoples under the guise of academic 'freedom.' He argued that the creation of an abstract and 'authentic' Indian as an object of knowledge enabled anthropologists to claim their own expertise, while excluding that of indigenous peoples (Deloria, 1969). Similarly, Sioux anthropologist Beatrice Medicine warned that to study 'the Indian point of view' was mere wordplay that allowed researchers to remain in control of the research and their title of 'expert' (Medicine with Jacobs, 2001). For both Medicine and Deloria, the products – the knowledge – of academic research was forged unethically through power relations

that continued the project of colonialism. As argued by Maori scholar Linda Tuhiwai Smith, '"[r]esearch" is probably one of the dirtiest words in the indigenous world's vocabulary'(1999:1).Instead 'Decolonization is a process which engages with imperialism and colonialism at multiple levels. For researchers, one of those levels is concerned with having a more critical understanding of the underlying assumptions, motivations and values which inform research practices' (Tuhiwai Smith, 1999: 20).

Geographers have only begun to draw upon the insights of indigenous and other communities, to frame our research in ways that may decolonize ethnography through research praxis and representational forms (e.g, Shaw *et al.*, 2006).

Cape Town, South Africa, 2004, with later reflections, 2007

KT: Ethnography and geography have unhappy histories in South Africa. I knew that my whiteness and Americanness might create problems with research relations before starting this project, but I didn't anticipate being the trigger for debates about internal power structures after my fourth research trip. When I arrived for the first of a series of workshops for which 'we' received a grant, no research assistants were hired, no contacts had been made with local groups, and internal uncertainty prevailed about allowing outsiders in. I knew from my previous research that if one does not live in the same place(s) in which one works, arrivals and departures are always a problem – internal hierarchies and local deadlines always mean that the calendars and priorities 'here' and 'there' are never the same. However, I never imagined I would be gendered through local power structures. When I was jokingly told I was 'one of the guys' from one of the board members, I didn't really know at the time what he meant. Later, I realized that some women viewed me as part of the(ir) problem because I had access to and attention from local (male) directors, and ultimately resources, that they did not.

Listening for hints that one is unwelcome is thus important even when one has an established collaboration. The kind of reciprocal interactions Karen envisioned, including exchanges and learning from one another, and the co-production of knowledges in multiple forms, did not mesh with local priorities and goals. While the project originated from within a participatory action research (PAR) design, she came to realize that unless one lives within and is a citizen of local environments, which include particular political and social relations, a well-intentioned research framework may be neither practical nor possible. Moreover, while she was initially welcomed by some host scholars as a geographer and ethnographer, rather than a historian, other hosts pointed out the negative legacies of both fields.

As both of our examples demonstrate, humility is an essential part of the practice of ethnographic participation. *Not* listening for refusals to participate constitutes poor research practice because it may rob individuals of their right to choose whether they wish to participate at all (England, 1994; Winders, 2001; Wolf, 1996). But it also remains an important way to engender trust and thus secure 'good data.' Without humility, the efficacy of the research may be jeopardized – and thus directly impact the researcher's career.

The goals of decolonizing ethnography, however, demand more than working reflexively to interrogate the topics of 'our' choosing. As argued by indigenous scholars, researchers must also take responsibility for our disciplines' intellectual trajectories. Geographers have their own colonial legacies that are difficult to escape. Annette's eventual field site, the homelands of Koyukon Athabascan Indians, for example, had also been 'observed' by nineteenth-century US explorers (proto-geographers) who produced the earliest English-language publications describing Alaska's geography (Dall, 1870). But their 'objects' of knowledge also included the indigenous people. Such early ethnographies produced by explorer-travelers explicitly *de*-humanized Indigenous peoples as either objects or petulant children (Tuhiwai Smith, 1999). One account described how an explorer snuck off to a grave to collect the skull of an Indian for his natural history collection:

I had long had my eye upon this grave, and had been waiting for weather which would cover up my tracks, in order to secure the skull. The Indians are very superstitious in regard to touching anything that has belonged with a dead body, and would have been highly incensed had it become known. (Dall, 1870: 67)

As this example suggests, geographers have been impacted even more subtly by our disciplinary history – the heroic accounts of explorers have influenced what topics are considered legitimate study. Critical of National Geographic Society funding priorities, Cindy Katz contends that geographers remain more concerned with producing knowledge that affirms a masculinist hero 'discovering' geographic frontiers, places like space and the Polar Regions, rather than work on geographies of 'home' places or of children's worlds in the global South (Katz, 1996).

Decolonizing ethnography means to consider research a process of collaboration rather than appropriation. When working with marginalized peoples, topics that the communities themselves would consider relevant should be carefully proposed and negotiated (Deloria, 1969; Tuhiwai Smith, 1999; Medicine, 2001; Stevens, 2001; Watson, 2007). In addition, participant-observers must accept that their written products do not have immediate relevancy to subaltern peoples, many of whom struggle daily with the legacies of colonialism and capitalism. 'Participation,' therefore, takes the form of providing pro-bono assistance to communities, such as writing grants for community organizations, sharing research skills, and writing policy documents based on their research, as well as providing community access to all research products for the purposes of self-representation.

Such decolonizing practices can be more often than not 'black boxed' when researchers actually write their ethnographies, which is why feminist researchers have troubled the very notion of authorship. Many scholars employ co-authorship strategies that question the format of either the 'single' author (e.g., The Sangtin Writers and Nagar, 2006) or a 'single' voice (e.g., Behar, 1994). Robert Rundstrom and Douglas Deur (1999) write explicitly about the problems associated with ethnographies conducted among Native peoples, arguing that '[e]thnographic facts are commonly decontextualized, and depicted as representative of a culture's collective worldview rather than being the words of a person or the intellectual property of an individual, a family, or a village' (1999: 242). Ethnographers thus try to establish responsible and respectful relationships with the peoples, communities, groups, nonhuman natures, and places they study through their writing as a practice of decolonizing methodologies (e.g., Benson and Nagar, 2006).

Jackie Huggins and colleagues, for example, described their distinctive experiences returning to Carnarvon Gorge National Park in Australia and responded to each other's experiences (2000). Jane Jacobs first encountered this place as a national heritage interpretive rock art trail, a view that stands in sharp contrast to Jackie and Rita Huggins' understanding of Kooramindanjee as a place of homecoming for them and other Bidjara peoples . Their co-authored text describes the colonial power relations that continue to shape the meanings and possibilities of dwelling. In quite a different form, Annette Watson and Orville Huntington wrote a collaborative account about an Athabascan moose hunt that also departs from the ethnographic tradition of a Western scholar reporting upon local forms of knowing (2008). They wrote a narrative that abruptly switches first-person voices, and shifts between descriptive narratives and theoretical insights. A kind of unresolved conversation highlights moments of revelation; their experimentation with co-authorship calls attention to how knowledge is actively co-produced.

Few works detail the difficulties of working collaboratively and for this reason *Playing with Fire*, by the Sangtin Writers, activists working in the Uttar Pradesh region of India, and Richa Nagar, an American-based feminist geographer, makes a particularly significant contribution to work critical of development ideology and to ethnography more generally. When members of the Sangtin group and Nagar identified their mutual frustrations about the problematic ways that outside agencies, non-government organizations (NGOs) and researchers appropriated the ideas and voices of grassroots activists for their own agendas, they decided to try out a longer-term relationship to explore their mutual interests. Their first book details this collaborative journey, as well as their personal struggles and group successes. The Hindi edition, moreover, led to controversial public discussions about the sexist and patronizing attitudes rural women face when interacting with officials of large NGOs.

As these works demonstrate, there are no clear steps that exist to assure a project is 'decolonized.' We can only continue to attempt to design ethnographic projects that help transform 'informants' to 'collaborators.' Indeed, decolonizing ethnography will never be complete, as the researcher can never escape the politics of her research (Shaw *et al.*, 2006; Tuhiwai Smith, 1999). Yet in the process of decentralizing research from the authoritative spaces of the academic institution to various communities, the very practice of conducting 'fieldwork' will by necessity come to encompass new research sites and strategies.

CONCLUSION

KT: Ethnography entails an unfolding process of learning and becoming – as researcher, writer, translator, creative communicator, intellectual curator, project manager, adopted local, and more simply and significantly, a responsible person in the world – and trying to come to terms with what those roles mean. Ethnography represents the intensity and passion that motivates my attempts to understand the many worlds through which I and others move between and learn from, as well as the peoples, things and places that have guided me on these journeys.

As we have discussed in this chapter, ethnography as a methodology raises significant questions about the status and situations of knowledges used and created in geography. An ethnographic approach to qualitative research complements geographers' concerns for understanding and depicting spaces, places, and local-global experiences.

Crucially, ethnographers do more than consider what methods would generate the best data in their research design, which is a common way that social scientists use multiple-methods, such as structured interviews, survey results, or census data. Projects can either begin with ethnographic research practices, to be later supplemented by other qualitative and/or quantitative research techniques, or can itself constitute a rich dissertation, academic text, or public creative project. Ethnography as a research practice is iterative, or non-linear – that is, we are concerned with writing as we observe and with how we participate as we write, all the while revisiting and thinking through our past participations and observations.

Ethnography makes explicit processes and power relations involved in knowledge creation through intersubjective and responsible approaches to research topics and research partners. Participating in the field means participating in creating knowledge, *with* people heretofore conceived of as 'subjects' – some of the co-writing we discussed in this chapter attest to the opportunity ethnographic depiction has to 'decolonizing' research representations more generally. In other words, ethnography is more about its 'doing' than it is about the procurement of 'facts.' For this reason, ethnography presents opportunities to reimagine the practice of research more generally and offers scholars the possibility of contributing to the world at large.

REFERENCES

Behar, R. (1994) *Translated woman: crossing the border with Esperanza*. Boston: Beacon Press.
Benson, K. and Nagar, R. (2006) 'Collaboration as resistance? Reconsidering the processes, products, and possibilities of feminist oral history and ethnography', *Gender, Place, and Culture* 13 (5): 581–92.
Bogdan, R. and Biklen, S.K. (1998) *Qualitative research for education: an introduction to theory and methods*, Third Edition. Boston and London: Allyn and Bacon.
Burowoy, M., Blum, J.A., George, S., Gille, Z., Gowan, T., Haney, L., Klawiter, M., Lopez, S.H., Ó Rian, S. and Thayer, M. (2000) *Global ethnography: forces, connections, and imaginations in a common world*. Berkeley: University of California Press.
Burowoy, M., Burton, A., Ferguson, A.A. Fox, K.J. Gamson, J., Gartrell, N., Hurst, L., Kurzman, C., Salzinger, L., Schiffman, J. and Shiori, U. (1991) *Ethnography unbound: power and resistance in the modern metropolis*. Berkeley and Los Angeles: University of California Press.
Butler, T. (2008) Memoryscape. http://www.memory-scape.org.uk/, date accessed: June 2008.
Butler, T. and Miller, G. (2005) 'Linked: a landmark in sound, a public walk of art', *Cultural Geographies* 12 (1): 77–88.
Carney, J. and Watts, M. (1991) 'Disciplining women: rice, mechanization, and the evolution of Mandinka gender relations in Senegambia', *Signs* 16 (4): 651–81.
Charmaz, K. (2006) *Constructing grounded theory: a practical guide through qualitative analysis*. Thousand Oaks, CA: Sage.
Clifford, J. (1988) *The predicament of culture: twentieth-century ethnography, literature, and art*. Cambridge, MA and London: Harvard University Press.
Clifford, J. (1997) *Routes: travel and translation in the late twentieth century*. Cambridge, MA: Harvard University Press.
Clifford, J. and Marcus, G. (eds) (1986) *Writing culture: the poetics and politics of ethnography*. Berkeley: University of California Press.
Crang, M. and Cook, I. (2007) *Doing ethnography*. Thousand Oaks, CA and London: Sage Publications Ltd.
Dall, W.H. (1870) *Alaska and its resources*. Boston: Lee and Shepard.
Del Casino Jr., V. (2001) 'Healthier geographies: mediating the "gaps" between the needs of people living with HIV and AIDS and health care in Chiang Mai, Thailand', *The Professional Geographer* 53 (3): 407–21.
Deloria, V. Jr. (1969) *Custer died for your sins: an Indian Manifesto*. New York: Avon Books.
DeLyser, D. (1999) 'Authenticity on the ground: engaging the past in a California ghost town', *Annals of the Association of American Geographers* 89 (4): 602–32.

DeLyser, D. (2001) '"Do you really live here?" Thoughts on insider research', *Geographical Review* 91 (1/2): 441–53.

Denzin, N. and Lincoln, Y. (eds) (2000) *Handbook of qualitative research*. Thousand Oaks, CA: Sage Publications.

Dickens, L. (2008) 'Finders keepers: performing the street, the gallery and the spaces in-between', *Liminalities* 4 (1), http://liminalities.net/4–1/finder-skeepers.htm, last accessed: June 2008.

Dowler, L. (2001) 'The four square laundry: participant observation in a war zone', *Geographical Review* 91 (1–2): 414–22.

Ehrkamp, P. (Forthcoming) '"I've had it with them!" public space and young Turkish women's everyday practices of resistance', *City and Community*.

Elder, G. (2003) *Hostels, sexuality, and the apartheid legacy: malevolent geographies*. Athens: Ohio University Press.

Emerson, R.M., Fretz, R.I. and Shaw, L.L. (1995) *Writing ethnographic fieldnotes*. Chicago and London: University of Chicago Press.

England, K. (1994) 'Getting personal: reflexivity, positionality, and feminist research', *The Professional Geographer* 46 (1): 80–9.

Escobar, A. (2001) 'Culture sits in places: reflections on globalism and subaltern strategies of localization', *Political Geography* 20 (2): 139–74.

Gallagher, R. (2007) 'Queering sex tourism: the geographies of gay, transgender, and female sex tourism in Southeast Asia in the time of HIV', Unpublished PhD Dissertation, Department of Geography, University of Cambridge.

Gilbert, M. (1994) 'The politics of location: doing feminist research at "home"', *The Professional Geographer* 46 (1): 90–6.

Glaser, B. and Strauss, A. (1967) *Discovery of grounded theory*. Chicago: Aldine.

Goldman, M. (2007) 'Tracking wildebeest, locating knowledge: Maasai and conservation biology understandings of wildebeest behavior in Northern Tanzania', *Environment and Planning D: Society and Space* 25 (2): 307–31.

Gupta, A. and Ferguson, J. (1997) *Culture, power, and place: explorations in critical anthropology*. Durham: Duke University Press.

Hannerz, U. (2003) 'Being there … and there … and there! Reflections on multi-site ethnography', *Ethnography* 42 (2): 201–16.

Hays-Mitchell, M. (2001) 'Danger, fulfillment, and responsibility in a violence-plagued society', *Geographical Review* 91 (1/2): 311–21.

Herbert, S. (2000) 'For ethnography', *Progress in Human Geography* 24 (4): 550–68.

Herbert, S. (1997) *Policing space: territoriality and the Los Angeles Police Department*. Minneapolis: University of Minnesota Press.

Huggins, J., Huggins, R. and Jacobs, J. (2000) 'Kooramindanjie place', in L. Johnston (ed.) *Placebound: Australian feminist geographies*. Oxford, Melbourne: Oxford University Press. pp. 167–81.

Huntington, O. (2008) 'Orville Huntington – it's a changing thing', *Polar-Palooza Podcast*. http://passporttoknowledge.com/polar-palooza/pp06.php, last accessed: June 2008.

Hyndman, J. (2001) 'The field as here and now, not there and then', *Geographical Review* 91 (1/2): 262–72.

Hyndman, J. (2000) *Managing displacement: refugees and the politics of humanitarianism*. Minneapolis: University of Minnesota Press.

Jackson, P., Crang, P. and Dwyer, C. (eds) (2004) *Transnational spaces*. London: Routledge.

Katz, C. (1992) 'All the world is staged: intellectuals and the projects of ethnography', *Environment and Planning D: Society and Space* 10 (5): 495–510.

Katz, C. (1996) 'The expeditions of conjurers: ethnography, power, and pretence', in D. Wolf (ed.) *Feminist dilemmas in fieldwork*. Boulder: Westview Press. pp. 170–84.

Katz, C. (2004) *Growing up global: economic restructuring and children's everyday lives*. Minneapolis: University of Minnesota Press.

Latour, B. and Woolgar, S. (1986) *Laboratory life: the construction of scientific facts*. Princeton: Princeton University Press.

Ley, D. (1974) *The black inner city as frontier outpost*. Washington, DC: The Association of American Geographers.

Malinowski, B. (1922) *Argonauts of the Western Pacific: an account of native enterprise and adventure in the archipelagoes of Melanesian New Guinea*. New York: Dutton.

Marcus, G. (1986) 'Contemporary problems of ethnography in the modern world system', in J. Clifford and G. Marcus (eds) *Writing culture*. Berkeley: University of California Press. pp. 165–93.

Marcus, G. (1995) 'Ethnography in/of the world system: the emergence of multi-sited ethnography', *Annual Review of Anthropology* 24: 95–117.

McLaren, H. (2008) 'Bordering', http://www.borderingart.org.uk/about.html, last accessed: June 2008.

Medicine, B. (ed.) with Jacobs, S-E. (2001) *Learning to be an anthropologist and remaining 'native': Selected writings*. Urbana: University of Illinois.

Moore, D. (1993) 'Contesting terrain in Zimbabwe's Eastern Highlands: political ecology, ethnography, and peasant resource struggles', *Economic Geography* 69 (4): 380–401.

Parr, H. (2001) 'Feeling, reading, and making bodies in space', Geographical Review 91 (1–2): 158–67.

Parr, H. (1998) 'Mental health, the body and ethnography', *Area* 30 (1): 28–37.

Richardson, L. (2003) 'Writing: a method of inquiry', in N. Denzin and Y. Lincoln (eds) *Collecting and interpreting qualitative materials*, Second Edition. Thousand Oaks, CA: Sage. pp. 499–541.

Richardson, M. (1998) 'Poetics in the field and on the page', *Qualitative Inquiry* 4 (4): 451–62.

Richardson, M. (2003) *Being-in-Christ and putting death in its place: an anthropologist's account of Christian performance in Spanish America and the American South*. Baton Rouge: Louisiana State University Press.

Rose, G. (2001) *Visual methodologies*. Thousand Oaks, CA: Sage.

Routledge, P. (2001) 'Within the river: collaboration and methodologies', *Geographical Review* 91 (1–2): 113–20.

Rundstrom, R. and Deur, D. (1999) 'Reciprocal appropriation: towards an ethic of cross-cultural research', in J. Proctor and S. David (eds) *Geography and ethics: Journeys in a moral terrain*. New York: Routledge. pp. 237–50.

Saldhana, A. (2007) *Psychedelic white: Goa trance and the viscosity of race*. Minneapolis: University of Minnesota Press.

The Sangtin Writers and Nagar, R. (2006) *Playing with fire: feminist thought and activism through seven lives in India*. Minneapolis: University of Minnesota Press.

Secor, A. (2004) '"There is an Istanbul that belongs to me": citizenship, space, and identity in the city', *Annals of the Association of American Geographers* 94 (2): 352–68.

Shaw, W., Herman, R.D.K. and Dobbs, R. (2006) 'Encountering indigeneity: re-imagining and decolonizing geography', *Geografiska Annaler* B 88 (3): 267–76.

Spinney, J. (2006) 'A place of sense: a kinaesthetic ethnography of cyclists on Mont Ventoux', *Environment and Planning D: Society and Space* 24 (5): 709–32.

Stevens, S. (2001) 'Fieldwork as commitment', *Geographical Review* 91 (1–2): 66–73.

Strauss, A. (1987) *Qualitative methods in social research*. Cambridge: Cambridge University Press.

Thomas, M. (2005) 'Girls, consumption space, and the contradictions of hanging out in the city', *Social and Cultural Geography* 6 (4): 587–605.

Till, K. (2001) 'Returning home and to the field', *Geographical Review* 91 (1–2): 46–56.

Till, K. (2005) *The New Berlin: memory, politics place*. Minneapolis: University of Minnesota Press.

Till, K. (2008) 'Artistic and activist memory-work: Approaching place-based practice', *Memory Studies* 1 (1): 95–109.

Tucker, A. (2009) *Queer visibilities: space, identity and interaction in Cape Town*. Oxford: Blackwell.

Tuhiwai, S.L (1999) *Decolonizing methodologies: research and indigenous peoples*. London: Zed Books Ltd.

Voight-Graf, C. (2004) 'Towards a geography of transnational spaces: Indian transnational communities in Australia', *Global Networks* 4 (1): 25–49.

Walsh, K. (2006) 'British expatriate belongings: mobile homes and transnational homing', *Home Cultures* 3 (2): 119–49.

Watson, A. (2007) 'Knowledges that travel: expertise and the "nature" of wildlife management in the Alaskan boreal forest', Unpublished PhD dissertation, Department of Geography, University of Minnesota.

Watson, A. and Huntington, O.H. (2008) 'They're here, I can feel them: the epistemic spaces of indigenous and western knowledges', *Social and Cultural Geography* 9 (3): 257–81.

Western, J. (1997) *Outcast Cape Town*. Berkeley: University of California Press.

Weston, H. (2003) 'Public honor, private shame and HIV: issues affecting sexual health service delivery in London's south Asian communities', *Health and Place* 9 (2): 109–17.

Weston, H. (2005) 'Seeking cultural safety: NGO responses to HIV/AIDS among south Asians in Delhi and London', Unpublished PhD dissertation, Department of Geography, University of Cambridge.

Willis, K. (2002) 'Conducting overseas fieldwork', in H. Viles and A. Rogers (eds) *Student's companion to geography*, Second Edition. Oxford: Blackwell Publishing. pp. 219–24.

Winders, J. (2001) 'On the outside of, in power, participation, and representation in oral histories', *Historical Geography* 29: 45–52.

Wright, M. (1999) 'The politics of relocation: gender, nationality, and value in a Mexican

Maquiladora', *Environment and Planning* A 31 (9): 1601–17.

Wright, M. (2006) *Disposable women and other myths of global capitalism*. London and New York: Routledge.

Wolcott, H. (1994) *Transforming qualitative data: description, analysis, and interpretation*. Thousand Oaks, CA: Sage.

Wolf, D. (1996) 'Situating feminist dilemmas in fieldwork', in D. Wolf (ed.) *Feminist dilemmas in fieldwork*. Boulder: Westview Press. pp. 1–55.

Yeoh, B. and Willis, K. (2005) '"Singapore unlimited"?: transnational elites and negotiations of social identity in the regionalization process', *Asian & Pacific Migration Journal* 14 (1–2): 71–95.

8

Autoethnography as Sensibility

David Butz

AUTOETHNOGRAPHY – BLURRED GENRES

The concept of *autoethnography* is best understood as a heuristic device, a metaphorical learning tool. The very term – auto-ethnography, auto/ethnography, aut*o*ethnography (with a dash, with a slash, with the wink of an eye) – suggests this sort of use. We all know what *ethnography* is: in a generic sense it is 'writing about or describing people and culture' (Ellis, 2004: 26); in a more politically and historically inflected sense it has been described as 'a means by which Europeans represent to themselves their (usually subjugated) others' (Pratt, 1992: 7). Imagine what possibilities emerge for linking self to the 'writing of culture' when 'auto' is tacked onto 'ethnography.' So far in its fairly short history the heuristic, exploratory and metaphorical exercise of attaching self to ethnography is still a field of open possibilities. In fact, we have not even settled definitively on what 'self' we are attaching to ethnography; what 'auto' is being driven by autoethnography (see Lambek, 2005, for an extension of the metaphor).

The existing literature describes a large variety of overlapping approaches to relating self to the description of culture. Carolyn Ellis and Arthur Bochner (2000: 739–40) list over 50 terms scholars have used to name their efforts in this regard. They conclude their list by noting that 'autoethnography, Native ethnography, self-ethnography, memoir, autobiography, even fiction, have become blurred genres,' and that 'in many cases, whether a social science work is called an autoethnography or an ethnography depends on the claims made by those who write and those who write about the work' (2000: 749). Deborah Reed-Danahay (1997: 2–9) provides a similarly extensive enumeration of more specifically anthropological uses of the term, which she boils down to a generic definition that encompasses her list and also the range of approaches described by Ellis and Bochner (2000). She says autoethnography is 'a form of self-narrative that places the self within a social context' (Reed-Danahay, 1997: 9).

Reed-Danahay's emphasis on the *narrative placement of self in social context* captures a central aspect of the range of autoethnographic work, and allows me to distinguish five main types of autoethnography from among the myriad 'blurred genres' she and Ellis and Bochner (2000) enumerate. These are (a) academics who reflect on their relations with research participants or the social context of their field work as a way to gain greater understanding of the social worlds they study or the epistemological characteristics of insights they take away from the field (e.g., McGee, 1995; Hyndman, 2001; Roth, 2001); (b) academics who study their own life circumstances intensely in order to illuminate a larger social or cultural phenomenon, and who often use experimental forms of personal narrative writing as a way to incorporate affect and emotion into their representations (e.g., Shrestha, 1995; Valentine, 1998; Moss, 1999; Cook, 2001); (c) 'insider' and 'complete-member' academic researchers who study a group or social circumstance of which they are a part, use their insiderness as a methodological and analytical resource, and may or may not understand themselves explicitly as subjects of their own research (e.g., Porteous, 1989; DeLyser, 2001; Saltmarsh, 2001); (d) 'Native' ethnographers, members of subaltern groups with metropolitan academic training who conduct research on their own groups, often from a position of opposition to existing metropolitan representations (e.g., Narayan, 1993; Mernissi, 1994; Sangarasivam, 2001; Sabra, 2005); and (e) non-academic members of subaltern groups – ethnographic others – who produce self-representations intended to intervene in dominant discourses about them, as a form of political claiming (e.g., Butz and MacDonald, 2001; Butz 2002a; Gold, 2002; Besio, 2005, 2006). A wide range of purposes, representational projects, and preoccupations are associated with these five autoethnographic positionings, and several of them overlap considerably in practice (e.g., Ghosh, 1998).

For the purpose of this chapter I have reduced this typology to three main orientations an autoethnographer may have to the production of authorized academic knowledge: inside, outside, or at the margins. The most familiar autoethnographic orientation is the *academic ethnographer* – the researcher. This narrating subject is positioned within academic knowledge, claims a degree of academic authority, and is therefore necessarily preoccupied with the epistemological and methodological implications of positionality, experiential knowledge, and narrative voice. In another much smaller literature, developed

most interestingly by Mary Louise Pratt (1992, 1994, 1999), the *ethnographic 'other'* – the researched, the ethnographically written-about – is the relevant autoethnographic subject. This subaltern narrating self is positioned firmly outside the institutions of academic knowledge production. Here, the task for researchers is not to produce such autoethnographies, but rather to receive them in epistemologically, politically, and ethically sensitive ways. Some autoethnographers, Native ethnographers and postcolonial researchers in particular, but also other sorts of 'insider researchers,' claim both self-positionings, simultaneously occupying an academic representational position and speaking against metropolitan academic representations of the group to which they belong. These *academic ethnographic 'others'* describe a third type of autoethnographic positioning, intermediate between the other two, and sharing characteristics of each.

In this chapter I describe each of these orientations, trace some of their differences and overlaps and explore how each may serve as a heuristic device – an expansion of possibilities – for the others. I aim to articulate some of the challenges and possibilities of approaching research with an *autoethnographic sensibility*. I should stress at the outset that autoethnography is not a methodology, nor even a set of methods united by a focus on self-representation. Rather, it is an epistemological orientation to the relationships among experience, knowledge, and representation that has a variety of methodological implications. I articulate some of the most important of these as the chapter proceeds and summarize them in the conclusion, but given the variety of these 'blurred genres' there is no coherent autoethnographic method. My ambition, rather, is to show why an autoethnographic epistemological orientation – an autoethnographic sensibility – is worth developing.

I began thinking in terms of autoethnography to help inform my own work on transcultural interactions in the rural community of Shimshal, northern Pakistan, in circumstances that resemble, in many ways, the colonial contact zones that concern Pratt, but I think the issues it addresses have relevance beyond this context. Asymmetrically constituted transcultural research interactions are not unique to former colonies, or to ethnographic research approaches. Many geographers study historically subordinated 'others' within their own Western societies, often in research circumstances that risk reproducing existing power relationships (Katz, 1994; Nast, 1994; Staeheli and Lawson, 1994; Elwood and Martin, 2000). But the representational issues broached by autoethnography are not limited to research with oppressed groups. Concerns about how to situate the narrating and experiencing self (whether researcher or researched) in relation to the production of knowledge are central to qualitative research more generally. Autoethnography, as practice and sensibility, is a useful resource for developing the critical reflexivity required to deal sensitively with these widespread concerns.

The chapter unfolds in four sections. The first section focuses on academic autoethnographies where social scientists write autobiographically about their own experiences in a social context in order to produce scholarly knowledge that incorporates the nuances of researchers' personal experience. By producing social texts that reflexively collapse the distinction between representing and performing experience, scholars attempt what Reed-Danahay (1997: 4) calls 'a rewriting of the self and the social.' I argue that this is an exercise in producing a self for the self (in performance) simultaneous to producing a self for an audience (through representation); a project that characterizes in different ways all three sorts of autoethnographic orientations discussed in the chapter. In the second section I discuss the autoethnographic practices of ethnographic 'others.' I argue that the motivation for such subaltern autoethnographies is primarily political (i.e., to gain a voice at the representational table in order to gain greater self-determination) rather than primarily epistemological (i.e.,

incorporating experience self-consciously into the production of knowledge). Having made this rough distinction I then discuss how both academic and subaltern autoethnographies are persuasive – and therefore political – endeavours, in that they aim to create a self for an audience of others to some extent in response to pre-existing representations; a comparison of the two helps to tease out some of the ways that each can be effectively persuasive. The third section explores the value for critical reflexivity of these two conceptualizations of autoethnography. I reference my work in Pakistan to show how understanding myself in autoethnographic terms sensitizes me to dimensions of the social setting I investigate and aspects of my own imbrication in the self-representations I receive from research subjects. Sensitivity to the autoethnographic characteristics of what we learn from research participants as well as to our situatedness in relation to the people and worlds we are studying constitutes an 'autoethnographic sensibility.' The fourth section focuses on autoethnographers who are simultaneously academic knowledge producers and members of the subordinated groups they study. I argue that the advantages of inhabiting the speaking position of both academic analyst and subjectively engaged member of the social world under investigation have less to do with conventional notions of the authenticity of insiderness than with the critical perspective gained by occupying a self-representational location at the unstable margins of dominant discourse and between disparate social worlds. The chapter concludes by summarizing the main insights of an autoethnographic sensibility.

NARRATIVES OF THE SELF – THE POETICS OF REPRESENTATION

Ellis and Bochner (2000: 740) describe the sort of autoethnography where 'social scientists take on the dual identities of academic and personal selves to tell autobiographical stories about some aspect of their experience in daily life' as:

> An autobiographical genre of writing and research that displays multiple layers of consciousness, connecting the personal to the cultural. Back and forth autoethnographers gaze, first through an ethnographic wide-angle lens, focusing outward on social and cultural aspects of their personal experience; then, they look inward, exposing a vulnerable self that is moved by and may move through, refract, and resist cultural interpretations. As they zoom backward and forward, inward and outward, distinctions between the personal and cultural become blurred, sometimes beyond distinct recognition. (p. 739)

Ellis summarizes her 'autoethnographic method' as follows:

> I start with my personal life. I pay attention to my physical feelings, thoughts, and emotions. I use what I call systematic sociological introspection and emotional recall to try to understand an experience I've lived through. Then I write my experience as a story. By exploring a particular life I hope to understand a way of life. (Ellis and Bochner, 2000: 737)

This sort of autoethnography is brilliantly exemplified in Ellis' own work dealing with the deaths of her brother (1993) and her spouse (1995), and her recent 'methodological novel' about teaching a graduate course on autoethnography (2004). The latter expands in considerable detail on the methodological, epistemological, and representational aspects of Ellis' approach.

This 'personal experience narrative' (Denzin, 1989) or 'narrative of the self' (Richardson, 1994) style of autoethnographic writing shares many characteristics with 'reflexive' and 'narrative' ethnography where researchers use their personal experience with a culture to illuminate their understanding of that culture (Ellis and Bochner, 2000), with 'ethnographic memoir' where the researcher reveals a personal, backstage tale of the field research experience (e.g., Malinowksi, 1967; Rabinow, 1977; Hardwick, 2001), and with autobiography (see Moss, 2001). Arguably, all but the latter are products (or precursors) of a 'shift in the 1970s from an emphasis on participant observation

to the "observation of participation" and to an emphasis on the process of writing' (Ellis and Bochner, 2000: 741; see also Tedlock, 1991). The key distinction between Ellis' 'narratives of the self' and reflexive or narrative ethnography, is that Ellis situates herself as the *primary* research subject – the main source of information – in her research, and reflects on her own experiences to understand and exemplify larger social or cultural circumstances. Two things distinguish what Ellis calls autoethnography from straight-up autobiography: the effort she makes to use a self-reflexive account of her own experience to inform her readers' understanding of a way of life that *exceeds* her individual experience, and her preoccupation with the relationship between truth and representation.

An important impetus for the sort of autoethnography Ellis advocates is the epistemological position that the slippery nuances and particularities of experience – emotions, feelings, bodily responses – are integral to the constitution, understanding, and representation of social or cultural phenomena. Autoethnography in this sense is a child of the twin crises of legitimation and representation (see Clifford and Marcus, 1986; Marcus and Fischer, 1986; Clifford, 1988; Denzin and Lincoln, 2005); it questions the legitimacy of knowledge that does not self-consciously incorporate the nuances of personal experience, and it doubts the ability of conventional academic writing to represent effectively the relationship between personal experience and larger social and cultural phenomena. Autoethnographers' response to the insight that researchers cannot directly capture lived experience, but rather create such experience in the social texts they write, has been to embrace forms of writing or other representational activities that collapse the distinction between representing and performing experience (see Corey, 1998; Lionnet, 1989; Alexander, 2005).

In blurring this distinction autoethnographers are engaged self-consciously in 'a rewriting of the self and the social' (Reed-Danahay, 1997: 4), a project of producing a self for the self simultaneous to producing a self for an other (the audience) (paraphrased from Pratt, 1999: 39). As articulated by Bryant Alexander (2005: 423), the 'act of showing in autoethnography is less about reflecting on the self in a public space than about using the public space and performance as an act of critically reflecting culture, an act of seeing the self through and as the other.' Hence the tendency to adopt an emphatically first person voice, and an emphasis on experimental, evocative forms of ethnographic writing, including 'short stories, poetry, fiction, novels, photographic essays, personal essays, journals, deliberately fragmented and layered writing' (Ellis and Bochner, 2000: 739).

A focus on producing a self through the process of writing often imbues the autoethnographic process with therapeutic value. Indeed, much autoethnographic work focuses on 'the narrative challenge one faces when an expected life story is interrupted by illness, violence or accident' and produces texts that act 'as an agent of self-discovery or self-creation' (Ellis and Bochner, 2000: 745). Autoethnography in the personal narrative style has been criticized for emphasizing the therapeutic at the expense of the analytical (e.g., Atkinson, 1997). Ellis and Bochner (2000: 746) respond by asking, 'Why should caring and empathy be secondary to controlling and knowing? Why must academics be conditioned to believe that a text is important only to the extent it moves beyond the merely personal?' and stress that what they are aiming for is an expressive and dialogic 'evocative social science' (p. 747) that gets beyond 'the trashing of emotion' (p. 746).

One of the challenges of an evocative mode of writing is to produce representations that have meaning and offer insights to the other who is reading the text, and not just to the self who is writing the text; representations that are not entirely *self*-referential. Part of the difficulty is that focused evocation is hard to achieve; Ellis and Bochner (2000: 738) say that 'most social scientists don't write well enough to carry it off,' and that

autoethnographic narratives are sometimes 'self-adoring or self-hating without being sufficiently self-aware or self-critical, and without taking into account cultural constraints and possibilities' (Ellis, 2004: 34).

For autoethnographic narratives to communicate across selves (i.e., to an audience) as an evocative genre, their self-reflections need to be situated in relation to a wider social field that includes, in some way, the audience. This is precisely what Gill Valentine achieves in the article 'Sticks and stones may break my bones' (1998), as she skillfully weaves together a description of sexual harassment she endured, a narrative of her emotional responses, a critical analysis of the part Geography as a set of disciplinary practices played in both the harassment and her capacity to deal with it, and important insights about the spatiality of social life. Reading Valentine's piece, geographers are compelled to reflect on their own involvement in a set of disciplinary practices that permit the forms of harassment she describes, as well as absorb the larger geographical insights her narrative evokes. She tells a very personal story, but avoids excessive self-referentiality by allowing other selves to find a place in her narrative. The result is effective autoethnography and insightful geography.

ETHNOGRAPHIC OTHERS AS AUTOETHNOGRAPHIC SELVES – THE POLITICS OF REPRESENTATION

Mary Louise Pratt introduced ethnographic others as autoethnographic selves in *Imperial Eyes: Travel Writing and Transculturation* (1992). She says 'if ethnographic texts are a means by which Europeans represent to themselves their (usually subjugated) others, autoethnographic texts are those the others construct in response to or in dialogue with those metropolitan representations' (1992: 7). She later expands as follows:

> Autoethnographic texts are not, then, what are usually thought of as autochthonous or 'authentic'

forms of self-representation… Rather they involve a selective collaboration with and appropriation of idioms of the metropolis or conqueror. These are merged or infiltrated to varying degrees with indigenous idioms to create self-representations intended to *intervene* in metropolitan modes of understanding. (Pratt, 1994: 28)

Kathryn Besio and I read the following implications into Pratt's conceptualization:

Autoethnography is not something researchers do, but something their research subjects do that they may want to study. It is an intentional process leading to an intentional representation (which may, of course, have unintended effects); the intent is to strategically alter the way an audience of dominant outsiders understands the subordinate group, and beyond that, to push back to some extent against the shove of domination. Thus, it has strategic ambitions beyond simple translation. It is an inseparable mix of accommodation and resistance: accommodation in terms of idiom; resistance in terms of at least some of its content. (Butz and Besio, 2004: 353)

In that article and elsewhere we use Pratt's conceptualization to analyze local people's self-representations to foreign explorers, adventure tourists, development workers, and researchers in northern Pakistan (e.g., MacDonald and Butz, 1998; Butz, 2001, 2002a; Butz and MacDonald, 2001; Besio, 2003, 2005, 2006, 2007; Besio and Butz, 2004; Butz and Besio, 2004.).

Pratt's autoethnography has a power relationship at its core: the capacity of one party to represent another, the capacity of that representation to affect the lives of the people being represented, and the constrained capacity of the people who are the objects of metropolitan representation to intervene in that representation. If for academic autoethnographers the crisis of representation is primarily a methodological crisis (a problem of effectively accounting for and evoking personal experience), then for the subordinated people who are Pratt's autoethnographic subjects it is primarily a *political* crisis (the problem of finding a voice that will be listened to in a transcultural representational space). In both cases autoethnographers are producing a self for the self and for the other. For Ellis, as I said earlier, this occurs as researchers

embrace forms of writing that collapse the distinction between representing and performing the construction of self. The subordinated autoethnographers imagined by Pratt, on the other hand, create a self for their metropolitan others by finding ways to insert self-representations into the discursive and institutional apparatus through which they are oppressed.

The example Pratt (1992) uses initially to develop her analysis is a 1200-page illustrated letter written in 1613, in a mixture of Spanish and Quechua, by an Andean named Felipe Guanam Pomo de Ayala and addressed to King Philip III of Spain. The letter 'began by rewriting the history of Christendom to include the indigenous peoples of America, then went on to describe in great detail the history and life ways of the Andean people … followed by a revisionist account of the Spanish conquest,' before finally proposing 'a new form of government through collaboration of Andean and Spanish elites' (Pratt, 1992: 2). In my work in northern Pakistan I distinguish between formal strategic autoethnographies such as the Shimshal Nature Trust Management Plan where the community adopts an environmentalist and developmentalist idiom to describe and justify local nature stewardship practices, and informal tactical autoethnographies like local trekking porters' conversational efforts to intervene in Western trekkers' understandings of transcultural portering labour relations as they walk together along the trekking path (Butz, 2002a, 2006; Butz and Besio, 2004). What emerges clearly in these works is that autoethnography is a *persuasive* art. In order to be successfully persuasive – to actually act on the actions of others – an autoethnographic representation has to concede something to the idiom, logic, and rhetorical style of the oppressors (see Butz and MacDonald, 2001). In this way, an autoethnographic representation is also a *product* of power; its content is influenced by those concessions it makes in order to circulate and persuade in the sphere of authorized knowledge. It must adapt itself to dominant discourse in order to gain an audience, and this has implications for the constitution of a self for the self. A self-representation that says, 'we are this' is also saying 'treat us as this,' and 'this is the us you will encounter when you engage with us.' Such a gesture may be purely tactical, but it nevertheless has the effect and intention of intervening in a host of potential actions, discursive and material, that force some version of it into being (Scott, 1990; Adams, 1996; MacDonald, 1998).

Ethnographic others as autoethnographic selves are engaged in an explicit *politics of representation*. Their efforts have more to do with getting a voice at the representational table in order to gain self-determination than with finding ways to represent personal experience more deeply or evocatively. Certainly, they are also interested in effective evocation as a resource for inserting themselves into dominant discourse, but are forced by a field of preexisting transcultural power relations to concede something aesthetically and substantively in order to gain an audience and insert themselves 'into the long road to hegemony' (Spivak, 1999: 310).

I do not want to draw too stark a differentiation here between the politics and poetics of representation. Nor do I want to suggest that the lessons of comparing these two types of autoethnographic practice flow more in one direction than the other. Both employ intensity of feeling, emotion and personal experience as sources of knowledge and resources of persuasion, even if these have received more attention in discussions of personal narrative autoethnography. Both also struggle to find a voice that reflects self-understanding effectively in an idiom that reaches the ears of an audience external to the self, even if that is more evident in the autoethnographies of ethnographic others. In both cases politics and poetics are intertwined and mutually constitutive. The difference is more of degree than kind.

Like the representational interventions of ethnographic 'others,' academic autoethnographies may be understood as attempts to intervene in authorized representations of

particular sorts of selves and lives they are talking about and performing. They are also necessarily responsive to the exercise of power, needing to concede something in terms of idiom, logic, rhetoric and content to the representational conventions they intend to disrupt. As Reed-Danahay says of this type of autoethnography, it is 'an act of writing against disciplines in a context molded by disciplines' (1997). Fred Corey (1998: 250) adds nuance to this evocative statement by suggesting that while 'the master narrative is an artillery of moral truth,' the personal narrative can be 'a mode of "reverse discourse"' that 'defixes the truth' of dominant discourses, giving voice to particularities that disrupt hegemonic and seamless representations of experience, its meanings, and its epistemological value. But only if it is successfully persuasive.

The effort to situate personal narratives explicitly in relation to authorized modes of knowing is a way to also situate them in relation to an audience, whose members are themselves positioned in some relation to authoritative knowledge. This enlarges the situational focus of narrative ethnography from an exclusive focus on the narrator's situation vis-à-vis the world to include the narrative text's situation vis-à-vis an audience and its positioning in relation to the dominant discourses in which the personal narrative hopes to intervene. Paying more attention to this politics of representation is one way out of the problem that some autoethnographic texts weave such a tight web of evocation and self-referentiality that it is hard to relate them to anything beyond themselves.

I think Nanda Shrestha's 'Becoming a development category' (1995) exemplifies how this may be done successfully. He narrates how his sense of self and life trajectory were colonized by development discourse, and in so doing provides an experiential rendering of his personal situation vis-à-vis the world of international development. By constructing his narrative in such a way that his experience demonstrates the power of development discourse while also disrupting the notion that he is one of development's success stories, Shrestha positions his auto-ethnography in relation to authoritative knowledge (i.e., development's narrative of itself), and thus folds his intended audience of international development scholars into the story. He engages in a politics of representation that relies heavily on a poetics of representation (i.e., collapsing the distinction between performing and representing the construction of a self) as well as on engaging directly with the idiom of development discourse.

AUTOETHNOGRAPHY – LESSONS IN CRITICAL REFLEXIVITY

Pratt's conceptualization of autoethnography provides academics, who work with subordinated groups involved in efforts to intervene in dominant discourses about them, with a useful *analytical* resource and a productive tool for *critical reflexivity*. It provides a frame for interrogating the motivations behind formal group self-representations, for analyzing their rhetorical shape, idiom and mode of address, and for situating them in a context of asymmetrical power relations. The concept is also useful for assessing the effects of specific autoethnographic self-representations in relation to their intentions. This analytical process can be especially useful for scholars who want to understand and support efforts by subordinated groups to establish, as Gayatri Spivak says, 'a line of communication … between a member of subaltern groups and the circuits of citizenship or institutionality' (1999: 310).

Kathryn Besio, Ken MacDonald, and I have found it helpful to expand the notion of autoethnography to include informal and less explicitly group-focused efforts by members of subordinate groups to communicate transculturally with their dominant 'others.' Expanding the concept in this way has sensitized us to the spontaneity and opportunism

of much autoethnographic expression, as well as to the interventionary intentions and effects of a wide variety of self-representational tactics our research subjects employ in their interactions with outsiders, and has helped us understand those tactics as part of a larger politics of (transcultural) representation. It also allows us to compare formal strategic self-representations of subordinated groups with the tactical autoethnographies of their individual members or internally subordinated sub-groups (Butz, 2002b). This analytical exercise helps to illuminate representational tensions and struggles within communities that are often understood to be homogenous in their stance towards metropolitan power, and provides a basis for assessing the representativeness of formal autoethnographies (see Besio and Butz, 2004).

An example from my research in Shimshal may help to clarify the point. About a decade ago a few Shimshalis began to read English language portrayals of them, and found that for over a century the village had consistently been represented by a long chain of foreigners in ways that bore little relation to community members' self-understandings, with sustained oppressive material effects (see Butz, 1998, 2002a, b). Using a largely environmentalist and developmentalist idiom, community elites responded to these largely denigrating portrayals by constructing their own formal narrative of what Shimshal is, designed to set the record straight. This is articulated in the 'Fifteen Year Vision and Management Plan of the Shimshal Nature Trust' (see Ali and Butz, 2003), which circulates internationally via the Internet. Villagers are instructed by community leaders to keep to the script of this formal strategic autoethnography in their conversations with outsiders, or preferably to refer outsiders to selected village elders. This directive conflicts with and threatens trekking porters' occasional practice of referring to well-known colonial-era travelogues (the source of some of the most egregious misrepresentations) in their descriptions of the community and its history to the tourists who employ them. Porters use such citations to demonstrate their familiarity with a Western idiom and Western renderings of the community, and also to gently remind tourists of the guilty similarities between colonial and tourist modes of travel/interaction. These conversations are subtle interventions in foreign visitors' easy assumptions about what they encounter in Shimshal, and are designed to 'guilt' tourists into paying porters better and treating them more humanely (see Butz and Besio, 2004). Comparing porters' tactical autoethnographic efforts with community elders' formal autoethnographies reveals much about the micro politics of representation in Shimshal, and the ways that formal group autoethnographies may undermine the interests and self-representational ambitions of some community members.

By expanding the concept of autoethnography from formal, group-focused, textual self-representations to include a range of informal, opportunistic, day-to-day representational tactics we are foregrounding the 'potential autoethnographic characteristics of all indigenous self-representations,' and advocating 'an autoethnographic sensibility: an attentiveness to the autoethnographic characteristics of things that are going on in our research settings' (Butz and Besio, 2004: 354). To speak of an autoethnographic sensibility is to expand the relevance of Pratt's conceptualization from a distanced study of the self-representations of ethnographic others to include a more intimate examination of the political and epistemological characteristics of relations between researchers and research subjects. Such an autoethnographic sensibility, which combines insights from the two conceptualizations of autoethnography I have discussed so far, provides a useful tool of *critical reflexivity* for academic researchers whether or not they work with systematically subordinated groups.

One of the central characteristics of personal narrative autoethnography is its committed reflexivity, its struggle to produce knowledge and representations that

self-consciously recognize the place of the researcher-self in the production of that knowledge; its requirement of 'those who are already embedded in particular cultural and social practices to subject themselves and their most intimate surroundings to the same forms of critical analysis as they would any other' (Young and Meneley, 2005: 2). For Ellis (2004: 45) this occurs as 'social scientists view themselves as the phenomenon and write evocative stories specifically focused on their academic as well as their personal lives.' Other genres of academic autoethnography also attempt some form of critical reflexivity: 'self-critical sympathetic introspection and the self-conscious *analytical* scrutiny of the self as researcher' (England, 1994: 82; see also McDowell, 1992; Schoenberger, 1992; Moss, 1995; Rose, 1997; Al-Hindi and Kawabata, 2002). What Ellis and Bochner (2000: 741) call reflexive or narrative ethnography, where 'the ethnographer's experiences are incorporated into the ethnographic description and analysis of others and the emphasis is on the "ethnographic dialogue or encounter" [Tedlock, 1991: 78] between the narrator and members of the group being studied' is another prominent autoethnographic approach to recognizing the place of the researcher-self in the production of knowledge.

These are efforts by researchers to situate themselves in relation to the people and worlds they are studying, and to the fields of power that constitute those relationships, and are ways to describe the situatedness and partiality of the academic knowledge that results. Bringing these struggles for critical self-reflexivity into communication with Pratt's efforts to understand autoethnography as an indigenous politics of representation allows researchers to consider how we are located in the web of power relations that mediate how the subordinate groups we work with insert self-representations into the realm of authorized knowledge. This can be a useful way to understand some of the epistemological characteristics of what we get from our research participants and what we do with it. More specifically, it leads to three fruitful avenues of reflexivity. The first is the path of imagining that what our research participants tell us is autoethnographic, the self-representation of people who have a political ambition, and for whom we as researchers are fields of possibility and constraint. Kathryn Besio and I describe this process as follows:

> We must attend to the ways that we, as researchers, are an audience to which autoethnographic representations are directed. Methods texts often give ethnographic field workers the advice to receive information from our Native informants with a mixture of trust and suspicion: trust that they are providing us with some slice of indigenous life/meaning, tempered by suspicion that they are telling us what they want us to hear or what they think we want to hear. A sensitivity to autoethnography suggests that these are mutually constitutive, rather than competing (or alternative), elements of transcultural knowledge production. It is in the interplay among these (only analytically separate) aspects of self-presentation that selves are produced as selves for the self, and others for the other. (Butz and Besio, 2004: 356)

This is an important epistemological insight that applies beyond the context of transcultural research interactions, to all individual or group self-representations that have a persuasive intent (including, for example, qualitative interviews). By definition self-representations are self-interested, and as such are responsive to the context of their reception. What we call autoethnographies are simply more self-consciously developed instances of a much more ubiquitous category of communication, and therefore what I am calling an autoethnographic sensibility is a widely applicable resource. We continue:

> To the extent that researchers are imbricated – as an attentive audience – in this process of autoethnographic knowledge production, we have a responsibility to become autoethnographers ourselves in the other sense of the concept; to engage in 'the process by which the researcher chooses to make explicit use of [their] own positionality, involvements and experiences as an integral part of ethnographic research' (Cloke et al., 1999: 333).

An important objective of this autoethnography will be to interrogate our own constitution (and

self-presentation) as a limited set of resources that our research subjects use productively in their efforts at transcultural self-presentation. This sort of exercise foregrounds our very practical, field-level, interventions in the ways subalterns speak transculturally. (Butz and Besio, 2004: 356)

A second opportunity for critical reflexivity is the exercise of imagining part of what we do as the analysis of autoethnographic material. Such a perspective provides an epistemological framing for treating the information we get from research participants less as primary data provided by 'Native informants' (Spivak, 1999), and more as secondary information, already worked-up, with a self-conscious perspective and purpose in the world. This framing adds clarity to the insight that rather than doing 'fieldwork *on* the unmediated world of the researched' we are actually working 'on the world *between* [ourselves] and the researched' (England, 1994: 86, first emphasis added, second in original; see also Katz, 1992, 1994; Denzin and Lincoln, 2005). It is well understood that as qualitative researchers we gather interpretations which we then interpret; both our research subjects' interpretations and our own emerge from that space of betweenness. To treat our participants' self-representations as secondary information means attending to the ways they are influenced by what they experience as the affordances and constraints of the world between themselves and us.

That leads to a third avenue of reflexivity. Pratt's autoethnography helps us to imagine the texts we researchers produce in relation to the autoethnographic ambitions of the people they represent:

> If it is true that the concept we're terming autoethnography begins to characterize our research subjects' most deliberate attempts to engage, on something like their own terms, with the globally-circulating discourses that underwrite their subordination, then part of our politics of research may be to facilitate these attempts, and the political project implicit in them. ... If an autoethnographic sensibility helps us to recognize our subjects as transcultural knowers, then it should be possible for us to respect the productive potential our research subjects are able to perceive in their interactions with us, and also to follow and support the

direction they set in their autoethnographic projects. (Butz and Besio, 2004: 356–7)

This way of thinking about our work and our subjects provides us with a means to situate ourselves in the production of knowledge without unduly shifting the focus of our representations to ourselves (see Crang, 2003, 2005; Bourdieu, 2003). In addition, this particular mode of critical reflexivity can help us assess how the ways we do field research and representation enable or constrain our participants' autoethnographic ambitions, and helps us to imagine a research politics of support for subordinate people's self-representations. We may interrogate our positioning in the self-representations of our research participants by writing about it auto-ethnographically, perhaps using some of the forms of experimental writing advocated by Ellis.

Kathryn Besio's 'Telling stories to hear autoethnography: Researching women's lives in northern Pakistan' (2005) provides an elegant example. Besio composes a series of interview conversations into a story that interweaves the narrative told by her interview participants (about circumstances surrounding the gift of a sewing machine) with the narrative of the interview encounter itself. She uses the genre of story telling to highlight ways that her participants shaped their narrative – and to some extent the interview encounter itself – to suit their understandings and ambitions regarding the interviewer and the transcultural interview context. According to Besio:

> Writing transcultural stories can be a powerful way of representing the complexities and problems of doing research … Moreover, story telling as a method of representation allows some of the women's knowledge to appear in the text I write, especially the extent of their participation in constructing 'my' narrative. This became more apparent upon rereading the story with an analytical ear for the autoethnographic. While my initial intentions of writing the stories were primarily reflexive and descriptive, an important outcome from returning to the story and rereading it here is a greater understanding of how the women inserted themselves in 'my' text and, conversely, inserted me into theirs. (2005: 328)

BOUNDARY DWELLERS – INSIDER RESEARCH, 'NATIVE ETHNOGRAPHY,' AND AUTOETHNOGRAPHY

Intermediate between the authorial positionings discussed so far is a diverse literature that understands academic 'Native ethnographers,' complete-member researchers and insider researchers as the relevant selves of autoethnographic research. The non-metropolitan subjects evoked by the term 'Native ethnographer,' especially, often share with Pratt's subaltern autoethnographers an intention to intervene in metropolitan representations of them, but from a position within or at the margins of academia (Bishop, 2005; Smith, 2005). Jamaica Kincaid's reflection on colonialism and tourism in Antigua in *A Small Place* (1988) is a good example of this sort of autoethnography. Kincaid begins her narrative with the sentence: 'If you go to Antigua as a tourist, this is what you will see' (Kincaid, 1988: 3). The book's first third sustains 'you' as its mode of address, telling prospective tourists what they will see when they visit the island, how they will understand it, and what their understanding will be missing. Kincaid, who was raised in Antigua but lives in Vermont as a writer and university teacher, draws on her positionality as an outsider to Antigua to tell readers what they will perceive when they visit the island, and on her insiderness when she explains how they will be wrong. In each case what tourists' understandings miss is the context of colonialism, imperialism and grinding poverty behind what they observe. The latter two-thirds of the book adopts a first-person voice to offer an alternately autobiographical and journalistic evocation of the effects of this context for life in Antigua. Kincaid uses her complex positionality as outsider/insider and academic/Native to write a self-representation that speaks back to metropolitan understandings of Antigua.

According to David Hayano (1979; see also Lejeune, 1989; Deck, 1990), authors' insider status increases the validity and authenticity of their work. It is argued from this position that Native ethnographers and other insider researchers are able to represent the non-academic social worlds of which they are a part more authentically than outsider researchers in two related ways. First, they are, in themselves, understood to be authentically representative of that world and its subjects. Second, they are understood through their insiderness to be well equipped to produce authentic representations of that world and its subjects. More recent reflections on 'insiderness' are less sanguine about its benefits and authenticity status as an academic research and representational location (Strathern, 1987; Narayan, 1993; Brettel, 1997; Herod, 1999; Spivak, 1999). Scholars have noted that insiderness may blind researchers to aspects of a social setting that are taken for granted and therefore limit their access to important insights (Bogdan and Biklen, 1998), as well as pose practical difficulties for interacting with and eliciting information from research subjects (Miles and Crush, 1993; DeLyser, 2001). Others observe that the very claim to insider status as a source of authenticity contributes to an oppressive (self-)essentializing of Native or indigenous groups (Motzafi-Haller, 1997), and fails to recognize that 'the "insider/outsider" binary in reality is a boundary that is not only highly unstable but also one that ignores the dynamism of positionalities in time and through space' (Mullings, 1999: 340).

Native ethnographers and other insider researchers exemplify Reed-Danahay's point that autoethnography is a boundary-crossing endeavour (1997: 3), in that they necessarily engage in projects of transcultural representation between non-academic and academic cultures (but see the essays in Meneley and Young, 2005), and also typically across linguistic, ethnic, class-based, or racialized boundaries of group identity. These insider researchers inhabit the subject positions and speak with the authorial voice simultaneously of academic analysts and subjectively engaged members of the social worlds they represent. In this way they are also boundary straddlers, subjects whose multiple positioning

presents complications for those who would attach a special 'insider' or 'Native' authenticity – and validity – to either their representativeness or their representations of those social worlds (see Bhabha, 1984, 1985; Griffiths, 1994; Slemon, 1995; Spivak, 1999). As a reviewer says of Pierre-Jakez Hélias' autoethnographic memoir *The Horse of Pride: Life in a Breton Village* (1978), he is 'no longer a representative of, but rather a spokesperson for his "otherness"' (Carrard, 1992, cited in Reed-Danahay, 1997: 129). The transition from representative to spokesperson results partly from a drift in subject positioning (hybridity, transculturation) and partly from a shift in representational idiom; both are implicit in writing ethnography from the inside out, and both undermine authenticity claims (Butz and MacDonald, 2001). The only alternative that can sustain claims to Native or insider authenticity is intolerable: to occupy the position of 'Native informant' (Spivak, 1999; see also Trinh, 1991; Motzafi-Haller, 1997; Butz and MacDonald, 2001).

If the boundary straddling positionality from which Native or other insider ethnographers write makes it difficult to sustain special authenticity claims for their representations, then it may be useful to understand them as boundary occupiers, less crossing or straddling boundaries than inhabiting them. The value of this transcultural positionality is not that it allows authentically Native forms of self-representation outside of dominant discourse, but rather that it provides a self-representational location at the unstable margins of dominant discourse and between social worlds that are assumed to be ontologically separate. Claims to authenticity may be replaced by critical reflexivity as ethnographic objects speak as autoethnographic subjects who intervene in essentializing discourses of authenticity by performing the experience of transcultural subjectivity through their use of idiom and the adoption of an authorial voice that dismantles the borders between the same and the other. Kincaid's *A Small Place* (1988), discussed earlier, is a good example.

It may be helpful to understand the auto-ethnographic endeavours of insider research-ers who are representing non-metropolitan or marginalized social worlds as comprising part of what Edward Said calls the 'voyage in': the effort 'to enter into the discourse of Europe and the West, to mix with it, trans-form it, to make it acknowledge marginalized or suppressed or forgotten histories' (1993: 216). Insider researchers, because of their explicit boundary occupying positionality, are in a good position to do this in a way that views metropolitan and non-metropolitan experiences contrapuntally, as overlapping, intertwined and belonging together because they are connected by historical and contem-porary relations of power. To work effec-tively, contrapuntal analysis must work from 'a decentred consciousness' (Said, 1985: 14) that can bring into association 'geographi-cally, temporally and culturally discrepant experiences that may otherwise have been closed to one another, perhaps even suppres-sive of one another' (Karpinski, 1993, paragraph 5). Kincaid's (1988) engagement with the perspective of tourists in Antigua, Shrestha's (1995) self-examination from the perspective of development discourse, and Shimshali porters' conversations with trek-kers about the colonial antecedents of their contemporary mode of travel all operate contrapuntally.

As a method that seeks a common ground of assembly among decentred truths rather than appealing to a common centre of author-ity, a contrapuntal mode of analysis/evocation is characteristic of subaltern autoethnogra-phies as conceptualized by Pratt and provides a productive way for academic knowledge producers to construct and receive insider research as autoethnography. The metaphors of the 'voyage in' and contrapuntal represen-tation also work productively for the sorts of autoethnographic narratives of the self that Ellis and Bochner advocate, in two ways. First, attempts to self-consciously incorpo-rate the nuances of personal experiences into scholarly accounts of a way of life that exceeds an individual's experiences may be

understood as efforts to 'acknowledge mar-ginalized or suppressed or forgotten histo-ries' (Said, 1993: 216), with implicit objec-tives of unsettling conventional academic understandings and master epistemologies of detachment, representativeness and objectiv-ity. Second, personal narrative researchers, like subaltern autoethnographers and insider researchers, are boundary dwellers. Their self-representations are produced from an authorial location between authorized knowl-edge and personal experience, and the forms of writing they employ to collapse distinc-tions between representing and performing experience show these sources of knowledge to be overlapping and intertwined because they are connected in the production and performance, simultaneously, of both a per-sonal narrative and a self.

CONCLUSION – AUTOETHNOGRAPHY AS SENSIBILITY

This chapter has discussed three loosely-configured understandings of autoethnogra-phy in order to show how bringing their distinctive orientations, preoccupations, and insights into conversation with one another may yield an autoethnographic sensibility. In approaching the chapter this way I have con-centrated less on how to do any of the various types of autoethnography than on describing how a sensitivity to the autoethnographic characteristics of much research practice and many of the representations we produce and analyze may serve as a productive epistemo-logical resource for a wide variety of qualita-tive research including, but certainly not limited to, research on geographical topics. Five main insights of an autoethnographic sensibility as they emerged in the preceding discussion are summarized below:

1. Autoethnography is distinct from everyday prac-tices of self-representation in that it is self-conscious, reflexive, concerned with intervening in conventional academic knowledge production,

and focused on understanding and exemplifying social circumstances or relations beyond the individual self. Qualitative researchers should recognize that an epistemological characteristic of the self-representations we receive from our research subjects is that they are self-conscious and have these autoethnographic attributes. They are exercises in rewriting the self and the social.

2. More than an exercise in representation – which personal narrative autoethnographers argue cannot directly capture lived experience – autoethnography as an academic practice seeks to perform experience textually. This deliberate process of producing a self for oneself simultaneous to producing a self for one's others highlights the extent to which all efforts by qualitative researchers to incorporate their own experiences, feelings and emotions into their analyses are self-constructions as well as self-representations; again, they are exercises in rewriting the self and the social that may be aided by using some of the forms of experimental writing advocated by personal narrative autoethnographers.

3. Autoethnography in all its forms is a persuasive endeavour that incorporates the intimacies of experience, emotion and self-reflection into self-representations that are designed to intervene in circuits of authorized knowledge. As attempted interventions – efforts to act on another's actual or potential actions – autoethnographies are political undertakings. As persuasive acts they must seek a receptive audience, and therefore be responsive to power relations, conceding something in terms of idiom, rhetorical style and content to the circuits of authorized knowledge they hope to influence. This means that autoethnographic self-representations cannot be too self-absorbed; to be effectively persuasive – and in order to succeed in rewriting the social – they must situate themselves in relation to a wider social field that incorporates an intended audience.

4. Autoethnographic representations are self-conscious and self-interested; authored truths that have a persuasive purpose in the world. By recognizing the autoethnographic characteristics of much communication, qualitative researchers may move beyond the untenable epistemological position that our research subjects are providing us with either naïve truth or instrumental deception. Rather, what we learn from research subjects about their experiences, emotions and opinions should be understood as sincere self-constructions that are produced in the micro social context of the research interaction, and influenced by their ambitions with regard to producing selves for themselves and selves for circulation and interpretation in the spheres of authorized academic knowledge. Much of what qualitative researchers do is interpret autoethnographic representations. This realization leaves us with the self-reflexive tasks of (a) questioning how our own positionality, comportment and self-representation in relation to our research subjects influences their self-representations, and (b) discerning whether and how we may (want to) facilitate or support our research subjects' persuasive intentions. Our 'field' is the world between ourselves and the people we research.

5. Autoethnographic representations strive to communicate across the space between inside/self and outside/other. The context of outside/other influences representations of inside/self, so the latter cannot be understood as autochthonous or authentic in any straightforward way. This is most evidently the case with insider and Native researchers, who clearly occupy subject positionings between academic and non-academic circuits of experience and knowledge. The epistemological advantages of insider research, therefore, have less to do with 'Native authenticity' than with a multiple positionality that facilitates the translation of experience and knowledge across social worlds, often between the periphery and the metropolis. Positioned as they are at the unstable margins of dominant discourse, insider researchers are in a position to deconstruct essentializing assumptions about the authenticity of Nativeness/otherness, and show autoethnographically how dominant and subjugated knowledges and experiences are overlapping, intertwined and connected by relations of power. The representations of academic ethnographic 'others' provide the most obvious example of a general characteristic of autoethnography: that it is always in some way a voyage into authorized knowledge intended to mingle with it, influence it and make it acknowledge marginalized or suppressed sources of (experiential and emotional) knowledge.

Finally, autoethnographic research should be appealing to geographers because its emotionally invested, experiential perspective is grounded in place, saturated with local specificity, the ebb and flow of daily life and what is going on behind the scenes.

It provides access to the affective qualities of place. To the extent that autoethnographies attempt a 'voyage in' from the margins of authorized knowledge they have additional appeal to geographers. Autoethnographers in each of the traditions discussed in the chapter are often able to provide a knowledgeable perspective on the metropolis from the margins, trace historical connections, flows of power and lines of association among places and describe relations of contact among geographically disparate groups. In so doing, they offer insights into transculturation, hybridity and other deeply geographical phenomena from perspectives that are not often acknowledged in Geography.

REFERENCES

Adams, V. (1996) *Tigers of the snow and other virtual sherpas: an ethnography of Himalayan encounters.* Princeton: Princeton University Press.

Al-Hindi, K. Falconer and Kawabata, H. (2002) 'Toward a more fully reflexive feminist geography', in P. Moss (ed.) *Feminist geography in practice: research and methods.* Oxford: Blackwell. pp. 103–15.

Alexander, B.K. (2005) 'Performance ethnography: the re-enacting and inciting of culture', in N. Denzin and Y. Lincoln (eds) *The Sage handbook of qualitative research.* Thousand Oaks, CA: Sage. pp. 411–41.

Ali, I. and Butz, D. (2003) 'The Shimshal governance model – A community conserved area, a sense of cultural identity, a way of life', *Policy Matters* 12: 111–20.

Atkinson, P. (1997) 'Narrative turn in a blind alley', *Qualitative Health Research* 7 (3): 325–44.

Besio, K. (2003) '"Steppin'" in it: postcoloniality in northern Pakistan', *Area* 35 (1): 24–33.

Besio, K. (2005) 'Telling stories to hear autoethnography: researching women's lives in northern Pakistan', *Gender, Place and Culture* 12 (3): 317–31.

Besio, K. (2006) 'Chutes and ladders: negotiating gender and privilege in a village in northern Pakistan', *ACME: An International Journal of Critical Geographies* 5 (2): 230–57.

Besio, K. (2007) 'Depths of fields: travel photography and spatializing modernities in northern Pakistan', *Environment and Planning D: Society and Space* 25 (1): 53–74.

Besio, K. and Butz, D. (2004) 'Commentary – autoethnography: a limited endorsement', *The Professional Geographer* 56 (3): 432–38.

Bhabha, H. (1984) 'Of mimicry and man: the ambivalence of colonial discourse', *October* 28 (1): 125–33.

Bhabha, H. (1985) 'Signs taken for wonders: questions of ambivalence and authority under a tree outside Delhi, May 1817', *Critical Inquiry* 12 (1): 144–65.

Bishop, R. (2005) 'Freeing ourselves from neocolonial domination in research: a Kaupapa Māori approach to creating knowledge', in N. Denzin and Y. Lincoln (eds) *The Sage handbook of qualitative research.* Thousand Oaks, CA: Sage. pp. 109–38.

Bogdan, R. and Biklen, S.K. (1998) *Qualitative research for education: an introduction to theory and methods,* 3rd Edition. New York: Allyn and Bacon.

Bourdieu, P. (2003) 'Participant objectivation', *Journal of the Royal Anthropological Institute* NS 9 (2): 281–94.

Brettel, C. (1997) 'Blurred genres and blended voices: life history, biography, autobiography, and the auto/ethnography of women's lives', in D. Reed-Danahay (ed.) *Auto/ethnography: rewriting the self and the social.* Oxford: Berg. pp. 223–46.

Butz, D. (1998) 'Orientalist representations of resource use in Shimshal, Pakistan, and their extra-discursive effects', in I. Stellrecht (ed.) *Karakorum – Hindukush – Himalaya: Dynamics of change (Part 1).* Köln: Rüdiger Köppe Verlag. pp. 357–86.

Butz, D. (2001) 'Autobiography, autoethnography and intersubjectivity: analyzing communication in northern Pakistan', in P. Moss (ed.) *Placing autobiography in geography: history, method and analysis.* Syracuse: Syracuse University Press. pp. 149–66.

Butz, D. (2002a) 'Resistance, representation and third space in Shimshal village, northern Pakistan', *ACME: An International Journal of Critical Geographies* 1 (1): 15–34.

Butz, D. (2002b) 'Sustainable tourism and everyday life in Shimshal, Pakistan', *Tourism Recreation Research* 27 (3): 53–65.

Butz, D. (2006) 'Tourism and portering labour relations in Shimshal, Gojal Hunza', in H. Kreutzmann (ed.) *Karakoram in transition – The Hunza valley.* Oxford: Oxford University Press. pp. 394–403.

Butz, D. and Besio, K. (2004) 'The value of autoethnography for field research in transcultural settings', *The Professional Geographer* 56 (3): 350–60.

Butz, D. and MacDonald, K. (2001) 'Serving *sahibs* with pony and pen: the discursive uses of native authenticity', *Environment and Planning D: Society and Space* 19 (2): 179–201.

Carrard, P. (1992) *Poetics of the new history: French historical discourse from Braudel to Chartier.* Baltimore: Johns Hopkins Press.

Clifford, J. (1988) *The predicament of culture: twentieth-century ethnography, literature and art.* Cambridge: Harvard University Press.

Clifford, J. and Marcus, G.E. (eds) (1986) *Writing culture: the poetics and politics of ethnography.* Berkeley: University of California Press.

Cloke, P., Crang, P. and Goodwin, M. (1999) *Introducing human geographies.* London: Arnold.

Cook, I. (2001) '"You want to be careful you don't end up like Ian. He's all over the place": autobiography in/of an expanded field', in P. Moss (ed.) *Placing autobiography in geography: history, method and analysis.* Syracuse: Syracuse University Press. pp. 99–120.

Corey, F.C. (1998) 'The personal: against the master narrative', in S.J. Dailey (ed.) *The future of performance studies: visions and revisions.* Annandale, VA: National Communication Association. pp. 249–53.

Crang, M. (2003) 'Qualitative methods: touchy, feely, look-see?', *Progress in Human Geography* 27 (4): 494–504.

Crang, M. (2005) 'Qualitative methods: there is nothing outside the text?', *Progress in Human Geography* 29 (2): 225–33.

Deck, A. (1990) 'Autoethnography: Zora Neale Hurston, Noni Jabavu, and cross-disciplinary discourse', *Black American Literature Forum* 24 (2): 237–56.

DeLyser, D. (2001) '"Do you really live here?" Thoughts on insider research', *The Geographical Review* 91 (1–2): 441–53.

Denzin, N.K. (1989) *Interpretive biography.* Newbury Park, CA: Sage.

Denzin, N.K. and Lincoln, Y.S. (2005) 'Introduction: the discipline and practice of qualitative research', in N.K. Denzin and Y.S. Lincoln (eds) *The handbook of qualitative research,* 3rd Edition. Thousand Oaks, CA: Sage. pp. 1–32.

Ellis, C. (1993) '"There are survivors": telling a story of sudden death', *The Sociological Quarterly* 34 (4): 711–30.

Ellis, C. (1995) *Final negotiations: a story of love, loss and chronic illness.* Walnut Creek, CA: Alta-Mira Press.

Ellis, C. (2004) *The ethnographic I: a methodological novel about autoethnography.* Walnut Creek, CA: Alta-Mira Press.

Ellis, C. and Bochner, A.P. (2000) 'Autoethnography, personal narrative, reflexivity: researcher as subject', in N.K. Denzin and Y.S. Lincoln (eds) *The handbook of qualitative research.* Thousand Oaks, CA: Sage. pp. 733–68.

Elwood, S. and Martin, D. (2000) '"Placing" interviews: location and scales of power in qualitative research', *The Professional Geographer* 52 (4): 649–57.

England, K. (1994) 'Getting personal: reflexivity, positionality, and feminist research', *The Professional Geographer* 46 (1): 80–9.

Ghosh, A. (1998) *In an antique land.* London: Granta Books.

Gold, L. (2002) 'Positionality, worldview and geographical research: a personal account of a research journey', *Ethics, Place and Environment* 5 (3): 223–37.

Griffiths, G. (1994) 'The myth of authenticity: representation, discourse and social practice', in C. Tiffin and A. Lawson (eds) *De-scribing empire: post-colonialism and textuality.* London: Routledge. pp. 70–85.

Hardwick, S.W. (2001) 'Identity, place and locale in Galveston', *The Geographical Review* 91 (1–2): 335–41.

Hayano, D. (1979) 'Auto-ethnography: paradigms, problems and prospects', *Human Organization* 38 (1): 99–104.

Hélias, P-J. (1978) *The horse of pride: life in a Breton village.* June Guicharnaud (Trans.). New Haven and London: Yale University Press.

Herod, A. (1999) 'Reflections on interviewing foreign elites: praxis, positionality, validity and the cult of the insider', *Geoforum* 30 (4): 313–27.

Hyndman, J. (2001) 'The field as here and now, not there and then', *The Geographical Review* 91 (1–2): 262–72.

Karpinski, E. (1993) 'Review of Edward Said's *Culture and imperialism*', *College Quarterly* 1 (2), http://www.senecac.on.ca/quarterly.

Katz, C. (1992) 'All the world is staged: intellectuals and the projects of ethnography'. *Environment and Planning D: Society and Space* 10 (5): 495–510.

Katz, C. (1994) 'Playing the field: questions of fieldwork in ethnography', *The Professional Geographer* 46 (1): 67–72.

Kincaid, J. (1988) *A small place.* New York: Penguin.

Lambeck, M. (2005) 'Our subjects/our selves: a view from the back seat', in A. Meneley and D. Young (eds) *Auto-ethnographies: the anthropology of academic practice.* Peterborough: Broadview Press. pp. 229–40.

Lejeune, P. (1989) *On autobiography.* Katherine Leary (Trans.). Minneapolis: University of Minnesota Press.

Lionnet, F. (1989) *Autobiographical voices: race, gender, self-portraiture.* Ithaca, NY: Cornell University Press.

MacDonald, K. (1998) 'Push and shove: spatial history and the construction of a portering economy in northern Pakistan', *Comparative Studies in Society and History* 40 (2): 287–317.

MacDonald, K. and Butz, D. (1998) 'Investigating portering relations as a locus for transcultural interaction in the Karakoram region of northern Pakistan', *Mountain Research and Development* 18 (4): 333–43.

Malinowski, B. (1967) *A diary in the strict sense of the term.* Norbert Guterman (Trans.). New York: Harcourt, Brace & World.

Marcus, G.E. and Fischer, M.J.M. (1986) *Anthropology as cultural critique: an experimental moment in the human sciences.* Chicago: University of Chicago Press.

McDowell, L. (1992) 'Valid games? A response to Erica Schoenberger', *The Professional Geographer* 44 (2): 212–15.

McGee, T. (1995) 'Eurocentrism and geography: reflections on Asian urbanization', in J. Crush (ed.) *Power of development.* London: Routledge. pp. 192–207.

Meneley, A. and Young, D. (eds) (2005) *Auto-ethnographies: the anthropology of academic practice.* Peterborough: Broadview Press.

Mernissi, F. (1994) *Dreams of trespass: tales of a harem girlhood.* Cambridge, MA: Perseus Books.

Miles, M. and Crush, J. (1993) 'Personal narratives as interactive texts: collecting and interpreting migrant life-histories', *The Professional Geographer* 45 (1): 95–129.

Moss, P. (1995) 'Embeddedness in practice, numbers in context: the politics of knowing and doing', *The Professional Geographer* 47 (4): 442–49.

Moss, P. (1999) 'Autobiographical notes on chronic illness', in H. Parr and R. Butler (eds) *Mind and body spaces.* London: Routledge. pp. 155–66.

Moss, P. (ed) (2001) *Placing autobiography in geography.* Syracuse: Syracuse University Press.

Motzafi-Haller, P. (1997) 'Writing birthright: on native anthropologists and the politics of representation', in D. Reed-Danahay (ed.) *Auto/Ethnography: rewriting the self and the social.* Oxford: Berg. pp. 195–222.

Mullings, B. (1999) 'Insider or outsider, both or neither: some dilemmas of interviewing in a cross-cultural setting', *Geoforum* 30 (4): 337–50.

Narayan, K. (1993) 'How native is a "native" anthropologist?', *American Anthropologist* 95 (3): 671–86.

Nast, H.J. (1994) 'Opening remarks on "Women in the field"', *The Professional Geographer* 46 (1): 54–66.

Porteous, J.D. (1989) *Planned to death: the annihilation of a place called Howdendyke.* Toronto: University of Toronto Press.

Pratt, M.L. (1992) *Imperial eyes: travel writing and transculturation.* London: Routledge.

Pratt, M.L. (1994) 'Transculturation and autoethnography: Peru, 1615/1980', in F. Barker, P. Hulme and M. Iversen (eds) *Colonial discourse/postcolonial theory.* Manchester: Manchester University Press. pp. 24–46.

Pratt, M.L. (1999) Apocalypse in the Andes. *Americas* 51 (4):38–47.

Rabinow, P. (1977) *Reflections on fieldwork in Morocco.* Berkeley: University of California Press.

Reed-Danahay, D. (ed.) (1997a) *Auto/ethnography: Rewriting the self and the social.* Oxford: Berg.

Reed-Danahay, D. (1997b) 'Introduction', in D. Reed-Danahay (ed.) *Auto/ethnography: rewriting the self and the social.* Oxford: Berg. pp. 1–20.

Richardson, L. (1994) 'Writing: a method of inquiry', in N.K. Denzin and Y.S. Lincoln (eds) *Handbook of qualitative research.* Thousand Oaks, CA: Sage. pp. 516–29.

Rose, G. (1997) 'Situating knowledges: positionality, reflexivity and other tactics', *Progress in Human Geography* 21 (3): 305–20.

Roth, R. (2001) 'A self-reflective exploration into development research', in P. Moss (ed.) *Placing autobiography in geography: history, method and analysis.* Syracuse: Syracuse University Press. pp. 121–37.

Sabra, S. (2005) 'From 1940s Fez to 1990s Paris: conceptualising contact zones and understanding autoethnography in a global arena of representation', Unpublished MA Thesis, Brock University, St. Catharines, Ontario.

Said. E.W. (1985) 'Orientalism reconsidered', *Race and Class* 27 (2): 1–15.

Said, E.W. (1993) *Culture and imperialism.* New York: Alfred A. Knopf.

Saltmarsh, R. (2001) 'A journey into autobiography: a coal miner's daughter', in P. Moss (ed.) *Placing autobiography in geography: history, method and analysis.* Syracuse: Syracuse University Press. pp. 138–48.

Sangarasivam, Y. (2001) 'Researcher, informant, "assassin" me', *The Geographical Review* 91 (1/2): 95–104.

Schoenberger, E. (1992) 'Self-criticism and self-awareness in research: a reply to Linda McDowell', *The Professional Geographer* 44 (2): 215–18.

Scott, J.C. (1990) *Domination and the arts of resistance*. New Haven: Yale University Press.

Shrestha, N. (1995) 'Becoming a development category', in J. Crush (ed.) *Power of development*. London: Routledge. pp. 266–77.

Slemon, S. (1995) 'Unsettling the empire: resistance theory for the second world', in B. Ashcroft, G. Griffiths and H. Tiffin (eds) *The postcolonial studies reader*. London: Routledge. pp. 104–10.

Smith, L.T. (2005) 'On tricky ground: researching the native in the age of uncertainty', in N. Denzin and Y. Lincoln (eds) *The Sage handbook of qualitative research*. Thousand Oaks, CA: Sage. pp. 85–108.

Spivak, G.C. (1999) *A critique of postcolonial reason: toward a history of the vanishing present*. Cambridge: Harvard University Press.

Staeheli, L. and Lawson, V. (1994) 'A discussion of "women in the field": the politics of feminist fieldwork', *The Professional Geographer* 46 (1): 96–102.

Strathern, M. (1987) 'The limits of auto-anthropology', in A. Jackson (ed.) *Anthropology at home*. London: Tavistock. pp. 16–37.

Tedlock, B. (1991) 'From participant observation to the observation of participation: the emergence of narrative ethnography', *Journal of Anthropological Research* 47 (1): 69–94.

Trinh, T.M. (1991) *When the moon waxes red: representation and cultural politics*. London: Routledge.

Valentine, G. (1998) '"Sticks and stones may break my bones": a personal geography of harassment', *Antipode* 30 (4): 305–32.

Young, D.J. and Meneley, A. (2005) 'Introduction', in Anne Meneley and Donna Young (eds) *Auto-ethnographies: the anthropology of academic practice*. Peterborough: Broadview Press. pp. 1–21.

9

Interviewing: Fear and Liking in the Field

Linda McDowell

You do not have to say anything. But it may harm your defence if you do not mention when questioned something you later rely on in court. Anything you do say may be given in evidence.

Police caution when arrested in the UK

WHAT MATTERS?

Words, stories, narratives matter. It is how we explain ourselves to others, how we justify our actions (or inaction), how we present ourselves to others. But interviews, like the classic police interview that starts with the verbal warning above, are also more than a straightforward or simple exchange of words. Relations of power and authority affect the nature of exchanges, most clearly in the police interview but in almost all social interactions. And body 'language' matters too: a suspect may sweat or twitch, and avoid eye contact with the interrogator. In job interviews, where we are a supplicant rather than a suspect, we tend to 'dress to impress'. In a recent UK guide to interviews for university candidates, for example, it was suggested that young women interviewees should avoid short skirts or large earrings which may distract the interviewer but in interviews

that I have undertaken with women working in merchant bankers, some of the more senior and successful women suggested that dressing to catch the eye, to stand out, is a better strategy when dealing with the banks' clients. Clearly assumptions about the gender of the people to be impressed are also embedded in this contradictory advice to women.

So language, bodies, clothes, gender, clearly matter in the sorts of exchanges that take place in interviews. Commonsense, I hear you muttering, everybody knows that. Yet in human geography and the social sciences more generally, the significance of the personal nature of the interaction and the consequent impact of embodied social characteristics was not widely accepted until relatively recently. Now, however, these questions of embodiment as well as the affects of language and questions about interpretation and representation have become central to philosophical discussions in the social sciences including human geography, as well as to the nature and practice of talking to people in a wide range of circumstances and locations (see for example Pryke et al., 2003). For human geographers interested in the difference that place makes to the public and private lives of individuals, households, social groups, communities, gangs, outcasts, hermits, wanderers, nomads, vagrants, professionals, workers, government officials, children, patients – the list is long – talking to people, some form of personal interaction between researchers and the people we are interested in is the most obvious method of collecting 'data'. But, as I have already intimated, this relatively simple statement hides a multitude of complex issues which are the focus of this chapter and of two related chapters – those by Jacquie Burgess on focus groups and Peter Jackson and Polly Russell on collecting life histories. With interviewing, these methods are now amongst the most common of the qualitative approaches utilised by human geographers in the collection of information about past and present lives and the circumstances that influence the course that they take. And because interviewing does involve personal contacts and interactions, it is perhaps the most exciting and the most challenging of the methods currently in wide use.

I have been interviewing people in the UK during my entire academic career so far – from steel workers in Corby New Town, local authority officials in Brighton, bankers in the City of London, young men in Sheffield and Cambridge, parents in London and Manchester, Latvian migrants in Leicestershire and elsewhere and, most recently, new migrants from the European Union and elsewhere working in service sector industries in Greater London. And yet each time, before I go to talk to the people I have identified as important to the aims of my work, my heart thumps, my palms sweat and I wonder whether I have the energy, confidence and the sheer check required to persuade them to share with me the sometimes intimate and occasionally painful details of their lives for what might seem to them to be very little return. The returns for me, perhaps unfairly, are much greater. I get to meet a range of interesting people often in circumstances that are new to me: people who tell me the most interesting and important things about their lives without necessarily expecting, or indeed wanting, reciprocal disclosures on my part. To add to this inequity, what they tell me

eventually appears as a scholarly paper in an academic journal or as a book that other people then ask me to talk about, raising more new and interesting questions for me to consider. In this process as I have outlined it, the emphasis shifts from an initial focus on the lives and stories of the people interviewed to a focus on the researcher who becomes responsible for both the interpretation and the reception of other people's lives.

Fieldwork, then, is often transformative for researchers but probably is much less often as exciting for those who are interviewed, although here too in recent years, we spend rather more time than previously thinking about the impact of an interview on the people involved than perhaps we used to (see for example Eyles and Smith, 1988; Limb and Dwyer, 2001). In this chapter I want to try and capture something of the fear and the delight of interviewing, as well as address the philosophical and ethical issues raised rather than provide a detailed technical guide to informant selection, question order or analysis and interpretation, although these questions will not be entirely ignored. There is already a whole series of useful articles, books, pamphlets, guides and on-line resources to turn too, that are easily available and accessible to novices, whether new researchers experimenting with different approaches or the lecturer who is asked to teach qualitative methods to beginners (Flowerdew and Martin, 1997; Kitchen and Tate, 2000; Mason, 2002; Silverman, 2000). Furthermore, many questions about data, confidentiality, analysis and interpretation that apply to interviews in general are addressed by Jackson and Russell in the succeeding chapter. So, this chapter is in a way an introductory exercise before their more detailed exposition.

WHY DO INTERVIEWS?

Perhaps the first question to think about is why interviews are a useful technique. As with all qualitative methods, the aim is to probe an issue in depth: the purpose is to explore and understand actions within specific settings, to examine human relationships and discover as much as possible about why people feel or act in the ways they do. In comparison to large-scale quantitative techniques, interview methodologies typically aim for depth and detailed understanding rather than breadth and coverage. Interviews are often associated with case study approaches rather than attempts to include a large sample, although short postal schedules or telephone interviews are a common way of collecting a limited range of material from a large population. As the interviewer and interviewee are not co-present in these encounters, as the scale of the work usually is large and the questions straight forward (to avoid misunderstandings), this type of interview methodology might more accurately be placed on the quantitative side of the methodological divide.

What distinguishes most interviews, however, is the scope they provide for probing meanings and emotions: interviewing is an *interpretative* methodology. It is this claim that has been at the heart of a fascinating philosophical debate about interviews as social encounters for the last three decades or so. I want to capture the main arguments in what follows. But first a brief reminder: interviews are often used in association with other methods – both qualitative and quantitative – in part as all social scientists who undertake interviews to explore what is going on in particular places and circumstance draw on a range of other methods to check our interpretations of what people tell them. Newspaper articles, census data, films, diaries may all be useful in providing both context and validation of the material collected through interviewing people.

WHERE TO START?

Undertaking interviews of any kind involves both a number of chronological decisions

and stages as well as a set of philosophical, political and ethical issues that underpin both the initial decision to adopt interviews as part of or the main methodological strategy and the practical issues that are important at different stages of the research. Thus, questions about identification, contacts, interactions, interpretation and representation are important at different stages in the process whereas issues of ethics, responsibility, equity, status and power underlie the whole process. It is these underlying issues about power and equality that I want to focus on in more detail, as well as arguments about the nature of knowledge constructed through fieldwork. It is here too that the debates in the social sciences about interviewing in particular and qualitative methods in general have been transformed in recent years.

When I first started interviewing migrant men working in the steel industry as part of an undergraduate project in the early 1970s, there was a widespread and strongly-held belief that such an approach should and must conform to what were then the key standards of scientific method – that is rigour, objectivity and replication. The social characteristics of the researcher about to go out into the city streets or the villages of an unknown rural area were completely ignored, seen as irrelevant to the whole process and talk revolved around the nature of the 'survey instrument' that was to be utilised in the proposed exchange. The extract below from Ann Oakley's book *Becoming a Mother Martin* (1979) lays out the advice she received as a social researcher planning to undertake interviews and the dilemmas it raised when she started interviewing pregnant women in the early 1970s for her doctoral research. At the time she was a mother of a small child and she became pregnant herself half-way though her project.

In the passage below Oakley (1979: 209) sets out the advice that was common at the time she began her research.

Regarded as an information-gathering tool, the interview is designed to minimise the local, concrete, immediate circumstances of the particular encounter – including the respective personalities of the participants – and to emphasize only those aspects that can be kept general and demonstrable enough to be counted. As an encounter between two particular people the typical interview has no meaning; it is conceived in a framework of other comparable meetings between other couples ... . (Denzin, 1970: 196)

But, as Oakley found, an interview is in practice a local and immediate encounter and the people involved in the exchange matter. 'Contrary to what the text-books say, researching and being researched are parts of *human* interaction' (Oakley, 1979: 310). The pregnant women whom she interviewed asked questions about her circumstances, about being pregnant and wanted advice when they discovered that she was already a mother. She answered as best she could and, as she found, 'there were times in the research when I began to confuse roles – researcher, pregnant woman, mother, feminist, participant observer and so on' (Oakley, 1979: 4). 'The point is', she concluded, 'that academic research projects bear an intimate relationship to the researcher's life, however "scientific" a sociologist pretends to be' (p. 4). Interviews are not and can never be 'typical' – one instance among comparable others, as the methods textbooks then insisted, but instead capture the variety of meanings and experiences. Thus, through interviews, difference rather than similarity in experiences is explored and so generalisations may be challenged, as well as allowing into both the encounter and the resulting text the emotions and feelings of the subjects, and more recently the researcher.

In the years since Oakley began her research, feminist arguments about power and responsibility, about rapport and positionality (Gluck and Patai, 1991; Bell *et al.*, 1993; Professional Geographer, 1994), work by radical anthropologists about dialogic writing and the politics of texts (Clifford and Marcus, 1986), and in the 1990s the wholesale impact of post-modern work in the humanities and the social sciences (Roseneau, 1992; Smart, 1993; Yeatman, 1994; Butler, 2002) have revolutionised understandings of

what is involved in interviewing, transforming the relationship between thought and materiality. Those older ideas that the exchange of information involved in an interview was independent of the social characteristics of those involved or of the place, time of day, the topics involved or whether payment was involved or not have now been overturned, although it is important not to exaggerate the extent of the shift nor its immediacy. Indeed, recent debates about affect in human geography seem unaware of the long debate within feminist theory about the place of emotions in social encounters.

At the same time as Oakley was struggling with the advice to be neutral and scientific in the 1970s, other social researchers had begun to recognise that personalities and opinions mattered, although their emphasis was on how structures of power and inequality influence research encounters rather than on issues of inter-personal interactions, emotions and feelings. Thus in a book published in the late 1970s based on ten personal accounts of doing research, it was argued that 'social research is political because the researcher has interests which may coincide with or contradict the interests of the researched. All social research has an end: the formulation of policy, the conservation, reform or radical transformation of the social situation being studied' (Cass *et al.*, 1978: 143) so social science is a *political* endeavour. Here we see links between methodological debates and some of the claims for a radical or critical practice of human geography that were evident in the 1970s and 1980s. I shall return to arguments about political purpose and transformative possibilities of qualitative research at the end of the chapter.

LANGUAGE MATTERS

From the late 1970s onwards, then, there has been a wholesale challenge to the notions of scientific objectivity in interviewing and to the transparency of the exchange of information through careful consideration of what James Clifford and George Marcus (1986) termed the poetics and politics of all cultural exchanges. Language, it is now recognised, is not a neutral instrument of communication but instead it produces, as Judith Butler (1993) has noted, 'the effects that it names' (p. 2). 'Reality' is no longer assumed to be 'out there', waiting to be discovered, named and described by social researchers but is itself constituted in and by discourse, and embodied interactions, as are the representations that we chose to construct from fieldwork and interviewing. Thus we construct questions to ask and make knowledge claims on the basis of what we discover though the already existing conventions of language and discourse within which we are working.

Here the work of Michel Foucault, the French historian and philosopher who was writing on the history of sexuality, the penal system, modern medicine and systems of classification in the second half of the twentieth century, has had a significant influence on geographical practice and scholarship. He argued that all knowledge is constructed within interrelated sets of statements or discourses that establish the ways in which it is possible to make statements about things. These discursive practices, he argues, are based in systems of power, in which it is possible only to make certain claims. Discursive practices thus establish what it is possible to speak about, to define and research. Such practices thus, Foucault (1977) argued, construct 'a delimitation of a field of objects, the definition of a legitimate perspective for the agent of knowledge and the fixing of norms for the elaboration of concepts and theories' (p. 23). It might help to think through this claim with an example.

Let's go back to Ann Oakley's work. Before she wrote her book on becoming a mother, she was responsible, almost singlehandedly, for putting the issue of housework on the social sciences agenda. Asking questions about and collecting information on who did what within the home had, before

the publication of her book *The Sociology of Housework* in 1974, barely appeared at all on the agenda of sociology or geography. Because work was defined solely as waged labour in the labour market, what went on in private (and here is a second contested term – you might like to think about why the home was seen as a private arena despite its penetration by all sort of capitalist goods and services and its regulation by state officials such as planners, health workers, and so forth), in the private sphere of the home was disregarded as a suitable subject for either theorisation or empirical investigation. In establishing how to explain this absence, views and opinions about the significance of women's place in the contemporary world then become important. Individualist explanations based on women's choices or their natural aptitude for certain types of repetitive work leave little to explain, whereas different philosophical positions – perhaps based on the necessity of housework for the functioning of a capitalist economy or in beliefs about male power and the oppression of women – open the possibility of empirical investigation based in part on interviews with the key actors that feature in the different explanatory frameworks. Nicky Gregson and Michelle Lowe's (1994) excellent book on commodified domestic work was one result of this re-conceptualisation of the significance of housework and has been followed by a long series of investigations of what goes on in the 'private' sphere of the home in which interviewing has been a key methodological strategy (for just two more recent examples of work by geographers see Blunt, 2005; Pratt, 2003).

It is clear then that starting a research project involving interviewing is a complex matter. The very issues that we decide interest us as well as the detailed questions that we plan to ask our interviewees are all set in the frame of already existing discourses, in our engagement in existing work and our commitment to a broader philosophical position that underpins our decision to do a certain type of work. These questions about power and poetics, about language, theory and context have become particularly significant for geographers as one of the effects of the post-structural and post-modern turn in the 1990s has been a growing interest in the theoretical significance of place, in diversity, difference and particularity, and its significance in the explanation of patterns of inequality. Some of these changes are captured in Doreen Massey's book *For Space* (2005) where she explores some of the complex philosophical origins in her commitment to theorising the significance of spatial diversity.

Rather than searching for law-like regularities in the lab or the library, the dominant purpose of those years of spatial science, many human geographers have (re)turned to fieldwork to explore difference and have adopted the interview as their main approach. However, theory, context and structures still matter. Like many theorists of the particularity of place, I see it as constituted in the coincidence of social process and flows/ interconnections across different spatial scales. As always, for social researchers, the relationships between structures and agency, about constraints and choice, and the adoption of different theoretical positions to explain these relationships influence our initial questions, our methodological strategies and how we interpret our findings. Although through interviews we often are searching for the difference that place makes, in interpretation we test these particularities against broader or more general theoretical explanations of how we think the world works. Thus although Denzin's advice to minimize 'the local, concrete and immediate circumstances' is now generally disregarded (and he has changed his own mind), for geographers the difference made by the local and concrete is often the very thing of interest. This local particularity or difference, however, typically is interpreted within a broader structural context. Indeed as I have argued elsewhere (McDowell, 2004), I believe that one of the key issues in contemporary theorising in human geography is how to combine a discursive relational approach to difference and particularity with the continuing significance of categorical inequalities.

TALKING TO WHICH OTHERS ABOUT WHAT?

I want now to assume that detailed reading and the development of an acceptable philosophical framework and a set of beliefs about what needs to be done has resulted in the identification not only of a research topic but a potential set or sets of people to interview. Actually identifying, contacting and arranging to meet interviewees often raises complicated logistical and ethical questions. And here too the philosophical notions that lie behind such encounters have also changed in recent years. Rather than being a transparent, straightforward exchange of information, the interview is a complex and contested social encounter riven with power relations. To a large degree, the social researcher is a supplicant, dependent upon the cooperation of interviewees, who must both agree to participate and feel willing and able to share with the interviewer the sorts of information on which the success of the work will depend. When interviewing the powerful – perhaps politicians, government officials, media 'stars' or whomsoever – the interviewer is frequently the less powerful party in the encounter but might also have in common social or educational background, class position or accent with the interviewees, leading to a sense of ease in the exchanges.

In other cases, however, interviewers are less obviously supplicants when the interviewees are much younger, less educated, or less socially skilled than they are and here care has to be taken not to intimidate or overwhelm potential participants. Even so, growing numbers of people have at least some experience of being interviewed: at school, for college entry, by their doctor, in applications for loans, as part of opinion polls and talk shows. Indeed, the interview is now such a ubiquitous feature of everyday life that some scholars have characterised the USA as 'the interview society' (Silverman, 1993; Atkinson and Silverman, 1997). The police interview that I began with or the research interview at issue here are now the norm rather than exceptions. As the contemporary media have become more and more intrusive it seems as if almost any member of the population is fair game for the most intrusive type of questioning. Indeed in their chapter on interviewing in a huge and comprehensive handbook on qualitative methods (interestingly co-edited by the same Denzin discussed by Ann Oakley: see Denzin and Lincoln, 2005), Andre Fontana and James Fey (2005) have suggested, drawing on Jaber Gubrium and James Holstein (1998), that 'the interview has become a contemporary means of storytelling in which persons divulge life accounts in response to interview enquiries' (p. 699).

Interviewers, nevertheless, often have to work hard to secure agreement and involvement and even harder to construct an encounter in which the exchange is both sufficiently collaborative to make the 'respondents' feel comfortable and that their participation is highly valued while at the same time not being overly intrusive or too focused on the interviewer's own life, values and beliefs. It has been suggested that revealing something of yourself, your own circumstances and feelings is a way to persuade interviewees of your good faith. However, getting personal should be more than just a way of squeezing more information out of people, but rather a way of creating both greater empathy and attempting to reduce the power differentials in the actual encounter, even if this is wishful thinking at the broader social scale. The idea that the interview exchange is more of a collaboration than an interrogation has now permeated geographical research and in common with anthropologists, geographers are now much more aware of the ways in which an interview is and should be an interactive and reflexive exchange wherever possible.

In establishing contact and arranging interviews, researchers must always follow the ethical code of their own institution and professional association. As a general rule, children and young adults under the age of 18 must not be interviewed alone and parental permission must be sought. In the UK, a police check is also necessary for those hoping to work with children. The ethical and practical issues that arise working with children and young people are discussed in more detail in papers by *inter alia* Stuart Aitken (see Aitken and Thomas, 1997; Aitken, 2001), Gill Valentine (1999) and Linda McDowell (2001). Similar issues are raised and codes of conduct apply in interactions with groups in the population who might be regarded as 'vulnerable' – the very elderly perhaps, people who are confused or ill, or those whose lives and livelihood are in other ways insecure.

A good guide for making the initial contact and deciding where to meet, assuming the interview involves face-to-face interaction rather than being either an e-survey or based on a telephone interview is to use empathy and try and imagine yourself in the pace of the interviewees. Will they be scared by your approach? How much will they know or understand about your work? Do you want to see them in their place of work or study, at home (theirs or yours?) or on neutral ground and why? What difference will these decisions make? How will the interviewees react to you? Will they take you seriously? Are you too different to be able to establish a connection? Here I often reflect on my naivety when as a young white undergraduate student I interviewed steel workers in Corby New Town. These were men from the former Yugoslavia, Latvia and Ukraine who had fled Soviet repression and, after a period in displaced persons camps in Germany, had become workers in heavy industry in the UK. What possible point of contact could I have with them? And yet my unthinking confidence and their courtesy made the encounter both possible and interesting (at least for me) as

I collected narratives of displacement that much later led to a new research project with women who had come to England as 'volunteer workers' at the same time (McDowell, 2005). In the 1970s, however, we did not use the word 'narrative' and much of the personal information these men told me about their hopes and fears for their lives in the UK disappeared in the eventual product – a dissertation based on a factorial ecology.

Although in this case my initial focus and aims and the eventual result coincided, partly I think because I was too inexperienced to realise the value of what I had actually collected, in the initial encounter with their research 'subjects', interviewers must be aware of the provisional nature of their intended research focus. The range and scope of the research may be open to re-definition or renegotiation once contact is made with the participants in the research endeavour. Here's Philippe Bourgois (1995), whose wonderful study of crack dealers in New York City is an inspiration for all qualitative researchers, talking about how his research focus identified itself:

> I was forced into crack against my will. When I first moved to East Harlem – 'El Barrio' – as a newlywed in the Spring of 1985, I was looking for an inexpensive New York City apartment from which I could write a book on the experience of poverty and ethnic segregation in the heart of one of the most expensive cities in the world. On the level of theory, I was interested in the political economy of inner-city street culture. From a personal, political perspective, I wanted to probe the Achilles heel of the richest industrialised nation of the world by documenting how it imposes racial segregation and economic marginalisation on so many of its Latino/a and African-American citizens. (p. 1)

So here, Bourgois makes clear both the theoretical assumptions that underlie his choice of subject and location as well as his own political position, illustrating my earlier arguments about how theory and politics structure the choice of what to study. When he and his wife arrived in NYC, however, he found rather than exploring a range of street activities, selling and smoking crack imposed itself as the focus because of its growing significance in the area.

> I had never even heard of crack when I first arrived in the neighbourhood – no-one knew about this particular substance yet … by the end of the year, however, most of my friends, neighbours and acquaintances had been swept into the multibillion-dollar crack cyclone: selling it, smoking it, fretting over it. (p. 1)

So crack took over both as Bourgois' focus and, to a large extent, his life, as he talked to his interviewees in a range of places including on the street and in crack houses and in his own apartment where their behaviour often repulsed his family. Furthermore, his field-work raised difficult ethical issues about, for example, his possible involvement in illegal activities and in the inevitable encounters with law enforcement agencies that were part of his time on the streets. His class, accent and skin colour all had to be negotiated not only with his informants but also in encounters with the police:

> I was almost never harassed by the street sellers; at worst they simply fled from me or ignored me. On the other hand, I was repeatedly stopped, searched, cursed and humiliated by New York City police officers on the beat. Form their perspective there was no reason for a white boy to be in the neighbourhood unless he was an undercover cop or a drug addict, and because I am skinny they instantly assumed the latter. (Bourgois, 1995: 30)

While Bourgois' work raises questions of access and the performance of identity in perhaps extreme forms in its focus on illegal street activities, all researchers must address similar issues of how to negotiate their identities, especially in the initial contact. In my own work, I have often made the wrong decision in, for example, how I contacted people or in the methods I used to elicit opinions. In the work in Corby New Town that I have already mentioned, I appeared unannounced on the doorsteps of eastern European migrants, wielding an officious looking clipboard and so appearing as a rather threatening 'official' despite my (then) youth. And to my surprise now, nobody challenged me or even asked how I had acquired their name, nor did they ask about the purpose of the research. More recently, in selecting and interviewing young men with little education, I over-estimated their literacy and embarrassed one or two by giving them a too-complicated newspaper cutting as a stimulus to talk about sex.

And like Bourgois, I too have had the experience of my research focus being changed by circumstances. In my case, it was in the study of migrant women's lives in post-war Britain (see McDowell, 2005). My initial aim was to critically explore the hegemonic image of domestic femininity that was established in post-war Britain and so I decided to explore the lives of a group of women who were clearly non-conformists, that is women in the labour market during the late 1940s and throughout the 1950s. I chose as possible interviewees a group of Latvian women who had come to the UK between 1946 and 1949 as migrant workers, recruited by the British Government to work in female-employing sectors that were short of labour – textiles, hospitals and various forms of institutional domestic service. I worked hard to produce an unstructured questionnaire schedule to explore the intersections and contradictions between their home and 'working' lives, but these women, when I began to talk to them, had a clear set of ideas about what they wanted me to know: about Soviet aggression in Latvia (one of the three Baltic states), about the German and Soviet occupations, about the years they spent in displaced persons' camps in post-war Germany. Only then would they turn to what was to them the relatively unimportant topic of their lives in the UK. And so my research changed and the eventual book is as much about the Second World War and about national memory as it is about divisions of labour in post-war Britain.

Times have changed, of course, and in the 'interview society', people are now more cautious and more savvy about being interviewed. In the work with bankers for example, I was subjected to intense cross-questioning about the research aims. Here is a further ethical dilemma: how much should/ must a researcher reveal about the purpose of the work to facilitate access? In general, I believe in honesty and openness but this principle might conflict with access and with the quality of the interview encounter. Was it reasonable of me to present myself to the gatekeepers in the merchant banks where I interviewed workers in the mid-1990s as interested in human capital and personnel policies or should I have admitted to a theoretical (and practical) interest in women's oppression, discrimination against women and members of minority groups, in sexualised workplace cultures and their effects? In all these examples, too, whether with male workers in heavy industry, with bourgeois bankers in the City of London, with working class young men and with elderly women of my mother's age, issues of class, gender, accent, previous experiences and shared (or not) knowledge make a difference to the encounter. There are no easy guidelines about establishing contact and rapport, although practice certainly helps and courtesy, a certain degree of persistence and open-mindedness are essential.

HOW TO DO IT?

One the difficult issues of what the focus of research should be and who to talk to in order to construct a detailed picture of what is going on, the more mundane details of what sort of interviewing to undertake tend to pale into insignificance. But here too questions about empathy, power and control, and the degree of mutual respect and collaboration that is achievable influence decisions. Interviewing ranges from the more to the less formal through the use of structured to unstructured sets of questions (sometimes grandly called the survey instrument) and what to chose depends both on the interviewees and on the skill and confidence of the interviewers. It is easier to administer a formal questionnaire survey than a less structured one but only if the respondents (and the interviewer) are prepared to stick to the themes. The best advice I was ever given at an early stage in my career was not to talk so much. Although it is hard advice to follow, allowing silences is often productive.

Doing interviews on your own is often harder than with a colleague, but two of you may seem intimidating. But then one of you can write notes while the other does the questioning, unless you decide to record the interview. Recording raises questions about unease and about confidentiality, as well as operating the machine and making sure it is still recording, as well as needing to transcribe the material afterwards. In the next chapter on life histories, Jackson and Russell provide an excellent guide to doing and analysing interviews so I shall not repeat their advice here. Instead, I want to return to the questions about power, language and representation I began this chapter with and conclude with some comments about multiple voices and the 'crisis' of representation.

WHOSE VOICES ARE/SHOULD BE HEARD? WHO'S LISTENING? WHO ARE YOU WRITING FOR?

As I argued in the introduction, doing interviews involves a set of political acts and negotiations of power differentials. This argument applies just as strongly to the analysis and interpretation of interviews and to deciding how and what to 'write up'. Representations and writing are also political acts. The researcher has to decide whose voices will be heard in the text (the majority of human geographers rely on textual representation although more recently visual and other forms of representation are becoming more common – see Crang, in this volume; Rose, 2001). Indeed, it might be that the interviewees themselves could/should be involved both in interpretation and writing, helping to select which parts of the interviews are include and which are excluded,

although to my knowledge such a method has never been used by geographers. Many of us, however, give our respondents draft texts to read, whether returning their own interview after transcription or involving them in reading drafts of future articles or policy documents. This opens up the prospect of producing a range of alternative discourses, which are (should be?) based in and on a collaborative encounter between researchers and their interviewees rather than on the straightforward transcription of transparent stories for an, usually academic, audience. But it also runs the risk of different degrees of censorship, from an interviewee perhaps refusing permission for a sensitive part of the interview to be used to outright refusal, perhaps by the more powerful, for the interviews to be used at all.

Even if less dialogic methods are possible or desirable, all interviewers are faced with the decision of whose voices and what claims should be heard in the text that eventually supersedes the interviews. In some cases, perhaps especially, although by no means always, in work with deprived or extremely disadvantaged groups, ethical questions about whether to include information about, for example, involvement in illegal activities, in tax fiddles, in working off the books for example, become important. It is also essential to avoid a 'warts and all' voyeuristic description, even a celebration, of the lives of the poor and desperation, ensuring that vulnerable participants are not exploited. Other groups – the policemen, for example, interviewed in East London by Michael Keith (1992), the young men in Cambridge and Sheffield to whom I talked and the crack dealers whose lives Bourgois portrayed so vividly – are often racist and sexist in their attitudes and speech. Interviewers may both find these views offensive and off-putting and may also want to avoid reinforcing popular stereotypes of young men and yet want to accurately portray the texture of people's lives. What sort of judgements face interviewers in these cases? In the extract below I repeat some of the questions that I found myself addressing as I interviewed young school leavers.

Is it appropriate, for example, to discuss semi-criminal and illegal activities at a time when young men are being demonised in the press as feckless or troublesome? What should be done with information about different ways of making a living if they involve tax or benefit fraud? How should the connections between troubling individual behaviours and attitudes (racist, sexist and homophobic acts for example) and macrosocial changes be represented when the participants of research expressly do not make these connections? What about naming acts as abuse if the informants do not call it this? Is it ethical, as Fine and Weiss (1996) ask to 'display the voyeuristic dirty laundry that litters our data base?' and further, 'how can we risk romanticizing or denying the devastating assault on poor and working class families launched by the state, the economy, neighbours and sometimes kin?' (pp. 258–9) (McDowell, 2001: 96–7).

To these questions, I now add another as well as suggest an appropriate response. If there is a possibility that interviewees might be prosecuted because of something they revealed, is the researcher obliged based on some abstract notion of truth to fully and accurately record, transcribe and publish the entire interview? These judgments are particularly hard in case where interviewees reveal that they have been victims of, say, bullying or other forms of verbal or bodily abuse. Here, recommended practice is to advise interviewees of appropriate sources of advice and help or to ask their permission to speak to someone on their behalf. At a more general level, however, all interviewers are faced with complex decisions about representation.

As well as deciding whom to include and what parts of their interview – or indeed as part of this decision – the intended audience and the purpose of the written piece (or less usually a video, an exhibition, or another form of performance) affects the nature of the argument and the ways in which it is presented. As Bourgois (1995) argued in his book, 'in the US there are few nuances in the popular understanding of the relationship between structural constraints and individual failure' (p. 15). As a consequence, he suggests that intellectuals typically have evaded their responsibilities, by either not addressing the devastating urban poverty that is still current in wealthy societies or by producing 'positive representations of the oppressed that those who have been poor, or who have lived among the poor, know to be completely unrealistic' (p. 15). Further, Bourgois argued that he often received a hostile reception among scholars when he presented the results of this work: his academic peers either reacted in outrage or suggested that his findings would be used against the poor.

In my work with white working class boys, I have been accused of denying the effects of racism on school achievement by not including young men of colour and, in a much earlier period, when feminist arguments about interpretative and contextual research were not acceptable within geography, my work has been dismissed as either lacking objectivity or being 'political'. While the world of scholarship has changed almost immeasurably, it is clear that careful thought about the audiences for and about the reception of different forms of text is remains significant. Most social researchers (most geographers) undertaking interviews tend to have a particular audience or audiences in mind, and write in light of their concerns, although sometimes it is hard to identify the multiple audiences who might be interested. The answer to the question 'For whom am I writing?' may include for, with and about the informants (which are not at all the same thing), for the funding body, for academic peers, for the next research assessment exercise, to improve one's own status, to gain promotion or more nobly to influence policy makers, even to change the world. Sometimes it is difficult to disentangle these audiences and motives and to address their implications.

REPRESENTING THE 'OTHER': ISSUES OF DISSEMINATION AND ADVOCACY

For student interviewers, the decision about audience and reception typically is more straight forward. The dissertation is usually the main or the most immediate output and so the audience is the examination panel. Here a set of conventions usually constrains the form of writing and presentation. Similar conventions operate when the final product is an academic article. But other outputs and different forms of presentation are also significant. The research may have been funded by a sponsor who expects a set of policy proposals. Alternatively, the researcher may be writing as an advocate of a particular group or point of view, with the aim of influencing political debate or decisions.

Many human geographers assert their belief in 'critical' research – research which, drawing on Nancy Fraser's (1989) definition, 'frames its research program and its conceptual framework with an eye to the aims and activities of those oppositional social movements with which it has a partisan, although not uncritical, identification' (p. 113). The usual aim of critical social research is to traverse the boundaries between research, policy, activism and theory construction (see for example Kobayashi, 2001), which raises the issues about advocacy but also whether and what extent interview-based research may have an impact not only in challenging the representation of social groups but also in the amelioration of inequality and injustice. In the case of my own work with under-educated young men, which I hoped fell into the category of critical research, I had four interconnected aims, all of which influenced the ways in which I designed and undertook the research, as well as how to write about it. This is what I argued at a time when I was just at the end of the second round of interviews:

First, I want to contribute to challenging the increasingly dominant and stereotypical designation of young working class men as 'yobs and thugs'1 that has become common in Government pronouncements on youth issues. Through both personal experiences and theoretical reading, I was aware that the ways in which young men behave and perform their masculinity were more varied than this singular view. This knowledge linked directly to my second aim: to contribute to the growing work in the broad area of scholarship in gender studies that attempts to combine a structural understanding of inequality and limited opportunities and discursive, post-structural analyses of identity (see for example Segal, 1999). Thirdly, although the young men with whom I talked were clearly at a transition in their lives, in the sense that they completed their compulsory schooling and moved into new forms of work or study during the year in which I interviewed them, I also want to contribute to recent youth debates that emphasise the variety and longevity in such transitions [rather than a singular view of a single successful transition] .... Finally, and perhaps of greatest importance, as the work was funded by the Joseph Rowntree Foundation which is a UK-based institution funding policy research, I hope to contribute to current policy debates about youth services, about raising the level of the minimum income and, indeed including presently-excluded 16 and 17 year old employees, about improving income support for the low paid and the provision of flexible forms of further education provision. In common with other critical studies of the attitudes and actions of less privileged groups, I hope to show that actions that are often seen as irrational or illegal are, in fact, economically rational given the ways in which the tax and benefit systems, for example, systematically discriminate against or exclude certain individuals, including young people. I wanted to demonstrate the huge efforts being made by these young men, in relatively adverse circumstances, to construct what appears to them to be a respectable life. (McDowell, 2001: 95)

Looking back, and after the publication of a book based on this work (McDowell, 2003), I not sure that I have been equally successful in achieving all these aims. I hope I achieved the academic aims, but I am much less certain that I have had any impact on policy formulation, although I have presented my work to a wide range of teachers in different types of schools, many, but not all of them dealing with 'difficult' boys. Complex questions about dissemination and influence are important as well as the willingness and opportunity to contribute in significant policy arenas and I do not think I tried hard enough to get politicians and other policy innovators to read my work. In part, my relative failure lies in not thinking hard enough about different forms of writing and multiple dissemination strategies. Sending an academic book to policy makers is seldom the best way to influence their debates.

A final issue that I grappled with in this and more recent work with women migrants (McDowell, 2005) is both how to involve the people to whom I talked in the process of representing their lives and to return the text to them. Informants are active participants in the initial stages of the research process and are able to (re)-direct the course of the conversations in which they are participants but they tend to have much less power in the later stages. Practices differ: some interviewers return transcripts to their interviewees, others send drafts of their text but this demands considerable time and resources from interviewees – much more than a simple commitment to take part in an interview.

Once the work is complete, it seems only courteous to send copies of papers and books to interviewees, as well as to the funding body and academic outlets. Yet, academic prose is often inaccessible and furthermore, re-presenting the lives of informants in the context of structural inequalities, especially if they are the victim of these forces, may seem brutal. Although many of the young men to whom I spoke recognised the poverty of the opportunities that faced them, I still shied away from presenting such an interpretation of their lives to them. I chose to talk to them because they were 'low achievers' at school and had little chance of a 'career' but it is a different matter to make this brutally plain in a written version of their lives. I did in fact send a short (four page) summary of my findings to each of them and although I spoke to them all again a year or so later, none of them commented on what I had written.

When I finished the book based on long life history interviews with women migrants from Latvia to the UK, I sent a copy to each woman as a gesture towards repayment of my huge debt to them. I also presented some of the 'findings' to an audience at the Latvian Embassy, finding it difficult to represent women's lives to an audience that included many of the women whom I had interviewed. But the response was generally good: many women appreciated having a concrete record of what they suggested was a largely 'forgotten history' and I was moved by the woman who told me she had given the book to her grandson: 'now he understands'. But some reactions surprised me – one woman hated the title of the book *Hard Labour*, suggesting it implied that she had been a prisoner in a Soviet labour camp. And at the Embassy, I found myself facing hostility from many of the men present who resented what they saw as the absence of their lives. Fine words about women's history, the perspectives of the Other and so on had limited effect.

Despite Bourgois's (1995) cynicism about contemporary practices and his belief in the need for committed academics, he ultimately left the judgement of his work to the reader of his book: 'I do not know if it is possible for me to present the story of my three and a half years of residence in El Barrio without falling prey to a pornography of violence, or a racist voyeurism – ultimately the problem and the responsibility is also in the eyes of the beholder' (p. 18). Is this a sufficient response? I value the comments from the women whose lives are at the centre of my book (our book?) perhaps more than the academic reviews but still want favourable responses from my academic peers.

A CRISIS/LIMITS OF REPRESENTATION?

In this final section I want to conclude by pursuing the question of the relationships between politically-inspired forms of work based on a notion of advocacy and issues of writing and representation in a little more detail. Bourgois included in his book a critique of the sort of work advocated by the anthropologists Clifford and Marcus. Clifford and Marcus in their championing of both 'poetics and politics' have embraced of a type of work that is complex, multiple and polyphonic – that includes not only multiple voices but different points of view. Bourgois (1995) believes that the form of writing that has characterised ethnographic and inter-view-based work in the last decade or so has been profoundly elitist and so relatively inaccessible to policy makers and almost entirely so to the people represented within these texts. Thus, Bourgois suggests that:

Although postmodern ethnographers often claim to be subversive, their contestation of authority focuses on hyperliterate critiques of form through evocative vocabularies, playful syntaxes, and polyphonous voices, rather than engaging with tangible daily struggles. Postmodern debates titil-late alienated suburbanised intellectuals; they are completely out of touch with the urgent social crises of the inner-city unemployed. (1995: 14)

While there may be force in this argument, I think Bourgois evades the question of multiple audiences for social research and the importance of different forms of writing. However, in the decade since his critique of postmodern playfulness, an even more seri-ous criticism has been levelled at social research and specifically at the (im)possibil-ity of representing the lives of others. In geography this critique has been summed up in a turn to non-representational theory. While Bourgois argued for a return to a sim-pler form of writing and what he saw as a more accurate representation of the lives of others, in the last decade or so, a number of influential critical theorists in the discipline of geography have developed a forceful analysis of the limits to representation. Nigel Thrift is a key figure in this critique (1996, 2003). In a useful (critical) summary of this non-representational turn, Noel Castree (2004) outlines the three charges that Thrift has levelled at work which relies on repre-sentational theory.

First, representation is about distance – a scholastic disposition that divorces putative 'observers' from 'objects'. Second, representation is about codifica-tion – it seeks to 'fix' or capture the represented as if it or they possess(es) some stable identity. Third . . . representation is about cognition, speech and vision, as if these were the only or privileged way of knowing things and, thus, of doing things. (p. 472)

Now, it is clear from what I have argued so far that these criticisms have all concerned qualitative researchers for many years. Ways of reducing distance, of emphasising inter-connection and the significance of the rela-tionship between 'observer' and 'object', and of recognising the fluidity, complexity and context dependence of social identity have all had a significant impact on practices. Ideas about more fluid, provisional encounters between subjects and analysts are important. Furthermore, as Steve Hinchliffe (2001; 2003) has argued, contingent and incomplete encounters in the world involve not only rela-tions between human subjects but the involve-ment of numerous corporal non-human and inorganic entities as we enter a 'cyborg' world (Haraway, 1991). This means that a wider range of 'actants' may have to be con-sidered in any research encounter, including the many non-human species and objects with which we have daily interactions and which even make life possible.

It is almost impossible, however, to imag-ine how any researcher might avoid represen-tation entirely, as well, I would suggest, impossible to evade the political implications of our work (although this is not what the non-representational theorists are arguing, but rather for a new form of less hierarchical politics). But however complex, fluid, multi-ple and contingent social relations are, the very act of naming something, perhaps even thinking about it, always, however temporar-ily, constitutes an ordering or a representa-tion of a relationship. Despite this 'fixing,' Thrift's (2003) advice to remain open to multiple possibilities in our research encoun-ters is useful. He advises researchers to work in 'a spirit of generosity towards the world' acknowledging 'people's increas-ingly extended and unexpected capacities' (p. 74), as new technologies reconfigure and make possible different types of encounters.

Even so, it still seems unavoidable that, as critical academics committed to engaged scholarship, we have to intervene in the sphere of and through representations of the world, which may extend beyond the text to various forms of artistic representations, including art and dance, writing about and representing the diversity of human and non-human interaction in place in ways that contribute to a politically-progressive agenda.

As interviewers, we cannot and should not evade the academic and political responsibility of speaking for/on behalf of others through interpretations of the world that start, if not end, with the personal interactions that take place in interviews and the ways in which we interpret these through the lens of our philosophical, theoretical and political frameworks. What may seem like a simple methodological approach has significant implications, as I hope I have made clear in this chapter. In the shift from accepting interviews as a supposedly objective method to the acceptance of their interpretative status, the responsibilities of researchers for their work has greatly increased, as has the significance of their own positionality. While we are no longer able to hide behind a veil of invisibility and objectivity, we are now able to assert and take responsibility for claims for change and greater social justice. This transformation in the status of interviews and interviewers has been both the initiator and effect of that range of new questions that has dominated human geography over the last three decades, from the position of women in the 1970s to the significance of a multiple others, including non-humans, in the new millennium. It is a far more exciting discipline to be working within than it was thirty years ago.

NOTE

1.   In a speech on 3 July 2000 Tony Blair referred to the shame of Britain's 'yobs', to 'drunken louts' and 'thug bars' and the need for 'zero tolerance on yobbery' (Coward, 2000). In the six years since then there has been a constant reiteration of this discursive construction. In January 2006, the British Government published a 'Respect Action Plan' to tackle the anti-social behaviour of young people (www.respect.gov.uk).

REFERENCES

Aitken, S. (2001) 'Shared lives: interviewing couples, playing with their children', in M. Limb and C. Dwyer (eds) *Qualitative methodologies for geographers: issues and debates.* London: Arnold. pp. 73–86.

Aitken, S. and Thomas, H. (1997) 'Gender, power and crib geography: transitional spaces and potential places', *Gender, Place and Culture* 4: 63–88.

Atkinson, P. and Silverman, D. (1997) 'Kundera's immortality: the interview society and the invention of self', *Qualitative Inquiry* 3: 304–25.

Bell, D., Caplan, P. and Karim, W.J. (eds) (1993) *Gendered fields: women, men and ethnography.* London: Routledge.

Blunt, A. (2005) *Domicile and diaspora: Anglo-Indian women and the spatial politics of home.* Oxford: Blackwell.

Bourgois, P. (1995) *In search of respect: selling crack in El Barrio.* Cambridge: Cambridge University Press.

Butler, C. (2002) *Postmodernism: a very short introduction.* Oxford: Oxford University Press.

Butler, J. (1993) *Bodies that matter.* London: Routledge.

Cass, B., Dawson, M., Radi, R., Temple, D., Wills, S. and Winkler, A. (1978) 'Working it out together: reflections on research on women academics', in C. Bell and S. Encel (eds) *Inside the whale: ten personal accounts of social research.* Oxford: Pergamon. pp. 141–51.

Castree, N. (2004) 'Old news: representation and academic novelty', *Environment and Planning A* 36: 469–80.

Clifford, J. and Marcus, G. (1986) *Writing culture: the poetics and politics of ethnography.* Berkeley: University of California Press.

Coward, R. (2000) 'Slurring the proles', The *Guardian* 4 July, p. 23.

Denzin, N.K. (1970) *Sociological methods: a source book.* London: Butterworths.

Denzin, N.K. and Lincoln, Y.S. (eds) (2005) *The Sage handbook of qualitative research.* 3rd ed. London: Sage.

Eyles, J. and Smith, D. (eds) (1988) *Qualitative methods in human geography.* Cambridge: Polity.

Fine, M. and Weis, L. (1996) 'Writing the "wrongs" of fieldwork: confronting our own research writing dilemmas in urban ethnographies', *Qualitative Inquiry* 2: 251–74.

Flowerdew, R. and Martin, D. (eds) (1997) *Methods in human geography: a guide for students doing a research project.* London: Longman.

Fontana, A. and Frey, J. (2005) 'The interview: from neutral stance to political involvement', in N. Denzin and Y. Lincoln (eds) *The Sage handbook of qualitative research.* London: Sage. pp. 695–727.

Foucault, M. (1977) *Language, counter-memory, practice.* Tr. D.F. Bouchard. Ithaca, NY: Cornell University Press.

Fraser, N. (1989) *Unruly practices: power, discourse and gender in contemporary social theory.* Cambridge: Polity.

Gluck, S. and Patai, D. (1991) *Women's words: the feminist practice of oral history.* New York: Routledge, Chapman and Hall.

Gregson, N. and Lowe, M. (1994) *Servicing the middle classes, class, gender and waged domestic labour in contemporary britain.* London: Routledge.

Gubrium, J. and Holstein, J. (1998) 'Narrative practice and the coherence of personal stories', *Sociological Quarterly* 39: 163–87.

Haraway, D. (1991) *Simians, cyborgs and women.* London: Routledge.

Hinchliffe, S. (2001) 'Indeterminacy in-decisions – science, policy and the politics of BSE', *Transactions of the Institute of British Geographers* 26: 182–204.

Hinchliffe, S. (2003) 'Inhabiting landscapes and natures', in K. Anderson, M. Domosh, S. Pile and N. Thrift (eds) *The handbook of cultural geography.* London: Sage. pp. 207–26.

Keith, M. (1992) 'Angry writing', *Environment and planning D: Society and space* 10: 551–68.

Kitchen, R. and Tate, N.J. (2000) *Conducting research into human geography: theory, methodology and practice.* London: Prentice Hall.

Kobayashi, A. (2001) 'Negotiating the personal and the political in critical qualitative research', in M. Limb and C. Dwyer (eds) *Qualitative methodologies for geographers: issues and debates.* London: Arnold. pp. 55–70.

Limb, M. and Dwyer, C. (eds) (2001) *Qualitative methodologies for geographers: issues and debates.* London: Arnold.

Mason, J. (2002) *Qualitative researching.* 2nd ed. London: Sage.

Massey, D. (2005) *For space.* London: Sage.

McDowell, L. (2001) 'It's that Linda again: ethical, practical and political issues involved in longitudinal research with young men', *Ethics Place and Environment* 4: 87–100.

McDowell, L. (2003) *Redundant masculinities? Employment change and white working class youth.* Oxford: Blackwell.

McDowell, L. (2004) 'Masculinity, identity and labour market change: some reflections on the implications of thinking relationally about difference and the politics of inclusion', *Geografiska Annaler: Series B. Human Geography* 86: 45–56.

McDowell, L. (2005) *Hard labour: the forgotten voices of Latvian migrant 'volunteer' workers.* London: UCL Press.

Oakley, A. (1974) *The sociology of housework.* New York: Pantheon.

Oakley, A. (1979) *Becoming a mother martin.* Oxford: Robertson.

Pratt, G. (2003) *Working feminism.* Edinburgh: Edinburgh University Press.

Professional Geographer (1994) 'Women in the field: critical feminist methodologies and theoretical perspectives special focus section', 46: 54–102.

Pryke, M., Rose, G. and Whatmore, S. (eds) (2003) *Using social theory: thinking through research.* London: Sage.

Rose, G. (2001) *Visual methodologies.* London: Sage.

Roseneau, P. M. (1992) *Postmodernism and the social sciences: insights, inroads and intrusions.* Princeton: Princeton University Press.

Segal, L. (1999) *Why feminism?* Cambridge: Polity.

Silverman, D. (1993) *Interpreting qualitative data: methods for analysing talk, text and interaction.* London: Sage.

Silverman, D. (2000) *Doing qualitative research: a practical handbook.* London: Sage.

Smart, B. (1993) *Postmodernity.* London: Routledge.

Thrift, N. (1996) *Spatial formations.* London: Sage.

Thrift, N. (2003) 'Summoning life', in P. Cloke, P. Crang and M. Goodwin (eds) *Envisioning human geography.* London: Arnold. pp. 65–77.

Valentine, G. (1999) 'Being seen and heard? The ethical complexities of working with children and young people at home and at school', *Ethics, Place and Environment* 2: 141–55.

Yeatman, A. (1994) *Postmodern revisionings of the political.* London: Routledge.

10

Life History Interviewing

Peter Jackson and Polly Russell

INTRODUCTION

Life history interviewing is a research method that is designed to record an individual's biography in his or her own words. It is part of a wide range of biographical methods that also includes reminiscence and autobiography. Life histories provide a means of accessing people's narrative accounts of their lives and of the changes that have occurred within living memory. Starting with a description of the origins of life history research, this chapter will detail the life history method and consider the issues associated with interpreting life stories. The chapter will place particular emphasis on the relationship between life history and narrative approaches to identity (cf. Somers, 1994). It will discuss the relationship between individual narrative accounts and the wider discourses within which those accounts are embedded. The chapter will also explore the tensions involved in respecting the integrity of each individual life story and the comparative analysis of multiple life histories in pursuit of an understanding of wider social change. A guide to the practice of life history research is included as an Appendix.

The chapter is written from the perspective of two researchers who have used life histories in a series of recent projects. We are enthusiastic advocates of the method and strongly endorse its capacity to shed new light on current geographical issues by demonstrating the importance of social change within living memory and by highlighting the role of memory in the narrative construction of personal identity.

ORIGINS AND DEVELOPMENT

Life history as a methodological approach may be situated within the wider tradition of oral history research.[1] Although oral history includes interviewing methods other than life histories, the attempt to record and assess an individual's life through a biographical account or life history is a key characteristic of much oral history work. The terms oral history, life story and life history are sometimes used interchangeably but for the purposes of clarity oral history is understood here to refer to a broad movement, described below, that draws from oral accounts. Oral history and oral historians tend to have a particular interest in oral sources for what they reveal about history and memory. Life stories and life histories are methods used by oral historians and other researchers interested in narrative and narrative identity. Oral history and life histories are of interest to geographers because of what they reveal about the past and the role of history, memory and tradition in the social construction of place. Where we refer to life histories we also recognise the relation of these to oral history as a broad theoretical and methodological project which has significant social and political origins.

Adopted as a means of recording the aspects of social life that are often omitted from the conventional (written) historical record, oral history has its roots in anthropology, sociology and social history (see Thompson, 1978). In anthropology, the method was used to counter the lack of documentary historical sources in pre-literate societies (Vansina, 1965). At the beginning of the twentieth century sociologists, including those belonging to the Chicago School, started taking an interest in everyday behaviour and deployed multidisciplinary research methods, including interviews, to inform their analyses. In social history, the method was adopted to counter the historian's reliance on archival and documentary sources and quantitative methods which had emerged during the nineteenth century with the development of history as an academic discipline. Post Second World War, a recognition of memory as a source for historical analysis emerged, leading to the development of radical movements such as the History Workshop, designed to counter top-down approaches to the past with an emphasis on 'history from below'. The History Workshop movement sought to examine social change by accounting for the experiences and memories of ordinary people rather than powerful groups or individuals (Samuel, 1975; 1977). A populist emphasis is still evident in much oral history research as practised by many local history groups and community-based historians.[2] The use of life histories within feminist accounts has a similar emphasis on recovering the experience of those whose lives were in danger of being 'hidden from history' (cf. Rowbotham, 1973; Gluck and Patai, 1991; Sangster, 1994).

In addition to being deployed in an academic environment as part of what might be broadly termed a radical historical project,

oral history provides museums and activists with an engaging way of presenting, interpreting and preserving the stories of those whose experiences might otherwise remain unheard. The Museum of London, for example, recently collaborated with over 15 different refugee groups and 150 refugees to produce an exhibition and website called *Belonging: Voices of London's Refugees* based on oral testimony detailing the refugee experience (see http://www.museumoflondon. org.uk/English/EventsExhibitions/Special/ Belonging/). According to the museum curator, refugee participants expressed their sense of empowerment and pride at being able to collaborate in 'telling their story' to a broad audience via a mainstream British institution. Oral history is also used, via oral testimony, as a political tool and for participatory action by development organisations such as Panos. Central to their work explicating the impact of global change on the majority world is The Oral Testimony Programme which trains and supports local organisations to 'record and disseminate the views and experiences of those usually excluded from international development debate' (http://www.panos.org. uk/global/overview.asp?ID=1004). The radical origins of oral history has meant the development of a practice which takes seriously an account of the everyday as temporally and spatially embedded and this has proved to have implications and application not only for historians but for a wide range of different intellectual, educational and political purposes. Oral history should be seen as a theoretical source and methodological tool for geographers interested in exploring place-based understandings of memory, identity and consciousness.

Early oral history work was concerned with the validity and reliability of oral history as a more-or-less accurate representation of the past (see Thompson, 1978; Lummis, 1983). In the introduction to *The Myths We Live By*, for example, Rafael Samuel and Paul Thompson describe the first historical investigations using oral history as a form of 'naïve realism' which attempted to replicate the historian's traditional focus on quantification, measurement and social structure:

> Inspired by the very abundance of the newly discovered sources in living memory which we had opened up, we made a fetish of everydayness, using 'thick' description, in the manner suggested by anthropologists, to reconstitute the small detail of domestic life: but we had little to say about dream-thoughts and the hidden sexuality of family relationships. (1990: 2)

By the late seventies and over the subsequent decade, oral history was marked by what Robert Perks and Alistair Thomson (2006) describe as a paradigm shift. Instead of being preoccupied with the reliability of oral sources, historians such as Alessandro Portelli and Luisa Passerini and the authors in Samuel and Thompson's edited collection argued that the characteristics of oral history such as narrative form, the interviewer and interviewee relationship and subjectivity were also worthy of study. As Passerini argues: '[We] should not ignore that the raw material of oral history consists not just of factual statements, but is pre-eminently an expression and representation of culture, and therefore includes not only literal narrations but also the dimension of memory, ideology and subconscious desires' (1979: 85).

Oral history research, therefore, is part of a wider concern with the nature of memory. Reflecting on the value of oral testimony, Alessandro Portelli argues that 'what is really important is that memory is not a passive depository of facts, but an active process of creation of meanings' (1991: 52). In his account of the Fosse Ardeatine massacre in Rome in 1944, Portelli establishes a plausible framework of verifiable 'facts' against which 'the creative work of memory and narrative can be measured and tested' (2003: 16). Portelli's account draws from over 200 interviews with former partisans and relatives of the men killed in the massacre. The testimony of these men is woven through Portelli's book and demonstrates how 'these events and the struggle over their memory and meaning illuminate the history and identity of Rome, the contradictions and conflicts of

Italian democracy, the ethics of armed resistance' (2003: 2).

In our own work researching the British poultry industry, life story interviews with Marks & Spencer employees responsible for developing a new brand of chicken illustrated the importance of memory in constructing, legitimising and articulating commercial practice. Common to many of the interviews we conducted was a shared notion of 'chicken the way it used to be'. As one of the key suppliers of Marks & Spencer chicken explained:

> Chicken's chicken, you know. I kept saying chicken is chicken, you know, and we need something different. That's when we said, well, what does the consumer want? And that's where we developed the Oakham breed. And the Oakham breed was a complete difference by, it's a slower growing strain by ten per cent, so it grows ten per cent slower, the feed was totally different ... It'll be fed on a maize diet, which changes the taste. You know, if someone said to me well how do you explain it in some very simple strap line, I'd say, 'Chicken the way it used to be', yeah? And that's what it is, it's chicken the way it used to be. So all we've done is, you know, every year chicken gets better and grows faster, you know. Remember ten years ago, it used to take us sixty days to grow a chicken to a two kilo live bird, today it takes us forty-two days. And it's getting to a stage where you can't carry on doing that. You've got to start going back the other way, and M&S are now, they've started doing that.
> *And what – I'm just gonna push this – why is that better for the customer?*
> It tastes better. It tastes better and also, we're not in the days of ration cards. Food is not something which you know, we've got full stomachs now so we can get a bit more pickier of how the welfare and how, what it's fed on, it's all British and a consumer's got a choice.
> *D'you feel that customers understand it?*
> I think customers are getting to understand it a lot more, and customers, if they was to choose between an Oakham and a standard chicken, they'd notice now.
> If they were to buy from another retailer they'd notice the difference straightaway. Succulence, tenderness, you know, and that's caused by the dieting and you know, the lifespan of the bird. And also we've gone for a different breed, backwards as well. And that's made a difference. So it's different breeds from the parent stock. So there is a noticeable difference. Now at first I thought it

was becoming a brand, rather than a perceived difference, but there is an actual difference and that's what our customers tell us as well. There is a difference, chicken tastes, is as it used to be, in the Oakham bird.

D'you have a sense of time when this used to be, or when was this, used to be?

Ten years. Fifteen years.[3]

The references here to 'chicken the way it used to be' assume a particular cultural memory and one that is used to serve commercial ends. This memory of chicken 'as it used to be' is complicated and contestable – the modern broiler industry has changed the consumption of poultry from a rare treat to an everyday occurrence within the space of about 50 years. Whether many people have a clear or first-hand memory of chicken 'as it used to be' is debateable. Whether poultry in the past – more often chickens sold at the end of their laying life and not bred primarily for consumption – tasted 'better' is questionable. But the accuracy of the memory here is of less significance than its widespread deployment and what it reveals about contemporary food production and the past as a terrain for the 'creation of meaning' with commercial implications.

Oral histories, therefore, are not regarded straightforwardly as representations of the past (with an emphasis on their historical veracity), but as a means of examining how individual narratives are socially and culturally constituted as part of an on-going explanatory and relational process.

Oral history has often been accorded a somewhat secondary status within the social sciences, reflecting an underlying suspicion about whether people's reminiscences can be treated as a reliable source of 'hard' evidence about the past (Bornat, 1994). Indeed, oral history has often been neglected within methodological texts (though see Plummer, 1983; Arksey and Knight 1999; Chamberlayne *et al.*, 2000). Geographers, in particular, have made a relatively modest contribution to oral history research, though there are some important exceptions. These include Linda McDowell's (2003, 2004, 2005a, b) inter-generational research with Latvian women in

Britain, Graham Smith and Peter Jackson's (1999) work on the 'imagined community' of Ukrainians in Bradford, and Anne Buttimer's (1983, 1993) commitment to recording the 'life-journeys' of geographical thinkers within her Dialogue project (1978–89). There have been some innovative attempts to re-think landscape through the practice of oral history, including Riley and Harvey's research, 'Landscape and Archaeology and Community in Devon: an oral history approach', which aims to augment and challenge traditional scientific approaches to understanding the changing landscape (see http://www.ex.ac.uk/geography/research/ hcgrg/oral.htm and http://www.ex.ac.uk/ geography/research/hcgrg/histE3BEA.htm). Other notable work includes Gavin Brown's (2001) examination of the city as a place of erotic pleasure and sexual danger which uses oral histories to create and examine mental maps of place. Work by Toby Butler (2005) explores the relation between place and memory by using oral histories to 'map' the memories associated with a stretch of the River Thames (see http://www.memoryscape. org.uk) as well as recent encouragement to supplement life history research with a geographical awareness of the biographical dimensions of people's life-paths (Nash and Daniels, 2004). There has been a proliferation of PhD research in geography using life history methods, including Polly Russell's (2003) study of British culinary culture and Joanna Roberts' (2005) exploration of men's narratives of health and place in a low-income neighbourhood in Sheffield.[4] There are also links between life history research and other methods practised by human geographers such as Steve Pile's (1990) 'depth hermeneutics' and Steve Herbert's (2000) ethnographic approach, focused respectively on British dairy farming and US policing methods.

As this brief description of the origins and development of oral history and life-story research suggests, the method raises a number of important issues for researchers including the growing number of geographers who are becoming aware of the method's potential. In the next section, we describe the life history method in more detail, drawing attention to some of the questions and complexities it raises.

THE LIFE HISTORY METHOD

Don Ritchie provides a pragmatic definition of the methodologies associated with oral history research:

> Simply put, oral history collects spoken memories and personal commentaries of historical significance through recorded interviews ... Tapes of the interviews are transcribed, summarised, or indexed and then placed in a library or archives. These interviews may be used for research or excerpted in a publication, radio or video documentary, museum exhibition, dramatisation, or other form of public presentation. (1995: 1)

As Ritchie's definition suggests, the collection and archiving of life history interviews may be the oral historian's primary purpose. Where this is the case, the methodological protocols of oral history focus on the process of recording and archiving, insisting that appropriate sound quality is maintained and that the interviews are archived in a professional manner with sufficient contextual material, as well as tape summaries and/or full transcripts of the interviews, to facilitate subsequent re-use of the material by other researchers at some point in the future.[5] For others, the collection of life histories is usually part of a wider process of interpretation. In this case the focus is on data analysis, including the use of software packages such as NUDIST and N.Vivo, designed to ensure that analysis is undertaken systematically and with appropriate rigour.[6]

Oral historians need to be aware that the interviews they record will provide primary sources for unspecified future audiences. Their emphasis is on recording the interviewee's life 'in the round', maintaining the integrity of 'the life' in any analysis or representation that follows. Social scientists are often more concerned with the systematic content of the interview and with its comparative potential. They may encourage interviewees to emphasize one or more aspects of their lives (as in our own recent work on food and culinary culture).[7] In reality, however, differences between social science and oral history approaches to collecting life stories may be less dramatic than this description implies. Where oral historians seek to collect an account of a 'life', they also work with time and funding constraints and research parameters that inevitably determine the scope, direction and focus of their recordings. Similarly, social scientists may approach their interviewees with clear research outlines but the life-story approach encourages detailed description and reflection and makes rigorous research boundaries difficult to enforce. Moreover, in the UK, the establishment of Qualidata (the Economic and Social Research Council Qualitative Data Archival Resource Centre) in 1991, aimed at advising on the safe archiving of qualitative research materials, has meant that there is an increasing body of qualitative social science material available for re-use by future researchers.[8]

Although bodies like the Oral History Society provide guidelines for oral historians about interviewing protocol, archiving and the issues raised by interpretation, there is no clear distinction made in oral history literature about the significance and implications of interviewing for posterity and interviewing for immediate interpretation. This absence may at first seem strange but the reality is that the distinction between collection and interpretation is both practically and theoretically overdrawn. Oral historians, museum practitioners and activists who use oral history to inform their analytical work are also likely to be involved in some form of data archiving. Moreover, the process of collecting oral histories, as we discuss in more detail later, is in itself seen as a form of interpretation – the material generated is not 'pure' or 'objective' data but is the result of a collaboration and agreed interpretative conversation between the interviewer and interviewee. To make a strong distinction between archiving 'pure' material and using this material as part of analysis fails to take serious account of the oral history practice and life-story method as processes which are in themselves interpretive.

Although closely related and sharing certain characteristics, there are important distinctions between the life history interview and those shorter more focussed interviews usually conducted by social scientists. These differences are discussed in detail below. The negotiated relationship between the interviewee and interviewer in a typical life history raises a number of important issues about authority and power in the research setting. The attempt to strive for 'objectivity' and 'detachment' in interview relationships has been widely seen by social scientists and oral historians as a flawed project. Instead, there has been a move towards making qualitative research processes more collaborative (see Oakley, 1981) but some have argued that 'sharing power' in an interview context does not equate to relinquishing privilege and its material consequences (Sangster, 1994). That said, there has been surprisingly little recognition of power as differentiated and the possibility, as we have experienced, of interviewees with cultural and economic capital on whom research may rely for funding or support potentially exerting the same if not more power than the researcher. While collecting life stories for her PhD thesis, Polly Russell recorded the life story of a prominent food entrepreneur. On arriving at the entrepreneur's business to start recording Polly was introduced to the company lawyer who then sat during the entire recording taking notes. Less explicitly, research conducted with Marks & Spencer has been reliant upon the goodwill of key people within the organisation. Power in an interview situation may make itself known explicitly or implicitly but either way it challenges a simplistic assumption that power always lies with the interviewer.

A key characteristic of life history research, and one that also relates closely to issues of power and control, is the intensely personal nature of life history material. The relationship between interviewer and interviewee builds up over a period of time and the trust that develops between them shapes the life history (see Yow, 2006). The life history method reduces the chances of the interviewee giving a purely sanitised version of events that rarely goes beyond what is already on the public record. While it can sometimes be difficult to persuade powerful interviewees to abandon the 'script' of what they are used to telling journalists and other interviewers, the life history interview works best where the public account is leavened with biographical detail and personal reflection.[9] In our research on the poultry industry a key focus for our analysis was on the relationship between shared, public and commercial narratives and the personal narratives of individual life histories. The life history method allowed us to explore the emotions, feelings and ambiguities associated with modern poultry production with people central to implementing change within the poultry business. The following extract is taken from an interview with a category manager for poultry and demonstrates the way that personal issues resonate with more strictly commercial concerns:

> The thing which I feel is because chicken is so cheap and so available now, I think people's aspirations and expectations of chicken have lowered in the course of the last number of years. And I describe chicken as a canvas upon which people paint because actually in itself it doesn't offer much. It's a source of protein, but in textural terms unless it's free range or organic, in flavour terms often, it doesn't really deliver. And what delivers is the sauce that you put on it or the way that you cook it. And I think because it's eaten so regularly and we eat such vast quantities of it, and you talked about it down to a unit or a commodity, I think that's a really good analogy because the other thing is that you know, chickens aren't the most appealing of things. I mean you know, you don't think of them as you do a robin or a swan, or something which is quite appealing, or a duck. They are, people think of them mostly in connection with either, when they think of them, and they still ask us the question about this, either in a cage as a caged battery egg, or as something they see scratching around on a farmyard, but they

would have a very different perception of the way that chickens are actually grown for in the modern broiler world. And I think that they don't want to think about it because they're not particularly easy to empathise with. Whereas I quite agree with you, people see a lamb outside, become a sheep and they see a calf become a heifer or a steer and they are much more visually appealing. The other big difference is, that you can see cows and sheep out in fields if you go to the countryside, you'll never see any chickens grown commercially, unless you happen to see a free range or organic, but often they're hidden away, so you don't see them. But you'll see cows and you'll see sheep all the time. And therefore there's a kind of connection isn't there, that they've been outside so they've had quite a decent life really haven't they? So I think people can make that connection a bit more with four-legged things than they can with chicken.

And just coming back to your comment to sort of push you a bit further, you said you don't think about it that much because you couldn't do the job if you did. Is that because, now I'm going to ask you to think about it, but is that because if you think about it, you don't fundamentally believe on some level that it's right?

Um ... that's a very interesting question and if you do push me, I would say the following. I think that it is right that we eat flesh, animals, because I think if you think back through tens of thousands of years, that's what we've done. The thing I struggle with – no, struggle's the wrong word – the thing if I were to think about it too much that I might struggle with is the way that we have exploited it and moved it to such a clinical and efficient way of doing things. The basic statistic is that the way that the breeders have worked – you may have heard this quote before – the way that the breeders have worked with chicken is that they have almost, in the last twenty years, taken a day off their life at the point of slaughter to achieve the same weight through genetic selection. So it means that you've almost got, I mean they are fully feathered, but you've almost got what would have been twenty years ago, baby chickens, they would have been a lot lower weight at that age, reaching the weight that we require to slaughter. That kind of, don't know, that kind of ... I'm obviously not that sentimental about it because I still eat chicken, I still do my job, but if you are pushing me, that kind of thing just doesn't quite feel right and natural. That was an admission wasn't it? I mean, with my job, but you have pushed me and I think that's where I would be on that.[10]

This extract involves the category manager in reflection and evaluation of an intensely personal nature. This individual is tussling with the ethical complexities of contemporary food production as part of a longer life-story recording. This highly evaluative extract is an important reminder that although individuals in large corporate organisations work within accepted structures and narratives, they nonetheless bring individual subjectivities to bear on these commercial environments. These, in turn, shape the decisions they implement. This extract was part of a seven hour interview recorded over four sessions. During this time the relationship between interviewer and interviewee developed to the extent that the interviewee expressed both interest in the life history process and a sense of trust in the interviewer's intentions and methods. Although not inconceivable, it is unlikely that a more focused or shorter interview would have provided the interviewee with the same security or scope to discuss his complicated feelings about poultry production with such openness or ease. Furthermore, the close relationship between the interviewee and interviewer meant that when this material has been used in different contexts, we have sought both written and oral confirmation from the category manager giving his consent for its use.

Life histories are usually based on a detailed interview schedule covering childhood, education, family and relationships as well as topical areas such as education, health and work.[11] But it is rare to follow a rigid sequence of questions and better for the interview to develop through a process of negotiation and collaboration (see Frisch, 1990). By sticking religiously to a set of prepared questions the interviewer's preconceived ideas about how different topics and events are connected is likely to shape the material gathered. Moreover, interviewer-driven approaches may conceal the ways that an interviewee remembers the past, concealing his or her historical or geographical consciousness. That said, many interviewees are more comfortable if they know they will be guided gently through the interview while others already have a clear sense of what they want to cover and need little prompting. Some oral historians advocate pre-interviewing potential participants in order to ensure that they will make 'good' life-story narrators, though this can favour those who are articulate and used to public speaking, further marginalising those whose voices are excluded from research using conventional documentary methods (Minister, 1991).

When a life history interviewee shares private, personal or sensitive information the interviewer finds themself in a position of trust which involves a delicate and sensitive understanding of the potential ethical issues at stake in sharing or disseminating their findings. Ethical life history research may well make it incumbent on researchers to withhold material from a wider audience. Moreover, life history recordings can elicit strong emotions on the part of both the interviewee and interviewer, and whether or when this might happen cannot necessarily be predicted. Sometimes a seemingly innocuous question can trigger strong reactions. Descriptions of schooling, for instance, often feature in the biographical explorations of Polly Russell's life history interviews but when she asked a London butcher to describe his school she stumbled unwittingly on an area of deep sadness associated with the butcher's sense of abandonment having been left in boarding school at an early age. In these circumstances oral historians have to be guided by an ethic of care, a strong sense of discretion and a recognition that they are probably not qualified to deal with deep-seated psychological issues. When conducting life history work with prostitutes, oral historian Wendy Rickard provides interviewees with the details of support groups and counsellors. Oral historians working on issues relating to trauma or abuse may face similar issues in processing the information they uncover. A large-scale oral history project with holocaust survivors initiated by the British Library involved employing a trained counsellor to assist interviewees with the distress they experienced listening to holocaust testimony.

These issues are no more pertinent to life history research than they are to other forms of qualitative research including short, focussed interviews or focus groups, but the personal quality of life history and the relationship established between researcher and researched brings them to the fore. The difficulties that life histories raise for the researcher in putting on display the process through which material is generated are, we contend, a strength of oral history.

While researchers may wish to negotiate maximum public access to the interview material (see section on confidentiality and copyright, below) with as few restrictions as possible, they must also be mindful of the moral and ethical responsibility they have to their interviewees. Although a researcher may be confident that the way they use life-story material will present no problems for an interviewee, they cannot police the subsequent re-use of material by others. Whatever the intended purpose of oral history material, whether for an archive, for immediate analysis or both, the use and possible re-use of oral history material raises a number of ethical and practical issues that oral historians are just beginning to consider. As Joanna Bornat (2003) explains, although historical sources have always been subject to reinterpretation at different times, the particular relationship between interviewer and interviewee and the significance of the context of an interview in shaping material collected makes oral history different and potentially more problematic when it comes to issues of re-use. Life-story recordings, therefore, bring to the fore issues of interviewee and interviewer power, control and vulnerability which need to be handled with sensitivity and awareness (see below and Borland, 1991; Thompson, 1998.)[12]

INTERPRETATION

Life-story recordings usually produce a large quantity and a wide range of material.

Interpreting this material can be a daunting task. To some degree, the form of analysis will be determined by the intended audience for whom research material is being produced – life stories are used in museum exhibitions, local community history projects and television or radio documentaries as well as academic research and each of these contexts has implications for how material is collected, sorted and analysed. Academic uses of life story and methods of analysis and presentation vary considerably.

Selecting extracts from a life story as part of a presentation or publication inevitably involves the selection of some material and the discarding of other material. For some, it is acceptable to cut and paste sections from different interviews in order to make a series of analytical points. For others, using lengthy interview extracts forms an important part of their commitment to retaining the integrity of an interviewee's life. As previously mentioned, Portelli's extensive study of the Fosse Ardeatine massacre involved the analysis of over 200 interviews. This testimony is woven throughout Portelli's book, with long, italicised sections of interview dialogue used to intercept the author's interpretation. Each chapter starts with a long extract from an interviewee called Ada Pignotti as a means of compensating for the fragmented representation of the personal narratives. As Portelli explains,

I made up for this limitation by opening each chapter with instalments of one story, which is thus reported almost in its entirety ... I hope that this will allow readers to know in depth at least one person and to obtain a fuller sense of the rhythm of the narratives. (2003: 18)

In our own project we are drawing from the life-story recordings of over thirty interviewees to reflect upon the politics and practices of food production. In sifting through our data we are drawn to key themes, anecdotes and descriptions about food production but we also attempt to incorporate a sense of the interviewee's biography as part of our analysis of their position in the food industry and the beliefs and opinions they hold. For some purposes the life-story recordings

of one individual may form the basis for a research project or publication. Lorraine Sitzia's collaborative research with the subject of her co-authored book, Arthur Thickett (a British soldier turned communist), involved a process of what she terms 'interactive dialogue' to interpret and order his life story (Sitzia and Thickett, 2002). This 'interactive dialogue' draws inspiration from Frisch's concept of a 'shared authority' where narrator and interviewer share the responsibility for producing final material. Involving considerable investments in time and emotion on the part of the researcher and subject, the notion of 'interactive dialogue' has important contributions to make in debates about power in qualitative research and the politics of representation and interpretation that are pertinent not only to oral historians but also to qualitative researchers in general.

Whatever the approach to collecting and interpreting life stories, the method brings to light the effect of the research context on shaping and determining any material generated. The influences that shape life-story interviews relate to both the conventions associated with method, the research context in which the story is collected and the internal dynamics between the interviewee and interviewer. Talking about the former, Yvette Kopijn argues that the oral history approach imposes particular constraints upon material collected in a cross-cultural setting:

My point is this: are oral historians sufficiently equipped to prepare and conduct an interview in a cross-cultural setting if they have been trained to work within the oral history frame? Such a frame teaches them to view Western communicative patterns as the norm, while others are denied; to regard the individual as more important than the group, and judge views of self which differ from this norm as deviant. It trains them to keep control of the interview: the interviewee is expected to take the floor, yet their contribution to the discussion is to be kept within the boundaries of the topics selected by the interviewer. These premises are highly problematic, for once they have been uncritically imposed on the interviewee they will transform any oral narrative that is produced in a cross-cultural interview situation into a mirror that simply reflects Western assumptions. (1998: 144)

The privileging of the individual voice rather than the communal voice is just one example of a methodological convention which might influence the interpretation of life history data. Others might include encouraging an interviewee to tell their life story chronologically or with thick description, a way of communicating with which they may well be unfamiliar or uncomfortable.

In relation to the research context, the question of who sponsors the research, who is selected for interview, who conducts the interview (and with what research agenda) and where the material is to be archived also shape the material collected. As Chris Mann states,

> the context within which life stories are collected may shape different presentations of self; may reveal different, even contradictory, life experiences; may affect the choice of the evaluative terms used to make sense of these experiences; and may even act as a catalyst that initiates the reassessment of a lived life. (1998: 81)

In addition to the broad conventions associated with the life-story method and the specific research agenda, life stories are a co-production, with authority shared between an interviewer and an interviewee (Frisch, 1990). Interviewees are sometimes described as informants, narrators or interview partners. The terms are significant as 'narrator' emphasizes the agency of the person telling the story (compared to the more passive role of 'interviewee'); 'informant' implies a degree of duplicity on the part of the narrator, providing the interviewer with privileged access to confidential material; and 'partner' emphasises the relational nature of the life history, produced in dialogue with the interviewer (though the 'partnership' may be far from equal). Social scientists have written at length about the reflexive nature of the research process and the potential influence of the researcher's positionality within research encounters such as life history interviews (see, in particular, Rose, 1997). In the following extract, for example, it is possible to see the effects of the researcher's positionality on the interview process where there is

an initial lack of understanding between interviewer and interviewee because each approaches the encounter with a different 'mindset'. The interviewer (Polly Russell) asks the farmer why he switched from intensive production of broiler chickens to selling free-range chickens at the local farmers' market. Her initial hesitation indicates that she was expecting a different kind of answer (driven by concerns of animal welfare, environmental issues and food quality, for example) rather than the purely commercial motivation that seems to have guided the farmer's decision:

> *So you, when you moved here, the sheds were here and you knew that you were going to go into poultry farming, chicken farming.*
> Mm.
> *How did you feel about that, I mean did you have any particularly strong feelings or did you...?*
> It just seemed like a good idea at the time. I mean, you go with the flow don't you..."
> *So the decision to go free-range, would you say it was primarily economic?*
> Economic probably. Yes, everything, any business is driven by economics isn't it. I mean whatever we do at the end of the day has got to turn a profit, and the bigger the profit the better obviously. But, obviously there's quality life for us and the animal as well, somewhere along the line, [inaudible] somewhere along the line. But yes. It was... And it was something different as well. And as I say, farmers' markets really came along just about the right time.[13]

Later in the recording Polly returns to the question of why the farmer decided to move into free-range poultry production:

> *Can you explain how long that decision process [to go free-range] took, and what the kind of transition was?*
> Well it just sort of slowly happened really. We, we'd started messing around with the sort of, the first farmers' markets when we were doing broilers, towards the end, then...
> *What were you selling at the farmers' markets?*
> Just doing whole chicken, yes.
> *Broiler whole chicken?*
> No, free range, we'd just taken some out of the broiler house and thrown them out in the field with a shed, you know, and, let them grow on ... just to sort of, you know, try it and see really, and see what happened. And there weren't many markets around ...
> *Why did you make that decision?*

We just felt that was probably what the public would perceive as better chicken, so, it's the same intensive argument again, isn't it really. They probably, the people, the market we were going to aim at would probably prefer free range.

And, just, I haven't got a sense of what you think of that.

Well I think ... I think we probably sell more as free range than if I had a broiler site here and I took out 50 every week or 100 every week.

So, the decision, so this, the first farmers' markets were when?

Well they were ... about sort of four, four and a half, between four and five years ago the first, the first sort of tentative steps were made with a few farmers' markets, trial markets round and about ....

How did you get to know about them, what was the ...?

Well it was, it was talked about from the local NFU [National Farmers' Union], and it was advertised, and you know, and we were all talking about, we had to improve our margins and cut the middle man out, and we ought to be selling directly to the public, and, you know, all the usual guff you hear. So, we just set to one Friday, or one, you know, Monday, and killed some chicken, and hoiked 'em on down to [the] market, and dumped them on the table, and the first couple weren't very good, because like any market, when the new guy turns up they look at you for a couple of weeks and then they'll try it, and then they come back. And we've been doing that on every Friday for nearly five years. And we've got a nice little customer base there down there now that come every week.[14]

In this extract the assumptions of the interviewer are as revealing as the explanation provided by the interviewee. Moreover, the interviewer's hesitations and apparent confusion shape and determine the direction of the interview and the material collected. The interviewer clearly had different ideas about the motivations for free-range production and the development of farmers' markets from the more purely commercial motivation of the poultry farmer. Reflexive interviewing and interpretation makes the constructed and negotiated nature of life-story material more apparent. But while it is possible to interview and interpret reflexively – understanding that the life-story method, the research context and the interviewer's personality or prejudices all shape the material collected – this is not the same as being able to account fully

for the effects of these influences. In other words, reflexive research always involves a recognition of both the inevitability of life stories being contextually determined and the impossibility of accounting for these in a final or complete sense.

This interview between Polly Russell and the chicken farmer can also be used to illustrate another key dimension of life history research and its interpretation: the distinction between narrative content and narrative style. Conventional social science interviews are often designed to elicit accurate information, with an emphasis on what people say (its narrative *content*). In life history research, there is more emphasis on questions of narrative *style*: on the ways that stories are told and the genres people draw from in making sense of their lives (see Ashplant, 1998; Chamberlain and Thompson, 1998). In other words, there may sometimes be less interest in the factual content of people's narrative accounts than in the way the story is told. This is what life-historians mean when they speak about 'trusting the tale' (Kreiswirth, 1992). When listening to the following extract, as much information is given by the mode of expression as by the actual content of what is said:

You were saying to me about the slaughter licence.

Yes, well technically, everybody ... with a slaughter premises, there should be a licensed slaughterman there, so, and they're licensed by the local Council. So [inaudible] it must have been about, five years ago I suppose, when this legislation came in, and we had a ... it was at Christmas, so everything was going swimmingly, and when this Ford Escort comes into the yard, and a young man of about twenty gets out, so we sort of, looked [inaudible] '[inaudible] mate, what are you up to?' And he said, 'Oh I'm from the local Council and I've come to license you for, your slaughter licence.' I said, 'Fine, OK, come on in.' So, he comes on in, he says, 'Right, so I need to see you kill a couple of turkeys.' Kill a couple of turkeys. And I said, 'Fine, 'I said, 'I've only been doing it for twenty-odd years, I'm not really sure how to do it, can you show me please?' And he said, 'No no no,' he says, 'I'm actually here to license you, so I just need...' I said, 'I can't do it, I don't know how to do it. I've got to make sure I know how to do it properly, you'll have to show me.' And he was there in this suit, and everything else, and he said, no he couldn't do it. So I said, 'Well, the best thing mate is, get in your car and disappear.' ... Which is what he did. So I assumed I'd probably be shut down the following day, but anyway...

Why wouldn't you just do it for him?

Well it was the principle, of sending obviously somebody who was straight out of college from what I could see, and in my opinion wasn't going to know, couldn't do it. So, you know, why should he be inspecting me, when he couldn't do the job himself? It was just lunacy. So anyway, he disappeared, and that was the last we heard of it. The following year, the following Christmas, same person comes back. So I said, you know, 'Have you learnt how to kill turkeys?' And he said, 'No.' I said, well, you know ... 'Can I see you kill ...?' So we went through the whole rigmarole again basically. And I sent him on down the road. And that was it, didn't see him again .... So I've never paid my £25 for my licence, and the [inaudible] never been back again.[15]

This anecdote is telling not so much for the facts of the event described, but in pointing us towards the farmer's narrative identity – how he sees himself and how he wishes to be seen. Told with an ironic and wry tone, the story establishes the farmer's sense of himself as practical and sensible and, ultimately, more quick witted than the so called 'expert' who arrived to licence his premises.

The next extract illustrates the importance of listening to recordings as well as reading transcripts for it is often the oral qualities of the interview that provide most insight into what is actually said (Anderson and Jack, 1998). In this extract, an agricultural technologist at Marks & Spencer, who had previously worked for the animal welfare charity the RSPCA, is talking about his uneasiness with slaughtering large animals and reflecting on how, ironically, the industrial scale of chicken slaughtering reduces his discomfort. Prior to this extract, he had spoken about the amount of waste within the industry and about consumers' reluctance to handle raw chicken. Asked about the scale and intensity of the slaughtering process, his answer is characterised by lengthy pauses and an inability to find the right words to express himself:

Are you thinking about the morality of it or, can you try and explain to me what it is that's uneasy for you, is it ...?

[Pause] ... What's uneasy about it? [Pause] ... I think it's just the whole process, just looks so alien at how quickly you can transform something which looks as easily recognisable as a, as a cow, a whole cow or a pig, and then ... almost ... not instantaneously but within, you know within thirty seconds, sixty seconds it's then just become ... almost something different hanging from a shackle line ... bleeding out, and I, it's bizarre. One of the things I always think about if you know, George Orwell Animal Farm, had things been different, or if you know ... we weren't, you know, we weren't in command, what would have ... What would it look like if it was just a line of humans being lined up and the same effect was done and how ...? I don't know, it's just a bizarre, and it's interesting because the more automated it is and the bigger the operation, so if you go into a chicken plant where you have got, you know a slaughter line of six hundred birds in a minute maybe, compared to a beef abattoir which might do one animal, depending on the abattoir or whatever, one animal every four or five minutes or three minutes or whatever ... it's less you know, the automation just takes again the whole thing is just completely ... more industrialised and ... less objectionable I think.[16]

This example indicates the difficulty of representing spoken language, with all its richness of accent, tonality, emphasis and pace, within the written form of a transcript or interview extract. Written language and oral language, after all, are clearly distinct and 'the spoken word can very easily be mutilated when it is taken down in writing and transferred to the printed page' (Samuel, 1971: 19). In using extracts of life history recordings as part of an educational website we have had opportunity to compare many examples of oral recording and transcripts. Tellingly, when selected extracts have been played to their interviewee authors, they have never objected to their spoken words but many been embarrassed by the verbatim transcripts of the same extracts. Wherein spoken language stutterings, word swallowing, 'errs' and 'ums' are expected, when these are presented in written form a person who is orally articulate and clear may seem inarticulate, muddled and confused.

For life-historians, the difficulty of accurately representing the spoken word in written form is a constant dilemma and there have been many attempts to convey these issues through the use of experimental forms of textual representation. Drawing on Catherine

Riessman's (1990; 1993) work on narrative analysis, for example, Joanna Roberts (2005) uses a variety of textual strategies in the analysis of her interview material which focuses on men's accounts of health and illness in a low-income part of Sheffield. She begins with a conventional thematic analysis of the material, drawing out themes such as 'roots' and 'insecurity' in her discussion of the interviewees' ambivalent attachments to place. She then moves through two further stages of analysis, described as prosodic and paralinguistic (looking for semantic, grammatical and phonological relationships within the text as well as issues of pitch, level, speed, volume, etc.) before undertaking a poetic restructuring of the text. Here, for example, she renders a short extract from one of her interviews in poetic stanzas:

I don't like I don't like
Sheffield
I hate it
I hate
Sheffield
I can't stand it.

There's just nothing
Nothing here to do
You can't do anything.

If you're going to do 'owt
You're going to be doing
Same thing.
You can go to the pub
That's it!
It finishes there.
Or bowling
You can go there
And bowling.
That's
It
Done.
What else can you do?
Sit at home,
Bored.

There's nowt here.

I went to Blackpool
And I'd love to live there
I could
Really
Live
At Blackpool
Cause there is so much
To do
There's LOADS.

They've got pubs
They've got arcade
They've got fairground
They've got golf course
They've got everything.
Bowling they've just got
They've got everything.
They've got
every
single
thing
You can't get bored!

That's me –
I'd live in Blackpool
I could live in Blackpool
I could live there

But Sheffield

There's nothing. (Roberts, 2005: 140–1)

Roberts's analysis of this extract draws out the significance of personal pronouns ('I' and the envied other, 'They'); the powerful use of repetition ('I don't like', escalating to 'I hate'); the splitting between Sheffield (that has 'nothing') and Blackpool (that has 'everything); the rhythmic isolation of the words 'They've got/every/single/thing'; and the dialogic moment of the narrator's conversation with himself. This is an innovative attempt to push the boundaries of textual interpretation that some researchers will resist, arguing that this is reading too much into the text and that the balance of power between the interviewer and the interviewee has slipped too far in favour of the former. But Roberts argues that this form of poetic representation is strongly guided by the interviewee in the sense that the line breaks and other poetic features of the text closely follow the qualities of the interviewee's oral account in terms of pauses, emphasis etc. She also provides an audio version of the interview extracts on CD-ROM so that readers can listen to the oral delivery of the material at the same time as they are examining its textual representation. While opinion may be divided as to the effectiveness of the experiment, it is a valuable exploration of the oral nature of life history interviews and of the limits of purely textual forms of representation. Ideally where material is drawn from oral sources, whether represented in conventional transcript or poetic form, an audience will have access to the original sound recordings from which these derive. With advances in digital technology this is becoming more feasible but with traditional publications remains a challenge.

Oral historians have also made great use of visual evidence in support of life history interviews both as props (to prompt memory) and as direct evidence of past events. Such an approach underlines the extent to which all life histories provide a recounting of past experience from the perspective of the present, where the significance attached to historical events reflects present-day concerns. An example would be the way that accounts of earlier generations of immigrants to Bradford from Eastern Europe take on new meaning in the context of more recent waves of immigration from the New Commonwealth and Pakistan (Jackson, 1992). In other cases, photographs are used to supplement the display of oral testimony in museum exhibitions or in popular books (see, for example, Bradford Heritage Recording Unit, 1987; 1994; Smith *et al.*, 1998). In most cases, the visual evidence is of much greater significance than its purely illustrative value. For example, the Bradford collection made great use of the photographs that were taken in the Belle Vue photographic studio in which immigrants posed for formal portraits that were sent 'home' to relatives and friends to demonstrate the social and economic success they had achieved in migrating to Britain. The theoretical and methodological tools are now available for undertaking a critical analysis of such visual material, aware of the 'burden of representation' (Tagg, 1988) that is involved in all forms of photographic practice (Rose, 2001).

NARRATIVE IDENTITY

In focusing on personal biographies, life histories may seem vulnerable to overstating individual agency. This tendency is, however, counteracted by the life history approach which emphasizes the interweaving of public and private narratives. Life stories situate an individual's description of events, memories, feelings and attitudes within and through the broad context of their lives. Individual accounts are also embedded within wider discourses. This is what Margaret Somers refers to in terms of narrative identity:

> Narrative identities are constituted by a person's temporally and spatially variable place in culturally constructed stories composed of (breakable) rules, (variable) practices, binding (and unbinding) institutions, and the multiple plots of family, nation, or economic life. Most importantly, however, narratives are not incorporated into the self in any direct way; rather, they are mediated through the enormous spectrum of social and political institutions and practices that constitute our social world. (1994: 635)

Any tendency towards privileging individual agency or overstating the 'heroic' qualities of an individual narrative are held in check by the detailed and sustained nature of the life-story interview that aims to bring to light the individual as a contextually, relationally and temporally situated subject. The emphasis on socially situated subjects is one of the strengths of the life-story approach. This can be illustrated in the following extracts from the life history of David Gregory, Head of Food Technology at Marks & Spencer. The interview began with a discussion of his childhood experiences of food shopping with his mother and progressed over the course of several hours to discuss the company's current approach to risk management within the context of increasing consumer anxieties about food safety. The following extracts illustrate this inter-weaving of personal and institutional narratives:

> The big revolution for me was that Sainsbury's changed their relationship with the customer I can remember this as a child because ... when you went in as a small child and you went to the old Sainsbury's stores, the way they structured the counters, they were high and it was quite hard to see over them and also, the people who served were on a platform, so they were high up over the

counter and they wore these very, very posh white coats and whatever and they were very domineering over you, and it was almost like you know, excuse me, this is a privilege. And if you look at lots of old photographs of old shops, and particularly old Sainsbury's shops, they were all up in the air, and if you look at them, they're all very high and they're all weighted very much towards the ceiling in terms of where goods are displayed and everything, rather than down, accessible to the customer. And this supermarket absolutely transformed that, because you'd go in as a child and pick things up and help yourself.[17]

David Gregory goes on to explain how his mother had worked for John Lewis and a number of other department stores. He remembers that she would point out the store manager to him and the fact that he wore a suit meant that it was a good job. He recalls reading food labels and other product information, sharing his mother's passion for retailing and selling food which later informed his own choice of career.

He goes on to explain the gradual shift within his job from a concern with food safety to an emphasis on risk management, responding to all kinds of institutional and technological changes:

The concept of risk management was just emerging in those days, although Marks and Spencer probably did it, but didn't quite understand the language. I say actually, there's a concept in food manufacture called HACCP which is – I don't know if you're familiar – Hazard Analysis and Critical Control Point identification and the idea is you break down every process into a series of blocks and you understand about each stage of the process. Is there a hazard related to it? For example has the food been cooked properly and how do you manage it? You know, you test the product to see what temperature it is. And that's a sort of simple description, and M&S always had those building blocks and was very comfortable to manage risk in that way.[18]

The life-story method draws our attention to life as storied. In this case, the account of shopping is inextricably related to and framed by the professional context Gregory reflects upon and situates himself within. Gregory situates his career within a specific personal context and sets up subsequent descriptions and explanations about career opportunities he has made. Both extracts, moreover, emphasize

Gregory as socially and historically situated. In the first, historical approaches towards shopping and retailing are described. In the second, Gregory relates his knowledge of historical developments within a specific retail organisation and broader approaches to managing food safety. In both accounts there is a dialectic between the social and cultural framework of retailing and David Gregory as a historically and socially situated individual. Although both accounts can be understood separately, together they serve to illuminate one another.

The social nature of individual life histories is also emphasised once it is recognised that each life story is never an entirely original or singular account. Most life-story narratives contain oft-repeated anecdotes, explanations and descriptions that are bound up with the everyday and on-going process of identity construction (see Andrews et al., 2000). According to the oral historian Simon Schrager, for example, memory and its relation to identity is sustained through the repetition of narrative as an everyday practice:

It is a common illusion to think that … narrators are creating their accounts for the first time in the course of the interview. In any such performance there is new and unique creation: in the combination of words, the association of ideas, the ordering of incidents, and much else besides, including, perhaps, the production of entirely new narratives. In all this the historian has a participatory role. But here, as in most circumstances of storytelling, most of what is told has been said before in a related form. (1998: 285)

That life stories are always 'relational' in the sense that what people say is related to the temporal, spatial and social context of its narration is illustrated by the way that life histories seldom conform to a strict chronology and are characterised by recaps, leaps forward and references across time and space. Indeed, chronological structure has been recognised as a peculiarly Western convention that has little meaning in other social contexts (see Skultans, 1995). Often, particular events or attitudes can only be described or explained with reference to other events. In telling their life story, people are being asked to arrange the events of their lives into some form of chronological narrative, however unwieldy, chaotic or contradictory it may seem. However loosely structured a life story may appear, the anecdotes and events that feature have been selected and highlighted because they explain and connect with other episodes or narratives as well as being shaped by the context of the recording or interview itself. A strict chronological account is not necessarily, therefore, a core objective of life history interviewing. Rather, life histories involve a dialogical relationship between past and present, where past events are viewed through the lens of the present and where present-day concerns shape what is remembered and forgotten from the past.

Indeed, it is in the connections and associations that people make when asked to recount their lives that life history methods can offer their most valuable insights. In Russell's work on British culinary culture, for example, some respondents simply saw their employment in the food industry as a job. For others, it was a core part of their identity, inseparable from their sense of self (Russell, 2003). It was when interviewees strayed from their central narrative about food that we learned most about their situated biography and the changing context of their working lives. During a series of interviews that lasted for 27 hours, for example, Rosamund Grant talked at length about her early educational failure as a result of childhood illness. This episode, though not ostensibly about food, situates the interview in relation to Ms Grant's academic family and, as later became clear, was embedded within a narrative framework in which her attitude towards food as a tool for education was explained. For Rosamund Grant, food was a vehicle for understanding her community's history including the impact of colonialism and slavery on Afro-Caribbean society. To teach people about 'West Indian' food was to show an appropriate respect for Caribbean culture. It was a personal and political commitment. Her decision to open a Caribbean co-operative restaurant was, by her own account, connected with the value her family placed on education as much as it was caught up in the politics of race and gender that characterised her involvement in the political life of Haringay in the 1980s (where her brother, Bernie Grant, was a Labour MP).

FUTURE DIRECTIONS

So far, geographers have had only a limited engagement with life history methods and the potential for further work in this area is vast. This chapter has sketched the origins and development of life history research, provided an outline of the methodology of life history interviewing and reviewed some of the current issues and debates within life history research. In particular, we have argued that life history interviewing provides a means of addressing the narrative construction of identity where the relationship between the individual life and the wider discourses within which individual narratives are set is a central theme. Indeed, the relationship between the individual life and a full appreciation of its social context is likely to remain at the heart of future life history research. On the one hand, we can anticipate a growing interest in questions of narrativity within oral history, where a closer encounter with literary theory may provide a key to future developments (see, for example, the recent work of the Centre for Narrative Study at Sussex University). On the other hand, we might expect further research on what has come to be known as social or collective memory (Halbwachs, 1992). Early work in this genre resorted to a rather mystical idea of a collective consciousness or *conscience collective* (see, for example, Samuel and Thompson, 1990). Today, however, researchers are using life history methods to address new ideas about the nature of memory and its diverse spatialities (see, for example, work reviewed in Green, 2004; Hebbert, 2005; Legg, 2005).

In its insistence on the situated and contextual nature of knowledge, life history research is entirely consistent with current methodological debates about positionality and calls for research to be more reflexive. To move forward, geographers would do well to engage more directly with their colleagues in oral history. For there is much to be gained by moving beyond the rather caricatured opposition between a localist oral history tradition with its emphasis on the integrity of the individual life and a disdain for social theory, and the rather cavalier attitude of geographers and other social scientists who have tended to subsume the individual subjectivity of each particular life history in their pursuit of a theoretically more ambitious comparative project.

Daniel Bertaux's (1981) insistence on the relationship between biography and society is one avenue through which such a dialogue between life history and social science may be progressed. But there are other models, too, and it is heartening to see recent work in oral history seriously interrogating the social context in which individual lives quite literally take place. Alessandro Portelli's (1991) work, for example, always uses individual accounts to complicate and politicise collective accounts, while Al Thomson's work on the Anzacs and on returning Australian migrants is theoretically informed and exemplary of the kind of truly social history to which many oral historians aspire (Thomson, 1994; Hammerton and Thomson, 2005). Above all, geographers should avoid the temptation to add life history research to their methodological arsenal without simultaneously engaging with the wider epistemological and conceptual questions with which oral historians have been grappling for many years.

We hope this chapter has conveyed our enthusiasm for oral history research, in general, and for life history interviewing, in particular. Life history methods have great value and unrealised potential for geographers interested in exploring the role of memory in the creation of place-based identities. They provide a vehicle for investigating the links between personal and collective identities, a means of understanding patterns of change within living memory, and a focus for thinking through the active links between past, present and future geographies.

APPENDIX: LIFE HISTORY INTERVIEWING: A PRACTICAL GUIDE

Getting started

There are no hard and fast rules for how to conduct life history interviews. Much depends on the context of the recording, the amount of time available and the relationship between interviewee and interviewer, both prior to the recording and as it develops. Persuading interviewees to participate in a research project may involve protracted discussion. The interview itself may take weeks to set up and record, frequently involving several sessions and lasting many hours.

Preparing for an interview

Some believe that prior to starting a recording session interviewers should prepare their ground thoroughly, ensuring, where possible, that they are well-briefed about the interviewee before undertaking the interview.[19] This has advantages in helping ensure key areas are covered. On the other hand, if an interviewee feels the interviewer is an expert in the subject they are being asked to talk about this may either inhibit them or mitigate the necessity to explain and go into detail about specific subjects. On occasion an interviewer's ignorance about a particular topic may encourage an interviewee to explicate in detail. In practical terms, where an interviewee is not in the public domain, it is likely that there is very little if any public material available to the interviewer. Either way, establishing with the interviewer a clear idea of how the interview will proceed, what sorts of areas are likely to be covered and how the recording will be conducted is an important step in ensuring interviewer trust. Preliminary work is also required in devising a list of interview questions.

Conducting the interview

Recordings should take place at a time and place that are convenient for both parties and it is good practice to send interviewees some prior information about the research, who will be interviewing them, how their material might be used and conserved and what copyright procedures will be followed. Ideally the interview will take place in a quiet room where interruptions are kept to a minimum. Although it is possible to record a life story in a single sitting over a period of a few hours this can be tiring for both the interviewer and interviewee. It is often useful to record interviews over a number of visits so that the recordings of earlier sessions can be listened to before subsequent meetings, where key issues can be taken up and developed. Researchers often keep an interview diary to record such information and to note other issues that may not be obvious from the tape recording (such as whether an interviewee seemed particularly anxious about specific issues). Recording interviews in people's homes or workplaces may provide useful additional information that can be noted in the interview diary (though they may also be more subject to interruption in such places). At the end of an interview, it is good practice to ask interviewees to reflect on the process of recording their life history. This can be an occasion for providing additional information on topics not covered so far or for returning to issues covered earlier that need clarification.

Confidentiality and copyright

Once the interview is complete interviewees should be asked to 'sign off' the interview, indicating their written consent for the recording to be archived and made available to future researchers.[20] Interviewees should be asked if they wish to place any restrictions on access to their interview. This can take a number of forms from open access to complete closure for a number of years. Interviewees may also request to close

certain sections of the interview or even, in extreme cases cut extracts out.[21] Reasons for such requests vary, including an unwillingness to make private, family matters available for public scrutiny through to doubts over the commercial sensitivity of particular extracts. Some forms of closure do not completely prevent future re-use. Even if interviewees wish to restrict public access, for example, they may still allow the person who recorded the life history to use specific extracts of the interview with their permission. It may also be possible to anonymise the material in certain ways (such as through the use of pseudonyms), though this is often problematic for prominent individuals or for those whose identities are revealed by circumstantial information in the interview.

Interpretation

Making sense of the data (Jackson, 2001) usually involves a process of coding, designed to make the analysis systematic and to prevent researchers from jumping to premature conclusions. Coding usually begins with lower-order codes, using the interviewee's own words and moving gradually towards more abstract codes that are often expressed in more academic language. At this stage, it is often valuable to tack back and forth between the text of the interview(s) and a series of wider theoretical issues and debates. It is also important to continue to listen to the recording rather than to rely on the transcript or tape summary in order to remain attentive to the interviewee's tone of voice and other oral evidence.

NOTES

1. For a review of 'critical developments' in oral history research, see Perks and Thomson (2006: 1–13).

2. The United Kingdom Oral History Society supports a regional network of oral history practitioners and projects (http://www.ohs.org.uk/network/), most of which are community based and locally focused.

A broad range of projects are listed in the Regional Networks annual reports. They include: *Burngreave Voices* a community project assisted by the Sheffield Galleries and Museum Trust; *Pit Voices*, which seeks to record the experiences of current and former miners in Burnley; Hampshire Coppice Craftsmen's Group recording experiences from the coppicing industry across the UK; and the London Chinese National Healthy Living Centre project which recorded the experiences of the London Chinese community (http://www.ohs.org.uk/network/2005.pdf).

3. Poultry supplier, interviewed by Polly Russell (July 2004).

4. Other recent geographical work using life history methods (much of it still unpublished) includes Caitriona Ni Laoire's work on Irish return migrants, Joanna Herbert's work on the role of memory in the life histories of South Asians in Leicester, Phil Hubbard's work on post-war British planning, Andrew Morrison's work on orphan children who migrated to Canada, Adrian Bailey's work on Bournville, Hayden Lorimer's work on the reintroduction of reindeer to Scotland, David Matless's work on the oral histories of British Soviet geography and Iain Robertson's work on crofting in Scotland. The journal *Social and Cultural Geography* recently published a special issue on geography and oral history (see Riley and Harvey, 2007).

5. In the UK, for example, some authorities such as the National Life Stories have insisted on the use of a Marantz tape recorder and TDK 60-minute cassette tapes, though they are current switching over to digital technology.

6. For an overview of current commercially-available software, see http://www.qsrinternational.com/products/productoverview/product_overview.htm. New technologies are re-shaping many aspects of life history research including the relationship between interviewer and interviewee where the Internet and video/DVD technology may offer interviewees more direct methods of dissemination that may potentially circumvent the researcher-as-expert-mediator.

7. Our research on 'Manufacturing meaning along the food commodity chain' was funded by the AHRC-ESRC Cultures of Consumption programme (award number RES-143-25-0026).

8. For a detailed description of the impetus and aims of Qualidata see Thompson (1998). The Qualidata project and archiving in general raises the question of how far it is possible to re-interpret material that was collected for one purpose in a different context, guided by new theoretical perspectives or in order to address different empirical questions (http://www.qualidata.essex.ac.uk).

9. For a discussion about interviewing 'elites' see Blee (1998) and McMahan (1989).

10. Poultry category manager, interviewed by Polly Russell (February 2004).

11. For a suggested list of topic areas and possible questions, see the 'model questions' section in Thompson (1978 and subsequent editions).

12. For the Oral History Society ethical guidelines, see: http://www.ohs.uk/ethics/

13. Poultry farmer, interviewed by Polly Russell (August 2003).

14. ibid.

15. ibid.

16. Agricultural technologist, interviewed by Polly Russell (January 2004).

17. David Gregory, interviewed by Polly Russell (February 2004).

18. ibid.

19. For a discussion about interviewing procedure and practice, see 'The interview' chapter in Thompson (1978 and subsequent editions). There is also a useful section on conducting the interview in Russell (2003).

20. For more detailed information about issues of copyright and ethics in oral history research, see http://www.ohs.org.uk/ethics/ .

21. The National Life Stories allow interviewees to embargo their recordings for up to 30 years, though it tries to encourage open access to all the material in its collections.

ACKNOWLEDGEMENTS

Thanks to Linda McDowell, Rob Perks, Graham Smith and Dydia DeLyser for their comments on an earlier draft and to the AHRC-ESRC for their funding of our research under the Cultures of Consumption programme.

REFERENCES

Anderson, K. and Jack, D.C. (1998) 'Learning to listen: interview techniques and analyses', in R. Perks and A. Thomson (eds) *The oral history reader*. London: Routledge. pp. 284–99.

Andrews, M., Sclater, S.D., Squire, C. and Treacher, A. (2000) *Lines of narrative: psychosocial perspectives*. London: Routledge.

Arksey, H. and Knight, P. (1999) *Interviewing for social scientists: an introductory resource with examples*. London: Sage.

Ashplant, T.G. (1998) 'Anecdote as narrative resource in working class life stories: parody, dramatization and sequence', in M. Chamberlain and P. Thompson (eds) *Narrative and genre*. London: Routledge. pp. 99–113.

Bertaux, D. (ed.) (1981) *Biography and society: the life history approach in the social sciences*. London: Sage.

Blee, K. (1998) 'Evidence, empathy and ethics: lessons from oral histories of the Klan', *Journal of American History* 80: 596–606.

Borland, K. (1991) '"That's not what I said": interpretive conflict in oral narrative research', in S.B. Gluck and D. Patai (eds) *Women's words: the feminist practice of oral history*. London: Routledge. pp. 63–75.

Bornat, J. (ed.) (1994) *Reminiscence reviewed: evaluations, achievements, perspective*. Buckingham: Open University Press.

Bornat, J. (2003) 'A second take: revisiting interviews with a different purpose', *Oral History* 31: 47–54.

Bradford Heritage Recording Unit (1987) *Destination Bradford: the history of migration into West Yorkshire*. Bradford: Bradford Heritage Recording Unit.

Bradford Heritage Recording Unit (1994) *Here to stay: Bradford's South Asian communities*. Bradford: Bradford Heritage Recording Unit.

Brown, G. (2001) 'Listening to queer maps of the city: gay men's narratives of pleasure and danger in London's East End', *Oral History* 1: 48–61.

Butler, T. (2005) 'Linked: a landmark in sound, a public walk of art', *Cultural Geographies* 12: 77–88.

Buttimer, A. (1983) *The practice of geography*. London: Longman.

Buttimer, A. (1993) *Geography and the human spirit*. Baltimore: Johns Hopkins University Press.

Chamberlain, M. and Thompson, P. (eds) (1998) *Narrative and genre*. London: Routledge.

Chamberlayne, P., Bornat, J. and Wengraf, T. (eds) (2000) *The turn to biographical methods in social science: comparative issues and examples*. London: Routledge.

Frisch, M. (1990) *A shared authority: essays on the craft and meaning of oral and public history*. Albany, NY: State University of New York Press.

Gluck, S.B. and Patai, D. (eds) (1991) *Women's words: the feminist practice of oral history*. London: Routledge.

Green, A. (2004) 'Individual remembering and "collective memory": theoretical presuppositions and contemporary debates', *Oral History* 32 (2): 35–44.

Halbwachs, M. (1992) *On collective memory*. Chicago: University of Chicago Press.

Hammerton, A.J. and Thomson, A. (2005) *'Ten pound poms': Australia's invisible migrants*. Manchester: Manchester University Press.

Hebbert, M. (2005) 'The street as locus of collective memory', *Environment and Planning D: Society and Space* 23: 581–96.

Herbert, S. (2000) 'For ethnography', *Progress in Human Geography* 24: 550–68.

Jackson, P. (1992) 'The racialization of labour in post-war Bradford', *Journal of Historical Geography* 18: 190–209.

Jackson, P. (2001) 'Making sense of qualitative data', in M. Limb and C. Dwyer (eds) *Qualitative methodologies for geographers*. London: Arnold. pp. 199–214.

Kopijn, Y. (1998) 'The oral history interview in a cross-cultural setting: an analysis of its linguistic, social and ideological structure', in M. Chamberlain and P. Thompson (eds) *Narrative and genre*. London: Routledge. pp. 142–59.

Kreiswirth, M. (1992) 'Trusting the tale: the narrativist turn in the human sciences', *New Literary History* 23: 629–57.

Legg, S. (2005) 'Contesting and surviving memory: "space, nation, and nostalgia in *Les Lieux de Mémoire*"', *Environment and Planning D: Society and Space* 23: 482–504.

Lummis, T. (1983) 'Structure and validity in oral evidence', *International Journal of Oral History* 2: 109–20.

McDowell, L. (2003) 'The particularities of place: geographies of gendered moral responsibilities among Latvian migrant workers in 1950s Britain', *Transactions of the Institute of British Geographers* 28: 190–34.

McDowell, L. (2004) 'Narratives of family, community and waged work: Latvian European Volunteer Worker women in post-war Britain', *Women's History Review* 13: 23–55.

McDowell, L. (2005a) 'Cultural memory, gender and age: young Latvian women's narratives of wartime Europe, 1944–47', *Journal of Historical Geography* 30: 701–28.

McDowell, L. (2005b) *Hard labour: the forgotten voices of Latvian migrant 'volunteer' workers*. London: UCL Press.

McMahan, E.M. (1989) *Elite oral history discourse: a study of co-operation and coherence*. Tuscaloosa, AL: University of Alabama Press.

Mann, C. (1998) 'Family fables', in M. Chamberlain and P. Thompson (eds) *Narrative and genre*. London: Routledge. pp. 81–98.

Minister, K. (1991) 'A feminist frame for the oral history interview', in S.B. Gluck and D. Patai (eds) *Women's words: the feminist practice of oral history*. London: Routledge. pp. 11–26.

Nash, C. and Daniels, S. (2004) 'Lifepaths: geography and biography', *Journal of Historical Geography* 30: 449–58.

Oakley, A. (1981) 'Interviewing women: a contradiction in terms', in H. Roberts (ed.) *Doing feminist research*. London: Routledge & Kegan Paul. pp. 30–61.

Passerini, L. (1979) 'Work ideology and consensus under Italian fascism', *History Workshop* 8: 82–108.

Perks, R. and Thomson, A. (eds) (2006) *The oral history reader* (second edition). London: Routledge.

Pile, S. (1990) 'Depth hermeneutics and critical human geography', *Environment and Planning D: Society and Space* 8: 211–32.

Plummer, K. (1983) *Documents of life: an introduction to the problems and literature of a humanistic method*. London: Allen & Unwin.

Portelli, A. (1991) *The death of Luigi Trastulli and other stories: form and meaning in oral history*. Albany, NY: State University of New York Press.

Portelli, A. (2003) *The order has been carried out: history, memory, and meaning of a Nazi Massacre in Rome*. New York: Palgrave Macmillan.

Riessman, C.K. (1990) Strategic uses of narrative. *Social Science and Medicine* 30: 1195–200.

Riessman, C.K. (1993) *Narrative analysis*. London: Sage.

Riley, M. and Harvey, D. (2007) 'Talking geography: on oral history and the practice of geography', *Social and Cultural Geography* 8 (3): 345–51.

Ritchie, D.A. (1995) *Doing oral history*. New York: Twayne.

Roberts, J. (2005) *Telling the tale: narratives of place, masculinity and health in Foxhill-Parson cross, Sheffield*. Unpublished PhD thesis, University of Sheffield.

Rose, G. (1997) 'Situating knowledges: positionality, reflexivities and other tactics', *Progress in Human Geography* 21: 305–20.

Rose, G. (2001) *Visual methodologies*. London: Sage.

Rowbotham, S. (1973) *Hidden from history*. London: Pluto Press.

Russell, P. (2003) *Narrative constructions of British culinary culture*. Unpublished PhD thesis, University of Sheffield.

Samuel, R. (ed.) (1971) 'Perils of the transcript', *Oral History* 1 (2): 19–22.

Samuel, R. (ed.) (1975) *Village life and labour*. London: Routledge.

Samuel, R. (ed.) (1977) *Miners, quarrymen and saltworkers*. London: Routledge.

Samuel, R. and Thompson, P. (eds) (1990) *The myths we live by*. London: Routledge.

Sangster, J. (1994) 'Telling our stories: feminist debates and the use of oral history', *Women's History Review* 3: 5–28.

Schrager, S. (1998) 'What is social in oral history?', in R. Perks and A. Thomson (eds) *The oral history reader*. London: Routledge. pp. 284–99.

Skultans, V. (1995) *The testimony of lives: narrative memory in post-Soviet Latvia*. London: Routledge.

Sitzia, L. and Thickett, A. (2002) *Seeking the enemy*. London: Working Press.

Smith, G. and Jackson, P. (1999) 'Narrating the nation: the "imagined community" of Ukrainians in Bradford', *Journal of Historical Geography* 25: 367–87.

Smith, T., Perks, R. and Smith, G. (1998) *Ukraine's forbidden history*. Stockport: Dewi Lewis.

Somers, M. (1994) 'The narrative constitution of identity: a relational and network approach', *Theory and Society* 23: 605–49.

Tagg, J. (1988) *The burden of representation: essays on photographies and histories*. London: Palgrave Macmillan.

Thomson, A. (1994) *Anzac memories: living with the legend*. Melbourne: Oxford University Press.

Thompson, P. (1978) *The voice of the past: oral history*. Oxford: Oxford University Press.

Thompson, P. (1998) 'Sharing and reshaping life stories: problems and potential in archiving research narratives', in M. Chamberlain and P. Thompson (eds) *Narrative and genre*. London: Routledge. pp. 167–90.

Vansina, J. (1965) *Oral tradition: a study of historical methodology*. London: Routledge and Kegan Paul.

Yow, V. (2006) '"Do I like them too much?" Effects of the oral history interview on the interviewee and vice-versa', in R. Perks and A. Thomson (eds) *The oral history reader* (second edition). London: Routledge. pp. 54–72.

11

Focus Groups as Collaborative Research Performances

Fernando J. Bosco and Thomas Herman

MAKING A CASE FOR FOCUS GROUPS

Inasmuch as this is a volume about qualitative methods, some readers may expect this chapter to be about how to collect qualitative data through focus groups. This is true to an extent, but stopping there would keep us from recognizing the tremendous value we see in using focus groups as a broader research approach both to build up and frame the knowledge and insights we carry forward from the act of research. We have developed an enthusiasm for the potential of focus groups as sites of two-way communication and cooperative knowledge formation, and as a research method useful to interrogate the multiple meanings that people attribute to relationships and to places (Cameron, 2000). Rather than seeing focus groups as quick ways to collect group data, we make a case for the use of focus groups as one of the most engaging research methods available to geographers working with qualitative data and approaching geographic questions from a critical perspective.

The focus group is often described as a research methodology that brings participants together to discuss topics that are of mutual interest to the participants but that are introduced by a researcher or moderator (Morgan and Spanish, 1984; Morgan, 1996). In practical ways, thinking about focus groups along these lines encapsulates well the kinds of activities carried out when one is working with groups of people: the goal certainly is to collect data, those data are generated through a group discussion where social interaction is the norm, and such interaction in turn is moderated by a researcher who keeps the group 'focused' through a set of prepared questions and prompts (Morgan, 1996). There is, however, more depth to the process of running a focus group. Researchers in geography and other disciplines (everything from sociology, to public health, to marketing research) have worried about things such as group size, the duration and composition of the focus group, the degree of flexibility allowed in the discussion, and the different ways to represent, report and interpret verbal and non-verbal expressions (things such as silences, attitudes, and emotions) that are part of the focus group experience. Discussions around some of these variables have led some to argue that there is a distinction to be made between 'traditional' focus groups commonly used in marketing studies and 'in-depth' groups, more useful for critical geographic research. According to James Kneale (2001), in-depth groups have the potential to shift the balance of power away from the researcher toward the participants and allow for supportive and reflexive encounters. Regardless of distinctions, providing guidelines for the organization of focus groups and for the analysis of focus group data has been an important theme in the literature (Bernard, 1995; Sim, 1998; Kidd and Parshall, 2000; Cameron, 2000; Bedford and Burgess, 2001), especially as researchers attempt to find the right balance of power relations among participants and researchers, and strive toward more ethical research practices (Kneale, 2001; Breen, 2006).

In this chapter, we think critically about some of the standard and accepted practices of focus group research and we offer what we hope are some valuable reflections, useful to those thinking about incorporating focus groups in their research design. Using examples from our own research experience, we discuss the process of working with focus groups. Our goal in this chapter is to do something more than to offer a list of recommendations and 'how-tos' in relation to practical matters such as setting up and managing focus groups. Instead, we position focus groups in the same critical perspective shared by other essays in this volume, taking into account issues of difference, reflexivity and positionality as well as of participation and collaboration. It is commonly accepted that focus groups are a valuable research method for exploratory and confirmatory reasons, including things such as '... gaining background information, clarifying ideas, developing questions, and understanding group reactions to particular problems, processes and patterns' (Skop, 2006: 114). Besides these points, we believe that focus groups are compatible with a socially embedded form of research that values the knowledge that participants have to offer and that has the potential to bring more transparency to the process

of knowledge production. Thus, the main thread that runs through this essay is an argument about focus groups as a research practice that can be used for reflexive, collaborative, and participatory geographic research. We also believe that focus groups are a good complement to the type of theory-rich and critically informed geographic research that has been prevalent in human geography during the last decades.

Our perspective on focus groups is closely associated with *in-depth groups* that generate dynamic conversations, provide a supportive atmosphere for participants, and shift power relations between researchers and those being researched (Kneale, 2001). Specifically, we understand focus groups as organized events in which researchers select and assemble groups of individuals to discuss and comment on, from personal experience, topics of relevance to different research projects (Powell and Single, 1996; Gibbs, 1997). Our definition and approach eschew the structural characteristics included in many other definitions of this technique, especially those related to the more traditional focus groups typically used in market and opinion research. Rather than placing parameters and constraints on the use of focus groups, our perspective emphasizes the ways in which focus groups appropriate, for the purpose of research, '...the kinds of everyday speech acts that are part and parcel of unmarked social life-conversations, group discussions, and the like' (Kamberelis and Dimitriadis, 2005: 887, following Bakhtin, 1986). For us, the distinguishing elements of focus groups are the *conversations among participants*. We see this in opposition to group interviews, which are often designed to generate multiple *individual* responses to a set of questions prompted by researchers.

Our understanding of focus groups as dynamic and in-depth conversations among participants hints at our ideas about *when* the use of focus groups is most appropriate for geographic research. We follow George Kamberelis and Greg Dimitriadis (2005) in understanding focus groups as a strategic approach to exploring the dynamics of social discourse and social practice in relation to the construction of collective meaning. As such, we believe that focus groups are particularly appropriate for examining the complex socio-spatial practices and discourses that are the focus of much contemporary work in human geography. For example, analyses of the spatiality of social life often require that human geographers deal with issues of difference and conflict in the performances of individual and group identity. Focus groups facilitate unearthing such issues through the dynamic conversations that they generate. As a technique, focus groups are also useful to help retain *within the data* the peculiarities and discontinuities that often emerge in such in-depth group discussions. In our research, focus groups have helped us examine internal conflicts among groups of activist mothers of 'disappeared' people in Argentina (Bosco, 2004, 2006). Focus groups have also helped us understand geographies of support and care among immigrant women of a community service organization in Southern California (Bosco *et al.*, 2007), as well as the negotiations of boundaries and meanings among children in an urban neighborhood (Herman, 2000).

We value focus groups as a research practice for different reasons. First, as we indicated above, there is a unique fluidity to the method. In a successful focus group experience the lines between researchers and participants become blurred and everyone comes a bit closer together and, through group synergy, engages with a set of topics and issues in-depth. Second, there is a kind of hybridity to focus groups. By this we mean that focus groups provide an opportunity to challenge traditional divisions between theory and methodology (and between data and interpretation) because there is the potential to revise and re-work theories and concepts from the ground up, together with participants, and to offer more clarity to the process of knowledge construction. For us, fluidity

and hybridity are important dimensions that make focus groups something akin to research *performances*. This performative view is about engaging focus groups as an active practice of simultaneously *doing* research and *being* in the research (Turner, 1985, 1992; Pratt, 2000; Castaneda, 2006), involving everyone as participants (regardless of their identification as researchers or subjects), collapsing the space-time dimensions of collecting and analyzing data, and being flexible in our ways of producing our research evidence and knowledge (Latham, 2003).

As scholars who have used focus groups in several of our research projects, we have come to experience how this coming together of people and ideas in specific settings is inseparable from the process of knowledge production. We see this as an advantage because through this process we have experienced the potential to produce critical knowledge. Such knowledge, we argue, can act as a liberating force and a creative push for all those involved in the experience. We are hardly the first scholars to make these points. In human geography, some scholars have already discussed the potential of focus groups as a critical methodology (Goss, 1996; Goss and Leinbach, 1996; Skop, 2006). Specifically, Jon Goss and Thomas Leinbach (1996) draw on Jurgen Habermas' (1988) thoughts on different forms of knowledge to argue that focus groups generate critical-emancipatory knowledge because such knowledge is produced by and for its subjects through the collective focus group experience – this is in contrast to the knowledge that is appropriated from research subjects through the more traditional methods of research in social science, such as surveys. Even outside the discipline of geography, and going back to the origins of focus group research, the method has been seen as an opportunity to generate some form of social change. This point can be better understood by reviewing some of the history of this research methodology and trying to learn something from Robert King Merton's original 'Sociology of Engagement' (Merton, 1987).

COMING TO TERMS WITH ONE GOOD WAY OF DOING CRITICAL RESEARCH

Our enthusiasm for focus groups as a potentially collaborative and participatory method can be connected to some extent to the original rationale for group interviews as represented in the ideas of Robert K. Merton, the recognized creator of the focus group. While Merton's work is not well represented in the writings of geographers, he achieved near rock-star status in the field of sociology in the post-war period. At Columbia University, he and Paul Lazarsfeld created the Bureau of Applied Social Research where groundbreaking studies of social life were carried out and Merton's so-called 'theories of the middle range' were developed. Merton's emphasis on relevant, accessible studies of contemporary social challenges helped to gain recognition for sociology as a discipline, and it also appealed to a new generation of Americans who saw sociology as an integrative and, more importantly, *consequential* field of study. Merton, after all, helped prepare Kenneth Clark's historic brief in *Brown v. Board of Education*, the Supreme Court case that led to the desegregation of American public schools.

In 1936, Robert Merton was working within the Works Progress Administration (WPA), a publicly funded effort that put millions of Americans to work during the Great Depression. As part of his job with the WPA, Merton was given the job of interviewing 'all the hoboes and homeless men and women that could be located in the Boston area' (1987: 553). Building on this experience, Merton was given an opportunity to reinvent the practice of interviewing after he presented to Lazarsfeld a critique of the method being used to predict audience response to radio programs. Merton thus began his quest for a better way of finding out what

was happening in the minds and worlds of research subjects separated from him by history, culture, and purpose. Merton's method was something he called the focused interview, used initially with individuals and groups, and it was a method developed against a backdrop of interest in the sociology of knowledge (1937). This backdrop ensured a depth to the method that is too often lost by modern practitioners, and this is what enabled Merton to move from prediction of audience response to examination of human behavior in the settings where education, paid work, and reproductive labor were carried out.

We recognize here the beginnings of a problem for focus groups being recognized as a method worthy of academic researchers. 'The term focus group is a barbarism that confused Merton's technique of an unstructured but "focused" interview and the traditional sociological technique of talking to a homogeneous group of people who stimulate each other under the interviewer's guidance' (Merton *et al.*, 1990: xxv). So we want to be clear here that the value we see in focus groups comes from the opportunities to have rich 'conversations with purpose' illustrated by Merton in his own research on contemporary American social issues and is not related to the detached and efficient, almost Fordist, approach to data collection that can characterize focus groups pragmatically administered in support of business and commercial pursuits.

The dilution of Merton's focused interview technique into the focus group model used by television network executives and advertising companies is driven in part by commercial interests. Despite the mainstreaming of the method, there are also some examples of focus groups being used to support critical research and activism among scholars (see Kameberelis and Dimitriadis, 2005). But within the academy, we argue that the lasting imprint of positivism on the social sciences has also intervened to keep geographers and others at arm's length from this valuable method and to limit the scope of its potential when it is used. It is our hypothesis, based on diagnosis of our own experiences, that focus groups are an especially challenging method for critical geographers to employ because the method compresses, in very personal time and space, the whole enterprise by which social scientists create meaning out of social phenomena. The more sensitive we become to the power imbalances that persist within the enterprise, the more we strive to account for our own position. And the more we recognize that the internal logic of our theories can exert an explanatory power that rivals that of our real world observations, the more we strive to disentangle and clarify the language that we use to describe the world. These are big challenges to be met by the responsible researcher, and it may be that they are challenges that many would not wish to try to come to terms with as part of a public performance. We, at least, have found it more comfortable to allow ourselves ample time (i.e., months of transcribing, analyzing, and interpreting) and space (i.e., the office and the library where we can work independently and without disruption) to accomplish the feat of appropriately positioning our knowledge claims. Perhaps, in our valuation of transparent positioning, empowerment, and democracy of knowledge, we have become too self-conscious to conduct our work in the light of day where others can see and understand what we are doing.

We feel everyone would be better served if we can bring out into the open the all-important step of data analysis or interpretation – the transformation of a researcher's limited access to diverse lived experiences into orderly insights aligned with or against prevailing theories aptly characterized by Mike Crang (2001) and, in this volume, by Sara MacKian. We suggest that focus groups can and should be used by researchers whenever possible to minimize the distance between the people whose stories are being represented and the researchers who aim to reposition those stories within their own stories of social and geographic meaning. In geography, Crang's (2001) work on group

understandings of neighborhood history in Bristol and Goss and Leinbach's (1996) earlier work on the experiences of transmigrants in Indonesia are exemplary of the approach we aim to embrace, a full engagement with the focus group as a method appropriate for critical research in human geography. These authors, as we do here, argue in some detail for focus groups or group interviews as a research practice closely aligned with larger trends and interests in ethnography, feminism, and post-structuralism. They look outside the discipline of geography to find models of research, like that presented by Judith Stacey (1988), where control of the process of knowledge production is yielded in favor of a truly collaborative project in which no one is ever asked to assume merely the very limited role of subject. Emily Skop (2006) also talks about the usefulness of focus groups for moving population geographers around the fixed, essentialist categories that are often used to define people. Given the more than half century long history of the focus group, and also in light of decades' long commitment of a cadre of geographers to critical research, we must ask why there are so few examples like these. We believe some of this is related to the ways in which the methodological literature on focus groups has adhered to guidelines that do not always mesh well with the critical conceptual approaches that many human geographers prefer. The topic of procedures and guidelines for running focus groups, then, also requires some critical examination.

WORKING WITH FOCUS GROUPS

Our argument is for a more critical approach to focus group practice in geographic research. This is an understanding that is fundamentally different from the approach that sees focus groups as tools for quick data collection for marketing research or political polling purposes. Approaching focus groups from such a critical perspective requires that we think about the different procedures involved in setting up and running focus groups. The goal is to effectively align the focus group experience with their participatory and collaborative potential. We find it important to clarify some of these points simply because much of the existing literature on the mechanics of focus groups makes assumptions and suggests procedures that might be incompatible with our view of focus groups as a collaborative research performance.

In the last decades much has been written about *how* to conduct focus groups. What is the appropriate size for a group? How long should a focus group last? How many focus groups should be held? What is the appropriate composition for a focus group? Should one look for homogeneity in participants to assure that data obtained is representative, or should one attempt to generate a diversity of opinions through a diverse group? Should the discussion be kept under control of the researcher all the time, or should one allow a group of people to run free with their ideas and discussion once a topic has been introduced? And what about power relations and ethical considerations? A survey of some of the existing literature suggests similar answers to these questions and specifies specific guidelines or 'fundamentals' to set up and work with focus groups (see for example Morgan, 1988; Krueger, 1994; Bloor *et al.*, 2001). Because we recommend flexibility in organizing focus groups and encourage researchers to use their commitments to ethical research practice and general social responsibility as their guides when conducting fieldwork (see Herman and Mattingly, 1999), a working knowledge of key parameters for focus groups is helpful.

The focus group 'fundamentals' include a preference for intra-group homogeneity, for medium-sized groups, and for styles of moderation that are focused but also flexible. For example, Harvey Bernard (1995) states that focus groups typically should have six to twelve members plus a moderator, and that eight people is a commonly used size for focus group experiences. Several scholars

emphasize that location is an important consideration when setting up focus groups, and that attention should be paid to the convenience of the participants (Breen, 2006). At the same time, most scholars agree that focus groups are well suited to formal settings that are specifically chosen for the focus group experience, as opposed to natural settings or environments where the populations being studied are likely to be found (Morgan, 1988). Other popular and commonly accepted fundamentals include advice about the frequency or quantity of group meetings. Pamela Kidd and Mark Parshall (2000), for example, suggest holding at least three focus groups so that knowledge obtained can be authenticated or verified. There are also different points of view regarding recruiting participants for focus groups. Scholars often suggest either recruiting participants through different variations of snowballing sampling techniques or in their natural environments – the settings where certain types of people are expected to be found, such as churches for churchgoers, sports clubs for athletes, and so on (Cameron, 2000; Kneale, 2001). We do not necessarily disagree with these fundamentals, but we also believe that many of them can artificially tie the way focus groups are conducted to an instrumental and positivist-influenced view of research that is more about collecting so-called 'representative' data than about doing collaborative research that is in turn dynamically informed by a critical conceptual framework and by a concern for the empowerment that focus groups participants could achieve through the research experience.

Focus groups have one key characteristic that we highlighted early on: an emphasis on participation and fluid interactions (Cameron, 2000; Skop, 2006). Through repeated social interaction, focus group participants generate different ideas and might even (publicly or privately) reconsider their own positions. Most scholars argue that a homogenous group is key to such group dynamics. For example, in a chapter on focus groups aimed at geography students engaging in the collection of primary data, David Conradson (2005: 113) explains that '… a general design principle in setting up focus groups is one of intra-group homogeneity (in terms such as gender, race, age, class, background or occupational sector).' Also writing for a geography student audience, Tracey Bedford and Jacquelin Burgess (2001: 124) echo this design fundamental by noting that 'each group is recruited to represent people of similar background, experience, or interest.' These ideas follow on the heels of work on focus groups outside geography, where seasoned focus group scholars such as David Morgan (1996) have argued that intra-group homogeneity contributes to a climate where participants can speak freely in an atmosphere of mutual respect, as people tend to feel more comfortable with others with whom they share particular similarities.

We do not fully embrace this fundamental for a number of reasons. While scholars argue that intra-group homogeneity does not mean necessarily finding people who think the same, there is still an implicit assumption that intra-group homogeneity equals something akin to a shared identity – as in an all black group in terms of racial homogeneity, an all women's group in terms of gender homogeneity, and so on. That shared identity, in turn, appears to validate the data obtained through the focus group as data that are representative of a particular group of people with certain characteristics. However, given the lessons that critical perspectives such as feminism and post-structuralism have taught us about the relationality of identities (the entangled web of social and power relations that go into the making and sustaining of personal and group identities), this seems misguided. One can never assume that power relations among people in a group of apparently similar characteristics are equal. This is particularly important if we are working with what Conradson (2005) and other scholars call 'natural' groups, that is, a pre-existing social group, based on clusters of relations such as a workplace, a neighborhood, or a social movement. For example, it *might* seem

appropriate to separate women from men in a study conducted out of a 'natural' group such as a specific workplace, but whether it is depends on the questions being asked. It *might* be the case that women will not discuss certain topics in front of their male coworkers, especially given what we know about gender inequality in the workplace, and patriarchy and sexism in society at large. So, if the research questions that guide the focus group are geared toward uncovering gender differences and conflicts in the workplace, a homogenous group in terms of gender could be advantageous. But such a group composition could be counterproductive if we are interested in finding out about other differences in the workplace, such as asymmetries in relations of power that might exist among women themselves. By relying on the fundamental of intra-group homogeneity, we could miss finding out what some women might share with some men in that particular workplace – as in, for instance, shared grievances among workers of the same rank that can be unrelated to gender. The general point here is that it is through a focus on difference that we might be able to uncover what Nancy Ettlinger (2004) calls 'untidy geographies' – contextual differences relative to variation in individual experiences across time and space. At the same time, we recognize that there might also be other cases in which intra-group homogeneity could be beneficial, as is the case when seeking an insider perspective, when trying to understand two sides of a social conflict, or when the participants recruited for a specific study are strangers. Again, decisions regarding group composition have to be weighed relative to the goals of the research and the questions being investigated, and this assessment must further be contextualized by ethical concerns.

In our own research experience, we have effectively conducted focus groups where intra-group homogeneity was the norm as well as groups where *difference* (in age, gender, perspectives, and so on) was prevalent. In a study about Latino immigrants' efforts in forging their own path to community participation, we conducted some focus groups in which the participants were all women, thus adhering to the principle of homogeneity that is discussed in the literature. Despite this social homogeneity, we were still interested in finding something about the types of community participation strategies that women *shared* as well as the obstacles that women encountered as a result of their *differences* – such as their migratory history, the composition of their households and other dimensions of their personal biographies. One of the focus groups we held featured one of us as the moderator, eight women and, interestingly, a man – the husband of one of the women who happened to show up by chance, and decided to stay once the women said they did not mind his presence (Figure 11.1).

During that particular focus group experience, the husband chose to stay at the sidelines and remained silent throughout the group discussion, sitting in a chair in the corner of the room. But whenever the conversation among the women turned to issues of gender differences (e.g., discussion of the work that women and men did around the house, the kinds of activities that women got involved in the community, and the lack of men's involvement in community work), the man gave different visual clues to the other man in the room (one of us), indicating his comfort or discomfort and approval or disapproval of some of the comments that the women were generating. His passive and yet persuasive way of participating gave us the opportunity to challenge and probe deeper into the issues that the women were raising. For example, women laughed together when we pointed out that, by the looks on his face, he seemed not to be agreeing with them on their comments about men's activities. So right at a time in the discussion when there appeared to be group consensus, new fractures and openings appeared in the discussion that made several of the women more strongly defend or reconsider their positions, either by confronting the man directly or by negotiating among themselves. Here, nonverbal clues, the interesting emotional responses generated by comments about gender differences in community participation, were crucial to reaching a high level of intimacy and depth in the discussion. Examining our notes and memories from the

Figure 11.1   In a study about Latina women's community participation in Southern California, an all-women focus group features an unexpected guest when one of the participants' husbands shows up to the meeting.

experience suggests to us that we would not have reached that level in the discussion if the group had been socially homogenous as was our original intention.

For the same study, we conducted focus groups where mostly monolingual women and their bilingual children came together to reflect on their own individual and family efforts regarding community involvement and participation (Figure 11.2). We asked children to reflect on the efforts they made on behalf of their mothers and other family members, and we asked the mothers to think about how the efforts of their children affected their own ways of seeing themselves as belonging in their new host community. This focus group was socially heterogeneous and it provided an opportunity for mothers and their children to reflect about dimensions of their lives that they rarely discussed among themselves. By exploring similarities and differences in their efforts to do things on behalf of their mothers (things such as translating for them at the bank, the doctor, or the post office) children gained a new understanding and appreciation of the important work that they do as members of their family and their community. Mothers, on the other hand, listened to their children and were proud of their work and achievements. They

also shared with each other their experiences as women who are mothers, workers, community activists, and migrants. During the focus group experience, mothers, their children, and researchers began piecing together all the ways in which immigrant families, through different practices, are forging a new kind of citizenship for themselves. The group was diverse and participants recognized and embraced their differences in the first place. This resulted in a participatory and creative endeavor where new understandings and appreciation of participants' commonalities and efforts were forged.

Another dimension that is not often critically discussed are the settings where the focus groups take place. Quite often, writing about focus groups emphasizes that meetings should take place in *formal* settings where there is little distraction to participants. Implicit in this piece of advice is an image of a plain conference room where people sit around a table waiting to be questioned by experts on a particular subject. This type of setting might be ideal for people engaged in marketing research, but it is hardly the only possible setting for social geographic research, especially since much geographic research is about understanding the multiple meanings that people attach to *places* and

Figure 11.2   A diverse focus group involving Latina immigrant mothers and their children in Southern California.

about the significance of *space–society relations* in different contexts. Ironically, some of the main advocates of focus groups find that the formal but 'unnatural' settings in which they are typically conducted are one of the key limitations of the methodology (Morgan and Spanish, 1984). As we pointed out before, even more peculiar is the advice to recruit participants from natural settings but to then hold focus groups in formal ones.

As geographers, we want to emphasize the importance of thinking about the *context* of focus groups relative to the group being assembled, the topic being discussed, and the broader foundations of the research project underway. Different settings experienced under different conditions could both enhance and detract from a successful focus group experience. For example, if a focus group involves students or office workers, perhaps a familiar setting such as a classroom or the office itself can enhance participants' feelings and insights during the focus group, as participants remain embedded in a familiar context. On the other hand, formal settings such as the ones mentioned above can be threatening or imposing, and participants might not feel comfortable discussing certain issues related to school or the workplace in such institutional environments. Sometimes, bringing participants to a different context (such as a public park where people might sit outdoors, or a comfortable place where people can sit as they please and share some refreshments or food) can enhance the focus group experience because the setting itself can contribute to participants' stepping outside their own boundaries or circumstances, which themselves could be constraining and might not allow participants to 'open up' and to freely express their impressions and opinions.

In our own experience in running focus groups, we have relied on a number of different settings. For example, in a project regarding women's public activism on behalf of human rights in Argentina, one of us found that talking with groups of women activists while sitting around in a park was a great setting for participants to discuss the public and performative dimensions of their activism (Bosco, 2006). Another focus group took place in an open-air street market where women set up a booth each Sunday to distribute fliers and information about their activism. Since their gatherings as human rights activists mostly took place in public spaces where their voices could be heard and their actions would be visible, it did not make much sense to take these women activists out of a context that was crucial for their success as a social movement. Asking these participants to meet in a formal setting, such as an office, simply for the purposes of our own research convenience and established protocols seemed manipulative and at odds with the participatory and performative nature of focus groups that we embrace and that we strive to follow whenever possible.

On the other hand, in the community participation research project that we described above, we relied on a more institutional setting (a classroom, after school hours) to meet the women and children who were going to participate in the focus groups. This experience was more in line with what is typically recommended as the appropriate setting for a focus group, but this particular setting was also the site of previous activities among the focus group participants. In this case, mothers and children were able to sit around tables and interact with us and with each other while sharing some food and refreshments (see Figure 11.2). For the children, the setting was comfortable since it was a familiar environment, allowing them to feel more at ease in the presence of their parents and other strange adults. For the mothers, the school was also a convenient place, since many of them lived close-by and regularly travel to the school to drop or fetch their children, to talk to the teachers, or to participate in school activities geared toward parents and families. But the classroom setting was also a relevant *context* for the research. The same qualities that made it a convenient place for the focus group have made it the location of prior activities and meetings among women in the group. In other words, we chose the school setting because it had meaning for our participants, because it worked relative to the goals of our research project, and because we thought it would be a good place where children and adults would interact. Much like the issue of group composition that we discussed above, it was our research questions and project and a concern for the participants themselves that aided us in choosing this particular setting.

Finally, there is something to be said about working with focus group data and about the processes of analysis and interpretation relative to the guidelines that populate much of the literature on focus groups. Focus groups are one of the least structured ways of collecting and generating data because participants have a much higher degree of control in discussions. We encourage this empowerment of participants that make the process of data collection inseparable from the process of knowledge production. Thus, we want to stay away from providing structured advice regarding how to handle focus group data because we do not see such recipes as productive for the kind of research approach that we are advocating. Several scholars provide advice on everything from how to record and transcribe focus group data to instructions on how to appropriately code and categorize such data using qualitative analysis software applications (see for example Sim, 1998; Kidd and Parshall, 2000; Conradson, 2005). However, a contribution in this volume by Sara MacKian provides in-depth reflections regarding the art of geographic interpretation that casts some doubt on such structured advice regarding the analysis of focus group data. As MacKian explains, qualitative data is messy and the whole research process is to some extent artificial, since for example, written transcripts are often not compatible with the spoken word so there is already idiosyncratic interpretation by the researcher from the moment a tape with recordings of a focus group discussion is transcribed. Moreover, Conradson (2005) rightly notes

that much of what goes on in a focus group are interactions that generate forms of communication that go beyond spoken exchanges of words, such as emotional responses to comments that might be communicated by facial expressions, bodily postures, and other embodied forms of both verbal and non-verbal representations that are almost impossible to capture on tape and even harder to represent. As a result, an exclusive focus on the textual and on transcripts in the interpretation of focus group data will always fall short. Here, our advice is to take some clues from the different efforts in human geography toward methodologies that try to get to the non-representational (Crang, 2003; Latham, 2003) and to embrace as fully as possible the notion of focus groups as research performances where *doing* and *being in* the research are always simultaneously data collection, analysis and interpretation.

It is easy and tempting indeed to fall back into the trap of thinking about the research process in terms of specific moments and spaces: the moments of data collection during a group discussion, and the moments of data analysis in our offices. Several chapters in this volume and our own examples in this chapter argue strongly against this separation. Earlier on we also said that we wanted to think about how to stay longer in those moments where we give our control and authority away and let our research be shaped by the exchanges between our knowledge and the knowledge of the participants. To do this, we think that it is crucial to begin from the recognition that our own positionality and situatedness influences the research process from early on (Rose, 1997). Moreover, the view of focus groups as research performances means that we are always interpreting data (even as the focus group is being conducted) and that such interpretations in turn are guiding the flow of the focus group itself – influencing the kinds of prompts we use to continue the conversation, shaping the direction of our discussions, and so on. It is not only that we (in our role as researchers) interpret data as we go along, but participants themselves listen, talk, challenge, and interpret everyone else in an iterative process. As our previous examples showed, unexpected opinions and statements lead to surprising discussions, and conversations emerge that could not have been anticipated. Analytically, paying attention to these changes is important, since one of the goals of working with group data is the identification of areas of agreement and controversy and of similarity and difference in order to understand how group interactions modify perspectives and produce new knowledge (Kidd and Parshall, 2000). Goss (1996) goes even further and argues that the stories that are collectively generated through the performance of a focus group are a better reflection of the social nature of knowledge than a collection of individual narratives that one can assemble through interviews. It is exactly at this juncture where we locate the emancipatory potential of focus groups in the process of knowledge production. It is through such unexpected discussions and surprising interpretations that it is possible to put abstract and often detached research questions in the context of the participants. It is also this type of research performance that allows researchers and participants to learn something about themselves and to create possibilities to challenge and inform theory from the ground up. This is not always easy to achieve, thus, we now want to acknowledge our own problems and missteps in trying to do our work this way.

AS A MATTER OF CONCLUSION: CONFESSIONS OF TWO GEOGRAPHERS

We are not too proud to say we have felt a level of discomfort every time we have gone into the field to conduct a focus group. A general discussion of this discomfort is appropriate here, before we discuss and dissect our specific research experiences. Like many other qualitative research methods,

focus groups can be an effective way for a researcher to 'get in' to a social space and a set of social relations and 'get out' with that much prized bounty: data from the field. We have each utilized focus groups in this fashion, reducing the abruptness of the data extraction as we could, of course, by using the rhetorical tools so well developed within post-structural, feminist, and self-reflexive paradigms of scholarship. But we want to acknowledge that our authorial caution and care – in how we represent the research we have done and the insight we have gained from it – do not alone help us to make more out of those wonderful opportunities; we have to be engaged in conversations with the very people we find interesting enough to write about. We want to think about how to stay in those moments for longer periods of time, to become more comfortable in these situations in which our control and authority are shared, and to expand the way in which we use those interpersonal exchanges to inform our research and writing.

If we are to improve our research practice, we must first reflect on and deconstruct our previous experiences. As if the usual dose of social anxiety were not enough, we carried with us into previously conducted focus groups a burden of guilt connected to our nagging feeling that we were going to put our interests ahead of those of our focus group participants. Even when participants are compensated for their time and thanked for their contributions, we knew a gulf of purpose regarding why we were there would likely separate us from our participants. One way to respect people's time and interests was not to attempt a comprehensive explanation of our purpose, providing instead a digestible version of our research questions and then moving into the conversation when no one had questions they wanted addressed. We showed our participants a great deal of respect, partly because we understood that we needed them to help us gain insight into their worlds, but also because we valued the opportunity to form new social bonds, as we would in any social situation.

We understood those opportunities to be precious, perhaps in part because they are so unlike the way we would go about data analysis and writing. After we felt we had collected enough data to allow us to move on to interpretation, we knew we would withdraw into the comparatively stiff and regulated spaces of the academy to make sense of what we had seen and heard. To be honest, this approach of extracting qualitative data and overlaying interpretations developed before and after our field work has seemed to be the approach best matched to the professional expectations placed on scholars, and that final withdrawal into a wholly academic conversation has been a crucial step to ensure that the results of a dynamic and uncontrolled field experience become of publishable quality. And even looking beyond academic projects to the community projects one of us has been deeply involved in for the past decade, the need for actionable and on-time information reliably trumps the idea of developing knowledge in deeper and more collaborative ways.

For each of us, there has been a conscious effort to align personal and professional commitments and to conduct research in places and on topics where we think we can make a positive difference in people's lives or at least call attention to their laudable efforts. This alignment positions us within our discipline and broader academic traditions and shapes the theories that we find useful. This alignment also redefines the field as a place where we seek solidarity and value, perhaps even more so than within the academic communities we now simultaneously inhabit. We find ourselves challenged, personally and professionally, to bring those environments, social discourses, and social practices together in a coherent and manageable way. While we expect that challenge to remain throughout our professional careers, we see focus groups as a means by which we can situate ourselves, our research practice, and our knowledge claims within the broader social contexts of which we seek to be part.

The research project we referred to earlier in the chapter examining community participation and models of citizenship among Latina immigrant women and children is a good example of how this challenge can play out. One of us had a long history of partnership in community service and activism with the women who were the focus of the study, having made contact with them through a community collaborative. The motivation behind the initial group involvement was a desire to share in an authentic community experience, support others who were trying to set examples for young people, and contribute to community projects. This motivation evolved into collaboration and mutual exchange, with the group becoming recognized in the community as a result of its achievements and durability. The group was successful in supporting its members as they became involved in their community and supported their children. This success made it an appealing topic for a research project aimed at illustrating the informal and creative pathways undocumented migrants and their US-born children use to perform citizenship and community membership.

In order to develop information for our study, we carried out a successful series of focus groups. We call them successful because we collected data that we used to construct a formal academic argument about different forms of citizenship and community participation. This resulted in several academic presentations and an article submitted to a peer-reviewed journal. This was in line with some of our professional goals. Yet, we did not give enough attention to other of our professional goals, which were related to opening up the ways knowledge is produced and sharing ownership of that knowledge. For example, even though we discussed our research interests with the participants and explained how such interests intersected with their own experiences, the women and children did not have enough opportunities to question our a priori concepts, add to our knowledge and contribute to our interpretations. This is our fault because in our position as group facilitators, we retained the privilege of organizing discussion topics and managing our time together.

At a personal level, the groups were also successful because researchers and participants had a positive socially bonding experience and everyone found the time to be usefully spent. This meets the minimum ethical standards for conducting research in community settings, but it falls short of our own goals. We wanted to reciprocate by giving some of our time and energy to the participants, in support of the projects and goals they have for themselves and for their families (e.g., given the age of their children, the women are interested in assisting their children in entering college.) Yet, a year after we finished the focus groups, our desire to give back has not been able to overcome our professional demands and personal time constraints. This is not an opportunity lost; it is a commitment that we have postponed so far but on which we hope to act. Despite these failings, we feel that we are coming closer to understanding how we can blend our personal and professional goals in order to achieve both more fully. During the focus groups, we experienced the type of collaboration that we feel can energize and inform our scholarship. Our challenge is to carry that energy and collaboration beyond the specific time and space of the focus group throughout the entire research practice.

We firmly believe in focus groups as a method for collaborative, participatory, and critical research in human geography. Focus groups allow the researchers to bring theory to the participants themselves. Through the conversations that emerge in a group, researchers can get inside the theories they are working with, and the participants can actively engage with some of the theories, concepts, and main ideas using different kinds of language. Through focus groups, there is the opportunity to bring theory to the ground level and to collaborate with others in the production and application of academic knowledge. It is also these conversations (between researchers and participants,

between participants themselves) that permit placing more abstract research questions in different social contexts and, in some cases, even in the context of struggles for social change. It is in all these ways that we believe that focus groups are useful in bridging the gaps between theory and methods and in demonstrating that it is possible, as part of a research project, to make theory and concepts accessible and useful to others outside our office halls, our universities, our journals, and our professional organizations.

REFERENCES

Bakhtin, M.M. (1986) 'The problem of speech genres' (V. McGee, Trans.), in C. Emerson and M. Holquist (eds) *Speech genres and other late essays*. Austin, TX: University of Texas Press. pp. 60–102.

Bedford, T. and Burgess, J. (2001) 'The focus group Experience', in M. Limb and C. Dwyer (eds) *Qualitative methodologies for geographers*. London: Arnold. pp. 121–35.

Bernard, H.R. (1995) *Research methods in anthropology: qualitative and quantitative approaches*. Walnut Creek, CA: Altamira Press.

Bloor, M., Frankland, J., Thomas, M., and Robson, K. (2001) *Focus groups in social research*. Thousand Oaks, CA: Sage Publications.

Bosco, F. (2004) 'Human rights politics and scaled performances of memory: conflicts among the Madres de Plaza de Mayo in Argentina', *Social and Cultural Geography* 5 (3): 381–402.

Bosco, F. (2006) 'The Madres de Plaza de Mayo and three decades of human rights activism: emotions, embeddedness and social movements', *Annals of the Association of American Geographers* 96 (2): 342–65.

Bosco, F., Aitken, S. and Herman, T. (2007) 'A kid has the right to speak to anybody they want in the world: children as institutional brokers in a border community', Paper presented at the Association of American Geographers' annual meeting, April 17–21, in San Francisco, CA.

Breen, R. (2006) 'A practical guide to focus-group research', *Journal of Geography in Higher Education* 30 (3): 463–75.

Cameron, J. (2000) 'Focusing on the focus group', in I. Hay (ed.) *Qualitative research methods in human geography*. Oxford: Oxford University Press. pp. 83–102.

Castaneda, Q. (2006) 'The invisible theatre of ethnography: performative principles of fieldwork', *Anthropological Quarterly* 79 (1): 75–104.

Conradson, D. (2005) 'Focus groups', in R. Flowerdew and D. Martin (eds) *Methods in human geography: a guide for students doing a research project* (2nd Edition). London: Pearson Prentice Hall. pp. 128–43.

Crang, M. (2001) 'Filed work: making sense of group interviews', in M. Limb and C. Dwyer (eds) *Qualitative methodologies for geographers: issues and debates*. London: Arnold. pp. 215–33.

Crang, M. (2003) 'Qualitative methods: touchy, feely, look-see?', *Progress in Human Geography* 27 (4): 494–504.

Ettlinger, N. (2004) 'Toward a critical theory of untidy geographies: the spatiality of emotions in consumption and production', *Feminist Economics* 10 (3): 21–54

Gibbs, A. (1997) 'Focus groups', *Social Research Update* 19: 1–4.

Goss, J. (1996) 'Introduction to focus groups', *Area* 28 (2): 113–4.

Goss, J. and Leinbach, T. (1996) 'Focus group as alternative research practice: experience with transmigrants in Indonesia', *Area* 28 (2): 115–23.

Habermas, J. (1988) *On the logic of the social sciences*. Cambridge, MA; MIT Press.

Herman, T. (2000) *Images of childhood, images of community*. Unpublished PhD dissertation, San Diego State University, San Diego, CA.

Herman, T. and Mattingly, D. (1999) 'Community, justice, and the ethics of research: negotiating reciprocal research relations', in J. Proctor and D.M. Smith (eds) *Geography and ethics: journeys in a moral terrain*. London and New York: Routledge. pp. 209–22.

Kamberelis, G. and Dimitriadis, G. (2005) 'Focus groups: strategic articulations of pedagogy, politics, and inquiry', in K.D. Norman and Y. Lincoln (eds) *The sage handbook of qualitative research* (3rd Edition). Thousand Oaks, CA : Sage Publications. pp. 887–914.

Kidd, P. and Parshall, M. (2000) 'Getting the focus group: enhancing analytical rigor in focus group research', *Qualitative Health Research* 10 (3): 293–308.

Kneale, J. (2001) 'Working with groups', in M. Limb and C. Dwyer (eds) *Qualitative methodologies for geographers*. London: Arnold. pp. 136–50.

Krueger, R.A. (1994) *Focus groups: a practical guide for applied research*. Thousand Oaks, CA: Sage.

Latham, A. (2003) 'Research, performance and doing human geography: some reflections on the diary-photography, diary-interview method', *Environment and Planning* A 35 (11): 1993–2017.

Merton, R.K. (1937) 'The sociology of knowledge', *Isis* 27 (3): 493–503.

Merton, R.K. (1987) 'The focussed interview and focus groups: continuities and discontinuities', *The Public Opinion Quarterly* 51 (4): 550–66.

Merton, R.K., Fiske, M. and Kendall, P.L. (1990) *The focused interview: a manual of problems and procedures* (2nd Edition). New York: Free Press.

Morgan, D. (1988) *Focus groups as qualitative research* (2nd Edition). London: Sage.

Morgan, D. (1996) 'Focus groups', *Annual Review of Sociology* 22 (1): 129–52.

Morgan, D. and Spanish, M. (1984) 'Focus groups: a new tool for qualitative research', *Qualitative Sociology* 7 (3): 253–70.

Powell, R.A. and Single, H.M. (1996) 'Focus groups', *International Journal of Quality in Health Care* 8 (5): 499–504.

Pratt, G. (2000) 'Research performances', *Environment and Planning D: Society and Space* 18 (5): 639–51.

Rose, G. (1997) 'Situating knowledge, positionality, and other tactics', *Progress in Human Geography* 21 (3): 305–20.

Sim, J. (1998) 'Collecting and analyzing qualitative data: issues raised by the focus group', *Journal of Advanced Nursing* 28 (2): 345–52.

Skop, E. (2006) 'The methodological potential of focus groups in population geography', *Population, Space and Place* 12 (2): 113–24.

Stacey, J. (1988) 'Can there be a feminist ethnography?', *Women's Studies International Forum* 11 (1): 21–7.

Turner, V. (1985) *On the edge of the bush: anthropology as experience*. Tucson: University of Arizona Press.

Turner, V. (1992) *Blazing the trail: way marks in the exploration of symbols*. Tucson: University of Arizona Press.

12

Visual Methods and Methodologies

Mike Crang

INTRODUCTION

In this chapter my aim is to suggest that an engagement with visuality is worthwhile, may be even necessary, for qualitative methods in geography. In doing this I want to push the case for these methods when despite sometimes warm words there are relatively few examples of their use. Indeed if one were to look at the methods covered in qualitative textbooks in geography, then the overwhelming dominance is of linguistic sources – be they written and/or spoken. I will focus upon methods connected to the production of what we might call visual ethnographies. In doing this I want to highlight not a set of techniques, as though they were some items on an *à la carte* menu, but also paradoxes in the ways visual material is treated in geographical work. That is, I want to highlight an ambivalence around visuality and its treatment in geography, and point to some theoretical critiques and slippages. I shall throughout this chapter be trying to position the visual as being used for more than just creating 'data' to be brought into accounts. Rather I am trying to suggest it may figure more prominently in finalised versions

and as outputs. In this I must confess my complicity as a long time cheerleader for visual research and new forms of visuality without really developing those forms. I shall effectively focus upon photographic and video work. This is not to deny the good work done in terms of other visual methods – such as respondent drawings and maps (see for example Young and Barrett, 2001). Partly my aim is to focus on visual media at a time when they are proliferating in society, and thus may form either (and I would argue both) a topic for study and a means for studies. It is also a time when visual ways of knowing have come under intense and refined critique within the discipline.

My starting point is a sense that 'visual methods' may almost have been killed off before they were born in qualitative geography by powerful arguments about the problematic elements of visual knowledge – and in geography especially. A variety of visual methods, and especially the long reliance on modes of observational practice in landscape work and visual tropes for truth and knowledge across the discipline, have been criticised for assumptions of detachment and objectivity of knower leading to objectification of the known. Recently the issue of representational knowledge has been challenged – and the visual seems perhaps inescapably bound to the representational. It has become common to hear the refrain that geography is a 'visual discipline' – and that this in some sense is a problem or limitation. But often 'those asserting the occularcentrism of geography, do so only as a prelude to other sensory articulations of knowledge' (Rose, 2003: 212) to produce what might be claimed as a more rounded version of the discipline. Just as classical anthropology positioned textual approaches against embodied experience (Csordas, 1993), so in geography the visual is said to have been opposed to the embodied. Vision is positioned as the problem both in how geographers know and a powerful locus of practice within the discipline. There is much to gain from taking this line of argument seriously and I will work with and through some of these problems below. And yet, as I browse through geographical journals, I am not exactly overwhelmed by the deployment of visual media. My contention is that we have allowed one sense of visuality, with a troubling past, to rather dominate our critical understanding of what visual methods might comprise or what they might do.

This chapter will begin with a review of some of the classic heritages of visual knowledge in geography, and their politics and legacies. It will develop an account of some of the deployments of visual methods, and different modes of visuality therein. The chapter will examine visual ethnographies that seek to offer an engaged, participatory form of seeing and set it against more ironic and perhaps even alienated, critical forms of seeing. It will conclude by trying to refigure how we think of seeing as representing rather than a medium of connecting and making present. It will thus ask about how we might show what is not seen, when it cannot be pictured and how we might think about vision not as the antithesis of touch but through a haptic register.

DISCIPLINARY VISUALITIES AND EXHIBITIONARY COMPLEXES

The phrase disciplinary visualities is used by Gillian Rose (2003) to point to the way disciplines have specific ways of looking at the world – shaping how we see, what we see and indeed what is visible, and, in geography's case, may be even defining knowledge as the visible (rather than the sayable). She points out that different academic communities have rather different visual cultures. For geography one could find numerous examples, from the technologies of visualisation in sections and maps to the most explicit statements by those such as Patrick Geddes and the Regional Survey Movement of the 1920s and 1930s. Geddes's 'outlook' tower mobilised a camera obscura and the regional surveys called for expeditions to elevated points to place sight in the service of regional synthesis via the gaze from above (Matless, 1992). These visualities are technologies, in the broad sense, that discipline both observer and observed. Indeed Irit Rogoff (2000) has used the phrase 'geography's visual culture' to highlight that vision is always geographically embedded so we might think of 'positioned spectatorship' as an 'understanding of geography as an epistemological structure, of visual culture as the arena in which it circulates' (p. 11). In this sense Tony Bennett (1988) uses 'exhibitionary complex' to talk about the rise of technologies of display. Here he is trying to move beyond simplistic readings of Michel Foucault that suggest the fall of spectacular and the rise of hidden modes of disciplinary power, to look at the mode of governmentality produced by new technologies of display and vision. Thus, if we are looking for archetypal devices framing society's way of seeing we should recall the moment in history that gave us the Panopticon also gave us the Crystal Palace and the Great Exhibitions. By 1893 the World's Columbian Exhibition in Chicago could have the motto 'To See is to Know'. These technologies of vision rendered the world knowable and controllable in a particular regime of truth.

In geography, critiques have highlighted how such an objectivised technology of vision rendered especially colonised landscapes and people into objects of an inquiring gaze. A gaze, that in nineteenth century accounts of the near east, 'rendered "Egypt" as a transparent space that could be fully known by a colonial, colonizing gaze' (Gregory, 2003: 196). Indeed in works such as the *Description de l'Egypte* it is clear 'that this was a *particular* vision of Egypt goes without saying, but it was also a particular *vision* of Egypt: the special significance of the *Description* … is that it valorized a visual appropriation of the Orient' (2003: 197). The landscape and people of Egypt were reduced, first, in scientific images then in popular ones to a series of abstracted spaces, framed through the lens. A visual regime defined places, people and things through typologies – each image exemplifying a type of person or scene – and provided a distanced and detached viewpoint from which to examine them. The connection of visual appropriation to colonial modernity was so strong that Zeynep Çelik (2004: 616–7) writes that in Algeria photography was a privileged means 'to convey the 'reality' of the colony to the metropole. The conquest was repeated by capturing Algeria visually'. Thus Félix Jean Moulin's 18-month expedition to Algeria in 1856–7, was reported in the weekly journal *La Lumière* as being commissioned to 'bring to France … precise documents on the little known habits and customs, on the habitations of diverse populations living in towns, on the monuments, sites, etc of our great African colony' (2004: 616–7).

The apparent facticity of pictures belied the development of a series of limited tropes and stock images that were both framed by colonial power and staged that power. Thus a genre of 'courtyard pictures' in North Africa offered a privileged glimpse into the 'interior' of indigenous society, a gaze whose desire to see feminised interiors of housing expressed a palpably gendered desire for mastery, with fantasies of unveiling and accessing the inaccessible, driving a colonial metaphysics of truth (Yegenoglu, 1998). Through depictions of exoticised and 'chaotic' old cities, to the interiors of 'local' houses, visual media enabled the progressive penetration of colonised spaces in a dialectic of mystery and mastery. If such spectacular systems of visual consumption reached their apogee with the World Fairs, Colonial Expositions and Expositions Universelle, then we can still trace the tropes and visual practices, spreading out and across intersecting practices. Thus the *ghawazi*, female dancers ('belly dancers') of Egypt had been a long established tradition (predating Islam) that comprised unveiled women performing in the street or in men's quarters or courtyards on special occasions. By the mid-nineteenth century performances in public were being suppressed and the dance was being hidden from view in Egypt. In Algeria, the dance performed by the Ouled-Nail's was moving from a rural to an urban event, with commercialisation tied to the growth of prostitution under the colonial regime. However, it became an increasingly popular, and singular staple of colonial expositions, Orientalist art and western imaginations – rapidly developing into a circulating industry of semi-pornographic representations of 'Moorish' dances, by then staged in Paris (Çelik and Kinney, 1990). Taken from its context, the visual economy made this a portable symbol of the exoticised and eroticised East. Indeed the colonial visual economies of ethnography and pornography come uncomfortably close to each other. Although ethnography proscribes the eroticisation of the Other, both show scopophiliac intentions while keeping the Other at a safe distance, both are governed by a desire to see and have highly developed codified systems to control this fascination (Russell, 1999).

This visual fascination is not isolated historically or geographically to the nineteenth century near-east. Similar patterns, though with inflections, can be traced across the globe. In the pacific islands, some 6500 glass plates of 'village life' taken by Beckes in the 1880s, not only conflated different cultures, but were then recycled through to the 1930s to produce postcards so that 'the "other" assumes a shocking portability' (Stephen, 1995: 64). The politics of the gaze remained aggressively gendered where to state the obvious for Polynesia, 'the foreign is feminised and regarded voyeuristically' with so many semi-clad women pictured amongst foliage as though 'Woodland Nymphs' (Thomas, 1995: 46). 'The women are thus overtly transposed into a radically remote domain of fantasy, a fairyland that is distant not only from the metropolitan societies, but also from the ordinary circumstances of Polynesian life' (1995: 49). Though we should note that while Polynesia was feminised and sexualised, Melanesia tended to be pictured as an aggressive masculine domain of rudimentary technology (Wright, 2003). More subtle and supple situations can be found, where the balance of fantasy, fascination and facticity are delicately poised. If we turn to Barton's photography in Papua New Guinea, his scientific imagery of semi-naked women studiously tries to avoid mentioning what it obviously depicts, where in one case a hand drawn box highlights the bare torso, and especially left breast, of a woman. Barton's stated purpose was to point out the location of tattoos. Tattoos that were to be recorded and conveyed thus realistically, yet also required his intervention–painting over the tattoos on the women's body to render them visible in the picture. Indeed here we might say 'ethnography is a pretext, a ruse that allowed Barton to indulge his voyeurism, the referencing of tattooing serving to veil what might otherwise make the photograph less acceptable' (Wright, 2003: 148). The controlling, apparently detached, yet deeply fascinated (and implicated) gaze that transforms people's bodies or places into fragmented attributes and details for a scientific gaze is a recurring motif in this colonial vision.

An ethnographic gaze aided by the new technologies of photographic reproduction could portray and indeed create 'specimens' with precision. It is also paralleled by other visual techniques where tourism brought the discourses of modernity, primitivism, visualism, and anthropology together with the commodification of new colonial possessions, such as Hawai'i, as pleasure zones (Desmond, 1999). The entanglement of the two scopic regimes of colonialism and tourism can be seen in a visual economy where photography is an incitement to a sort of interrogative vision (Bourdieu, 1990) which drives an accumulatory economy of experience (Sontag, 1977). The parallels of practice between colonising vision and leisured photography are many and multi-layered. They feed into each other as images are produced and circulated that relate promiscuously to these registers of science and pleasure. Nor is this purely a historical connection, with colonial tropes persisting in touristic visuality (Bate, 1992). Indeed the constellation of knowledge, vision, desire, race, gender and power remains depressingly robust. The art critic Lucy Lippard was lead to remark that after ploughing through heaps of travel magazines with a sort of 'dead eye' that: 'Tourism is about desire – desire for change, but also a more sensuous desire to become intimate with the unfamiliar. The exotic other is most often female. Gender joins race on the manipulated bottom line of tourism. [With seduction and adventure both] embodied as male goals in female flesh' (1999: 50–1). Olivia Jenkins likewise looking through brochures would point to the continual, blatant offering up of female bodies as part of the scenery of desire – often western women tourists framing the picture, sharing a gaze directed onto the same scene but positioned slightly ahead so they are gazing subjects, but also objects of a gaze in this 'rear view' (2003).

This history of visual technologies suggests their vital role in disciplining and controlling both the subjects of knowledge but also the modes of knowing. The notion of visuality stresses that it is how things become 'seeable', and are made visible that is important not just what we see (Foster, 1988).

That is, we need to see technologies and techniques creating a field in which certain things become apparent, and some things are occluded. This is a scopic regime of knowledge which 'imposes a systematicity on the visual field; a structuring effect on who sees, through the constitution of the viewing subject, and on what is seen, through the production of a space of constructed visibility that allows particular objects to be seen in determinate ways' (Gregory, 2003: 224). Moreover, things become apparent only in ways specific to that way of seeing and an attendant regime of knowledge. Thus the flat, fragmenting colonial gaze hides hosts of histories of entanglement and power between coloniser and colonised. Of course there are also more inflections on this process, the emptying of some landscapes, the naturalising of others, the feminising of different ones. My purpose here was to illustrate why, having established the power and historical importance of visual methods in some rather unsavoury ways of knowing, it might seem the best thing to do is move away from the visual altogether.

The above account has in many ways become familiar – though not to the extent that it does not bear repetition. To it, and in part because of it, we might add a general theoretical hostility to modes of knowledge that depend upon an optical register (Jay, 1993; Jenks, 1995). There have indeed been well made criticisms of correspondence theories of truth, of the classic model of visual knowledge ordering an exterior and detached world from a privileged interior (Crary, 1990). Indeed from Martin Heidegger onwards we can trace a fundamental ontological critique of the visual as being a representational practice that means a separation from our world and a distancing from experience. Jacques Derrida developed a critique of what he termed the 'heliopolitics' of truth models founded on 'photology' – notions of light and seeing (Levin, 1997: 405) – building from how he saw 'Levinas describing the interconnected concepts of vision, sun, light, and truth as functioning to abolish the otherness of the face-to-face or ethical relation in

the works of philosophers from Plato to Heidegger' (Taylor, 2006: 4). Derrida argues that the 'ancient clandestine friendship between light and power, the ancient complicity between theoretical objectivity and technico-political possession. ... To see and to know, to have and to will, unfold only within the oppressive and luminous identity of the same' (136: 91–2 cited in Taylor, 2006: 5).

Drawing from these kinds of critiques, work using visual methods in geography has been criticised for an implicit notion of 'pure vision – vision that is uncorrupted by secondary connotations of knowledge and cognition' (Kearnes, 2000: 338). That is, visual methods that imply an appeal to the authority, indeed facticity, of vision (in photography) as somehow ontologically prior to the troublesome and difficult issues of knowledge and epistemology – that seeing is prior to saying. Thus David Dodman argues that whereas the 'research voice is often intrusive and imperial', the 'use of self-directed photography as a research method can therefore help to prevent many of the problems associated with representing the viewpoint of another person' (2003: 294). Matthew Kearnes in contrast suggests a reliance on the 'obviousness' of vision allows one to imply a transparency about world and picture, that can suggest the visual offers 'raw data' as if bypassing troublesome issues of constructing knowledge (2000: 333). Such a critique means that getting people to take pictures of their environments can lead to accusations of a sort of empiricism (the object of Kearnes critique was work by Markwell, 2000a ; the response was Markwell, 2000b). Indeed it might discourage using visual methods at all, as when Sara Kindon comments that 'given the tensions associated with "the gaze", it is not surprising that few geographers have used video within their research to date' (2003: 143). However this critique of 'pure vision' seems to me to rather miss the details shown by more scrupulous histories which suggest that the model of vision portrayed is historically contingent (Crary, 1990) and that different historico-geographies of an embodied vision embedded in worldly practice can be retrieved (Atherton, 1997) offering different spatial formations for knowledge.

DISRUPTIVE VISIONS, PLAYFUL PICTURES AND WITHDRAWING SIGHT IN ABYSSAL GEOGRAPHIES

Let me first suggest that a sensitive use of visual methods is important precisely to access some of the above problematics. That is, far from using a notion of transparency or objectivity we can use the visual to stage precisely those assumptions about knowledge. So we might sketch out a variety of strategies which range from attempts to gain inclusion to those that seek to disrupt the assumptions of visual truth, or use aesthetic registers to emphasise a creative knowledge founded not on verisimilitude but artistic interpretation, to approaches that focus on what cannot be shown and finally those who point to limits of representation. These latter trends I am badging with notions of withdrawal or the 'abyssal' to suggest that far from vision functioning as a naturalistic, foundational form of knowledge, it as a gap or an absence.

We might begin with precisely that orientalist vision that objectified and fixed people. This has been actively countered by attempts to become subjects, rather than objects, of vision. Projects such as *Arab Women Speak Out* have focused on producing videos documenting the unseen lives of Arab women, produced by Arab women for audiences of other Arab women – to render their struggles visible and through becoming seen, to build solidarity and commonality (Underwood and Jabre, 2003). Participatory video work may give a 'photovoice' (McIntyre, 2003) to represent what is important to people, partly by what they choose to picture but also by allowing respondents to edit the output and document their own lives according to their own lights (Dodman, 2003). For instance in

work with children, using pictures as the basis of discussion or activities may offer an engaging process that offers a means to express their own ideas not so keyed to verbal skills (Cappello, 2005). Indeed embedding visual production in a local culture, enabling participants to represent themselves according to their own priorities, to become producers of their own images rather than objects of others has been one of the abiding aims of Participatory Video and Indigenous Media initiatives (for examples see Thede and Ambrosi, 1991; Turner, 1991; Aufderheider, 1993; White, 2003). For instance, the *Raíces Mágicas* (Magic roots) project in the 1990s, in Ocána in Colombia, worked with youngsters capitalising on their dreams of access to glamorous mass media, to get them to conduct oral histories with local elders as a means on strengthening community cohesion and intergenerational understanding – in both directions. Two upshots were clear. First 'even though the formal history or the pervasive violence in the region would not be changed by the workshop, Raíces Mágicas was having a definite impact on the children's sense of belonging to their collective roots, and on their individual perceptions of themselves' and second that the video was less a product than a pretext to engender community activity (Gómez, 2003: 217–18). Similar participatory work with the Maori *Te Iwi o Ngaati Hauiti* led to the establishment of a Community Video Research Team with academics and locals as collaborators who together researched, designed, shot and edited a short video about *waahi tapu* (sacred places) in their *rohe* (territorial area of influence) and set it to one of their *waiata* (songs) (Kindon, 2003). Again this is about locating control of process and representation with respondents.

The dangers in this visual method are fourfold. First, that we are in some senses operating with a Faustian pact. These images are not made in a visual vacuum. They can be taken up and recirculated by other media and we risk asking people to become collaborators in their own visual commodification. It may be that if this was going to happen anyway participatory approaches are the most benign form. It may also be that the additional impact of visual media is a consideration in presenting materials for policy makers (McIntyre, 2003). Second, these interventions focus on video as process. We have to be aware of the full effects – for instance anthropologists have been wary that supplying selected people with cameras and the consequent power to define the group image changes or strengthens internal group power relations and dynamics. It can also impact on cultural dynamics as formerly evolving oral or performed traditions are now recorded and 'fixed' for posterity (Turner, 1991). Third, the pressure to document can produce a sort of confessional effect. Thus work with video diaries offers people a chance to narrate their own lives and events (for a discussion see Lomax and Casey, 1998; Holliday, 2000; Pink, 2001). They also though produce a compulsion to document. In a Foucauldian sense we are producing a particular kind of subjectivity here. Fourth, there is a risk that it can fall back on a sort of realism. While the urge to allow people to document their conditions is a powerful and important motivation, the risk is that these recordings do get 'treated simply as "visual facts"' (Kindon, 2003: 147). Now that may be a risk of all qualitative methods, where hearing people's 'real' voices and giving a sense of ethnographic immediacy have long been problematised, but with visual media the pitfalls of realism seem especially profound. As Kindon (2003: 149) notes, 'All uses of video, including those that are participatory, build in specific ways of seeing; there is no unmediated image only, "highly specific visual possibilities, each with a wonderfully detailed, active, partial way of organising worlds"' (Haraway, 1991: 190)'. To qualify these 'facts' then we might draw upon the scopic regime from portraiture – where the depiction is always partial and reflects the artists interpretation of salient aspects of those depicted (Dixson et al., 2005).

An alternate response is to use visual documents to throw into focus contradictions and tensions, so that rather than representing a seamless whole or way of life they offer a 'trangressive validity' by confronting the limits of representations (Guba and Lincoln, 2005). Thus Karin Becker (2000) in a project on the community gardens of Stockholm – that are used by people from Finland, SE Asia, Turkish muslims, Turkish Syrians/Assyrians, people from Syria and Lebanon – spent six years on and off in interviews and walking tours producing 900 colour prints, 30 black and white rolls of film. Her pictures had first a documentary role (recording her visits, recording what was there, and over time recording change), second, were a tool for establishing relations with respondents (photography facilitated contact with South East Asian gardeners but actually inhibited that with older middle eastern women) and, third, produced a form of output for analysis and presentation. In this area of open public sight it seemed a useful strategy, and one which over the years revealed what was not seen as much as seen. Not one picture recorded intercultural activity, unless led by the researcher. Indeed the pictures were used in a public exhibition to present this as a challenge to locals. Despite this an editor in the media reporting the exhibition spliced together photographs to make a layout headlined 'A Botanical UN' which repeated 'a popular view of what community gardening represents also in Swedish society' mobilising a blooming backdrop, linked to clear signs of ethnic difference to suggest some harmonious natural ecology (Becker, 2000: 119).

So perhaps the challenge is to move from a formation looking *at* people to one which, adapting Trinh Minh-ha's notion of speaking nearby rather than speaking for, would be one of 'looking nearby' as a kind of indirected gaze (Kaplan, 1997: 21–22). As Kindon explains the formulation it would be a

looking that reflects on itself and comes very close to a subject without, however, seizing or claiming it. A looking in brief, whose closures are only moments of transition opening up to other possible moments of transition…[…] an attitude in life, a way of positioning oneself in relation to the world'. (Chen and Minh-ha, 1994: 443 cited in Kindon, 2003: 149; see also Trinh, 1990)

This indirect gaze shows the conditions of vision as much as what can be seen, that does not create objects of an all powerful vision nor does it posit autonomous subjects wielding a neutral technology of representation. To see the possibilities for such indirection, one might look at Edward Said's and Jean Mohr's (1986) *After the Last Sky* where Said's memories of Palestine and Mohr's photographs are set together. Here both words and pictures are allowed to fail on various occasions – where Said cannot offer a personal experiential side to women's experiences in pictures, reflecting the gendered politics of Palestinian society, but also where a picture happens to capture someone he knew and Said is left mourning that so much of her is inaccessible or lost in the picture. While the book overall fulfils a demand or indeed a compulsion to testify, to offer a picture of life, indeed not just their lives but his, and a living people, yet in the end what the pictures evidence is an impossibility – the impossibility of homecoming because it no longer exists.

If we look at the persistence of colonial optics, we might look at the spatial imaginary of tourism. The effects of tourism's scopic regime play out in a geography of the visual, the seen and unseen, where, for instance, in Baltistan in Northern Pakistan, 'travel photography and travelers' dress reflect, inform, and produce narratives of modern and not modern' (Besio, 2007: 54). There restrictions on picturing, in the name of cultural sensitivity, reproduce a category of non-modern located around the female body. The conflicting definitions here of western travellers' defining traditional as veiled, while urban baltistanis may define modern as wearing a *hijab*, and rural unveiled women in public thus as 'traditional', are all set against 'Western travelers' physical presence in the village and the possibility that they may take photographs' which contributes 'to local productions of tourist spaces that contain travelers and exclude women' for fear of being pictured (Besio, 2007: 56). One interpretative strategy or visual method to deal with tension of depiction, truth and concealment might be putting the regime of visuality itself on display. Thus to return to Hawai'i, David Prochaska (2000) staged an exhibition of postcards of the islands through four rooms. The first showed the production of postcards including the relabelling of a chicken coop as 'grass hut', the retouching and redrawing of pictures. The second confronted the viewer with the sheer volume of postcards from the early twentieth century. The third took them to the site of reception with a bourgeois drawing room, showing the collation into albums and indeed what was written on the reverse of them that might contradict the apparent image. It also showed the same image successively recaptioned in a variety of periods. Finally the last room showed the curators mounting the exhibition, and included the notes and annotations showing the uncertainties about a variety of aspects.

A different undercutting of the adage that seeing is believing can be found in ethnographic film. Marlon Fuentes' film *Bontoc Eulogy* (1995) uses archive footage, in flickering black and white, to recount an ethnography of his grandfather, who was brought to the USA as a member of the Igorot 'tribe' from the Philippines to be exhibited in a 'native village' at the St. Louis world fair for popular visual consumption. So at a first level of undercutting colonial visualities, instead of 'showing' him as an 'untouched' example of premodern life, his grandfather is depicted enmeshed in circuits of power and knowledge that produce him as an 'exhibit' – deliberately restaging and destabilising the ethnographic gaze. The film however has a further sting in the tail, since at the very end it puts up a disclaimer that all events and people portrayed are fictional – it thus asks the audience why they might trust such archive footage and about their need to believe in the authority of ethnographic film

(Rony, 2003). This is not to say the film is untruthful in broad terms but rather that it might encourage audiences to think about the events portrayed and how they come to (dis) believe in stories about them. It reminds us that all ethnographies are fictions, as in they are all fabricated worlds, and that, to rework the literary theorist Frank Kermode, 'fictions are for finding things out' to which we might add 'they are also for being found out' (Kamberelis, 2003: 693). In this sense might we think of this as an abyssal representation of what was not (quite) there, and a refusal to represent in the terms of the scopic regime of ethnographic knowledge?

In that vein we might look at the deployment of the visual to depict global entanglement. One approach is clearly the insertion on pictures into a fairly normal narrative text of global commodity flows. Thus works like Deborah Barndt's (2002) use pictures to humanise narratives, to give otherwise invisible workers faces, in a large scale commodity chain. Rather more ambitious might be a strategy that deploys the visual as part of the intellectual argument. Allan Sekula's (1995) book on the real and imagined geographies of global trade, *Fish Story*, is a case in point. Sekula deliberately shows the surreal and surprising conjunctions of forces in his work. Thus, by hanging around docksides where strange combination of goods were being placed on ships crewed by people of diverse national origins, he was looking to frame photographs where 'for one moment the global supply network is comically localised' (1995: 32). In looking for the 'surreal' in the 'real', taking pictures which jar, Sekula has used photography to critique, rather than to reproduce, disembodied and despatialised knowledges and ways of seeing.

A similar and explicit refiguring of global visions can be found in the video essay *Remote Sensing* by the Swiss artist Ursula Biemann. Among its aims is an explicit reworking of the visual mode of knowledge so that 'going beyond a critique of capitalism and a deconstruction of encrusted gender models towards a geographic and video-theoretical perspective, the text reflects on the aesthetic strategies that reorganise and visually recode the space in which we write femininity, female sexuality and its economy in the global context' (Biemann, 2002b: 71). Taking up the story of the exotic Other rendered up in a sexualised and eroticised visual economy, Biemann starts to connect this to 'the visual regime involved in setting up the relation between a desirable geography and the desiring gazer with a travel budget' that enacts a 'male gaze of desire from a distance, a gaze that can evaluate, compare, book and buy. This gaze operates as a remote control of the male imaginary over a sexualised and racialised geography; it is a situated, gendered gaze with buying power' (2002b: 74–6). Biemann rejects a representational strategy that would contrast seductive imagery of women as available and desiring to serve with images of enslavement or immiseration since both these representations of female sexuality (seduction and incarceration) function at the poles of a masculine economy of desire and depend upon each other for effect. Her aim instead is to enlarge the space of representation for the feminine. She also wishes to challenge the technological, distanced visualisation usually available for global flows and trade:

> Geography is understood as a visual culture in this context. Satellite media and other geographic information systems are generating profuse quantities of topographic images to be interpreted for scientific, social and military use. Increasingly they make their way into our daily lives, inform the way we think about the world and code our concept of globality. I make it my project to explore how these satellite visions of globality are producing a sexual economy in which it has become thinkable to reorganize women geographically on a global scale. (Biemann, 2002a: 77)

Thus she offers a critique of 'optical technologies [that] monitor, control and visualize the globe and its topographies from an orbital, distanced perspective' but one that 'does not target primarily the intervention in the production of the image but in the production of the knowledge derived from the visual data. The idea is to infuse the technological images with highly charged and sexualized human stories. What seems to be an abstract geophysical representation slowly turns into a densely human experience' (2002a: 79). To do this she produces screens with multiple frames focused around women and landscapes of and in motion (roads, signage, people travelling), overlain by locational data (relative times, sunrise, latitude, longitude, passenger ticket numbers, stops on the itinerary). She thus renders visible the traces of global movements of women driven by a sex trade, and mobilises a dialectic of global surveillance and imagined data shadows of hidden movements. The layering of women in different spaces and times tries to bring together the disparate yet linked moments in a visual geography. As she describes the intended effects for one part of the video focusing on one woman:

> Caroline, who comes from a slum neighborhood in Manila and now works at the Bunny Club in Hong Kong, confesses how exhausted she gets from "entertaining" customers for the rest of the night after she finishes her long hours of dancing on stage. Her close-up is mounted on a satellite image looking down on slowly rotating Pacific Islands, next to a video clip of the pulsing city traffic moving over a bridge at sunset, overlaid with Chinese Characters signifying the word "Observatory". The surface is overloaded with signs. As Caroline speaks, textual information on Hong Kong's exact data on Sunrise, Sunset, Moonrise, Civil Twilight and Tidal Changes rolls up suggesting the entanglement of the hardship of a sex worker with factual scientific information. The potentially romantic moment of the sun setting or the moon rising above the Hong Kong bay is somewhat thwarted by both the sober figures of astrophysics and the compromising survival strategies of a slum girl. (2002b: 81–2)

Powerful visual imagery can, in this way, help to unpack fantasies of stable places and pure cultures in a world of global flows, dislocation and proliferating hybridity. Moreover, it attempts to dislocate visual knowledge rather than produce further fixed objectifying images (Biemann, 2002a). So this strategy of dislocation offers a play of paradoxical elements – the totalising, global gaze with fragmented experiences, and then

the sense of invisible and marginal people evading borders with locational technologies to make their trajectories visible. This vision is not participative nor is it indirect, looking askance or nearby as a way of illuminating its topic. It is reportage yet one that destabilises that reportage through the very technologies of facticity.

GRASPING VISION, TOUCHING THE LIGHT

One answer to the strong critiques of occularcentrism is that a careful analysis would disentangle critiques about the relationship of vision and knowledge and those about techniques of vision. The two are clearly related but perhaps more complexly than often suggested. Much of the weight of Derrida's critique for instance is about the use of visual language to describe processes of knowledge, not about visual processes *per se*. In other words a starting point for an answer is that, while critics find an all too easy set of slippages from seeing to knowing, and a circumscription of the knowable to the visible, there is then an often over-quick jump into talking about different bodily senses – which does not itself necessarily change the 'heliocentric' form of knowledge as say Derrida would have it. Valid critiques of seeing *all* knowledge as a visual activity do not mean that some arenas of knowledge are not properly visual – what might be a classic case of baby and bath water. However, I do not think that is really adequate as a position. One of the reasons for beginning this piece with a critique of one form of visuality was to remind us that vision and knowledge do not walk innocently in the world. Rather more importantly we should surely be able to suggest that specific sorts of visual knowledge have become dominant but equally then that other forms are possible. The implication is not then that we should abandon visual methods and techniques but find new ways of thinking them, with new senses of vision of that avoid some of the problems outlined in the first section. Thus in his

> critique of heliological philosophy, Derrida stresses the manner in which vision itself is given to us through language, and thus that the problematic features of vision are problems not intrinsic to the sense of sight but rather embedded in metaphysical discourse. It is not so simple a matter, therefore, as positing language as an ethical alternative to seeing, for sight only comes to us through its discursive constructions. As such, if we wish to change the violent ways in which we see, we must first change the language of vision. (Taylor, 2006: 15)

It is not about abandoning the visual and seeking other senses but recasting the visual. We can trace a different sense of sight back via the seventeenth century work of George Berkeley who in his most famous work, largely a rebuttal of Descartes, saw 'vision as a language, in which visual ideas derive their meaning predominantly by suggesting to us ideas of touch' (Atherton, 1997: 154). Berkeley's theorem challenged the notion of vision as being about representation, that is about the production of images first and foremost. Rather than a binary spatial configuration of images inside and of a world outside, Berkeley saw visual stimuli that are tangible and connective. Such a connective sense then draws us to think about light as touching rather distancing. This in many ways is counter intuitive since touch has often been set up as the antithetical form of knowledge of sight – the two hardly coexisting.

> A significant aspect of light's texture is that it implicates touch in vision in ways that challenge the traditional differentiation of these senses within the sensible/intelligible binarism of photology. Conceived of in terms of this binarism, vision has the distance required for theoretical knowledge and gives the sense of objective certainty and freedom, while the subjective immediacy of contact in the tactile faculty gives the sense of qualitative alteration and intuitive irrefutability. In its sensible indeterminacy as both feeling subject and object being affected, tactile perception is defined as a loss of objectivity in relation to the infinitude of vision's scope. (Vasselu, 1998: 12)

Resisting this binary sees the gaze as capable of caressing the beheld where, following Aristotle and Bacon, vision acts through sensation occuring in the *organs* of sense in the beholder in a reciprocal, corporealised form of sight (Biernoff, 2005). In essence then this is seeking a form of visual knowledge that is not founded on the principle of representation. As Kevin Hetherington puts it:

> touch in our culture assumes a form of knowledge that is often more proximal than distal in kind. ... Proximal knowledge is performative rather than representational. Its nonrepresentational quality is also context-specific, fragmentary, and often mundane. This contrasts with distal knowledge, which generally implies a broad, detached understanding based on knowledge at a distance or on a concern for the big picture'. (2003, page 1934)

Distal knowledge implies objects are finished and complete beings whereas proximal understandings see them as continuous, becoming, and indeed partial and precarious. Hetherington develops a notion here of something inside and outside of representation that he wishes to call praesentia: 'a way of knowing the world that is both inside and outside knowledge as a set of representational practices. It is also performative and generative of knowledge communicated other than through representation. Both a form of the present and a form of presencing something absent' (2003: 1937). Hetherington seeks to produce an impure sense of the scopic regime of touch. My purpose is perhaps the converse, to look at the haptic regime of optics. But still to think through the practices that make 'place as an encounter rather than a representation, one where the distinction between the experiencing subject and experienced object dissolves in the idea of praesentia' (Hetherington, 2003: 1933).

If then we return to tourism photography and think through the practice of picturing we might see it less as about representing the destination than about doing tourism. Nor is it an activity that simply privileges the visual – though it clearly valorises that in particular ways – we can also locate it and use it to access a wider sensorium. To illustrate this take tourism to the Greek island of Kefalonia. This island, unlike some others, is marketed on the basis of its scenic charms. It has also been connected with the book and film of *Captain Corelli's Mandolin* (de Bernières, 1995). One might argue it has been inserted into a global imaginary and powerful set of visual technologies that are trading on romantic and scenic qualities. Despite the generally hostile reviews of the movie, visual consumption of the island was reemphasised as many acerbically suggested the best actor was the scenery. But this is not to tell a story of a 'disneyfied' destination. For sure, the odd tourist has their picture taken in front of 'Captain Corelli's bar'. More though stay away as it seems so kitsch. Rather we might look at the pictures as attempts to presence something which is absent – and which was in many ways never there. So if we look at perhaps the canonical site, and sight, of the island – Myrtos Beach – this is quite often reduced to a moment of visual consumption. It is reputedly one of the

most photographed beaches in the world, and has a long history of appearing in Greek tourist promotional material. More than that nearly every time what is reproduced is one view from above and to the north of the bright white beach and blue shelving sea wrapped around by great cliffs. This visual imagery feeds into tourist practice. Announced some kilometres before you arrive (in fact the signs start on the other side of the island), it is set up as a 'must see' and, generally, must photograph, often en route elsewhere. Tour buses disgorge visitors on a specially widened viewing platform, from where they can see the beach as pictured in so many brochures. The platform is a good 5km trip from the beach. Typically they take a picture (see Figure 12.1) – the vision of the beach is recorded not the sensate experience of being on a beach. One might say the circle is complete.

Figure 12.1   The sign announcing 'The famous Greek Beach' of Myrtos is on the other side of the island, the view of the beach reproduced in many promotional materials, tourists taking pictures of the view of the beach.

And yet this easy story hardly sums up vision in tourism. One simple start is the use of pictures precisely as mementos of presence. Most pictures even of this scenic island do not comprise landscape views. They are records of places visited and moments of action. Do they record what people did? Not entirely, they rather offer us moments where people try to hang on and keep alive the times and spaces of holidays. One strategy is to use pictures then as prompts for stories to get people to talk (see for example Harper, 2002; 2003). Pictures do not simply function as visual detachment but rather stand for moments of imaginative contact. They are the basis for reminiscence and recall. What they recall can be varied. So for Kefalonia, people would occasionally seek and take pictures to echo the movie. And yet very often the sites of the movie were hard to find, the pictures might be of the wrong place or wrongly attributed. Does this show that they were in some way failures or alienated from the encounter? Maybe, but more often such pictures are about the 'atmosphere'. Something that is not visual at all. People were inspired by the romantic ambience of the novel and film, the island is beautiful and often this is what pictures might try and

capture – the emotive and affective response of people. The ghost in the pictures is often that absent presence of emotional meaning. These pictures are much more about touching or grasping something, that in that grasping slips away. They do not offer complete closed happenings, but rather are perforated by the sense of connection to the island and the memories of the visit.

However, the possibilities of visual media as a tool to interrogate tourist practice surely suggest going a little farther. More than that though it allows us to probe some of the silences and absences by trading on the visual currency of tourism. Thus producing pictures or footage of this process serves to puncture or ground the circulation of the iconic image. It serves to reinscribe the photographer and re-embed an otherwise detached vision. One might reinsert the researcher as photographer (Figure 12.2) which begins to raise the issues of who pictures who in what ways. As tourists are in public and taking pictures legally one may be able to photograph them, but placing them at the centre of gaze restages the power relations that see tourists assuming the right to picture anything and everything. Just as tourists all too often turn people's everyday lives

Figure 12.2   Taking pictures of tourists taking pictures of Myrtos.

into spectacles so too the researcher here may end up 'objectifying' tourists, rendering their banal practice a spectacle and both tourist and researcher play out what Derrida calls the 'right of inspection' ('*droit de regard*') (Taylor, 2006: 17). So Figures 12.1 and 12.2 offer a double alienation, objectifying an objectifying form of vision, that is perhaps the opposite effect from participatory video. Alternately, one could collaborate with the photography by visitors – indeed the ability to send pictures from phones and post them on photo sharing sites offers more collaborative moments. But what they also allow is using pictures to open out the inevitable failure of touristic vision to capture the presence of place, and indeed the limits of the visual discourse of the island's marketing (Figure 12.3) where the romantic is both undercut yet preserved. In Figure 12.3, the picture taken by the researcher suggests the need to emulate and replicate the ideal picture from the movie discourse (above it), yet played across it is the ironic recognition of its lack of impact on the children playing. The aim is not then to set up a detached or 'real' vision but rather to work at undercutting the visual truths and facts of tourism. The ethnographic image might restage the discourse as haunting the image rather than the image confirming the discourse.

CONCLUDING REMARKS

In this chapter I have tried to suggest that using photographic and visual media in geography means being aware of the history of such approaches. That is that these methods come freighted with legacies about desires to see, and assumptions about who has the right to see whom and what. There seems at the moment to be a trend to move from such critiques to dismiss visual media altogether. Alongside this are theoretical critiques of how visual approaches function as a representational metaphor for knowledge. The critique focuses around notions of representation and objectivity and their lure for visual media. I have tried to suggest that taking initiatives like participatory video offers a partial answer – it embeds vision and changes the will to knowledge and desire to see from being solely the researchers' prerogative. It does though often still trade upon a notion of facticity and realism – sometimes to politically strategic effect. It also plays with a desire to be seen and a politics of visibility. We might regard this as regrettable but pragmatic cases have been made that given the power of global scopic regimes, this represents the best political strategy to engage audiences and control some of the knowledge generated.

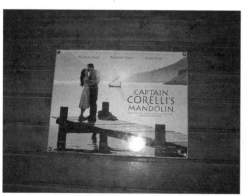

(a)

(b)

Figure 12.3 Left: a movie poster depicting the romantic theme and scenery, redisplayed in a restaurant in Kefalonia. Right: the jetty in the poster being used by children playing.

However, I have tried to return to these issues to suggest that visual methods offer some opportunities to highlight and package precisely scopic regimes themselves. This essay has worked through the picturing of Otherness in touristic and ethnographic discourses to try and show how some of these issues might be reframed. Picking some techniques that undercut the objectifying power and realism of pictures it has tried to find ways of destabilising the association of pictures with the evident. Thus it looked at Biemann's work conjoining global and local happenings – using visualisations more usually associated with locationary and surveillant technologies alongside desires—to make hidden suffering visible, and in so doing tried to reframe a space of the Asian feminine that evades standard visual tropes. A variety of more or less ironic strategies then showing the staging the visual seem to offer some ways of playing around this. More fundamentally, it then tried to make some connections to thinking about vision differently. The last section endeavoured to think about it as a way of (also) touching and connecting, rather than (only) detaching and representing. Twisting the work of Hetherington, the aim was to suggest thinking of the visual haptically. My aim was to thus recover the visual by suggesting it is not what we have often thought it to be. I do accept the backdrop of an historic ontological assumption that what is observable is what geography is about, and its elision into observation as method, visual media as recording and envisioning (be that maps or pictures) as technique. And that it seems to me does rumble through the epistemological claims of geography using correspondence theories of truth. But that it seems to me is to accept one form of vision as the model for knowledge and indeed for visuality tout court.

Instead I hope to have shown one can think of other scopic regimes both through specific historic-geographic configurations of spaces of viewing, practices of seeing and ways of presenting but also through thinking about the visual not as detaching and enframing but

connective and performative. At a time of the expansion of visual media into new and more portable formats, and the emergence of technologies for sharing pictures it would seem bizarre to choose to reject visual methods. These new media are likely to be offering new scopic regimes, as well as enlarging and energising old ones. It would seem a field into which we could look for some exciting developments. In a discipline that is rediscovering an urge to visualise data, the popular dissemination of global imaging systems that were formerly the domain of experts that seem to offer openings for participatory work in a variety of visual genres and medias. Add to this the profusion of visual devices that are recording the social world and it seems an issue of some importance that we should be looking and thinking about how we move our visual practices forward.

REFERENCES

Atherton, M. (1997) 'How to write the history of vision: understanding the relationship between Berkeley and Descartes', in D. Levin (ed.) *Sites of vision: the discursive construction of sight in the history of philosophy.* Cambridge, MA: MIT Press. pp. 139–65.

Aufderheide, P. (1993) 'Latin American grassroots video: beyond television', *Public Culture* 5 (3): 579–92.

Barndt, D. (2002) *Tangled routes: women, work and globalization on the tomato trail.* Lanham, MD: Rowman & Littlefield.

Bate, D. (1992) 'The occidental tourist: photography and colonizing vision', *AfterImage* 20 (1): 11–3.

Becker, K. (2000) 'Picturing a field: relationships between visual culture and photographic practice in a fieldwork setting', in P. Anttonen (ed.) *Folklore, heritage politics and ethnic diversity.* Stockholm, Sweden: Botkyrka Multicultural Centre. pp. 100–21.

Bennett, T. (1988) 'The exhibitionary complex', *New Formations* 4: 73–102.

Besio, K. (2007) 'Depth of fields: travel photography and spatializing modernities in Northern Pakistan', *Environment and Planning D: Society and Space* 25 (1): 53–74.

Biemann, U. (2002a) 'Remotely sensed: a topography of the global sex trade', *Feminist Review* 70 (1): 75–88.

Biemann, U. (2002b) 'Touring, routing and trafficking female geobodies: a video essay on the topography of the global sex trade', *Thamyris* 9: 71–86.

Biernoff, S. (2005) 'Carnal relations: embodied sight in Merleau-Ponty, Roger Bacon and St Francis', *Journal of Visual Culture* 4 (1): 39–52.

Bourdieu, P. (1990) *Photography: a middlebrow art*. London: Polity Press.

Cappello, M. (2005) 'Photo interviews: eliciting data through conversations with children', *Field Methods* 17 (2): 170–82.

Çelik, Z. (2004) 'Framing the colony: houses of Algeria photographed', *Art History* 27 (4): 616–26.

Çelik, Z. and Kinney, L. (1990) 'Ethnography and exhibitionism at the expositions universelle', *Assemblage* 13: 34–59.

Crary, J. (1990) *Techniques of the observer*. Cambridge, MA: MIT Press.

Csordas, T.J. (1993) 'Somatic modes of attention', *Cultural Anthropology* 8 (2): 135–56.

de Bernières, Louis (1995) *Captain Corelli's Mandolin*. London: Vintage.

Desmond, J. (1999) 'Picturing Hawai'i: the "ideal" native and the origins of tourism, 1880–1915', *Positions: East Asia cultures critique* 7 (2): 459–501.

Dixson, A.D., Chapman, T.K. and Hill, D.A. (2005) 'Research as an aesthetic process: extending the portraiture methodology', *Qualitative Inquiry* 11 (1): 16–26.

Dodman, D.R. (2003) 'Shooting in the city: an auto-photographic exploration of the urban environment in Kingston, Jamaica', *Area* 35 (3): 293–304.

Foster, H. (ed.) (1988) *Vision and visuality*. Seattle: Bay Press.

Gómez, R. (2003) 'Magic roots: children explore participatory video', in S. White (ed.) *Participatory video: images that transform and empower*. London: Sage. pp. 215–31.

Gregory, D. (2003) 'Emperors of the gaze: photographic practices and productions of space in Egypt, 1839–1914', in J. Ryan and J. Schwartz (eds) *Picturing place: photography and the geographical imagination*. London: I.B.Tauris. pp. 195–225.

Guba, E. and Lincoln, Y. (2005) 'Paradigmatic controversies, contradictions and emerging confluences', in N. Denzin and Y. Lincoln (eds) *The sage handbook of qualitative research*. London: Sage. pp. 191–216.

Harper, D. (2002) 'Talking about pictures: a case for photo elicitation', *Visual Studies* 17 (1): 13–26.

Harper, D. (2003) 'Framing photographic ethnography: a case study', *Ethnography* 4 (2): 241–66.

Hetherington, K. (2003) 'Spatial textures: place, touch, and praesentia', *Environment & Planning A* 35 (11): 1933–44.

Holliday, R. (2000) 'We've been framed: visualising methodology', *Sociological Review* 48 (4): 503–22.

Jay, M. (1993) *With downcast eyes: the denigration of vision in twentieth century French thought*. Berkeley, CA: California University Press.

Jenkins, O. (2003) 'Photography and travel brochures: the circle of representation', *Tourism Geographies* 5 (3): 305–28.

Jenks, C. (1995) 'The centrality of the eye in Western Culture', in C. Jenks (ed.) *Visual culture*. London: Routledge. pp. 1–25.

Kamberelis, G. (2003) 'Ingestion, elimination, sex, and song: trickster as premodern avatar of postmodern research practice', *Qualitative Inquiry* 9 (5): 673–704.

Kearnes, M. (2000) 'Seeing is believing is knowing: towards a critique of pure vision', *Australian Geographical Studies* 38 (3): 332–40.

Kaplan, E.A. (1997) *Looking for the other: feminism, film, and the imperial gaze*. New York, London: Routledge.

Kindon, S. (2003) 'Participatory video in geographic research: a feminist practice of looking?', *Area* 35 (2): 142–53.

Levin, D. (1997) 'Keeping foucault and derrida in sight: panopticism and the politics of subversion', in D. Levin (ed.) *Sites of vision: the discursive construction of sight in the history of philosophy*. Cambridge, MA: MIT Press. pp. 397–465.

Lippard, L. (1999) *On the beaten track: tourism, art and place*. New York: The New Press.

Lomax, H. and Casey, N. (1998) 'Recording social life: reflexivity and video methodology', *Sociological Research Online* 3 (2). http://www.socresonline.org.uk/socresonline/3/2/1.html.

Markwell, K. (2000a) 'Photo-documentation and analyses as research strategies in human geography', *Australian Geographical Studies* 38 (1): 91–8.

Markwell, K. (2000b) 'Seeing is believing is knowing: towards a critique of pure vision: a rejoinder', *Australian Geographical Studies* 38 (3): 341–3.

Matless, D. (1992) 'Regional surveys and local knowledges: the geographical imagination in Britain, 1918–39', *Transactions of the Institute of British Geographers* 17 (4): 464–80.

McIntyre, A. (2003) 'Through the eyes of women: photovoice and particpatory research as tools for reimagining place', *Gender, Place & Culture* 10 (1): 47–66.

Pink, S. (2001) 'More visualising, more methodologies: on video, reflexivity and qualitative research', *Sociological Review* 49 (4): 586–99.

Prochaska, D. (2000) 'Exhibiting the museum', *Journal of Historical Sociology* 13 (4): 391–438.

Rogoff, I. (2000) *Terra infirma: geography's visual culture*. London: Routledge.

Rony, F. T. (2003) 'The quick and the dead: surrealism and the found ethnographic footage films of *Bontoc Eulogy* and *Mother Dao: the Turtlelike*, *Camera Obscura* 18 (1): 128–55.

Rose, G. (2003) 'On the need to ask how, exactly, is geography "visual"?', *Antipode* 35 (2): 212–21.

Russell, C. (1999) *Experimental ethnography: the work of film in the age of video*. Durham, NC: Duke University Press.

Said, E. W. and Mohr, J. (1986) *After the last sky: Palestinian lives*. London: Faber and Faber.

Sekula, A. (1995) *Fish story*. Dusseldorf: Richter Verlag.

Sontag, S. (1977) *On photography*. London: Penguin Books.

Stephen, A. (1995) 'Familiarising the South Pacific', in A. Stephen (ed.) *Pirating the pacific: images of travel, trade and tourism*. Sydney: Powerhouse Publishing. pp. 60–77.

Taylor, C. (2006) 'Hard, dry eyes and eyes that weep: vision and ethics in Levinas and Derrida', *Postmodern Culture* 16 (2). http://muse.jhu.edu/journals/pmc/toc/pmc16.2.html.

Thede, N. and Ambrosi, A. (eds) (1991) *Video the changing world*. New York: Basic Books.

Thomas, N. (1995) 'The beautiful and the damned', in A. Stephen (ed.) *Pirating the Pacific: images of travel, trade and tourism*. Sydney: Powerhouse Publishing. pp. 42–60.

Trinh, T. M.-h. (1990) 'Documentary is/not a name', *October* 52: 76–99.

Turner, T. (1991) 'Social dynamics of video media in an indigenous society: the cultural meaning and personal politics of video making in Kayapo communities', *Visual Anthropology Review* 7 (2): 68–76.

Underwood, C. and Jabre, B. (2003) '*Arab women speak out*: self-empowerment via video', in S. White (ed.) *Participatory video: images that transform and empower*. London: Sage. pp. 235–51.

Vasselu, C. (1998) *Textures of light: vision and touch in Irigaray, Levinas and Merleau-Ponty*. London: Routledge.

White, S. (ed.) (2003) *Participatory video: images that transform and empower*. London: Sage.

Wright, C. (2003) 'Supple bodies: the Papua New Guinea photographs of Captain Francis R. Barton, 1899–1907', in C. Pinney and N. Peterson (eds) *Photography's other histories*. Durham: Duke University Press. pp. 146–72.

Yegenoglu, M. (1998) *Colonial fantasies: towards a feminist reading of orientalism*. Cambridge: Cambridge University Press.

Young, L. and Barrett, H. (2001) 'Adapting visual methods: action research with Kampala street children', *Area* 33 (2): 141–52.

13

Doing Landscape Interpretation

Nancy Duncan and James Duncan

INTRODUCTION

What's so important about landscape? How has it survived over the last hundred years as one of the central concepts in Anglo-American geography? This chapter addresses these questions as it traces various geographical approaches to landscape research. We look at contrasting definitions of landscape and the methods most appropriate to these differing definitions. The point of the chapter is not to advocate one or more conceptual or methodological approaches to the analysis of landscape, but to point to some of the methodological implications of choosing particular ways of conceptualizing landscape. We trace these conceptualizations and methodological commitments from the early twentieth century forward because we believe that there are certain merits to earlier approaches that contemporary researchers may wish to consider.

Richard Hartshorne (1939: 65) defined landscape as a 'restricted piece of land.' David Lowenthal states that 'landscape is all-embracing – it includes virtually everything around us' (1986: 1). Alternatively, landscape has been defined as a way of seeing. Yi-Fu Tuan (1979: 89) sees landscapes as the imagination,

representation or sensory perception of the land: 'an image, a construct of the mind, a feeling.' Many landscape researchers, however, assume that the materiality and human experiences (cerebral, affective and sensory) of landscape are best explored simultaneously. D.W. Meinig (1979b: 33–4) states, 'Any landscape is composed not only of what lies before our eyes but what lies within our heads.' In a similar fashion, Stephen Daniels (1989: 218) says that landscape is both material and ideological. He warns against trying to resolve landscape's contradictions: 'rather we should abide in its duplicity.'

Although, as we will show, there have been attempts to formulate post-humanist landscape studies which radically de-center the human perspective, most definitions of landscape continue to assume a focus on human agency, culture and vision. Landscape is seen as an object of perception, 'nearly everything we see when we go outdoors' (Lewis, 1979) or 'what the eye embraces with a look' (Vidal as quoted in Ross, 1988: 86). Simon Schama (1995: 10) traces the English word landscape to the Dutch *landschap*, 'a unit of human occupation, a jurisdiction, as much as anything suggesting a pleasing object of perception.' As a historian interested in memory and landscape as a way of looking at nature and culture, he finds the complexity and ambiguity of the double concept appealing. Landscape research ranges from structural semiotics in which the researcher is an expert decoder of landscape to post-structural studies of historical and cultural differences in meaning, emphasizing ambiguity, multi-vocality, instability of meaning practices, the productive slippage and interplay of unpredictable power relations. While most landscape researchers emphasize vision, some explicitly work to counter the 'ocular-centrism' of much landscape analysis.

Given the diversity of definitions of landscape, it is useful to ask a few conceptual questions before choosing the most appropriate research methods. For example, is landscape most usefully defined so as to clearly distinguish it from related concepts such as place, environment, ecology and region? In making such distinctions, might it not make sense to retain the relative narrowness, human scale and vantage point of some of the more common definitions? Differing ways of answering the question 'What are landscapes?' will lead to differing ways of studying them. Methodologies should ideally be open-ended and empirically grounded such that the resulting research will offer fresh perspectives on ontological issues while pointing to refined methods of research.

MORPHOLOGICAL LANDSCAPE ANALYSIS

Much late nineteenth century geography was based on morphological as opposed to causal analysis: the phenomenological study of forms and relations as they naturally occur. This holistic approach to science that refuses to dissect and abstract its subject matter was resistant to, and increasingly isolated from, mainstream science that deals with the social, economic, political or physical processes that underlie the landscape. Nevertheless, it maintained a strong presence in geography

through the influence of the Berkeley School under the leadership of Carl Sauer. More recent versions of phenomenological landscape analysis in geography have grown up fairly independently of Sauerian morphology and are far more radical in their methodological implications. The subject matter differs from Sauer's as well. However, the principal goal of an unmediated, presuppositionless encounter with the landscape remains.

Sauerian claims to a scientific morphology were forfeited by later phenomenological geographers who accepted the widespread twentieth century view of science as necessarily abstract and positivistic. While Sauer believed that a well-trained eye supplemented by archival backup was necessary to discovering the ways cultures had shaped the natural landscape historically, his approach has been considered too analytical and cognitive for later, more thoroughly phenomenological geographers. Sauer's view of science can be traced in large part to his devotion to Goethe's humanism and the historicism of German geography. In his 'Morphology of Landscape' written in 1925, Sauer approvingly cites Goethe's argument that morphology is phenomenological in that 'one need not seek for something beyond the phenomena' (1963: 327). For him, Goethean science involved close attention to direct experiential encounters with nature. Sauer (1963: 327) describes morphology as 'a purely evidential system, without prepossession regarding the meaning of its evidence, and presupposes a minimum of assumption.'

In contrast to more recent versions of phenomenology which downplay vision, Sauer (1963: 393) describes what he refers to as 'the "morphologic eye," a spontaneous and critical visual attention to form and pattern.' His 'Morphology of Landscape' set the course for several generations of American students who studied landscape as a product of human activity that shaped the natural environment. His often cited dictum, 'culture is the agent, the natural area is the medium, the cultural landscape is the result' was intended to lead geographers to see culture as an active force not reducible to human decision-making (Sauer, 1963: 343). In this respect, his approach bears a resemblance to more recent work on landscape such as actor-network theory, which also wishes to shift the focus away from individual human agency. However, as we shall see, there are significant differences between these perspectives stemming from the need Sauer felt to maintain disciplinary boundaries and more recent theorists' urge to trace out all types of connections regardless of whose disciplinary toes they may step on.

While, Hartshorne (1939: 65) had defined landscape as a region or bounded piece of land, he also recognized that the concept, having been derived from the German word *landschaft* (shape of the land), retained a double meaning that includes the aesthetic appearance of the land. He therefore rejected it as insufficiently objective for his vision of a new, more rigorous scientific geography (Olwig, 1996). For him the idea of landscape was imprecise and dangerously pleasurable. This early view prefigured a major split within geography between those who favored spatial science and those such as Sauer who made no apologies for taking aesthetic pleasure in uncovering secrets hidden within the visible landscape which only those with trained eyes and a background in comparative regional histories could possibly uncover. Pleasure in looking and its enhancement or detraction from successful analysis remains a more or less explicit theme throughout the history of landscape geography.

Sauer writes, 'One should go down into the field again and again.' He considered landscape interpretation to be a practice with cumulative dividends. For example, his interpretation of the landscape along the road to Cibolla (Sauer, 1963) was based on five field seasons during which he covered the area multiple times and in different seasons. This in-depth observation was then backed up by library and archival work (West, 1979). There are obvious cost implications of his methodology in terms of both time and money.

Although Sauer was inductive in his approach, he nevertheless formulated testable hypotheses and took contradictory evidence

seriously. Robert West (1979: 12) writes, 'Much of the time, being in the field with Carl was rather like a continuous seminar, for as he saw new country, he tied observations to the data he had dredged out of his readings.' Sauer stated, 'No science can rest at the level of mere perception' (1963: 322). However, he stressed the importance of 'personal judgment' and an assessment of that which is of value to us. (Sauer, 1963: 324).

Sauer saw geography as a science founded on a 'naively given' section of reality to which 'the experience of mankind' was naturally drawn (Sauer, 1963: 316). This 'common curiosity' alone justified the visible landscape as a self-evidently important enough topic for a science to be based upon. He viewed landscape study as objective, unpretentious, and 'value free or nearly so' (Sauer, 1963: 327). The idea that interpretation should be data-led, without recourse to the mediation of theoretical statements, has been the hallmark of Berkeley School landscape research. A strength of such an approach is that it takes data seriously. This is in contrast to much of cultural geography during the past three decades which has been theory-driven, with too little research yielding only thin empirical examples, and much of the theoretical apparatus underutilized. Having said this, we believe (as has been argued in relation to Sauer's reified, superorganic theory of culture (Duncan, 1980)) that all interpretations are necessarily theory-laden, and that to be unaware or uncritical of one's theoretical borrowings is highly problematic.

Sauer used interviewing, but purely as a supplemental method to enhance his own powers of observation and interpretation of evidence. Sauer then systematically checked out his informants' information against standard scientific references. Over the decades, as the focus of Berkeley school landscape study shifted towards contemporary landscapes, the methodological repertoire was exposed as unnecessarily limited by a generation of critical cultural geographers wishing to broaden the study of landscape to include political, social-psychological and economic practices and processes.

LANDSCAPE AS A PALIMPSEST FOR CULTURE HISTORY

Of course, Sauer and members of the Berkeley School were not the only scholars who read landscapes as evidence of the past. Landscapes were seen as palimpsests (documents partially erased and overlain with newer forms and patterns) holding a wealth of information and clues to their histories by those who were able to recognize significant features and relate these to a larger system of landscape features. American cultural and historical geographers such as D.W. Meinig and Michael Conzen, geographer-journalist J.B. Jackson, folklorists such as Henry Glassie, British geographers and historians, H.C. Darby, Oliver Rackham, W.G. Hoskins, and Richard Muir in their varied ways all see landscape as a deeply layered palimpsest, 'a priceless archive' (Zelinsky, 1993: 1295), 'a record of change' (Darby, 1948: 426), 'a continuous process of development or of dissolution and replacement' (Sauer, 1963: 333) that can reveal past cultural/environmental histories to those with 'trained eyes.' Muir (2000) offers his readers some guidelines for learning to read the English countryside. He suggests familiarizing oneself with historical changes in architectural styles, considering the geographical placement of buildings such as churches in relation to present day settlements and in relation to evidence of past settlements, using various archeological techniques to survey and inventory landscape features such as old walls, and field patterns.

A similar approach to landscape as a palimpsest can be found in the French historical geography of Vidal de La Blache, founder of modern French academic geography. Vidal saw landscapes as visual indicators of holistic relationships among humans and natural environments, each stamped with a particular *genre de vie* or way of life. Like Sauer, Vidal was concerned 'not to break apart what nature has assembled,' to understand the correspondence and correlation of things, whether in the setting of the whole surface of the earth, or in the regional setting where things are localized (Martin and James, 1977: 193). Kristin Ross (1988: 86), however, claims to find in Vidalian historical landscape study,

> an undercutting of Vidal's own fetishization of visual criteria ... Vidal's landscapes cannot, in fact, be seen; his masterful ... literary style masks the fact he is concerned not with precise, localized landscapes – the observed landscape – but rather with the typical landscape that he constructs from abstract and derivative cliché formulations.

In a similar vein, American historical geographer Meinig (1979a: 164–92) writes of symbolic landscapes that serve as 'idealizations of American communities.' Examples include 'The New England village,' 'Main Street of Middle America,' and 'Suburbia.' These are not actual locations, but ideal types or models with which observers summarize and identify actual scenes that are seen as reflective of cultural values. The methodological implications of such work can seem mysterious to those trained in more scientific approaches. Meinig refers to his work as art, rather than science. Methods include the slow process of collecting fragmentary evidence from scattered local records and weaving these together into ambitious narratives of culture history. For Sauer, it was the reconstruction of the landscapes of Mexico at the moment of Spanish conquest and for Meinig, it was 500 years of the historical development of the United States. Both put forward broad generalizations based on the observation of particular places; both were similarly inductive. They viewed landscape as a rich historical record, which could be read with the help of archival records, novels, paintings, postcards and other popular images of symbolic landscapes.

Glassie describes landscape reading as 'cultivating the habit of attention' (1971: 2). He says

> students need to develop and cultivate the habit of using their eyes and asking non-judgmental questions about familiar, commonplace things. ... Students need to get the habit of trusting the evidence of their eyes – of looking and asking some very elementary descriptive questions. 'What

is that?', 'Why does it look the way it does?' (1971: 3)

Aesthetic pleasure is seen as more than an incidental benefit of the research process. For many landscape researchers the appreciation of landscapes was the original basis of their interest and desire to acquire fieldwork expertise.

POST-SAUERIAN PHENOMENOLOGICAL APPROACHES TO LANDSCAPE ANALYSIS

A diverse group known as humanistic geographers began writing in the 1970s. (Ley and Samuels, 1978). Some were drawn to phenomenology, not through reading Sauer, but by looking beyond the traditional boundaries of geography to find a philosophical critique of the positivism and spatial analysis dominating the field at the time. Bypassing Sauer's version of Goethean science, they drew directly from Husserl and Goethe. David Seamon (1998, 2000) carries the Goethean tradition forward into the present. Whereas Sauer had described geography as 'a science of observation' (1956: 290), Seamon (1998: 2) goes further urging observers to 'plunge into the looking.' To do this one must disengage the rational half of the mind and adopt what phenomenologists call the 'natural attitude.' In daily life people tend to take the landscapes in which they are immersed for granted. Although this natural attitude is largely unarticulated and uncritical, attention is often heightened by care and intentions.

Whereas Sauer looked to natives to point out landscape features that he might miss calling this 'the education of attention,' humanistic geographers of the latter half of the twentieth century elaborated this methodology, suggesting far more radically that researchers could best learn to adopt a native dweller's point of view by suspending their own knowledge. Tim Ingold (2000) points out that landscape observers can learn to

see by asking others to guide their attention. This idea has led some researchers to experiment with giving informants, often children or teenagers, cameras so that they can record the elements in their own landscapes that are meaningful to them. In this way it is hoped that they can escape their own preconceived ideas about what is important in a particular setting and come to see the world through the eyes of others.

STRUCTURAL AND POST-STRUCTURAL APPROACHES TO LANDSCAPE AS A TEXT

The idea of landscape as a text or palimpsest written, partly erased and over-written, has been around for a long time. Pierce Lewis (1979: 12) speaks of the landscape as 'our unwitting biography.' While some landscape elements, such as monuments, are designed intentionally to communicate and celebrate values, many of the material traces of everyday life are indeed unwitting. Nevertheless, these can reveal much about values, power relations and material circumstances. Gay Gomez (1998) is an example of an activist's approach to landscape. She writes a wetland biography in which she dons hip boots and becomes a participant in the routine activities of people who live in the Chenier Plain along the US Gulf Coast. Diaries and letters help her understand the intricacies of its marshy landscape. Her notion of reading a landscape is reminiscent of Sauer's in that it is measured by the keenness of her powers of observation and her ability to relate this to an outsider's over-view of the region's complex ecology. Her interest in local lives is, however, driven by a desire to communicate their local knowledge and insider's point of view to those who will make decisions regarding the future of this landscape.

Kevin Lynch (1960) sees city landscapes in terms of their legibility and believes that creating legible cities is an important goal for planners. His work on mental maps, although influential in planning and cognitive geography, has been considered reductionist in its emphasis on the individual perception of spatial forms such as paths, nodes, edges districts, and landmarks and on psychological issues of way-finding which excludes sociological issues of communication and ideological connotation in the built environment. Although the work raised a useful set of issues for planners interested in making improvements in the quality of life of urban residents, Lynch's approach has been dismissed as behaviourist in that it is limited to sense perceptions with no way to include the social or cultural discourses that mediate cognition. However, as we will describe below, recent work in neuro-science and 'place cells' in the brain may re-introduce new life into the idea of mental maps.

Marwyn Samuels (1979) refers to the landscape as authored by individuals who intentionally shape landscapes that accordingly reflect their own individual biographies. Denis Cosgrove (1992: 7), on the other hand, points out that landscapes are not normally the product of the single, coherent policy of an individual or a state, but 'rather a function of myriad individual and corporate decisions.' 'But', he continues 'at a deeper level, a level which becomes more apparent once we consider seriously the various ways in which those involved represented what they were attempting and achieving ... we can discern another and more coherent discursive field' (1992: 7). In order to research this deeper discursive field, it is necessary to look into the intertextuality of landscapes, in other words, the textual context within which landscapes are produced and read, which includes various other media, such as novels, films and popular histories. Raymond Williams's (1982) notion of culture as a signifying system provides a framework in which to understand the transformation of ideas from one cultural production to another. The idea of a coherent discursive field or system implies structured practices which as we will see contrasts with other more individualistic or culturally diffuse practices.

Post-structural approaches to reading the landscape as a text, such as James Duncan and Nancy Duncan (1988), James Duncan (1990), Trevor Barnes and James Duncan (1992) refer to a greatly expanded definition of text which includes all sorts of cultural productions and is intended to convey 'the inherent instability of meaning, fragmentation or absence of integrity, lack of authorial control, poly-vocality and irresolvable social contradictions that often characterize them'(Barnes and Duncan 1992: 3). If meanings shift according to discursive contexts, then they cannot faithfully mirror any reality outside themselves; they are, however, productive of changing meanings. Post-structuralism takes very seriously the idea that 'a view from nowhere' does not exist. In other words, no perspective is thoroughly objective; all perspectives are partial in significant and interesting ways. Given this belief, post-structural research on landscapes tends to focus on different readings or interpretations. These readings are not only individual, but can be understood as shaped by cultural discourses with multiple and complex histories that can only be very partially traced. The meanings that landscape researchers seek in this case can only be speculatively reconstructed. The principal expertise required would not be in decoding artifacts in the field, but in broad-based research into the material (including textual) conditions of the social and political production of meanings. The latter would require much archival research including both primary and secondary written texts as well as in-depth interviewing. Competing meanings may be of interest in and of themselves or for the roles they play in politics. Some of the most obvious examples are environmental and other planning issues. In our own research we have found that the materiality and apparent stability of landscapes tend to naturalize the status quo. Deeply embedded in landscapes are class relations, diffuse and unwitting complicity and social costs invisible to the eye. Landscapes are usually not as innocent as they appear (Duncan and Duncan, 2004).

Richard Schein (1997), Duncan and Duncan (1988), and Duncan (1990) look at how landscapes are read inattentively in the course of daily life. The idea of the researcher as an expert decoder is replaced by a hermeneutic methodology in which reception and audience is of primary interest and expertise is based on critical sociological, psychological or ethnographic research concerning the unarticulated conditions of individual actions. For example, Liz Bondi (1992: 57) states, 'I am interested in whether it is possible to "read" the urban landscape for statements about, and constructions of, femininity and masculinity, and if so, what versions of femininity and masculinity are being articulated in contemporary forms of urban change.' She suggests that, 'suburbia itself resonates with assumptions about the beneficence of nuclear family living, "complementary" gender roles, and heterosexuality' (1992: 160). The evocative term, 'resonate,' signals methodological challenges. The question arises, 'Resonates for whom?' Bondi suggests that non-experts, ordinary dwellers of cities and suburbs regularly 'read' the landscape, unconsciously absorbing cultural messages about social relations. The approach she signals is critical. It assumes the possibility of standing apart from the people who live and work in a landscape in order to see what is encoded in the everyday urban landscape and the difference this makes materially and psychologically in their lives. It assumes also that it is possible to gain an understanding of power structures whose interests are made to seem natural and thus legitimized in the signifying environments that surround people.

The processes by which powerful interests manage to establish the naturalness of the status quo cannot be assumed, as these are historically and culturally specific. Nor would it be valid to presume too much intentionality on the part of those who participate in designing the landscape. It is incumbent on the researcher to figure out how certain interests are served without assuming coordination of efforts or conspiracy. In her study of a gentrifying neighborhood, Bondi signals the question of whether – and to what extent – the people who inhabit the landscape are victims of patriarchal discourses and to what extent their responses to their environments can be resistant. In order to illustrate the complexity of these issues, she proposes a critical feminist analysis of gentrification.

In the case of such critical research, interviewing, focus group discussions and other methods of discovering the opinions and beliefs of individuals cannot provide all of the necessary data. These methods however, cannot stand alone. They must be balanced with other methods that can analyze the larger structures and unacknowledged conditions of action. Bondi cites research which documents women's spatial activities effectively exposing male bias in planning decisions, however, she cautions against a priori assumptions that often characterize ideological critiques. This type of research utilizes archival research into planning decisions and negotiations over the production of urban space, observation of unconscious behaviour, participant observation, and critical analysis of values and hierarchical relations embedded in spatial arrangements and visual signs. However, as Bondi points out, such work is too often underpinned by a 'radical opposition between makers and users, between doers and done to … casting agents as professional men, the victims as women, with male inhabitants appearing as beneficiaries, and perhaps, via patriarchal ideologies, as indirect agents' (1992: 162). Bondi's own work suggests that the aesthetic refashioning of conventional gender oppositions can reinscribe these oppositions in subtle ways if they are 'detached from any challenge to the power structures that underpin these relations' (1992: 167).

Both structural and post-structural approaches to reading the landscape as a text can be traced back to the semiotics of American philosopher C.S. Pierce and the French linguist Ferdinand de Saussure. A formal decoding of the denotative function of signs in the built environment can be found in the work of social scientists such as

Claude Lévi-Strauss (1992) on the Bororo village. Connotation, then, came to the fore in the ideological critique in *Mythologies* by the early Roland Barthes (1986) which sought to expose the connotative meaning of signs, streets, buildings, planning texts, advertising and the political interests which these meanings help to reproduce. In the most radical versions of post-structuralism, as we will see, signification came to be considered an infinite regress, a play of signifiers unconstrained by material reality.

Under the influence of Lévi-Strauss's research on the structural linguistic basis of human cultures, European and some Anglo-American geographers and urban semioticians began to apply Saussurian principles to the study of cultural productions such as landscapes as systems of conventional signs. Signs are formed by the junction of a signifier (material form – verbal or visual) and a signified (mental concept evoked by the signifier whose relation to the signified is conventional or cultural rather than natural. Meaning then arises from relations of arbitrary, but conventional, difference among signs.

Lévi-Strauss and structural semioticians such as Umberto Eco (1976) and Barthes (1967) (in their earlier writings) decoded cultural practices according to rules of combining, substituting and juxtaposing signifieds. They looked not only for fairly straightforward denotative meanings, but also for connotations or second order meanings in which a sign can encapsulate a whole system of ideas (as when a flag stands for the idea of a nation and nationalism). Barthes drew on the insights of Saussure's structural linguistics to go beyond a static notion of signs whereby elements of a landscape or other cultural production are seen as signs with stable, intrinsic meanings. Barthes looked for structured systems of signs in the environment that could be deciphered to reveal the complexity and instability beneath the apparent obviousness of the everyday environment. His ambition was to shatter what appears to most observers (professional researchers and non-professionals alike) as

innocent, natural and inevitable. In this sense, Barthes' work can be considered critical, requiring an expert, distanced perspective.

His methodology is based on close analysis of the processes by which myths naturalize historically and culturally contingent, class-specific practices, values and moralities. He traces the way particular signs have become emptied of their straightforward denotative function and subsequently acquired second-order connotations. Jon Goss (1993) uses such a method to study the way designers of American malls have attempted to stimulate consumption by manipulating shoppers' behaviour through the design of a symbolic landscape that promotes associative moods in shoppers. Goss demonstrates how the landscape of the mall works to modify emotions, thoughts and behaviour.

Saussure had based his semiotics on structured, relatively static differences between signifiers, especially binary oppositions that depend on each other for their meaning. Later semioticians such as Greimas then continued to look at binary oppositions such as public-private, sacred-profane, masculine-feminine, rural-urban, here versus elsewhere, self and other as principal structuring discourses of landscape. Here the landscape is seen as a text with a grammar that people in the course of their everyday life are unaware. It can be analyzed only by experts who discover the deep structure of its narratives. For such semiologists, signifiers and their relations are seen to shift, but the range of meanings is constrained by cultural structures. If landscape meanings are concealed behind what is visible to passers-by then the decoding process requires expertise in formal grammars rather than ethnographic methods. A classic example of the expert decoding of landscape is the early, more structural, work of Pierre Bourdieu (1970). In this research Bourdieu was less concerned with fluid, meaning practices than he was in his later work. In his structural period, he analyzed Berber houses in Algeria as embodying gender roles in ways that the inhabitants were unaware. Gender for him was the important binary structuring Berber domestic life.

The Saussurean disjuncture between signification and reality also lies behind such varied post-structural developments as the philosopher, Judith Butler's notion of performativity, which we will discuss further below, and Jean Baudrillard's notion of simulation. In Baudrillard's (1988) study of hyperreality in America, we witness the turning of the crisis of faith in representation into a celebration of the play of signifiers largely unconstrained by material reality. Baudrillard shows how immaterial representations of reality begin to blur with material reality especially in highly commodified societies such as contemporary America which depend heavily upon advertizing and image manipulation. Hyperreality is the term Baudrillard uses to refer to these images, simulations and signifiers which effectively become more real than 'reality' itself. He encourages his readers to question the concepts of authenticity and the aura of an original. In fact, he argues that all that exists is the circulation of images.

Baudrillard's view that contemporary culture is highly mediated by self-referential signs that are increasingly detached from any sort of independent reality differs significantly from ideology critique in that there can be no unmasking or exposing of myths. For Baudrillard there are only simulations, images and connotations, but no authenticity. There can be no simple decoding of signs to reveal a hidden reality, because consciousness cannot distinguish between simulations and reality in the contemporary world of highly mediated spectacles. He describes hyper-real American landscapes as so commodified that they have become depthless, signifying only other signs in an endless deferral of meaning. Eco, however, worries about the idealist implications of this perspective. There is always a feedback, he argues from the material world, the power relations which constrain the play of signifiers. Mark Gottdiener (1995) agrees that objects in the landscape are unstable signifiers, but sees them as linked to both use value

and exchange value through what he terms the exo-semiotic system of capitalist accumulation. He believes that Baudrillard has been led into a methodological impasse where his analysis can only consist of 'impressionistic observations and sweeping generalizations'(Gottdiener, 1995: 34). For us, many methodological questions arise. How do we to analyse hyper-real landscapes or document the assertion that all that is left is pure simulation?

One of the best examples of hyperreality as the blurring of reality and imagination in a landscape is found in Dydia DeLyser's *Ramona memories* (2005). In this study, DeLyser settles for a less radical view of the hyperreal, but manages to demonstrate the blurring of representations and reality nevertheless. She therefore successfully avoids Gottdeiner's critique. Hers is a study of a fictional character, Ramona, and the places in southern California where thousands of visitors came each year because they believed they were Ramona's real birthplace, home, marriage place, and grave (even though they knew Ramona to be a fictional character). Tourists' emotional attachment to the imaginary makes some sense in a contemporary capitalist culture that places a high degree of value on images, spectacles and simulations that may provide a fuller experience than that which they are simulations of.

In Butler's view, reality cannot be represented linguistically; it is made anew each time it is enacted. Discursive practices perform that which they name (Butler, 1993). Conventions are enacted through repeated bodily and discursive practices. These conventions appear natural and necessary, even though they take shape only through such repeated performances. Repeated (albeit each time somewhat different) readings of cultural productions such as landscapes produce new realities. Post-structural semiotics sees the multi-vocality of all such cultural productions as undermining any conscious attempts at stablizing representation.

Jacques Derrida, whose influence has been strongly felt in geography and in many other disciplines well beyond his own field of philosophy, has consistently undermined the idea of structured binary oppositions by exposing the implicit value hierarchies embedded within them. Like Baudrillard, he assumes an endless deferral of signification. Deconstruction, his method of analysis, looks for slippage in the continual coding and decoding which is brought about by repetition, because changing circumstances mean that exact reproduction of meaning is impossible and contradictions will be exposed. Derrida argues against what he calls the 'metaphysics of presence' by which he means the privileging of that which is present, visible and knowable. Instead he argues for a permanent state of undecidability. This critique of the visible has interesting implications for the study of landscape which, as we have argued, has historically been heavily dependent on vision.

We see anti-foundationalism and celebration of ambiguity at work in writings of Butler on performance which she says creates difference, not as structured oppositions, but as the instability of meaning through repetition. Repetition entails difference and creativity because meaning is fluid. Contexts change, producing unending chains of signification. Landscapes (and the practices which reproduce them) are performative in this sense of creating new forms and meanings. They can be seen as signifying assemblages that are like written texts, cut off from the intentions of their authors, and open to new interpretations by readers who become their authors. Butler states that 'places only operate through constant and iterative practice. ... Indeed they are performed' (Butler as quoted in Cresswell, 2002: 23). Over the years in our own work on landscape we have adopted such an approach. Our early work on landscape and identity stressed how people performed their identities through landscape. Drawing on symbolic interactionism and structuration theory, we were keen to stress that landscapes are not merely symbolic, but that they are 'performed' as members of various groups act out their identities. These performances are shaped not individualistically, but in continuous social interaction. People invest hugely in landscapes in terms of money, time, political power and other resources not to make them merely symbolic, but to make them useful. And very often much of this use value comes from the role of landscapes in the performance of group identities.

Many examples of contested landscape meanings can be found in our book *Landscapes of Privilege* (2004). Here we trace the iterations between identities, contested aesthetics and social justice in the politics of landscape in a suburb of New York. We show the unwitting complicity in social injustice on the part of many concerned with historic preservation and environmental conservation. For example, we show how aesthetic concerns shape the social relations between Latino immigrants and the receiving communities. Racism and abjection dominate the political struggles in one town which attempts to clear all public spaces of immigrants who socialize or wait for day jobs, while in an adjoining town the presence of day labourers maintaining the landscape in clearly marked service roles is naturalized as white privilege. The rich who, as they say, 'can't live with them, but can't landscape without them,' manage to keep their landscape unspoilt by the Latinos whose labor maintains its valuable aesthetic. We also show in other ways how social identities and status claims are negotiated between families who have lived in a town for generations and those who are newly arrived. Dirt roads that are considered the finest and most valued of landscape features to some, are seen as a symbol of poverty and backwardness to others. Reproductions of old colonial style houses built by newcomers to town are often considered ostentatious because the scale of certain features such as columns, or increasingly the whole house, is considered wrong. What seems a beautiful copy to one person is called a 'McMansion' or 'starter castle' by others. The performance of taste and its relation to social class is a very important, but sensitive, topic to many Americans in large part because they believe it is an impolite topic which is fundamentally un-American.

LANDSCAPE AS A WAY OF SEEING

Landscape is seen by some researchers as a form of visuality. Tuan (1979) argued that it is not landscape as a bit of land that is of interest to humanistic geographers, rather it is landscape as the visual and aesthetic human experience. Cosgrove (1984) and Cosgrove and Daniels (1988) draw on the works of Marxian cultural historians, Raymond Williams (1973) and John Berger (1972) in specifying the idea of landscape as a particular elitist, distanced way of gazing upon the land which plays an ideological role in symbolizing and legitimating capitalist class relations and political power. They refer to a historically and culturally particular, painterly way of seeing land that began during the sixteenth century transformation from feudalism to capitalism in Italy. Landscapes were sketched and painted in order to sharpen active seeing as a form of knowledge. John Barrell (1980) argues that in the eighteenth century having a commanding view over an estate was associated with a liberal-minded, upper-class, male with the ability to abstract, generalize and separate the general interests of humanity from private interests. Williams (1973: 120) states, 'A working country is hardly ever a landscape. The very idea of landscape implies separation and observation.' Gillian Rose (1993) points out that this painterly, distanced way of seeing is not just classed, but also a gendered way of seeing.

Mikhail Bakhtin (1986: 217) writes:

When collective labour and the struggle with nature had ceased to be the only arena for man's encounter with nature and the world – then nature itself ceased to be a living participant in the events of life. Then nature became, by and large, a 'setting for action', its backdrop: it was turned into landscape ....

Along similar lines, Schein describes a shift in nineteenth century American lithographic representations of the emerging urban industrial-capitalist order from pictorial to 'bird's eye view' scenes. These were not quaint or innocent documents of the built environment, but hugely popular constructed images embodying nineteenth century urban ideals. They 'contributed to changing the definition and direction of a modernizing, industrializing America' (Schein, 1993: 8). Views shifted from pictorial evocations of the moral, holistic community to map-like urban spectacles emphasizing geometric order and control over the urbanization process on the part of the wealthy, powerful and the civic minded. In a similar way, Michael Crang (1997: 360) looks at tourist photography's 'conventions of how to look, such as in framing of the picturesque through the canons and techniques of painting.' He says that through tourist photography, the world is experienced as a series of iconic sights 'marked in terms of their adequacy to pictures' (1997: 360).

Barthes and Michel de Certeau both write about twentieth century distanced viewing from above. Barthes (1979: 8) writes, 'To visit the (Eiffel) Tower is to get oneself up onto the balcony in order to perceive, comprehend, and savor a certain essence of Paris.' The viewer feels both cut off from the world and owner of that world. The distanced survey allows the observer to comprehend, to order and to control the landscape. De Certeau writes of the view from the World Trade Center as a powerful experience in which 'elevation transfigures one into a voyeur. It puts you at a distance. It transforms the bewitching world by which one is "possessed" into a text that lies before our eyes. It allows one to read it, to be a solar Eye, a divine gaze' (1988: 140). He continues, '[t]he fiction of knowledge is related to this lust to be a viewpoint and nothing more' (1988: 92). He describes the view of the whole as illusory, with no comprehension of the highly mobile, intertwining daily practices down below, but only 'imaginary totalizations produced by the eye' (1988: 93). However, he says, if the view from above is alienated, the view from below is equally blind. Those who live below the threshold at which visibility begins 'follow the thicks and thins of the urban 'text' they write without being able to read it. The networks of these intersecting writings compose a manifold story that has neither author nor spectator, shaped out of fragments of trajectories and alterations of spaces' (De Certeau, 1988: 93). The distinction between close-up readings of landscape and distanced viewing raises difficult theoretical, methodological and ethical issues about insider versus outsider perspectives, the nature of incomprehensively large structures, the limits to consciousness, and the unknown and unintended consequences of one's actions.

The types of expertise and modes of analysis implied by the definition of landscape as a way of seeing are multiple. If landscape is a historically and culturally specific way of seeing, then intertextuality becomes important. Intertextuality refers to the textual context within which a text (be it a landscape or any other form that can be read) is understood. Discourse analysis is perhaps the most relevant methodology because it seeks to relate ways of seeing landscape to the larger discursive fields, the various ideologies, practices, institutions, texts and concepts which structure a specific way of looking. This type of analysis requires the use of various primary and secondary historical sources to gain an understanding of the relevant institutions, texts, practices and power relations that make up the larger discursive field. One needs to look beyond what people may say about their beliefs, values and attitudes. It is necessary to supplement the data from interviews and questionnaires, to find other ways to analyze the taken-for-granted socially produced 'regimes of truth' that enable and constrain the way people construct their accounts. In the case of landscape, visuality or cultural ways of seeing can sometimes be explained with reference to images, especially images of landscapes. The researcher

can look at a range of relevant images to find out what rhetorical strategies are used to produce what Michel Foucault called 'effects of truth.' It is important to look for what is unspoken, especially when there appears to be a silence about values that are assumed to be unquestionable.

In our own work we have found that there is always an interesting history to the way landscapes are understood. The histories of the discourses that people draw upon in their interpretations are largely unknown by most of the people themselves. In *Landscapes of Privilege* (2004) we attempt to trace historically, culturally and politically, the taken-for-granted textual context within which various groups of people tended to read, construct, maintain and more generally perform their home landscapes. This proved to be quite challenging as the textual context of landscapes in contemporary American culture is very diffuse, far more so, for example, than that described by Duncan (1990) in the Kandyan Kingdom of Ceylon which was a small, highly textualized and centrally controlled, albeit bitterly contested, religious landscape.

THE CRITIQUE OF VISUALITY

We have seen that Hartshorne rejected landscape for its pleasurable visual qualities, fearing that it would seduce geographers away from rigorous science. Much more recently, Gillian Rose (1993: 10) argued that 'the landscape which geographers hope to know but whose pleasures escape their mastery is a construct of masculine power and desire.' In response, however, Catherine Nash (1996) questions the premise that visual pleasure is necessarily dependent upon a position of domination or that such pleasure is inherently oppressive. She says that 'looking is never innocent, but its politics is always contextual and never only or just masculine' (1996: 167). Nevertheless, as Rose shows, the romanticism of much landscape description and the heroic tone of geographers' reminiscences of fieldwork in the 'remote corners' of the world appear to reveal their seduction by landscapes. Due to the work of Edward Said and others whose critiques have resulted in a widespread 'crisis of representation' in social science, geographers have become critical of representations of landscape and fieldwork that appear orientalist, romantic, or nostalgic. As we will describe below, Duncan and Duncan (2004) and Don Mitchell (1996) extend this argument, attempting to understand how popular (rather than just academic) aesthetic appreciation of landscape in everyday life can lead to the aestheticization of social relations and the naturalization of privilege.

While vision is the biologically based sense of sight, visuality refers to the dependence of vision on culture. John Walker and Sarah Chaplin (1997) point out that vision provides about 70% of all information to the brain – more than all other senses combined. The eyes convert light rays into electrochemical signals that are sent to the brain through optic nerves. The brain then integrates color, motion, depth, and shape into perception of a pictorialized landscape. 'The fact that we perceive one world rather than five (corresponding to each of five senses) suggests that inside the brain/mind visual information from the eyes merges with information arriving from the other senses, and with existing memories and knowledges, so that a synthesis occurs' (Walker and Chaplin, 1997: 18). Because such memories and knowledges are historically, socially and culturally specific, a critical discourse analysis will be required to show how vision is mediated.

In her book, *Visual Methodologies*, Rose (2001: 128) states that the Lacanian notion of the gaze 'is a form of visuality that pre-exists the individual subject; it is a visuality into which subjects are born ... the Gaze is culturally constituted.' Again this formulation of visuality requires that the researcher develop a knowledge of discourses well beyond that consciously understood by the subjects of the research. Rose (2001: 130) says, 'Since the Gaze looks at everyone, men as well as women are turned into spectacles through it.' She says that this formulation of the dominant scopic regime breaks down the binary distinction between 'woman as image and man as bearer of the look' pointing towards a more complex feminist approach to the question of visuality open to the idea of shifting and contestable signifiers (Rose, 2001: 123). In terms of methodology, theories such as Jacques Lacan's assume that discourses mediate vision through unconscious motives. This again requires a strongly critical, distanced view in which the researcher believes that he or she can recognize contradictions, slippages in signification, and power structures that are not normally be visible to the subjects of study. It also requires that the researchers be critically self-reflexive, open to their data, and avoid assertions or overinterpretation.

THE ROLE OF LANDSCAPE IN SOCIAL AND POLITICAL PROCESSES

W.J.T. Mitchell suggests that landscape should be used as a verb rather than a noun. Researchers should ask, 'not just what landscape "is" or "means" but what it "does," how it works as a cultural practice' (Mitchell, 1994: 1). This approach investigates below and beyond the visible surface of landscapes to reveal the complex history of embedded labor (Mitchell, 1996) and the social and economic relations that are materialized in the landscape (Harvey, 1985; Zukin, 1991; Anderson and Gale, 1992; Schein, 1997; Mitchell, 2003; Duncan and Duncan, 2004). Cultural landscapes play a central role in the practices and performance of place-based social identities, community values and social distinction (Lowenthal, 1991; Cosgrove, 1993; Daniels, 1993; Matless, 1998; DeLyser, 2003, 2005). Distinctive landscapes work to establish place-based senses of community and can be mobilized to maintain and contest individual and collective identities and to

advance the attainment of political or economic goals. Landscapes are normally
viewed in a practical, non-discursive, inatten-
tive manner and tend to be interpreted as
physical evidence of social standing and
material success as when a large house and
garden are seen to represent the economic
and/or moral worth of its occupiers.
Landscapes have an important inculcating
effect as they tend to be taken for granted as
tangible evidence of the naturalness of the
social, political and economic practices and
relations.

Duncan's (1990) study of the landscape of
royal capital of Kandy in the highlands of
Sri Lanka investigated the role it played in
the practice of politics in the early years of
the nineteenth century. He analyzed the landscape itself for evidence of symbolism that
had been intentionally incorporated into the
building of the Temple, palace, walls and
lake. However, his primary objects of inquiry
were the competing meanings that the landscape had for different groups of people in
Kandy and the way these were mobilized.
His work can be considered both hermeneutic and intertextual in that, he offers *his* interpretations of *their* interpretations of the
landscape with reference to religious/politi-
cal discourses which were known to all,
including illiterate peasants, through various
interpretative communities. These textually
and politically based interpretations, he
argues, were concretized in the landscape in
explicit, allegories of kingship, thus opening
up the texts to multiple meanings and political struggle.

Although there is little extant material on
landscape interpretations, and especially
little on the interpretations of peasants, it was
possible to use discourse analysis on what
little material remains. British spies and
ambitious nobles had gathered information
on the peasants' discontent each for their own
political reasons. This material can be analyzed for information about the attitudes of
both nobles and peasants. Because claims to
the throne were made through poetry that
outlined opposition to the kings' landscape

transformations and his exploitation of the
labor of the peasants, poetry was an important source of information. Although the
peasants' views are difficult to get at directly,
rituals and poetic allegories about the building program of a king can be interpreted as
reflecting the people's political opposition in
a veiled way (Duncan, 1990). The methods
of getting at a subaltern point of view is far
more difficult than many commentators
whose work is primarily theoretical wish to
believe. A good deal of detective work, piecing together of disparate bits of information
written in various different languages and a
degree of well informed speculation is often
required.

In our long-term ethnographic research in
a contemporary American suburban community (Duncan and Duncan, 2004), we investigated the role landscapes play in the
aestheticization of politics. Here we found
that the effect of the landscape was less well
articulated and the readings more naturalized
than in Kandyan society where the landscape
was more explicated textualized. We looked
at how the materiality of landscape tends to
naturalize social relations, concretizing the
status quo. The town is a site of aesthetic
consumption practices in which the residents
perform their social status by preserving and
enhancing the beauty of their town. They
accomplish this through highly restrictive
zoning and environmental protection legislation. We demonstrate how romantic anti-ur-
banism, and an anglophilic, class-based
aesthetic lend a political dimension to the
seemingly innocent desire to live in a beautiful place. We show how a mélange of views
on the natural environment, historic preservation, and the claimed uniqueness of a local
landscape all work to divert attention away
from interrelated issues of exclusion, exploitation and subsidies for the rich. We attempt
to demonstrate that the seemingly innocent
pleasure in the beauty of landscapes acts as a
subtle, but highly effective mechanism of
exclusion.

The methods necessary for such a study
include semi-structured interviewing, archival

research, focus groups, participant observation and discourse analysis. The approach, however, does not privilege vision; neither we nor the residents can see the social and political implications of the landscape by merely looking at it. The difference between us and many of our informants is that we do not have a personal stake in maintaining the landscape; on the contrary, we have an interest in exposing the inequities brought about by its maintenance. It is this difference of standpoint that led us to investigate the history of the landscape, in particular the political struggles that have produced it with an eye to tracing the effects the maintenance of the landscape has on potential residents who are excluded. We argue against an essentialist interpretation of standpoint theory, however, as we encountered many interviewees who, in our opinion, fail to see the structural biases that exclude them. In this, they are blinded by the American individualist 'hidden injuries of class' still in evidence thirty or so years after Richard Sennett and Jonathon Cobb (1972) wrote so perceptively about this problem. Again, this blindness is by no means inevitable. In fact, we found significant variation among people in terms of their awareness.

This type of landscape analysis entails a critical perspective on the views of one's informants. Informants are, of course, often far more knowledgeable about many aspects of the landscape than a researcher coming in from the outside. In this particular case, while many of the residents know that their landscapes depend upon a politics of anti-development, they tend to naturalize their privilege, having no reason to trace the far reaching, unintended consequences and unacknowledged conditions of that privilege. Our object of study is not to the landscape per se, but the socio-political relations that, although inextricably bound to the materiality of the landscape, are not visible to the eye. Therefore, archival and ethnographic research are the primary methods. One of the most important is discourse analysis. In our case, we traced the institutionalized ideas and

ideals that insulated residents from uncomfortable questions of race and poverty. These included such discourses the English country gentlemen, owner of all he surveys, which appears to sit comfortably alongside the democratic pastoralism of the Jeffersonian small farmer. A whole complex of competing, sometimes contradictory narratives, appears to be amalgamated into a general moral geography widely shared, but subscribed to with differing emphases and connotations.

THE SOCIO/NATURAL LANDSCAPE

Most definitions of landscape are founded on an ontological nature-culture duality. There have, however, been some interesting attempts to unsettle this dualism by rethinking (with the aim of enacting and experiencing) the multiplicity and relational materiality of the socio/natural landscape. These include various combinations of Deleuzean phenomenological, non-representational, actor-network and performative theories of landscape all of which emphasize materiality and embodiment, prediscursive knowing and fluidity, rather than adopting a critical stance towards the more stabilizing forces that structure and constrain landscape processes and practices as discussed above.

Non-representational theory is currently popular among certain, mainly British, geographers who seek an alternative to conceptualizations of landscape which they consider too cognitive, alienated, arrogant, expert, critical and concerned with vision at the expense of other senses (e.g. Wylie *et al.*, 2002). An underlying phenomenology is evident in many of the key concepts which include dwelling, pre-cognitive perception, affect, care and intentionality. However, as we will show, this work is more radically phenomenological than that of Sauer or the humanistic geographers of the 1970s. For instance, although Cosgrove (1984) and Barbara Bender (1993) had acknowledged the experience of pre-capitalist peasants who actively engage with and 'dwell' (in the phenomenological sense) upon the land, they made a clear distinction between this and the patrician, distanced contemplation of landscapes. In contrast, the radical ontology of non-representationalism sees *all* human beings as *inherently* entangled with non-human elements of landscape. Ingold (2000: 191), for example, is keen to collapse the distinction between the seeing and the seen: 'I reject the division between inner and outer worlds – respectively of mind and matter, meaning and substance – upon which such distinction rests. The landscape is not in the mind's eye nor is it a formless matter waiting for humanly imposed order.'

Note the language here; they specify *neither/nor* not *both* as in earlier formulations mentioned above such as Daniels's (1989). Non-representationalism aims to dissolve commonsense boundaries in the search for what Nigel Thrift envisions as 'uncommon sense' assemblages of heterogeneous material and immaterial elements (2004: 89).

Thrift (2004), Mitch Rose (2006), Steve Hinchliffe, (2003) and Paul Harrison (2007) promote the idea that the autonomous human subject should not be privileged over processes and flows, connections and assemblages of culture/nature. Hinchliffe approaches landscape through the concept of inhabitation which he describes as 'not simply a matter of adding in non-humans' (2003: 206). 'Indeed,' he says, 'it is not about 'social interactions between already constituted objects' (Hinchliffe, 2003: 207). The goal is to extend the ideas of performativity to cover human entanglement with nature. For Hinchliffe, the goal is very different from denaturalizing landscape, critiquing aestheticization or analyzing the power relations among historically situated human subjects as we have described above. Rather it is about what he calls 'inhabiting' human and nonhuman landscapes so as to bring about significant changes to all parties.

Nigel Thrift and J.D. Dewsbury (2000: 424) critique what they see as the limited repertoire of qualitative methods saying that these normally 'boil down to semi-structured interviews, focus groups, and generally short-term ethnographies.' They argue that 'co-performance' with non-academics offers a whole new range of techniques for creating new experiential knowledge about embodiment, which will 'give flesh' to theories of the body. We wonder whether such small-scale 'co-productions' would have an effect on anyone except those directly involved?

Thrift wants to enact a non-cognitive (or more-than-cognitive) realm in which one can create new openings, creative spaces, resonances, and landscapes 'where words cannot take you' (Thrift, 2004: 90). Description from this perspective is not simple re-presentation; it is creation. Methods are seen to enact what they describe (Law, 2004). The term non-representation (Lorimer, 2005 uses the term 'more-than-representational') refers to the idea that while representations cannot mirror reality, they *do* have affective force as practices. This force is largely, but not wholly, non-cognitive. Thrift thinks of landscape representation as a patrician, 'know and tell' politics. In its place, he proposes what he calls a more modest, democratic, and practical engagement that allows 'space for new things to thrive' (2004: 83). He compares this method to types of psychotherapy that reject the privileged role of the therapist in favour of a mutual client-therapist construction of reality. Researchers aim to discover the 'unseeable' by becoming attuned to their bodily, visceral emotions; they strive to achieve a deep, participatory immersion in the landscape. They are struck, enchanted and seduced by the landscape. Jane Bennett (2001) argues that the joy and wonder they experience will promote care and hence more ethical practice.

It is not the content of landscapes that landscape researchers are urged to investigate, but the sensible affects that they activate. Affect here, is given a Deleuzian spin referring to an intensity of unarticulated feeling (as opposed to cognitively organized emotions). Because this perspective on landscape looks at practices that cannot be conveyed in words, it presents difficult methodological challenges. In their review of non-representational methods, Claire Dwyer and Gail Davies (2007) point to experimental modes of experiencing the city drawn from work by the Situationists (Pinder, 2005) and psycho-geography (Bassett, 2004; Philips, 2004). They point to various other methods of research that 'foreground embodied experience' including working alongside participants to understand manual labour in India (phenomenologically rather than discursively) (Davies and Dwyer, 2007: 259). On recent urban fieldtrips we have experimented with the use of blindfolds to give our sighted students an opportunity to experience an unfamiliar city with heightened (non-visual) senses.

One important methodological challenge is how to devise methods that have an impact beyond a few participants. Possibly this can be achieved through evocative writing about the emotions which a writer feels in the presence of particular landscapes with the hope of sensitizing readers' conscious attention to their own affective experiences of landscapes. John Urry (2007) summarizes a growing body of literature on forms of mobility as active engagement with one's environment which he believes should not be contrasted with the stasis of place or landscape as these should be seen as actively performed. He suggests various methods of studying the corporeal experience of mobility such as walking through landscapes. However, these are generally vague and most of his references to what he terms 'mobile methods' are to unpublished work. His principal suggestion is walking ethnography and other ways of participating in patterns of movement in order to gain a deeper, more bodily experienced, understanding of the lives of others as they move through and perform landscapes Jon Anderson tries to produce geographical knowledge by having conversations while walking in order to 'trigger knowledge recollection and production.' He calls this 'a collage of collaborative knowledge' (Anderson, 2004: 254). John Wylie (2005) attempts a Heideggerian self-immersion in nature while walking in a

southern English coastal landscape in order to discover his own bodily sensations and emotions. He says that walking is 'irreducibly multiple' and not conducive to coherent narrating. However, the fact that he did in fact narrate his experience suggests that it is difficult to avoid re-presentation. On the other hand, had he not tried to make his experiences public, his efforts could have been criticized as merely solipsistic.

Although interviews yield primarily cognitive data, some recent researchers have proposed what they call 'a walked interview.' Phil Jones and James Evans (2007) have suggested that particular places trigger memories and moods not always detectable by the interviewee or interviewer at the time of the interview, but which may be reconstructed afterward through a combination of methods. For example, in order to better understand interviewees' embodied experience of a regenerating Birmingham landscape, they combined walked interviews with GIS. Content analysis of interview transcripts was used to examine whether different themes emerge from stationary and walked interviews. Interviews were analyzed to expose the way themes develop through the two different interview forms. They also used tablet PCs enabled with GPS technology during the interviews

> to record the extent to which comments about particular spaces/buildings are made in/adjacent to them. Combining these tracks with 'contour' maps of ambient noise permit an examination of whether certain areas are explored in less detail because of the noise from traffic and other sources interfering with the interview process. (Jones and Evans, 2007: 1)

The researchers hope that by matching qualitative data and spatial context they will be able 'to give a "voice" to the otherwise impersonal traces left by GPS tracking' (Jones and Evans, 2007, 1).

LANDSCAPES AND EMOTION

Much of the work on emotions and geography focuses on memory (Nora, 1989;

Johnson, 2003; Legg, 2005; Till, 2005) and some on the psychoanalysis of unconscious desire (Rose, 2001; Callard, 2003; Philo and Parr, 2003). Material landscapes can be emotive, that is, they can have constitutive or transformative effects on people's memories and bodily level reactions (Reddy, 2001; Connolly, 2002). New work in neuro-biology may shed light on emotional attachment to places as a bio-cultural phenomenon (Wilson, 1998). While the phenomenological notion of the lived body and the psychoanalytic idea of the unconscious may resonate with contemporary neuro-science, these approaches pre-exist and remain unmodified by neuro-imaging techniques. Furthermore, most landscape researchers are ill equipped to do the biological research necessary to discover exactly how cultural responses become embodied.

One fairly basic technological approach to measuring emotions, however, has been used by artist Christian Nold (www.biomapping. net) who has developed an extensive bio-mapping project in various cities in Europe, the USA, India and Japan. He collaborates with local residents to discover how they react emotionally to aspects of their local landscape. Over the last several years he has wired up thousands of people with GSR (galvanic skin response) devices which work like lie detectors to measure the high and low points of their emotional arousal as they walk around their own neighborhoods. They then annotate these mapped journeys explaining why they reacted emotionally in particular places. Nold believes that this technology is useful in helping us to understand how landscapes shape emotional and psychological states.

Cognitive and affective processes and multiple neuro-chemical systems have mutual impacts. Neurochemicals can enhance or reduce susceptibilities and dispositions to engage the environment. The relation between the world outside the body and emotions is especially complex and difficult to study when it comes to long-lasting (background) emotions such as attachment to landscapes or feelings of security associated with

places (Clark, 1999; Nussbaum, 2001). Emotions focus attention on the salient features of an environment and thus landscape plays a role in memory. Neurological research suggests that there may be cells in the hippocampus known as 'place cells' thought to become active when a person is in a particular known place (Redish, 1999; Rolls, 1999). These are thought to help to focus and integrate memories, making them coherent. Mechanisms by which both nature and culture deliver their effects (the wiring up of synapses) are the same. What is important from the point of view of landscape researchers is how malleable the human brain is. The synaptic organization of the brain is pre-programmed for cultural learning. The organization of neural pathways is constantly being reconfigured; synapses and their transmission properties are altered by experience of the environment.

Both conscious and unconscious memory processes require that memories be continually re-remembered and reshaped to facilitate the development and maintenance of a coherent self in relation to one's social and physical environment. (Note how the idea of re-remembering, which can never be the same – due to changing contexts – parallels the creativity that has been posited by performance theories.) Emotions are to a degree 'hardwired,' but innately open to being translated cognitively into conscious, subjective experiences that have cultural content, historical and place specificity. Culturally available emotional responses to landscapes shape and are shaped by discourses concerning place-based identities, including nationalism. Landscapes are used as 'memory theaters,' synecdoches, or *aides-memoires*, in other words, imagined spaces that can 'hold' images, desires, collective memories and ideologies. The concrete spatiality of particular places allows them to be experienced in unconscious, practical, sensual, unarticulated and naturalizing ways. Collective memories are constructed socially not individually and must be stored in communal spaces, in public landscapes, not just written texts.

The new neuro-imaging technology and expertise required to carry out research into the embodiment of cultural responses to landscape is largely unaccessible to most landscape researchers except through collaborative research with neuro-biologists. However, as it would be a mistake to arbitrarily narrow one's conceptual framework based on the limits of one's own research expertise, it might be useful to revise psychoanalytic and phenomenological conceptualizations of the emotions, the unconscious, and desire in light of new neuro-biological conceptualizations of embodiment.

One could look at the role of cultural narratives in the translation of a complex and unstable array of cognitive (discursive) material, unconscious thought and bodily states into coherent orientations towards places. Lasting emotions need vivid imaginings and unconsciously processed stimuli. These are enhanced by the materiality of places as sites of memory. The smells and sounds of places as well as visual landscapes can provide this density and can trigger emotional responses to and through places. Gaston Bachelard (1969: 9) says, 'Thanks to the house, a great many of our memories are housed.' He says, 'Memories are motionless, and the more securely they are fixed in space the sounder they are' (1969: 9). Bachelard speaks of the memory of outdoor spaces of home: 'How precise the familiar hill paths remain for our muscular consciousness!' (1969:10). Despite the epistemological and philosophical chasm between such phenomenological writings and contemporary neuro-biology, we can see that the idea of 'muscular consciousness' is not entirely unlike the 'procedural memory' or 'over-learned cognitive habits' or 'pre-coded neural pathways' genetically programmed to be shaped by the physical and cultural environment in which an individual lives.

Attachment *to* places can be thought of as attachment *through* places to the people, events and ideas one has built one's life around. Places become synecdoches for people, family, memories, security and cultural values. An example drawn from Duncan

(2007: 53) shows a young Scotsman in Ceylon who expressed his home sickness in letters written home shortly after he assumed his post as a superintendent on a coffee estate in 1852. He asked for more letters from home which, 'would be a great comfort to me in this lonely wilderness.' He greatly missed the landscape of his native Scotland. 'As yet I mind everything as distinctly as though I had left yesterday – every cut in the road and every large stone and all the blue hills and knolls.' He sought in each small detail of the remembered landscape emotional links to his previous life.

Building on this common tendency to 'place' memories, many landscape features are deliberately designed to commemorate events and collective memories. Pierre Nora (1997) describes how societies use museums, monuments and iconic places not just to represent, but to perform and construct, collective memories. He believes that memories are enhanced with landscape features; they 'adhere' to objects and entire landscapes. With globalization and migration, as communities fragment and can no longer spontaneously keep memories alive through traditional rituals and shared customs, it is necessary to deliberately construct special public 'lieux de memoires' or memory places. The fact that landscapes give memories a material form demonstrates the emptiness of such conceptual dualisms as representation versus materiality.

Recent neuro-biological research actually shows how the associations between landscapes and memory work at the synaptic level of neural pathways, just as they do at the level of consciousness; conscious and unconscious thought work together as part of the same system with a person's unconscious thought processing a huge amount of environmental information which it may or may not call to the attention of his or her conscious thought. One can see why research on emotions and landscape is very difficult as clearly such common ethnographic techniques as interviewing need to be supplemented by methods that are not readily available to most geographers. In our own research on landscape we have discovered that emotions and aesthetic judgments are particularly difficult for informants to articulate because they think of them as intuitively obvious, widely shared therefore unnecessary to explain. The 'cultural turn' in geography and other social sciences has been charged with over-emphasizing the 'discursive' while neglecting the material. However, as these dimensions are not mutually exclusive, it is possible that they will be most profitably considered in their reciprocal formation.

CONCLUSION

As we stated in the introduction to this chapter, our intention has not been to advocate one or more conceptual or methodological approaches, but to point out the methodological implications, difficulties and possible contradictions associated with the differing ways of conceptualizing landscape. We think that some approaches, especially the non-representational, are especially difficult methodologically with the result that the development of theory is far more sophisticated than the development of methods. Furthermore, the ideal of grounded theory in which the theory arises from the data and data can resist that theory can rarely be successful as non-representational methodologies tend to be weakly developed in relation to theoretical formulations.

There is a strong phenomenological strain running throughout the history of landscape geography. Many geographers are 'struck' by the sensual pleasure of wild or exotic landscapes. While, members of the Berkeley School saw such aesthetic pleasure as compatible with expert, scientific analysis, others, such as Hartshorne, warned against seduction by the beauty and wonder of landscapes. Feminists critique the masculine pleasure of heroic field exploration and call for more self-reflexivity. Historical geographers consider themselves expert decoders. Still others critique aestheticization, attempting to de-

naturalize by tracing the underlying power relations and exploitation of labor in the production of landscapes. In the 1970s humanistic geographers rejected the position of the distanced, scientific perspective; they tried to bracket out rationality and adopt a 'natural attitude.' Today anti-humanists (or post-humanists) try to avoid what they see as alienated, abstract analysis, but also reject the privileging of a human viewpoint. Recent foci in the geography on mobilities and affect can leave traditional ideas of landscape looking static, bounded and overly cerebral (Sheller and Urry, 2006). For that reason, Tim Cresswell (2003: 269) suggests abandoning the term, which he finds 'too much about the already accomplished and not enough about the processes of everyday life.' He says that although the concept of landscape could be made to 'grow and adapt, to colonize the dynamism of living geography,' he wonders what of value would be saved in the process (Cresswell, 2003: 269). We take his point, however we believe that the idea of landscape can be useful especially if one sharpens and narrows its analytical and critical focus. We also do not believe that critical landscape analysis need be static or that it cannot deal with the non-cognitive. In fact, ideas of materiality, performativity and practice, fragmentation, ambiguity and fluidity now predominate in much of contemporary landscape geography, in critical as well as non-critical approaches. Methodological choices will have to be made, however, – especially over whether the researcher will adopt a critical perspective or not. Although empathic or hermeneutic methods can be critical, the more radical phenomenological approaches are clearly incompatible with a critical perspective which necessarily distances researchers from the objects of their research.

REFERENCES

Anderson, J. (2004) 'Talking while walking: a geographical archaeology of knowledge', *Area* 36 (3): 254–62.

Anderson, K. and Gale, F. (eds) (1992) *Inventing places.* Melbourne: Longman Cheshire.

Bachelard, G. (1969) *The poetics of space.* Boston: Beacon Press.

Bakhtin, M. (1986) *The dialectic imagination.* Austin: University of Texas Press.

Barnes, T. and Duncan, J. (1992) *Writing worlds: discourse, text and metaphor in the representation of the landscape.* London: Routledge.

Barrell, J. (1980) *The dark side of landscape: the rural poor in English painting 1730–1840.* Cambridge: Cambridge University Press.

Barthes, R. (1979) *The Eiffel tower.* New York: Hill and Wang.

Barthes, R. (1967) *Elements of semiology.* Trans. A. Lavers. New York: Hill and Wang.

Barthes, R. (1986) *Mythologies.* Trans A. Lavers. New York: Hill and Wang.

Bassett, K. (2004) 'Walking as an aesthetic practice and a critical tool: some psychogeographic experiments', *Journal of Geography in Higher Education* 28 (3): 397–410.

Baudrillard, J. (1988) *America.* Trans. C. Turner. New York: Verso.

Bender, B. (ed.) (1993) *Landscape: politics and perspectives.* Oxford: Berg.

Bennett, B. (2001) *The enchantment of modern life: attachments, crossings, ethics.* Princeton: Princeton University Press.

Berger, J. (1972) *Ways of seeing.* Harmondsworth: Penguin.

Bondi, L. (1992) 'Gender symbols and urban landscapes', *Progress in Human Geography* 16 (2): 157–70.

Bourdieu, P. (1970) 'The Berber house, or the world reversed', *Social Science Information* 9 (2): 151–70.

Butler, J. (1993) *Bodies that matter: on the discursive limits of 'sex'.* London: Routledge.

Callard, F. (2003) 'The taming of psychoanalysis in geography', *Social and Cultural Geography* 4 (3): 295–312.

Certeau, M. de (1988) *The practice of everyday life.* Berkeley: University of California Press.

Clark, A. (1999) *Being there: putting brain, body and the world together again.* Cambridge, MA: MIT Press.

Connolly, W.E. (2002) *Neuropolitics: thinking, culture, speed.* London: Minnesota University Press.

Cosgrove, D. (1984) *Social formation and symbolic landscapes.* London: Croom Helm.

Cosgrove, D. (1992) *Water, engineering and landscape: water control and landscape in the modern period.* New Delhi: CBS Publishers.

Cosgrove, D. and Daniels, S. (1988) *The iconography of landscape: essays on the symbolic representation, design, and use of past environments.* Cambridge: Cambridge University Press.

Crang, M. (1997) 'Picturing practices: research through the tourist gaze', *Progress in Human Geography* 21 (3): 359–67.

Cresswell, T. (2003) 'Landscape and the obliteration of practice', in K. Anderson, M. Domosh, S. Pile, N. Thrift (eds) *Handbook of cultural geography.* London: Sage. pp. 269–81.

Daniels, S. (1989) 'Marxism, culture, and the duplicity of landscape', in R. Peet, and N. Thrift (eds) *New models in geography vol. II.* London: Unwin-Hyman. pp. 196–220.

Darby, H.C. (1948) 'The regional geography of Thomas Hardy's Wessex', *Geographical Review* 38 (3): 426–43.

Davies, G. and Dywer, G. (2007) 'Qualitative methods: are you enchanted or are you alienated?', *Progress in Human Geography* 31 (2): 257–66.

DeLyser, D. (2003) 'Ramona memories: fiction, tourist practices and the placing of the past in Southern California', *Annals of the Association of American Geographers* 93 (4): 886–908.

DeLyser, D. (2005) *Ramona memories: tourism and the shaping of Southern California.* Minneapolis: University of Minnesota Press.

Duncan, J. (1980) 'The superorganic in American cultural geography', *Annals of the Association of American Geographers* 70 (2): 181–98.

Duncan, J. (1990) *The city as text.* Cambridge: Cambridge University Press.

Duncan, J. (2007) *In the shadows of the tropics: climate. Race and biopower in 19th century ceylon.* Aldershot: Ashgate.

Duncan, J. and Duncan, N. (1988) '(Re) reading the landscape', *Environment and Planning D: Society and Space*, 6 (2): 117–26.

Duncan, J. and Duncan, N. (2004) *Landscapes of privilege.* London: Routledge.

Eco, U. (1976) *A Theory of semiotics.* Bloomington: Indiana University Press.

Glassie, H. (1971) *Pattern in the material folk culture of the Eastern United States.* Philadelphia: University of Pennsylvania Press.

Gomez, G.A. (1998) *Wetland biography: seasons on the Chenier plain.* Austin: University of Texas Press.

Goss, J. (1993) 'The magic of the mall: an analysis of form, function, and meaning in the contemporary retail built environment', *Annals of the Association of American Geographers* 83 (1): 18–47.

Gottdienner, M. (1995) *Postmodern semiotics: material culture and the forms of postmodern life.* Oxford: Blackwell.

Harrison, P. (2007) 'The space between us: opening remarks on the concept of dwelling', *Environment and Planning D: Society and Space* 25 (4): 625–47.

Hartshorne, R. (1939) *The nature of geography: a critical survey of current thought in light of the past.* Association of American Geographers, Washington, DC.

Harvey, D. (1985) *Consciousness and the urban experience.* Oxford: Basil Blackwell.

Hinchliffe, S. (2003) '"Inhabiting" – landscapes and natures', in K. Anderson, M. Domosh, S. Pile and N. Thrift (eds) *Handbook of cultural geography.* London: Sage. p. 2.

Ingold, T. (2000) *The perception of the environment: essays in livelihood, dwelling and skill.* London: Routledge.

Johnson, N. (2003) *Ireland, the great war and the geography of remembrance.* Cambridge: Cambridge University Press.

Jones, P. and Evans, J. (2007) *Rescue geography: developing methods of public geographies.* Economic and social research council (ref. RES-000-22-2375). School of Geography, Earth and Environmental Sciences, University of Birmingham and School of Environment and Development, University of Manchester.

Law, J. (2004) *After method: mess in social science research.* New York: Routledge.

Legg, S. (2005) 'Contesting and surviving memory: space, nation and nostalgia in les lieux de mémoire', *Environment and Planning D: Society and space* 23 (4): 481–504.

Lévi-Strauss, C. (1992) *Tristes tropiques.* New York: Penguin.

Lewis, P. (1979) 'Axioms for reading the landscape', in D. Meinig (ed.) *The interpretation of ordinary lndscapes: geographical essays.* New York: Oxford University Press. pp. 11–32.

Ley, D. and Samuels, M. (1978) *Humanistic geography: prospects and problems.* London: Croom Helm.

Lorimer, H. (2005) 'Cultural geography: the busyness of being more than representational', *Progress in Human Geography* 29 (1): 83–94.

Lowenthal, D. (1986) *The past is a foreign country.* Cambridge: Cambridge University Press.

Lowenthal, D. (1991) 'British national identity and the English landscape', *Rural History* 2 (2): 205–30.

Lynch, K. (1960) *The image of the city.* Cambridge, MA: MIT Press.

Martin, G. and James, P. (1977) *All possible worlds: a history of geographic ideas.* New York: John Wiley and Sons.

Matless, D. (1998) *Landscape and Englishness.* London: Reaktion Books.

Meinig, D.W. (1979a) 'Symbolic landscapes: some idealizations of American communities', in D.W. Meinig, (ed.) *The interpretation of ordinary landscapes: geographical essays.* New York: Oxford University Press. pp. 164–92.

Meinig, D.W. (1979b) 'The beholding eye: ten versions of the same scene', in D.W. Meinig, (ed.) *The Interpretation of ordinary landscapes: geographical essays.* New York: Oxford University Press. pp. 33–48.

Mitchell, D. (1996) *The lie of the land: migrant workers and the California landscape.* Minneapolis: University of Minnesota Press.

Mitchell, D. (2003) 'California living, California dying: dead labor and the political economy of landscape', in K. Anderson, M. Domosh, S. Pile, and N. Thrift, (eds) *Handbook of cultural geography.* London: Sage. pp. 233–48.

Mitchell, W.J.T. (1994) 'Imperial landscape', in W.J.T. Mitchell, (ed.) *Landscape and power.* Chicago: University of Chicago Press. pp. 5–34.

Muir, R. (2000) *The new reading the landscape: fieldwork in landscape history.* Exeter: University of Exeter Press.

Nash, C. (1996) 'Reclaiming vision: looking at the landscape', *Gender, Place and Culture* 3 (2): 149–69.

Nold, C. *BioMapping.* www.biomapping.net.

Nora, P. (1989) 'Between memory and history: les lieux de memoire', *Representations* 26 (Spring): 7–25.

Nora, P. (1997) *Realms of memory.* New York: Columbia University Press.

Nussbaum, M. (2001) *Upheavals of thought: the intelligence of emotions.* Cambridge: Cambridge University Press.

Olwig, K. (1996) 'Recovering the substantive nature of landscape', *Annals of the Association of American Geographers* 86 (4): 630–53.

Philips, P. (2004) 'Doing art and doing cultural geography: the fieldwork/field walking project', *Australian Geographer* 35 (2): 151–59.

Philo, C. and Parr, H. (2003) 'Introducing psychoanalytic geographies', *Social and Cultural Geography* 4 (3): 283–93.

Pinder, D. (2005) 'Arts of urban exploration', *Cultural Geographies* 12 (4): 383–411.

Redish, A. (1999) *Beyond the cognitive map: from place cells to episodic memory.* Cambridge, MA: MIT Press.

Reddy, W. (2001) *The navigation of feeling: a framework for the history of emotions.* Cambridge: Cambridge University Press.

Rolls, E. (1999) 'Spatial view cells and the representation of place in the primate hippocampus', *Hippocampus* 9 (4): 467–80.

Rose, G. (1993) *Feminism and geography: the limits of geographical knowledge*. Cambridge: Polity.

Rose, G. (2001) *Visual methodologies: an interpretation of visual materials*. London: Sage.

Rose, M. (2006) 'Gathering dreams of presence: a project for the cultural landscape', *Environment and Planning D: Society and Space* 24 (4): 537–54.

Ross, K. (1988) *The emergence of social space: Rimbaud and the Paris commune*. Minneapolis: University of Minnesota Press.

Samuels, M. (1979) 'The biography of landscape', in D.W. Meinig (ed.) *The interpretation of ordinary landscapes: geographical essays*. New York: Oxford University Press. pp. 51–88.

Sauer, C. (1956) 'Education of a geographer', *Annals of the Association of American Geographers* 46 (3): 287–99.

Sauer, C. (1963) 'Morphology of landscape', in J. Leighly, (ed.) *Land and life: a selection of writings of Carl Ortwin Sauer*. Berkeley: University of California Press. pp. 315–50.

Schama, S. (1995) *Landscape and memory*. New York: Knopf.

Schein, R. (1993) 'Representing urban America: nineteenth century views of landscape, space, and power', *Environment and Planning D: Society and Space* 11 (1): 7–21.

Schein, R. (1997) 'The place of landscape: a conceptual framework for interpreting an American scene', *Annals of the Association of American Geographers* 87 (4): 660–80.

Seamon, D. (1998) 'Goethe, nature, and phenomenology', in D. Seamon and A. Zajonc (eds) *Goethe's way of science: a phenomenology of nature*. Albany, NY.: State University of New York Press. pp. 1–14.

Seamon, D. (2000) 'A way of seeing people and place: phenomenology in environment–behavior research', in S. Wapner, J. Demich, T. Yamamoto and H. Minami (eds) *Theoretical perspectives in environment–behavior research*. New York: Plenum. pp. 157–78.

Sennett, R. and Cobb, J. (1972) *The hidden injuries of class*. New York: Vintage.

Sheller. M. and Urry, J. (2006) 'The new mobilities paradigm', *Environment and Planning A* 38 (2): 207– 26.

Thrift, N. (2004) 'Summoning life', in P. Cloke, P. Crang and M. Goodwin (eds) *Envisioning human geographies*. London: Arnold. pp. 81–103.

Thrift, N. and Dewsbury, J.D. (2000) 'Dead geographies and how to make them live', *Environment and Planning D: Society and Space* 18 (4): 411–32.

Till, K. (2005) *The new Berlin: memory, politics, place*. Minneapolis: University of Minnesota Press.

Tuan, Y. (1979) *Landscapes of fear*. New York: Pantheon Books.

Urry. J. (2007) *Mobilities*. Cambridge: Polity Press.

Walker, J. and Chaplin, S. (1997) *Visual culture: an introduction*. Manchester: Manchester University Press.

West, R. (1979) *Carl Sauer's fieldwork in Latin America*. Dellplain Latin American studies volume 3. Ann Arbor: University Microfilms.

Williams, R. (1973) *The country and the city*. London: Chatto and Windus.

Williams, R. (1982) *The sociology of culture*. New York: Schocken Books.

Wilson, E. (1998) *Neural geographies: feminism and the micro-structure of cognition*. London: Routledge.

Wylie, J. (2005) 'A single day's walking: narrating self and landscape on the South West Coast path', *Transactions of the Institute of British Geographers* NS 30 (2): 234–47.

Wylie, J., Dewsbury, J.D., Harrison, P. and Rose, M. (2002) 'Enacting geographies', *Geoforum* 32 (4): 437–40.

Zelinsky, W. (1993) 'Landscapes', in M. Clayton and E. Gorn and P. Williams (eds) *Encyclopedia of American social history*. New York: Charles Scribners's Sons. pp. 1289–97.

Zukin, S. (1991) *Landscapes of power*. Berkeley: University of California Press.

14

Caught in the Nick of Time: Archives and Fieldwork

Hayden Lorimer

INTRODUCTION

Dust, as academic convention has it, is an impediment to good archival scholarship. Dust coats surfaces. Dust obscures print. It is dust that renders already bad handwriting illegible. Dust is the irritant in the historian's otherwise discriminating eye. Unless care is taken, dust can be the cause of itching and reddening. Such vocational discomforts acknowledged, dust is quintessentially the scholar's choice of dirt. It is a research phenomenon to be quietly gloried in as might the scientist fieldworker take the grimmest sort of pleasure in oppressive heat or swarming insects. Dust blackens palms and gets under fingernails. But at day's end, on having departed the scene, it can be brushed off and washed clean away. For others in the business of preserving or reclaiming the past, the prevention of dust's over-accumulation is a task to which many working hours are dedicated. It is on dust that archivists, from time to time, wage their very own form of chemical warfare (Amato, 2003; Ogborn 2004a). And yet, dust is still, at least for the more romantically-inclined, part of the archive's atmospheric appeal. It bestows upon the research exercise an unmistakable aura.

Dust suddenly becomes visible before us. It drifts across rays of light, appearing as if from thin air. Dust, we convince ourselves, gathers on those texts which have remained the longest undisturbed or are as yet unknown to rival scholars. And thus it is possible to find in dust's proliferation, a seeming authenticity in our encounter with the past. To blow off a thick cloud of dust from a leather-bound book is a universal signifier – endlessly rehearsed in modern cinema – of the existence of secrets awaiting discovery. No matter how unique the document or manuscript over which it has formed a blanket, it is dust itself that remains the commonest of all matter to survive from the past. Born of the printed word and the velum page, the microscopic creatures and the storage facilities that are their host environment, dust settles down as an undifferentiated, and perennially troublesome, trace from the passing of time.

In a new wave of creative historical research, dust is no longer to be regarded as simply a distraction from the work-at-hand, or at best an ambient side-effect to be enjoyed in wistful moments before attentions return to the proper matters of scholarship. Of late, dust has become noteworthy in and of itself, substantially present, *and* symbolic of the greater ecologies, social conditions, transformative processes and physical textures of historical research practice. Carolyn Steedman can be positioned at the vanguard (2001), a cultural historian for whom dust is muse, the stuff of which telling words might conceivably be spun. For others like her (see DeLyser, 1999), dust represents an invitation to speak up imaginatively for the archive's existence as site as much as source, and for those social contexts orbiting steadfast consultation of documentary content. To do so, is to assert a version of archival hermeneutics extending beyond print culture and the written word, to include the context, encounters and events that constitute research practice. By implication, it is to seek out possible methodological means to evoke more of archival life: as a particular kind of place where complex subjectivities, and working relations, are created through the act of researching the past. And – pushing further still – it is to reconsider the limits and location of any set of materials determined as an 'archive'. Figured expansively, archives can exceed the darkened catacomb and civically-administered collection, and be sought out in physical landscapes, or still less likely sorts of locale. Mike Pearson and Mike Shanks (2001: 157) present a roster of fundamental questions concerning method, mode and manner: 'What is to be recorded, how and why? How is the past to be written and on whose behalf? What are the politics of interpretation and representation? How might contested interpretations of the past be embraced and presented? They may therefore be susceptible to those practices which are aware of their plurality of motive, which pay attention to the local and particular and which are bound to be subjective, emotional and provocative, which are as unafraid of poetry as they are of politics'. We might frame this as a possible manifesto for the experimental archivist wishing to work in the nick of time.

This chapter is an occasion to consider the parameters and potentials of such an approach to the past, for highlighting examples of methodological innovation and non-conformism in an expanded archive, and ultimately a consideration of the nature of the stories and accounts being crafted of times gone by. Efforts are made here to shift attention to versions of the past being created beyond geographers' home constituency. Novel academic research *is* cited, showing up affinities between geography and reference points spanning music, visual art, creative writing, investigative journalism, film-making and performance. Before that, I want critically to consider the methodological trajectories followed in disciplinary scholarship to date. To do so, it is necessary to take a few steps back before beginning to consider possible ways forward. In this task, it is the field of historical geography that is reckoned the natural home of archival inquiry and associated landscape researches.

ARCHIVAL INQUIRY AND THE TRAJECTORY OF METHOD IN HISTORICAL GEOGRAPHY

Where then to begin? The standard issue checklist, the all-encompassing instruction manual and the methodological handbook hold considerable appeal: laying out the breadth of geographical and interpretive scholarship which is possible in the archive. Alas, these are few. John Fines' (1988) step-by-step introduction might well stand alone in this regard. Granted, specialist guides to local sources, notable collections and annotated bibliographies exist in great number. These texts treat strict empiricism as the practitioner's benchmark, and are designed to aid the use of very particular sorts of historical source: civil registers of births, deaths and marriages; censuses; field books; ledgers; personal papers; municipal, civic and court records; city directories; deed records; medical records; maps; committee minute books. In each instance there are, for sure, precious nuggets of advice to be quarried. Suggestions on mechanistic and systematic ways to search records are of undoubted functional use, but oftentimes so particular, and so bespoke, that they can only be a niche interest for the tight community of researchers for whom they will ever actively come to matter.

In geography's corner of the academic publishing market, to date methodological textbooks dutifully dedicate a chapter to archival research. Mostly designed for an undergraduate readership, these have tended to advocate a fairly instrumental approach to archival inquiry and tasks of interpretation (Hannam, 2002a, b; Hoggart *et al.*, 2002; Blunt *et al.*, 2003; Ogborn, 2003; Roche, 2005). Methodological commentary, exchange and review at a more advanced level remain relatively rare (Harris, 2001), and commonly eschew the identification of unifying concerns. Recently, Robert Mayhew (2008) has remarked on a quarter of a century having passed since an assembly of historical geographers last subjected their methods, and use of source materials, to critical consideration. Echoing Alan Baker and Mark Billinge's original choice of title, *Period and Place* (1982), the volume in question now stands as a historical marker in the field. Certainly, critical questions of method seldom feature prominently in regular reports on historical geography appearing in *Progress in Human Geography*. A special issue of *Historical Geography* (2001) presents one notable (and commonly overlooked) exception. Essays herein – alighting on oral history (Cameron, 2001; Winders, 2001), visual sources (Domosh, 2001), emancipatory intervention (Duncan, 2001) and material encounters (Gagen, 2001; Kurtz, 2001; Till, 2001) – ought to be regarded forerunners for a new collection exploring the diverse and increasingly hybrid nature of historical research practice (Gagen *et al.*, 2008). Though the tradition of methodological overview has been patchy, more narrowly directed contributions and commentaries do crop up, tending to be circumscribed by the temporal and spatial co-ordinates of empirical research, or quite tightly-defined scholarly fields. This varied literature already includes work on the nature

of archival practices (Rose, 2000, 2002; Withers, 2002; Lorimer, 2003a, b), the materiality of historical 'texts' (Ogborn, 2004b; Livingstone, 2005; Ogborn, 2007; Mayhew, 2008), the study of visual records (Rose, 2001; Schwartz and Ryan, 2003; Schwartz, 2004), the encounter with historical objects both human and non-human (Featherstone, 2004; DeSilvey, 2006; Hill, 2006a, b; DeSilvey, 2007a, b; Hill, 2007; DeSilvey, 2008), the historical spaces of biography (Livingstone, 2003; Daniels and Nash, 2004; Thomas, 2004; Lorimer, 2006; Matless and Cameron, 2006, 2007), and the *eventfulness* of historical embodiment and performance (Lorimer, 2003a, b; Gagen, 2004; Cresswell, 2006; Vasudevan, 2006).

The long-standing absence of summative reviews of historical method in geography is, on the face of it, a little puzzling and worthy of further consideration, in part as it enables me to more fully rehearse how dominant understandings of reasoning in historical research method have been shaped according to sub-disciplinary traditions of inquiry. What is covered in this introductory overview can only ever be a thumbnail sketch of the development of modern historical geography (and thus, in places, runs the risk of caricature). Historiographical qualifications aside, my remarks hang on a vexed question: Why is it that historical geographers – a community of practitioners for whom the archive is 'bread-and-butter' – have so seldom gone in for instrumental descriptions of archival method, or, ethical reflections upon archival conduct or the founding epistemic principles and schema underlying the nature of their practice? Possible explanations are various. The first is rooted in a blunt, matter-of-fact worldview that seems still to prevail, at least in certain fields of historical inquiry. According to a normative logic, complicated explanations of practice are unnecessary, since, in essence, the task at hand is eminently straightforward (see also Schein, 2001). It works as follows: in any given archive informed searches of sources are undertaken and, as a result, data about the past is uncovered. In this regard, it might not be incidental that archival research has, almost always, been figured a solitary, self-directed undertaking. Arguably, collaborative programmes of research – a perfectly common arrangement in many other geographical fields – produce fulsome methodological commentaries *because* dialogue, exchange and conciliation are necessary to ensure that things actually get done. By contrast, the lone researcher, sequestered in the archive, can 'just get on with things'; and, in so doing, renders reflexive commentary on practice as superfluous. In search of a dictum and provocation, I'm tempted to offer: 'historical geographers seldom do practice'. Many of us seem comfortably assured that the beginning researcher will somehow intuit what must be done once having entered the archive. Or, failing that, that archival awareness will be self-taught.

I argue the case from bitter experience. In the earliest stages of my doctoral research I paid an exploratory visit to the University Library in Cambridge. My memories are vivid enough to remind how, with the formalities of visitor registration completed, feelings of disorientation and confusion quickly overwhelmed me. Tellingly, I recall a great deal more of the building's physical fabric and the social introductions that took place over the course of that first morning, than I do of the archival work undertaken. Steering me around and showing me the ropes, my doctoral supervisor occasionally bumped into scholarly acquaintances, respected veterans of the field of historical geography. Conversations suggested that they knew the building and the cataloguing system inside-out. All seemed to share a confidence, born of experience and evident in manner, that I felt myself so obviously lacking. Left to my own devices after lunch, I spent a very long time seated several floors up staring out of a window wet with condensation from the mild Autumnal weather. I had the distinct impression that 'the archive' was somewhere between a labyrinth and an impregnable fortress. Escape was not an option. My surviving notebook records a series of searches attempted, each too tightly circumscribed, hunting for items unlikely to surface, or perhaps even exist.

Undoubtedly, there *is* much about the mechanics of archival research that remains unchanging, and reassuringly predictable. Not the least being the necessity of patient labours to understand and unravel a topic, or to grub-up long forgotten facts. However, the thin and patchy record of critical review and reflexive commentary by historical geographers must also be understood to reflect a particular intellectual heritage. The research parameters, the specialisms, and the generally preferred tone of archive-based research during the post-war era developed amongst a relatively small, dynastic – though in some respects international – community of historical geographers. Generally speaking, their work was founded on an objective, positivist mode of inquiry where the researcher's neutrality and detachment from the subject was a matter of principle, and thus s/he could not feature as a willful, political or emotional agent in its midst. In recounting this episode of scholarship, it should not go unsaid that the assembly of historical geographers was, in greatest number, a gentlemanly fraternity. When statements on method did emerge these tended to adapt a broad-based scientific model to the specific requirements of historical inquiry. As such, age-old empiricist research skills seem to have pertained, variously: subjecting as many evidentiary documents and source materials as possible to a forensic level of scrutiny; cross-referencing between documentary sources to ensure the triangulation of evidence; the need for pinpoint precision backed by an awareness of social bias and the 'tainting' of data; the systematic consideration of possible relations between different variables and the setting up of multiple working hypotheses; and, the use of supposition only until a pressing case for falsification emerged. In these respects, the historical geographer was, for Alan Baker (1997) among others, not unlike the most exacting of detectives working around a difficult case by sifting the available evidence for clues. The suite of sleuthing skills was upheld in the service of maintaining robust and rigorous methodological measures for archive-based scholarship. By implication, conjecture, speculation and inference were faulty modes of reasoning to be avoided wherever possible. The methodological approach was underpinned by an unwavering, foundational belief that buried in the sources there were facts which could be dislodged by the enquiring mind, verified by the lateral thinker. Once quarried, and synthesized, those same facts could be pressed into the service of model-building (see Harley, 1982), as the preferred scientific device to explain, and compare, spatial patterns of social and economic changes in the countryside, town or city. Since the data amassed could be quantitative in nature, synthesis enabled statistical forms of analysis. For this task, the researcher had to be numerate, sometimes to an advanced level. Commonly the results of archival research took summative expression in tables, graphs, cartograms and accompanying maps.

Acknowledgement of the archive's existence was limited to that of a research resource by which to better assemble more accurate and fuller versions of past geographies. Those worlds, societies and landscapes existed *outside* the archive's bounds. The archive did not merit comment as a part of that world, as a site with its own population of human subjects (archivists and researchers), or as a resource with its own history of production. It was stifled, rendered as passive, reduced to no more than a storage space. In this sense, much published research can be said to have been immaculate in its conception; none of the vulgar labour of production was revealed. One textual device allowing for controlled forms of confession, and positioned at one step remove from the voice of objective detachment is, of course, the footnote – which can be deployed for a parallel or oblique form of commentary, voiced as if from the sidelines of research, and on occasion directed as if to you 'Dear reader ...'. Towards the bottom of the page,

time-honoured rules of use continue to apply; and, the complex underworld of the footnote has its own venerable traditions of subversion, retort and feedback (Grafton, 1999).

Methodological approaches to archive-based research did not alter noticeably during sub-disciplinary forays into Marxist, world-systems and structuration theory in search of a greater philosophical framework to bolster (and sometimes embellish) the conception of historical geography (Baker and Billinge, 1982; Baker and Gregory, 1984a, b). Instead, it was the later encounter with theoretical constructs emerging from post-structuralist thought and post-colonial studies that delivered the most significant jolt to historical geographers' collective nervous system. In this respect, Brian Harley (2001; see also Brothman, 1993; Edney, 2005) was a pioneer, leading efforts to problemitize cartographic sources through a quasi-Derridean system of deconstruction. Others found inspiration in Michel Foucault's genealogical approach to the epistemic construction of power arrangements and spatial regimes running across history epochs, others still in Edward Said's invitation to rehabilitate forgotten voices and marginalized identities. Related literatures emerging from New Historicism offered examples from the humanities of greater conceptual freedoms to be enjoyed. Even so, this paradigm shift later attributed to 'new cultural geography' has tended to be figured in terms of theoretical, rather than explicit methodological, advance: variously, the search for cultural, social and political meaning in the representation of landscape; the discursive constitution, and contestation, of knowledge, language and power in different space and sites; and the new focus on different registers of identity (gender, ethnicity, sexuality, nationality, embodiment). Significantly for historical geographers, the first flush of social and critical theory had a centripetal effect. An emerging generation of researchers directed new ideas *outwards* by charting the great diversity of spatial imaginaries and worldviews produced according to period, place and colonial regime, and by demonstrating how examinations of the social construction and moral classification of different groups in society could herald in geographies previously unknown to historical research (Graham and Nash, 2000). In its practical operation, this pioneering school of historical-cultural research was certainly multi-lateralist in voice, was catholic in its choice of sources materials, and so can be understood to have quietly legitimated the greater use of such source materials as paintings, photographs, films, documentaries, commercial advertisements, postcards, cartoons, recorded music and sounds, even household objects and personal effects. In the process, and without terrific fanfare, the limits of the geographers' archive were unbound.

In a handful of notable instances, having been awakened to the complex cultural politics of authorship and claims to representation, critical attentions turned *inwards* to consider the status and organization of the archive, and researcher's possible treatment of it. Historical geographers' introduction to a feminist critique of knowledge production, and of the need for greater reflexivity and a transparent situating of the researcher within research, is most attributable to Gillian Rose. Her account of the process and practice of working on a collection of photographic portraits of women (2000, 2002) is remarkable for its unfamiliarity of tone, where archival research is rendered uncanny because it is more assertively emplaced, and yet resultantly, becomes much less certain of its self. Held under the steady glare of the desk light the very fabric and texture of the photographs are brought to the reader's attention, and Rose's self-conscious, inter-textual deliberations about what might possibly be said of them are candidly explained.

That the effect of Rose's work – and others since written that follow its lead (Yusoff, 2007) – has been slow-burning seems to say something of the continuing legacy of the modern historiography of the sub-discipline. *En masse* historical geographers are still not much given to anxious bouts of introspection,

at least in published work. 'And a good thing too', some might yet bridle. Where the shift from interpretation to self-interpretation is most marked, experimental and non-conformist types of historical research practice have resulted. The appetite for efforts to narrate archival practice and chronicle the messiness of process is sure to differ. An excess of subjectivity can prove just as discomforting reading as the earlier untroubled objectivity assumed by the researcher. For critics, the willingness of some researchers to mine identities, or episodes of *their* experience, for material seems only to distract from the actual topic under investigation; since *who* it is that they think they are, or how it is that research makes them *feel*, can have no causal relation to events that happened in the, sometimes very distant, past. When it is least effective, the approach can succeed only in indulging a cult of personality. Undoubtedly there is a careful balance to be struck since a reflexive approach seems more comfortably suited to some historical topics and subjects than to others. How to deal with subjectivity – whether kept at arm's length or allowed just that little bit closer – is *the* meaningful tension disclosed in the archive. If *reflexivity* has not been accepted throughout as common currency, arguably, among historical geographers there is a more widespread acceptance of the need to critically interrogate the *historicity* of the archive as sited repository, and a space of knowledge. The very idea of the archive – its origins, scope, layout, composition, content and treatment – has been stirred up and shaken, and in the process, the status of the information it holds, been rendered more provisional, indeterminate and contestable.

Three thematically-organized sections that follow later draw attention to particular methodological approaches which speak to this continuing episode, and expose the closer coupling of manner and method, and inventive entangling of content and context where research is caught in the nick of time. Before that, however, it is necessary to consider how any project to humanize the archive also makes necessary a proper acknowledgement of how today, pressing practical, managerial and technological issues in the archive impinge directly on research method.

CHANGING LOCAL CULTURES OF SITE AND SOURCE

Were there space permitting it would be tempting to re-introduce the archive using the schema of a pocket field guide, this version designed for the 'great indoors'. Though it would be unwise to push the analogy too far, something of the classic conventions of the geographical genre of handbook-to-foreign-lands-and-other-societies would offer a possible structure: preparedness for terrain, local population, social organization, ritual and custom, equipment and technical expertise, even climatic conditions and ecologies. Alas, abbreviated dispatches will have to suffice. In this regard, archivists themselves ought to be researchers' key informants, having been the practicing community most active in re-creating the social and institutional conditions by which (sometimes ossified approaches to) archival method might be extended and re-invented.

Archival advances

For those still tempted to reduce the role of the professional archivist to one of simple information provision, or at best the proficient execution of a fairly drab civil service, Kathleen Marquis (2006) has some salutary reflections to offer from the 'other side' of the Inquiries Desk. In her experience the role of archivist is daily a multi-faceted one: 'we play the roles of tour guide, teacher, consultant, salesperson, matchmaker and certainly mediator' (p. 38). In spite of the diverse demands of the role, archivists' skills are sometimes judged by the older currency of 'librarianship'. Unthinking scholars beware: archivists are no longer so ready to accept such unfair diminution. While 'search-based

exasperation' is a common enough condition among historical scholars, archivists too harbour their own professional frustrations. In ordinary dealings with archive users, Marquis explains how she and fellow archivists draw on considerable reserves of patience and tolerance: 'If the past is a foreign country, then educating researchers about using archives can feel like conducting a Berlitz course' (2006: 39). Mutual incomprehension can result, and matters-of-fact crucial to shaping or directing a search can get lost in translation. Commonly, the researcher wants to be directed along the shortest, quickest and easiest search routes likely to lead to the desired archival object, or anticipated 'find'. Anxious to save precious time, paradoxically the researcher can feel encumbered by technical knowledge that *could* only *potentially* prove time-saving. Offers of a 'Reference Interview', guided tour' or 'Orientation Session' might conceivably have been turned down as either 'too intrusive' or 'surplus to requirements'. For the single-minded researcher, awareness of the archive's 'undercarriage' is dealt with on a strictly need-to-know basis. The average scholar may brush-up against such pressing archival considerations of containment, deposition and mobility – and on occasion become active decision-makers in such matters (Withers and Grout, 2006) – but in large part the practical day-to-day considerations of maintaining an archive are not their immediate concern. Figured either as 'gatekeeper' or 'facilitator', it is the archivist who must decipher and interpret readers' requests, and it is the archivist who can navigate the local terrain. Similarly, it is the archivist who understands an unfamiliar technical language which must turn on a proper understanding of key terms. For example, how many researchers will truly know how to discriminate between search processes based on 'scope and content notes', 'EAD's', 'finding aids' and 'provenance' (Cook, 2003; Yakel, 2006); certainly not this one!

Whenever and wherever they persist, and however mundane in expression, practical instances of disconnect between archivists and researchers may not simply be inter-personal, but instead borne along on structurally uneven working relationships. For Terry Cook, the systematic fashioning of servile status for archival staff within the bureaucratic infrastructure of the modern state was something that historians *and* archivists themselves were too long complicit in. Persistent labelling as the 'handmaidens of historical research' was revealing of sharply gendered relations and male power at work in the archive, and equally problematic for the reproduction of a hierarchy of knowledge claims (Cook, 2006). Traditionally, subservience, neutrality, silence and invisibility in the execution of archival duties were those 'qualities' that managers and users most valued in staff. The archivist's meekness and lowliness stands in striking opposition to the (image of the) lofty, imperious scholar, high of brow and embedded in *his* archive.

It is in this institutional context that the systematic management of archives attained the status of a science, though a reputation as a rather dismal one at that. Commentators at the leading edge of a post-modern turn in the re-theorisation of archival science – hotly debated in the pages of *Archivaria* – have argued that there were intellectual costs, as well as practical-methodological implications, arising from the prevailing professional culture of passivity (Cook, 2001a, b). For Brothman (1993) it allowed among many historians 'a peculiar form of disciplinary repression of blindness' where narratives of the past could be written with barely a mention of the archive as an actual place and archiving as an active process necessary for the preservation of the past. Having been subject to such erasure, Cook (2006) likens the archivist to a spectral presence; a shadowy keeper, but crucially not a creator, of the past. Returning to day-to-day interactions in the reference room, Marquis finds greater comfort (and levels of respect) promoting the idea of archivist as skilled consultant, without whom users' enquiries, however well-conceived, can prove rudderless or ultimately fruitless. Aiming for

best practice – where any putative scholar-archivist opposition collapses through commitment to shared, congenial endeavour – she envisages conditions where 'research partnerships' are forged.

Archival equipment and conduct

To the self-enclosed researcher, these changes to working conditions and relations may go unnoticed. However, of late, the archive's cherished atmosphere as the most concentrated of working environments has undergone significant (perhaps even seismic) change. Archival handiwork is a changed business. The pencil's place as a humble and transportable implement for record work has been challenged and, in truth, largely overhauled by the ubiquity of the laptop computer. Aside from altering the nature of data collection in the archive, the consequences of this technological shift are sensational: the sound of the reading room is no longer one of silence, punctuated occasionally with whispered readers' requests, coughs stifled into handkerchiefs and the creak of straining furniture. Listen today and you hear the continual soft chatter of competing keyboards, and closely repeating hard thumb strikes on the space bar. For many 'readers' the acts of reading and writing no longer rank as the primary function of their archival visit. Increasingly, specialized digital cameras are used to photograph the textual and pictorial contents of books, folders and filed materials. And so, backs once hunched over documents are straightened up since researchers now stand as often they sit. Eye strain comes from checking on lens focus and light levels, rather than deciphering difficult handwriting. The rise of this personal reprographic technology means that the scholarly method of close-grained study and consultation no longer need happen *in situ*. The task of transcription is all but removed, and interpretation is forestalled. Eventually, and intermittently, study is undertaken from the comfort of home or office. In this fashion, a personally-compiled version of the archive is amassed and made mobile. But for the sentimentalist in any historical researcher (and we can be a fairly traditional bunch), the archive's hermetic seal has been punctured still more fundamentally. For a new generation of researchers thoroughly-schooled in the use of information and communications technologies (ICTs), the adoption and widespread use of electronic search engines and digital storage formats in archive management systems, will almost certainly revolutionize the nature of historical research and the manner in which it is conducted.

Information and communications technologies have already opened up a multitude of archival resources for virtual consultation and study. At its most rudimentary, the technology allows for the main catalogues and indices of national archives to be explored in advance of a planned visit; and preliminary or contextual queries to be submitted by e-mail. In certain scenarios (research using genealogical source data being an excellent example), it is no longer absolutely necessary (as it still was only five or ten years ago) to travel in-person to an archive (quite conceivably located on another continent) for the purposes of examining source documents on-site. More and more documentary sources and photographic collections have been digitized, and graphics-based representations of the originals made available on-line. At magnified scales, forensic inspection is now computer-aided, and historical verisimilitude generated in high definition, ideally by the greatest possible number of pixels. Among the professional archival community, ever conscious of the need to protect *and* provide source materials, one key advantage of virtual consultation is that it avoids the steady deterioration of documents through regular use, and the greater threat of permanent physical damage to the rarest and most prized manuscripts. In the process, both the founding idea and the practical operation of 'the visit' – to say nothing of its evidentiary claims – have been placed in question. On-line versions of public access (albeit sometimes coming at an institutional fee and also dependent on the availability of a high-speed broadband connection) can happen at any time, and in any place. There are undoubted virtues to the virtual version of search method: the geography of archival consultation can extend such that claims to confidently 'know' are triangulated at a trans-continental scale, perhaps even to have global reach; and, locally, certain inconsistencies and idiosyncrasies experienced in-the-thick of institutional cultures are ironed out, made generic, or simply removed. However, if the demands of archive-oriented travel itineraries are many and the financial costs to be incurred sometimes punitive, then the intellectual and social rewards that come of a conventional mode of 'presenteeism' are very often greater still. Consequently, it is impossible to generalize about what might be lost, missed, overlooked or simply put beyond reach if the scope of archival study is limited to those documents available to view on-line. Though there will never be verifiable evidence to support the claim, the likelihood of making that serendipitous (and all-important) archival discovery would seem to be greatly reduced for the remote researcher. There is, for sure, a case to be made for the creative possibilities of being present, spending time *in situ*. For archivists, the implications of technological advance are far-reaching too. The emergence of the 'post-custodial' archive has been a subject of intense debate, and design-based dialogue, within the profession (see *Archivaria* for a wide selection of commentaries). The pooling of digitized archival resources seems, for many, the best means to give off-site users a computer-generated simulacrum of the authentic item. Academic research is itself productive of new archives. Increasingly (if the situation in the UK is considered exemplary), it is an expectation of research councils that in agreeing to fund a project, one of the deliverable outcomes will be a digitized and electronically-accessible resource base of key source documents (http:www.ahrc.ac.uk).

ARCHIVING EXTENDED OUT-OF-DOORS

An inner life, elsewhere

The spatialities and styles of archival research are still shifting. In light of recent technological developments and styles of information management, it is now inaccurate to figure archival work as an entirely sedentary exercise. However, on reflection, this was never so. While the body is ever present on site, thoughts are restless and nomadic. The great multitude of ideas that spring out from archival materials have a rich inner life, journeying hither and thither. Oftentimes, and without any great act of will, researchers call on their geographical imagination to picture, to populate and to personalize the pasts to which they are dedicating such time, effort and thought. In the mind's eye, unknown aspects of subjects' identities are coloured in, the outlines of unseen faces are etched, landscapes settled, and key scenes set and staged so that events might dramatically unfold. The urgent workings of the mind take the researcher on travels, perhaps even offering the co-ordinates for them to lead a second life. In this respect, it might be said that archival method is boosted by a vivid imagination and an ability to inhabit imaginary, or parallel, worlds.

Further complications exist within any positing of a simple relation between spaces of knowledge that are to be found *indoors* and *outdoors*. Travel in real-time begins with the inclination to step-outside, and to variously encounter the places, practices and politics of the past. For many geographical researchers, landscape is the arena where pasts seem to pass through the present, and where forms of fieldwork are entwined with archival inquiry. For these researchers, staggered or shuttling movements are sometimes necessary between sites, conveniently recognizable and demarcated as 'archive' and 'field'. And, of course, documents, objects and knowledge from the past were themselves highly mobile, sometimes passing

repeatedly through both orbits. Their eventual place of deposition can have been the result of an arbitrary stranding, as well as a most carefully planned bequest. It can become evident that there are archives to be found embedded within the field, and, unsurprisingly, the inverse of this occurs, when elements or aspects of a fieldsite's past can sometimes only be accessed in the archive. Perhaps, whether fieldwork is an activity that takes place open to the skies or with a roof overhead is itself a moot point.

That crossover work in archives *and* field sites takes place, is in part borne of inquisitiveness; a curiosity to discover 'What the place might have been like?' The yearning to pay a visit in person to *that* place in which so much thought has been invested is surely commonly felt (Harris, 2001). Claims to authenticity of experience matter; though, the urge to follow in old footsteps is all too easily read into others' actions, rather than those of the researcher. Pilgrimage and homage might seem too strong a vocabulary, though forms of spiritual connection and feelings of intimacy are privately conceded. Spending time where others did so in the past might forge new kinds of connection, and throw out new leads; even perhaps attempting to shadow, in practice, just a little of what was once laboured over or enjoyed at leisure (Lorimer, 2007). Hip-high, shoulder-deep or skein slim, past landscapes are about coming to the spot. Details of location can be cross-referenced. Things can be scooped up, delved into, even dug up. A less settled phenomenon than the historian's palimpsest (of clean-cut layers resting level upon level) and enlivened by presence, landscapes promise depth and disruption. Certain experimental archaeologists-cum-anthropologists are expert in the gleaning of fragments. Generously outward-looking and experimental in their methods, they continue to rework longer histories of technique: finding in aerial mapping, documentary sources, phenomenological apprehension and modern-era salvage operation, new sorts of creative opportunity and combination (Bender, 1993; Tilley, 1994; Pearson and Shanks, 2001; Tilley, 2004; Hicks and Beaudry, 2006; Holtorf and Williams, 2006; Joyce, 2006; Wilkie, 2006).

Three thematically-arranged forays into these hybrid archival-field spaces – and their inventive expression of method – follow below: first, the rehabilitation of historical fragments; second, the performance of landscape and personal memory; third, the archive as launch-pad for political and social activism.

MAKE-DO-METHODS: RENEWABLE AND FRAGMENTARY CRAFT WITH THE PAST

Amidst any cross-disciplinary traffic of ideas and techniques concerning the fragmentary past, the specifics of method can still be hard to pre-plan. More likely, they are fallen upon, or opportunistically designed. To do so requires that faith be kept in immediate surroundings and our human abilities to perceive them. With exploratory mapwork, educated guesswork and direct observation, things from the past issue forth, and begin to connect up. In places, they abound: to saturation point, or standing proud. In others, they remain concealed, squirreled away, needing to be chiselled out. 'Findings', as poet and writer Kathleen Jamie (2005) has it, exist both as verb and noun, they are the process and the culmination of any quest; however modest in ambition. Activities take shape on-the-hoof, are improvised according to circumstance, conditions underfoot and things to hand. Jamie's key injunction is to turn in again, and then once again, to what exists, there, then, in the moment. To ask, what yet can be grubbed up and snuffled out? With whom can conversations be struck? What living memories remain? What kinds of return can be made? Whether she is traipsing after cultural artefacts, rooting out natural specimens, or divining more numinous qualities, Jamie is an appropriate role-model for fieldwork practice. She enters into the spirit of sites, happily shedding trained sorts of

conservatism, loosening off the moorings and allowing for unlikely affinities to crop up. We might respectfully recognize this as a poet's soulful ease with the qualities of a place, but acknowledge too that elsewhere, comparable skills were once known by an older coinage of geographical appreciation and emotional apprehension as *genre de vie*.

Methodologically, what this all actually amounts to can still be hellish hard to determine or render systematic. In some respects, arguably the strongest comparisons hold with the old-fashioned crafts employed by natural historians in the field. They would, for sure, know all about getting your eye (or ear) in, about learning to take a longer look and to listen hard. But perhaps it's more besides. By taking that second glance, waiting and watching wide-eyed, there are chances to see normality differently; even just a little squint. I'd like to cast this as a receptive state, combining an attitude of mind, heightened powers of observation and an openness of manner. During the slow crafting of such a position, the influences that work away are diverse; variously empirical and theoretical, academic and personal, sometimes suffocating in their site-specificity. When revisited they seem always to crop up in different arrangement and relation. Nevertheless, in forming what I have gradually come to recognize and refer to as 'make-do-method' my own greatest debt of gratitude is owed to a humane pairing. The only previous acknowledgement of Edwin and Ann Wakeling was a sparing one; shrunken in scale to superscript text (Lorimer, 2006). A fuller explanation of their methodological influence is overdue, and I hope will prove instructive.

Make-do-and-Mend, 8 Milton Park

The Wakeling's house is one of a clutch of properties on a 1950's local authority housing estate in Aviemore, Invernesshire. 'Make-do-and-Mend', the name tagged on to the postal address, hints at an older design for life with its cultural origins in the straightened circumstances of post-war British society.

The Wakelings are members of a generation that came to know a doughty, domestic resourcefulness; those who did not waste would not want. Rather than finding nostalgia in the strictly rationed household economies of the austerity years, paying the Wakeling's a visit is to encounter a continuing ethic of self-sufficiency, grooved out of shared habits for raising a family, running a home and keeping a garden. At Make-do-and-Mend decades of dwelling are everywhere apparent, and take diverse but always practical expression in a willingness to repair, re-connect, redeploy and retread. This material culture of home drew my attention at a particular time; I was busy researching the landscape history of a herd of reindeer. Fortune was kind in this regard. The Wakelings were principal characters internal to the story of the herd's early years, and would prove just as pivotal in the shaping of research praxis. No mean local historians-cum-antiquarians, their home-grown techniques for living extend to a foraging sort of field method when exploring the surrounding landscapes of Strathspey. Outings and rambles in their company are eclectic affairs; variously enterprising, resourceful, independent, unhurried, experimental, conversational, dignified and holistic. Covering traditional routes through the herd's grazing grounds at walking pace, stories were told of passage and of place, found items stashed away, trails of animal spoor followed, impromptu workshops held on animal husbandry, rudimentary instruments fashioned and tried out, and edible things gathered up for later consumption. Moving through a landscape in this fashion was a salutary reminder of the adaptable wisdom and place-based 'commons-sense' often learned in childhood; but for me at least, long since in abeyance. On returning home, the haul of fragments from the field was drawn into longer conversations about the contents of Edwin's personal herding archive. Against a backdrop of local area maps, disparate objects and elements (stones, stories, topographical features, photographic portraits and herd kinship diagrams) could be grouped. Description, matter and medium were held together.

Edwin's tales and my speculative theories juxtaposed. Peculiar and particular assemblies of stuff jogged new memories. Narrative threads emerged in unexpected ways, by twists and turns. It was according to these collaborative conditions, that I came to know the rich landscape history and life pattern of the reindeer herd.

Transferable skills

This situated example of 'making-do' offers a motif for the re-design of method and ethics of conduct with possible appeal and application beyond the bounds of any one geographical or cultural setting. Making-do might usefully be thought of as collagist and chthonic, in character and, being of earthly making, considered portable to all manner of other places besides Strathspey. As such making-do can be understood as an adaptive mode of inquiry, variously indebted to environmentalism (where a personal commitment can be made to sustainable research practice), to protectionism (played out in the common urge felt to conserve and commemorate), and to vitalism (suggesting a set of values for renewal, retrieval, practical action and animation). Under this billowy canopy of thought, it is the massing of remainders, redundant objects, fragments and discarded substances dating from the past that seems to offer a renewable resource for the undertaking of historical research (see Lorimer and MacDonald, 2002; Neville and Villeneuve, 2002; DeSilvey, 2008). Consider this, if you will, a creative form of cultural recycling that aims, wherever possible, to tread lightly and respectfully. In such a fashion, the principles of beachcombing and 'freeganism' – reclamation and accumulation by other, less wasteful means – can be turned back on the exercise of research. Cultural by-products, junk, ephemera and leftovers become a treasure trove and staple resource. Hereabouts, significance and enchantment exist in a found sound, a chance field trip, thrift store scouring, a successful dumpster dive or spell of crate digging, vintage recording and reprographic technologies, an enlightening trespass, an overgrown ruin or the parcels of 'edgeland' past the point where the path gives out. Such a fusion of ecological thought and modes of intensive local field study was undertaken as an audacious experiment by Laura Cameron (1997) in *Openings: a meditation on history, method and Sumas Lake*. More recently, Caitlin DeSilvey (2006; 2007a; b; 2008) has observed the slow morphing of an abandoned Montana homestead through processes of decay, decomposition and overgrowing. Given the recombinant, wild ecologies that now prosper where once a vulnerable and threadbare human order held sway, the true nature and full extent of any collaborative homestead salvage project has created thorny questions for its curators. Entropy has become the very source for their creative unsettling of landscape history. Instances of making-do need not only stir Walden-like in the backwoods or while trundling through open country. Tim Edensor's (2005) ventures in the derelict wastelands of the post-industrial city are an unlikely field guide to "nowheresville". These geographies occupy a strange country, where unauthorized access is forbidden and transgressive land-use continues. Amidst abandonment, rust, shattered glass, asbestos, oozing chemicals, graffiti and twisted metalwork, Edensor finds secret depths and elusive networks. Methodologically, this represents the academic edge of psychogeographical literatures (Seabrook, 2002; Sinclair, 2003, 2006;), contemporary experimentalism and surrealism (Fenton, 2005; Pinder, 2005) and the self-styled dark pastimes of a new generation of urban explorer (Ninjalicious, 2005). The fragments that hold the attentions of these urbanists are as likely to be gestural, immaterial or epiphenomenal as they are classically architectural.

Auto-assemblage

Without habitual thoroughness on the researcher's part, collections of bits and pieces are destined to remain just that. Accumulating fragments (in the hope that their sum will add up to more than the parts) can be as much a personal compulsion as it is a controlled expression of method. In truth, collecting old things (be these books, maps, artefacts, memorabilia, souvenirs, curiosities, pamphlets or photographs) is a predictably studious sort of extramural pastime, where research *may* emerge as a spin-off, but quite probably only in the long term. The focus of the geographer-collector's attentions might be variously biographical, bibliographic, regional or place-based. The symptoms of their condition might be diagnosed as an expanded form of bibliophilia, or a strain of archive fever (Derrida, 1996) where acquiring becomes a solitary quest, rather than an institutional or civic project. Hoarding – in an attic or study depository – is commonplace. However voluminous its holdings the thirst to amass just a little more can seem sometimes unquenchable. When personal expenses are incurred these are often justified by the promise of prospective studies (on *that* project forever stalled at the larval stage). Or, by the practical need for a reference library near at hand. Or, indeed, by the sanctuary offered by shelving packed tight with faded spines. As tools of the trade, books comfort, console and inspire during the lonely, isolated hours of research. Objects produce feelings of close association with earlier periods or past places. In the strictest sense, crude accumulation is no research method, and nor is a lifestyle enthusiasm for retrospectives, historical re-enactment or cultural revivalism. Nevertheless, the private passions that revolve around collecting act as powerful forces in the production of research expertise and know-how.

Underlying any research interest, there is, without question, an addictive quality to the ideal of recovery and rehabilitation. In Henry James's novella, *The Aspern Papers* (1909) an avaricious historical scholar undertakes a search for a highly-prized series of letters, in the process he loses all perspective and with it his moral compass. Great personal sacrifices are made, loyalties and confidences betrayed, and all in vain. The archival bounty, and cause of such trouble, is ultimately destroyed. At the story's end, he is bereft. With caution, I submit to having been left similarly forlorn by an archival 'find', only to quality that its occurrence (and recurrence) was in my dreams. The setting was all too familiar: a second-hand bookshop and favourite neighbourhood haunt. The scenario entirely predictable: while innocently browsing the shelves I would chance upon an unmarked box-file and to my amazement discover inside the personal papers of a photographer in whose biography I had a long-standing research interest. Up until that point all my research inquiries had drawn only blanks; reflecting, of course, my actual experience in waking searches. Blessing my luck, I agreed on a price with the bookseller. At this point, inevitably and abruptly, the dream sequence ended. I would awake with a start. But the feverish sense of loss lasted for days; and I still feel a touch rueful whilst typing this out. However pitiful or tragic-comic, an undeniable ache remains for the find that never was. Unconscious desires, archival imaginings and a longing to accumulate yet more can quickly outflank the starched, more presentable and sane version of our selves. Whether we express this need through ethically questionable conduct or commodity fetishism, disparate stuff remaining from the past a, figured as fragmentary in status, *can* produce intense kinds of affective response. Care is necessary here. Certainly by critical feminist readings (Parr, 1995; Smith, 1998), affording the past a mystical power to seduce the avid researcher with the possibility of togetherness – or alternatively to jealously guard and withhold secrets – is to become a victim of hubris, and put nothing more than a scholarly gloss on familiar tropes of masculine conquest.

The creation of internet auction sites with customized search engines (e-Bay being the most omnipresent) has made the individual accumulation of specialist archival material an altogether easier task. In some instances (DeLyser 2003; DeLyser *et al.*, 2004; DeLyser, 2005; Lorimer, 2007), the purchase of original documents and second-hand goods has shaped the design of historical studies to such an extent that web-based shopping can quite properly be regarded a research method, and e-Bay a validated methodological device for global sourcing. Among historical scholars, I suspect there are mixed feelings about an accelerated and competitive version of intellectual consumption that allows for the purchase of 'ready-made' archives, and for the most arcane of inquiries to be immediately sated; bank-balance permitting. There are worries too that it is more than the concept of the centralized archive that has gone to pieces. Scare stories circulate about large collections broken up for quick sale, and of once publicly available materials entering into private hands. Other objections sound as easily antediluvian as is innocent any rejoicing at the wonder of technology, or celebration of accumulation for the sake of accumulation. Almost all new agglomerations of unwanted old stuff are entirely harmless. Indeed, the trend might actually speak of a contemporary version of antiquarianism: kitschy, none-too-choosey, and indulging the sentimental "pack-rat" in all of us. In the lyrics for 'Teenage Winter', recording artists and cultural commentators St. Etienne (2005) wryly capture the habits of a rising generation, schooled the e-Bay way: 'Holding on to something, and not knowing what you're waiting for'.

IT'S ALL AROUND YOU: PERFORMANCE, TOPOGRAPHY AND MEMORY

I've chosen to open this section with a harmless thought experiment, in order to consider the potentially enlivening effect of performance and personal memory on more traditional modes of field method in historical study. Imagine, if you will, an encounter between Mike Pearson, artistic director and performance studies scholar and practitioner, and W.G. Hoskins, standard-bearer for studies in English local history. Photographic portraits appear below as an aid to picturing the scene. Ideally their paths would cross at a gap in a hedgerow marking the boundary of two English shires, those of Lincoln and Leicester. At different times, they have called these counties home and study area (Hoskins, 1967; Pearson, 2007). Hoskins (Figure 14.1) is remembered and celebrated as a masterful reader of landscape; finding in trace elements such as ancient roadways, agricultural and ecclesiastical buildings, remnant woodlands and water-meadows, the kind of physical evidence necessary to interpret and understand the formation of places in the past. Fieldwork was fundamental to his basic philosophy for historical reconstruction, though always pinned to the closest inspection of surviving source materials (Pearson offers his own thoughts on the legacy of Hoskins's 'naturalism' in Pearson and Shanks, 2001: 152). The methodological relationship was reciprocal and iterative:

> There is no opposition between fieldwork and documents. Both are essential to the good local historian. Behind a good deal of work in the field and in the street are documents that help to throw more light on what is being studied; and behind a good many documents lies much valuable

fieldwork if only the unimaginative "researcher" had the wit to see it. Most academically-trained historians are completely blind to the existence and value of visual evidence. Visually speaking, they are illiterate. (Hoskins, 1967: 183)

Hoskins's resulting work – exemplified in his accepted classic, *The Making of the English Landscape* (1955) – was rural in its geography, largely pastoral in character, and offered reconstructive explanations of how the countryside had been settled. Pearson's (Figure 14.2) approach to landscape is similarly committed to exploring a vernacular past. Though his attentions might be drawn similarly to earthworks, field patterns, grazings, drove roads or the like, greater emphasis falls on those lives once lived that give meaning to place. The continuing local significance of sites, their oral history, collective memory, folklore and festive rites, are for Pearson, an invitation to perform. Inventive techniques are deployed in the choreographing of landscape as a theatre open to the skies.

Although fanciful (and a little mischievous) the convergence of Hoskins and Pearson is full of intriguing possibilities. Over which matters would dialogue and debate be pitched out? Perhaps the particulars

Figure 14.1   W.G. Hoskins (with permission from the staff at the Centre for English Rural History, University of Leicester).

Figure 14.2   Pearson's approach to landscape (with permission from Professor Mike Pearson, University of Wales, Aberystwyth).

of place names, or, questions of local dialect, or perhaps just the relative merits of one landmark over another? Who would be the more frightened, or flummoxed, or informed and entertained, in the presence of the other? Divergence and stark contrast need not be assumed. Variously, they can be said to occupy common methodological terrain: in a form of research where raking over the material remains and graphic representations of landscape is a primary means to disinter aspects of the past; in the region as the preferred scale of analysis, and optic for understanding social change wrought through the transformation of landscape; and, in their own authoritative presence as researcher-performer. Take Pearson's appearance. He is properly turned out as a field researcher. Formally attired in shirt-and-tie, offset by a pair of Wellington boots, he observes traditional standards for dress and practical footwear. In this respect, Pearson's presentation of self is likely to have met with the approval of Hoskins, latterly in his career a television presenter and trusted guide to the nation's origin story.

But, methodological parallels drawn should not be strained. In four important and connected ways, respective claims to intimacy of knowledge and depth of field experience take contrasting expression. For Pearson, the researcher's own body is the yardstick by which landscape is paced out, and episodes from his own life story are treated as a source of narrative and means for orientation. The emergence of such a self-consciously performative register, connecting then and now, marks a significant departure from established traditions of landscape interpretation. By reviving the ancient figure of the troubadour, Pearson's theatrics might be read as an imaginative reworking of a still older kind of chronicling. There are dangers here. If meticulous craftsmanship is anywhere lacking, the poise of performance can slip towards a "see-me" sort of enterprise, where critics bridle that the past features merely as backdrop to personality. Second, if this new vein of work is less conservative in conduct, likewise it is not so censorious about the nature of data sources suitable for the interpretation of meaning; though skeptics might contend it is not censorious enough, too often departing from 'historical realities' in favour of a free-for-all with former times. Third, it does not seek to clean-up content or shear off context, instead making room to speak of, and reflect on, the full operations of research. In collaborative writing, Pearson incorporates an open and refreshingly frank commentary on methodological options considered (Pearson and Shanks, 2001). Explanations are given for steps *not* taken, as well as paths travelled. By such a code of conduct research becomes its own road-movie, framed as a journey, with diversions, stops for re-fuelling, periods of drift or frantic navigation. Fourth, it is as concerned with transience as it is with permanency, with absence and loss as much as presence and preservation: 'By this we mean an ecology of interpenetration between past and present, with the visit treated as a performance event which witnesses absence'. (Pearson and Shanks, 2001: 155). Productive comparisons can be drawn with geographer Owain Jones's (2005) moving account of family history and the passing of presence in place, inspired directly by autobiography and personal memory. On this occasion, less a researcher and more a ruminator, Jones becomes a blotting paper, porous to the possibilities of encountering and soaking up aspects of his own past.

That there is a greater acceptance of the place of personal memory – and its umbrella method, oral history (Perks and Thomson, 2006) – in historical-geographical research (McDowell, 2004; Harvey and Riley, 2005; Andrews *et al.*, 2006; Harvey and Riley, 2007) opens up a range of sites and sources, as yet only partially explored. Though the source material for much historical research remains squarely located in the great national archives of the world, a vein of inquiry finds its home in family archives, lodged in out-of-the-way places and according to private conditions of storage and unexpected forms of cataloguing or display. The work of locating previously unheralded or informal archives is, in itself, a task worthy of note. To be granted permission to consult personal papers, handle precious keepsakes, heirlooms and forget-me-nots, or leaf through family photograph albums is to come to appreciate the emotional charge, vulnerability and tactility of the archive, and the significance of reliquaries. In his arresting memoir, *In the Dark Room: A Journey in Memory* (2006) Brian Dillon offers the closest of descriptions of the shape, form, function and feel of personal effects, thus exposing a tender history

of childhood grief and slow recovery. Comparably sensual considerations of the rich mnemonic worlds stashed away in rooms, caskets, closets, cupboards, drawers, shoe boxes, even perspex IKEA storage solutions, are all possible (see also, Batchen, 2004; Edwards and Hart, 2004a, b; King, 2006). Elsewhere, Matthew Kurtz (2001) has been sidetracked by the history of the filing cabinet while searching through office archives. In the domestic setting, archival research can unfold as a wholly different kind of undertaking. Crowded houses, musty attics, 'empty' rooms and the archival caches therein create their own kinds of phenomenal intensities, and practical considerations (Lorimer, 2003a, b; 2006). When consulted in the company of a family member-cum-host-cum-curator, and interleaved with reminiscence, archival materials play with the appearance of historical events, and alter the eventual conditions of its narration. Generosity of reception is a value that can be traded by respective parties, in either direction. The delicacy demanded in negotiating publishable versions of the past, in person, with next-of-kin or more distant descendents renders the researcher as loss-adjuster with a difference (Lorimer and Spedding, 2005).

Conceding that lives are always a fiction offers to historical research a greater degree of latitude. The intimacies of the self – receding time horizons, muddled chronologies, forced erasures, passionate relations, brief encounters and withering judgements – are what make the *partiality* of reconstruction so appealing. If once all life *was* there, that which remains presents the means to craft more emotionally sensitive geographies.

DISPOSSESSION, ADVOCACY AND ACTIVISM

The archival record can present a powerful evidential resource for militancy, agitation, protest, dissent, civil disobedience and diverse public campaigns set on securing greater social justice, emancipatory action and establishing proof of dispossession. The politicization of present landscapes can occur by dredging the documentary record. In aggregate, we might then usefully recognize the form as 'advocacy/activist archiving', a collection of research actions understood by activists to have beneficial impacts on the lives and identities of those who appear as subjects therein, or of their friends and family, even if sometimes several generations removed. In certain instances, disclosing little known, previously classified and even suppressed documentary evidence can enable the correction of wrongs once committed in the name of state and local authorities, or if not that then at least the recovery and construction of an opposing view to challenge, and sometimes undermine, received wisdom about the events surrounding past geographies and histories. Clearly, projects of this nature which are undertaken by the scholar working single-handedly or researcher collaborating with local community groups will never match for scope and depth of coverage, or for supporting bureaucratic machinery, those of the public inquiry, government commission, or Committee for Truth and Reconciliation. It is not investigative exercises on the grand scale that I want to consider here. Rather, I want to profile two investigative inquiries, based on advocacy archiving, that are concerned with past events and peoples *and* seek on others' behalf to make a difference in the present. The examples of work chosen are non-academic and as such are intended to show the creative approaches and campaigning practice employed by activist musicians and journalists that might offer methodological leads for those wishing to build bridges between the material contents of the archive and the continuing social and political life of the world outside its bounds.

Ry Cooder, guitarist, composer, producer and musical activist, is best known today for his efforts to salvage Cuban musical traditions from cultural obscurity and enforced geo-political isolation by helping establish the *Buena Vista Social Club*. However it is another of his projects in cultural restoration and remembrance that merits consideration here. Cooder's album *Chávez Ravine*, released in 2005, takes its name and creative focus from the area of land used to build the Los Angeles Dodgers baseball stadium in the early 1950s. Previous to this landmark project in urban redevelopment, Chavez Ravine was the hillside home to a large number of the city's thriving Chicano community. Subject to the view one take's of past events, the Los Angeles City Council initiated either a land-grab, or a slum clearance, or a scheduled demolition in the ravine with the stated intention of constructing new low-rent housing. Financial coercion, eviction orders, orchestrated campaigns of violence, racial prejudice and political harassment – the latter executed with the complicity of the House Un-American Activities Committee (HUAC) – were deployed to ensure the removal and dispersal of the mostly American Mexican inhabitants, and the ultimate erasure of the irregular landscape of tin-roofed shacks, yards and woods that comprised a *barrio* slum town or a 'poor man's Shangri la'; two opposing views according to differing political persuasion. Of the two descriptions, the latter is offered by Don Normark who in 1948, as a young man with a passion for photography, accidentally 'discovered' the neighbourhood whilst 'looking for a high point to get a postcard view of Los Angeles' (2003: xx). Subsequent visits resulted in his unwitting production of a social document for a community soon-to-be disappeared. The ravine was bulldozed. The promised low-rent housing never got off the ground. The city's new home for baseball was raised instead. Normark's original collection of black-and-white photographs set the mood for Cooder's subsequent dramatisation of events, part-fact part-fiction, re-worked according to different Chicano musical traditions. The result is a bittersweet geographical tribute to a forgotten place. The album's accompanying booklet, and detailed liner notes, are a composite of Cooder's own memories of youthful travels around his native city, surviving archival materials from the City Public Library, residents' family portraits and oral histories: 'Ravine old-timers locate themselves by a memory plum line, straight down through the playing field of Dodgers stadium, to the town underneath all that cement. "I'm from 3rd base", "we're from home plate" etc'. For those still living there is a memory, and through them the story-map of Cooder's lyrics unfolds. But, there is no credible promise of return. 'In their minds, they are still a community', Normark asserts, 'They have formed a group called *Los Desterrados* – "The Uprooted" – that meets each year to picnic at Elysian Park, the playground of their childhoods'. Cooder's example of artistic exchange and community collaboration suggests one sort of response to recent calls for more inclusive 'public geographies', of a sort that cast backwards into the past to shed light on the present. In search of an apposite term, projects such as this might be considered 'public historical geographies'. Advocacy, lobbying and campaigning, over a more pressing humanitarian issue, that carries with it a long history, offers another means of activating the archive through direct intervention. In this respect, the investigative work of John Pilger, journalist, broadcaster and activist, is exemplary.

A different dream of homecoming is as yet unresolved for the Chagossian Islanders, one-time residents of the Pacific atoll, Diego Garcia. In 1961, the Britain government struck a bi-lateral agreement with the United States allowing for the open-ended lease of Diego Garcia for the purposes of establishing a strategic air base, and (having undermined any legal claim to permanent residency) engineered the deportation of the entire population to the 'neighbouring' island of Mauritius. Now elderly, the Chagossians remain exiled, along with their extended families. They still claim a right of return. In 2006, a British High Court decision found in their favour, and against the actions of the British government. A major aspect of the Chagossian's case centres on establishing

credible testimonies of dispossession and forced removal. Their plight and welfare has been researched, and their on-going campaign for justice taken up as a popular cause, by John Pilger (2004, 2006). In his documentary, *Stealing a Nation* (2004), Pilger draws an assortment of classified government material, archive film footage, and location-based oral testimonials into service as rhetorical weaponry and as evidence for legal advocacy. Investigative archiving has pieced together a papertrail of correspondence and memoranda produced by the British diplomatic service chronicling government officials' efforts to cover-up the island's clearance, or explain events away as an unfortunate local difficulty. In interview footage, politicians, retired and currently serving, answer Pilger's charges, their responses are shown as an indictment of Anglo-American geopolitics, in the past and the present. Geographical research is even enlisted as supporting evidential resource. Professor David Stoddart submits the findings of bio-geographical science and field survey experience earlier in his career in support of the argument that Diego Garcia remains an island where sustainable community life could easily be revived; in the process making plain his disdain for the instruments of a neo-imperial British state.

Pilger's career, meanwhile, has been defined by a highly mannered form of investigative method. Elements of his research style might not present an acceptable template for the academic researcher to borrow from directly. Previously, he has been accused of sloppily sourcing evidence, and of skillfully editing and juxtaposing material to advance a cause; though the judicious arrangement or 'touching-up' of evidence in the construction of a compelling argument is not limited to the field of journalism. Critics mock his eagerness to turn the camera back onto himself. Monomania aside, Pilger's confrontational style, hanging on the sensational scoop or hard-won expose of hidden agendas, is largely unknown to historical research in academic communities, and certainly seems less well suited to longer publishing timescales. Although the vein of hot-blooded, angry writing that Pilger (2006) has long favoured is increasingly in evidence in human geography, sharp-edged 'op-ed' reportage by a strident and partisan voice can seem at odds with the unpoliticized, even-handed treatment often expected of the historian. Expediency can give occasion for the simplification of key arguments understood to serve a greater good, and thus might be sanctionable, but can also rub up against the task of constructing a subtle, multi-layered analysis. Finally, the task of crusading for truth can prove a controversial and cut-throat business on which reputations and claims to legitimacy are staked, and where enemies are easily made.

Consciously lower in profile though arguably no less worthy of mention, examples of archival advocacy in the academy do exist. Social anthropologists have an extensive track-record of advocacy in land claims made by indigenous communities, extending to making sworn statements at state tribunals and legal proceedings. Here it is very often the absence of a conventional textual archive that prompts anthropologists to act, aiding in the production of oral testimonies or 'memory-maps' chronicling land use and ancestral knowledge of presence in place (Cruikshank, 2005). Such efforts are lesser known in human geography, though Caitlin DeSilvey (2003) is one notable exception. She explains how a campaign to save an area of allotments threatened by urban development, when brought before a parliamentary hearing, was galvanized by evidence dredged up from city council records. More generally, calls for 'historical geographies of the present' (Smith, 2002; Gregory, 2004; Pred and Gregory, 2005; Kearns, 2008) suggest that the survival of public memory, the defense of public space and protection of rights of protest are almost always contingent on a keen awareness of the historical conditions that were fundamental in their making. As such they represent a contemporary re-working of a tradition of dissenting radicalism in histori-

cal inquiry first shaped by members of the New Left (Thompson, 1963). Cautionary words aside, there is something of Cooder and Pilger to be detected in recent investigative research projects designed to pick away at the secretive workings of the North American military-industrial complex (Paglen, 2005), or to expose how the rudimentary sovereign rights of subjects have been undermined by different imperial regimes (Kearns, 2008), or to study the scorch marks left in urban communities by processes of gentrification. Each recall Alan Berger's (2007) provocative new visual taxonomy of 'drosscapes' and show the dividends that come from fusing archival inquiry with situated action, and coupling historical consciousness with contemporary human rights campaigning.

CONCLUSION

In a little over two decades, historical scholarship in geography has shifted in methodological inclination from the predominantly arithmetical to the knowingly artful. The diversity of topics researched by geographers' reveal no common thread running through archival work. Needless to say, varying blends of empiricism, interpretation and experimentation continue to be accommodated in a community of practitioners generally accepting of contrast. Where continuing differences over style of approach exist, these speak to greater epistemic truths about the nature, scope, manner and methods of archival scholarship. Changes in the specifics of technique, or in attitudes to practice, need not fray the edges of any case made for a common or unifying purpose. If anything, a growing focus on lower worlds – composed of fragments, emotions, gestures and memories – can be most effectively fused with less personal, sometimes global, historical geographies of economic transformation, social change, spatial dislocation, and shifting relations between society and environment.

Shifts in methodological approach can create their own distinctive writing cultures, and representational styles. The inverse of this relation also applies, where the attractions of different forms of writing and formatting can shape the bounds of a project, the manner of its methods, and specific design of data collection techniques. As outlined earlier, post-structuralism provided historical geographers with a theoretical apparatus to explore the plurality of identities and the spatial particularity of their situation. Only more recently have historical geographers returned to the post-structural canon and found in the writings of the likes of Bakhtin and Benjamin a means to critically reflect on the fragmentary nature of work on the past, the possibilities of assemblage as a motif, and the creeping doubts that partiality seems to cultivate. Crafting a different kind of writing about the past where demonstrating mastery of site, scale or period is *not* the ultimate objective might at first seem heretical. In fact, claims to having only partial, provisional and incomplete knowledge can afford to research an allure and shroud of mystique. That gaps in source material consciously be held open, rather than closed up, might well seem like a dereliction of the historian's duty. In *Rodinsky's Room* (2000) Iain Sinclair, writer, and Rachel Lichtenstein, artist, search London's East End for a missing person according to the traces found in the domestic detritus of his life. David Rodinsky, their subject and quarry, is presented as a shape-shifter, haunting their every move, always one step ahead of the pursuit. The authors' willingness to chronicle a topography of chance occurrences, inadvertent meetings and the following of crooked leads has dramatic effect, producing the thrill in the chase. That they do so is, of course, a stylistic choice and most witting device. They create an unsettling, spectral mood and an enigmatic account of a man-hunt. Inexorably, the researchers are enveloped, and the question posed of just who is in control. In the twilight hour, *Rodinsky's Room* can be read as a cryptic sort of methodological manifesto that invites comparable kinds of transitive inquiry. Of course, the idea of scholars, writers and antiquarians being engulfed by the past itself is not new. Intrigue and mystery has been plotted by, among others, A.S. Byatt (*Possession; The Biographer's Tale*), Evelyn Waugh (1957) (*The Ordeal of Gilbert Pinfold*), M.R. James (1971) (*Ghost Stories of an Antiquary*) and Henry James (1917) (*The Sense of the Past*). Though not quite in clover, geography is enjoying a fine spell of experimentation in form and tone where fragmentary data is being turned towards more imaginative styles of composition and expression. Forgotten or previously untried formats such as diary entries, photo documentation, montage, scrapbooks, essays, websites, field sketches and drawings, working notes, art installations and soundpieces, now crop up with increasing regularity. Notably, the form of archival record with the greatest hold on geographers' attentions remains the ream rather than the reel. Genres of film (home movies, documentaries) and sound formats (vinyl, wax cylinders, reel-to-reel) hold huge promise, as yet largely untapped.

Many experimental formats invoke, or allude to, the working style of the bricoleur (Denzin and Lincoln, 2000; Crang, 2003). Mostly, these have had liberating and leavening effects. In this regard, the possible scope of work, inventive technique and formatting of findings has been advanced and stretched through recent collaborative research aligning historical-cultural geographers and practitioners in the creative and performing arts (Driver *et al.*, 2002; Rose and Dorrain, 2004; Hampson and Priestall, 2005; DeSilvey and Yusoff, 2006; Foster and Lorimer, 2007). Works by Bryndis Snaebjorndottir and Mark Wilson (2006), Jeremy Deller and Alan Kane (2005), Gair Dunlop (www.cumbernauld.nu; www.tompro.co.uk), Kate Foster (www.meansealevel.net) and Mark Dion (Coles, 2001) make mysterious and playful cross-cuts through scientific and expeditionary traditions of amassing and classifying archives, and their associated image banks and exotic fieldwork collections. Methodologically-speaking, aspects of historical geography research are undertaken increasingly as a field art and a field craft; though, for good strategic and historiographical reasons, a toehold is kept in the field sciences too.

A related trend equally worthy of note is the use of narrative to structure the telling of past geographies. Geographers can make some reasonable claim to having re-discovered the power of the story, ushering in more thickly descriptive – sometimes lyrical, highly decorative – prose. The current preference for the personalized, micro-scale inquiry – and the relative unpopularity of macro-scale survey – produces a miniaturized version of research subjects well suited to the unfolding of narrative. Biographies – of people, animals, objects, and ideas – are a template for the attractive tailoring of 'tellable' tales. These take the shape of 'research miniatures' or 'mini-epics' – though sometimes still research monographs (Ogborn, 2007) – disclosing how in minutia it is possible to find small kingdoms of worldliness, and to craft short stories as outcrops of global history. The continuing challenges presented, in respect of methodological approach and narrative form are considerable, not least of discovering composite states for an acceptable fusing of poetics and politics in our research on the past.

ACKNOWLEDGMENTS

For helpful comments on earlier drafts of this work, my thanks to the editors, and to Simon Naylor, Chris Philo, Jo Norcup, Merle Patchett and Allan Lafferty.

REFERENCES

Amato, J. (2003) *Dust: a history of the small and invisible.* Los Angeles: University of California Press.

Andrews, G.J., Kearns, R.A., Kontos, P. and Wilson, V. (2006) '"Their finest hour": older people, oral histories, and the historical geography of social life', *Social and Cultural Geography* 7(2): 153–77.

Baker, A.R.H. (1997) '"The dead don't answer questionnaires": researching and writing historical geography', *Journal of Geography in Higher Education* 21 (2): 231–43.

Baker, A.R.H. and Billinge, M. (eds) (1982) *Period and place: research methods in historical geography.* Cambridge: Cambridge University Press.

Baker, A.R.H. and Gregory, D. (eds) (1984a) *Explorations in historical geography: interpretive essays.* Cambridge: Cambridge University Press.

Baker, A.R.H. and Gregory, D. (1984b) 'Some *terrae incognitae* in historical geography: an exploratory discussion', in A.R.H. Baker and D. Gregory (eds) *Explorations in historical geography: interpretive essays.* Cambridge: Cambridge University Press. pp. 180–94.

Batchen, G. (2004) 'Ere the substance fade: photography and hair jewellery' in E. Edwards and J. Hart (eds) *Photographs, objects, histories: on the materiality of images.* London: Routledge pp. 32–46.

Bender, B. (1993) *Landscape: politics and perspectives.* London: Berg.

Berger, A. (2007) *Drosscape: wasting land in Urban America.* Princeton: Princeton University Press.

Blunt, A., Gruffudd, P., May, J., Ogborn, M. and Pinder, D. (eds) (2003) *Cultural geography in practice.* London: Arnold.

Brothman, B. (1993) 'The limits of the limits: Derridean deconstruction and the archival institution', *Archivaria* 36: 205–20.

Byatt, A.S. (1991) *Possession: a romance.* London: Vintage.

Byatt, A.S. (2001) *The biographer's tale.* London: Knopf.

Cameron, L. (1997) *Openings: a meditation on history, method and Sumas Lake.* Montreal: McGill-Queens University Press.

Cameron, L. (2001) 'Oral history in the Freud archives: incidents, ethics and relations', *Historical Geography: An Annual Journal of Research, Commentary and Review* 29: 38–44.

Coles, A. (2001) *Archaeology: Mark Dion.* London: Black Dog Publishing.

Cooder, R. (2005) *Chavez Ravine.* Audio CD, Nonesuch Records.

Cook, T. (2001a) 'Archival science and postmodernism: new formulations for old concepts', *Archival Science: International Journal on Recorded Information* 1 (1): 3–24.

Cook, T. (2001b) 'Fashionable nonsense or professional rebirth: postmodernism and the practice of archives', *Archivaria* 51: 14–35.

Cook, T. (2003) 'Mind over matter: towards a new theory of archival appraisal', in B. Craig (ed) *The archival imagination: essays in honour of Hugh A. Taylor*. Lanham, MD: Scarecrow Press. pp. 38–70.

Cook, T. (2006) 'Remembering the future: appraisal of records and the role of archives in constructing social memory', in F.X. Blouin and W.G. Rosenberg (eds) *Archives, documentation and institutions of social memory: essays from the Sawyer seminar*. Ann Arbor: University of Michigan Press. pp. 169–81.

Crang, M. (2003) 'Telling materials', in M. Pryke, G. Rose, and S. Whatmore (eds) *Using social theory: thinking through research*. London: Sage. pp. 127–44.

Cresswell, T. (2006) '"You cannot shake that shimmie here": producing mobility on the dance floor', *Cultural Geographies* 13 (1): 55–77.

Cruikshank, J. (2005) *Do glaciers listen? Local knowledge, colonial encounters and social imagination*. Vancouver: University of British Columbia Press.

Daniels, S. and Nash, C. (2004) 'Lifelines: geography and biography', *Journal of Historical Geography* 30 (3): 449–58.

Deller, J. and Kane, A. (2005) *Folk archive: contemporary popular art from the UK*. London: Book Works.

DeLyser, D. (1999) 'Authenticity on the ground: engaging the past in a California ghost town', *Annals of the Association of American Geographers* 89 (4): 602–32.

DeLyser, D. (2003) 'Ramona memories: fiction, tourist practices, and placing the past in southern California', *Annals of the Association of American Geographers* 93 (4): 886–908.

DeLyser, D. (2005) *Ramona memories: tourism and the shaping of Southern California*. Minneapolis: University of Minnesota.

DeLyser, D., Curtis, A. and Sheehan, R. (2004) 'Using e-Bay for research in historical geography', *Journal of Historical Geography* 30 (4): 764–82.

DeSilvey, C. (2003) '"When plotters meet": cultivated histories in a Scottish allotment garden', *Cultural Geographies* 10 (4): 442–68.

DeSilvey, C. (2006) 'Observed decay: telling stories with mutable things', *Journal of Material Culture* 11 (3): 317–37.

DeSilvey, C. (2007a) 'Art and archive: memory-work on a Montana homestead', *Journal of Historical Geography* 33 (4): 878–900.

DeSilvey, C. (2007b) 'Salvage memory: constelling material histories on a hardscrabble homestead', *Cultural Geographies* 14 (3): 401–24.

DeSilvey, C. (2008) 'Practical remembrance: material and method in a recycled archive', in E. Gagen, H. Lorimer and A. Vasudevan, (eds) *Practicing the archive: reflections on methods and practice in historical geography*. London: Historical Geography Research Group Monograph Series. pp. 37–46.

DeSilvey, C. and Yusoff, K. (2006) 'Art and geography', in I. Douglas, R. Huggett and C. Perkins (eds) *Companion encyclopaedia of geography: from Local to Global*. London: Routledge. pp. 573–88.

Denzin, N.K. and Lincoln, Y.S. (2000) 'Introduction: the discipline and practice of qualitative research', in N.K. Denzin and Y.S. Lincoln (eds) *The handbook of qualitative research*. London: Sage. pp. 1–29.

Derrida, J. (1996) *Archive fever: a Freudian impression*. Chicago: University of Chicago Press.

Dillon, B. (2006) *In the dark room: a journey in memory*. London: Penguin.

Domosh, M. (2001) 'Visual texts in historical geography', *Historical Geography: An Annual Journal of Research, Commentary and Review* 29: 68–9.

Driver, F., Nash, C. and Prendergast, C. (eds) (2002) *Landings: eight collaborative projects between geographers and artists*. London: Royal Holloway.

Duncan. J. (2001) 'Notes on emancipatory collaborative historical research', *Historical Geography: an Annual Journal of Research, Commentary and Review* 29: 65–67.

Dunlop, G. (2007) http//:www.tompro.co.uk; http//www.cumbernauld.nu

Edensor, T. (2005) 'The ghosts of industrial ruins: ordering and disordering memory in excessive space', *Environment and Planning D: Society and Space* 23 (6): 829–49.

Edney, M.H. (2005) 'The origins and development of J.B. Harley's cartographic theories', *Cartographica* 40 (1 & 2) Monograph 54.

Edwards, E. and Hart, J. (2004a) 'Mixed box: the cultural biography of a box of "ethnographic" photographs', in E. Edwards and J. Hart (eds) *Photographs, objects, histories: on the materiality of images*. London: Routledge. pp. 47–61.

Edwards, E. and Hart, J. (2004b) *Photographs, objects, histories: on the materiality of images*. London: Routledge.

Featherstone, D. (2004) 'Spatial relations and the materialities of political conflict: the construction of entangled political identities in the London and Newcastle port strikes of 1768', *Geoforum* 35 (6): 701–11.

Fenton, J. (2005) 'Space, chance, time: walking backwards through the hours on the left and right banks of Paris', *Cultural Geographies* 12 (4): 412–28.

Fines, J. (1988) *Reading historical documents: a manual for students.* Oxford: Blackwell.

Foster, K. (2007) http//:www.meansealevel.net.

Foster, K. and Lorimer, H. (2007) 'Some reflections on art-geography as collaboration', *Cultural Geographies* 14 (3): 425–32.

Gagen, E. (2001) 'Too good to be true: representing children's agency in the archives of playground reform', *Historical Geography: an Annual Journal of Research, Commentary and Review* 29: 53–64.

Gagen, E. (2004) 'Making America flesh: physicality and nationhood in turn-of-the-century New York schools', *Cultural Geographies* 11 (4): 417–42.

Gagen, E., Lorimer, H. and Vasudevan, A. (eds) (2008) *Practicing the archive: reflections on methods and practice in historical geography.* London: Historical Geography Research Group Monograph Series.

Grafton, A. (1999) *The footnote: a curious history.* Cambridge: Harvard University Press.

Graham, B.J. and Nash, C. (eds) (2000) *Modern historical geographies.* London: Prentice Hall.

Gregory, D. (2004) *The colonial present: Afghanistan, Palestine, Iraq.* London: Blackwell.

Hampson, D. and Priestnall, G. (eds) (2005) *Chat moss.* Nottingham: CMG.

Hannam, K. (2002a) 'Coping with archival and textual data' in P. Shurmer-Smith (ed.) *Doing cultural Geography.* London: Sage. pp. 189–98.

Hannam, K. (2002b) 'Using archives' in P. Shurmer-Smith (ed.) *Doing cultural geography.* London: Sage. pp. 113–22.

Harley, J.B. (1982) 'Historical geography and its evidence: reflections on modeling sources', in A.R.H. Baker and M. Billinge (eds) *Period and place: research Methods in Historical Geography.* Cambridge: Cambridge University Press. pp. 233–43.

Harley, J.B. (2001) *The new nature of maps.* Baltimore: Johns Hopkins University Press.

Harris, C. (2001) 'Archival fieldwork', *Geographical Review* 91 (1–2): 328–34.

Harvey, D. and Riley, M. (2005) 'Narrating landscape: the potential of oral history for landscape archaeology', *Public Archaeology* 4 (1): 15–26.

Harvey, D. and Riley, M. (2007) 'Talking geography: on oral history and the practice of geography', *Social and Cultural Geography* 8 (3): 345–51.

Hicks, D. and Beaudry, M.C. (2006) 'Introduction: the place of historical archaeology', in D. Hicks and M.C. Beaudry, (eds) *The Cambridge companion to historical archaeology.* Cambridge: Cambridge University Press. pp. 1–9.

Hill, J. (2006a) 'Globe-trotting medicine chests: tracing geographies of collecting and pharmaceuticals', *Social and Cultural Geography* 7 (3): 365–84.

Hill, J. (2006b) 'Travelling objects: the wellcome collection in Los Angeles, London and beyond', *Cultural Geographies* 13 (3): 340–66.

Hill, J. (2007) 'The story of the amulet: locating the enchantment of collections', *Journal of Material Culture* 12 (1): 65–87.

Hoggart, K., Lees, L. and Davies, A. (2002) 'Behind the scenes: archives and documentary records', in K. Hoggart, L. Lees and A. Davies (eds) *Researching human geography.* London: Arnold. pp. 119–68.

Holtorf, C. and Williams, H. (2006) 'Landscapes and memories', in D. Hicks and M.C. Beaudry (eds) *The Cambridge companion to historical archaeology.* Cambridge: Cambridge University Press. pp. 235–54.

Hoskins, W.G. (1955) *The making of the english landscape.* London: Hodder.

Hoskins, W.G. (1967) *Fieldwork in local history.* London: Faber.

James, H. (1909) *The aspern papers.* London: Penguin.

James, H. (1917) *The sense of the past.* London: Collins.

James, M.R. (1971) *Ghost stories of an antiquary.* New York: Dover Publications.

Jamie, K. (2005) *Findings.* London: Sort of Books.

Jones, O. (2005) 'An emotional ecology of memory, self and landscape', in J. Davidson, L. Bondi and M. Smith (eds) *Emotional geographies.* Oxford: Ashgate. pp. 205–18.

Joyce, R. (2006) 'Writing historical archaeology', in D. Hicks and M.C. Beaudry (eds) *The Cambridge companion to historical archaeology.* Cambridge: Cambridge University Press. pp. 48–65.

Kearns, G. (2008) 'Taking theory for a walk in Ireland' in E. Gagen H. Lorimer and A. Vasudevan (eds) *Practicing the archive: reflections on methods and practice in historical geography.* London: Historical Geography Research Group Monograph Series. pp. 9–22.

King, J.A. (2006) 'Household archaeology', in D. Hicks and M.C. Beaudry (eds) *The Cambridge companion to historical archaeology.* Cambridge: Cambridge University Press. pp. 293–313.

Kurtz, M. (2001) 'Situating practices: the archive and the file cabinet', *Historical Geography: An Annual Journal of Research, Commentary and Review* 29: 26–37.

Lichtenstein, R. and Sinclair, I. (2000) *Rodinsky's room.* London: Granta.

Livingstone, D. (2003) *Putting science in its place: geographies of scientific knowledge.* Chicago: University of Chicago Press.

Livingstone, D. (2005) 'Text, talk and testimony: geographical reflections on scientific habits', *British Journal for the History of Science* 38 (1): 93–100.

Lorimer, H. (2003a) 'Telling small stories: spaces of knowledge and the practice of geography', *Transactions of the Institute of British Geographers* 28 (2): 197–217.

Lorimer, H. (2003b) 'The geographical fieldcourse as active archive', *Cultural Geographies* 10 (3): 278–308.

Lorimer, H. (2006) 'Herding memories of humans and animals', *Environment and Planning D: Society and Space* 24 (4): 497–518.

Lorimer, H. (2007) 'Songs from before: creating conditions for appreciative listening', in L. Gagen, H. Lorimer and A. Vasudevan (eds) *Practicing the archive: reflections on methods and practice in historical geography*. London: Historical Geography Research Group Monograph Series. pp. 57–74.

Lorimer, H. and MacDonald, F. (2002) 'A rescue archaeology, Taransay, Scotland'. *Cultural Geographies* 9 (1): 95–103.

Lorimer, H. and Spedding, N. (2005) 'Locating field science: a geographical family expedition to Glen Roy, Scotland', *British Journal for the History of Science* 38 (1): 13–34.

Marquis, K. (2006) 'Not dragon at the gate but research partner', in F.X. Blouin and W.G. Rosenberg (eds) *Archives, documentation and institutions of social memory: essays from the Sawyer seminar*. Ann Arbor: University of Michigan Press. pp. 36–42.

Matless, D. and Cameron L. (2006) 'Experiment in landscape: the Norfolk excavations of Marietta Pallis', *Journal of Historical Geography* 32 (1): 96–126.

Matless, D. and Cameron L. (2007) 'Geographies of local life: Marietta Pallis and friends, Long Gores, Hickling, Norfolk', *Environment and Planning D: Society and Space* 25 (1): 75–103.

Mayhew, R. (2008) 'Denaturalising print, historicising text: historical geography and the history of the book', in L. Gagen, H. Lorimer and A. Vasudevan (eds.) *Practicing the archive: reflections on methods and practice in historical geography*. London: Historical Geography Research Group Monograph Series. pp. 23–36.

McDowell, L. (2004) 'Cultural memory, gender and age: young Latvian women's narrative memories of war-time Europe, 1944–1947', *Journal of Historical Geography* 30 (4): 701–28.

Neville, B. and Villeneuve, J. (eds) (2002) *Waste-site stories: the re-cycling of memory*. New York: State University of New York Press.

Normark, D. (2003) *Chavez Ravine: 1949, a Los Angeles story*. Los Angeles: Chronicle Books.

Ninjalicious (2005) *Access all areas: a user's guide to the art of urban exploration*. London: Coach House Press.

Normark, D. (2003) *Chavez Ravine: 1949, a Los Angeles story*. Los Angeles: Chronicle Books.

Ogborn, M. (2003) 'Finding historical data', in N. Clifford, and G. Valentine (eds) *Research methods in human and physical geography*. London: Sage. pp. 101–15.

Ogborn, M. (2004a) 'Archives', in S. Harrison, S. Pile and N. Thrift (eds) *Patterned ground: entanglements of nature and culture*. London: Reaktion. pp. 240–1.

Ogborn, M. (2004b) 'Geographia's pen: writing, geography and the arts of commerce, 1660–1760', *Journal of Historical Geography* 30 (2): 294–315.

Ogborn, M. (2007) *Indian ink: script and print in the making of the english East India Company*. Chicago: University of Chicago Press.

Paglen, T. (2005) 'Groom Lake and the imperial production of nowhere', in A. Pred and D. Gregory (eds) (2005) *Violent geographies: fear, terror and political violence*. London: Routledge. pp. 237–54.

Parr, J. (1995) 'Gender, history and historical practice', *Canadian Historical Review* 76: 354–76.

Pearson, M. (2007) *In comes I: performance, memory and landscape*. Exeter: University of Exeter Press.

Pearson, M. and Shanks, M. (2001) *Theatre/archaeology: disciplinary dialogues*. London: Routledge.

Perks, R. and Thomson, A. (eds) (2006) *The oral history reader*. London: Routledge.

Pilger, J. (2004) *Stealing a nation*. DVD. ITV/Granada Television.

Pilger, J. (2006) *Freedom next time*. London: Bantam Press.

Pinder, D. (2005) 'Arts of urban exploration', *Cultural Geographies* 12 (4): 383–411.

Pred, A. and Gregory, D. (eds) (2005) *Violent geographies: fear, terror and political violence*. London: Routledge.

Roche, M. (2005) 'Historical research and archival sources', in I. Hay (ed) *Qualitative research methods in human geography*. Oxford: Oxford University Press. pp. 133–146.

Rose, G. (2000) 'Practising photography: an archive, a study, some photographs and a researcher', *Journal of Historical Geography* 26 (4): 555–71.

Rose, G. (2001) *Visual methodologies: an introduction to the interpretation of visual materials*. London: Routledge.

Rose, G. (2002) 'Working on women in white, again', *Cultural Geographies* 9 (1): 103–9.

Rose, G. and Dorrian, M. (2004) *De-territorialisations: revisioning landscape and politics*. London: Black Dog Publishing.

Schein, R. (2001) 'Re-placing the past?', *Historical geography: an annual journal of research, commentary and review* 29: 7–13.

Schwartz, J.M. (2004) '*Un beau souvenir du Canada*: object, image, symbolic space' in E. Edwards and J. Hart (eds) *Photographs, objects, histories: on the materiality of images.* London: Routledge. pp. 16–31.

Schwartz, J.M. and Ryan, J. (2003) (eds) *Picturing place: photography and the geographical imagination.* London: Reaktion.

Seabrook, D. (2002) *All the devils are here.* London: Granta.

Sinclair, I. (2003) *London orbital.* London: Penguin.

Sinclair, I. (ed) (2006) *London: city of disappearances.* London: Hamish Hamilton.

Smith, B. (1998) *The gender of history: men, women and historical practice.* Cambridge: Cambridge University Press.

Smith, N. (2002) *American empire: Roosevelt's geographer and the prelude to globalization.* Berkeley: University of California Press.

Snaebjornsdottir, B. and Wilson, M. (2006) *Nanoq: flat out and Bluesome: a cultural life of Polar Bears.* London: Black Dog Publishing.

St. Etienne (2005) *Tales from Turnpike house.* Audio CD, Sanctuary Records.

Steedman, C. (2001) *Dust.* Manchester: Manchester University Press.

Thomas, N. (2004) 'Exploring the boundaries of biography: the family and friendship networks of Lady Curzon, Vicereine of India 1898–1905', *Journal of Historical Geography* 30 (3): 496–519.

Thompson, E. P. (1963) *The making of the english working class.* London: Victor Gollancz.

Till, K. (2001) 'Fragments, ruins, artifacts and torsos', *Historical Geography: an Annual Journal of Research, Commentary and Review* 29: 70–3.

Tilley, C. (1994) *A Phenomenology of landscape: places, paths and monuments.* London: Berg.

Tilley, C. (2004) *The materiality of stone: explorations in landscape phenomenology.* London: Berg.

Vasudevan, A. (2006) 'Experimental Urbanisms: *psychotechnik* in Weimar Berlin', *Environment and Planning D: Society and Space* 24 (6): 799–826.

Waugh, E. (1957) *The ordeal of Gilbert pinfold: a conversation piece.* London: Penguin.

Wilkie, L. (2006) 'Documentary archaeology', in D. Hicks and M.C. Beaudry (eds) *The Cambridge companion to historical archaeology.* Cambridge: Cambridge University Press. pp. 13–33.

Winders, J. (2001) 'On the outside of "in": power, participation and representation', *Historical Geography: an Annual Journal of Research, Commentary and Review* 29: 45–52.

Withers, C.W.J. (2002) 'Constructing the geographical archive', *Area* 34 (3): 303–11.

Withers, C.W.J. and Grout, A. (2006) 'Authority in space?: creating a web-based digital map archive', *Archivaria* 61: 27–46.

Yakel, E. 'Archival representation', in F.X. Blouin and W.G. Rosenberg (eds) (2006) *Archives, documentation and institutions of social memory: essays from the Sawyer seminar.* Ann Arbor: University of Michigan Press. pp. 151–64.

Yusoff, K. (2007) 'Antarctic exposure: archives and the feeling body', *Cultural Geographies* 14 (2): 211–33.

15

Textual and Discourse Analysis

Jason Dittmer

INTRODUCTION

Over the past 25 years, the analysis of discourse has opened up new dimensions within human geography, providing tools through which to interrogate the 'situatedness of knowledge, the contextuality of discourses and the active role which spatial images play in political life,' (Hakli, 1998: 333). One possible origin for the discursive turn can be found in the work of Edward Said (1978), who outlined the role of 'imaginative geographies' in constituting ontological categories such as Orient and Occident. Since then, papers in human geography that draw on discourse analysis either explicitly (through methodology) or implicitly (through the postpositivist philosophy associated with discourse) have become almost innumerable. For example, in political geography the discursive turn allowed a move away from 'realist' accounts of the role of the nation-state that reify and naturalize the status quo in which political actors other than governmental elites are marginalized. Now, scholars have shown not only alternative geopolitical imaginations enunciated and lived by marginalized voices all around the world (Adams,

2004; Dalby, 1993; Megoran, 2006) that are often critical of the territorial state system, but have also analyzed the processes by which these geopolitical imaginations are mobilized vis-à-vis each other (Dalby, 2003; Dittmer, 2007b).

Similar shifts have been made in sub-disciplines throughout human geography, with urban geographers incorporating discourse into their analyses of arts and entertainment district-led development (Eisinger, 2000) and urban policy (Davoudi and Healy, 1995), economic geographers studying cultural aspects of firms (Schoenberger, 1997) as well as the role of performance in retail location (Miller *et al.*, 1998), and human-environment geographers have studied discourses of the environment in areas such as safari tourism (Norton, 1996) and land development (Whatmore and Boucher, 1993). What all of this work recognizes is the fundamental role of language and discourse in enabling virtually all social activities. As James Paul Gee puts it, '[the] primary function of human language [is] to scaffold the performance of social activities (whether play or work or both) and to scaffold human affiliation within cultures and social groups and institutions,'

(1999: 1). If a researcher is interested in the ways in which knowledge is formulated and validated by society as truth, then discourse analysis is likely an excellent methodology to use.

The connection between the literary and the political has long been accepted, but the discursive turn brought broader significance to fields such as grammar and rhetoric and their newfound political importance enabled their liberation from the academic ghetto. The ability to frame debate through the use of rhetoric, however, has long been understood as political at the scale of person-to-person interaction. The discursive turn's potentially greatest success has been in recognizing the meso- and macro-scale importance of language – most obviously through engagement with the concept of discourse. This engagement has borne tremendous fruit already, as witnessed in the plethora of empirical work done within human geography, studying how the taken-for-granted geographies of the world are constructed and performed. Geography's discursive turn has in some ways been emancipatory to a greater degree than other disciplines' engagement with discourse. Geography, in part because of modernity's obsession with history and progress, has been traditionally stigmatized as being static and boring. Recent changes in geography, including this increasing attention to discourse, give it a dynamism and 'now-ness' that the discipline often appeared to lack in the past.

This chapter will begin by introducing the idea of discourse, and then outlining the various meanings and theoretical perspectives associated with discourse. After grounding the discussion in these specifics, the chapter will then move on to discuss a method for linking together the various scales at which discourse operates in one substantive research project, using my own dissertation research as an example. Those interested in smaller scale projects will be able to pick and choose from the material provided, but the overarching goal will be a fully-integrated project, including recent trends

toward social practice as being performative of discourse.

WHAT IS DISCOURSE?

Discourse is a notorious term within human geography and other social sciences because of the messy multiplicity of meanings associated with it. There is of course the everyday colloquial definition, roughly equivalent to conversation on a specific topic. In an academic sense discourse has yet more meanings, which can be distinguished through the terminology of discourse and Discourse (Alvesson and Karreman, 2000; Gee, 1999). At the more human scale, discourse (intentionally lower case) refers to the phrasing and word choice that is associated with 'language-in-use' (Gee, 1999: 7). The ways in which issues and spaces are framed through this textual form of discourse are of importance, as this is the most empirically observable aspect of language's impact on, and constitution of, the social world. Newspapers (Dalby, 1996; Myers *et al.*, 1996; Dittmer, 2005, 2007a), magazines (Sharp, 1996), debates among government figures (Sparke, 1996; Dixon and Hapke, 2003), and cartoons (Dodds, 1996) have all been analyzed at the textual level to uncover the various modes of representation that result in certain geographies becoming self-evident.

However, it is the leap from the linguistic, or textual, discourse to the much larger Discourse that gives such great purchase on the processes through which these 'truths' become embodied and enacted. The fusion of material texts with other forms of communication, such as body language, interactions, symbolic acts, technologies, and the like constitutes a Discourse, or a culturally-specific mode of existence. It is through the recognition and interaction of the various discourses in which we are embedded that meaning is created, power is conveyed, and the world is rendered recognizable. 'All life for all of us is just a patchwork of thoughts, words, objects, events, actions, and interactions in Discourses,' (Gee, 1999: 7).

Theoretical evolution

Discourse, with its many different meanings, has yet another fork in the path to understanding for us to navigate. There are two major strands of thought within discourse analysis, structuralist and poststructuralist (Lees, 2004), which differ largely in the extent to which they think discourse constitutes 'reality.' The structuralist strand is mostly strongly associated with Marxism, the work of the Frankfurt School in Discursive analysis (Adorno and Horkheimer, 1972), and the political thought of Antonio Gramsci (1992). This perspective views discourse as a mechanism for inculcating ideology among populations, and it is the importance of ideology that gives discourse its political relevance. As Claire Sutherland (2005: 188) wrote, '[a]n ideology is an adaptable but internally coherent belief system that offers an interpretative explanation of society coupled with practical measures for maintaining or changing the political status quo.' Ideologies can be viewed as either normatively neutral in that every perspective is equally ideological, or negative in that only oppressive or 'wrong' ideas produce ideologies. Generally speaking, the neutral perspective is aligned with most forms of poststructuralist work using discourse theory (see below), while the negative perspective is more commonly associated with the structuralist perspective, which typically (but not always) views ideology from a Leftist vantage point.

The structuralist version of discourse presupposes a subject that is ontologically prior to the effect of the discourse of the subject, largely a result of this formulation of discourse's early connections to Marxism and its class-based ontology. Gramsci (1992) outlined his concept of ideology in response to the seeming failure of socialist revolution to take place as per Marx and Engels. Gramsci argued that this 'cultural hegemony' by the capitalist class over the more numerous working class was the effect of the colonization of the workers' Discourse by the ruling class, and that the hegemony of capitalist values and perspectives would preclude the expected revolution. Thus, the concept of cultural hegemony is not only a description of how ideology and discourse work, but also leads to a political proscription: any political or economic revolution must be preceded by a revolution of class consciousness, or whatever kind of consciousness is required for the cause. For instance, a nationalist rebellion would require the development of a nationalist sensibility.

Richard Peet (2002) operationalizes Gramscian notions in his work on development in South Africa, in which he addresses what he refers to as 'globally hegemonic discourse.' Peet outlines two dimensions to discourse – hegemonic depth and hegemonic extent. Hegemonic depth refers to 'its intensive regulatory power – [which] resides in its ability to restrict serious, 'responsible' consideration to a limited range of topics and approaches or, more generally, an ability to specify the parameters of the practical, realistic, and sensible among linked groups of theoreticians, policy-makers, and practitioners,' (Peet, 2002: 57). Hegemonic extent refers instead to the geographic distance across which a discourse becomes hegemonic, especially in places where the discourse contradicts regional experiences. Peet identifies three dimensions to the enforcement of depth and extent on populations (2002: 57).

- The imposition of theoretical legitimacy, in terms of linking formalized systems of ideas with a recognized interpretation on a dominant, regional experience, set down in a hegemonic textual tradition, and widely accepted as proven and universally applicable.
- The establishment of a more directly realistic legitimacy, in terms of a prevailing sense of technical viability as adjudicated by expert opinion; several kinds of institutional legitimacy, in terms of the labeling of ideas as 'mature and responsible' in a social accounting process controlled

by conventions derived from dominant 'proven' practices of wealth accumulation.

- Popular processes of the carrying of conviction from experts to people through cultural practices developed by established media that marshal broad patterns of consent.

The operation of Gramscian hegemony in practice is not as nefarious as Peet's description makes it sound: instead of a group of elites dictating to the masses what to think, hegemony is produced through an almost infinite number of small, local interactions. Miniscule in isolation, these interactions together become cohesive in the form of social structures that oppress the very working class individuals who participate in them. Having said that, certainly Gramsci believed that capitalist elites foster this false consciousness; he equally believed that they could not impose it unilaterally. Gramsci also thought that achieving this kind of Discursive hegemony is a natural choice for would-be hegemons, as ruling by consent is infinitely easier and less costly than ruling by coercion: once hegemony is achieved, the capitalist perspective of the underclass precludes the consideration of the overturning of the status quo. To summarize the ontological implications of Gramscian hegemony, the working class is caught between (at least) two groups of elites in a tug-of-war for their consciousness; the working class is passive, and pre-existent. This tug of war for hegemony is discursive, which is to say that 'discourse is almost synonymous with hegemony itself in so far as it functions to conceal the power of vested interests and to induce the consent of the dominated to their own domination,' (Lees, 2004: 102).

Poststructuralist perspectives on discourse in human geography have less of a focus on political economy and class and more of an interest in power and the work of Michel Foucault (1974, 1977, 1989). The key difference between these two perspectives on discourse is that Foucault's formulation does not take the (usually) class-based ontology of the structuralist perspective as a pre-given; rather, he saw individual subjectivities, as well as collective identities such as economic classes, nations, etc., as being formulated through discursive processes. 'In Foucauldian terms, discourses are not simply reflections or (mis)representations of "reality"; rather they create their own "regimes of truth" – the acceptable formulation of problems and solutions to those problems,' (Lees, 2004: 102–3). In other words, it is impossible to imagine or discover what a pre-discursive world might be like. While 'it' may be 'out there,' it is impossible to know anything about 'it' (or even 'me') without resorting to language as a mediating agent that classifies, subjectifies, and objectifies. 'Thus, from a post-structuralist perspective we can understand gendered subjectivity in terms of multiple, shifting, and potentially contradictory subject positions, which individuals take up through engagement with a range of discourses and social practices,' (Mehta and Bondi, 1999: 69).

Foucault's notions of power are rooted in his term 'governmentality.' Governmentality 'describes the development of a philosophy of governance based less on territorial administration and more on the management of every aspect of people's lives through successive discursive formations,' (Sutherland, 2005: 189). Hence, Foucault's perspective brings the scale of analysis to the microscaled, diffuse interactions that compose everyday life. This is often overstated as a major difference between Gramscian and Foucauldian discourse – as described earlier, Gramsci demonstrates real knowledge of the microscaled nature of discourse. However, his followers have tended to focus more on the macro-scale structures and so it is Foucault who reintroduces the microscale as the basis for analysis. Because governmentality is an impossible totality to engage with analytically, it requires the breakup of governmentality into hierarchical layers of governmental discourse, such as the psychiatry and sexuality (among other things) that Foucault studied. This concern with power and governmentality shows a connection to the structuralist view of discourse and ideology, but Foucault himself is famously agnostic regarding the normative qualities of that power, believing that there is no truth, rather only truth effects. Gayatri Chakravorty Spivak (1988) has criticized this as an abdication of responsibility on the part of poststructuralist academics, who uncover these archaeologies of discourse yet refuse to acknowledge some forms of discourse as superior to others. Spivak argued that traditional Marxist concerns of social justice and the international division of labor should provide a politically normative element to poststructuralist discourse analysis and that these analyses can 'lead to an incisive critique of ideology by revealing the "mistakes" that found knowledge, the contradictions within discourses, and the things that are left unsaid or cannot be said,' (Pratt, 1999: 218).

This potential for social change through discourse analysis relies on the intervention of the individual, as 'the relationship between discourse and material reality/action is mediated by the social power of the discursive agent,' (Schoenberger, 1998: 6). This return of the active agent introduces practice as a more important part of the creation of social 'reality' than in Gramscian formulations: 'from a post-structuralist perspective, practice is not the product of rules internalised by actors; rather it is fundamentally improvisatory, inventive, and creative,' (Mehta and Bondi, 1999: 69). This improvisational process prevents any universalist, essentialized understanding of society from taking hold. Instead, society is seen as eternally in process, with any perceived regularities being the result of moments of discursive fixation that attempt to create the illusion of their own timelessness. This, then, is the role of discourse: it is 'the means used to organize a society into a structured totality, in order to give it stability and meaning,' (Sutherland, 2005: 191). Given this broad role for discourse, it makes sense that Ernesto Laclau and Chantal Mouffe (1985) use the broader Discourse, including language, social practices, and institutions within its domain (Laclau, 1995). Thus, ideology is under the umbrella of discourse, one element among many. This is in contrast to the structuralist view, in which ideology and discourse were synonymous; it also implies the contextuality of ideology, as it is ultimately part of a larger discursive structure, or system of difference-making.

Laclau and Mouffe (1985) take up the same issues that Spivak was concerned with, namely the use of discursive analysis to enact social change, but borrow heavily from Foucault's ideas of discourse. 'According to them, power struggles reveal points of friction between rival political projects and ultimately, between antagonistic world-views. Furthermore, challenges to the received wisdom of a given society are depicted as sources of identity crises, in which notions generally accepted to be "common sense" are re-evaluated,' (Sutherland, 2005: 190). Avowedly post-Marxist, Laclau and Mouffe discard all the structuralist baggage associated with Gramsci's formulation of hegemony and discourse, such as the focus on class identity, but nevertheless infuse Foucault's 'regime of truth' with Leftist political sensibilities. Class struggle is seen as but one type of struggle among many of interest to those of these sensibilities, hence the appellation post-Marxist. Thus, Laclau and Mouffe distance themselves from Gramsci, but also distance themselves from Foucault by interesting themselves in legitimacy and the consent of the governed.

The political sympathies between Gramsci and Laclau and Mouffe take the form of a mutual interest in ideology. However, where Gramsci saw ideology *in* hegemony, Laclau and Mouffe turn to conflict over terminology and language as a sign of the contestation between competing ideologies. The focus then is on the contingent and flexible; hegemony now has to share the stage with resistance. The analytical unit for this new focus is the discursive articulation: 'any practice establishing a relation among elements such that their identity is modified as a result,' (Laclau and Mouffe, 1985: 105). However, practice here is seen as a diffuse activity, not the effect of an individual's agency: 'a shared poststructuralist tendency can be discerned [between Foucault and Laclau and Mouffe], however, in the fact that discourse theory subordinates the attributes of the actor to the role it plays in constructing a discursive reality,' (Sutherland, 2005: 190). Drawing from Jacques Derrida (1984), Laclau and Mouffe see discursive articulations as composed of linguistic elements, themselves floating signifiers, that are momentarily stabilized through the act of articulation. The emphasis here is on the flexibility and processual nature of these discourses, which in turn makes their deconstruction a potentially political endeavor.

Despite all these variations in what scholars mean when discussing 'discourse', 'ideology', and the like, they are united in their belief that language matters; indeed, this is at the core of Foucault's famous proclamation of the unity of power/knowledge. Similarly, there is a great deal of tacking back and forth among these perspectives within human geography. The term 'poststructuralist' should not be taken as meaning that structuralism and Gramsci have been superceded. Rather, these two perspectives exist alongside each other, and not always uneasily. 'Indeed, perhaps the most influential example of discourse analysis is Edward Said's (Said, 1978) *Orientalism*, which tried to blend Gramscian ideology critique with poststructural understandings of discourse as constitutive' (Lees, 2004: 103).

Despite the blurring of theoretical boundaries during many discourse analyses, it is nonetheless important to be explicit about the theoretical background that the researcher brings to any project, as that background then has bearing on the methodology undertaken in the project.

METHODOLOGY

Conducting a discourse analysis for the first time is notoriously difficult, because while there are many fine examples of discourse analysis in the human geography literature, there are very few explicit discussions of how that research was undertaken. This is, in part, because it is not a stable process, done in a laboratory with infinite iterability, but rather it is more artisanal (Hoggart *et al.*, 2002). Still, there are two touchstones for conducting a discourse analysis (Lees, 2004). The first is attention to context; because the social setting in which language is deployed makes a tremendous difference in how it is understood. The second touchstone is the text itself: its rhetorical stance, its claims to authority, its organization. In this way, both Discourse and discourse are accounted for. Norman Fairclough (1992) offers a different model, taking these two touchstones and breaking them into a three-pronged approach to discourse analysis. The first prong is textual analysis, such as the second touchstone described above. This would include word choice, grammar, etc. The second prong is that of discursive practice, which includes the immediate context in which language and discourse are employed. The final prong is that of social practice, which includes the larger ideologies within which the social context is located. Effectively in Fairclough's system, Discourse is divided into meso- and macro-scales.

One of the problems with discourse analysis is a lack of explicit reference by many practitioners to what scale of discourse they are directing their attention. Textual analyses are often disconnected from any of the surrounding discursive context, even other related texts. Similarly, discourse analyses at the macroscale of Discourse often seem to lose their grounding in anything empirical whatsoever, but rather in vague currents floating through the aether. Making the connections between the micro-, meso-, and macro-scaled discourses is one of the real methodological challenges associated with full-fledged discourse analysis.

Discourse theorists consider ideas and their linguistic expression to be one aspect of the complex web of institutions, customs and practices, which together constitute a society. The question then arises as to how to design a piece of research adapted to the study of ideology within a world of Discourse. If an ideology is defined as a belief-system in the abstract it is, of course, structured conceptually and expressed linguistically. [...] In turn discourse theory demands that research design take account of context when interpreting data. Further, a theory which rejects a view of ideologies as dogmatic or immutable requires research methods capable of rendering the subtleties of conceptual manipulation and ambiguity. (Sutherland, 2005: 197)

This section of the chapter will describe a methodology for conducting a discourse analysis at all scales (two or three, depending on whom you ask), with recognition that there are many ways of undertaking an analysis such as this and it is, to a certain extent, artisanal and dependent on the discourse you are analyzing. Each step in the methodology will be set alongside a description of how I undertook my dissertation project, an analysis of the discursive representation of 'Eastern Europe' in newspaper coverage of NATO and EU expansion.

Textual analysis

Textual analysis, as described earlier, describes the attempt to understand the content, mode of address and authority, organization, and other aspects of language-in-use, specifically for the purpose of understanding their contribution to the intellectual scaffolding of our existence that Gee has described (1999). This has led to an enhanced appreciation for rhetoric which, while significant from the times of ancient Greece through the medieval era, was sent into the intellectual ghetto by Cartesian doubt (Lentricchia and McLaughlin, 1995). Rhetoric's retrieval from the dustbin coincides with its rejuvenation as the study of discursive and ideological efficacy. Through effective rhetoric, a truth regime may be set in place that produces self-evidence and a semi-fixity that makes it seem as if other perspectives are unnatural and flawed from the beginning. It is this process that interests the scholar conducting textual analysis.

When analyzing texts it is important to have foremost in your mind what you are looking for while reading. David Cooper (1993: 198) identified four distinct rhetorical features in an argument:

(i) [T]he deployment of tropes, like metaphor and metonymy; (ii) the deployment of persuasive techniques other than 'straight' logical argument; (iii) unity of style and content, and what I shall call (iv) the deferral of reference ... the strategy whereby an author's or speaker's reference to the real world is indirect, because refracted through an imaginary, or imaginatively presented one, which he sets up.

Cooper's rhetorical features are useful when considering persuasive argumentation, but in a more abstract sense textual analysis can be used to deconstruct texts that are less explicitly about rhetoric, such as newspaper articles or academic papers.

However, many texts are meant less for argumentation than for other purposes. What should a researcher look for when analyzing these texts? Gee (1999) identifies six building tasks that language (and other systems of meaning) accomplishes. The first, semiotic building, refers to the basic identification of epistemologies that are relevant to the current situation, whatever that may be. The second building task is that of world building, which refers to the subsequent identification of ontologies that describe the current situation: 'what is here and now (taken as) present and absent, concrete and abstract, "real" and "unreal", probable, possible, and impossible,' (p. 85). The third task of language is activity building, creating a situated meaning of ongoing processes. This is followed by socio-culturally-situated identity and relationship building, in which collective groupings relevant to the current situation are produced and attributes, proper behavior, and values given to each: these identities often take the form of 'us' versus 'them.' The fifth building task of language is political building, in which power is attributed or invested in various material or intangible goods. The final activity, connection building, is about establishing a topology of values, people, and places: 'using cues or clues to make assumptions about how the past and future of an interaction, verbally and non-verbally, are connected to the present moment to each other – after all, interactions always have some degree of continuous coherence,' (p. 85). While it would be a Sisyphean task to try to document all six building tasks for anything other than a tiny scrap of language, they are all important functions of discourse. A scholar should identify which of the six tasks are most important to them theoretically so that they know what they are looking for. Any textual analysis, depending on whether or not it is interested in methods of argumentation (as per Cooper) or a comprehensive, deeper, analysis (as per Gee) has a set of objectives to complete a thorough analysis. Of course, this is all very fine in the abstract; what does it mean to actually undertake an analysis of this type?

The first question to be asked by anyone considering textual analysis is, why am I considering textual analysis? Like any methodology, it should flow from a project's theoretical assumptions (which have been outlined above in respect to discourse and textual analysis) as well as from the object of your analysis. For my dissertation, the starting point in my analysis was an interest in the role of perception in NATO and EU expansion. A personal sympathy for Russian sensibilities regarding American/Western broken promises (generated through my graduate study of international affairs), combined with my naïve belief in the innocence of American intentions (generated through innumerable avenues over the span of my life), led me to confront two contradictory discourses I had internalized during my youth and schooling – those of American exceptionalism and 'sphere of influence'-based geopolitics. I had (somewhere) gained a poststructuralist sensibility that led me to compose research questions that focused on truth regimes, language, and geopolitics.

That question having been satisfactorily answered, the next question is one of texts – what to analyze? The texts must be linked to

your research objectives in a direct fashion. For instance, Deborah Dixon and Holly Hapke (2003), interested in discourses associated with U.S. agricultural legislation, conducted a textual analysis of US Senate debate records. This direct instrumentality in the selection of texts to analyze is important for demonstrating the rigor of the analysis. This is stated in sympathy with Jamie Baxter and John Eyles (1997: 505), who are interested in the evaluation of qualitative research: 'We recognize that there is an apparent tension between the creativity of the qualitative research process – which implies contingent methods to capture the richness of context-dependent sites and situations – and evaluation – which implies standardized procedures and modes of reporting.' Nevertheless, as Baxter and Eyles thoughtfully point out, that does not mean that qualitative research has no standards. A great deal of the legitimacy of research conducted with this methodology comes from the research design (i.e., choice of texts, sampling procedures, etc.), as it is expected that there will be some changes mid-stream regarding the way in which the research is actually conducted. Some texts may prove more fruitful than others, thus leading what had been a 'random' sample of appropriate texts into new 'less random' directions in search of relevant data.

In my dissertation I chose to follow Garth Myers and colleagues (1996) by studying newspaper accounts of geopolitical events (their work was in comparing the media discourses associated with Bosnia and Rwanda). This allowed me to directly address my primary concern: the method through which Western audiences came to understand their governments' actions and those of Russia during a time of intense geopolitical alignment following the Cold War. Newspapers during the 1990s were already losing their role as the primary news medium to 24-hour news channels, but at the time I did the research (2001–2003) there was no central database of news channel transcripts (now you can get them on Lexis-Nexis, the same database I used to get the news articles).

Therefore, the news articles represented the best, most tangible, form of data for my research questions from which I could base my analysis. I then loaded the text of these articles into a qualitative analysis computer program (a very helpful, but not necessary addition – the program creates a network topology of similar quotes for ease of collation) and coded the articles, which is to say I used the program to mark any description or representation of the countries seeking admission to NATO and the EU as well as Russia. I deliberately coded everything that met those qualifications, no matter how trivial, and no matter how apolitical it appeared at first glance. In retrospect, I was probably too militant on this point, but I was still tied up in quantitative definitions of validity that had been the centerpiece of my education up until that time. Nevertheless, this overly-inclusive coding process helped generate insights, for example in the importance of physical landscape description (which seems apolitical at first) in geopolitical 'othering.'

There are a variety of ways to assess the validity of textual analysis. Peter Jackson (1985) argues that alternatives to quantitative validity are required, particularly an emphasis on the logic of connections that are claimed by the researcher. This logic can only be uncovered by comparison of the researcher's claims to the surrounding context in which the project is embedded. Similarly, Linda McDowell (1992) argues that qualitative validity is not inherent to a researcher's claims but is instead conferred upon the claims by the research's intended audience. This social constructionist perspective on validity is contradicted by Baxter and Eyles (1997), who argue that a more public form of validity must be constructed, allowing for qualitative research to be deemed valid and acceptable by those outside the intended audience (usually qualitative researchers themselves). Certainly both perspectives are important – many researchers have attempted to increase the validity of their work by not only passing it through a peer review committee, but also showing their conclusions to the community studied:

Do the authors and audiences of the texts analyzed recognize the discourses found by the researcher (even if they had not noticed it themselves)? If so, that is an important confirmation of the validity of the project's findings. If not, perhaps the researcher should revisit the texts. In the context of my research, I had the validity confirmed by my dissertation committee and later through the traditional peer review publication process (Dittmer, 2005, 2007a).

Discourse analysis

As a project moves away from the intimate interaction with texts themselves it begins to take on more abstract overtones; one hears of structures, power, identities. It is important while undertaking research of this type to make sure that in this leap from the micro- and meso-scale to the meso- and macro-scale that the data is not decontextualized. Thus, the shift from textual analysis to discourse analysis (or if you prefer, from discourse to Discourse) is about connecting the data set analyzed earlier to the broader realm of geographical practice. This is complicated, because as with the textual analysis, things are often not as explicit as we would prefer. Geographical practice often masks the power relations that are inherent to them.

Perhaps the first step in contextualizing the 'language-in-use' studied in the textual analysis is to approach the topic of symbolic power (Bourdieu, 1983). Symbolic power refers to the access to discursive resources held by various actors. In other words, not every person has the same ability to influence discourse. In the so-called 'marketplace of ideas' some people are rich and some are poor; as in real markets, those who are rich can influence what is on sale more than the poor. Some examples of those with heightened levels of symbolic power include politicians, media elites, academics, bosses, etc. These people not only have access to mass media or other 'soapboxes' but also generally have linguistic resources that give them enhanced power. Tuen van Dijk (1993: 256) outlines an analytical tool for studying symbolic power.

> An analysis of the various modes of discourse access reveals a rather surprising parallelism between social power and discourse access: the more discourse genres, contexts, participants, audience, scope and text characteristics they (may) actively control or influence, the more powerful social groups, institutions or elites are. Indeed, for each group, position or institution, we may spell out a discourse access profile. Thus, top business managers have exclusive access to executive board meetings, in which the most powerful is usually associated with the chair, who also controls the agenda, speech acts (e.g. who may command whom), turn allocation (who is allowed to speak), decision-making, topics and other important and consequential dimensions of such institutional talk. At the same time, managers have access to business reports and documents, or can afford to have those written for them; they have preferential access to the news media, as well as to negotiations with top politicians and other top managers.

Thus, by contextualizing the act of text-creation by combining it with the institutional ability of the creator to disseminate his/her text (i.e., their symbolic power) a researcher can 'profile' the overall significance of a text. In the case of my dissertation, this part was relatively easy – there is an abundant literature on the power of media to shape political attitudes through the combination of professional writing styles and symbolic capital associated with the journalism industry itself. Further, Myers *et al.* (1996) went into detail about the journalistic practices that produce near-identical commonsense geographic representations in the pages of ostensibly competing newspapers. Others have similarly illustrated the dominance of the government as a source of free, 'authoritative' information for the media and the processes by which that generates media representations that are tied to governmental perspectives. Thus, it was easy for me to show the union of the material texts I was analyzing and governmental practices within overarching discourses, such as Orientalism and *Realpolitik*.

Of course, missing in this focus on the text and its context (both in this chapter thus far and in my dissertation) is the context of the audience that receives the text and ultimately provides meaning. Tuen van Dijk (1993: 257) does this by introducing social cognition as the process that bridges the personal to the collective in regards to discourse.

> Hence social cognitions mediate between micro- and macrolevels of society, between discourse and action, between the individual and the group. Although embodied in the minds of individuals, social cognitions are social because they are shared and presupposed by group members, monitor social action and interaction, and because they underlie the social and cultural organization of society as a whole.

Unfortunately, there has been very little uncovered in research on the technicalities of these processes and they remain shrouded in mystery. They nevertheless appear to be influenced by ideology, which socializes the cognitive process, thereby connecting the individual to collective textual interpretative processes. While these processes have thus far been opaque, the outcomes of these processes have finally begun to be systematically studied within human geography. Klaus Dodds (2006: 120) approaches these outcomes using reception theory to conduct research on the ways in which audiences make sense of texts (in this case, cinematic texts): 'The role of particular interpretative strategies is therefore critical because it helps to better understand what films mean to viewers and the types of emotional investment that they bring to bear[.]' There are a multiplicity of ways to approach these interpretive strategies. Dodds notes both spectatorship (associated with film theory) and audience research as two different traditions that attempt to understand interpretive processes. Methodological decisions made by the researcher will necessarily be dependent on the type of text in the study, the type of audience being incorporated into the study (i.e., die-hard versus passing fans), and the types of questions being asked. It is beyond the scope and capability of this chapter to go into all the methods associated with this type of research; needless to say, it is a critical step to take in contextualizing the textual analysis and looking beyond the text.

Beyond discourse?

Another step to be taken in conducting a thorough discourse analysis is to begin to make a bridgehead from the results of your textual analysis and your subsequent contextualization to the critically important questions of how these discourses impact the material world. As Tim Richardson and Ole Jensen (2003: 17) say, 'Put crudely, one could say that the textually oriented discourse analytical frame work can be used to study "how" something is constituted as an object of knowledge formation and planning, whereas theories of socio-spatial transformation are used to study "what" is created and under "which" material and societal conditions.' Their interest leads them to policy discourse, which almost inevitably becomes manifest in material practices by the state – thus showing the material implications of the discourse analysis described above. Indeed, as Andrew Sayer (2000: 44) puts it, 'Discourses in society can be performative as well as descriptive because they are embedded in material social practices, codes of behaviour, institutions and constructed environments.'

This performance of discourse is perhaps the most recent turn in the short history of discourse analysis. Adding to the indeterminacy at the margins of discourse (e.g., the social cognition described above) is the now contested boundary between the physical and the cognitive: 'The source of the subject's understanding of the world is a practical knowledge, which is not only linguistic. Thus, it becomes difficult to know how to make the distinction between practical and discursive knowledge,' (Mehta and Bondi, 1999: 69). Poststructuralists remind us that the creation of a singular, cognitive sense of self separate from the physical body is itself a discursive creation. Thus, even the boundary of what can be called 'discourse analysis' is called into question.

My dissertation lacked an appreciation of this role of performance in the constitution of discourses, but it is not difficult to envision what I could have written. An important,

repetitive performance that helped develop the discourses surrounding NATO and EU expansion could be the highly-ritualized State Department press conference, in which members of the press meet with a spokesman to hear the official perspective of the U.S. government on various geopolitical events, enunciated in an environment that drips with bureaucratic authority and American prestige. The State Department representative is shackled by his role and its expectations, as are the members of the press. At the other end of the mediation process, the ritualized daily performance of newspaper-reading assumes a certain subjectivity of those consuming the printed words, assuming membership in the collectivity to which the newspaper is marketed. Of course, the most important performance associated with these discourses would be the inclusion of new member states into NATO defense exercises and EU governmental conferences. These rituals show the material effects of discourse and their subsequent performance, from the deployment of nuclear weapons to the diversion of East European tax money to pay for American-produced weapons systems.

CONCLUSIONS

The chapter began by introducing the terminology and theory associated with discourse analysis, showing how complex it is, and creating some simple definitions with which the chapter could move forward. Then, an outline of how to conduct textual analysis was offered, followed by a discussion of how to broaden that linguistic approach with a more broadly contextualized (or discursive) approach.

Taking on a project utilizing discourse analysis can sometimes seem overwhelming because of the fuzziness of the concepts, the time-intensive nature of the method, and the fluidity of the results. A methodology that is rooted in a belief in the open-endedness of social processes, like this one, does not provide a satisfying 'Truth' at the end of the research, but rather a situated reading of life's phenomena. However, the same philosophical elements that make this research difficult also make conducting research like this important. Appropriately disseminated research, using discourse analysis, intervenes directly in the discourses that it studies. Thus, Spivak's expectation that this kind of scholarship can politically intervene in social injustices around the world is entirely within reach. While much academic writing tries to describe the world, discourse analysis seeks to show how alternative geographies are foreclosed while the status quo is perpetuated. As James Sidaway once reminded me, the powerful have an innate sense of the power of discourse and language because they know it is the basis for their rule. Simply writing about the role of discourse is thus to de-naturalize the power relations that prevent a more just future.

While other related perspectives have begun to emerge within the academy, discourse analysis is far from being displaced from its role as one of the cores of contemporary human geography. As Sayer (2000: 183) puts it, 'Our insistence on the material and spatial embedding of social relations in no way implies that discursive relations can be ignored, for communicating and representing are of course actions in themselves.' In other words, rather than being a paradigm to be overturned, discourse analysis is being built on, tweaked, and reworked. It is likely to remain an integral part of human geography for many years to come.

REFERENCES

Adams, P. (2004) 'The September 11 attacks as viewed from Quebec: the small-nation code in geopolitical discourse', *Political Geography* 23 (6): 765–95.

Adorno, T.W. and Horkheimer, M. (1972) *Dialectic of enlightenment*. London: Verso.

Alvesson, M. and Karreman, D. (2000) 'Varieties of discourse: on the study of organizations through discourse analysis', *Human Relations* 53 (9): 1125–49.

Barnes, T. and Duncan, J. (eds) (1992) *Writing worlds: discourse, text, and metaphor in the representation of landscape*. London: Routledge.

Baxter, J. and Eyles, J. (1997) 'Evaluating qualitative research in social geography: establishing "rigour" in interview analysis', *Transactions of the Institute of British Geographers* 22 (4): 505.

Bourdieu, P. (1983) *Ce que parler veut dire*. Paris: Fayard.

Cooper, D. (1993) 'Rhetoric, literature and philosophy', in R. Roberts and J. Good (eds) *The recovery of rhetoric*. Bristol: Classical. pp. 193–202.

Dalby, S. (1993) 'The "kiwi disease": geopolitical discourse in Aotearoa/New Zealand and the South Pacific', *Political Geography* 12 (5): 437–56.

Dalby, S. (1996) 'Reading Rio, writing the world: the New York Times and the "Earth Summit"', *Political Geography* 15(6–7): 593–613.

Dalby, S. (2003) 'Calling 911: geopolitics, security and America's new war', *Geopolitics* 8 (3): 61–86.

Davoudi, S. and P. Healy (1995) 'City challenge: sustainable process or temporary gesture?', *Environment and Planning C: Government and Policy* 13 (1): 79–95.

Derrida, J. (1984) *Signâeponge = Signsponge*. New York: Columbia University Press.

Dittmer, J. (2005) 'NATO, the EU and central Europe: differing symbolic shapes in newspaper accounts of enlargement', *Geopolitics* 10 (1): 76–98.

Dittmer, J. (2007a) 'Changing American metanarratives of Russia in NATO expansion debates, 1993–2002', *National Identities* 9 (1): 49–66.

Dittmer, J. (2007b) 'The tyranny of the serial: popular geopolitics, the nation, and comic book discourse', *Antipode* 39 (2): 247–68.

Dixon, D. and Hapke, H. (2003) 'Cultivating discourse: the social construction of agricultural legislation', *Annals of the Association of American Geographers* 93 (1): 142–64.

Dodds, K. (1996) 'The 1982 Falklands War and a critical geopolitical eye: Steve Bell and the if ... cartoons', *Political Geography* 15 (6–7): 571–92.

Dodds, K. (2006) 'Popular geopolitics and audience dispositions: James Bond and the Internet Movie Database (IMDb)', *Transactions of the Institute of British Geographers* 31 (2): 116–30.

Eisinger, P. (2000) 'The politics of bread and circuses: building the city for the visitor class', *Urban Affairs Review* 35 (3): 316–33.

Fairclough, N. (1992) *Discourse and social change.* Cambridge: Polity.

Foucault, M. (1974) *The order of things: an archaeology of the human sciences.* London: Routledge.

Foucault, M. (1977) *Discipline and punish: the birth of the prison.* London: Allen Lane.

Foucault, M. (1989) *The archeaology of knowledge.* London: Routledge.

Gee, J.P. (1999) *An introduction to discourse analysis.* London and New York: Routledge.

Gramsci, A. (1992) *Prison notebooks.* New York: Columbia University Press.

Hakli, J. (1998) 'Discourse in the production of political space: decolonizing the symbolism of provinces in Finland', *Political Geography* 17 (3): 331–63.

Hoggart, K., Lees, L. and Davies, A. (2002) *Researching human geography.* London: Arnold.

Jackson, P. (1985) 'Urban ethnography', *Progress in Human Geography* 9 (2): 159–76.

Laclau, E. (1995) 'Discourse', in R. Goodin and P. Pettit (eds) *A Companion to contemporary political philosophy.* Cambridge, MA: Blackwell. pp. 431–43.

Laclau, E. and Mouffe, C. (1985) *Hegemony and socialist strategy.* London: Verso.

Lees, L. (2004) 'Urban geography: discourse analysis and urban research', *Progress in Human Geography* 28 (1): 101–7.

Lentricchia, F. and McLaughlin, T. (eds) (1995) *Critical terms in literary study.* Chicago and London: University of Chicago Press.

McDowell, L. (1992) 'Valid games? A response to Erica Shoenberger', *The Professional Geographer* 44 (2): 212–15.

Megoran, N. (2006) 'For ethnography in political geography: experiencing and re-imagining Ferghana Valley boundary closures', *Political Geography* 25 (6): 622–40.

Mehta, A. and Bondi, L. (1999) 'Embodied discourse: on gender and fear of violence', *Gender, Place and Culture* 6 (1): 67–84.

Miller, D., Jackson, P., Thrift, N., Holbrook, B. and Rowlands, M. (1998) *Shopping, places and identity.* London: Routledge.

Myers, G., Klak, T. and Koehl, T. (1996) 'The inscription of difference: news coverage of the conflicts in Rwanda and Bosnia', *Political Geography* 15 (1): 21–46.

Norton, A. (1996) 'Experiencing nature: the reproduction of environmental discourse through safari tourism in East Africa', *Geoforum* 27 (3): 355–73.

Peet, R. (2002) 'Ideology, discourse, and the geography of hegemony: from socialist to neoliberal development in postapartheid South Africa', *Antipode* 34 (1): 54–84.

Pratt, G. (1999) 'From registered nurse to registered nanny: discursive geographics of Filipina domestic workers in Vancouver, BC', *Economic Geography* 75 (3): 215–36.

Richardson, T. and Jensen, O. (2003) 'Linking discourse and space: towards a cultural sociology of space in analysing spatial policy discourses', *Urban Studies* 40 (1): 7–22.

Said, E. (1978) *Orientalism.* Harmondsworth: Penguin.

Sayer, A. (2000) *Realism and social science.* London: Sage Publications.

Schoenberger, E. (1997) *The cultural crisis of the firm.* Oxford: Blackwell.

Schoenberger, E. (1998) 'Discourse and practice in human geography', *Progress in Human Geography* 22 (1): 1–14.

Sharp, J. (1996) 'Hegemony, popular culture and geopolitics: the Reader's Digest and the construction of danger', *Political Geography* 15 (6–7): 557–70.

Sparke, M. (1996) 'Negotiating national action: free trade, constitutional debate and the gendered geopolitics of Canada', *Political Geography* 15 (6–7): 615–39.

Spivak, G.C. (1988) 'Can the subaltern speak?', in C. Nelson and L. Greenberg (eds) *Marxism and the interpretation of culture.* Urbana: University of Illinois Press. pp. 271–313.

Sutherland, C. (2005) 'Nation-building through discourse theory', *Nations and Nationalism* 11 (2): 185–202.

van Dijk, T. (1993) 'Principles of critical discourse analysis', *Discourse & Society* 4 (2): 249–83.

Whatmore, S. and Boucher, S. (1993) 'Bargaining with nature: the discourse and practice of "environmental planning gain"', *Transactions of the Institute of British Geographers* 18 (2): 166–78.

16

GIS as Qualitative Research: Knowledge, Participatory Politics and Cartographies of Affect

Stuart C. Aitken and Mei-Po Kwan

Most of us live complex daily rounds that are more often than not experienced through varied competing auditory and visual representations. It is often difficult to sift through the genuine from the dross, the stuff we need to know from the stuff other people want us to know. Powerful media technologies are designed to sway our opinions about the ways political events unfold or to help us decide what to consume or how to play. And, as researchers, we use powerful technologies and representational tools to delve, to understand, to explain, and to sway. These actions are not devoid of emotion and artifice. There is an undeniable 'wow' factor associated with new technologies, and this is especially the case if the output of the technology stimulates or heightens acuity in one or more of our senses. Using a combination of animations, maps, audio and video we can, for example, squeeze interviewees' daily lives onto three dimensional space-time trajectories. These geo-visualizations may inspire new insights and can entrance an audience if presented well. There is an affective politics to this kind of work that is inspirational.

These affective politics have been around since before the Greek medical/theatre practitioners at Epiduras used the auditory technology of their amphitheatre to reach a host of attending patients without raising their voices. This kind of power is palpable to the extent that centuries later listeners at the amphitheatre in Epiduras still wonder at the technology that produced the architecture. The representational effects of geographic information systems (GIS) can be equally mesmerizing. In what follows, we focus on the power behind the ways these representations affect both researchers and researched. To do so, we explore issues of knowledge generation and representation through the technology of GIS from a qualitative perspective.

We make the rather outrageous opening that GIS are qualitative methods with the intent to turn some conventional wisdom on its head. To a large extend our discussion focuses on the representational technology of GIS. Although we broach the related contexts of Geographic Information Science (GIScience) and Geovisualization, we avoid some of the pithier issues of science and qualitative methods that are dealt with much better elsewhere (see Herbert, in this volume). Rather we focus on the qualitative possibilities of GIScience, and the affective components of geovisualization. As part of our arguments, we examine how places are put together through local geographies and local politics so that we may highlight the ways local knowledges and GIS are often at odds with each other.

GIS are 'massive software packages providing a range of functions for creating, acquiring, integrating, transforming, visualizing, analyzing, modeling and archiving information about the surface and near-surface of the earth' (Goodchild, 2006: 251). We want to argue that there is an important non-representational component to GIS that goes beyond the 'wow' factor and provides a key, at least in part, to understanding the software and its potential from a qualitative perspective. Given the rampant and sometimes de-humanized use of GIS in geography and planning, this is an important issue to broach and so, to get to it, we focus on four critical issues: (i) Qualitative methods and GIS, (ii) GIS as a qualitative method, (iii) Qualitative visual methods and GIS and, (iv) community-integrated or public participatory GIS (CiGIS). These issues are a foil against which we elaborate GIS through cartographies of affect. In her *Atlas of Emotion* (2002), Guiliana Bruno talks about affective forms of cartography as ways to get beyond maps and technology that are in the service of capital, militarism and empire.

It is important at this time to provide a brief sketch of the arguments that we make through the four critical issues. We begin with an overview of qualitative methods and GIS; our arguments are derived from an epistemology that favors feminist and post-structural theories. A more focused look at these theories as a basis for GIS research is elaborated later in the chapter where we turn to (non-representational) cartographies of affect. With this epistemology in mind, we argue for GIS to be considered as a qualitative method. This is followed by a discussion

of the science of visualization and qualitative visual methodologies, and examples of projects where visual and remotely sensed information fail to elaborate local geographies. We then engage a critique of planning and spatial decision-making as it is currently constituted in GIS. An important issue that relates to geo-visualization concerns the representation of places and people's knowledge and perceptions about them. Of particular concern is the hegemony of thoughtless mechanistic GIS practices in the planning process. In our concluding section, we elaborate the limits (and potential) of GIS as part of qualitative knowledge with a particular focus on ways of knowing that move from text and objects to images, movement and affect. We argue that for this move toward the cartographies of affect then there is a need for a reflexive, situated rethinking of how GIS specialists view not only spatial decision-making but also data. GIS produces data in the form of representations, but there are quirky politics to these representations. Planning and spatial decision-making is almost always a discursive, emotive practice, which, we argue, requires some consideration of non-representational perspectives. And so, at the end of the paper we point beyond mechanistic GIS representations to what Giles Deleuze (1986; 1994) calls 'modes of encounter,' and argue for the ways that GIS might promote cartographies of affect.

QUALITATIVE METHODS AND GEOGRAPHIC INFORMATION SYSTEMS

Geography is first of all knowledge gained by observation, that one orders by reflection and re-inspection the things that one is looking at ... The mode of locomotion should be slow, the slower the better, be often interrupted by leisurely halts to sit at vantage points and stop at question marks. (Sauer, 1956: 296)

... [our] subject position is constituted in spaces of betweenness ... a position that is neither inside nor outside ... By operating within these multiple contexts all the time, we may begin to learn not to displace or separate so as to see and speak, but to see, be seen, speak, listen and be heard in the multiple determined fields that we are everywhere, always in. (Katz, 1994: 72)

As several chapters in this volume point out, qualitative methods have been used widely in human geography throughout the twentieth century. The last two decades of the century, however, witnessed a vibrant phase of renewed development and use of qualitative methods in geographical research. Beginning largely as a response to the dominance of the objectivist and quantitative methodologies associated with the rise of spatial science in the late 1960s, the value of interpretive (e.g. phenomenology and hermeneutics) and qualitative methodologies was first re-asserted by humanist geographers, who were later joined by feminist, poststructuralist, postcolonialist and other critical geographers (Dwyer and Limb, 2001). This notwithstanding, the quantitative methodologies of the 1960s gained significant impetus for renewal and redevelopment over the last half century with the creation of GIS and its broad acceptance amongst spatially-based professions (e.g. urban planning, spatial data management, regional governance and development) (Goodchild, 2006). To a large degree during its embryonic years, growth in GIS was driven by technological advances to the extent that qualitative assessments and infusion of critical debates are recent considerations. In the early 1990s, critical geographers and GIS specialists came together for the first time to discuss the relations between GIS and society (cf. Pickles, 1995a; Shepherd and Poiker, 1995). Critiques at this time focused on (i) the limitations of GIS representations and (ii) the implications of those limitations for power relations (Goodchild, 2006). Since then, the conjoining of qualitative methods and GIS has arisen as an approach to creating geographical knowledge (particularly within the realm of grassroots, community based GIS) and critical GIS has become a crucial theoretical basis (and watchdog) for the technology.

The two quotes that begin this section suggest not only that qualitative methods in geography have been around for some time but that they are different today from what they were in the time of Carl Sauer. Today, qualitative methods are about using ourselves as a research tool and understanding our position as 'subjects in spaces of betweenness'. To do so, we are involved in knowledge creation and practical research, which takes us into places, into often intimate contact with the people who occupy those places, and into our part in the creation of whatever knowledge foments from that contact with people and places. This is where we believe there is an important intersection with GIS, but we are concerned that the nuanced positions of researcher and researched are often lost in mechanistic procedures. To understand this more fully requires some care over the ways qualitative methods and spatial technologies create knowledge.

Knowledge creation through qualitative and quantitative methods

As geographers, we seek to understand and interpret human experience in its sociospatial settings (Dwyer and Limb, 2001). Hilary Winchester (2005: 5–6) notes that qualitative methods strive to answer two sets of questions: the first relates to the shape of societal structures and the processes through which they are constructed, maintained and reworked; the second set probes individual experiences of places and events. One important reason for using qualitative methods is that they may help us recover the silenced voices of marginalized individuals and social groups whose feelings and thoughts have been ignored by the dominant societal discourses of powerful groups in society (Nagar, 1997; Dunn, 2000; Cope, 2003). It is a highly political process. The experiences of women, ethnic minorities, poor people and children are often omitted in official historical records and planning data and, it may be argued that the focus on GIS in planning and policy-making creates the possibility of complicity with dominant, hegemonic discourses (Aitken, 2002; Elwood, 2002). In a very real sense, those who adopt GIS as a platform for planning advocacy become tied to a particular way of knowing the world.

As an important context for monitoring and resisting mechanistic ways of knowing, qualitative methods can help place 'non-dominant' knowledges at the center of geographical research (Dwyer and Limb, 2001). Is it possible, then, for GIS as a qualitative method, to do likewise?

As outlined in detail elsewhere in this book, techniques that come under the rubric of qualitative research include ethnography, participant observation, in-depth interviews, focus groups, archival documentation and historical analysis, landscape interpretation, and visual and discourse analysis. It is beyond the scope of this chapter to go into any of these techniques with any kind of thoroughness (but see chapters by Watson and Till, McDowell *et al.*, Lorimer *et al.*, Ditmer, and Crang in this volume). Our purpose is mainly to explore the intersection of qualitative methods and GIS rather than to provide a detailed treatment of these techniques.

Qualitative researchers often talk about using multiple methods, or triangulating methods with the idea of producing a relatively comprehensive outcome that includes quantitative data. The French term *bricolage* applies well to the task of the qualitative/ quantitative researcher who gathers to herself or himself all and sundry methods to hand with the purpose of discovery, of answering questions, of taking a road less traveled. Alternatively, some researchers like to think of qualitative methods in opposition to quantitative methods (see the Introduction, as well as chapters by Cope and Aitken, in this volume), despite the admonition from contemporary feminist and post-structural thinkers that worrying within the confines of dualisms is not very productive. Qualitative methodologies are characterized by an in-depth, intensive approach rather than an extensive or numerical approach. They seek

'subjective understanding of social reality rather than statistical description or generalizable predictions' (Dwyer and Limb, 2001: 6). Whilst quantitative methods often focus on things that can be measured, qualitative methods elaborate more ephemeral, perhaps deeper and more personal meanings. Whilst the former focus on generalizing across a statistical norm, the latter are predisposed to individual perspectives, unique contexts and specific renderings. Whilst the former are concerned with mathematical and logical connections, and hypothetico-deductive reasoning, the latter sit in a well of senses, speculations and interpretation. Whilst the former seek to smooth out and normalize, the latter embrace difference and contradictions.

Stewart Fotheringham (2006: 237–8) argues that quantification in geography is primarily about 'provid[ing] useful evidence towards a better understanding of spatial processes.' Of course, this is true also of qualitative research to the extent that it is interested in probing questions that relate to a deeper understanding of the way spaces are produced and maintained. Toward this goal, Fotheringham avers, quantitative methods focus on the exploration and reduction of large spatial data sets, the examination of the role of randomness in generating observed spatial patterns of data and testing hypotheses about such patterns, and the mathematical modeling and prediction of spatial processes. Mike Goodchild (2006: 253) extends these points to GIS, noting that because 'numerical analysis of geographical data is too tedious, inaccurate and costly to perform by hand … [q]uantitative geographers were quick to recognize the power of GIS for spatial analysis.' He goes on to point out that, unlike qualitative geographers, GIS users subscribe to the notion that objectivity in knowledge creation is an important goal, and that every effort should be made to adhere to the norms of science. It is only through the acceptance of these norms, he argues, that one person's work may be understood by another and accepted in the broader community (Goodchild, 2006: 256).

Qualitative researchers, on the other hand, are often suspicious of the hegemonic status of any norm that becomes a dominant discourse. Some argue that the mechanistic practice of GIS and its concomitant cartographic displays lend themselves to acceptance of an insidious default 'black-box' that is easily manipulated by political interests (Aitken, 2002; Elwood, 2002). An argument is often made for clarity in the underlying theories and 'ways of knowing' in the practice of research (cf. Aitken and Valentine, 2006).

Theories as methods

Qualitative methods, in and of themselves, eschew mechanistic, menu-driven approaches, while at the same time embracing appropriate theoretical perspectives and using them as methodological approaches. Indeed, of late, some researchers argue that qualitative methodologies, with their penchant for deep process work, are more likely to provide explanation when compared with descriptive and multivariate statistics. Ethnographies and participant observation are about looking, immersing, contemplating and conversing and they are also, often, underwritten explicitly by process theories of narrative and culture. In-depth interviews and focus groups are about asking questions and facilitating discussion and they may be underwritten by explanatory theories of discourse. Archival research is often about pouring over old documents, numbers, texts and photographs but it is also about establishing links with remembered and actual places in the real-world (see Lorimer, in this volume). Visual methods are about viewing and thinking about what you are seeing and are often informed by structured and semi-structured representational theories. Landscape interpretation involves hanging out and, to whatever degree possible, immersing yourself in a people and a place with a concomitant ability to communicate what that feels like. Without doubt there are skills required to initiate and guide focus group discussions and, like hanging out, this kind of research requires a consideration of situatedness and positionality as discussed in feminist theory (see below). Talking to people is no simple matter and when you are a researcher trying to probe an interviewee's thoughts on topics that are sometimes innocuous and sometimes emotionally charged. Feelings are encountered that run the gamut from boredom to anger, which takes theorizing situatedness to understandings that are, perhaps, pulling from the affective and non-representational theories of post-structuralism.

While a course in quantification methods focuses on scientific norms while teaching students to cluster, factor, kriege, regress, bound (in fuzzy or clear-cut ways), combine and condense data or extract eigenvalues, components and Moran coefficients in multivariate ways, qualitative methods courses focus on interpretation and explanation through the lenses of social theory. When compared to the mechanistic and seemingly atheoretical methodological devices of GIS – multi-spectral scanners, digital overlays and drapings – qualitative methodologies may appear structurally unsophisticated. Our argument here is that qualitative sophistication and rigor is not derived solely from methodological structure (cf. Baxter and Eyles, 1997) but, rather, from theoretical engagement. For example, while researchers using quantification go to great lengths to secure a statistically valid and representative sample to generalize from, those who favor qualitative methods may also seek saturation, a point after which gathering more information simply will not add new information or lead to new theoretical insights. The decision to stop belongs to the researchers. Similarly, when computer aided qualitative data analysis (see MacKain in this volume) is used to manage and code textual and visual data, there is no structured output or statistical summary as such. Rather, it is incumbent upon the researcher to stick themselves in the middle of the qualitative information and say something about it. This may seem severely unsophisticated to some, but it always takes a coherent strategy (and luck and happenstance) to get yourself firmly ensconced (stuck if you will) in information that engages a set of research questions and it takes a coherent engagement with (and sometimes purposeful disengagement from) theory to make sense of that information.

So what is the academic worth of combining qualitative methods with GIS? Do the two perspectives not collide more than they cohere? Where is the finesse? Where is the reasoned elegance? Without denigrating the importance of the latter, we are suggesting that the *savoir faire* of qualitative methods lies in the theories that drive them, and not only in their practice or analysis. As noted above, there is a myriad of different theoretical approaches to the analysis of qualitative information (it is probably not appropriate to call it data), and we argue that it is vital to theoretically contextualize the ways that GIS and qualitative methods are integrated. What we offer below is not some elegant fit, but rather some possible pointers to an uneasy epistemological integration. This edgy coalescence begins to find form for us in feminist and post-structural ways of knowing.

Feminist and post-structural theories as methods

Qualitative methodologies are widely used in feminist geographies since they are congenial to feminist epistemologies and politics. Many qualitative researchers reject the view that there is a pre-existing world that can be known or measured. They instead consider the social world as changing and dynamic, 'always being constructed through the intersection of cultural, economic, social and political processes' (Dwyer and Limb, 2001: 6). This corresponds closely to the feminist perspective that any claim to transcendent objectivity or truth is untenable - since all knowledge must be acquired through knowers situated in particular subject positions and social contexts (Haraway, 1991; Harding, 1991). Feminist geographers recognize the

partiality and situatedness of all knowledge, and the importance of critical reflections on our subject position relative to research participants, the research process, and the knowledge produced (reflexivity) (England, 1994; Gibson-Graham, 1994; Gilbert, 1994; Rose, 1997; Nast, 1998). They emphasize the need to challenge the unequal power relations between researchers and research participants through critical and reflexive research practices.

Feminist geographers also hold that the material and discursive construction of gendered identities is crucial for understanding difference in the lived experiences of individuals. Research in feminist geographies often draws upon cultural, post-structural, post-colonial and psychoanalytic theories, and these perspectives place considerable emphasis on the highly complex and dynamic nature of gendered experiences. Since qualitative methodologies seek to understand and interpret the richness and complexities of people's lived experiences, they are particularly suitable for exploring issues pertinent to the construction of gendered identities and subjectivities across multiple axes of difference (e.g. race, ethnicity, age, sexuality, religion and nationality) (Rose, 1993; McDowell, 1999). Further, as feminist geographers emphasize methodological approaches that are non-exploitative, qualitative methodologies such as in-depth interviews are often used in feminist geographic research because of the empathetic research encounter that these approaches tend to engender (Dwyer and Limb, 2001). Post-structural perspectives also speak to the embeddedness of our lives, our embodied experiences and the emotions that go with them. Methodologically, it is difficult to interpret, let alone write about or represent visceral experiences, such as the reactions individuals might have to GIS-informed planning decisions. We'll have more to say about this at the end of the essay.

Susan Smith (2000) groups qualitative methods into three broad types: in-depth interviews with groups and individuals; direct engagement with subjects through participant observation and related ethnographic techniques; and the interpretation of a variety of 'texts' including landscapes, archival materials (e.g. diaries), maps and visual images. Hilary Winchester (2006) identifies three main types of qualitative research: the oral (primarily interview-based), the textual (creative, documentary and landscape) and the observational; where documentary sources may include maps, newspapers and planning documents. Although Smith (2000) and Winchester (2005) include maps and visual images as materials for qualitative research and GIS methods are constantly used to produce visual images, GIS is seldom discussed in the rubric of qualitative methodologies in geographical literature until recent years (Kwan and Knigge, 2006; Pavlovskaya, 2006). Rather, researchers in GIS are more likely to talk about how qualitative methods may be used along with GIS (Craig et al., 2002).

We want to turn this thinking on its head by considering how GIS is a qualitative method with specific emphasis on the ways it is embedded in feminist and post-structural ways of knowing. We do so because we believe that this is an important move away from GIS in the service of capital, militarism and empire. We do so also in part because we are concerned about the propensity for students and beginning researchers to 'tag on' qualitative methods in order to 'fill out' a GIS project, perhaps by interviewing a few so-called end-users. What follows is a discussion of the ways that GIS may be considered a qualitative method, with special reference to visualization and community-integrated GIS. Throughout the discussion we try to hold central the feminist and post-structural imperative of understanding the situated and visceral experiences that contextualize all research practices, including those that use GIS.

GIS AS A QUALITATIVE METHOD

When GIS is discussed in the context of computer assisted qualitative data analysis, it is often used to reveal the weakness of current computer assisted qualitative data analysis software relative to GIS software. More specifically, discussion focuses on their limited capabilities for linking qualitative materials with spatial data (e.g. Crang et al., 1997; Peace, 2000). In this context, Mike Crang and his colleagues (1997) make the important point that computer assisted qualitative data analysis may not be as suitable for geographic research as many have assumed, but they do not consider the possibility of extending current GIS as a tool for handling and analyzing qualitative information in geographic research or, rather, to follow our outrageous proposition, they do not consider the ways GIS may be embraced within qualitative discourses. In what follows we defend this proposition by looking at the relations between qualitative information and what comprises a GIS and GIS within the framework of qualitative analysis before returning to a consideration of knowledge creation but this time with a specific focus on representation.

Qualitative information and GIS

Although GIS can be used as a tool for collecting qualitative information from research participants, using GIS as a data collection tool is not a very common practice in qualitative research to date. Instead, GIS is more often used for the storage and analysis of qualitative (and quantitative) information, and a data conversion process is necessary in order to render the original data suitable for use in GIS. Recent development of digital technologies has greatly expanded the kind of qualitative information GIS can handle. Indeed, any type of information that can be 'digitized' and stored in a computer can be linked to or accessed by a GIS. For instance, with the recent availability of a wide variety of low-cost digital technologies (e.g. scanners, digital cameras and video recorders), qualitative materials such as digital photos, video and voice clips can be converted to digital form and incorporated into GIS. Similarly, handwriting, hand-drawn maps and other sketches collected through semi-structured interviews and ethnographic methods can also be incorporated in a GIS. This not only means that today's GIS allows for a much wider array of representational possibilities than before, it also means that the use of GIS does not necessarily preclude the use of qualitative materials collected from research participants or locales.

The most common form of linking qualitative information with a GIS is through establishing 'hyperlinks' for accessing various qualitative 'objects' in a manner similar to using object linking and embedding technology. These hyperlinks are basically file-location pointers that enable the user to access linked objects through particular actions (e.g. clicking on a geographical feature with a hyperlink). Using the built-in hyperlink features of a GIS or specially developed hyperlink capabilities, the user can access various types of qualitative information associated with particular geographical features in a GIS (e.g. Lancaster and Bodenhamer, 2002). In addition, various actions can be initiated through hyperlinks. For instance, a voice or video clip can be launched using the media program with which media files are currently associated, or a web page can be launched in the default web browser through a universal resources locator (URL). Hyperlinks have been used in ethnographic research to incorporate qualitative data into geographic databases. For example, in a multi-site study of low-income and welfare recipient families and their children, family ethnographic field notes are linked with neighborhood field notes and other contextual data in a GIS (Matthews *et al.*, 2005). The integration of GIS and ethnography enabled researchers of the project to visualize and better understand the complexity of the lives of low-income families and the strategies they adopt in negotiating the welfare system.

Qualitative analysis and GIS

To a certain extent, GIS may be considered a special kind of computer aided qualitative data analysis software. This kind of software has specific capabilities for analyzing textual, visual and aural materials. GISystems, for example, correspond quite well to qualitative analysis software such as NVivo's capabilities for coding qualitative data, identifying relationships between concepts, and building models based upon grounded theory (Strauss and Corbin, 1998). Like ArcView GIS, NVivo's central element is the 'project', which holds and organizes all the relevant qualitative data items such as interview transcripts, memos and notes for a particular study (Bazeley and Richards, 2000; Gibbs, 2002). NVivo uses three systems for managing qualitative data: documents, nodes and attributes. Documents in NVivo are plain or rich text files, which can include embedded links to pictures, video, audio, spreadsheet, database, web pages or other data items stored in the computer but outside the program. Any part of a document can be coded at any number of nodes, which are containers of categories and coding. Nodes can represent any categories, including concepts, people, abstract ideas, places and anything else that is important to the project. They are stored as free nodes or are organized hierarchically in trees or linked networks. Both documents and nodes have attributes whose values represent any of their properties and can be used in searches. Users of NVivo can combine or bring these three systems together in a project by: (a) linking - documents can be linked to other documents or nodes in the project, and nodes can be linked to other nodes or documents; (b) coding - creating categories and placing at them references to data; (c) shaping - building 'trees' to link nodes or using 'sets' to group nodes and documents; (d) searching; and (e) modeling - building visual models by drawing, diagramming or representing ideas and relationships visually.

A comparison of GIS software such as ArcView GIS or ArcGIS with computer assisted qualitative data analysis software such as NVivo or ATLASi reveals many similarities between them (although the latter focuses mainly on the coding and analysis of textual data). Both types of program adopt a highly visual approach, provide links for accessing various types of qualitative data outside the program (photos and voice clips), support a suite of query and model building tools, and emphasize exploratory data analysis. In this light, many common procedures performed with GIS are quite similar to those found in computer assisted qualitative data analysis software. In addition, when different types of data (both qualitative and quantitative) are transformed into visual representations (e.g. 3D scenes), GIS allows a more interpretive mode of analysis than what is possible in conventional spatial analysis (Harris, 2002; Kwan, 2002a). This suggests that GIS can be used as a critical visual method for the creation, analysis or interpretations of GIS-generated visual images.

For example, 3D GIS is used by one of us to trace and visualize women's life paths in space-time and to examine the impact of space-time constraints on their spatial mobility and job location (Kwan, 1999). In another study using similar GIS-based 3D visualization methods, the racialized geographies of Portland, Oregon – which show the spatially restricted life spaces of African-Americans throughout the day – was revealed (Kwan, 2000). When visual representations of individual daily space-time paths are presented together with an interpretative textual narrative that incorporates other information collected from personal interviews, rich and scale-sensitive spatial stories about what a person goes through in a particular day can be told (Aitken, 1999, 2002). For example, an NVivo figure in Stuart Aitken and colleagues's 2006 research findings elaborates more fully the complexity of focus group transcriptions as they relate to the complexity of the daily routines of child workers in Tijuana. These examples suggest that GIS and computer assisted qualitative analysis can be used to create and interpret visual images in a manner drastically different from that of conventional GIS-based quantitative spatial analysis. With this interpretive and

visual mode of analysis, GIS can be used in qualitative research in which visual images (albeit generated and composed with digital technology), words and numbers are used together to compose contextualized visual narratives elaborated through geographical discourse (Kwan, 2002a).

Knowledge creation/representation and GIS

Despite GIS's capabilities in handling and analyzing qualitative data, how to represent human knowledge, meanings and emotions in a GIS still remains a major challenge for qualitative researchers who want to avoid the seduction and artifice of the 'wow' factor. Another problem arises largely from the vagueness, imprecision and nuances in people's representations and expressions, which are used by research participants to convey their experiences, ideas and feelings during their interaction with the qualitative researcher. Current GIS has very limited capabilities for handling qualitative data like these although there is some recent research that seeks to address this limitation (e.g. Gahegan, 1995; Shariff et al., 1998). This research attempts to develop a geospatial semantics for handling geographical notions expressed in natural language (e.g. near, far, next to, east side of the city) through set-theoretical frameworks and fuzzy logic. But thus far these functions for handling qualitative geographical information are not yet readily available in current GIS; researchers who use qualitative methods need to find other ways to handle this kind of qualitative data in their research.

One possible solution is to use methods that facilitate and encourage direct input from research subjects. For example, in a study of CiGIS for land reform in Mpumalanga Province in South Africa, Trevor Harris and Dan Weiner (2002) incorporate views and local knowledge of different groups of subjects into a multi-media GIS using sketch maps compiled through participatory mental mapping workshops. They admit that incorporating people's local knowledge in a GIS is very difficult because it is usually imprecise spatially. They suggest that the collection of visual, graphical, aural, and narrative forms of qualitative information and its integration within a GIS calls for the use of spatial multimedia (Shiffer, 2002).

SCALING THE VISUAL

Some of the first studies of geography and film criticized the discipline's unwillingness to look beyond the material world to visual culture and the ways it influences our lives (Aitken and Zonn, 1994; Benton, 1995). Recently, visual methods have received considerable attention in several disciplines (e.g. visual sociology and visual anthropology: Banks, 2001; Pink, 2001; van Leeuwen, 2001), but as yet geographical research and work in this area is in its infancy (Rose, 2001; Kwan, 2002b; Aitken and Craine, 2005, 2006; Knigge and Cope, 2006). Discussions of visual methods in geography have mainly focused on the interpretation of visual images (Benton, 1995; Robins, 1996). These discussions do not address critical issues pertinent to the creation of visual images with geospatial technologies such as GIS and remote sensing. One exception is a paper by Aitken (1999), which focuses on the scale dependencies of GIS images and then uses narrative theory as a way of understanding the impact of these geovisualizations. In this study, a GIS produced for Catalina Island, off the coast of California, is critiqued for the ways that it produces a story of preservation and construction of a so-called pristine natural environment while at the same time hiding larger neoliberal issues of privatization and limited access. Other geographers working with visual methods such as Kevin Robins (1996), Gillian Rose (1996, 2001) and Rob Bartram (2003) do not consider visual images produced by geospatial technologies. Although critical geographers

have examined cartographic and GIS images (Pickles, 1995b; Roberts and Schein, 1995), they tend to ignore the possibility for geographers to appropriate geospatial technologies as media of critical visual methods.

This section moves our discussion of how GIS can be a qualitative method in general by focusing specifically on its potential as a critical visual method. It focuses more on using GIS for creating and interpreting visual images and understanding people's lived experiences (e.g. local knowledge, feelings and emotions), rather than on using GIS as a tool for performing quantitative spatial analysis (e.g. surface modeling or geostatistics). These issues are explored in terms GIS's capabilities for illuminating people's experiences of places and landscapes across geographical scales.

Aitken and James Craine (2006) argue that the very heart of geography and GIS is constituted in large part by the practice of looking and is, in effect, the stuff of images. If this is so, then geovisualization is highlighted as an important disciplinary and practical endeavor. The last two decades witnessed increasing recognition of the power of articulate, moving images to intervene in the ongoing transformations of everyday geography and yet there remains a reticence within the geovisualization community to fully embrace the emotive non-representational power of images. Aitken and Craine (2006) argue for a recognition in GIS circles of the intensification of emotional life that is possible through moving spatial images. Their primary assumption is that while data visualized through GIS can be provocative, there is often a tendency for the program to overwhelm the content. Even the best GIS-visualized data is more interesting to *think* about than to *experience*, more interesting to *create* than to *comprehend*.

A fruitful direction for addressing the difficulty in representing human knowledge, meanings and emotions in a GIS is through a detailed comparison of the knowledge provided by GIS and visually-based remote sensing data with the personal knowledge and perceptions of research subjects collected through qualitative methods (e.g. in-depth interviews or oral histories). As several recent studies show (e.g. Jiang, 2003), there are significant discrepancies between the 'objective' knowledge represented by visual images generated with GIS or remote sensing technologies and people's partial and situated knowledge. These studies used mixed methods to show that a careful comparison of these two types of knowledge may yield significant insights into people's partial knowledge and perceptions, as well as the underlying social, cultural and political processes. Local knowledge stands not so much as a means to 'ground truth' data in a GIS but rather to empower emotively knowledge that is distanced from those who are part of it because it is derived from satellite imagery or census surveys. Three such studies are discussed below to illustrate this important direction for addressing the limited capabilities of current GIS in representing human knowledge.

In her study on community forestry in Nepal, Andrea Nightingale (2003) sought to interrogate nature–society relations by examining how cultural understandings of forestry and the social-political contestations embedded within forest use impact the implementation of a resource-based development program. Her study challenges dominant representations of forest change (i.e., aerial photo and other remote sensing data) through demonstrating how they provide only a partial story of forest change in the study area. She accomplished this through an analysis of the discrepancies between the story told by aerial photos and the stories told by local villagers (ecological oral histories). The oral histories reveal that the forest was over-harvested after the village lost control in 1976 as the district forest office (DFO) took over management of the forest, but conditions have improved in recent times. This suggests a pattern of decline under the DFO and improvement after the establishment of the community forestry in 1991. On the other hand, the aerial photos show that the areas

with the most improvement are those closest to the villages but that overall forest cover has not changed much. These discrepancies between local knowledge of the villagers and the photos indicate that the villagers know the more accessible areas of the forest better. These areas are of great value and importance to them and the improvement they see in these areas represents a dramatic change to them. Further, the dramatic improvements the villagers talk about actually referred to small areas of significant improvement in key places, while the images captured by the aerial photos were devoid of local meaning. Her study highlights the partiality and limitations of GIS or remote sensing data as representations of local knowledge. It also demonstrates that the use of qualitative methods and GIS data can yield rich insights by analyzing the discrepancies between the stories told by different sources of materials, including oral histories, participant observation, in-depth interviews, aerial photos and quantitative vegetation inventory.

Similarly, Paul Robbins (2001, 2006) studied the discrepancies between remotely sensed images and local knowledge in what he calls the colonial ambiguity of research with a focus on how much forest change there is in southern central Rajasthan in India. He describes aspects (demarcation, instutionalization, etc.) of the energy and momentum from the colonial period to the present, which resulted in dramatic landscape change. To answer the question of how much forest change, his discussions with foresters and work in colonial archives were supplemented with analysis of satellite imagery and extensive interviews with local people living in and around conservation areas. These two modes of inquiry produced a curiously contradictory picture of forest cover change, which sheds light onto the post-colonial condition of regional forests. Satellite imagery was unambiguous; forest canopy cover in the 900 km^2 region facing the Kumbhalgarh reserve had increased dramatically between 1986 and 1999, on the order of 50 percent in just a few years. He notes, however, that a walking ground survey of these emergent forests reveals complications. The trees in this emergent forest represent a relatively narrow range of species in plantation, including trees from the Americas and the Near East. Because they grow quickly and form a thick canopy, they often crowd out other important local species. Robbins (2006: 317) goes on to point out that the problems experienced by people living in 'the material shadow of someone else's forest imaginary are manifold.' For example, new thorn scrub discourages the growth of grassy ground cover for grazing, the leaves of the new trees are poor fodder, the new trees charcoal reasonably well but make poor materials for local construction. While the new forest cover is not exactly a nuisance, it by no means represents the return of 'forests' in any meaningful way for most locals (Robbins, 2001): not so for foresters or for state level statistical reporting, which defines as forests all lands under the control of the Forest Department, who continue to insist that this land cover is successful forestry (Robbins, 2006).

Hong Jiang's (2003) study of pastoralists' knowledge of the pastureland in Uxin Ju (Inner Mongolia, China) combines remote sensing analysis with local ecological knowledge. Her research aims at understanding the meanings and perceptions of Mongolian pastoralists about land use and landscape change through an analysis of the differences between the stories told by remote sensing data and local people's ecological knowledge. Through methods including ecological oral histories and ethnographic interviews, Jiang found that research participants in general agreed that natural shrub has significantly decreased and that the lowland grass has become degraded. Most of them agreed that enclosed pastureland around their houses has significantly improved, but the contracted sand dunes located away from their homes have not seen much improvement. Her analysis of remote sensing data, however, reveals the limitations of local ecological knowledge at the landscape scale. For instance, spatial diversity has decreased and over time the

landscape has become more homogeneous, but this increase in homogeneity has eluded local people's perceptions of the landscape. Further, the rich store of groundwater in the study area has supported the increase of tree and shrub planting and irrigated cropping since the early 1980s, but such increase has also caused the lowering of the shallow groundwater table. She suggests that the concurrent trends of landscape improvement and degradation are closely related through the dynamics of groundwater – that is, landscape improvement in certain locations has exacerbated or caused landscape degradation in other locations.

Jiang's study shows how stories told by remote sensing images may lead to significant insights into landscape change that are not revealed through ethnographic methods. Results highlighted the partiality of human knowledge and experiences, which need to be triangulated or complemented by other accounts (e.g. those from remote sensing data) in order to provide insights into human life. The study demonstrates that each account is only a partial interpretation of the landscape, and large-scale geographical processes and meanings of landscape change are often hidden and can only be revealed through comparing multiple stories told by different data sources.

These three studies suggest that there are multiple ways to represent landscapes, and no one perspective (e.g. human experience or remotely sensed data) creates infallible knowledge. Some feminists argue that remotely sensed images enable experts to take on positions as disembodied master subjects, what Dona Haraway (1991) calls the 'god-trick.' This trick is embellished with technical and instrumental discourses that do not necessarily serve local needs. This is certainly Robbins (2006) point, and yet Jiang's (2003) study suggests that this is not always the case. Nonetheless, Nightingale (2003) and Robbins' (2006) point out that the scale of remotely sensed data may hide the nuances of local knowledge. Moreover, local knowledge engages an emotional realism that pushes a particular politics of place and scale. Robbins's (2006) post-colonial project points to this politics of scale that pit locals against state officials, and begs the question of whose knowledge is considered appropriate for making planning and policy decisions. The question that we finish with focuses on how well local and remote knowledges can co-create appropriate ways of being and knowing. It takes our preceding discussion of methods and knowledge into the planning and decision-making realm and introduces post-structural concerns over what is representable and what is not.

PLANNING, POWER AND CARTOGRAPHIES OF AFFECT

In an attempt to disrupt the mechanistic logic of GIS modeling and say something about how it might aid planning and spatial decision-making, one of us argued with Patsy Healey (1992) and John Forester (1989) that because day-to-day planning is inherently qualitative it requires appropriate technologies (Aitken and Michel, 1995; Aitken, 2002). At the level of day-to-day decision making, planning depends on the way people communicate with each other, on their abilities to form consensus and compromise, rather than on their rationality and their abilities to analyze quantitative data. In the previous section, we argued that GIS is also inherently qualitative. How then may it aid emancipatory forms of planning?

Community participation and GIS

In their conclusions to a volume that collects together a number of essays on community participation and GIS, William Craig and colleagues (2002: 368) aver that as a platform for integrating qualitative and quantitative information, CiGIS highlights '*place* … in ways that conventional GIS systems do not.' Their italicization of the word "place" suggests perhaps the concept's importance, and perhaps also its elusive nature. Reading

the term within the context of the previous section, we understand it to relay the importance of locale, of place-specific political struggles. Protracted discussions of the ways place is constituted have a long history in geography and as the notions of space, spatiality and place are tortuously elaborated throughout the humanities and the social sciences, it is now perhaps one of the most ill-defined concepts in contemporary academic discourse. We do not attempt to engage elusive notions of place here; such a project is beyond our scope and, we would argue, somewhat futile from a political standpoint. Rather, we accept the importance of place-based political struggles and instead focus on their elaboration through GIS. Ultimately, with this section, our focus is on the legitimacy of place-based political struggles that generate qualitative data for spatial decision-making and GIS practitioners. Questions raised by this practice foment around epistemological issues although the ontological issues discussed previously also apply here. What kind of knowledge is legitimate for spatial decision-making? What kinds of visual and archival data are acceptable? What kinds of knowledge are lost to the Boolean logic that is the foundation of all GIS? What other ways of knowing are missing and yet important?

Of interest here is that Craig and his colleagues (2002) believe that CiGIS offers a solution to the historical schism between qualitative and quantitative researchers and because of this it contributes to more inclusive spatial decision making. We believe that this issue turns on how things are represented. For example, from the left and the right, concepts such as community integration and place are ill-defined but are almost never used unfavorably. And yet CiGIS, like all GIS systems, requires that its knowledge base, its objects, be defined. The place from which the public participates in a GIS and in decision-making systems must be known precisely. It is a particular kind of representation, but to understand the politics we need to get beyond the representation.

Knowledge creation and planning

In the previous section we suggested the importance of creating and visualizing multiple knowledge bases at multiple scales. From a feminist perspective, Nancy Fraser (1989, 1997) contends that we need to focus on the power differentials between these multiple knowledge bases. Fraser refers to multiple public spheres, or counterpublics – such as women's groups, gay/lesbian caucuses, immigrant activists, local farmers in India, students and so forth – that become political to contest the exclusionary norms of a singular hegemonic knowledge base. She argues that planning's knowledge base is not only problematically singular, it also presupposes the desirability of separation between civil society and the apparatus of the state. This divide between local practice (consent, dissent, argument and feeling) and state ideology (knowledge bases and guiding beliefs) is extremely problematic from a feminist and post-structural perspective. Fraser argues that this distinction promotes weak publics where action consists exclusively of opinion formation through knowledge that does not influence decision-making, which is left to the state. We want to argue in a moment that it does much more than silence certain points of view, because it also silences the drama and emotions that accompany opinion formation and by so doing reproduces a mechanistic form of justice/ideology. Strong publics, argues Fraser, encompass both opinion formation and decision-making. They are hegemonic and authoritative because they are able to set the terms of debate for weaker publics and, more often than not in GIS decision-making, that debate is supported by the reasoning and logic of an argument derived from representations of spatial data and less so from emotional arguments and nonrepresentable data (cf. Dewsbury in this volume).

The question of what is representable (numerics, visuals, texts) and what is not representable (meanings, feelings) bears heavily on a discussion of how GIS and qualitative methods collide. Drawing on our previous discussion of the ways GIS can be constituted as a qualitative method, we argue that this collision may elaborate a creative tension rather than a schism.

MOBILE KNOWLEDGES AND CARTOGRAPHIES OF AFFECT

Qualitative methods influenced by feminist and post-structural perspectives are now looking beyond what is representable to knowledge based on corporeality and emotions. This shift into bodies and affect was facilitated by concern over emotional space as an intensely political issue. Kay Anderson and Susan Smith (2001: 7) claim that the neglect of emotions in social science research suppresses 'a key set of relations through which lives are lived and societies made.' Emotions are highly political and sexual, and they are rarely enframed and emblazoned by academics as an important component of public action and responsibility. To paraphrase Anderson and Smith (2001), there are times and places where lives are explicitly lived through pain, love, shame, passion, anger and so forth to the extent that it is hard to discount the ways emotional relations dictate social practices. When we go to planning meetings or when we participate in a decision-making situation that is supported by GIS, we invariably witness underlying feelings and tensions that go beyond communicative reasoning and action. Fraser has little to say about the thrown-chairs, the put-downs, the red-faces and the hugs; about the anger, the frustrations, the sadness, the joys; and yet these emotions figure hugely in the ways decisions are made.

With his criticism of representational theories, his focus on affect, his relevance to theories of the body, and his writing on the centrality of maps and spatial metaphors, Giles Deleuze's work is now fairly well known to geographers (Thrift, 1996; Doel, 2000; Kingbury, 2003; McCormack, 2003; Harker, 2004; Lulka, 2004). Recent writing on embodied, emotional geographies and their relations to empowering the celebration of difference and enabling social transformations open the door for a reappraisal of the uses of representational and visual theories that underlie GIS practices. The core criticism of representations is their lack of connections to the material world and for Deleuze (1986, 1994; Deleuze and Guattari 1987, 1993), in particular, it is their uselessness for understanding embodied affects. Derek McCormack (2003: 493–6) points out that Deleuze reworks Spinoza's cartography of affect in ways that are crucial for attending to the unrepresentable, and especially for attending to the body and emotion in geographical research.

Importantly, Deleuze's treatment does not supplant or denigrate thinking or communicative reasoning. Rather, it extends the field in which thinking and speaking emerges by making more of those affective capacities and bodily reactions that are less representational. Christopher Harker (2004) argues that with Deleuze's insight, a new practical-theoretical grammar is produced; one which recognizes the roles that embodiment and emotions play in our lives, and which does so without colonizing or claiming to fully represent those roles. GIS theorists who embrace representational ways of knowing – and particularly those who embraced the 'GIS and Society' debate's (Pickles, 1995a, b; Shepherd and Poiker, 1995) penchant for lauding the power of the visual – often avoid the visceral, the embodied, the unimaginable, the unwritable.

In an important sense, Deleuze's theorizing is not about understanding identity but about understanding difference. As such, it ties closely with Fraser's project to raise the efficacy of weak publics. Deleuze's project recognizes more fully the need for a flat ontology that moves beyond nested hierarchical scales of power. As such, it embraces some of the important aspects of feminism and post-structuralism that we discussed earlier. Deleuzian theory suggests relations with the material world that challenges static representations of reality and identity, which

effectively reinstate vertical hierarchies rather than generating ideas about as yet unrealized horizontal spatial relations of autonomy. To augment differentiated capacities, static representations of people must be discarded in favor of approaches that foreground the embodied, visceral nature of existence, and encourage fluid affective relations (Smith 1998). Yet, as David Lulka (2004) suggests, even this specific form of revisualization serves merely as an improvisation in redefining difference. In actuality, a further push towards a non-representational theory is ultimately needed to dissolve hierarchies that currently separate. Approaching people and their places from different angles of encounter rather than modes of representation begins to open new options. The examples articulated earlier suggest modes of encounter rather than modes of representation. Robbins's modes of encounter in India, for example, included archival research, talking to locals, walking around, and studying satellite imagery. All three studies show that 'objective' knowledge of places and landscapes produced by GIS and remote sensing data often does not reflect people's knowledge and perceptions of them. Importantly, they demonstrate that no one mode of encounter has legitimate claims to truth. Focusing on dynamic and multiple modes of encounter, we argue, is an important re-theorization of qualitative methodologists' problematic commitment to triangulation as a way to converge on something that looks like truth. GIS as a qualitative method comprises its own inherent ground-truth.

REFERENCES

Aitken, S.C. (1999) 'Scaling the light fantastic: geographies of scale and the web', *Journal of Geography* 98 (3): 118–27.

Aitken, S.C. (2002) 'Public participation, technological discourses and the scale of GIS', in W.J. Craig, T.M. Harris and D. Weiner (eds) *Community participation and geographic information systems*. London: Taylor & Francis. pp. 357–66.

Aitken, S.C. and Craine, J. (2005) 'Visual methodologies: what you see is not always what you get', in R. Flowerdew and D. Martin (eds) *Methods in human geography*, 2nd edn. Harlow: Longman. pp. 250–69.

Aitken, S.C. and Craine, J. (February 7, 2006) 'Guest editorial: affective geovisualizations', *Directions Magazine: The Worldwide Source for Geospatial Technology, http://www.directionsmag.com/article. php?article_id=2097&trv=1.*

Aitken, S., Lopez Estrada, S., Jennings, J. and Aguirre, L. (2006) 'Reproducing life and labor: global processes and working children in Tijuana', *Childhood* 13 (3): 365–7.

Aitken, S.C. and Michel, S. (1995) 'Who contrives the "real" in GIS?: geographic information, planning and critical theory', *Cartography and Geographic Information Systems* 22 (1): 17–29.

Aitken, S.C. and Valentine, G. (2006) 'Ways of knowing and ways of doing geographic research', in S. Aitken and G. Valentine (eds) *Approaches to human geography: philosophies, people and practices.* London: Sage. pp. 1–12.

Aitken, S.C. and Zonn, L. E. (eds) (1994) *Place, power, situation and spectacle.* Lanham, MD: Rowman and Littlefield.

Anderson, K. and Smith, S. (2001) 'Emotional geographies', *Transactions of the Institute of British Geographers* 26 (1): 63–88.

Banks, M. (2001) *Visual methods in social research.* London: Sage.

Bartram, R. (2003) 'Geography and the interpretation of visual imagery', in N. Clifford and G. Valentine (eds) *Key methods in geography.* London: Sage. pp. 149–59.

Baxter, J. and Eyles, J. (1997) 'Evaluating qualitative research in social geography: establishing "rigour" in interview analysis', *Transactions of the Institute of British Geographers* 22 (4): 505–25.

Bazeley, P. and Richards, L. (2000) *The NVivo qualitative project book.* London: Sage.

Benton, L. (1995) 'Will the reel/real Los Angeles please stand up', *Urban Geography* 16 (2): 144–64.

Bruno, G. (2002) *Atlas of emotion: journeys in art, architecture and film.* London and New York: Verso.

Cope, M. (2002) 'Feminist epistemology in geography', in P. Moss (ed.) *Feminist geography in practice: research and methods.* Oxford: Blackwell. pp. 43–55.

Cope, M. (2003) 'Coding transcripts and diaries', in N. Clifford and G. Valentine (eds) *Key methods in geography.* London: Sage. pp. 446–59.

Craig, W., Harris, T. M. and Weiner, D. (2002) *Community participation and geographic information systems.* London and New York: Taylor & Francis.

Crang. M. (1997) 'Analyzing qualitative materials', in R. Flowerdew and D. Martin (eds) *Methods in human geography.* Harlow: Longman. pp. 183–96.

Crang, M., Hinchliffe, S., Hudson, A. and Reimer, S. (1997) 'Software for qualitative research: 1 prospectus and overview', *Environment and Planning A* 29 (5): 771–87.

Deleuze, G. (1986) *Cinema 1: the movement-image.* Tr. H. Tomlinson and B. Habberjam. London: The Athlone Press.

Deleuze, G. (1994) *Difference and repetition.* New York: Columbia University Press.

Deleuze, G. and Guattari, F. (1987) *Anti-Oedipus: capitalism and Schizophrenia.* Minneapolios: University of Minnesota Press.

Deleuze, G. and Guattari, F. (1993) *A thousand plateaus: capitalism and Schizophrenia.* London: Athlone Press.

Doel, M. (2000) 'Un-glunking geography: spatial science after Dr. Seuss and Gilles Deleuze', in M. Crang and N. Thrift (eds) *Thinking space.* London and New York: Routledge. pp. 117–35.

Dunn, K. (2000) 'Interviewing', in I. Hay (ed.) *Qualitative research methods in human geography.* South Melbourne, Australia: Oxford University Press. pp. 50–82.

Dwyer, C. and Limb, M. (2001) 'Introduction: doing qualitative research in geography', in M. Limb and C. Dwyer (eds) *Qualitative methodologies for geographers: issues and debates.* London: Arnold. pp. 1–20.

Elwood, S. (2002) 'GIS and collaborative urban governance: understanding their implications for community action and power', *Urban Geography* 22 (8): 737–59.

England, K.L. (1994) 'Getting personal: reflexivity, positionality, and feminist research', *The Professional Geographer* 46 (1): 80–9.

Forester, J. (1989) *Planning in the face of power.* Berkeley: University of California Press.

Fotheringham, S. (2006) 'Quantification, evidence and positivism', in S. Aitken and G. Valentine (eds) *Approaches to human geography: philosophies, people and practices.* London: Sage Publications. pp. 236–62.

Fraser, N. (1989) *Unruly practices: power, discourse and gender in contemporary social theory.* Minneapolis: University of Minneapolis Press.

Fraser, N. (1997) *Justice interruptus: critical reflections on the 'postsocialist' condition.* New York and London: Routledge.

Gahegan, M. (1995) 'Proximity operators for qualitative spatial reasoning', in A.U. Frank and W. Kuhn (eds) *COSIT '95 proceedings: spatial information theory: a theoretical basis for GIS*. Berlin: Springer-Verlag. pp. 31–44.

Gibbs, G.R. (2002) *Qualitative data analysis: explorations with NVivo*. Philadelphia: Open University Press.

Gibson-Graham, J.K. (1994) '"Stuffed if I know!" Reflections on post-modern feminist social research', *Gender, Place and Culture* 1 (2): 205–24.

Gilbert, M.R. (1994) 'The politics of location: doing feminist research at "home"', *The Professional Geographer* 46 (1): 90–6.

Goodchild, M. (2006) 'Geographic information systems', in S.C. Aitken and G. Valentine (eds) *Approaches to human geography: philosophies, people and practices*. London: Sage. pp. 251–62.

Haraway, D. (1991) *Simians, Cyborgs, and women: the reinvention of nature*. New York: Routledge.

Harding, S. (1991) *Whose science? Whose knowledge? Thinking from women's lives*. Ithaca, NY: Cornell University Press.

Harker, C. (2005) 'Playing and affective times-spaces', *Children's Geographies* 3 (1): 47–62.

Harris, T.M. (2002) 'GIS in archaeology', in A.K. Knowles (ed.) *Past time, past place: GIS for history*. Redlands, CA: ESRI Press. pp. 131–43.

Harris, T.M. and Weiner, D. (2002) 'Implementing a community-integrated GIS: perspective from South African fieldwork', in W. J. Craig, T. M. Harris and D. Weiner (eds) *Community participation and geographic information systems*. London: Taylor & Francis. pp. 246–58.

Hay, I. (ed.) (2005) *Qualitative research methods in human geography*, 2nd edn. South Melbourne, Australia: Oxford University Press.

Healey, P. (1992) 'Planning through debate: the communicative turn in planning theory', *Transportation Planning Research* 63 (2): 143–62.

Jiang, H. (2003) 'Stories remote sensing images can tell: integrating remote sensing analysis with ethnographic research in the study of cultural landscapes', *Human Ecology* 31 (2): 215–32.

Katz, C. (1994) 'Special edition on "Women in the Field"', *Professional Geographer* 46 (1): 1–140.

Kingbury, P. (2003) 'Psychoanalysis, a gay spatial science?', *Social & Cultural Geography* 4 (3): 347–67.

Knigge, L. and Cope, M. (2006) 'Grounded visualization: integrating the analysis of qualitative data through grounded theory and visualization', *Environment and Planning A* 38 (11): 2021–37.

Kwan, M-P. (1999) 'Gender, the home-work link, and space-time patterns of non-employment activities', *Economic Geography* 75 (4): 370–94.

Kwan, M-P. (2000) 'Interactive geovisualization of activity-travel patterns using 3D GIS: a methodological exploration with a large data set', *Transportation Research C* 8: 185–203.

Kwan, M-P. (2002a) 'Is GIS for women? Reflections on the critical discourse in the 1990s', *Gender, Place and Culture* 9 (3): 271–79.

Kwan, M-P. (2002b) 'Feminist visualization: re-envisioning GIS as a method in feminist geographic research', *Annals of the Association of American Geographers* 92 (4): 645–61.

Kwan, M-P. and Knigge, L. (2006) 'Doing qualitative research using GIS: an oxymoronic endeavor?', *Enviornment and Planning A* 38 (11): 1999–2002.

Lancaster, L.R. and Bodenhamer, D.J. (2002) 'The electronic cultural atlas initiative and the North American regional atlas', in A.K. Knowles (ed.) *Past time, past place: GIS for history*. Redlands, CA: ESRI Press. pp. 163–77.

Limb, M. and Dwyer, C. (eds) (2001) *Qualitative methodologies for geographers: issues and debates*. London: Arnold.

Lulka, D. (2004) 'Stablizing the herd: fixing the identity of nonhumans', *Environment and Planning D: Society and Space* 22 (3): 439–63.

Matthews, S. Detwiler, J. and Burton, L. (2005) 'Viewing people and places: conceptual and methodological issues in coupling geographic information analysis and ethnographic research', *Cartographica* 40 (4): 75–90.

McCormack, D. (2003) 'An event of geographical ethics in spaces of affect', *Transactions of the Institute of British Geographers* 28 (4): 488–507.

McDowell, L. (1999) *Gender, identity and place: understanding feminist geographies*. Minneapolis: University of Minnesota Press.

Moss, P. (ed.) (2002) *Feminist geography in practice: research and methods*. Oxford: Blackwell.

Nagar, R. (1997) 'Exploring methodological borderlands through oral narratives', in J.P. Jones III, H.J. Nast, and S.M. Roberts (eds) *Thresholds in feminist geography: difference, methodology, representation*. Lanham, MD: Rowman and Littlefield. pp. 203–24.

Nast, H. (1998) 'The body as "place": reflexivity and fieldwork in Kano, Nigeria', in H. Nast and S. Pile (eds) *Places through the body*. London: Routledge. pp. 93–116.

Nightingale, A. (2003) 'A feminist in the forest: situated knowledges and mixing methods in natural resource management', *ACME* 2 (1): 77–90.

Pavlovskaya, M. (2006) 'Theorizing with GIS: a tool for critical geographies?', *Environment and Planning A* 38 (11): 2003–20.

Peace, R. (2000) 'Computers, qualitative data and geographic research', in I. Hay (ed.) *Qualitative research methods in human geography.* South Melbourne, Australia: Oxford University Press. pp. 144–60.

Pickles, J. (ed.) (1995a) *Ground truth: the social implications of geographic information systems.* New York: Guilford.

Pickles, J. (1995b) 'Representations in an electronic age: geography, GIS, and democracy', in J. Pickles (ed.) *Ground truth: the social implications of geographic information systems.* New York: Guilford. pp. 1–30.

Pink, S. (2001) *Doing visual ethnography: images, media and representation in research.* London: Sage.

Robbins, P. (2001) 'Tracking invasive land covers in India or why our landscapes have never been modern', *Annals of the Association of American Geographers* 91 (4): 637–59.

Robbins, P. (2006) 'Research is theft: Environmental inquiry in a postcolonial world', in G. Valentine and S. Aitken (eds) *Approaches to human geography: philosophies, people, and practices.* London: Sage. pp. 311–24.

Roberts, S.M. and Schein, R.H. (1995) 'Earth shattering: global imagery and GIS', in J. Pickles (ed.) *Ground truth: the social implications of geographic information systems.* New York: Guildford. pp. 171–95.

Robins, K. (1996) *Into the Image: culture and politics in the field of vision.* New York and London: Routledge.

Rose, G. (1993) *Feminism and geography: the limits of geographical knowledge.* Minneapolis: University of Minnesota Press.

Rose, G. (1996) 'Teaching visualised geographies: towards a methodology for the interpretation of visual materials', *Journal of Geography in Higher Education* 20 (3): 281–94.

Rose, G. (1997) 'Situating knowledges: positionality, reflexivities and other tactics', *Progress in Human Geography* 21 (3): 305–20.

Rose, G. (2001) *Visual methodologies: an introduction to the interpretation of visual materials.* London: Sage.

Sauer, C. (1956) 'Presidential address', *Annals of the Association of American Geographers* 46: 287–99.

Shariff A.R., Egenhofer, M. and Mark, D. (1998) 'Natural-language spatial relations between linear and areal objects: the topology and metric of English-language terms', *International Journal of Geographical Information Science* 12 (3): 215–46.

Shepherd, E. and Poiker, T. (1995) Special journal issue on GIS and society. *Cartography and GIS (CaGIS)* 22 (1).

Shiffer, M.J. (2002) 'Spatial multimedia representations to support community participation', in W.J. Craig, T.M. Harris and D. Weiner (eds) *community participation and geographic information systems.* London: Taylor & Francis. pp. 309–19.

Smith, D. (1998) 'The place of ethics in Deleuze's philosophy: three questions of immanence', in E. Kaufman and K. Heller (eds) *Deleuze and Guattari: new mappings in politics, philosophy and culture.* Minneapolis: University of Minnesota Press. pp. 251–69.

Smith, S. (2000) 'Qualitative methods', in R.J. Johnston, D. Gregory, G. Pratt and M. Watts (eds) *The dictionary in human geography,* 3rd edn. Oxford: Blackwell. pp. 660–2.

Smith, S. (2001) 'Doing qualitative research: from interpretation to action', in M. Limb and C. Dwyer (eds) *Qualitative methodologies for geographers: issues and debates.* London: Arnold. pp. 23–40.

Strauss, A. and Corbin, J. (1998) *Basics of qualitative research: techniques and procedures for developing grounded theory.* Thousand Oaks, CA: Sage.

Thrift, N. (1996) *Spatial formations.* Thousand Oaks, CA: Sage.

van Leeuwen, T. and Jewitt, C. (2001) *Handbook of visual analysis.* London: Sage.

Winchester, H.P.M. (2005) 'Qualitative research and its place in human geography', in I. Hay (ed.) *Qualitative research methods in human geography,* 2nd edn. South Melbourne, Australia: Oxford University Press. pp. 1–22.

17

"A Little Bird Told Me ...": Approaching Animals Through Qualitative Methods

Mona Seymour and Jennifer Wolch

EPISTEMOLOGICAL AND ONTOLOGICAL CHALLENGES IN ANIMAL GEOGRAPHIC RESEARCH

Contemporary human geography has witnessed a revived interest in animals over the past decade (Wolch and Emel, 1995, 1998; Philo and Wilbert, 2000a). The rise of animal geography stems from several factors, including growing awareness of conditions in factory farms and research laboratories, habitat loss due to land development and extractive economic activities, and theenvironmental impacts of toxic waste and pollutants. Animal suffering, species endangerment, environmental degradation, and general fears about 'the end of nature' have spurred resistance to modes of animal treatment and environmental management, through legal battles, public opinion campaigns and activism. Within the academy, developments in social theory, particularly feminism and postmodern theory, have led geographers to rethink the human–animal divide, and to question the 'human' in human geography (Whatmore, 1999). The result has been an effervescence of animal geographic research, mobilizing

conceptual frameworks variously drawn from political economy, political ecology, actor-network theory, cultural ecology, and ecofeminism.

How do animal geographers actually go about their research? The study of human-animal relations presents considerable epistemological challenge. A major decision to make in the process of designing and executing a project is choosing how to conceptualize not only humans of different sorts, but also animals. Are they a marginal social group, faceless commodities, ecosystem service providers or valued companions? Unsurprisingly, our personal characteristics and experiences as researchers – cultural and class background, race/ethnicity, gender, religion, urban or rural upbringing, exposure to institutional messages and media, and past experiences with animals – mediate roles in human–animal relationships and how we think about the relationships we study.

Epistemological commitments inform this decision to some extent. Feminists might see human–animal relations as characterized by a power imbalance created and reinforced by patriarchy, and conceptualize animals as powerless, disenfranchised beings within patriarchal society; the goal of feminist research on animals might be emancipatory or educational. A Marxist, in contrast, might conceptualize animals as exploited laborers and resources, and understand their issues as externalities of capital accumulation. Self-reflexivity about epistemological standpoints to animal geographic research not only illuminates for our own benefit why we may be approaching our project and analyzing our data in particular ways, but also clarifies for readers why we researched, analyzed, and drew conclusions in the way that we did.[1]

There are also ontological particularities about animals that warrant some degree of self-reflexivity in research and analysis. Early humans relied on animals for food, companionship, and spiritual inspiration, and predator-prey interactions precipitated selection pressure for a larger, more complex brain (Bonner, 1980; Shepard, 1996) and social skills that some believe were honed by the need for collaborative hunting (Stanford, 1999). Though the nature of human–animal interactions has changed significantly over the history of our species, animals remain deeply entrenched in the human psyche, personal identities, and daily lives. While we cannot be certain how such a developmental history and ontology might shape our perceptions of and attitudes toward animals, it is important to consider how these may affect research frameworks and strategies.

Aside from personal and intellectual self-reflection, animal geographers must grapple with the issue of how various types of research participants think about animals – participants who are subject to geographic, developmental, institutional, and interpersonal variables that may be similar to or wildly different from the ones that inform our own understandings of animals. Whether individual informants, or representatives of corporations or the state, all participants will have formal and informal perspectives and attitudes about animals, informed by institutional and group agendas, societal norms, and other factors.

The study of human–animal relations also presents methodological challenges for the minority of animal geographers who focus on the animal experience rather than on the human perspective in the interspecies relationship. How can we as scholars examine the life and death situations of animal others, and their interactions with people? How do we approach an animal as a research subject or participant – through the people they live with or are controlled by, or on their own terms – and if we try to approach them on their own terms, what would that mean in terms of research design? Indeed, the standard toolkit of qualitative methods in human geography – including interviews, focus groups, ethnography, surveys, archival research, textual analysis methods – clearly privileges the human side of the human–animal relationship.

This chapter offers a review of the traditional qualitative research methodologies used in animal geographic research. Throughout this discussion, we point out the challenges that animal geographers face in qualitative research given the central role of nonhuman subjects. We then introduce two additional qualitative approaches that animal geographers may wish to add to their methodological toolkits. These methods promise to enrich animal geographic work and hone its findings. This is followed by a brief section that looks at different ways of presenting research. Finally, we end with general observations on the advantages and limitations of qualitative methods for animal geographic research.

TRADITIONAL QUALITATIVE APPROACHES TO THE STUDY OF HUMAN–ANIMAL RELATIONS

Geographers exploring human–animal relations come from various theoretical and methodological traditions within the field. Thus not surprisingly, they have employed a wide range of methodological approaches, of which most have been qualitative in nature.[2] In what follows we assess animal geographic work undertaken with qualitative techniques that have dominated the subfield, including ethnography, interviews, focus groups, surveys, and document analysis conducted as part of a historiography or case study. The assessment draws on original research to explicate ways in which particular methods may help researchers to address some of the challenges described above, and also to discuss ways in which particular methods are especially valuable to or problematic for animal geographic research in general. We begin with arguments in favor of using document analysis to construct past and present animal geographies. We then discuss survey research, results from which can be incorporated into qualitative studies of people's attitudes and beliefs about animals. Next we look at the ways interviews and focus groups elucidate meanings of animals and, finally, we discuss ethnography as a method for elaborating the experiential contexts of animal geographies. After providing this assessment, we critique the body of animal geographic research in terms of its transparency in data collection and analysis methods.

Documenting past and present animal geographies

Working with written-source documents has emerged as the most common way to conduct animal geographic research, either as part of historiographic research or the development of contemporary case studies. The latter range widely, focusing on, for example, particular places, species, human–animal conflicts, animal-based industrial sectors, or heterogeneous networks. Animal geographers may look to archives, museum collections, media outlets, or the internet to find old or current newspapers, personal letters, court proceedings, and private industry records for their analysis; and they may incorporate reference books, academic research papers, government reports, and other information sources to build an argument or support a claim.

Documents are typically vital resources for researchers aiming to reconstruct historic public discourses about animals. Historiographic methods also allow a researcher to probe private, underground, or closed social worlds of the past, or see behind the scenes of public or well-known events (Hoggart *et al.*, 2002; Cloke *et al.*, 2004). For example, Kay Anderson (1995) worked with over a century's worth of Royal Zoological Society of South Australia (RZSSA) annual reports, along with RZSSA council minutes and local newspaper articles and ads, to create an account of the evolution of the several discursive frames including race and nation through which zoo animals were deliberately fashioned and delivered to the public.[3]

Structuring an analysis within an actor-network framework, another way of looking at the evolution of animal geographies over time and space, can involve use of a wide mix of document types. Due to its recognition of a heterogeneous social network composed of people, places, animals, documents, and devices, it is an approach that is especially advantageous for animal geographers hoping to draw out the animal experience in an interspecies relationship. Drawing on published work on animals in Roman life, art, and entertainment, Sarah Whatmore and Lorraine Thorne (1998) attempted to reconstruct the trade network that enmeshed big cats in Roman gladiatorial times, and also tried to reveal the cats as active, subjective beings that experienced the network. These historical accounts allowed them to envision the capture conditions of the felines, which in turn contributed to a more vivid understanding and explication of the animal experience.

Studies of contemporary animal geographies have relied on vastly different resources and analytic methods. While Jennifer Wolch and colleagues (1997) performed a content analysis on *Los Angeles Times* items to understand what types of public attitudes about cougars this widely-circulated newspaper was shaping and reflecting, Michael Woods (2000) analyzed a wider array of materials pertinent to another contemporary wildlife issue: fox hunting. He examined parliamentary debate transcripts, newspaper letters and articles, leaflets, and advertisements to elucidate the tactics and types of 'evidence' (e.g., anecdotes, scientific knowledge, and emotional appeals) that interest groups used to represent quarry animals as competitors, pests, and victims in a high-profile 1997 British hunting debate. These studies illustrate that analysis of written records can shed light on the nature of structural influences (e.g., the media) on attitudes about animals.

Another use for documents is to elucidate the political economy of animal-based industries. Studies of livestock movements, slaughter procedures or genetic engineering draw on an eclectic assortment of sources. Geographers who have looked at agro-industrial trends have utilized published statistical data on agriculture, newspaper articles, the US census, and animal industry trade publications (e.g., Furuseth, 1997; Ufkes, 1998). Recently Richard Yarwood and Rick Evans (2000: 103) have suggested that research on farm animal geographies could be improved using more 'culturally sensitive approaches' that capture cultural linkages between livestock and place in addition to explications of changes in spatial distribution attributed to financial imperatives and/or consumer demand.

Finally, documents are useful for animal geographic researchers seeking to make applied contributions. Scholars interested in welfare and conservation issues, for instance, can do applied research using documents as a springboard. James Wescoat (1998) studied Pakistani precolonial, colonial, and postcolonial law via secondary sources, performed interviews with local Pakistani Society for the Prevention of Cruelty to Animals staff, and consulted US federal law and state case law and statutes. He then forged a comparative analysis of US and Islamic water laws, asking what relevance Islamic 'right of thirst' law, essentially a moral imperative to provide water for animals, has in the contemporary Pakistani and US legal landscapes. Yarwood and Evans (2003) considered the feasibility of implementing European Union (EU) policies that subsidize farmers who keep rare indigenous breeds. They mapped data from herd and flock books compiled by breed societies to determine Welsh livestock distributions across Britain, and used Rare Breeds Survival Trust data to determine breeds in danger of extinction. Their analysis indicated that there were several very rare breeds clustered outside of their indigenous range which consequently would be ignored by EU policies.

Representing attitudes and beliefs

Survey research methods have been used infrequently in the animal geographic literature. They are, nonetheless, an excellent method for generating representative data on values, beliefs, attitudes, and experiences as related to animals. Though not a qualitative method per se, they may comprise part of a mixed methods strategy – for instance, surveys can be a useful first cut at understanding attitudes and perceptions about animals, enabling the construction of a preliminary narrative about human–animal relationships that can be explored further with additional methods (e.g., Wolch and Zhang, 2005). Also, wildlife managers increasingly value local public opinions on topics like deer culling (Lauber et al., 2001; Miller and McGee, 2001), making surveys a useful tool for animal geographers interested in applied work.

One criticism of the use of surveys in animal geographic research has been that the instruments tend to oversimplify attitudes and fail to capture the complex, contradictory feelings, and ideas that people have about animals (Wolch et al., 2000). Survey instruments designed with open-ended questions or innovative exercises, and written to grasp nuanced attitudes, can begin to address this criticism. Susan Simpson (2005) included an informative mapping exercise along with closed, semi-open, and open-ended questions in her survey of general public and conservation professional perceptions of human and wildlife spaces in Tucson, AZ. Participants were provided with a map of the Tucson area onto which they were instructed to delineate areas where they believed humans, nuisance animals, and threatening animals presently exist, should be, and should be during drought, allowing participants to express space-, time-, and species-dependent attitudes. The maps (98 from the public, 27 from professionals) were later digitized and analyzed with responses to survey questions. Maps were also analyzed against themselves, to produce response ranges for the delineation questions and to compare public and professional responses for each question.

The method is problematic in at least one additional way, namely with respect to how survey instruments are discursively constructed. Depending upon research aims, vocabulary may be problematic as respondents are confronted with conceptualizations of animals and human–animal relationships that they may find unfamiliar or confusing, or that they misinterpret. Chris Philo and Chris Wilbert (2000b) present thoughts on what may constitute an animal, a 'proper animal', animate things, and so forth, as influenced by particular cultural, social, psychological, political, and economic understandings. Paul Carter (2006) points out that the noun 'parrot' conjures up drastically different species and even genera in respondents' minds. Therefore failing to qualify the very topic of one's research can result in misinterpretations of the survey instrument.

Elucidating meaning and experience through interviews

In light of these issues most qualitative geography has focused upon the spoken and sometimes written word to expand our access to the rich array of meanings associated with society-animal relations. A more common

method in animal geographic research, and often used in tandem with ethnographic studies or document analysis, interviews allow for a dialogue between researcher and participant that surveys do not. This provides opportunities for on-the-spot probing about comments of interest and for clarifications. More enticingly, interviews present an opportunity to partially confront the methodological challenge of understanding interspecies relationships and animal experiences through a human informant alone by asking interviewees questions that can elucidate aspects of the animal's life experiences – such as, 'Where are they kept during the winter?', 'Do you let him out every time he goes to the door?', and 'Will you spay her?'

For example, Lewis Holloway (2001) interviewed English and Welsh hobby-farmers to learn about human–animal relationships on these small farms. His respondents reflected on their role in the geographies and experiences of the animals they raise, sharing information about letting their pigs run free in the woods rather than keeping the animals in cages, and about refusing to ear-tag their cattle to spare the animals some perceived pain. Holloway also discovered that the identities of his hobby-farming informants seemed to have formed as a rejection of commercial farming practices, and guided the hobby-farmers in their embrace and treatment of their animals as individuals who have the potential to be happy and fulfilled. In general, then, answers to queries about respondent handling of animals can aid a researcher in constructing an account of an animal's situation by using the actions of its human counterpart as data.

Alternatively, a researcher can query his or her participants for their own observations of the animals' experiences and behaviors. Hayden Lorimer (2006) relied on reindeer herders for examples of deer behaviors that belied 'sentient geographies,' such as a herd's propensity to collectively perform a 'snow dance' when they sensed via environmental cues the approach of a cold front. There is considerable probability that informants will respond with anthropomorphized descriptions of an animal's behaviors. Holloway's (2001: 301) results, for example, were presented with a note of caution to the reader that his respondents' 'ascription[s] of identity, desires and character [were] frequently anthropomorphic.' Interview transcript analysis will require a researcher to critically separate objective and subjective elements of the descriptions in order to approach the animal experience apart from any emotional state that a participant may attribute to the animal.

Like interviews of individuals, focus groups – often termed group interviews – offer the opportunity to pose questions that inform the researcher about an animal's life experiences. An important aspect of focus group methodology is group composition, since gender and class have been pinpointed as important variables in shaping attitudes toward animals (Driscoll, 1995; Kellert, 1996; Lockwood, 1999; Munro, 2001). Focus group demographics in animal geographic research generally have reflected consideration for these variables.

Groups of uniform composition have benefits past supplying the participants with common ground from which to depart. One advantage of single-gender focus groups is that participants may feel freer to criticize gendered animal practices than they would in mixed company. A series of focus groups undertaken to elucidate links between attitudes toward animals and racialization, and to understand the roles of cultural difference and geographical context in attitude formation, supports this claim. In each of the five groups, composed of low-income Los Angeles, CA women of diverse racial/ethnic backgrounds, gender as well as class and race were held constant (Griffith et al., 2002; Lassiter and Wolch, 2002, 2005; Wolch et al., 2000). Unna Lassiter and Jennifer Wolch (2005) reported that women in their Chicana focus group expressed disapproval of bullfights, cockfights, and dogfights, animal practices that play a social role for men. The participants made some derisive comments about these sports and their role in

men's lives, leading the authors to surmise that 'such shows of masculine bravado' are unimpressive to the women (Lassiter and Wolch, 2005: 277). These remarks perhaps would not have been made in the presence of male participants.

The set of Los Angeles focus groups also provides fodder for a brief reflection on data analysis. Marci Griffith and colleagues (2002) describe the development of a 'coding tree' or 'index tree' with three general categories – practices; perceptions and knowledge; and values and attitudes. Focus group text was coded, assigned to a particular conceptual 'node' (individual; family/friends; cultural; cross-cultural; and gender), and linked to one of the three general categories. This analytic framework demonstrates one way in which to break down a discussion, differentiating between what people do to animals, what people think about animals, and what people feel about animals. In creating nodes or other like structures, concepts touched on so little that they do not merit a node can also be important to reflect on. For instance, it is perhaps significant that 'class' was absent from Griffith et al.'s conceptual nodes, indicating that the participants either did not perceive class differences to be important in human–animal relationships or conversely they perceived class differences to be so essential that they were assumed rather than vocalized.

Exploring emotional geographies in place and over time

A noticeable increase in the use of ethnographic or participant observatory methods[4] to study animal geographies mirrors the general surge in the use of ethnography in human geographic research. This method is particularly appropriate for studies of the human–animal bond and of the role or significance of animals in a group's culture. Ethnography allows the researcher to personally witness human–animal interactions in place and over time, whereas survey, interview, and focus group methods garner for the researcher accounts of past or potential events as perceived by respondents.[5]

By its nature, ethnographic work is conducted in the setting relevant to the interactions and relationships that the researcher seeks to understand. This immersion enables researchers to observe the emotional primacy of human–animal encounters. Paul Cloke and Harvey Perkins (2005) participated in multiple whale-watching and dolphin encounter trips off Kaikoura, New Zealand, to observe tourists' physical and emotional reactions to the mammals at the moments of encounter, and also to conduct conversations and interviews immediately thereafter. Their presence on the boats also allowed them to understand the heavily mediated context of these trips – crew members' instructions on how best to enjoy and photograph the animals significantly impacted some tourists' expectations and experiences.

Collaborative fieldwork between an academic geographer and a tribal hunter allowed Annette Watson and Orville Huntington (2008) to achieve a complex and contextualized understanding of the practice of Indigenous Knowledge (IK) and the social and spiritual relations between Koyukon Athabascan hunters and prey. Watson accompanied her coauthor, an Athabascan hunter, into the field, living and breathing a moose hunt with him. Participation in the hunt allowed both authors to intimately experience the spaces, senses, intuitions and interspecies connections and communications that inform the practice of IK, and to then construct an ethnographic account informed by these experiences and their drastically different cultural backgrounds. This cross-cultural collaborative ethnographic method addresses some of the epistemological and ontological challenges we face in studies of human–animal relations, by facilitating in-depth and introspective conversations between co-authors aware of fundamental cultural differences in ways of seeing and knowing animals.

Suzanne Michel (1998) used her fieldwork not only to witness the connections between her human and animal research participants, but also to put herself in the emotional shoes of her informants. This is an immensely important part of field methodology when working on a project with humans and non-human animals, allowing the researcher to understand what it is that motivates human informants to perform with, for, or against animals in specific contextual settings. By interacting with debilitated golden eagles she experienced first-hand the emotion that mobilized small children and retired adults alike to become political on behalf of helping eagles. Both the participants' and her own visceral experiences with the birds allowed her to more deeply understand the birds' agency in garnering help for their cause.

Ethnography also provides perhaps the most opportunities to cope with the challenges of performing fieldwork on taboo or illegal animal practices – namely, the difficulty of obtaining information from participants if they anticipate danger or a negative reaction from disclosure. Lisa Naughton-Treves (2002) relied on local farmers and hunters as informants for the portion of her field study that addressed local use and perceptions of wildlife in Peru's Tambopata Province. Cognizant of regional political struggles over land and wildlife and of illegal hunting activity, she seemed to use the length and depth of her involvement in the region to her advantage. After an initial round of interviews, she continued conversations with farmers on an informal basis to gain additional insight on local perspectives on wildlife and hunting; and also pinpointed and interviewed other community members familiar with hunters' activities to corroborate data from hunter interviews and hunting diaries. Hiring local people as part of the research team may also have increased trust in and acceptance of her and her co-workers.

Critique

Reflecting on the work we have just reviewed, we wish to make some overarching observations about the standards for methodological rigor in our subfield. Published research on animal geographies often minimizes or excludes entirely discussions of methodology. Many studies fail to describe data sources, collection, and analytic techniques – our review of the literature made this all too clear to us! The inclusion of a detailed 'Methods' section in publications has fallen out of fashion in human geography as a whole, and few would embrace a return to past practices which too often downplayed the importance of research context. But we concur with Jamie Baxter and John Eyles (1997), who contend that by explicitly detailing data collection and analysis methods, a research audience can among other things recognize a study's findings as credible; generalizeable or transferable; dependable or having minimized idiosyncrasies in interpretation; and confirmable or having been determined by the respondents and the inquiry conditions rather than by the investigator's biases, interests, and perspectives. Thus in our emerging subfield it is particularly vexing to encounter so few in-depth presentations of methods and data. Moreover, as we have pointed out above, there are issues specific to doing work on animal geographies that will require a dialogue amongst researchers if innovative approaches that address these challenges are to be discovered and fleshed out. In short, a dialogue on methods cannot completely materialize unless we are forthcoming about our research designs and techniques.

It is useful to point to gaps and inconsistencies in discussions of basic data collection frameworks. Most of the contributions that involve interview, survey, focus group, or ethnographic work make mention of their methodology somewhere in the text. Such 'mentions,' however, vary from brief descriptive endnotes (e.g., Michel, 1998; Waley, 2000) to details scattered throughout the article (e.g., Cloke and Perkins, 2005) to descriptive paragraphs buried within the text (e.g., Griffiths *et al.*, 2000) to sections including information such as justifications of the method, recruitment procedures, and demographic breakdowns of the participants (e.g., Lassiter and Wolch, 2002; Naughton-Treves,

2002). Those who work with documents are often lax in describing the sources that have been compiled for analysis (though see, e.g., Yarwood and Evans, 2000 and Hintz, 2003 as exceptions). Works cited lists and footnotes become the referents for this type of information, but do not explain to the reader why particular documents were utilized or identify their limitations as data sources, nor do they allow readers to judge what sources were not consulted and why.

Our broad criticism also extends to the dearth of descriptions of data analysis methods. Researchers working with documents for historiographies or case studies, for example, generally fail to present an analytic framework that would explain to a reader how official documents, private letters, travel brochures, magazine articles and other written texts are analyzed. Thus a significant gap emerges between the paper's purpose and sources on one hand, and detailed findings on the other. This lack of information on data analysis is not restricted to historiographic or other research based on archives or other documents, but is common across the board in this subfield.

Overall, we are left with the impression that methods of data collection and analysis are obscure to the point of being counterproductive to the advancement of research in animal geography. While we do not intend to question the integrity of any contributor's data or rigor of their analyses, we do wish to highlight the fact that in order to advance the field, we need to be able to model new research on robust existing research designs, as well as data collection and analysis methods, and to constructively criticize weaker ones if our goal is to produce a strong body of literature.

EXPANDING THE ANIMAL GEOGRAPHER'S TOOLKIT

Three additional avenues of research bring a fuller complement of artifacts and practices under the scrutiny of animal geographers. The first that we discuss is ethology, the study of animal behavior. We suggest that incorporating ethological methods into any animal geographical study that asks about human–animal relationships and animal experiences will only produce a more complete understanding of the topic. Ethology is a way for us to engage animals on their own terms in addition to interpreting their experiences through documents and other accounts from humans. The second and third avenues come from cultural studies, and focus, in particular, on visual and popular cultural studies. Topics in these fields can be approached with many of the methods already familiar to geographers, including interview and content analysis. Cultural studies topics are not foreign to human geography, but few animal geographers have yet engaged with those topics and methods.

Studying animal behaviors

Ethology – the study of animal behavior – and geography have been linked before, in the humanistic and behavioral traditions of our discipline, though the suggested application of ethological practice was to human behavior rather than nonhuman animals. As Yi Fu Tuan (1976) suggested, ethological knowledge is part of the ideal education for the humanist geographer, as a means of ensuring that rigorous techniques of observation were used in research. With the emergence of the new animal geography, and 'post-human' geographies (Castree and Nash, 2006), Tuan's advice now applies to those of us who seek a better understanding of the heterogeneous situations of animals.

Ethology is a particularly enticing methodology to consider given the interests and agendas of some animal geographers. A number of animal geographers have an ethical purpose for their work, intentionally exploring animal suffering, animal rights, animal welfare, and moral landscapes. Ethology – which has been associated with

animal welfare issues for decades (Gonyou, 1994) – is thus a salient addition to the animal geographer's methodological toolkit. And even for projects without an interest in animal welfare, ethology constitutes an opportunity to supplement findings from focus groups, interviews, content analyses, and other qualitative endeavors, by 'asking the animals' what *they* think or how *they* feel about their situation, and receiving answers in the form of animal movements, calls, and social interactions.

For instance, Eric Laurier *et al.* (2006) recently combined ethnography and ethology in their observational fieldwork in Swedish parks, examining the types of intentional human and dog behaviors and interactions that occur in order to accomplish a walk in the park (e.g., glancing at each other, trying to initiate play, indicating by example which direction the walk should proceed). Michael Campbell (2007) envisions practical applications for research that draws on observations of animal and human behavior. Similar to Laurier *et al.* (2006), he conceptualizes urban birds and humans as co-actants, negotiating urban life in response to each other. He observed instances of intentional bird feeding by humans in Glasgow parks, recording inter- and intraspecies avian interactions and human–bird interactions, in order to write 'a more dynamic geography of animal and human interactions' (Campbell, 2007: 85) that addresses the need to base urban conservation decisions on understandings of human–animal–landscape interactions.

Lorimer (2006) has also incorporated ethological research into his own work on herding memories of animals and humans, in order to address the question of what a deer herd knows or cares about geography. He relied on another scholar's research on a reindeer herd to inform his discussion; F. Fraser Darling (1937) concluded that the herd's sensed experiences with its environment informed ways of living in the landscape – that thedeer interacted with their surroundings with insight and even foresight, and did not simply reflexively respond to environmental stimuli. Indeed, utilizing ethology means tapping into the perceptual world of the organism – Jakob von Uexkull's *umwelt* (1957) – in order to understand the animal's experience through its own eyes, ears, nose, antennae, and skin.

Understanding the utility of ethology, we suggest that human geographers are probably well-suited to employ ethological methodology in their work. Indeed, ethology is an inherently geographical concept, with place or environment being a major behavioral variable. Eighteenth- and nineteenth- century ethologists realized that animal behavior is intimately tied to place, as they debated over the virtues of studying animals in laboratories, menageries, zoos, or natural habitats in the discipline's formative years (Burkhardt, 1999). Geographers may prove to be adept ethologists, coming into behavioral research endowed with an education that emphasizes the importance and particularity of place. The geographer's eye for landscape, for environmental attributes, thus could be a boon to any human geographer who elects to study animal behavior and interactions with people.

In most cases, using ethological methodology for descriptive purposes (e.g., use of a well-developed ethogram to code seagull behavior in an urban park) should require less training than would studying behavior within a primarily ethological framework (e.g., asking questions about proximate causes of behavior, such as 'How did seagulls learn to exploit garbage in urban parks?'). Realistically, human geographers are constrained in their use of ethological methodology according to the resources (time, expertise) available to them, since ethology unlike the other qualitative methods discussed in this chapter is not a traditional method in human geography research and as such geography faculty and peers are unlikely to be able to provide adequate guidance. But *supplementing* animal geography research with ethological methodology is entirely within reach. Building an interdisciplinary research team is another avenue to combining ethology and geography.

Animals in visual and popular culture

Though uncommon in animal geographic studies, examinations of the forms and practices of culture are far from new to the discipline of geography as a whole. Out of the broad realm of cultural studies we wish to hone in on two fields that we feel would be especially beneficial to animal geographic research – visual culture studies, whose subjects are embodied by a diverse range of visual texts (Walker and Chaplin, 1997), and popular culture studies, whose subjects are practices, processes, and broader trends in society, not limited to any particular sort of medium (Storey, 2003).

The utility of cultural studies for animal geographers lies in the information that cultural materials and practices give us about the perceptions, attitudes, practices, and social relationships existing and being reproduced in a certain place. Studying visual culture can tell us both how the creator (whether private citizen, working artist, corporation, or organization) conceptualizes animals and how viewers are supposed to understand the animal subject – with the image often producing multiple and contradictory readings (e.g., van Stipriaan and Kearns, unpublished 2002). Understanding the roles of animals within popular culture can elucidate the ways in which popular trends and lifestyles have shaped the geographies of many animal groups and the nature of human–animal relations. Cultural studies topics and artifacts encompass the highly personal – video diaries, family snapshots – to participatory practices open to anyone and mass communication images meant for every eye (Banks, 2001).

Four directions in cultural studies offer particularly fruitful directions for future animal geographic research. Advertisements, including billboards, television commercials, and newspaper ads, are riddled with animal imagery and constitute promising target for analysis. Television advertisements, for instance, use animals (live and animated, named and anonymous) to promote a vast number of products, such as insurance (geckos and ducks), breakfast cereal (tigers and rabbits), and pet food (domestic cats and dogs). Interesting for a different set of reasons is the use of live animals to sell their own bodies or products, such as the happy cows of Real California Cheese, the very much prodded and shaken cow for Carl's Jr.'s milkshakes, and the western gunfighting chicken for a Carl's Jr.'s grilled chicken sandwich; and the use of animal parts to sell animal products, such as El Pollo Loco's sizzling chicken breasts and Carl's Jr.'s quarter pounder patties.[6]

Mona Domosh (2003) suggests the analysis of advertisements – documents that shape and reinforce public culture – to reveal normative patterns of gendered, racialized, and sexualized social relationships, cultural anxieties and desires, and the construction of various identities (corporate, regional, more). Blair van Stipriaan and Rose Kearns (unpublished 2002), for instance, looked into the gendered, sexualized, and localized cultural discourses that fed into and grew out of a controversial urban New Zealand billboard posting that encouraged the public to 'de-sex [one's] bitch' (spay their female dog) and pictured a dog dressed in a bra, skirt, and pumps. They analyzed the billboard, interviews, spaying campaign leaflets, correspondence, and media coverage to discover the multiple ways in which the message was interpreted. What could advertisement discourse analysis or viewer focus groups tell us about the relationship between society and animals represented in and interpreted from the television commercial images mentioned above?[7]

Animal geographers may also want to focus on popular consumption. Materials bought and used in everyday life are made of, come from, or copy animals – leather and fur clothing and accessories, meat and dairy food items, and pet toys are only a few examples. Pet care practices, human diets, and fashion trends impact animal geographies in significant ways, and the influences of class, gender, race/ethnicity, and place on these merit

investigation. We can also raise questions about the ways in which shifting attitudes toward animals influence consumption patterns, and where. Where is fur popular and why? Where is a shift away from meat consumption happening the fastest and why? Where are people most likely to make connections between embodied animals and products? How and why have pets become the objects of escalating financial, emotional, and cultural investment?[8] Data for studying animals as objects of mass consumption could conceivably come as much from interviews and focus groups as from statistical databases such as the CITES Trade Database.

Television programs, including syndicated shows and news programs, are our third suggested topic.[9] Content analyses of a sample or series of television programs that features animals can speak to corporate and organizational interests in or about environmental issues, conservation, education, and the lives and fates of particular species. What nature–human relationships are portrayed in these programs? What are the dominant discourses about animal others? And how do they influence and reflect the attitudes of viewers? Gail Davies (1999, 2000a–c, 2003) has approached television differently, focusing on the people, wildlife, and technologies behind the scenes of natural history programs to lay bare the representational practices that culminate in the particular visions of wildness, wilderness, and nature being brought to the small screen. This issue of representation is seen as so critical in shaping attitudes that the Humane Society of the United States gives an annual 'Genesis Award' to major news and entertainment media that have done the most to raise public understanding of animal issues.

Finally, we suggest that animal geographers turn to personal effects such as family photographs, home videos, and other personal texts to study place-based human–animal relationships. We imagine that analysis of such personal artifacts would be particularly salient for studies of relationships between humans and companion animals. For instance, tombstone epitaphs at a

Victorian-era pet cemetery enhanced Philip Howell's (2002) understanding of grieving owners' senses of affection and loss, and also their hope for a future reunion in the afterlife. James R. Ryan's (1997) work demonstrates that human–wildlife relations (as well as international relations) can be derived from photographs. He used photographs to inform his work on British imperialism and wildlife photography in African countries, noting that the photos were as much about capturing moments in time as about capturing and controlling nature.

APPROACHES TO PRESENTATION

Though the focal points of this chapter have been fieldwork and analytic methods, we now make brief remarks on methods of writing up qualitative research in animal geography. Traditional social science reporting, involving the orderly presentation of findings via data tables and select quotes, is the 'industry standard.' However, some work in animal geography, and perhaps especially ethnographic work, begs to be presented in a different way. The use of narrative strategies to present results is a promising way to illuminate the animal experience uncovered via research and also to engage the reader in an animate text. The qualitative research experience is a subjective one in the first place, and limiting our write-ups to conventional quasi-objective presentations seems to deny that subjectivity. We also contend that narrative may be a more translucent form of reporting, by virtue of presenting the author's positionality more clearly than does a traditional write-up.

We offer two examples of the use of narrative strategies to present findings, one employing an approach that melds autobiographical narrative and theory, and the other presenting results through an interpretive narrative. Watson and Huntington (2008) use a moose hunting event to demonstrate that indigenous knowledge is produced through the epistemic spaces in which it is performed. They tack

between their respective points of view in order to describe 'from the perspective of the 'middle'' (Watson and Huntington, 2008: 259) how this knowledge is assembled through the hunt's space and actors (human and non-human). The resulting co-narrative illustrates intimate emotional geographies, revealing the spiritual connections between hunter (Huntington) and animal, and Watson's personal reactions to an unfamiliar human-animal geography. The reader is rendered privy to the complex intra- and trans-species relations of the hunt. Kristin Stewart (2006) takes a different approach, with a composite narrative, creating an ethno-fiction. With data from interviews and a participant-observatory experience on a dolphin encounter trip off the Florida coast, Stewart consolidates many participants' perspectives in a few fictionalized characters; and with data from her own observations, interviews, and the research literature she crafts a dolphin perspective. The narrative then presents an encounter event, as experienced both by humans and dolphins that is meant to convey the embodied experiences of both human and animal participants. These examples suggest that narrative strategies as presentation method allow animal geographies to come to life on the page for the purpose of relating a subjective experience to the reading audience in a way that is both engaging and informative.

CONCLUDING OBSERVATIONS

To conclude, we offer some general observations on the strengths of qualitative research methods in animal geography. As Hilary Winchester (2005) indicates for qualitative methods in general, qualitative research can elucidate both the societal structures that influence the ways that animals live out their lives, and animals' individual or group experiences of place and events as well as human experiences of 'animated' places. Clearly, qualitative work can shed light on these structures and experiences in ways that quantitative work cannot, producing findings about meanings, perceptions, attitudes, beliefs, and ethics.

Qualitative methods are invaluable tools for animal geographers for at least four reasons. First, methods that embrace subjective experiences assist us in producing research that takes seriously the lived experiences of animal others, recognizing that animal lives are important in their own right and hold an important place in human culture and society. Indeed, qualitative methods can be an activist's tool, allowing researchers to assert that oft-overlooked groups can be studied and show that there are important things to be said about them and about their subjective experiences. Expressing interest in or striving to care about marginalized groups of nonhumans or human–animal relationships is facilitated in important ways by qualitative research methods. The style in which qualitative studies can be written up is an added opportunity as well – the use of narrative strategies to present results is a promising way to illuminate the animal experiences uncovered via research and also to engage the reader in the text.

Second, research using qualitative methods can shed light on the ways in which human–animal relationships affect the positioning of human social groups and animal groups within broader society. The goal here is the illumination of discrimination and marginalization, by highlighting the abuses animals suffer as the result of human attitudes toward them, and the prejudice encountered by human outsider groups as the result of what some might consider their controversial animal practices.

Third, qualitative methods serve practical, socially relevant purposes. Public and group discourses about animal practices and animal lives can be distilled through qualitative research and this knowledge is quite valuable for purposes, such as understanding whether particular management strategies are likely to be embraced or subverted by target communities and interest groups. Such methods can capture public opinions on policy issues, glean information on human activities that impact landscapes and wildlife in detrimental and/or unsustainable ways, and elucidate tolerance levels and tipping points with respect to human–animal interactions and the sharing of space within a landscape.

Last, qualitative methods are particularly useful in exploring the ways that emotions are woven into the fabric of space and place. Because emotions are deeply imbricated in human–animal relations, qualitative research strategies are thus especially powerful tools for understanding individual human, animal, or organizational behavior. In short, attention to the emotional geographies of human–animal relations via qualitative research can not only elucidate a wide range of research questions centered on humans, but also – given their rich emotional lives – on animals too (Bekoff and Goodall, 2002). It may also help us better understand and perhaps shape the evolution of public policies and practices toward animals (Anderson and Smith, 2001).

In closing, we look at the qualitative methods already in use by animal geographers and see much potential for scholarly dialogue designed to develop innovative ways to better capture relationships between space, place, animals, and humans. This will require commitment and fidelity to reporting data collection and analysis methods. We also urge geographers to look toward cultural studies and animal behavior studies to round out our methodological toolkit. Indeed, we have much yet to do in exploring the geographies of the 'other' members of the animal kingdom, be they tame or wild, pests or pets, common or rare, all in the family or cash-on-the-hoof bound for slaughter.

NOTES

1. Jody Emel's (1998) chapter on wolf eradication in the United States is probably the best example of qualitative animal geographic work contextualized within an author's life experiences and epistemological positionality.

2. Quantitative work has generally characterized biogeographical studies that focus on animal population distributions, habitat suitability modeling, and the role of particular species in ecosystems.

3. Also see work by historian Robert Darnton (1984) for an important example of research into past human–animal relations. Darnton used sources including the memoirs of a printer's apprentice to contextualize an eighteenth-century cat massacre within French culture and class relations.

4. While we recognize that there are important differences between ethnography and participant observation, in terms of level of involvement and depth and length of relationship, we use the term 'ethnography' loosely throughout this section to denote a methodology that involves any level of participatory research with a study group.

5. Of course, this matter of participant-as-filter is not always problematic – the many studies of human perceptions of animals require exactly this type of data.

6. All of these commercial images have aired recently or continuously on US television.

7. Instructive examples of animal advertisement studies exist in other social science disciplines, such as Arnold Arluke (1994), Nancy Spears *et al.* (1996), and Jennifer Lerner and Linda Kalof (1999). Also see Steve Baker (1993), who has used advertisements, along with materials such as political cartoons and posters, as touchstones in his extensive exploration of animals, symbolism, and human identity.

8. Heidi Nast (2006a; b) has begun to explore this and similar questions.

9. See Jacquelin Burgess (1990) for a complete and classic agenda for media research in geography, including television programming, that recognizes the production and consumption of environmental meanings.

REFERENCES

Anderson, K. (1995) 'Culture and nature at the Adelaide Zoo: at the frontiers of "human" geography', *Transactions of the Institute of British Geographers* 20 (3): 275–94.

Anderson, K. and Smith, S.J. (2001) 'Editorial: emotional geographies', *Transactions of the Institute of British Geographers* 26 (1): 7–10.

Arluke, A. (1994) '"We build a better beagle": fantastic creatures in lab animal ads', *Qualitative Sociology* 17 (2): 143–58.

Baker, S. (1993) *Picturing the beast: animals, identity and representation*. Manchester and New York: Manchester University Press.

Banks, M. (2001) *Visual methods in social research*. Thousand Oaks, CA: Sage.

Baxter, J. and Eyles, J. (1997) 'Evaluating qualitative research in social geography: establishing "rigour" in interview analysis', *Transactions of the Institute of British Geographers* 22 (4): 505–25.

Bekoff, M. and Goodall, J. (2002) *Minding animals: awareness, emotions, and heart*. New York: Oxford University Press.

Bonner, J.T. (1980) *The evolution of culture in animals*. New Jersey: Princeton University Press.

Burgess, J. (1990) 'The production and consumption of environmental meanings in the mass media: a research agenda for the 1990s', *Transactions of the Institute of British Geographers* 15 (2): 139–61.

Burkhardt, R.W., Jr. (1999) 'Ethology, natural history, the life sciences, and the problem of place', *Journal of the History of Biology* 32: 489–508.

Campbell, M.O. (2007) 'An animal geography of avian ecology in Glasgow', *Applied Geography* 27 (2): 78–88.

Carter, P. (2006) *Parrot*. London: Reaktion Books Ltd.

Castree, N. and Nash, C. (2006) 'Posthuman geographies', *Social and Cultural Geography* 7 (4): 501–4.

Cloke, P., Cook, I., Crang, P., Goodwin, M., Painter, J. and Philo, C. (2004) *Practising human geography*. London, Thousand Oaks, CA and New Delhi: Sage Publications.

Cloke, P. and Perkins, H.C. (2005) 'Cetacean performance and tourism in Kaikoura, New Zealand', *Environment and Planning D: Society and Space* 23 (6): 903–24.

Darling, F.F. (1937) *A herd of red deer*. Oxford: Oxford University Press.

Darnton, R. (1984) *The great cat massacre and other episodes in french cultural history*. New York: Basic Books.

Davies, G. (2003) 'Researching the networks of natural history television', in A. Blunt, P. Gruffudd, J. May, M. Ogborn, and D. Pinder (eds) *Cultural geography in practice*. London: Arnold. pp. 202–17.

Davies, G. (2000a) 'Narrating the natural history unit: institutional orderings and spatial strategies', *Geoforum* 31 (4): 539–51.

Davies, G. (2000b) 'Science, observation, and entertainment: competing visions of postwar British natural history television, 1946–1967', *Ecumene* 7 (4): 432–60.

Davies, G. (2000c) 'Virtual animals in electronic zoos: the changing geographies of animal capture and display', in C. Philo and C. Wilbert, (eds) *Animal spaces, beastly places: new geographies of human–animal relations*. London and New York: Routledge. pp. 243–67.

Davies, G. (1999) 'Exploiting the archive: and the animals came in two by two, 16mm, CD–ROM and BetaSp', *Area* 31 (1): 49–58.

Domosh, M. (2003) 'Selling America: advertising, national identity and economic empire in the late nineteenth century', in A. Blunt, P. Gruffudd, J. May, M. Ogborn and D. Pinder (eds) *Cultural geography in practice*. London: Arnold. pp. 141–53.

Driscoll, J.W. (1995) 'Attitudes toward animals: species ratings', *Society and Animals* 3 (2): 139–50.

Emel, J. (1998) 'Are you man enough, big and bad enough? Wolf eradication in the US', in J. Wolch, and J. Emel, (eds) *Animal geographies: place, politics, and identity in the nature-culture borderlands*. London and New York: Verso. pp. 91–116.

Furuseth, O.J. (1997) 'Restructuring of hog farming in North Carolina: explosion and implosion', *The Professional Geographer* 49 (4): 391–403.

Gonyou, H.W. (1994) 'Why the study of animal behavior is associated with the animal welfare issue', *Journal of Animal Science* 72 (8): 2171–77.

Griffith, M., Wolch, J. and Lassiter, U. (2002) 'Animal practices and the racialization of Filipinas in Los Angeles', *Society and Animals* 10 (3): 221–48.

Griffiths, H., Poulter, I. and Sibley, D. (2000) 'Feral cats in the city', in C. Philo and C. Wilbert (eds) *Animal spaces, beastly places: new geographies of human–animal relations*. London and New York: Routledge. pp. 56–70.

Hintz, J. (2003) Grizzly conservation and the nature of essentialist politics. *Capitalism, Nature, Socialism* 14(4): 121–45.

Hoggart, K., Lees, L. and Davies, A. (2002) *Researching human geography*. London: Arnold.

Holloway, L. (2001) 'Pets and protein: placing domestic livestock on hobby-farms in England and Wales', *Journal of Rural Studies* 17 (3): 293–307.

Howell, P. (2002) 'A place for the animal dead: pets, pet cemeteries and animal ethics in late Victorian Britain', *Ethics, Place and Environment* 5 (1): 5–22.

Kellert, S.R. (1996) *The value of life: biological diversity and human society*. Washington, DC: Island Press.

Lassiter, U. and Wolch, J. (2005) 'Changing attitudes toward animals among Chicanas and Latinas in Los Angeles', in W. Deverell and G. Hise (eds) *Land of sunshine: an environmental history of metropolitan Los Angeles*. Pittsburgh, PA: University of Pittsburgh Press. pp. 267–87.

Lassiter, U. and Wolch, J.R. (2002) 'Sociocultural aspects of attitudes toward marine animals: a focus group analysis', *The California Geographer* 42: 1–24.

Lauber, T.B., Anthony, M.L. and Knuth, B.A. (2001) 'Gender and ethical judgments about suburban deer management', *Society and Natural Resources* 14 (7): 571–83.

Laurier, E., Maze, R. and Lundin, J. (2006) 'Putting the dog back in the park: animal and human mind-in-action', *Mind, Culture, and Activity* 13 (1): 2–24.

Lerner, J.E. and Kalof, L. (1999) 'The animal text: message and meaning in television advertisements', *The Sociological Quarterly* 40 (4): 565–86.

Lockwood, R. (1999) 'Gender differences in the perpetration of animal cruelty'. *Proceedings of the Fifth Interdisciplinary Conference on Human Relations with Animals and the Natural World*. Philadelphia, PA.

Lorimer, H. (2006) 'Herding memories of humans and animals', *Environment and Planning D: Society and Space* 24 (4): 497–518.

Michel, S. (1998) 'Golden eagles and the environmental politics of care', in J. Wolch and J. Emel (eds) *Animal geographies: place, politics, and identity in the nature-culture borderlands*. London and New York: Verso. pp. 162–87.

Miller, K.K. and McGee, C.T.K. (2001) 'Toward incorporating human dimensions information into wildlife management decision-making', *Human Dimensions of Wildlife* 6 (3): 205–21.

Munro, L. (2001) 'Caring about blood, flesh, and pain: women's standing in the animal protection movement', *Society and Animals* 9 (1): 43–61.

Nast, H.J. (2006a) Critical pet studies? *Antipode* 38 (5): 894–906.

Nast, H.J. (2006b) 'Loving … whatever: alienation, neoliberalism and pet-love in the twenty-first century', *ACME* 5 (2): 300–27.

Naughton-Treves, L. (2002) 'Wild animals in the garden: conserving wildlife in Amazonian agroecosystems', *Annals of the Association of American Geographers* 92 (3): 488–506.

Philo, C. and Wilbert, C. (2000a) *Animal spaces, beastly places: new geographies of human–animal relations*. London and New York: Routledge.

Philo, C. and Wilbert, C. (2000b) 'Animal spaces, beastly places: an introduction', in C. Philo and C. Wilbert (eds) *Animal spaces, beastly places: new geographies of human–animal relations*. London and New York: Routledge. pp. 1–34.

Ryan, J.R. (1997) *Picturing empire: photography and the visualization of the British Empire*. Chicago: University of Chicago Press.

Shepard, P. (1996) *The others: how animals made us human*. Washington, DC: Island Press.

Simpson, S.L. (2005) 'Perceptual boundaries between human and wildlife spaces and their changes due to drought', Tuscon AZ. MA Thesis, University of Arizona.

Spears, N.E., Mowen, J.C. and Chakraborty, G. (1996) 'Symbolic role of animals in print advertising: content analysis and conceptual development', *Journal of Business Research* 37 (2): 87–95.

Stanford, C.B. (1999) *The hunting apes: meat-eating and the origins of human behavior.* Princeton: Princeton University Press.

Stewart, K.L. (2006) 'Human–dolphin encounter spaces', Ph.D. dissertation, Florida State University.

Storey, J. (2003) *Cultural studies and the study of popular culture.* Athens, GA: The University of Georgia Press.

Tuan, Y.F. (1976) 'Humanistic geography', *Annals of the Association of American Geographers* 66 (2): 266–76.

Ufkes, F.M. (1998) 'Building a better pig: fat profits in lean meat' in J. Wolch and J. Emel (eds) *Animal geographies: place, politics, and identity in the nature-culture borderlands.* London: Verso Press. pp. 241–55.

van Stipriaan, B. and Kearns, R.A. (2002) 'Bitching about a billboard: advertising, gender, and canine (re)presentations'. Unpublished manuscript,The University of Aucklund.

von Uexkull, J. (1957) 'A stroll through the worlds of animals and men', in C.H. Schiller (ed.) and transl. *Instinctive behavior: the development of a modern concept.* New York: International Universities Press. pp. 5–80.

Waley, P. (2000) 'What's a river without fish? Symbol, space, and ecosystem in the waterways of Japan', in C. Philo and C. Wilbert (eds) *Animal spaces, beastly places: new geographies of human–animal relations.* London and New York: Routledge. pp. 159–81.

Walker, J.A. and Chaplin, S. (1997) *Visual culture: an introduction.* Manchester: Manchester University Press.

Watson, A. and Huntington, O.H. (2008) 'They're here – I can *feel* them: the epistemic spaces of indigenous and western knowledges', *Social and Cultural Geography* 9 (3): 257–81.

Wescoat, J.L., Jr. (1998) 'The "right of thirst" for animals in Islamic law: a comparative approach', in J. Wolch and J. Emel (eds) *Animal geographies:*

Place, politics, and identity in the nature-culture borderlands. London: Verso Press. pp. 259–79.

Whatmore, S. (1999) 'Hybrid geographies: rethinking the "human" in human geography', in D. Massey, J. Allen, and P. Sarre (eds) *Human geography today.* Cambridge: Polity Press. pp. 22–39.

Whatmore, S. and Thorne, L. (1998) 'Wild(er)ness: reconfiguring the geographies of wildlife', *Transactions of the Institute of British Geographers* 23 (4): 435–54.

Winchester, H.P.M. (2005) 'Qualitative research and its place in human geography', in I. Hay (ed.) *Qualitative research methods in human geography* (2nd ed.). Melbourne: Oxford University Press. pp. 3–18.

Wolch, J., Brownlow, A.C. and Lassiter, U. (2000) 'Constructing the animal worlds of inner-city Los Angeles', in C. Philo and C. Wilbert (eds) *Animal spaces, beastly places: new geographies of human–animal relations.* London and New York: Routledge. pp. 71–97.

Wolch, J. and Emel, J. (1998) *Animal geographies: place, politics, and identity in the nature-culture borderlands.* London and New York: Verso.

Wolch, J. and Emel, J. (1995) Themed issue on 'Bringing the animals back in,' *Environment and Planning D: Society and Space* 13 (6): 631–760.

Wolch, J.R., Gullo, A. and Lassiter, U. (1997) 'Changing attitudes toward California cougars', *Society and Animals* 5 (2): 95–116.

Wolch, J. and Zhang, J. (2005) 'Siren songs: gendered discourses of concern for sea creatures', in L. Nelson and J. Seager (eds) *A Companion to feminist geography.* Oxford: Blackwell Publishing. pp. 458–85.

Woods, M. (2000) 'Fantastic Mr Fox? Representing animals in the hunting debate', in C. Philo and C. Wilbert (eds) *Animal spaces, beastly places: new geographies of human–animal relations.* London and New York: Routledge. pp. 182–202.

Yarwood, R. and Evans, R. (2003) 'Livestock, locality and landscape: EU regulations and the new geography of Welsh farm animals', *Applied Geography* 23 (2–3): 137–57.

Yarwood, R. and Evans, R. (2000) 'Taking stock of farm animals and rurality', in C. Philo and C. Wilbert (eds) *Animal spaces, beastly places: new geographies of human–animal relations.* London and New York: Routledge. pp. 98–114.

18

Performative, Non-Representational, and Affect-Based Research: Seven Injunctions

J.D. Dewsbury

All of old. Nothing else ever. Ever tried. Ever failed.
No matter. Try again. Fail again. Fail better.
(Beckett, 1987: 7)

INTRODUCTION

All of old: interview and record voices, transcribe and represent 'authentic' opinions of those whose everyday life we want to capture; or locate an event, time and space specific, and with video camera and an ethnographic eye, ear and turn of phrase, report back in prose and supporting image that which has just happened as something that is so ritually at the heart of the social formation that is our study. Performative, non-representational, and affect-based research pauses on the frightening thought: nothing else ever. Of course all methodological endeavour is creative in that we never quite get at what is going on in the interviewee's head, nor are we ever so prepared not to be surprised by some revelatory event; so

without a perfect representation at the end of it all there has always been some improvisation at the edges. Researching then, whatever the methodology, has always been and is always about ever trying and ever failing: the difference of a performative approach is that it relishes this failure, 'no matter', and uses it to mount a serious political critique of the restrictions that methodological protocols might impose on what can count as knowledge. It therefore advocates resolute experimentalism – 'try again, fail again, fail better'. Whether to fail better is to fail ever more spectacularly or to fail less worse than last time is something we return to at the end of the chapter. For now, the point is that performative, non-representational and affect-based research is all about cutting into the 'dogmatic image of what counts as thought' (Thrift, 2004: 81) and destabilizing the 'know-and-tell' politics of much sociological methodology. There are going to be a series of injunctions in this paper, so here is the first: (1) don't fret about the risks of

experimenting, it is a justifiable way of proceeding that works better if you really
embrace it.

> To create or to represent: in the Deleuzian universe
> this is a stark alternative. (Hallward, 2006: 69)

In part I strive to make this chapter a performative enactment itself and therefore in
setting this up a number of caveats need to be
aired. Firstly, whilst in this chapter I lean on
the many insights, successes, failures and
frustrations of qualitative research carried
out by scholars in geography and beyond,
I reference these sparingly. I do this because
across these legacies I try to enact the push of
a non-representational and performative critique in order to emphasize that performative
research methodology more often than not
works best as a singular disposition to disrupt
research habits and pare things down to the
immediate and the embodied. However, at
the start of each section I provide a referen-
tial coda to give some indication of the necessary context.

Secondly, I accept that this pared down
stance, or way of doing research, is also
'impossible'. However, whilst it is impossible to escape such legacies and ways of
thinking, I also believe that in this failure a
particular creativity is achieved, which is
crucially creative of problems not solutions.
The performative act of this chapter is therefore to 'strongly' advocate the argument that
problems over solutions or accounts count.
A lot of what I argue is then by no means
new, but something about the emphasis perhaps is. And that is that this ethos of disrupting by striving to think the unthought has to
take place at every step of the research – at
the moment of thinking, then sensing, then
presenting (although of course these overlap
at times, they do have their distinct place in
the overall process to make the chronology
stand for the argument's sake here).

Thirdly, the argument is staged around the
double-bind of representational and non-
representational modes of thought, and whilst
both need each other, the stress here is placed
on the non-representational. In this it

addresses the practice-based thinking,
embodiment, present-moment focus, and
distributed agency that conceptually underpins the wider non-representational project
(for full definitions see Thrift, 2008). This set
of concepts, dispositions and dissemination
tactics, which encompass but are not
exhausted by non-representational theory and
affect-based understandings, will be referred
to as performative research. So whilst this
will not include all performative methodological approaches, many of which use the
representational, it should not preclude them.
The representational is not the enemy.

Fourth, part of my performative act in the
chapter is also to starkly stage the danger of
scientism. Qualitative methodologies have
long exercised and exorcized this threat –
that in answering to the demand for validity
and rigour towards reasonably transparent
means of evaluating the standing and efficacy
of research done, the research (not just the
findings but the modes of engagement) inevitably becomes reductive of the world (for
clear expositions see Baxter and Eyles, 1997
and Bailey et al., 1999, and for a performative and personal staging of an incident of
this threat see Rose, 1997).

For this reason I stylized the chapter both
in tone and proscription. The tone is set in an
attempt to convey the consistent demand to
rethink the frames of thought by which we
stage our research. The injunctions that are
made in this chapter act as proscriptions (as
opposed to prescriptions which would suggest a formula or a known or better way to
proceed in performative methodological
endeavour). The point is that procedure is not
known. The point is rather, that something
performative in research itself, something
experimental and creative, and above all
problematic, will occur if certain proscriptions are raised instead. These proscriptions
then take place as a series of injunctions,
as temporary antidotes to the inevitable
scientism in which our research is staged
(we too often, but not always, have to affirm
certain outcomes in advance, acknowledge
certain literatures to found and contextualize

our own research, we have to encounter the world through familiar modes of conduct and communication, we have to confirm existing representations as we attempt to express others we have encountered, and we have to be certain especially when we conclude). Whilst we all know and face this, and as already intimated we do have to proceed intelligently and effectively, my beef here is with the 'too often'; let this be a moment of 'not always' to ensure that the spark of those 'unthought' moments have as long a duration and affect as possible. *And* they will inevitably fail, but that is not as bad as we think. Fail again. Fail better.

Justification is often the name of the game in setting out methodological choices for research, and in the last ten years performative research has increasingly got aired in journal interventions that act like case law. These open doors enabling future research to justify experimentalism, but cracks need to be made wider. Let us consider one key area, that of the progress report on cultural geography made by Hayden Lorimer in 2005 in which he skilfully gestures support and critique towards the non-representational in equal measure:

> The focus falls on how life takes shape and gains expression in shared experiences, everyday routines, fleeting encounters, embodied movements, precognitive triggers, practical skills, affective intensities, enduring urges, unexceptional interactions and sensuous dispositions. Attentions to these kinds of expression, it is contended, offers an escape from the established academic habit of striving to uncover meanings and values that apparently await our discovery, interpretation, judgement and ultimate representation. (Lorimer, 2005: 84)

Let us proceed with crow bar in hand by pivoting off the central nub of the quote above: 'it is contended'. Not to read the 'contended' as a striving against nor as in competing as if there were a better way for doing research (and certainly not as some race to find the 'best way' of doing things as if there were ever a way of capturing all that we want to get at). Difficulties are rife and are often the focusing point of research which tries to capture 'fleeting encounters, embodied

movements, precognitive triggers', and these difficulties get ever more difficult when brought into confrontation with 'established academic habit'. So instead let us see this 'contended' as a result of an open community, a metaphorical laboratory testing out theories or a studio for flexing embodied modes of empirical apprehension that exist by the ethos of *stretching* the means by which research is done and *striving* to continue as experiments fail or always fall short in the attempt. This latter striving is not against difficulties; rather it embraces the difficulties as the constitutive point of its mode of engagement in the first place – i.e. it is akin to artistic *experiment*. Here a warning: as we know, we need a passion for art for it often leaves the artist poor, gets valued in an untimely way after the artist is dead, is often thought to be easy to achieve until attempts are made to do so, and when it fails, it really fails. Injunction (2): make sure you have conviction to stretch and strive to the full.

Setting forth on actually conducting a piece of research, be that interviewing a lay practitioner, conducting an ethnographic study of specific place or practice, or being a participant observer with our own eyes and body or through some form of digital capturing technology, it should be immediately apparent that one has always already begun researching by implicitly setting up research questions in relation to an economy of knowledge. By such economies, which exist as ways of making knowledge function, specific sets of relation between modes of speech, forms of visibility, and protocols of intelligibility get produced (see Rancière, 2007: 73). So quite a lot is at stake when staking out a performative methodology because implicitly we accept and enact the fact that our choice of mode of speech, what we deem to be worthy of visibility, maintains existing, or produces alternative, intelligibilities (see particularly in relation to politics Butler, 1997, and in relation to performative art, Phelan, 1997, and in philosophy, Deleuze, 1988). Methodology is far from dull: it is extremely political. As such, a performative methodology explicitly follows Michel Foucault (1966, 1972) in neither determining transcendental a priori conditions of knowledge, nor in striving towards a social science as something which is ever more objective and pure, but instead studies *and enacts* the very condition of possibility for social-scientific knowledge. In its non-representational aspect, performative methodology is so much more than choice of method (video camera, interview, ethnography, etc.) and the standard of carrying out these methods, and much more about questioning how we are going to configure the world, and how we question in practice to what extent we are able to configure different worlds. In being affect-based, this methodological questioning is further complicated by no longer being scripted by disembodied contemplation but rather being apprehended by the very open sensations and connections of the body itself. Taken together, the object of study for performative research literally comes into being through being enacted in the practice of the research itself.

This challenges us to consistently and vigilantly align our perspective or mode of research with an awareness that every methodological choice we make has an implication for the management of meaning that we are making. In other words, to be acutely aware that making meaning is precisely what we are doing, and that this takes place through a whole number of interconnected empirical encounters (readings of philosophy, a material site, a research problematic) which develop (maintaining or critiquing) academic networks at conferences, seminars, in teaching and in text, in ways that destabilize or do away with territorial disciplinary anchorage (whether that be adherence to a particular 'name' or movement in the discipline). Nobody need do qualitative or quantitative methods as such. Part of the ethos of this type of research then is to keep the researcher alive to change and chance, to prevent the researcher from stopping their travels and forging a safe methodological territory to re-use again and again impervious to new twists and turns of direction and focus.

Above all the performative research advocated here emphasizes, and it is simply this emphasis that is key, a methodological stance that is rigorously experimental in singularising the abilities and capacities of thought, locution, and action in the location where they take place. This chapter thus proceeds by arguing that the underlying principle of performative research is to put theorizing first at each step of the research process: at the point of the conceptualization of the research, at the juncture of doing the actual empirical research, and as the research culminates as thought and data become written text or conference exposition. Performative research can thus be thought through three key agendas – thinking, sensing, and presenting; and it is these agendas that structure the chapter.

THINKING

Perhaps the world resists being reduced to a mere resource because it is but coyote, a figure for the always problematic, always potent tie of meaning and bodies. (Haraway, 1995: 201)

In many ways, performative research thinks its way towards a form of expressionism – problematic new folds of meaning and body – that is often accused of being productive of uncritical subjectivism. Respectful of the struggles of qualitative methodologies since their conception, performative research likewise sits at the site of these struggles, namely that space between essentialism and constructionism (see Taussig's 'Report to the Academy' (1993)). As such it rejects the idea of the interiority and purity of the individual subject, the rationality and economy of reason dominating notions of shared knowability, and the idea that communication re-presenting the field research as knowledge, whether written or spoken, is merely the transmission of information. In this it rests on the legacy of the ground broken by feminist theory in the 1970s and 1980s (see as indicative example, Irigaray, 1985, and

Haraway, 1995, and as overview into the text of the performative Elam, 1994), and specifically the critiques therein made of disembodied, objectivist, and universalizing representations (see for critical augmentation within geography Rose (1993) and Moss (2007), and with performance studies Phelan (1993)).

What this means for us now is that we have more open space to think about what kinds of knowledge we are trying to produce. This immediately raises the theoretical question of what knowledge is in the first place. Given that the overall injunction of this chapter is to push research into resolute experimentalism, we need to address straight away that fear which holds us back and thus pull the carpet from under our feet: knowledge is not science. Injunction (3): don't fear the judgement that tethers social science, especially that which is in close proximity to the humanities, to scientific values of efficacy and rigour.

A particular guide for this is the work of Gilles Deleuze who reminds us that: 'Knowledge is not science and cannot be separated from the various thresholds in which it is caught up, including even the experience of perception, the values of imagination, the prevailing ideas or commonly held beliefs (Deleuze, 1988: 51).

Our task, if we wish to follow Deleuze, is to push

> the experience or experimentalism of thought into a zone before the establishment of a stable, intersubjective 'we' … making it a matter of not recognizing ourselves or the things in our world, but rather of encounter with what we can't yet determine – to what we can't yet describe or agree upon, since we don't yet have the words. (Rajchman, 2000: 20)

In short, begin, even before thoughts have been put down onto paper and moulded into those first tentative research questions, by pausing and thinking upon the empirical metaphysics we are working on. Often when confronted with the desire to do performative research the knee-jerk reaction is to speed fast into devising a research project that involves animating knowledge by using video capture of one form or another: the 'only way' to get at practice and performance, and any other present-tense action. This is ill-thought-out, and I will use this stereotypical example to illustrate how important the pre-cursive set-up of thought and conceptualization is to research: and to argue rhetorically that this is doubly so with performative research precisely because of this misconceived trend to turn to moving images. Remember resources for research can only go so far: it is a video camera, it records moving images with different effects for sure which can then be edited and superimposed in imaginative ways but still. Think instead, at least for a moment before proceeding along this route, upon a productive empiricism in order to rediscover the vitality of empirical methods not reduced by or to a pre-given theoretical schema. A well conceived set of interview questions might well be far more effective at capturing the tension of the performing body as witnessed by the body of the interviewee.

To this end, and to end this first section, Richard Shusterman's book (2000), 'Performing Live', is an excellent starting point for thinking through the implications of dismantling our propensity for already framing in thought our research questions and design, and ultimately the means by which we make what we research, and what we find through research, meaningful. In part the book pivots on a simple question: Do we ever refrain from interpreting, and if we do, do we do so without thereby refraining from intelligent activity altogether? Is this just another philosophical quagmire that gets us nowhere? No, for whilst we might never be able to 'talk (or explicitly think) about things existing without their being somehow linguistically mediated, it does not mean that we can never experience them nonlinguistically' (Shusterman, 2000: 129). In other words, experience doesn't need to be coded to be appreciated and understood, it needs to be presented and treated as being just what it is. This doesn't need video capture, although that might work; nor do words fail us in presenting the 'what-it-is-ness' of experience, although they might steer us more forcibly to the habitual, and specifically reductive, means of rendering meaningful especially given that we academics are far more proficient in articulating our point in words than in images. But this is all missing the point: by breaking down the processes of research and being explicit about the conceptualizations used by the research to make meaning, we might allow some capture of the experience in itself to edge into view. After all, any method operates by way of a trained blindness: How aware are we of what our particular vision overlooks or brings into view? The video camera might well be perfect not least because it brings in view literally as well as metaphorically the frames we use to capture our research. The point to be made here is to think this awareness at every step of the way, treating the research as an ongoing process which 'means the materials' – the feelings, the codes, the awkward intensities, the architected space, the architecture of time, to name but a few – 'are understood and allowed to develop with intelligence and intuition in every direction' (Knowles, 2006: 105).

Remember, 'something in the world forces us to think' (Deleuze, 1994: 154) but also, and this is Injunction (4), remember we are producing an understanding of the world because the world is not already out there as such (if it were why would we be in such a bother about the methods we chose to capture some aspect of it – it would just be transparently obvious and everyone would see it and get it, and there would be no need for books like this!)

SENSING

If bodies are objects or things, they are like no others, for they are the centers of perspective, insight, reflection, desire, agency. They require quite different intellectual models than those that have been used thus far to represent and understand them. (Grosz, 1994: xi)

This is perhaps the most expansive and important aspect of performative research: that it takes the body seriously. A vast array of papers within geography have emerged over the last decade and a half that all go some way in taking the body more seriously as a key locus and thus focus of research (see Longhurst, 1995; Nast and Pile, 1998). Further, the body features prominently in work advocating a turn to emotional and affect-based geographies (see McCormack, 2003, Davidson and Milligan, 2005) and in the recent return to more explicitly phenomenological accounts of geography (Wylie, 2005, Simonsen, 2007). However, the connective potential of the body taken as a volatile subject as opposed to an object of knowledge, and as an experience achieved through the sensation of a spacing that is both material and immaterial, human and animal, organic and non-organic, is still rarely synthesized or risked in the setting up process of research questions or as the key author of the research findings in their 'final' presentation (see the untapped theoretical concerns of Grosz, 1994).

The directive here is to move into the empirical site with an allegiance towards exposing ourselves towards:

> A kind of energetics, an interest in moments of indeterminacy, undecideability and ambivalence, the abandonment of subject-predicate forms of thought, an orientation to thought as inclusive of affect, and, in general, a sense of the 'tone' of any situation, the play of singularity, which *might* (and only might) produce new virtualizations. (Thrift, 2004: 85)

The idea is to get embroiled in the site and allow ourselves to be infected by the effort, investment, and craze of the particular practice or experience being investigated. Some might call this participation, but it is a mode of participation that is more artistic and, as with most artistic practices, it comes with the side-effect of making us more vulnerable and self-reflexive. It is not however an argument for losing ourselves in the activity and deterritorializing ourselves completely from our academic remit, but nor does it mean sitting on the sidelines and judging. Rather the move, in immersing ourselves in the space, is to gather a portfolio of ethnographic 'exposures' that can act as lightening rods for thought. It is then in those key 'times out' as we set upon generating inventive ways of addressing and intervening in that which is happening, and has happened, as an academic, that such a method produces its data: a series of testimonies to practice. This is of course the flipping over of 'participant observation' to 'observant participation' that Nigel Thrift made (2000) to emphasize the serious empirical involvement involved in non-representational theory's engagement with practices, embodiment and materiality. This was made in part to caution against the ease with which non-representational theory's conceptual bent could become dismissed as engineering a distance from actual hand-to-mouth, flesh and blood, living matters (see also Laurier and Philo, 2003: 91). Not so – it is more a question of a localized tactics for research that operates a close proximity to its object either by tracking and questioning intently the role of object-to-body relations themselves and/or more precisely because it is achieved through the body itself. One difficulty is that this methodological engagement really does expose the body to, or in, us. Not only does it really take the body seriously, it does so with a microscopic intensity and attention to its borderless and controlling fluidity that unfolds it and continually places it within the ecology of its material surroundings. This is disarming and alarming in suggesting further that the body does not choose to think but is rather forced to think in its 'serially self-orgainizing generative movement' (Massumi, 2002: xxxi).

One consistent feature of this method is then its address of the minutiae of import enacting, moving through, and being dispersed by the body itself. Mike Crang ends the last of his progress reports on qualitative methods with this exact provocation: that whilst the body has become 'an important topic of work' it is 'not yet something *through* which the research is often done'

(2005: 232). So whilst there are many aspects that get played up, a key and consistent feature of performative research is a concentrated interest in the somatic and the quality of immediate experience. Untethered from the corset of interpretation, the focus and the sense making of this research comes from thinking through explicit bodily dispositions – feelings and movements or 'intelligence-as-act' (Melrose, 1994) – such as 'the endorphin-enhanced glow of high-level cardiovascular functioning, the slow savouring awareness of improved, deeper breathing, the tingling thrill of feeling into new parts of one's spine' (Shusterman, 2000: 137). The body is then definitively thought through and presented in the research itself as the locus of sensory appreciation prior to the resulting sensation's interpretation via existing knowledge, discourse, practice and bodily discipline that structure the somatic experience (Shusterman, 2000). Deleuze's book on the paintings of Francis Bacon, *The Logic of Sensation*, exhibits one way of presenting such body thought. Of particular note is how Deleuze writes sensation in its 'excessive and spasmodic appearance' as something 'immediately conveyed in the flesh through the nervous wave or vital emotions' (2003: 44). Armed with this mode of expression, and its expressive vocabulary, the researcher can have the confidence of using her or his body directly in the field as a recording machine itself, knowing that writing these nervous energies, amplitudes and thresholds down, is feasible as such jottings become legitimate data for dissemination and analysis.

Such a methodological approach is not without critical tensions but it does not try and smooth these out; rather it embraces the cut of these tensions as the very constitutive heart of what performative research is about. Perhaps the key tension, and let's face it the unique tensions are not that extensive, is how to deal with any performance's flawed materiality: in other words, its present tenseness or its presence and movement as formal disappearance. The problem has its solution, and that is to stage aggressively and with

confidence this appearance and disappearance, and not to worry about maintaining
coherence outside that which is in evidence
in the very act of appearing and disappearing.
The point is now to engage in the research
and move towards creating presentations of
the experience that we encounter and create.
Significantly, these presentations can, and
should, be bookended: 'prologued' by the
explicit thinking and intentions that lead
us into the enterprise in the first place, and
'epilogued' by an explicit accounting of what
we hope our mode of dissemination is trying
to show as a trace of the empirical experience
itself.

Further, performative research asks what
practical engagement we as researchers have
with the world. Whilst this is not always so
directly involved with political intervention
with policy outcomes, it is practical as it
engages precisely with thinking and experiencing thought itself, and as such can make
important interventions in the world. Derek
McCormack's work, in particular his 2002
'A paper with an interest in rhythm', is
exemplary of this stance towards research.
Here he shapes, within the black-and-white
parameters of the classic journal page, movement 'with and through the expressive and
theoretical spaces of an interest in rhythm'
(2002: 469). McCormack simply presents,
albeit in a theoretically nuanced way, the
space-time, spacing-timing, experiences of a
body-environment assemblage (in his case, a
dance workshop). What is important to note
is that it is purposefully expressive and
experimental, that it considers the practical
spaces of the empirical encounters on show
to be equally and simultaneously theoretical,
and that what is being researched as such is
not a body, dance or a dance, nor a particular practice or an individual expertise or historical biography, but 'an interest in rhythm'
itself. This 'interest in rhythm' is just that; it
is not mine, nor McCormack's, nor a definitive accounting of or for rhythm itself, but
rather an immediate and emergent and real
practical-theoretical engagement that produces particular space-time connections and

thus particular modes for manifesting such
connections, for manifesting 'an interest in
rhythm'. The injunction here is that the arguments and diagrams of such space-time connections that McCormack presents are a
quite legitimate space to justify a research
agenda: let's use it to experiment ourselves.
In that paper, McCormack offers up his own
criteria for judgement, that all he is trying to
do is 'enliven the repertoire of ways in which
geographies are creatively enacted' (2002:
483). Why not? If we want to dispute this, we
might as well start arguing against going to
the theatre, or engaging with, and hence validating, any work of art. Injunction (5): diagram quite straightforwardly the space-time
connections you experience with a palette
and sensibility akin to the artistic. The arts
matter: that we don't know for sure how or
why they matter is the point behind their
creative mattering.

Works of art – yes, this whole project is
productive of something, and is of course
contextualized by the historical, political
context of that production. But 'The play's
the thing/Wherein I'll catch the conscience
of the King' (Shakespeare, *Hamlet*, c1600;
Act II, Scene II, 600–1). It is all about being
productive of apprehension, of catching the
overlooked conscience behind what is going
on; and being herein productive of thought,
of manifesting differently conscious beings.
Human beings, let us argue, do so much in
the doing, far more than in the sense making
they have of what they think they were doing
or thought they did: 'There is no 'being'
behind doing, effecting, becoming ... the
deed is everything' (Nietzsche, 1967: 45).
Whilst that much may be true, and whilst that
might be a stance for considering research
that can be labelled non-representational,
work done in performance studies places the
singularity and purity of this standpoint – the
attention to the immediacy of the somatic,
the physiological and the images of those
body-brain-culture relays (Connolly, 2002) –
with the sociological, the political and
the imaginary in order to make apparent the
'performative interfaces occurring between

history, corporeality, power, language, and the sensorial' and thereby 'investigate processes where history and body create unsuspected sensorial-perceptual realms' and 'alternative modes for life to be lived' (Lepecki and Banes, 2006: 1).

So whilst the somatic experience should be prioritized, it is not left hanging as something incongruous and ephemeral. Andre Lepecki and Sally Banes implicitly indicate four ways of focusing research into the sensing post the sensation itself. Modifying these for our purposes, and signalling them as spaces for micro attention in research, they are as follows: where the corporeal meets the social, the somatic meets the historical, the cultural meets the biological and the imagination meets the flesh. When witnessing such performances, whether in being a member of a theatre audience or as a passerby in the street just literally encountering another body, we intuit more or less localized, more or less momentary, more or less material, constructions of body and sense, such that we have either a fairly clear socially defined response with a sense of its meaning-making or a more affective and felt response that whilst not so tangibly clear still disposes us to a course of action. Performative research addresses this meaning-making precisely in its localized, momentary and materially constituted existence, researching and valourizing the need to research the politics of appearing it facilitates such that:

> Whether this appearing, this stepping of the sensed object or subject into the fore of perception, happens visually, or happens rather as an olfactory, or tactile, or proprioceptive, or gustary, or aural experience (or as a combination of, or synthesis between, different sensory organs), the imbrication of sensory perception with language and memory makes the senses a matter of urgency for understanding the conditions under which the body interfaces with and assigns privileges to certain modes of the perceptible while condemning other modes to the shadows of the imperceptible and the valueless. (Lepecki and Banes, 2006: 2)

Ultimately the recording project of the empirical data is one which operates by allowing the research to grow and acquire a coherence of its own. As it grows, the research doesn't become more 'whole' but more complex and multiple in its implications (after Rajchman, 2000: 24). Thus it is rhizomatic: it is connective, and therefore not merely happenstance, but in these connections, and the implications of its findings, it is not hierarchical and overwrought in asserting definite results. The implications are in effect an encounter for their next user. Performative research, perhaps more than other methodologies, demands that we generate the 'next users' of our research: in many ways our body has been used as the witness of the empirical experience and now we have to convince, or at least make problematic easy judgement (dismissal), by the nature of our testimony – and it is to that that the chapter turns in its final section.

PRESENTING

> The critic in me could read this text, elaborate its essentialisms, mediate its mystifications ... but the rest of me prefers to give it to you unprotected. Another fragile dream of a not-yet built body still beckoning for image. (Phelan, 1997: 22)

How to present performance when it is not a performance any longer, and then, as so often, in another medium altogether – (you cannot write dance)? As academics we mediate most things in text, and there have been many examples of performative research being disseminated in performatively tuned accounts whether that be as ethnographies of self-in-performance as performer (see Smith, 2000; Morton, 2005), within the politics of performing research (Pratt, 2000), in other ethnographies akin to our anthropological inheritance (see Crang, 1994), or within the frames of video ethnographic investigation (Jacobs *et al.*, 2008). And we have *Cultural Geographies in Practice* as journal space for more experimental exhibitions in text. But perhaps it is not to art per se, and its other modes of presenting (dancing a research paper for example (see Conquergood, 1998)), but rather the thinking behind the artistic that matters most here: fragile unprotected not-yet fully discernible images have cause.

To begin with, whilst it has long been accepted that the author is not a neutral vector for the conveying of information, the performative method utilizes this fact up front exposing it to open up the possibility of experimenting with the manner and mode of the statements through which the research can be made 'known'. Any methodology is troubled by the imperative to capture and then evidence the empirical sites of research. In this the form of showing chosen, be that an interview transcript or a photograph, is often selected on the basis of being better able to reflect back the world – but, contra an overwrought essentialism, we now take for granted that there is no one world out there. Therefore we all try to do as best we can in the time we have whatever method and research design we have chosen. But here, in relation to doing performative research, we want to be explicit about the creative possibilities in this move from capturing to evidencing research. We want to prise it open and indulge it a little in order: 'To tend to the stretch of expression, to foster and inflect it rather than trying to own it … to enter the stream, contributing to its probings: this is co-creative, an aesthetic endeavour' (Massumi, 2002: xxii). What part of this 'stretch' entails, and it is not easy to swallow, is, as Stephen Zagala notes in commenting on 'Deleuze and Guattari's frequent attention to modernists such as Paul Klee, Jackson Pollock, Claude Debussy and Samuel Beckett', a move towards the creation of 'abstract languages that have a certain autonomy from representational systems of reference' which are then seen as an 'engagement with the 'new' as something which is essentially disruptive, rather than a desire for transcendence and aesthetic idealism' (2002: 22).

So what does this mean for us? The social-science mode might be to use video or powerpoint or sound playback as a tool for straightforwardly presenting ideas or 'evidence'; there is nothing wrong with that as long as no greater claim is made for what is on show. In the humanities, often having had training towards gaining an eye for productive creative arts, such technologies of presentation are used for precisely that, presentation, to hold attention, entertain or to offer up as a means of communication an embodied experience there and then in the time of the presentation itself. Here we would be making rather than using video, manipulating words and sentences rather than taking a word or image merely as a fixed container of an accepted idea. Now expression is rather more tortured and unbound, and its content is no longer viewed 'as having an objective existence prior and exterior to the form of its expression' (Massumi, 2002: xv). In other words, the mode and/or form of expression conveys as much of the message or point being conveyed as the so-called content of that which is expressed. An excellent example of this open dialogue between expression and meaning (or art and inquiry) is the work of Inkeri Sava and Kari Nuutinen (2003) where they stage explicitly between themselves, one a writer/academic the other a painter/artist, how word and picture meet each other, and do so towards a performance to an audience as the mode of dissemination. So in effect we can solicit and co-opt the audience to make the presentation meaningful. In other words, the audience can be used far more effectively, productively, and explicitly, to help us script the meaning and findings of the research (which will probably be a series of further questions for research based upon the problematics raised and staged). But crucially this is not just participation for it is far more disruptive arguing that what is staged is the fact that modes of expression are also modes of registration: therefore it is the mode of registration that makes something visible and shared.

However a further step is still to be made, for the modes of expression that most rely upon immediate presentation can of course be the only means for making and sharing some phenomena. What this means is that the mode of expression also constructs quite explicitly the audience that is being 'expressed' to. Thus: 'How we think of an audience is a function of how we think about ourselves, social institutions, epistemological processes, what is knowable, what not, and how, if at all, we may accommodate the urge for collective experience' (Blau, 1990: 28). In no small part, what is being signalled here is how what we audience as our research, and when we do so, contributes to the making of the relationship between the individual and the collective; or rather the researcher and the wider research community that validates the efforts of the research. We thus constitute what makes up that relationship by our choice of means of expression; and we valorize those things that do make up that relationship even if that means confronting the difficulty of giving account of ephemeral and intangible experiences. But isn't it often the case that such intangible experiences are precisely the bridges between individuality and communicability in the face of a shared experience? Instead of representing some fact about a given event or phenomena, the issue is to point to the co-presencing that comes about in sharing the same physical space and the same temporal frame in a direct and immediate relationship through a broadly similar physicality (i.e. we are human animals who communicate in all manner of ways through our body). This acceptance composes the cultural habitus through which we construct the meaning-making of our lives; it means we give credence to, and wish to track as research, those moments when something 'happens' that glues us together – moments like 'the buzz of anticipation' in a large gathering, or 'the heightened attention' resulting from a mutually directed gaze, or 'the sense of shared tension and subsequent relief'. We are of course active interpreters of experience and not passive recipients – so on this methodological path we must acknowledge that we confront a classic chicken-and-egg dilemma: which comes first, sensation or representation? Perhaps the single point to take home from this chapter, and from the conduct of

performative methods, is that we can as easily emphasize sensation over representation in the first instance, whereas it is perhaps the habitual status quo to start with representation which thus avoidably but unwittingly relegates the import of sensation itself. Injunction (6): instead of concentrating on the cultural product, concentrate on the cultural experience.

There is though no prescription as to how to carry out the presentation of performative research. We can do it as usual as is more often the case. But we can, and this is crucial, we can experiment as if it were a performance, by asking much more explicitly a series of performative questions. So for example, if we are using video playback in our presentation, what are we using the technology to say? And who are our audience? Will they get it? Do we want them to immediately get it? Perhaps we want them to go away discussing, dissenting, and probing, thereby animating further the talk or paper in a space of perplexion. Challenge an audience to take the research presented to task, but challenge knowingly. So who do we want our audience to be – on side, bored, agitated, enthused? What demands do we want to make of our audience and to what ends? We thus have to be extremely vigilant as we frame our research and select our findings and mode of dissemination. In all of this, it is not a question of 'why not' to every which way we can manipulate rhetorically the presentation of our research, but an explicit attention, and freedom, to be much more artistic in that attention. So it is to question 'why so', and even to question our own means of presenting the research as a live performance; thus the dissemination of research becomes a further part of the research itself. 'Why so' then: 'Why do the research in this way, and why present in the manner that we are doing'?

If we are explicit in our attentions we can of course be judged to fail more easily. Again that is the point: expose our presuppositions to be tasked to that disruptive rethinking again. The point is that the presentation of research for performative methods is also research in itself, if not even a continuation of the research. So fail again, and fail better: that is research. Research here then means questioning 'how information and interaction are 'framed' so as to allow for common sense' (Rajchman, 2000: 11); and to continue this questioning as we frame our own research in the mode of presentation we use. So these caveats and uncertainties said, what purpose and purchase is there for performative presentations of our research findings, be they in writing, video playback or theatrical presentation of one form or another including jazzed up powerpoints? If in such presentations the aim is to 'enact the affective force of the performance event again', following Peggy Phelan (1997: 8) we must be acutely aware at all times that these re-presented events will 'sound differently' in the new presentations of them than in the 'experiencing' of them. Therefore, like Phelan, 'it is the urgent call of that difference that' we need 'to amplify here' (1997: 12), and not some nervous sense of being inferior to science in seeking to understand the social by covering up the difference that does so much to make the social alive, political, invigorating, dangerous and wonderful: that difference of not knowing what the other is thinking, of not knowing whether it is a feeling rather than a thought that is moving us, because in micro what is at stake here is the cosmological difference between now and then, ever on.

Or the difference in the heartbeat of the next moment, and the question of whether we can plan for the next encounter, or whether we find our body forced into some new unforeseen connection that we will shortly give some sense to (albeit that there are many sense-making possibilities). And then the difference of what sense we chose to make of it, and how that in turn frames how we make sense of it; it then 'sounds differently' and bifurcates life's path. In achieving this amplification as legitimate knowledge, one needs above all to be confident in presenting this difference with a faith of being 'solicitous of affect' whilst 'nervous and tentative about

the consequences of that solicitation' (Phelan, 1997: 12). It is worth remembering as we set about this task that it is not a transparent representation that we are after, nor is it about the representation being a true reflection of the empirical experience or event being investigated (given that we are playing up the difference of that impossibility, that being the more 'truthful' aspect here), rather it is a stance that 'wishes all the same to say' in that it is the attempt at articulation rather than its success that counts, and where the articulation made will always be performative in itself. As such our presentations after non-representational and affect-based research are 'alternately bold and coy, manipulative and unconscious' pointing both to themselves 'and to the "scenes" that motivate' them (Phelan, 1997: 12). The injunction here is (7): remember you cannot directly signify that which is past, so be more acute and cute in the research stories that you tell.

CONCLUSIONS: THERE IS A RUB

It is not a question of anything going, for when conducting performative methods with a non-representational theoretical, practice, and affect-based bent, the thinking, sensing, presenting aspects should be all specific interferences – interferences in problematizing how we think the world and how the world forces us to think, in attending intensely to the fluid, nervous, fleshy dispositions of our body's agency, and in how the world records itself on its surfaces both on the skin and in the cell, and in experimenting with the images we produce in disseminating our research across an open and mutually transforming nexus of expression, content, form and audience effect.

The new normative question therefore becomes which of these interferences are good ones. And when, where, in which context, and for whom they are good. Good knowledge, then, does not draw its worth from *living up* to reality. What we should seek, instead, are worthwhile ways of *living with* the real. (Mol, 2006: 121)

As such there is a political and strategic weight to the methodological pointers outlined here. This is important, for all along it has been the case that the way research is framed matters more than any other aspect, and perhaps nowhere is this framing more sharply felt and orientated than in the end-game point of the research's application. And let us be clear about that here: conducting performative research aims and justifies its endeavours by being about trying to manifest 'the not-yet-captured ontological condition of limit-attractions' (Caspao, 2007: 136). Now whilst this advocates embracing uncertainty through experimentation in a way that might seem frivolous and self-indulgent to some, the point is precisely about 'giving way to the eruption of singular-sense combinations that don't necessarily fit in with the consensually established ones' (2007: 139). We can miss a trick if we solely task ourselves in our research to live up to reality, when it is precisely about finding alternative methodological strategies for living with reality. Our 'task is then not only to reconfigure the limits of each of our senses and their relations to one another, but also to constantly push those limits to tensional thresholds of dis-sensus, to produce a crisis in consensus' (Caspao, 2007: 139).

So think then upon what we produce in the name of research as tableaus which offer up operative openings through specific bodily engagement for particular spheres of concern. If artistic expression matters, then so does proximity to their methods matter in social science. This politically affirms another way of going on, another way of going about the business of making research interferences that matter, that create, that affirm full stop. This is the endgame this chapter has been working towards – a resolute experimentalism that is productive, that proliferates, and creates such interferences, for:

Yes, I believe that there is a multiple people, a people of mutants, a people of potentialities that appears and disappears, that is embodied in social events, literary events, and musical events. I'm often accused of being exaggeratedly, stupidly, stubbornly optimistic, and of not seeing people's wretchedness. I can see it, but ... I don't know, perhaps I'm raving, but I think that we're in a period of productivity, proliferation, creation, utterly fabulous revolutions from the viewpoint of this emergence of a people. (Guattari, 2008: 9)

REFERENCES

Bailey, C., White, C. and Pain, R. (1999) 'Evaluating qualitative research, dealing with the tensions between "science" and "creativity"', *Area* 31 (2): 169–83.

Baxter, J. and Eyles, J. (1997) 'Evaluating qualitative research in social geography: establishing "rigour" in interview analysis', *Transactions of the Institute of British Geographers* 22 (4): 505–25.

Beckett, S. (1987) *Westward ho!*. London: John Calder Publishers.

Blau, H. (1990) *The audience*. Baltimore, MD: Johns Hopkins University Press.

Butler, J. (1997) *Excitable speech: a Politics of the Performative*. London: Routledge.

Caspao, P. (2007) 'Stroboscopic stutter: the not-yet-captured ontological condition of limit-attractions', *TDR: The Drama Review* 51 (2): 136–56.

Connolly, W. (2002) *Neuropolitics: thinking, culture, speed*, Minneapolis, MN: University of Minnesota Press.

Conquergood, D. (1998) 'Beyond the text: toward a performative cultural politics', in S.J. Dailey (ed.) *The future of performance studies: visions and revisions*. Annadale, VA: National Communication Association. pp. 25–36.

Crang, P. (1994) '"It's showtime!" On the workplace geographies of display in a restaurant in South East England', *Environment and Planning D: Society and Space* 12 (6): 675–704.

Crang, M. (2005) 'Qualitative methods: there is nothing outside the text?', *Progress in Human Geography* 29 (2): 225–33.

Davidson, J. and Milligan, C. (2005) 'Editorial – embodying emotion sensing space: introducing emotional geographies', *Social and Cultural Geography* 5 (4): 523–32.

Deleuze, G. (1988) *Foucault*. London: The Athlone Press.

Deleuze, G. (1994) *Difference and repetition*. London: The Athlone Press.

Deleuze, G. (2004) *Francis Bacon: the logic of sensation*. London: Continuum Press.

Elam, D. (1994) *Feminism and deconstruction*. London: Routledge.

Foucault, M. (1966) *The order of things: an archaeology of the human sciences*. London:

Foucault, M. (1972) *The archaelogy of knowledge*. London: Tavistock Publications.

Grosz, E. (1994) *Volatile bodies: toward a corporeal feminism*. Bloomington, IN: Indiana University Press.

Guattari, F. (2008) *Molecular revolution in Brazil*. Los Angeles: Semiotext(e).

Hallward, P. (2006) *Out of this world: Deleuze and the philosophy of creation*. London: Verso.

Haraway, D. (1995) *Simians, Cyborgs, and women: the reinvention of nature*. London: Free Association Books.

Irigaray, L. (1985) *The sex which is not one*. New York: Cornell University Press.

Jacobs, J.M., Cairns, S.R., and Strebel, I. (2008) 'Windows: re-viewing Red Road', *Scottish Geographical Journal* 124 (2): 165–84.

Knowles, A. (2006) '"Process" in "A lexicon"', *Performance Research* 11 (3): 105.

Lepecki, A. and Banes, S. (2006) 'Introduction: the performance of the senses', in A. Lepecki and S. Banes (eds) *The senses in performance: 1 (worlds of performance)*. London: Routledge. pp. 1–7.

Laurier, E. and Philo, C. (2003) 'The region in the boot: mobilising lone subjects and multiple objects' *Environment and Planning D: Society and Space* 21 (1): 85–106.

Longhurst, R. (1995) 'The body and geography', *Gender, Place and Culture* 2 (1): 97–105.

Lorimer, H. (2005) 'Cultural geography: the busyness of being "more-than-representational"', *Progress in Human Geography* 29 (1): 83–94.

Massumi, B. (2002) 'Introduction: like a thought' in B. Massumi (ed.) *A shock to thought: expression after Deleuze and Guattari*. London: Routledge. pp. xiii–xxxix.

McCormack, D.P. (2002) 'A paper with an interest in rhythm', *Geoforum* 33 (4): 469–85.

McCormack, D.P. (2003) 'An event of geographical ethics in spaces of affect', *Transactions of the Institute of British Geographers* 28 (4): 488–507.

Melrose, S. (1994) *A semiotics of the dramatic text*. London: Saint Martin's Press Inc.

Mol, A. (2002) *The body multiple: ontology in medical practice*. Durham: Duke University Press.

Morton, F. (2005), 'Performing ethnography: Irish traditional music sessions and new musical spaces', *Social and Cultural Geography* 6 (5): 661–76.

Moss, P. (2007) *Feminisms in geography: rethinking space, place, and knowledges*. Lanham, MD: Rowman & Littlefield.

Nast, H. and Pile, S. (1998) *Places through the body*. London: Routledge.

Nietzsche, F. (1967) *On the genealogy of morals*. New York: Vintage.

Phelan, P. (1993) *Unmarked: the politics of performance*. London: Routledge.

Phelan, P. (1997) *Mourning sex: performing public memories*. London: Routledge.

Pratt, G. (2000) 'Research performances', *Environment and Planning D: Society and Space* 18 (5): 639–51.

Rajchman, J. (2000) *The Deleuze connections*. Cambridge, MA: The MIT Press.

Rancière, J. (2007) *The future of the image*. London: UK: Verso.

Rose, G. (1993) *Feminism and geography*. Cambridge: Polity Press.

Rose, G. (1997) 'Situating knowledges: positionality, reflexivities and other tactics', *Progress in Human Geography* 21 (3): 305–20.

Sava, I. and Nuutinen, K. (2003) 'At the meeting place of word and picture: between art and inquiry', *Qualitative Inquiry* 9 (4): 515–34.

Simonsen, K. (2007) 'Practice, spatiality and embodied emotions: an outline of a geography of practice', *Human Affairs* 17 (2): 168–81.

Shusterman, R. (2000) *Performing live: aesthetic alternatives for the ends of art*. New York: Cornell University Press.

Smith, S.J. (2000) 'Performing the (sound)world', *Environment and Planning D: Society and Space* 18 (5): 615–37.

Taussig, M. (1993) *Mimesis and alterity: a particular history of the senses*. London: Routledge.

Thrift, N. (2000) 'Afterwords', *Environment and Planning D: Society and Space* 18 (3): 213–55.

Thrift, N. (2004) 'Summoning Life' in P. Cloke, P. Crang and M. Goodwin (eds) *Envisioning human geographies*. London: Arnold. pp. 81–103.

Thrift, N. (2008) *Non-representational theory: space/politics/affect*. London: Routledge.

Wylie, J. (2005) 'A single day's walking: narrating self and landscape on the South West Coast Path,' *Transactions of the Institute of British Geographers* 30 (2): 234–47.

Zagala, S. (2002) 'Aesthetics: a place I've never seen', in B. Massumi (ed.) *A shock to thought: expression after Deleuze and Guattari*. London: Routledge. pp. 20–43.

PART III

Making Sense

Making Sense: Introduction

Mike Crang

Writing and communicating our research is painful for many of us; making sense can be a significant challenge, especially when there's something to be said for messiness itself, for not reducing the complex world to a few tidy research findings. My own first attempt to write about making sense as messy and unstable and as itself just as theoretically and epistemologically loaded as any other stage in the research process, appeared as a chapter called 'Telling Materials' (Crang, 2003), whose draft text is still labelled 'D834' in my files – the course number of the Open University postgraduate research methods training module in geography for which it was written. And as one of the other editors of this volume told me, the collection based on that module baffles students since it refuses to box the theory away at the start. Thankfully they did not seem to have noticed my contribution to that bafflement.

The chapters in this section are all concerned in varying ways with the outcomes and outputs of qualitative work. In their various ways they work to destabilise two prevalent assumptions about the concluding stages of qualitative research. First, they challenge the awful phrases we have to learn to use in funding-body reports and university management plans – outputs and deliverables. Second they challenge the notion of simple temporal stages of research – moving predictably from

idea to fieldwork to findings, through a macabre set of spatial steps in a circular dance from academy to world and back to the cloisters. They challenge the dreadful model of linear stages whereby research is conceived, executed and then results are disseminated as 'outputs' of some research machine. Third, they then develop from this to point out that the understandings we ground and gain through qualitative research are in the most profound way created, fabricated and produced – we are *making* sense, not finding it out. Finally, they also point to the fragility of that sense not in terms of robust logic or clever ideas but rather how the notion of what sense is made, needs to be complicated – questioning not only the process of *making* sense but the nature and stakes in the *sense* that is made.

First, then, in the auditable, accountable neoliberal university, we are increasingly disciplined to speak in terms of measurable outcomes, preferably predictable in advance. Through the earlier chapters in this book we can see that such a discourse drains the contingency and eventfulness from research, and positively silences the revelatory and transformatory moments of research processes – especially, but by no means exclusively, qualitative work. The chapters in this section do not though simply make clear that great research, of all kinds, by definition, very often produces ideas we did not have at the start. Nor do they take the line that somehow qualitative methods are singularly unamenable to these constraints – a line of argument that is dangerously open to the marginalisation of such methods in the eyes of funders and managers. Instead, they raise queries over the position of outcomes and their nature, and how our work sits ambivalently and uncomfortably within a world where outcomes are measured, and projects delivered.

Dydia DeLyser's chapter offers an elegant refutation of the idea that findings are out there and are then 'written up'. She illustrates how writing becomes a way of doing and a way of thinking – not a final phase. Similarly, Sara MacKian offers an insight into going beyond the mechanistic notions of interpretation as analysis and stressing it is a transformative process. She points to the need to go beyond the data to look at silences, to read into it and restore a sense of the creativity, contingency, to offer work that does not just speak to the richness of its materials but their hesitations and unclarities as well. Both though unpack the sense of mystique around making sense of qualitative work, that Sara MacKian and others elsewhere have pointed out exists around analysis – reduced either to a mechanistic and soulless vision of 'coding', or instead depending upon inspiration or some exceptional insight which emerges mysteriously (Schiellerup, 2008). While textbooks trying to offer guides generally are content to follow the old saw that most things are 99% perspiration and 1% inspiration (e.g. Crang and Cook, 2007: 145), DeLyser's chapter instead refuses this division of creativity versus arduous work, and instead embeds practices of creativity in writing, through training oneself to develop ideas and think through material. Her chapter looks at the different modes of expression that might speak to different audiences, making room for styles from the formal, the experimental to the realist. Instead of focusing upon written outcomes, Paul Routledge looks at those that are performative and processual between the researcher

and the participants. The notion of academic outputs being conveyed to represent participants to some state actor (in both epistemological and political senses) that subtends many of the calls for 'relevant research' is neatly subverted. It raises new problems to be sure but we can also see here the way this upends the linear logic of research outputs when the research practice here is meant to prefigure and create openings and possibilities rather than produce fixed results.

The second issue about the circular spatiality assumed in a linear and productivist model of research flows from this. Thus for Routledge the idea of separating the academy is politically troubling. He specifically aims not to withdraw from the fray to some contemplative ivory tower. Indeed, the point of the clown army is to suggest that far from the chaos of research being made sense of in the groves of academe, it is the fieldwork that highlights the ordinary everyday madness of the world, and the academy within it. The conflicts and compromises of working between the two settings raises many issues for activist work, issues that also resonate far more widely. Thus in the situation Garth Myers recounts in his chapter, a collaboration in the field is complicated by two very different and distant sets of institutional positions and politics over the production of knowledge. His chapter addresses the issues of who gains and who might suffer in a complex world where outcomes are unsure, and where the spatial circularity of fieldwork, academic work and more fieldwork, results in outputs circulating back amongst the field – which itself is not so easily localisable or bounded – as collaborators move and indeed audiences for his work feed material back there.

If the field is thus expanded and promiscuously entwined with the academy, both Myer's chapter and Deb Martin's then unpack the academy. Myer's chapter looks at the relationships his fieldwork creates for him with different communities of scholars and indeed the relations of communities at home with those in his field site. Martin's chapter focuses on the way qualitative research itself feeds back as practice into the academy. Her autoethnographic account of qualitative teaching in a US graduate school returns us to some of the pressures for outcomes and milestones, as she looks at the demands of differently positioned students who want a model that promises linearity and predictability, whilst her teaching uses methods to illustrate the plurality of theoretical ontologies and epistemologies that compete in the academy in order to undercut those very notions of research. In many ways her pedagogy tries to carry through the moves highlighted in this introduction and, in ways that will be familiar as well to those outside the US who teach qualitative methods, the destabilising and unpredictable nature of qualitative work engenders excitement and fear in often equal measure, encountering student enthusiasm for sure but also resistance and desire for an orderly model of knowledge production.

Such ambivalent responses and the recursivity of pedagogy, methods, and theory resonate painfully for many of us. That Open University course for which I wrote 'D834' was designed to meet UK research council requirements for graduate methods training which offers a counterpoint to Martin's account of the US. Indeed her reflections on the quarter of US graduate programmes providing qualitative courses raises clear issues of the geography of postgraduate education, and indeed the geographical variation of geographical traditions.

The third thing all these papers thus reveal is that knowledge is made, not found. Through the practices of writing, the creative moves of rendering the field encounter alive, or the consideration of needs of collaborative workers for different kinds of work with different effects, the chapters show how qualitative research is indeed about crafting a work whose form and effects are contingently produced through the researcher's own subjectivity, inter-subjective understandings and institutional structures. No form of work necessarily follows from a given type of topic, fieldwork or materials. Indeed we

might perhaps turn the linear sense of research around to say (qualitative) research seeks not to present results *to* the world but to produce results *in* different audiences and spaces in which they are encountered – from academic peers, to academic assessors, to policy makers (or those who may have access to them), to students, to participants and many, many more. Knowledge is made in the web of audiences and expectations and intentions of different actors. Those multiple contexts and forms of knowledge and competing claims may conflict or collide. Knowledge is always partly a work of translation between contexts and criteria. As the papers suggest, sometimes, if you are lucky, it might just also be a moment of transformation.

In this way the papers offer a final challenge to the notion of making *sense* as the end point of research. There is something commonsensically appealing to geographers about making sense of the world. Perhaps a relic of injunctions to plain writing, that DeLyser shows are so freighted with assumptions, perhaps connected to realist models and correspondence models of truth, and ever so popular with students as Martin's work suggests, a logic of demystification and rendering clear pervades much of geography of all methodological flavours. But one of the aphorisms I like to quote to students is where Walter Benjamin rather (un)helpfully pointed out that there is all the difference in the world between a confused presentation and the presentation of confusion. That latter, the presentation of the madness of the world, of its messiness, of its vitality comes through in Routledge's performative art, in Mackian's engagement with artists themselves connected to groups like the Guerrilla Geographers. The creation of new meanings and effects in audiences perhaps offers a counterpoint to the logics of demystification where our work holds up some clear mirror to the world, where our good representations counter the world's confusing ones (Morris, 1992). Instead, these chapters point to sense making as contingent yes, but also open to new senses beyond the cognitive, beyond the reductive, for which qualitative work might open up space.

REFERENCES

Crang, M. (2003) 'Telling materials', in M. Pryke, G. Rose and S. Whatmore (eds) *Using social theory.* London: Sage.

Crang, M. and Cook, I. (2007) *Doing ethnographies.* London: Sage.

Morris, M. (1992) 'The man in the mirror: David Harvey's "Condition of postmodernity", *Theory, Culture and Society* 9: 253–79.

Schiellerup, P. (2008) 'Stop making sense: the trials and tribulations of qualitative data analysis', *Area* 40: 163–71.

19

Writing Qualitative Geography

Dydia DeLyser

In 1903 the Czech-born poet Rainer Maria Rilke penned words of advice to a young man then aspiring to a life of writing but who, like Rilke before him, was faced instead with the prospect of life in the military. Rilke (1934: 16–17) counseled,

> Go into yourself. Investigate the reason that bids you write; find out whether it is spreading out its roots in the deepest places of your heart, acknowledge to yourself whether you would have to die if it were denied you to write. This above all: ask yourself in the stillest hour of your night: must I write? Delve into yourself for a deep answer. And if this should be affirmative, if you may meet this earnest question with a strong and simple 'I must,' then build your life according to this necessity; your life even into its most indifferent and slightest hour must be a sign of this urge and a testimony to it.

Rilke wrote from his own true conviction, and his words, published in one of his most famous prose works (*Letters to a Young Poet*, first translated into English in 1934 and today still in print), have served as inspiration for generations of poets, artists, and writers.

Still, for many academics, geographers included, the call to write seems frankly often understood not through the profundity of its personal need but instead through a professional need: most frequently the need to publish, understood as linked to the need

for tenure and promotion. As anthropologist Harry Wolcott (1990: 10) has observed, most of us (academics) are not professional writers but 'professionals who must write'; we often write 'because others expect [us] to contribute to the field.' And, while Rilke, who struggled with poverty for much of his life, might have understood the economic motivations that are partly behind such academic 'needs,' in this chapter I attempt to understand both Rilke's advice and academics' needs to write, more richly. As scholars engaged in active conversations with other scholars, as researchers engaged in active programs together with the people and the communities where we place our work, and as academics who seek, in multiple ways, to create links between those worlds – and importantly to shed light and proffer benefit on both – writing is our most frequent, our most lasting, and our most profound opportunity to accomplish those goals. Furthermore, writing is not only our most important means of communicating our research, it is itself a way of thinking, and a way of thinking through our research – writing, as this chapter will show, is a significant research method in itself.

Nevertheless, not two decades ago, Trevor Barnes and James Duncan (1992: 1) declared that 'Very little attention is paid to writing in human geography.' This chapter, along with a number of others in other books as well as articles in journals, is an active effort to remedy that oversight. In fact, in the years since Barnes and Duncan's observation, geographers writing about writing have changed that situation considerably, until nowadays books on research methods and methodologies for geographers (like this one) nearly always include a chapter on writing (see, for example, Bennet and Shurmer-Smith in Limb and Dwyer, 2001; Cloke *et al.*, 2004; DeLyser and Pawson in Hay, 2005; Mansvelt and Berg in Hay, 2005; Crang and Cook, 2007; DeLyser in Jones *et al.*, 2010), journal articles at least in significant part about writing seem more common (see, for example, Katz, 1992; Keith, 1992; Pratt, 1992; Doel, 1993; Smith, 1996; Bondi, 1997; Rose, 1997; Valentine, 1998; Barnett, 1999; Pratt, 2000; DeLyser, 2003; Mitchell, 2006) and whole books have paid attention to writing geography (see, for example, Barnes and Duncan, 1992; Cloke *et al.*, 1994; Curry 1996; and Duncan and Gregory, 1999). But paying attention to writing is only the beginning.

In this chapter I urge qualitative geographers to think of ourselves as writers, and explore what I mean by that and what that implies for writing as a qualitative method. Throughout the chapter I engage the words and advice of geographers known for their writing, as well as those in other fields – like anthropology, sociology, and political science, but also literature, poetry, and screen writing – known for theirs. I begin by examining why we write and what engaging the writing process as an active, embodied part of our research can do for our research. I next examine the writing process, what lies behind it, and review sound advice about how to make it productive. I then scrutinize debates within geography about the way geography should be written, taking in as well important debates that reach beyond our field alone to address why the way we write is so important. And, since writing, though in some ways problematic as a means of expression, is the chief form of scholarly communication,

I also present what I consider good counsel, like that of Rilke's but some of it less daunting, about how to make writing a positive part of our lives, in order to gain a deeper understanding of the writing process, a process that, I argue, is a formative part of our research itself. My goal is to convey writing as I understand and live it: as a product and a process, as well as a practice and a praxis, and as an embodied, more-than-representational act.

ENGAGING WRITING AS A QUALITATIVE-RESEARCH METHOD

As students and former students, most of us were probably trained in the 'writing it up' school of writing, where writing is a simple, even almost mechanical act that comes (often hurriedly) at the very end of research in order to link that research (the data we gathered and created) with the analysis we perform in our offices or labs and in our brains. Writing, in this understanding, is the simple way of conveying 'results,' results revealed by the data and otherwise understood only in our minds: to make those results more broadly known we have to write them 'up.' Because research results (and the research process itself) in this model are straightforward and unproblematic, writers who live by the writing-it-up model often also believe that there is only one way of expressing what they've learned from that research: once you've completed everything else you quickly write up your findings in the way that the findings themselves dictate. Writing is a simple, mechanical output directed by the research 'results.' Language theorist and philosopher Richard Rorty (1978: 145) calls this writing as an 'unfortunate necessity' – writing that seems an irritating-but-required interference in the transmission of research findings.

But, as other chapters in this handbook have detailed, qualitative geographers have come to recognize research as anything but a simple or unproblematic undertaking. Each biographically situated qualitative researcher will see, hear, and feel different things, have different interactions with people in the field, and create different understandings. Writing, of course, is no different: each person will write differently, even about the same events and experiences.

Not only that, in qualitative research, the writing, in an important way, is the research. Unlike quantitative research, the 'results' of qualitative research cannot be summarized in a table, re-presented by a map, or, for that matter, effectively encapsulated by an abstract or a 'conclusions' section. Just as a reader cannot expect to 'get' *Ulysses* from only a plot summary, qualitative research must be conveyed in its written entirety (see Richardson, 2000). The voices of those with whom we work, as well as the voice and interpretation(s) of the researcher, and the very telling of the tale itself – the ways those voices are conveyed – are all critical, essential to qualitative geography (and qualitative research more broadly; see Richardson and St. Pierre, 2005).

But understanding these two points about writing qualitative research compels a third: the writing process itself is formative. Indeed, as this section will show, it is an embodied, mindful process that shapes the research itself. As sociologist and writer-about-writing Laurel Richardson (2003: 923) explains, 'Writing is not just a mopping up activity at the end of a research project.' Instead, writing must be understood and engaged as a 'way of "knowing" – a method of discovery and analysis' (Richardson, 2000: 923). This, as Wolcott observes, is different from what one might have been led to believe: 'The conventional wisdom is that writing reflects thinking,' but actually 'writing is thinking' (1990: 21).

Though we were perhaps not trained to understand writing in this way, a diverse group of scholars have come to see it so. 'Writing can be a time for learning,' observes Larry Ford (2006: 130). 'By writing passionately about what you see, feel, and experience, you can teach yourself a lot, even about old, familiar topics' (Ford, 2006: 130). Even the otherwise dispassionate writers-about-writing William Strunk Jr. and E.B. White

(1970 [1959]: 56) agree: 'writing is one way to go about thinking.' And Paul Cloke and colleagues (2004: 338) put it succinctly: 'research is actively constructed through the process of writing.' But what does this view of the writing process suggest, and what does it lead to for qualitative geographers?

Perhaps to a more sophisticated, and more engaged way of understanding writing – both the product and the practice. The written work, after all, is not just a product of research, but is also a physical trace of an embodied act and process, that of writing. Thus, while most have understood written works as mere representations – the inevitably impaired attempts to engage a multi-dimensional affective world and convey it on a two-dimensional page – we can also look further. We can, by attempting to understand and engage the lived practice of writing, attend to the 'non-representational act of writing' rather than just its final product on the finished printed page (Carton, 2007: 1). As Jenny Carton (2007: 1, 2) suggests, we can 'take representation seriously' and 'radically reengage with the act which writing performs.' Understanding literary writing (and I extend this to our academic writing as well) as more than representation, Carton (2007: 4) proposes that we think of writing as something beyond just a finished product, as a literary act, and of writing itself as a 'space of self emergence.' Indeed, rather than viewing writing only as representational product, we can also engage writing as part of an embodied practice that actively shapes both our lives and our research (both the practice and the product).

In fact, as J.D. Dewsbury *et al.* (2002: 438) point out, representations themselves 'are transformers, not causes or outcomes of action but action in themselves.' Casting our research – our thoughts, our interactions, our observations, and those of the people we work with – in written form in part shapes, even creates the work itself. As Cloke *et al.* put it (2004: 336), 'writing is a form of representation (or indeed re-presentation) which helps to create, rather than simply reflect, our geographical experiences.'

Some, like Marcus Doel (1993: 378), would take a stronger stance: 'there is no separation, real or imagined, between existence (things) and writing (words)....' Extending existence to events and observations, we can understand that, from Doel's perspective at least, fieldwork and writing are not separated – writing, as a way of thinking and a part of the research process, cannot be fully separated from the research we do in the field. And that, in turn, can be a productive way to understand the role of writing in our research.

Writing, reading, and research are interlinked as interdependent, iterative processes (Cloke *et al.*, 2004; DeLyser and Pawson, 2005; Mansvelt and Berg, 2005). Writing informs research just as it is informed by research. Engaging writing as an active, embodied process leads not just to the reporting of research results, but to new understandings of what it is the research reveals, understandings gleaned while we write.

These are not new observations. Socialist and political scientist Graham Wallas (in Boyle, 1997: 238) put it bluntly back in 1926, 'How can I know what I think till I see what I say?' Or, as Richardson (2000: 925) phrases it, 'I write in order to learn something that I did not know before I wrote it.' But however we choose to understand writing, and the writing process, for those of us with academic careers, writing will likely become the most important, most significant way we communicate with our peers. That makes the choices we make about the role writing will play in our research, and the ways we will incorporate writing into not just our research but also our lives, among the most significant choices we face as scholars. The choice is ours, each time we write.

BEYOND THE ELUSIVE MUSE

Engaging writing as a part of our research and our lives involves an active, embodied awareness of the writing process – a process that for centuries has seemed elusive, as writers struggle to bring clarity to the complexity of our world. It is possible that Rilke's insistence about the fundamental importance of a 'call' to writing described above may have come from his own particular experiences. Partly, to be sure, from his against-his-wishes experiences with the military. But, importantly for the course of Rilke's writing, throughout his writing life he relied on a muse (in particular, mostly a series of different women) for poetic inspiration as well as, at various times, for emotional and financial sustenance. And this makes Rilke, the physically fragile, emotionally enraptured, penniless (white, male, European) poet, an archetypal example of the romanticized writer (see Freedman, 1996). But for all his brilliance, the romanticized image of the writer Rilke helped inspire and, can be seen to constrict the world of the possible for other (aspiring) writers. The absurd purity of an idealized poverty and fragile health aside, the perceived need for an inspirational muse itself hinders the ability to write, since it proffers the inspirational core of the writing ability to the muse, removing from the writer that essential agency and control over the writing process.

Still, the compelling need (or desire) for a muse, that magical person who inspires great writing, lingers – in poetry, in literature, and in scholarly writing. Seen from a less romanticized viewpoint, the writer's muse falls into the same category as many of the rituals writers often put ourselves through before we write – the perhaps more prosaic but equally compelling needs to have the house in order, to listen to particular music, to write with a special pen, to write only at a particular time of day, or only in a certain room. Sociologist and writer-about-writing Howard Becker (1986) understands such widely shared 'crazy writing habits' as 'magic rituals' of the sort that, cross-culturally, many people feel compelled to engage in order to influence something over which they fear they have no control. Whether our fears focus on the absence of rain, the hazards of an airline flight, or 'getting it wrong,' many of us share a reliance on a variety of 'magic rituals.' Though 'crazy writing habits' in themselves may not be harmful, un-critically engaging in them conflates the writing process over which we, as writers, have control and agency, with processes and events over which we have no influence (rain, an airline crash). Important then, is not to throw out the 'magic' pen, but to take control of the writing process. To bodily understand that writing is different from those other events: we can write at will, and we have agency over its outcome.

But such an embodied relationship to the writing process does not come automatically – it must be cultivated. Writing counselor Joan Bolker (1998) advises we carve fifteen minutes out of each and every day as a way to accustom our minds and bodies to writing. Indeed, writing for fifteen minutes is vastly better than not writing at all precisely because it topples the wall of the blank screen, and reclaims agency over the writing process. Writing daily, even for just fifteen minutes, conditions the body and mind to writing.

With daily practice, writing – the agility needed to create and craft thoughts while we write – can be nurtured like a habit or what Bolker terms a positive addiction, until we want to write, until time set aside for writing becomes a sought-after time for reflection and discovery. Often writers cultivate their craft by setting aside writing time at the same time each day. Some, for example, prefer to begin writing before dawn, when the world around them is at rest, and they condition themselves to this habit until the habit itself, the embodied practice of writing at that time every day, becomes empowering in itself, inspiring the 'feel' for writing at that hour (see Bolker, 1998). But if habits and patterns can be cultivated, they can also be broadened and challenged, stretched to serve wider range. As writers we can train ourselves to write whenever, and wherever the opportunity is available – not just at the magic hour or in the otherwise-appointment-free day, with or without the gentle suasion of favorite music, and not just under the whisper of the

muse. As academics with multiple demands on our time, consciously stretching our abilities and training ourselves to adaptable writing practices can be both productive and empowering.

This, too, is old advice, and still just as valid as ever it was – writer and writing teacher Brenda Ueland declaimed its benefits in 1938 (quoted in Richardson, 2003: 379): 'Writing, the creative effort, should come first – at least for some part of each day of your life. It is a wonderful blessing if you will use it. You will become happier, more enlightened, alive, impassioned, … [and you will lose] all the … ailments of discouragement and boredom.' Further still, she declared (2007 [1938]: 22–3), creative work is 'like a faucet: nothing comes unless you turn it on, and the more you turn it on; the more comes.' Committing oneself to writing regularly is the first step to writing productively and to writing well.

CONVEYING CONCEPTS IN STRAIGHTFORWARD PROSE

Even with a commitment to daily writing, however, writing well does not always follow. 'One of the many problems besetting the academic left (and indeed most of academia),' Katharyne Mitchell (2006: 205) has declared, 'is the miserable quality of our writing. With few exceptions we write for each other [rather than for a broader audience] and we do it with dense, turgid and usually mind-numbingly boring prose.' In efforts to remedy this problem, human geographers have long sought to write in prose simple and straightforward – prose uncomplicated by too much specialized language – in order to communicate effectively with the relatively small community of academic geographers, but also to convey our insights so that an educated non-expert could gain from them.

Behind such efforts often lies the notion that, through straightforward prose what

William Clark calls our 'careful scientific work' could be 'attractive to a wide audience' (2006: 108). Or, as Mitchell (2006: 205) puts it, because 'the point of scholarship … is not just to interpret the world but also to change it … it is imperative that our writing … reaches a wider audience.' We should, she suggests (Mitchell, 2006: 205), 'write better, and write for audiences outside of academia.' This is a notion appealing not only to those (like Clark) with a quantitative orientation, or (like Mitchell) with a leftist liberatory commitment. As urban geographer Larry Ford (2006: 122, 119) has observed, at least since the 1970s, skilled writers have shown that a 'lively "journalistic" style could be not only acceptable but also appreciated by academics as well as a more general public' and some geographers (himself included) have striven for a 'casual and accessible style with a minimum of big words.' While the term 'journalistic' can be received by some academics as an insult, for those like Ford (2006: 123), the 'challenge remains: How can we as geographers combine the appeal of the arts [and humanities] and the concerns of social science to create [written works] that are both readable and useful?'

First, accessible writing is not necessarily casual. Formality and accessibility need not exclude one another (and certainly should not be suggested as another false dichotomy; compare Mansvelt and Berg, 2005), but can rather be understood as mutual contributors to the way written work is understood. For different audiences, and different subjects, a certain formality may be required – but even then, understanding the audience and carefully crafting the prose, can lead to ready accessibility. Here, for example, is a passage (quoted in Williams, 1995: 159) where political scientist George Kennan describes in his memoirs the formally elegant American diplomat Averell Harriman:

> Unique in his single-mindedness of purpose, it was his nature to pursue only one interest at a time. When we were associated with each other in Moscow this interest was, properly and commendably, the prospering of the American war effort

[in WWII] and American diplomacy, as President Roosevelt viewed and understood it. To the accomplishment of his part in the furtherance of this objective he addressed himself with a dedication, a persistence, and an unflagging energy and attention that has no parallel in my experience.

Here Kennan uses the very formality of his prose to convey, in more than just his description, the formality of the man he describes. Accessible, yes. But also more: the formality of the style reaches the audience as more than a pretense of form, but as part of the substance of what Kennan describes, as part of the man, Harriman, himself.

So penning accessible prose need not demand a casual tone, but it does demand an understanding of audience, an understanding of the world beyond the mind of the writer, and a careful attention to how the written words will be received (Williams 1995).

THE CRISIS OF REPRESENTATION AND STRAIGHTFORWARD-SEEMING LANGUAGE

Even with a commitment to straightforward prose, the relationship – as ethnographer and writer-about-writing John Van Maanen has observed (1990: 7) – 'between words and worlds is anything but easy or transparent.' Still, as Cloke *et al.* point out (2004: 348), 'For much of its history, human geography has rather unproblematically accepted the conventional view of language which sees words as mirrors of the worlds they represent.' In other words, we have embraced a naïve realism thought to link ideas, people, actions, objects, and words in direct, 'right and incontrovertible ways' (Eagleton, 1983: 134). Geographers – and so many others – long simply did not question the myriad disjunctures between the 'world out there' and its portrayal on the printed page. In so not-doing, we ignored significant power relations in how we chose to represent that 'world out there' in our work, and we simultaneously reduced writing to a disembodied, mechanical process of 'bolting words together in the right order' (Barnes and Duncan, 1992: 2). This section examines what that implies for writing as a qualitative-research method.

The link between a (quantitatively based) view of both research and researcher as objective, and the objective-seeming language produced by 'plain,' scientific prose was established in the Western scholarly community by the seventeenth century when a second kind of writing, literary writing, was separated from writing scientific and identified with fiction, rhetoric, and subjectivity (Richardson, 2000; Richardson and St. Pierre, 2005; see also Clifford and Marcus, 1986). 'Fiction was false because it invented reality, unlike science, which was "true" because it purportedly "reported" "objective" reality in an unambiguous voice' (Richardson, 2000: 925). What scholars have since realized, as Richardson explains (Richardson and St. Pierre, 2005: 960), is that 'no textual staging is ever innocent' – all writing is written from somewhere, by someone, and no writing can ever be purely objective.

In fields across the social sciences and the humanities, by the 1980s this awareness grew into what has been termed the 'crisis of representation' (Marcus and Fischer, 1986), as scholars engaged seriously with what it meant to write about others, and examined sincerely the power relations involved in such endeavors. What emerged was a 'new theoretical and critical attitude to writing' that influenced the ways people thought about their writing as much as it influenced how they wrote (Barnes, 2000: 588). Scholars began to understand 'ourselves reflexively as persons writing from particular positions at specific times' (Richardson in Richardson and St. Pierre, 2005: 962). Further, once writing was understood as more than a mechanistic and mimetic conveyance of reality, scholars in many fields began to critically examine the intertanglings of writing, language, and power in issues of 'social power, cultural norms, [and] interpretive and rhetorical strategies' (Barnes, 2000: 588), and

we came to understand writing (and all forms of representation) as active, constitutive practices that help shape the realities we endeavor to depict (Duncan, 2000). The result has been that writing is today understood as 'constitutive, not simply reflective [of reality]; new worlds are made out of old texts, and old worlds are the basis of new texts' (Barnes and Duncan, 1992: 3). We not only shape our thinking by writing, but we also in part shape the world by what we write about it.

This has led human geographers (along with scholars in other fields across the social sciences and humanities) to take writing seriously: to carefully consider the ways we represent others in our work; to critically examine who we are, and where we come from, and how that informs our representations of others and ourselves (see Aitken and Myers, in this volume). Such care and caution are well placed, but the debates around issues of representation grew, for some, tiresome, even to the point where some considered the 'crisis of representation … in danger of becoming a cliché' (Keith, 1992: 559) – reflexivity was accused of descending into solipsism. But if, to some, self-reflexive writing can become a self-indulgent act that forces upon the reader superfluous information about the author, when thoughtfully engaged it is an essential part of qualitative research. Essential because all qualitative researchers are humans interacting with other humans, and our readers deserve to understand the basis of our claims to knowing, as well as how we 'position ourselves as knowers and tellers' (Richardson in Richardson and St. Pierre, 2005: 962). In qualitative research that goes beyond superficial notions of objectivity to embrace the unfolding positionality of each researcher in each research-engaged community; careful reflexivity is an obligation of the writer to the community, to the readers, and to her- or himself.

That obligation extends beyond an awareness of the self and the self-in-the-field, to a responsibility to the people with whom we work, over whose representations we, as writers, often have power. Indeed, Pamela

Shurmer-Smith (Bennett and Shurmer-Smith, 2001: 259) has suggested a broader understanding of representation, one that may lead to a deeper insight into the writer's engaged and reflexive task of representing:

> That word 'represent' is also used in the context of standing in for. A defense lawyer is not expected to reveal what really happened; she is supposed to draw upon specialist knowledge to put the best possible interpretation on things and will give explanations the accused would not generate. This representing implies taking responsibility for what one says for someone else and comes quite close to what I believe a piece of academic writing based on qualitative research methods should aim at. Representation is not just presenting again what was already presented; it is about coming up with new thinking about human relationships.

As skilled and trained qualitative researchers, we take responsibility for what we write about ourselves and others, and we rely on our skill, training, and personal insights to forward – rather than hinder – our research-and-community obligations.

Significantly, too, engaging discussions of how language represents (and fails to represent) the complex realities and peoples we study by focusing on issues of representation neither rejects nor privileges the importance of form or style. So discussion of critical representational issues should not preclude equally careful attention to the details of writing itself.

In fact, as US Supreme Court Justice Benjamin Cardozo observed, 'Form is not something added to substance as a mere protuberant adornment. The two are fused into a unity. ... The strength that is born of form and the feebleness that is born of lack of form are in truth qualities of substance. They are the tokens of the thing's identity. They make it what it is' (quoted in Williams, 1995: 80). Or, put differently (by economist Donald (Dierdre) McCloskey), 'By style we mean properly the details of substance. ... Style is not a frosting added to a substantial cake. ... [because] the substance of a cake is not the list of basic ingredients. It is the style in which they are combined' (McCloskey, 1988: 286 quoted in Cloke et al., 2004: 349). Style,

in other words, is a formative part of substance; the way we write is intimately bound to what our writing can convey and how we can convey it (see also Sayer, 1989; Richardson, 2000; Cloke et al., 2004).

Thus, no matter how vexing are issues of representation, cloaking them in poor writing, or writing ill-crafted, leads us no closer to resolution. And, while clear prose and prose well-crafted may similarly not resolve issues of representation, such writing will, at least, convey its content and, if reflexively oriented, can hope to convey with honesty the representational issues at hand.

HARD WRITING

Even while many scholars (geographers included) have striven to write straightforwardly, others have maintained suspicion of such efforts. Evocative writing, in particular, semanticist Samuel Ichiye Hayakawa cautioned more than sixty years ago (1941: 187), can cause the reader or listener to lose critical ability: 'Like snakes under the influence of a snake charmer's flute, we are swayed by the musical phrases of the verbal hypnotist.' Fine writing, in other words, misleads.

Indeed, even in our seemingly simplest statements, we may (perhaps inadvertently) speak untruths. Untruths, according to Richard Symanski (1976), masked by the straightforward language in which they are phrased. The 'success of certain geographic and scholarly works may be as much a function' he wrote (1976: 606), 'of the way in which ordinary language is used as is the application of careful scholarship and the profundity of the analysis undertaken.' To prove his point Symanski undertook a carefully harsh analysis of Donald Meinig's widely acclaimed scholarly works and proclaimed them so peppered with hyperbole (chiefly in modifiers: quickly, severely, greatly, simply; in categoricals: all, any, always, only; in words that magnify: so, most, many, very) that they could not be trusted. In the service of writing well, Symanski insisted, Meinig had sunk to continual exaggeration. Exaggeration likely to go unnoticed by the average reader; exaggeration that, to Symanski, undermined Meinig's very scholarship. Perhaps, Symanski suggested (1976: 614), 'one ought to approach the use of ordinary language ... with the same suspicions which are brought to the evaluation of statistical and mathematical models.'

Beyond such suspicion (whether motivated by hostility or not), one response to the power of fine prose and narrative persuasion has been to deliberately craft demanding prose, prose that will force the reader to focus on every word and concept. To some, this strategy emerges from the recognition that 'textual representations create rather than reflect the world of experience,' a recognition that leads 'some analysts to adopt textual strategies which are explicitly designed to get a particular message across' (Smith, 2000: 661). Prose 'purposely obfuscated' to deliberately challenge readers and 'weed out all but the most committed' is what others call it (Ford, 2006: 119). This challenging strategy has many critics – as Michael Keith (1992: 563) has declared, 'Impenetrability wins few friends and obscurantism is hardly to be welcomed.'

But writing that challenges the reader can also expand her horizons, and draw new connections between word and text. Allan Pred, for example, has engaged montage, poetic form, and alternative spellings to link his rich empirical research with his theoretical insights and keep the reader's taught attention (see, for example, Pred, 1990, 2004). He writes, for example, about the aim of his own book thusly (2004: xi):

This is a book that attempts
to show,
by way of telling Swedish example,
    the (con)fusions of fact and fiction
    the fiFcAtCiTonS,
    through which racializing stereotypes are
    perpetuated
        and reenacted at dispersed sites; ... .

His creative engagements of language, research, and theory have earned him both

praise and imitation (see Soja, 1994 who wrote his own review in Pred-like verse), as well as derision (Olwig, 1991) and likely also misunderstanding. Despite Pred's direct challenge to academic writing styles, some academics seem unwilling to accept scholarly presentation in such alternate forms: reviewer Richard Breaux wrote that '... much of this story and even Pred's analysis is obscured by the book's organization and postmodernist form' (2005: 696); while Ken Olwig (1991: 551) suggested that 'By making use of poetic license, [Pred] is able to make socio-linguistic semiotic assertions that give color to his argument but which the empirical evidence does not always seem to be able to sustain.'

Perhaps because academics are accustomed to a particular style of work, we may be at times reluctant to welcome efforts by those in our ranks who seek to write differently. Or, perhaps because we are trained and skilled at writing in certain formats, we may be less well able to write in others. But the form/format of an academic text need not hinder our abilities to express ourselves (see DeLyser and Pawson, 2005): as Pam Shurmer-Smith (in Bennet and Shurmer-Smith, 2001: 260) observes,

I don't think it matters whether the vehicle is a poem or a play or a formal report. If what one is trying to say is exciting, it will shine through any medium (even tables of statistics). If it is not exciting, poetry will only make it more embarrassingly banal. A poem from someone involved – great; a poem from someone who wants to look involved – cringeworthy. New modes of representation from mere amateurs – forget it! The best you will get in response is politeness.

Though Pred avoids jargon, others engage it, and deploy it deliberately as part of a difficult writing style to draw readers into focus on their content without getting lost in their form. Philosopher, social theorist, and literary critic Roland Barthes, for example, developed a style 'intentionally difficult to read' in an effort to call readers to become 'active participant[s] in the overturning of taken-for-granted assumptions' that he understood as flourishing in the passive reading of polished prose and which could, to Barthes, enable the bourgeois culture and politics he sought to struggle against (Duncan and Duncan, 1992: 24; see also Smith, 1996).

Nor is it only those on the left who have advocated hard writing. Leo Strauss, now considered the intellectual father of neoconservatism in the US, endorsed what he called 'esoteric writing' as an important way for a writer to avoid potential political or religious persecution. As Earl Shorris (2004: 68) has observed of Strauss, he 'advised his readers not to write in plain English [and] followed his own advice, [crafting] convoluted, contradictory, arcane, [and] clubfooted writing' and advocated 'telling the truth to the wise while at the same time conveying something quite different to the many.' Thus Strauss mustered difficult writing explicitly to create an audience of disciples or insiders, mustering obscurantism as elitism in the guise of escaping persecution (Shorris, 2004).

Clearly, whatever the political motivations behind hard writing, the readerly challenges of such writing can have an 'exclusionary effect' (Duncan and Duncan, 1992: 24) that will limit and hamper audiences – this is an issue, therefore, on which each writer, each time he or she writes, must take a stand.

While writers and teachers of writing have long eschewed purposely difficult writing (Strunk and White, 1970 [1959]; Becker, 1986; De Souza, 1988; Wolcott, 1990; Williams, 1995; Williams, 2006; Biklen and Casella, 2007; Golden-Biddle and Locke, 2007), clearly not all writing need be simple or straightforward, and some writing cannot be. Some written works must, by their nature, be complex and will, therefore, at times, require of their readers a specialized understanding. The challenge is that, as linguist and writing teacher Joseph Williams (1995: xi) points out, though some complex writing 'precisely reflect[s] complex ideas,' other complex writing may 'gratuitously complicate complex ideas' or 'gratuitously complicate simple ideas.'

And, tempting for academic readers/writers, specifically those new to a particular field or area, is the often-mistaken tendency to 'defer to what seems difficult' (Williams, 1995: xii) – we tend to assume that difficult writing is difficult because we can't understand it, not because it's poorly written or poorly thought out (Becker, 1986; Williams, 1995). For students in particular, Becker (1986: 30) observes, 'Learning to write like an academic [seems to move them] toward membership in that elite,' but in mimicking the prose style of published academics, they may inadvertently be aspiring to an obfuscatory writing style that masks their content in prose delirium.

Still, for some, the temptation to 'resort to theoretical obscurantism' (Keith, 1992: 561) in order to convey complex and intense issues in a suitably lofty and theoretically engaged manner remains irresistible. Keith (1992) explained his own nervous endeavors to present his research in such form: Sometimes, he reported (Keith, 1992: 561–2), this strategy

> seemed to impress. Impress some. Maybe they were impressed by the assiduously calculated appearance of erudition, maybe they were afraid to admit they understood barely a word. Maybe both. But others were alienated and resentful, I could not help but think at times sophistication and tortuous argumentation were a convenient defense.

Whether used as a defensive strategy or not, just as some argue that fine writing may mislead, others argue just as vociferously that it is difficult writing that deceives. Writer George Orwell (1961 [1950]: 363) explained the temptation of difficult writing as one of duplicitous intentions: 'The great enemy of clear language is insincerity. When there is a gap between one's real and one's declared aims, one turns as it were instinctively to long words and exhausted idioms, like a cuttlefish squirting out ink.' Behind the mask of jargon and turgid sentences, such writers claim, lies nothing – or worse, only lies (see, for a heated example, Sokal, 1996a–c; Ross, 1997).

The issue of purposely turgid prose today remains a difficult and complicated ethical issue because, since form and content are profoundly intertangled, it involves much more than merely 'style' of writing. As Williams (2006: 130) explains it, how should we

> respond to those who know they write in a complex style, but claim they must, because they are breaking new intellectual ground[?] Are they right, or is that just self-serving rationalization? This is a vexing question, not just because we can settle it only case-by-case, but because we may not be able to settle it at all, at least not to everyone's satisfaction.

Is murkily complex writing 'babble,' or is it 'the expression of a thought so complex, so nuanced, that what it says can be expressed only as written?' (Williams, 2006: 130). We can make no blanket judgment. But if we understand ourselves as writing for our readers, writing for a specific audience, then we can change the question: Is it our readers who are obligated to try to understand our prose, or we who are obligated to craft that prose so that readers can understand it? To Williams (2006: 130–1), 'We owe our readers an ethical duty to write precise and nuanced prose, but we ought not assume that they owe us an indefinite amount of their time to unpack it.' Williams (2006: 131) quotes Ludwig Wittgenstein, philosopher and proponent of ordinary language: 'Whatever can be thought can be thought clearly; whatever can be written can be written clearly,' and then adds, 'Whatever can be written can usually be written more clearly, with just a bit more effort.'

In fact, despite the observations of writers and writing teachers that we seem to favor complex prose for its 'classy' and erudite tone – often favoring a long, complicated-sounding word over a short, simple one (Becker, 1986; Williams, 1995; Cloke *et al.*, 2004), and leaning toward big words when we feel most insecure (Pennebaker and Lay, 2002) (as when we first learn new terms) – psychologist Daniel Oppenheimer (2006) found his subjects well able to discern when prose was needlessly complicated, and then reject it. While the Stanford students in his study did indeed strive for complexity in

their own written work, they simultaneously down-graded the intelligence of those whose written work demonstrated complexity needlessly. The point, his research showed, was that despite the compelling call of complexity, writers who wish to communicate seem indeed better served when they make the effort to write straightforwardly.

ON CLARITY AND COMPLEXITY

Of course, since we write for different audiences at different times, it is also possible – even likely – that the same person will write in a weighty and complex style using targeted jargon in order to best convey her ideas to a particular audience, but that, on another occasion she will choose to express her ideas in comparatively jargon-free straightforward prose rich with specific examples – and anything in between (see Richardson, 1988). Significantly, we should avoid reducing writing as an expressive medium and formative process to a binary of simple and complex, and instead engage the form and format of writing appropriate for the circumstances and audience (Cloke *et al.*, 2004). Neil Smith (2004: xxi–xxii) explained it well:

> In my book *Uneven Development* [1990], I attempted to derive a theory of uneven global geographical development. ... It was a book of heavy abstractions and theory, economic logics, and grand geographical processes, with little human touch inspiring even the geographies it sought to explain. The present book [*American Empire*] is very much the other side of the same coin. It is light on logics and abstractions, and theory is generally unobtrusive; in contrast ... it is heavy on historical detail and human drama. The story told here looks strikingly different from that of *Uneven Development*, but I hope readers will agree that it is sympathetic with that earlier argument.

The bottom line may be that, no matter how we choose to write, if we wish our work to be readily understood, we must carefully consider who our audience is, what their understanding is of the subject, and then how to craft our work to best meet and extend that understanding. Balancing the needs of an audience with our own commitments to the communities and individuals with whom we work, with our own notions of what it is we wish to convey and how we wish to convey it, is a challenging task to be sure. But it is one made no less challenging by ignoring it.

Writing, after all, is not only an embodied practice, but also the result of a series of unfolding, always-emergent decisions about how to communicate. A thoughtful decision to write straightforwardly, using simple terms (like Larry Ford or Neil Smith) is as important as the equally thoughtful decision to write in a complex style that attempts to disrupt the reader's expectations of academic prose (like Allan Pred), particularly when underlying them both is an equally thoughtful consideration of how a chosen style will be received by an intended audience. Neither extreme necessarily attaches to a particular form of fieldwork or research, to a particular method or methodology, or to a particular politics.

But writing, as a personal and conscious process of language crafting, is embedded with issues of power, politics, and ideology. That holds equally for prose clear, or prose complex. Indeed, writing itself has long been used to exclude the illiterate, just as specialized vocabulary is used to exclude the less educated, or those not insiders (Williams, 1995, 2006) – it is not only complex prose that can be exclusionary.

And indeed, as noted above, some argue that clear writing is used deliberately to disable critical thought; sociologist Stanley Aronowitz (1991: 91) is one of those:

> [T]he 'language of clarity' plays [a significant role] in a dominant culture that cleverly and powerfully uses 'clear' and 'simplistic' language to systematically undermine and prevent the conditions from arising for a public culture to engage in rudimentary forms of complex and critical thinking. ... [L]anguage and power often combine to offer the general public and students subject positions that are cleansed of any complex thought or insight.

But, as Williams (2006: 132) points out,

> those who attack clarity [of writing] as part of an ideological conspiracy to oversimplify complicated

social issues are as wrong as those who attack science because some use it for malign ends: neither science nor clarity is a threat; we are threatened by those who use clarity (or science) to deceive us. It is not clarity that subverts, but the unethical use of it.

The same can be said for turgidity. But the choice, and the ethics, reside with the writer. With each writer, each time he or she writes.

REVISION

In fall of 2007, the fiftieth anniversary of the publication of the beat saga and seemingly improvised explosive prose work *On the Road*, Jack Kerouac's publisher released a hardcover edition of the novel in an effort to acknowledge the way Kerouac first typed it – as a continuous, single-spaced paragraph on a 120-foot-long scroll (Kerouac, 2007). Kerouac, inspired (but aided by caffeine and speed), had typed the entire *On the Road* manuscript at a pace of as much as 100 words a minute over a period of just three weeks. And, significantly, 'three weeks' had been Kerouac's famous answer to talk-show host Steve Allen's 1959 question about how long it took to write *On the Road*. That answer, in turn, fueled a myth (cultivated by Kerouac himself) about Kerouac's allegedly spontaneous writing style, where a complete book manuscript flowed, revisionless, to perfection on the page. In fact, Kerouac had been making notes for the novel for years before typing the scroll, and then the text of the scroll itself underwent multiple revisions over a many-year period before Kerouac could interest a publisher. Some of Kerouac's brilliance lay in his pumped-up spontaneity, but only some of it; much of what today seems spontaneous was actually long thought-over, carefully crafted, and painstakingly revised (Weinreich, 1987; Cresswell, 1993; NPR, 2007).

The power of Kerouac's myth though, is that it appears to reveal a particular purity of genius, one achievable only by a few uniquely talented individuals who reach straight to their inspirational pinnacles and never turn back to tamper with so much as a comma (and that, in fact, was essentially Kerouac's advice for writing what he termed 'spontaneous bop prosody;' see Weinreich, 1987). It is a myth that obscures the nature of writing as a carefully cultivated craft involving formative phases of editing and revision as much as drafting. A myth that clouds the nature of writing as actually practiced by thousands of writers – Kerouac himself among them. It is a myth that masks the labor that writing well entails.

But for academics who most likely learned to write under the limitations of undergraduate and then graduate course structures, who honed our skills on quick term papers the research for which could easily be captured in the brain at one time, and who trained ourselves through bursts of long-haul, late-night surges timed to meet a morning deadline, the Kerouac myth can all-too-often approximate a strived-for reality: hopefully a brilliant (or good enough) work cranked out all at once in near perfection; a case where revision never enters the mind. Indeed, journalist, novelist, and screenwriter Nora Ephron (1986: 7) acknowledges that, for her, the revision process emerged as a 'developmental stage' she entered after her college years of submitting unrevised term papers. In college, she later reflected, 'it would never have crossed my mind that what I had produced was only a first draft and that I had more work to do; the idea was to get to the end, and once you had got to the end you were finished.' After years of writing professionally with tight deadlines (as a journalist and screenwriter), Ephron learned to move beyond her first drafts and, in fact, to spend as much time as possible revising and continually re-crafting her work.

In fact, of course, few well-thought-of published writers adhere to the kind of writing practices Kerouac advocated. On the contrary. Just as Kerouac himself went through as many as 6 drafts of *On the Road* (NPR, 2007), most writers understand revision as far more than comma correction,

and rather as a formative part of the writing process – as itself an intimate part of the creative endeavor. And, while Kerouac sought to emulate the free form of bebop in his prose (Weinreich, 1987; Cresswell, 1993), that free-form feel is not necessarily achieved by free-form drafting alone. Ephron, for example, seeks to get the feel for her prose by beginning each new revision with the manuscript's very first words, exerting as many as 400 pages of typescript, all tolled, to craft a completed 6-page essay (Ephron, 1986). Not all begin at the beginning: Ernest Hemingway, before he was satisfied with his work, rewrote just the last page of *A Farewell to Arms* 39 times (see Bolker, 1997). And US National Book Award winner Don DeLillo pours over paragraphs at different points in his highly crafted novels, writing and rewriting a single paragraph over and over often a dozen times before moving onward to the next paragraph (Max, 2007: 67).

For them, the perfection of their expression is achieved as much in the revision, as in the initial inspiration. It is not, in other words, that editing and revision provide an 'antidote for the lack of giftedness among the huge corpus of us who recognize that we had better write but are not among the better writers' (Van Maanen, 1990: 13). Rather, the process of revision extends the creative practice of writing itself, helping us to develop, clarify, and focus our insights – as well as to improve its presentation. Because writing is a formative process, we create, shape, and hone ideas while we write, ideas we did not know or did not have before we sat down to write – and that happens equally with the time we spend revising (DeLyser and Pawson, 2005). As Anthony De Souza (1988: 2) put it, 'Rewriting is re-vision.'

What this suggests is a productive way to understand writing: as a skill or a craft rather than an inborn talent (see also Cloke *et al.*, 2004; DeLyser, 2010). The completed work on the published page masks the effort and the revisions that went into it, but that need not keep us from appreciating or understanding that labor. In fact, of course, much of what we are presented with masks its own labor – the gymnast's perfect routine masks his years of training and practice, the carpenter's perfectly hung door masks her efforts at shimming and planing that enable its proper (often unremarked) function. Like good writing, his perfect routine and her perfect door are the fruits of revision – of trying again and again until it's right, or as good as it can be. But the revision process for writers is simultaneously about more than repetition or shimming. Because we think while we write, because the writing process itself is formative, revising our work is as productive, as creative, as writing the first draft.

Thus, we need not think less of ourselves for the time we spend revising our prose. Indeed, rather more. Particularly since first drafts tend to reflect the 'rough' understanding of the writer, they may not clearly articulate the writer's goals, or appeal to the needs of the reader. Thoughtful and formative revision can help the writer with both issues. By engaging the revision process we can discover what it is we really wish to say, we can sharpen our focus, and then better say (or write) what we think. Once our ideas are clear to us, by continuing to engage with the revision process, we can then also hone and re-craft our prose with the audience in mind so that our readers will better understand what we have written.

Formative revision, clearly, is a multi-layered and time-consuming process. So why spend so much time crafting and re-crafting our prose? Once we've used the revision process to discover what we want to say it becomes a matter of how we consciously decide to treat our audiences. Do we expect them to be willing and able to mine for meaning, or do we feel committed to making that meaning readily accessible? That, in part, is an aesthetic choice, but it is also a profoundly philosophical – and political – one, depending upon how we, as writers, understand our engagements with language, knowledge, and audience.

Nowadays, as literate academics writing for a literate audience, we often take that literacy for granted. In the early days of books and printing (and well into the nineteenth century), however, that was not the case, and writers addressed their works to the 'gentle reader' with words, phrases, and passages meant explicitly to lead the reader through the text (Chartier, 1994). Those academics who write clearly today often write with a similar frame of mind: one of leading the reader, consciously, through a presentation of our research, research only we ourselves know intimately, but research we wish to share with others. It is a frame of mind that seeks to make the path ahead, and the point of the prose, clear to the audience, even if the writer knows it so well already (Williams, 1995). When writers do so, their writing becomes inviting, engaging, and accessible to their audience, regardless of their political, philosophical, or theoretical persuasions.

CONCLUSION

For all of Rainer Maria Rilke's devotion to the need to write (which I discussed in the context of his advice to an aspiring poet at the opening of this chapter), he understood also the risk involved in writing. In counseling the young poet he wrote, 'Being [a writer] means, not reckoning and counting, but ripening like the tree which does not force its sap and stands confident in the storms of spring without the fear that after them may come no summer' (Rilke, 1934: 28; see also Ueland, 2007 [1938]). What he meant, I think, was that though some passages, some pages, may come harder than others, we should not fear. But Rilke's poetic understanding of the process may seem ill-adapted to academics with deadlines and other career imperatives. Still, when writing is understood and engaged as an embodied practice, as a discipline – one familiar to Rilke who took writing as his calling – it is the discipline and practice itself that will urge (not force) the 'sap.' Rilke, in his words above, did not overlook, but rather presupposed an acceptance of the discipline and practice, the praxis of writing.

What Don DeLillo wrote to David Foster Wallace about their shared field of contemporary novel writing is apropos of academic writing praxis as well:

> I was a semi-conscious writer in the beginning. Just sat and wrote something, or read the newspaper, or went to the movies. Over time I began to understand, one, that I was lucky to be doing this work, and, two, that the only way I'd get better at it was to be more serious, to understand the rigors of novel-writing and to make it central to my life, not a variation on some related career choice. ... [E]ventually discipline no longer seemed something outside me that urged the reluctant body into the room. At this point discipline is inseparable from what I do. (quoted in Max, 2007: 68)

I believe both Rilke and DeLillo would agree about the foundational component of discipline in one's writing praxis: you force yourself until that force becomes a part of your natural motion; the discipline becomes part of your praxis, and writing becomes part of your life.

The point though is to build writing into our lives in a positive way, not a painful one. Writing time can become an expressive and enjoyable time, a time we look forward to—both a refuge and a key to creativity. And even on difficult writing days, once the time commitment is fulfilled, we have kept our promises to ourselves. As Bolker advises, by making writing a daily part of our lives, it becomes our 'practice' in the Buddhist sense of that term – an embodied, engaged, and essential part of our lives, one not ephemeral but lasting. Bolker, for one, favors such a life: 'Perhaps I'm prejudiced,' she writes (1998: 150), 'in believing you're very lucky if writing has become part of you for life, the craft you now naturally go to in order to think, feel, and clarify problems of all sorts.'

And in this sense, Rilke's advice to the young poet about the need to write was wise counsel. Once we cultivate a writing praxis, accept and nurture writing as a way of thinking – as a formative part of our research and our lives – writing itself, as a form of thought and expression, becomes a need. A need for the embodied practice, for the engaged praxis that shapes our research – a need far beyond that for the printed output of that praxis. Then we will build time for writing into each day, and into each phase of our research projects. We will engage the writing process as a creative and formative praxis that shapes our research and our ideas themselves, along with the ways we present them. We will strive to prudently represent both ourselves and the people with whom we work. We will conceive of and carry out our prose with the needs of our audiences carefully in mind. We will thoughtfully revise our prose, re-crafting the words along with the concepts and ideas, even as new ideas emerge through the revision process. We will share that work with our students and colleagues, as well as among the people in the communities with whom we work, thus casting our writing farther and encouraging further engagement with our written ideas. We will have made ourselves writers.

REFERENCES

Aronowitz, S. (1991) *Postmodern education: politics, culture, and social criticism.* Minneapolis: University of Minnesota Press.

Barnes, T. (2000) 'Poetics of geography,' in R.J. Johnston, Derek Gregory, Geraldine Pratt, and Michael Watts, (eds) *The dictionary of human geography*, 4th edition. London: Blackwell. pp. 588–9.

Barnes, T.J. and Duncan, J.S. (1992) 'Introduction: writing worlds,' in T.J. Barnes and J.S. Duncan, (eds) *Writing worlds: discourse, text and metaphor in the representation of landscape.* London: Routledge. pp. 1–17.

Barnes, T.J. and Duncan, J.S. (eds) (1992) *Writing worlds: discourse, text and metaphor in the representation of landscape.* London: Routledge.

Barnett, C. (1999) 'Deconstructing context: exposing Derrida,' *Transactions of the Institute of British Geographers* NS 24 (3): 277–93.

Becker, H.S. (1986) *Writing for social scientists. how to start and finish your thesis, book, or article.* Chicago: University of Chicago Press.

Bennet, K. and Shurmer-Smith, P. (2001) 'Writing conversation,' in M. Limb and C. Dwyer, (eds) *Qualitative methodologies for geographers: issues and debates.* London: Arnold. pp. 251–63.

Biklen, S.K. and Casella, R. (2007) *A practical guide to the qualitative dissertation.* New York: Teachers College Press.

Bolker, J. (1997) *The writer's home companion: an anthology of the world's best writing advice from Keats to Kunitz.* New York: Owl Books.

Bolker, J. (1998) *Writing your dissertation in fifteen minutes a day: a guide to starting, revising, and finishing your doctoral thesis.* New York: Owl Books.

Bondi, L. (1997) 'In whose words? On gender identities, knowledge and writing practices,' *Transactions of the Institute of British Geographers* 22 (2): 245–58.

Boyle, P.J. (1997) 'Writing up – some suggestions,' in R. Flowerdew and D. Martin, (eds) *Methods in human geography. a Guide to students doing a research project.* Harlow: Addison Wesley Longman. pp. 235–53.

Breaux, R.M. (2006) '*Review of the past is not dead: facts, fictions, and enduring racial stereotypes* by Allan Pred', *Biography* 28 (4): 695–6.

Carton, J. (2007) 'Narrating space, self, and the body: the strangeness between us: writing the self after non-representational theory,' Paper presented at the meetings of the Association of American Geographers', San Francisco, California. Text available from the author.

Chartier, R. (1994) *The Order of Books: readers, authors, and libraries in Europe between the fourteenth and eighteenth centuries.* Stanford: Stanford University Press.

Clark, W.A.V. (2006) 'Writing for the public/writing for the academy: competing goals with uncertain outcomes,' *Yearbook of the Association of Pacific Coast Geographers* 68: 108–18.

Clifford, J. and Marcus, G.E. (1986) *Writing culture: the poetics and politics of Ethnography.* Berkeley: University of California Press.

Cloke, P., Cook, I., Crang, P., Goodwin, M., Painter, J. and Philo, C. (2004) 'Representing human geographies,' in P. Cloke, I. Cook, P. Crang, M. Goodwin, J. Painter and C. Philo (eds) *Practicing human geography.* London: Sage Publications. pp. 336–63.

Cloke, P., Doel, M., Matless, D., Phillips, M. and Thrift, N. (eds) (1994) *Writing the rural: five cultural geographies.* London: Paul Chapman Publishing Ltd.

Crang, M. and Cooke, I. (2007) *Doing ethnographies.* London: Sage Publications.

Cresswell, T. (1993) 'Mobility as resistance: a geographical reading of Kerouac's "On the Road"',

Transactions of the Institute of British Geographers NS 18 (2): 249–62.

Curry, M. R. (1996) *The work in the world: geographical practice and the written word.* Minneapolis: University of Minnesota Press.

DeLyser, D. (2003) 'Teaching graduate students to write: a seminar for thesis and dissertation writers,' *Journal of Geography in Higher Education* 27 (2): 169–81.

DeLyser, D. (2010) 'Writing it up,' in J.P.Jones III and B. Gomez, (eds) *Research methods: a first course.* London: Blackwell.

DeLyser, D. and Pawson, E. (2005) 'From personal to public: communicating qualitative research for public consumption,' in I. Hay, (ed.) *Qualitative research methods in human geography*, 2nd edition. Melbourne: Oxford University Press. pp. 266–74.

De Souza, A.R. (1988) 'Writing matters,' *The Professional Geographer* 40 (1): 1–3.

Dewsbury, J.D., Harrison, P., Rose, M. and Wylie, J. (2002) 'Introduction,' *Geoforum* 33 (4): 437–40.

Doel, M.A. (1993) 'Proverbs for paranoids: writing geography on hollowed ground,' *Transactions of the Institute of British Geographers* NS 18 (3): 377–94.

Duncan, J.S. (2000) 'Representation,' in R.J. Johnston, D. Gregory, G. Pratt and M. Watts, (eds) *The dictionary of human geography*, 4th edition. London: Blackwell. pp. 703–5.

Duncan, J.S. and Duncan, N.G. (1992) 'Ideology and bliss: Roland Barthes and the secret histories of landscape,' in T.J. Barnes and J.S. Duncan, (eds) *Writing worlds: discourse, text and metaphor in the representation of landscape.* London: Routledge. pp. 18–37.

Duncan, J.S. and Gregory, D. (1999) *Writes of passage: reading travel writing.* London: Routledge.

Eagleton, T. (1983) *Literary theory: an introduction.* Minneapolis: University of Minnesota Press.

Ephron, N. (1986) 'Revision and life: take it from the top – again,' *The New York Times* 9 November 1986, section 7 (Book Reviews), p. 7.

Ford, L. (2006) 'Writing books for a general audience: motivations, goals, and challenges,' *Yearbook of the Association of Pacific Coast Geographers* 68: 119–31.

Freedman, R. (1996) *Life of a poet: Rainer Maria Rilke.* New York: Farrar, Strauss, and Giroux.

Golden-Biddle, K. and Locke, K. (2007) *Composing qualitative research.* Thousand Oaks, CA: Sage Publications.

Hay, I. (ed.) (2005) *Qualitative research methods in human geography*, 2nd edition. South Melbourne, Australia: Oxford University Press.

Hayakawa, S.I. (1941) *Language in action.* New York: Harcourt Brace.

Jones, J.P. III and Gomez, B. (eds) (2010) *Research methods for geographers: a first course.* London: Blackwell.

Katz, C. (1992) 'All the world is staged: intellectuals and the projects of ethnography,' *Environment and Planning D: Society and Space* 10 (5): 495–510.

Keith, M. (1992) 'Angry writing: (re)presenting the unethical world of the ethnographer,' *Environment and Planning D: Society and Space* 10 (5): 551–68.

Kerouac, J. (2007) *On the road: the original scroll* with introduction and critical commentary by Howard Cunnell, Joshua Kuppetz, George Mouratidis, and Penny Vlagopoulos. New York: Viking.

Limb, M. and Dwyer, C. (eds) (2001) *Qualitative methodologies for geographers: issues and debates.* London: Arnold.

Mansvelt, J. and Berg L.D. (2005) 'Writing qualitative geographies, constructing geographical knowledges,' in I. Hay, (ed.) *Qualitative research methods in human geography*, 2nd edition. Melbourne: Oxford University Press. pp. 248–65.

Marcus, G.E. and Fischer, M.M.J. (1986) 'A crisis of representation in the social sciences,' in G.E. Marcus and M.M.J. Fischer, (eds) *Anthropology as cultural critique: an experimental moment in the human sciences.* Chicago: University of Chicago Press. pp. 7–16.

Max, D.T. (2007) 'Letter from Austin. Final destination: the a-list archive,' *The New Yorker* 11 and 18 June 2007, 54–71.

Mitchell, K. (2006) 'Writing from left field,' *Antipode* 38 (2): 205–12.

NPR (National Public Radio) (2007) 'Jack Kerouac's famous scroll, "On the road" again,' All Things Considered, 5 July 2007. Transcript at www.npr.org.

Olwig, K. (1991) 'Review of *lost words and lost worlds: modernity and the language of everyday life in late-nineteenth-century Stockholm* by Allan Pred', *The Professional Geographer* 43 (4): 550–1.

Oppenheimer, D.M. (2006) 'Consequences of erudite vernacular utilized irrespective of necessity: problems with using long words needlessly,' *Applied Cognitive Psychology* 20 (2): 139–56.

Orwell, G. (1961) [1950] 'Politics and the English language,' in *The George Orwell Reader* with an introduction by Richard H. Rovere. San Diego: Harvest Books/Harcourt Brace Jovanovich. pp. 355–66.

Pennebaker, J.W. and Lay. T.C. (2002) 'Language use and personality during crisis: analysis of Mayor Rudolph Giuliani's press conferences,' *Journal of Research in Personality* 36 (3): 271–82.

Pratt, G. (1992) 'Spatial metaphors and speaking positions,' *Environment and planning D: Society and space* 10 (3): 241–4.

Pratt, G. (2000) 'Research performances,' *Environment and planning D: Society and space* 18 (5): 639–51.

Pred, A. (1990) *Lost words and lost worlds: modernity and everyday language in late-nineteenth century Stockholm.* Cambridge: Cambridge University Press.

Pred, A. (2004) *The past is not dead. Facts, fictions, and enduring racial stereotypes.* Minneapolis: University of Minnesota Press.

Richardson, L. (1988) 'The collective story: postmodernism and the writing of sociology,' *Sociological Focus* 21 (3): 199–208.

Richardson, L. (2000) 'Writing: a method of inquiry,' in N.K. Denzin and Y.S. Lincoln, (eds) *Handbook of qualitative research*, 2nd edition. Thousand Oaks, CA: Sage Publications. 923–48.

Richardson, L. (2003) 'Writing: a method of inquiry,' in N.K. Denzin (ed.) *Turning points in qualitative research: tying knots in a handkerchief.* Walnut Creek, CA: Rowman Altamira Press. pp. 379–96.

Richardson, L. and St. Pierre, A.E. (2005) 'Writing: a method of inquiry,' in N.K. Denzin and Y.S. Lincoln, (eds) *Handbook of qualitative research*, 3rd Edition. Thousand Oaks, CA: Sage Publications. pp. 959–78.

Rilke, R.M. (1934) *Letters to a young poet.* Translated by M.D. Herter Norton. New York: W.W. Norton and Company, Inc.

Rorty, R. (1978) 'Philosophy as a kind of writing: an essay on Derrida,' *New Literary History* 10 (1): 141–60.

Rose, G. (1997) 'Situating knowledges: positionality, reflexivities and other tactics,' *Progress in Human Geography* 21 (3): 305–20.

Ross, A. (1997) 'Reflections on the Sokal affair,' *Social Text* 50: 149–52.

Sayer, A. (1989) 'The "new" regional geography and problems of narrative,' *Environment and Planning D: Society and Space* 7 (3): 253–76.

Shorris, E. (2004) 'Ignoble liars. Leo Strauss, George Bush, and the philosophy of mass deception,' *Harpers Magazine* June 2004, 65–71.

Soja, E. (1994) 'Review of *reworking modernity: capitalisms and symbolic discontent* by A. Pred and M.J. Watts', *Annals of the Association of American Geographers* 84 (1): 168–9.

Sokal, A.D. (1996a) 'Transgressing the boundaries: towards a transformative hermeneutics of quantum gravity,' *Social Text* 46–47: 217–52.

Sokal, A.D. (1996b) 'A physicist experiments with cultural studies,' *Lingua Franca* May–June: 62–4. Available at: http://physics.nyu.edu/~as2/.

Sokal, A.D. (1996c) 'Sokal's reply to social text editorial,' *Lingua Franca* July–August. Available at http://www.physics.nyu.edu/faculty/sokal/#debate (last accessed 5 January 2009).

Smith, J.M. (1996) 'Geographical rhetoric: modes and tropes of appeal,' *Annals of the Association of American Geographers* 86 (1): 1–20.

Smith, N. (1990) *Uneven development: nature, capital, and the production of space.* London: Blackwell.

Smith, N. (2004) *American empire: Roosevelt's geographer and the prelude to globalization.* Berkeley: University of California Press.

Smith, S.J. (2000) 'Qualitative methods,' in R.J. Johnston, D. Gregory, G. Pratt, and M. Watts, (eds) *The dictionary of human geography*, 4th edition. London: Blackwell. pp. 660–2.

Strunk, W., Jr. and White, E.B. (1970) [1959] *The elements of style.* New York: Macmillan Paperbacks.

Symanski, R. (1976) *Annals of the Association of American Geographers,* 66 (4): 605–14.

Ueland, B. (2007) [1938] *If you want to write: a book about art, Independence, and spirit* with introduction by Andrei Codrescu. Saint Paul, MN: Graywolf Press.

Valentine, G. (1998) '"Sticks and stones may break my bones": a personal geography of harassment,' *Antipode* 30 (4): 305–32.

Van Maanen, J., with P.K. Manning and M.L. Miller (1990) 'Editor's introduction,' in Harry F. Wolcott, *Writing up qualitative research.* Newbury Park, CA: Sage Publications. pp. 7–8.

Weinreich, Regina (1987) *The spontaneous poetics of Jack Kerouac: a study of the fiction.* Carbondale: Southern Illinois University Press.

Williams, J.M. (1995) *Style: toward clarity and grace.* Chicago: University of Chicago Press.

Williams, J.M. (2006) *Style: the basics of clarity and grace*, 2nd edition. Chicago: University of Chicago Press.

Wolcott, H.F. (1990) *Writing up qualitative research.* Newbury Park, CA: Sage Publications.

20

The Art of Geographic Interpretation

Sara MacKian

Our interpretations are our claims to the independent creation of new knowledge. Arrogant work, indeed.

(Wolcott, 1994: 258)

So what is this 'arrogant work' we are involved in? What *is* the art of geographic interpretation? Interpretation in qualitative research is variously (and often unhelpfully) described as something that relies on 'mysterious procedures' (Agar, 1980), a process of 'transformation' (Wolcott, 1994), or allowing the 'emergence' of key themes or issues from materials (Bennett and Shurmer-Smith, 2002). But is this continuing air of mystery around qualitative inquiry necessary in an era when this range of methods has seemingly come of age (Crang, 2002, 2003, 2005)? Phrases such as these have in common a sense of 'going beyond' the categorising, ranking, correlating, rationalising of the scientific method. Indeed it is now commonly assumed amongst practitioners of qualitative methods that such objective detachment and distancing from our data is not possible. Nonetheless accounts of interpretation often offer little more than somewhat superficial 'analysis of text'. Surely interpretation *has* to be something more?

It has been acknowledged that the experience of fieldwork 'has been trivialised as the "collection" of data by a dehumanised machine' (Okely, 1992: 3); but we hear much less about the silence of interpretation and hence the dehumanisation of the experience of analysis. In terms of guidance available for the qualitative geographer, a great deal of emphasis is placed on getting the fieldwork element 'right'. It often then seems left to chance what happens back 'at the desk'. Indeed there is still this clinging to the idea that we *do* 'bring back' the data in this simplistic way (Thrift, 2000), despite the reality that we have really been 'in the field' all of our life (Tuan, 2001), and are always inevitably *still* there (Katz, 1994; Hyndman, 2001).

The reality is we analyse and interpret from the minute we decide to tackle a particular research topic, and bring with us an outsize range of baggage prior to even reaching that point. All of which will influence the final interpretation and presentation of our 'finished work'.[1] Thus the mysterious gap between fieldwork and 'final report' hides much. Firstly it obscures the process of analysis and interpretation that is going on by not speaking openly and clearly about it. Secondly it implies that interpretation is limited to that space and time when, as I argue throughout this chapter, it is something that saturates our entire practice from the first spark of an idea to the final consumption of outputs by our audiences.

At the heart of interpretation is the aim of 'going beyond' the data (Wolcott, 1994). If we do go beyond our data, What can we legitimately bring to that process to help us? What gives us the right and the ability to make these decisions? Is it training, experiences, intuition, initiation? In this chapter I will be exploring these questions and others, by looking at the art of interpretation in a range of contexts, and investigating whether geographers' attempts at creating new knowledge can indeed be described as 'arrogant work'.

ANALYSIS AND INTERPRETATION: WHICH WAY IS OUT?

[T]he real mystique of qualitative inquiry lies in the processes of using data rather than in the processes of *gathering* data. (Wolcott, 1994: 1)

One problem is perhaps that whilst we are trying to 'get at' worlds which are in some sense 'external', our interpretations are always inevitably 'internal' and projected out (Wylie, 2002) – and it is difficult to get this 'internal' comfortably displayed in the 'external'. In order to explore this I want to start by outlining the distinction between 'analysis' and 'interpretation'. Analysis may be seen as the 'external' presentation in-the-world and the physical act of coding, cutting, grouping, tallying this 'out-thereness'; whereas interpretation is the 'internal', something that hides deeper and lingers longer in many

ways. Therefore I will be talking about much more than the act of cutting and filleting out data on the butcher's slab of our desk.

The problem is a frequent confusion between 'analysis' and 'interpretation'. Whereas analysis might be seen to be addressing the key features from the data, interpretation attempts to move beyond the data, not to be restricted by it, 'to reach out for understanding or explanation beyond the limits of what can be explained with the degree of certainty usually associated with analysis' (Wolcott, 1994: 10–11); what Harry Wolcott describes as his 'third way' (see Table 20.1).[2]

The very act of constructing data is in itself an act of interpretation. We choose what to observe, what to record, what to render invisible. There is no such thing as 'immaculate perception'. After that we start the 'analysis'. We sift and sort, select, discard, code and recode, categorising, comparing and contrasting. Analysis thus, suggest Dewsbury *et al.* (2002), involves a certain kind of 'vampirism', draining events for the sake of extracting order, structure and process. Interpretation goes beyond this 'curious vampirism'. Rather than stripping the data of its essential messiness, the aim is to capture this messiness in all its glory and say something about it. Thus an element of reflexivity, on the part of researcher (and perhaps, as we shall see, researched) moves *analysis* into *interpretation*.

As there are already numerous eloquent texts detailing the 'techniques of analysis' for qualitative researchers (see for example Crang and Cook, 2007; Hay, 2005; Shurmer-Smith, 2001; Silverman, 2004), this chapter

Table 20.1   Which way?: Layers of interpretation (developed from Wolcott (1994))

	What	How	Wolcott's way
Description	Descriptive account of data in original form 'What is going on?'	Observations reported Data 'speaks for itself'	First way
Analysis	Identifies key factors and relationships 'How do things work?'	Systematic description of interrelationships Data 'talks amongst itself'	Second way
Interpretation	Meanings and context explored 'What is to be made of it all?'	'Theory and speculation' We enter a 'conversation' with the data	Third way

is primarily concerned with taking that *extra* step; the leap into the unknown; Wolcott's 'third way'. Of recognising, acknowledging and reflecting upon the fact that interpretation is *not* something confined to the space and time sandwiched neatly between 'field' and 'output'.

Qualitative methods, as this volume indicates, are numerous and diverse, from traditional ethnography, interviews and focus groups, to archive analysis, landscape interpretation and visual methodologies. However the common ground for all is their interpretivist epistemology: the belief that we can only know the world through examining *interpretations of it*. Nonetheless, if you thumb through the indexes of many key texts in qualitative research, the very idea of interpretation is not something that appears to feature heavily. Does this invisibility imply that interpretation is not something we as qualitative researchers do? Or is it just something we as qualitative researchers find it hard to write about? If all knowledge takes the form of interpretation (Sontag, 1978), then why do we seemingly shy away from making it more clearly central and explicit in our final outputs? Perhaps Allison Blunt and colleagues have one answer:

> Most pieces of published work … are presented as completed, neat and tidy arguments with all the loose ends tied away and all the evidence pointing in the same direction … On one side is an orderly, well-composed picture. On the other side is a tangle of threads. (2003: 3)

In this chapter we turn therefore to the tangle of threads, to explore this 'art' I speak of in the title. In doing so I turn first to reading between the lines of my own journey to this point, to interpret why I am here now, writing this, and engulfed yet again in the very act and art of interpretation.

INTO THE VOID?

[A] 'postmodern' ethnographer, concluding an informant interview, says to the interviewee, 'Well,

that's the story of my life. Do you have anything to add?' (Wolcott, 1994: 44)

When I was lost in the depths of analysis for my PhD thesis I found I became completely lost in the *process* of interpretation. Not lost in the sense of having no direction, but lost in terms of being fully immersed, embedded in the material I was seeking to understand. All the conventional accounts of 'analysing' qualitative data at my disposal seemed to me to be missing out a fundamental part of what it is to be engaged in the process of interpretation as a qualitative human geographer. The researcher's presence often becoming 'a ghostly absence' in published papers (Crang, 2003). So convinced was I of a 'conspiracy of silence' around this part of the research process, that I even subtitled the first of my methodology chapters 'or being honest about qualitative analysis'.[3]

There was a time when 'men of geography' would stride the narrow world, mapping faithfully the borders they crossed, the mountains they climbed and the rivers and seas they navigated. For those parts still unknown – those great expanses of watery blackness, beyond which lay they knew not what – artistic interpretation had free reign. 'There be monsters' may not have been proved empirically or even be verifiably accurate, but it captured the essence of the unknown, the danger of countless lives lost at sea, and the terror of things we were yet to understand. An apt interpretation which served a point, said something about the knowledge of the time, a lot about the culture and beliefs, and enough for us to still understand and interpret meaning from it several hundred years later.

Following this art and science separated, the enlightenment brought with it a certainty and rationality based on scientific principles. Maps were 'stripped of all elements of fantasy and religious belief' and became abstract and functional (Harvey, 1989: 206). At the end of the twentieth century however, the postmodern turn forced academics to once more question what they knew, how they knew it and how they presented it (Tierney, 2002).

Starting out on my academic career at the time, I felt myself in a climate still coloured by the certainty of the quantitative revolution, with the discipline in some senses still clinging to the coat tails of the statistician. More than a decade later and undoubtedly the discipline has come far. No longer is there the sense of outsiderness, otherness and difference for a young researcher starting out on the journey of discovery into qualitative methodologies. Certainly in a British context it is now almost *de rigueur* to throw one's lot in with the qualitative camp. But it seems to me it is no clearer what we are doing. No easier to get to the bottom of precisely what it is these eminent geographers are doing when they 'transform' their data produced from ethnographies, interviews, explorations of performativity and visual deconstructions. The act of interpretation is still one performed behind closed doors, despite more honesty and openness about researcher positionality and the difficulty of representation, the more creative aspect of what we do to make sense of our data remains too often cloaked in silence. Should we not finally be celebrating that art of interpretation as being a fundamental part of what we are creating and not something that we should be keeping quiet about?

To perhaps oversimplify it a little, it seems that what many qualitative researchers seem to end up doing is analysing 'text' (gained from interview transcripts, etc.), rather than the *experience or phenomenon* under investigation. Although often our data is restricted to 'texts' gained from interviews, fieldwork diaries or participant observation, I am not convinced this limits us to working solely with words on paper (MacKian, 2000; 2004). With even the most basic of raw materials there is more to the art of interpretation than most conventional accounts of analysis might have us believe.

Some words about words: The example of interviews

Although interviewing receives widespread attention and is a commonly used qualitative method in human geography, most of the attention is focused on interview structure (i.e. structured, semi-structured and unstructured) and the use of various forms of thematic analysis. Far less attention has been given to alternative strategies for understanding and interpreting interviews. (Wiles et al., 2005: 89)

The very existence of the *research process itself* means the resulting information is a *focused reality*. A negotiated creation *based upon* some event under investigation, guided by expectations and conventions, which in terms of the reality of the original experience is somewhat unreal. It is therefore an intersubjectively constructed interpretation already. Interviews, for example, have predetermined formats in which the event being investigated will be presented, due to the simple fact that we arrange a particular time, grouping, venue and setting. The whole research process is 'shot through' with 'incompleteness and eventness' (Latham, 2003: 2005) and is to a greater or lesser extent 'articifial' (McGregor, 2005).

This artificiality continues with the production of 'transcripts'; with italics, pauses and intonations added to the spoken word, we represent our research encounters in written form. The usual rules or constructs applied to the written word are often not compatible with the spoken word. We seldom speak in 'sentences' with capitals at the beginning and a fullstop at the end. Therefore each idiosyncratic interpretation by the researcher of the spoken word into textual format begins the process of presenting that data to the end reader. At this stage the gaps, the pauses, changes in direction, detours and interruptions in conversation are seen and interpreted primarily pragmatically in ordering the flow of the interview into a visually convenient format (the same way we *type* paragraphs but do not *speak* them). Thus a 'typographical interpretation' is the first step to battering 'dynamic oral and aural performances' (Wiles *et al.*, 2005: 90) into static texts on the page. There is then little guidance 'out there' beyond variations on the theme of thematic analysis.

Having conducted the interview (be it unstructured or otherwise), the researcher is left with a wealth of data in the form of tapes and transcripts, notes and fieldwork diaries. The commonly accepted norm is then to 'code' and 'categorise', searching for 'themes', be this with pen and paper, word processing, or apparently more sophisticated software packages. It may seem an obvious conclusion that repeated and dominant topics or constructs be drawn out, but does such splicing of words constitute interpretation? Is that repeated theme *central* to the individual's lived experience, or are there more important themes being overlooked because they are not clearly portrayed repeatedly running through the text? Any interior designer will tell you it is the occasionally appearing 'accent' colour which completes the picture, not the dominant base palate. Do we run the risk of overlooking the 'accent' if we focus on obvious base?

How do researchers *know* they've found the essence of the experience and hence the 'right' themes by purely relying on the *words* participants give us? 'Talk is "messy"' (Wiles *et al.*, 2005), and I am not alone in questioning whether 'the wordy practices that we encounter are representational events after all' (Laurier and Philo, 2006: 355). Winchester (2000) points out there is often a numerical significance attached to 'representative' quotes, indicating idiosyncrasies or majorities. However, we must remember numerical superiority is still no reason to believe in representativeness. I am reminded of the peculiarly British habit of discussing the weather. It is invariably the opening gambit in a conversation, an ice-breaker with a new acquaintance, or we may even use it in an attempt at jocularity. Whereas the true intention of those lines might more accurately be revealing of our innermost thoughts and desires.

These 'weatherisms' are not always so simple or so blatant, but they illustrate nicely how often we might say one thing and mean another (Table 20.2). Therefore I suggest that methods which code the words or themes used *may* be doing little more than analysing the *text of the transcript*, when it is in fact the experience or story told by that research encounter which we *really* want to understand. It may be my concerns are unfounded, but I am not alone (see for example Laurier, 1998). Apart from a conventional sentence or two about coding and recoding it is not always indicated in final reports, academic articles and presentations precisely *how* the interpreter got at the experience and not the text alone.

The interview text in itself reveals little more than the respondent's ability to use the spoken word to convey messages and the interviewer's ability to grasp the meaning of these words and from them pose further questions and facilitate the art of conversation. For Janine Wiles and colleagues (2005) the challenge now lies in deciding what elements of the interview are 'important', and how these are to be 'recorded'. Thus the danger of moving too far down the coding avenue, is that we lose the 'many layers of meaning' (Wiles *et al.*, 2005) that were present in the original encounter. We also lose the 'narrative' of the tale being told, the 'whole' of how the respondent wanted to be heard. Furthermore we run the risk of assuming the 'whole story' is visible in the text.

But because we are only human, and computers are merely machines, we have to do

Table 20.2   Intentions and weatherisms: The art of not saying what we mean

Words uttered	What they wanted to say
'Freezing isn't it!?'	'I'm terrified of this meeting we're going into but don't know how to broach the subject with you.'
'Did you get caught in the downpour?'	'You look great with wet hair!'
'Nice time of year for the weather!'	'I'd like to ask you for a drink but we've only just met, honestly I'm a fun person, stop and talk to me…please….'

what we can. And so we fall back on scientific concepts of 'frequency', or on theoretically informed ideas about what *should* be important from prior knowledge. As the text stands however these themes remain *sequentially* ordered in terms of the interview process, but are not yet related to the *whole lived experience* of the subject. Since it is this lived experience and not the structure of the interview we are aiming to elucidate and understand it is vital to interpret the significance of these constructs. We must determine whether or not a recurrent theme is integral to that lived experience or indicative of another process or relationship not revealed to us through the text alone; or perhaps it is nothing more than a 'weatherism'. Themes at this stage are little more than random points on a number line we cannot see. We must develop a method of interpretation that is sensitive to this 'partial-ness and moment-ness of the accounts offered' (Latham, 2003: 2005), to uncover what that number line *looks* like and how the points fit together along it.

Yi-Fu Tuan (2001) suggests there are active and passive elements to experience, and although we can analyse the 'active' through the words the respondent tells us, it is more difficult to interpret the 'passive' – what they are *not* telling us. Research respondents do not theorise or problematise their everyday experiences in the same way we do, and so may find it difficult to answer questions asking them to reflect on the taken-for-granted (Latham, 2003) or 'largely happenstance' nature of everyday experience (Tuan, 2001). Hence we may end up illuminating commonly accepted modes of 'talk', certain commonplace intersubjective actions or experiences, and not *yet* be touching upon the subjective world of the respondent As researchers we are clearly aiming for more than proof that we are good conversationalists; so where to now? The crucial issue is 'how we move from treating the elements of interview talk as discrete units to be codified, counted and depersonalized, to a more contextual analysis and *interpretation*' (Wiles *et al.*, 2005: 97 Italics added).

It is necessary to try and fathom out how the blocks of texts, the identified 'constructs' or 'themes', are ordered *in the subjective world of the respondent*, and how this subjective ordering informs that person's relationship and interaction with the social and physical worlds. It must be realised that it is therefore not the blocks of text themselves which are integral to elucidating the lived experience. They are in fact little more than interpretations used to depict that experience in the interview situation. Our job is to try to find the essence of their interpretation of their reality, from their representation of it to us in the research encounter. So how might we move beyond the text and 'imbue traditional research methodologies with a sense of the creative' (Latham, 2003: 2000)?

IMAGINING OTHERWORLDS: INTERPRETATION AS AN ART

> So, coding has made me do some laborious interpretative work and, most painful of all, I've summarized hundreds of pages of speech into key codes. But then, I just cut and paste a nice quote as a lone representative voice into my text. (Laurier, 1998: 38)

> We simply do not have the methodological resources and skills to undertake research that takes the sensuous, embodied, creativeness of social practice seriously. (Latham, 2003: 1998)

Mike Crang (2005) suggested that with the maturing of qualitative approaches there has emerged a 'certain conventionality' to our methods. My concerns so far have reflected this trend. However, alongside this conformity, we are also witnessing the emergence of some geographers who *are* treating their data more creatively. Here I want to explore three particular examples of qualitative geographers who are critically and artistically opening the process of interpretation up beyond the strictures of conventionality. Through the arts of storytelling, performance and idle speculation, we will see how interpretation can open us up to more aesthetic, less wordy, dimensions of experience in place.

Telling tales: Once upon a journey...

Tierney called for a more protean and engaged portrayal of our research subjects, suggesting we should 'broaden the narrative strategies we employ so our texts are built more in relation to fiction and storytelling, rather than in response to logical empiricism' (2002: 385). Rather than getting bogged down in the minutiae of codes and words, some qualitative geographers are acknowledging more explicitly the research encounter as creating a story itself. This is seen in the literature on two levels: firstly the text itself is *interpreted* as a story; secondly the research experience is *presented* as a story.

Firstly, Wiles *et al.* (2005) offer an example of using of narrative analysis as an alternative to thematic coding and analysis of interview transcripts. Here, instead of focusing on the words and themes covered in the interview, the narrative structure of the transcript is uncovered. The text is interpreted as a story being told, with an 'abstract' to frame the story, 'orientation' features to set the stage, elements of 'evaluation' and resolution to complete a 'fully formed narrative' (Labov, 1972). Narrative analysis is therefore acknowledging that 'talk is used strategically as well as to represent ideas' (Wiles *et al.*, 2005: 91). Merely focusing on the words used will not necessarily uncover the true meaning of those words in the story being told. This method allows the interpreter to understand *how* people talk as well as *what* they actually say, and hence to 'access the nuances of interview talk' (Wiles *et al.*, 2005: 89). Something which, as I suggested earlier, is often overlooked or simply ignored.

Narrative analysis therefore does at least offer a chance to get beneath the 'weatherisms' and offer an interpretation of the context in which they are being used. However, as a strategy for interpretation it is, for some, a little too structured and formal and I therefore wish to concentrate here on the second use of storytelling – the use of narrative to interpret and represent the research encounter.

In his analysis of embodied interaction with nature John Wylie uses narrative to structure the presentation of his research process and analysis together, leading the reader by the hand up Glastonbury Tor (2002), along the coastal path (2005) or 'in and around Smoothlands' (2006). Here interpretation is clear from the outset and the careful weaving of prior expectations, traditional 'research evidence' and his reflections 'in-action' and 'on-action' (Schön, 1991), provide a 'story' that is perhaps far more 'artistic' in a literary sense than the average geography paper.

Wylie's papers are indeed far from pedestrian. His work aims to explore 'the possibilities of deploying a fragmentary and narrational rather than thematic or schematic structure' (Wylie, 2005: 235). Rather than seeking coherent analysis, his use of narrative style allows for 'contrast and progression to emerge' (2002: 245) in the same way as it would in the experience itself. Thus he overcomes my criticisms in the earlier parts of this chapter, as he strives to maintain a sense of 'fidelity to the original research' (Wylie, 2005: 235). Indeed this use of the narrative to 'invent writing strategies' (Tierney, 2002) took a further leap forward in Wylie's 2006 paper on Smoothlands. Rather than using text to follow the narrative of his research encounter, the page is dominated by carefully placed images of the landscape, metaphorically representing the striations and topographies of the landscape. Short bursts of text spew forth – predominantly quotes from three key authors – interspersed with reflective retreats. There is no bibliography, no labels for the pictures, no deference to any of the conventionalities of academic publishing. I have no idea what the central message of the paper is, if there is one at all, but I am left with a sense of awe, a feeling of having been there, on the edge of the world, buffeted by wind and waves, and mesmerised by the rhythms of the all-surrounding sea.

This sort of kinetic description (Kneale, 2003) and interpretation has its value in terms of revealing the inner workings of the researcher's mind (and the outer workings of the body), but is it really work at all or simply 'the casual, unstructured sensing of our surroundings' (Zelinsky, 2001: 7)? This can occupy all our working hours, but most of us would seldom choose to write about it for our peers. Should we? The examples from Wylie's work illustrate his drive to deploy both 'critical and creative registers'. For some, his literary style – 'a secluded, silent idyll, cupped in the green hands of the enclosing forest' (2002: 239); evocative imagery – 'he was naked to the waist and his leathered, lean torso writhed with tattoos' (2002: 239); and clear disregard for many of the formalities of the academic game (2006) – may represent a step too far in his walk away from the critical. Nonetheless, his 'ache, ennui and enervation' (2005: 240) certainly serve to bring alive the relation between self and landscape, and his linguistic and visual evocations of the places he visits are as legitimate a claim to interpreting the English landscape as such classics as WG Hoskins's *Making of the English Landscape* (1977).[4]

Performance and embodiment

> The idea of day-to-day life as involving an element of performance is pervasive in contemporary popular culture. (Latham, 2003: 2003)

If we can accept the research encounter and our 'data' as 'stories', it is a small step to opening the creative door a fraction wider. Traditionally qualitative researchers have shied away from explicitly acknowledging or utilising the body, its messy subjectivities and unpredictability, in favour of adopting the stance of 'detached' disembodied observer as analyst, effectively removing themselves from the picture (Wolcott, 1994). 'It is still unusual for geographers to acknowledge the body and its use as a research tool in geographical research' (Parr, 2001: 166). The reality of everyday experience is often the memories of 'materials, movements, shapes, gestures' (Dewsbury *et al.*, 2002: 437), rather than the words we encountered around them.

And it is such subtleties we sense not through intellect alone, but through the *body*. Hence there are some qualitative geographers who do explicitly use and explore the nature of embodiment in their interpretations and I wish to turn to them now.

Claiming that human geography needs to be 'more imaginative' Alan Latham (2003) suggests reframing what we do as researchers as something more creative allows us to address novel questions and access experience that conventional methods fail to address adequately. He suggests the 'performative' turn in geography allows us to view the research process itself as a performance, allowing for 'a more experimental and more flexible attitude towards both the production and interpretation of research evidence' (2003: 1993).

Reflecting my earlier suggestion that the interview is a negotiated relationship Latham (2003) warns that if we fail to acknowledge this in our interpretations we fail to take *practice* seriously. He chooses to use diaries to act as 'proxy observer' to enable his research participants to map out their daily movement through and use of public space. However, with a layering of evidence, rather than adopting the sort of 'hit and run' style of subsequently taking these off the respondent and 'analysing them', he moves on to use the diaries as the basis of further interviews. It is the following step which is the one of key interest here, however. In interpreting these various layers of evidence, Latham then produces what he calls 'time-space collages' – an amalgamation of material from interview, diaries, photographs and researcher reflection. The result is a highly creative visual representation which captures the flow and movement of the respondent's day, their reflections upon it – in the form of photographs and comments – as well as the researcher's interpretations. It is artistic, lively, informative and fun! Not to mention incredibly straightforward to navigate, through the use of different styles of text to distinguish who is 'talking' or 'reflecting'. In this way we see before us the negotiated relationship presented as a collage of movement, moments, actions, reflections and 'analysis'.

Here I am reminded of a conversation between friends over the harvest from a digital camera. For one the 'horrible' pictures, the ones with irretrievable red eye, smudged faces and awkward angles, would be deleted immediately. Possibly never even making it to the inbox of the computer. For the other, each random shot of the excessive capturing that digital photography allows would be carefully filed along with the 'presentable' pictures of the story. To be returned to in order to remember the 'real' story obliterated by time and vanity from the fallible human memory, but always undeniably present on the hard-drive. James Kneale (2003: 50) reminds us when reading a text, to 'do the text justice often means acknowledging that it doesn't just mean one thing'. The list of photos remaining on the memory stick will tell one story. The gaps obliterated between might tell another. The co-presence of the gaps and presences, tells a story not just about the event being depicted, but about the photographer's views on what counts as legitimate representations of that story to an external voyeur. How has Latham accounted for the photos deleted, or not taken, and the gaps that are left behind, both visible and invisible? In acknowledging the co-production of the interpretative process, by both respondent and researcher, Latham's time-space collages perhaps go some way to answering this common concern of qualitative geographers who have to rely on what our respondents choose to show us!

Incidents and speculations

Impasses, silences and aporias … These are the points at which language finds its limits. (Laurier and Philo, 2006: 353)

By 'rediscovering' the body (Longhurst, 1997; Parr, 2003) – the 'vehicle of being-in-the-world' (Merleau-Ponty, 1962) – geographers are opening up not just to a new research tool,

but also a *site of and tool for* interpretation in qualitative research. Indeed, for some all they need is to take their body out into space and speculate on the incidents around them. Without recourse to the artistic tendencies of Latham or Wylie, other geographers have continued to use the written word to portray interpretations of 'other' than the things we hear from interviews or view through observations. There are sounds, smells, moments of touch, flashes of déjà vu, all of these inform the experience and thus all legitimately hold a claim to a stake in interpretation.

Although there are many examples of this I wish to concentrate on the way in which one author (sometimes with co-authors) has allowed this art of speculating on the everyday to direct the nature of his interpretation in such a way that it subsequently dictates the style in which his research and interpretations are presented. I borrow from one of his conventions in order to set the scene:

Vignette: Quite a stir was caused over our departmental coffee one morning with the arrival of Area Volume 38 Number 4. The first article – some thought rather aptly entitled 'Possible Geographies' – appeared to be little more than the idle speculations of one of the authors whilst he sat waiting in a café. Some colleagues threw their noses in the air, others feigned indifference, whilst one launched into an eloquent tirade of abuse at the unsuspecting article.

The piece was one by Eric Laurier and Chris Philo, whose message was that '[s]cholars of social life can, scepticism contained, learn much from taking seriously how any encounter unfolds' (2006: 353). Laurier has spent some years taking everyday encounters seriously and creating publications out of events that might pass most of us by (1998, 2001; Laurier et al., 2002). His reasoning for doing so is not to limit himself by the requirements and performances of cultural geography to such an extent as to miss the point of what is really 'going on' (Laurier, 2001).

The focus on the everyday and 'just-this-ness' (Laurier and Philo, 2006) lends itself clearly to alternative forms of interpretation and hence the focus on them here. Instead of

cutting out quotes from a transcript and forcing us to take at their word the context and
interpretation of these, Laurier and his co-
workers pick out whole 'events', placing
them in the text complete with 'evidence' of
interpretation at work. This may be in the
form of various symbols used to depict contextual 'things' we cannot 'see' in the words
(Laurier, 2001), 'Vignettes' drawn from a
variety of 'instants' and put together in such a
way as to aid the reader's understanding of
the authors' interpretations (Laurier et al.,
2002), or detailed footnotes explaining both
analysis techniques and the style of interpretation (Laurier, 1998). Whilst this breaks with
convention, as it 'creates' fabricated coali-
tions from the data and reveals very clearly
the 'knife' used by the analyst, it makes the
interpretation transparent and that much more
human. As Laurier himself says, it brings the
way we write closer to the way we talk and
understand in context. 'Although interpreting
the text might be the exemplary discursive
analysis to do, we … look at how the text is
used procedurally in its setting rather than
isolated lying on the desk of an academic
researcher' (Laurier et al., 2002: 361).

Laurier and Philo maintain 'there is much
to learn from continuing to revisit the places
that (we assume) we already know (about)'
(2006: 356). Whilst some might beg to differ,
such revisiting forces the researcher into an
introspective level of interpretation which by
definition has to get beneath the obvious
external, because we already 'know' about
that. Thus whilst I might agree with my
vociferous colleague, that the *focus* of the
paper was perhaps somewhat inconsequen-
tial, the idea of uncovering the 'seen but
unnoticed' (Laurier et al., 2002) *is* worth
pushing home if we are to encourage more
qualitative human geographers to dig deeper
in their interpretations.[5]

You've been framed: The limits to interpretation

[O]ur projects are often unstable entities which are
not only presented, but actually exist, in multiple
versions given to funders, colleagues, friends,
family, peers and (different) respondents, none of
which need be necessarily the 'true one.' (Crang,
2003: 497)

Are there limits to the possibilities of
interpretation, given the 'abstract intellectual
goals' of research (Wylie, 2003)? Who frames
our art and how? Our outputs are measured
predominantly by journal publications – and
these are predominantly restricted to the
written word and a limited number of those.
Perhaps the odd black and white photograph,
map or diagram might break up the flow of
text, but how true to the original experience
can these really be? For those of us straddling the border between 'soft' humanities
and 'harder' sciences, for example medicine,
education or environmental concerns, how
do we tame our beasts of interpretation to fit
the standard rules of presentation for scientific publication? The 'structures in which we
are placed' (Tierney, 2002) have profound
implications for the type of interpretational
avenues open to us, and how far down them
we may travel. We are also in part framed by
the time limits of necessity imposed upon us.
Interpretation has to be brought to a halt at
some stage. Or does it? A colleague, over
coffee, once said to me 'There is a final stage
[to interpretation] which has as much to do
with producing a report/paper/article as it is
the narrative of the sample'.

This chapter has been curiously silent on
the final act of writing, and how it is itself a
part of the interpretive process. Undeniably it
is, and my silence has more to do with the
brief I was given for the chapter and a respect
for the running order of the book, than any
indication that it is not a part of the art of
interpretation we are engaged in. However
artificial it may seem to separate the end
'writing' stage from the ongoing 'interpretive' process, the very practice of conveying
our art to an audience demands that somewhere we 'invoke boundaries and blur borders' to use Cindi Katz's (1994) phrase. This
chapter has its borders and hence I had to
draw the act of interpretation to a halt somewhere, even if the reality is that it is ongoing
through the written word and beyond.

REFLECTIONS: INTO THE FUTURE...

Thus numerous frames limit our ability to learn something from the investigations of our research beyond the words which we use to represent it. 'These are the points at which language find its limits … things, events, encounters, emotions and more that are unspeakable, unwriteable and, of course, unrepresentable' (Laurier and Philo, 2006: 353). Perhaps eschewing academic conventions, becoming more open and writing less formally will open the discipline to the possibilities beyond 'advice to authors' and research assessment ratings (Sibley, 2003). 'The real voyage of discovery consists not in seeking new landscapes but in having new eyes' (Marcel Proust).[6]

I have offered three examples of work as possible solutions to demystifying the interpretive process and taking it 'beyond the text'. By 'reshaping the existing all-too-narrow conventions' (Latham, 2003: 2009) the examples illustrate that by 'transgressing norms' (Tierney, 2002) qualitative researchers can put interpretation centre stage, rather than relegating it to the implicit 'something' that we never hear about. In particular we have seen how using the body provides us with the interpretive lens to understand and experience space in ways which might ordinarily be hidden. Latham's 'time-space collages', Wylie's at times rather baroque accounts and Laurier's vignettes, take one undeniably into the thick of the moment in question. Nonetheless these accounts remain, as Wylie admits, 'angled towards academic narratives' (2005: 244). So what might the 'next step' be? If ideas of the visual, the performative and everyday incidents were developed by qualitative geographers as a way to enable our audiences to *interpret with us* the material we have gathered, the 'texts' that emerge may be very different to the ones we might choose to write for routine academic consumption (Figure 20.1).

> Do we really know anything and, if so, what? And how do we know it? And how do we know that we know it? And how do we know that we know that we know it? (Jones and Wilson, 1987: 302)

Claims of truth are simply about the different ways in which people construct their understandings of the world; i.e. their interpretations. In this chapter I have suggested that the art of interpretation is often invisible. 'Analysis' is privileged and interpretation rarely discussed. As a result what ends up being *called* interpretation is really 'the analysis of text'. Text is 'lifted out' – frequently based on quantitative principles – and then labelled interpretation. Thus a positivist logic underpins much qualitative research, using quantitative indicators to suggest that meaning is something that can be 'counted up' from the words we gather.

My aim has been to encourage a certain barefoot irreverence to some of these more structured tools, and to highlight the work of some who are exploring more arresting and meaningful ways of interpreting their data. To paraphrase Wiles *et al.* (2005), all approaches reduce the richness and messiness of human experience. But there are ways to recapture some of that messiness and reveal the noise which is so often ironed out. Therefore I suggest we need to continue our attempts to 'disrupt' the text (Wiles *et al.*, 2005), to 'open things up rather than seal them up' (Wolcott, 1994: 260). I cannot hope in the scope of a single chapter to explore fully how we might do this, I hope instead to have offered a flavour of the options available, and some inspiration to take these further. The rest I will leave up to the reader.

Reality is indeed 'contested and up for grabs' (Tierney, 2002: 393). And having completed this exercise I know one thing: Interpretation in all its forms, hinges upon the researcher allowing themselves and their data some leeway. We are undeniably in the business of telling stories – let's throw ourselves into them and make them good ones!

NOTES

1.   Although of course I have to say at this point, that the 'final' piece of work will itself of course be open to further deconstruction and interpretation

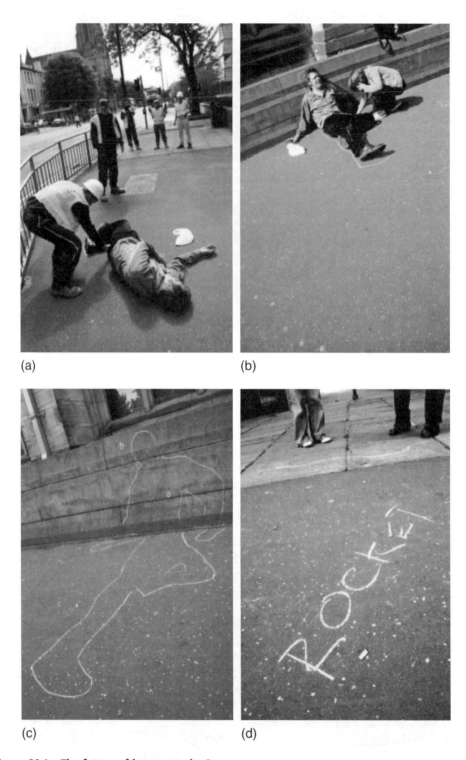

(a)   (b)

(c)   (d)

Figure 20.1   The future of interpretation?

ad infinitum: 'What is really going on in things, what is really happening, is always to come' (Caputo, 1996: 31).

2. It is important to stress that this should not be thought of as a linear progression, but rather as Wolcott says three ways to 'do something' with qualitative data.

3. I say 'the first' because the process of interpretation and how it informed the whole practice of research seemed to me to warrant at least two chapters before the chapters which actually dealt with the 'data' itself.

4. Although the photograph of his blistered foot was too much for even me!

5. Indeed the authors themselves stress this is not just for 'comfortable cafés'.

6. http://www.quotationspage.com/quote/31288.html.

7. Michael Mayhew holds a Leverhulme Artist in Residence with the Geography Discipline in the School of Environment and Development, University of Manchester, England.

REFERENCES

Agar, M.H. (1980) *The professional stranger: an informal introduction to ethnography.* London: Academic Press.

Bennett, K. and Shurmer-Smith, P. (2002) 'Representation of research: creating a text', in P. Shurmer-Smith (ed.) *Doing cultural geography.* London: Sage. pp. 211–22.

Blunt, A., Gruffudd, P., May, J., Ogborn, M. and Pinder, D. (eds) (2003) *Cultural geography in practice.* London: Arnold.

Caputo, J.D. (1996) *Deconstruction in a Nutshell: a conversation with Jacques Derrida.* New York: Fordham University Press.

Crang, M. (2002) 'Qualitative methods: the new orthodoxy?', *Progress in Human Geography* 26 (5): 647–55.

Crang, M. (2003) 'Qualitative methods: touchy, feely, look-see?', *Progress in Human Geography* 27 (4): 494–504.

Crang, M. (2005) 'Qualitative methods: there is nothing outside the text?', *Progress in Human Geography* 29 (20): 225–33.

Crang, M. and Cook, I. (2007) *Doing ethnographies.* London: Sage.

Dewsbury, J.D., Harrison, P., Rose, M. and Wylie, J. (2002) 'Enacting geographies', *Geoforum* 33 (4): 437–40.

Harvey, D. (1989) *The condition of postmodernity.* Oxford: Basil Blackwell.

Hay, I. (2005) *Qualitative research methods in human geography.* 2nd Edition. Australia: Oxford University Press.

Hoskins, W.G. (1977) *The making of the English landscape.* London: Hodder and Staughton.

Hyndman, J. (2001) 'The field as here and now, not there and then', *The Geographical Review* 91 (1/2): 262–72.

Kneale, J. (2003) 'Secondary worlds: reading novels as geographical research', in A. Blunt, P. Gruffudd, J. May, M. Ogborn and D. Pinder (eds) *Cultural geography in practice.* London: Arnold. pp. 39–51.

Labov, W. (1972) *Language in the inner city: studies in the black English vernacular.* Philadelphia: University of Pennsylvania Press.

Latham, A. (2003) 'Research, performance, and doing human geography: some reflections on the diary-photograph, diary-interview method', *Environment and Planning A* 35 (11): 1993–2017.

Laurier, E. (1998) 'Geographies of talk: "Max left a message for you"', *Area* 31 (1): 36–45.

Laurier, E. (2001) 'Why people say where they are during mobile phone calls', *Environment and Planning D: Society and Space* 19 (4): 485–504.

Laurier, E. and Philo, C. (2006) 'Possible geographies: a passing encounter in a café', *Area* 38 (4): 353–63.

Laurier, E., Whyte, A. and Buckner, K. (2002) 'Neighbouring as an occassioned activity: "finding a lost cat"', *Environment and Planning D: Space and Culture* 5 (4): 346–67.

Longhurst, R. (1997) '(Dis)embodied geographies', *Progress in Human Geography* 21 (4): 486–501.

MacKian, S. (2000) 'Contours of coping: mapping the subject world of long-term illness', *Health and Place* 6: 95–104.

MacKian, S. (2004) 'Mapping reflexive communities: visualising the geographies of emotion', *Journal of Social and Cultural Geography* 5 (4): 615–31.

McGregor, A. (2005) 'Negotiating nature: exploring discourse through small group research', *Area* 37 (4): 423–32.

Merleau-Ponty, M. (1962) *The phenomenology of perception.* London: Routledge and Kegan Paul.

Okely, J. (1992) 'Anthropology and autobiography: participatory experience and embodied knowledge', in J. Okely and H. Callaway (eds) *Anthropology and autobiography.* London: Routledge. pp. 1–28.

Parr, H. (2001) 'Feeling, reading, and making bodies in space', *The Geographical Review* 91 (1/2): 158–67.

Parr, H. (2003) 'Researching bodies in virtual space', in A. Blunt, P. Gruffudd, J. May, M. Ogborn and D. Pinder (eds) *Cultural geography in practice*. London: Arnold. pp. 55–68.

Schön, D. (1991) *The reflective practitioner: how professionals think in action*. Aldershot: Ashgate.

Shurmer-Smith, P. (ed.) (2001) *Doing cultural geography*. London: Sage.

Sibley, D. (2003) 'Geography and psychoanalysis: tensions and possibilities', *Social and Cultural Geography* 4 (3): 391–99.

Silverman, D. (2004) *Doing qualitative research: a practical handbook*. 2nd Edition. London: Sage.

Sontag, S. (1978) *Illness as a metaphor*. Middlesex: Penguin.

Thrift, N. (2000) 'Dead or alive?', in I. Cook, D. Crouch, S. Naylor and J. Ryan (eds) *Cultural turns/geographical turns: perspectives on cultural geography*. Harlow: Prentice Hall. pp. 1–6.

Tierney, W.G. (2002) 'Get real: representing reality', *Qualitative Studies in Education* 15 (4): 385–98.

Tuan, Y-F. (2001) 'Life as a field trip', *The Geographical Review* 91 (1/2): 41–5.

Wiles, J.L., Rosenberg, M.W. and Kearns, R.A. (2005) 'Narrative analysis as a strategy for understanding interview talk in geographic research', *Area* 37 (1): 89–99.

Winchester, H. (2000) 'Qualitative research and its place in human geography', in I. Hay (ed.) *Qualitative research methods in human geography*. Oxford: Oxford University Press. pp. 1–22.

Wolcott, H.F. (1994) *Transforming qualitative data: description, analysis and interpretation*. London: Sage.

Wylie, J. (2002) 'An essay on ascending Glastonbury Tor', *Geoforum* 33 (4): 441–54.

Wylie, J. (2005) 'A single day's walking: narrating self and landscape on the South West Coast path', *Transactions of the Institute of British Geographers* 30 (2): 234–47.

Wylie, J. (2006) 'Smoothlands: fragments/landscapes/fragments', *Cultural geographies* 13 (3): 458–65.

Zelinsky, W. (2001) 'The geographer as voyeur', *The Geographical Review* 91 (1/2): 1–8.

21

Representing the Other: Negotiating the Personal and the Political

Garth Myers

If we no longer think of the relationship between cultures and their adherents as perfectly contiguous, totally synchronous, wholly correspondent, and if we think of cultures as permeable ... a more promising situation appears ... To see Others not as ontologically given but as historically constituted would be to erode the exclusivist biases we so often ascribe to cultures, our own not least. Cultures may then be represented as zones of control or of abandonment, of recollection and of forgetting, of force or of dependence, of exclusiveness *or of sharing, all taking place in the global history that is our element.*

(Said, 1989: 225; my italics)

So, why not be more reflexive? At least make a stab at explaining where you're coming from. *Your* position in all of this. Talk about your research as partial, in both senses of the word. It's not the whole story and it's impossible to be 'impartial.' Give your reader something to think with. Include other voices. Position but de-center your own. No single, straightforward conclusions.

(Cook *et al.*, 2005: 22)

INTRODUCTION

I'm not normally carried away by thoughts about postcolonial debates on representing 'The Other' when I eat my lunch. Yet sitting in the lunch room of the University of Kansas Geography Department on a Saturday afternoon in 2005, postcolonial theory invaded my brain right about the time I started in on my stash of peanut butter cookies. Admittedly, this was not a normal workday lunchtime, for I was engaged in a drawn-out meeting of a Task Force formed, with my help, between the Tanzanian Association of Wichita and the Serengeti Association [for Tanzanians] of Kansas City. Still, it was a rather ordinary grant-making meeting, to say nothing of my mundane food.

It was the reactions of the crowds of people I saw passing by the window, on their way to a football match, which really stirred my mind. All of the throngs, it seemed, were white – probably unsurprising in a state and at a university that are both nearly 95 percent white. All of the young men and women in the lunch room vigorously debating the contents of a grant proposal were, with the exception of me, black. Our meeting was clearly out of place to many gaping onlookers. I was caught off guard as some people shook their heads, or a few caught themselves staring and looked away quickly – whether for no real reason or out of inexpressible fear or out of embarrassment at their unconscious racial profiling I cannot say.

In any case, my positionality, the question of *me* representing *Others*, suddenly became very personal and political, to echo my title in this chapter, as the 'exclusivist biases' Said alludes to in the quotation above crept across the faces of onlookers who did not seem to see this scene – to see *us* – on *their* map of global – or even local Kansas – history. Our conversation at the lunch table slipped into a discussion of how frequently my colleagues on the community task force had experienced racism, racial profiling, or a simple accumulation of assumptions about them in their five to ten years of living in the US. Everyone had had multiple experiences of exactly this sort, in effect a feeling of being a specimen in a zoo, so frequently that many of my friends seemed outwardly inured to the fact of their difference as Africans in the land of the Wizard of Oz. The conversation caused me to decide to open this chapter about representing Others in publications from field research with this story, rather than any other ones, because it offered me as vivid a reminder as any map or book or chart or painting that the sometimes airy, distant, or abstract realms of theoretical analyses of the politics of representation are actually very much alive, lived spaces all around us. Like university lunch rooms.

In this chapter, I would like to use my 15 years of experience with qualitative research in, about, or with eastern and southern African people, and the experience of generating three books and a few dozen articles or book chapters from this research, as departure points for discussion of three themes in the negotiation or navigation of the Other, the personal, and the political. The first of these is the balance of representing self and representing others, particularly in publications that emerge from conversations and collaborations. The second concerns the politics of contentious findings – how to represent or not represent the uncomfortable or

discomfiting parts of the story in an age of information overload. Finally, I examine the question of how to manage one's loyalties, in balancing empathy and distance. These are three somewhat intertwined themes, but I try to separate them out and discuss each in turn in the three sections below.

SELF/OTHER/CONVERSATION/ COLLABORATION/CONTESTATION

This is meant to be a chapter dealing with how to represent the Other in published work based on qualitative research, and we'll get there. But there are philosophical, personal, and political issues that crop up before the fieldwork starts and continue through the writing, revision, and publication. Hence these philosophical, personal, and political issues are my starting point here. The greatest of these concerns the researcher's relationships to, and with, the people s/he is researching, and then how to re-present those in publications that anyone in the world might see. When these are relationships fraught with obvious imbalances, tensions, or inequalities, as they have nearly always been for me, the philosophical issues actually have no solution outside of political and strategic decisions. They may develop into a workable ebb and flow, but this is an ongoing conversation that does not stop even with the publication of a work about it.

I have conducted field research in Kenya, Tanzania, Malawi, and Zambia over the last two decades, with the majority of my time in the field spent in the semi-autonomous polity of Zanzibar. Zanzibar is part of Tanzania, but it has its own President, House of Representatives, laws, national history (including its own status as a separate British Protectorate from 1890–1963), and its own convoluted ways of telling that history. The grandest convolution in its history is its Revolution of January 1964, when socialist rebels overthrew its very new (one-month-old) independent government, only to unite, in April 1964, with Tanganyika to form Tanzania. I completed a dissertation on the history and politics of urban development in the city of Zanzibar, where about 40 percent of the polity's population of 1 million lives, and I have returned to Zanzibar regularly in the 15 years since that project, on grants funded by the US National Science Foundation, the National Geographic Society, the US Fulbright program, and the Association of American Geographers, as well as the universities at which I have worked. Out of these research projects in Zanzibar and elsewhere, I have published two books on African cities (while co-editing a third) and three dozen academic journal articles or book chapters.

Unsurprisingly given the balance of time that I have spent there, Zanzibar is the primary empirical setting for much of my published work. Zanzibar is a place with a richly evocative imagery attached to it, to say nothing of a growing tourist economy. It is also a very complicated place. It is torn apart by political divisions, wracked by a bitter history of racial and regional strife, deeply sophisticated socially, deeply poor economically, deeply unjust politically. It has become a place, for me, of love, memory, passion, friendship, football, beauty, wonder, and dreams, but also of nightmares, where my friends have buried their children, where I've seen first-hand the traumas and scars of botched illegal abortion, wife abuse, child abuse, drug abuse, armed robbery, political repression, brutal police interrogation, chronic and endemic terminal disease, mental illness, general depravity, and almost every other thing one would generally conclude to be 'not good' about the place, such that when I add everything up, I feel I understand it as a home, with the whole range of ordinary human experiences we call life within it. Yet it is not home, I do not belong, and I am inevitably confronted by relationships that involve, force, question or subvert the representation of Zanzibar and Zanzibaris as Other.

David Harvey (1989: 47) once complained about geographers and urbanists being 'seduced' by what he termed 'the most liberative and therefore most appealing aspect of postmodern thought – its concern with "otherness."' I understand and to some extent agree with Harvey's complaint about the facile and potentially relativistic tendencies of deconstructionism, but this 'concern with otherness' he wrote about is as much, or more, a conundrum as it is something seductive, liberative, or appealing. Otherness is a mess that does not easily sort itself out. It is 'The Thing That Wouldn't Leave' of qualitative research, an inescapable personal and political knot, like so many knots that tie up qualitative researchers.

Part of the reason that this business of representing otherness is such messiness has to do with its perplexing depth. Human geography owes its existence at some level to the question of areal difference, of how and why one place is different from another. So, for instance, in our discipline I can, if I so wish, professionally pontificate all of the ways that Zanzibar is not Wilkes-Barre, Pennsylvania, the Rust Belt coal town in which I was born and raised. Part of that pontification would be easy, for it might 'be read adequately and directly out of the politics and economics of social inequality' (Pile, 1996: 88). Other *Other* stuff is not so easy. Personal and social boundaries 'carry deep emotional resonances' and so much of our 'knowledge about ourselves and about the world is constituted in the ambivalences of intrapsychic processes' (Pile 1996: 94). Even the physical and biological functions of our brains seem to involve a lot of work in the amygdala to try and separate an us and a them (Schumann, 1993). In representing others we are representing *ourselves* and all the confusion, insecurity, ego, sexuality, love, fear, anger, and entanglement that come with the research and the writing (Cupples, 2002). Throw colonialism, imperialism, racism, sexism, and classism back in to the research context, have a look at the 'ambivalent desiring machine' (Young, 1995: 167) that such a context emerges from, and it seems apparent we are – I am – in for an unsettling negotiation across the chasms from Wilkes-Barre to Zanzibar in my head.

Moreover, the increasing pace of globalization and the flows of communication, culture, and exchange that have come with it complicate things still further, because they annihilate the space-time separating researcher and researched. Where Western researchers once went off to a place like Zanzibar on a long slow boat and perhaps saw the people they worked with there a decade later, with a scattering of letters in between, today, there is no exoticizing distance in these encounters. The email inboxes, cell-phone logs, and Western Union money trails alone tell us a very different story, one of inextricable intimacy and complexity. When we follow Said and 'no longer think of the relationship between cultures and their adherents as perfectly contiguous, totally synchronous, wholly correspondent' (1989: 225) we do find ourselves in a 'promising' time of 'sharing,' but this makes other aspects of the strategic choices that confront us more daunting still. Once we give up on the notion of a Truth that somehow separates us and Others and therefore a faithful, mirror-like representation of that Truth as our publication, the best we can aim for is an incomplete 'tracing' of the 'links between the dispersed fragments of the mirror' (Söderström, 2005: 14). We have only Cook's 'partial' account, with 'no single, straightforward conclusions' from the quotation at the head of the chapter.

It is thus a constant struggle to place oneself in a fieldwork project or any publications that come from it, particularly when the projects and publications involve a Westerner like me researching and writing about people in marginalized countries. Edward Said (1989: 216) wrote that there 'is no vantage outside the actuality of relationships between cultures ... that might allow one the epistemological privilege of somehow judging, evaluating and interpreting free of the encumbering interests, emotions, and engagements of the ongoing relationships themselves.' He meant this as a criticism of Western anthropologists who conduct fieldwork in countries

that are under the oppressive thumbs of the Western governments that often sponsor their research, but it actually lingers much longer on the landscape of this handbook. Pamela Shurmer-Smith (2002: 12) writes that for cultural geographers this encumbrance 'requires that one becomes self-reflexive, conscious of one's own viewpoint when trying to understand viewpoints in general.' This can be inspiring and enlightening in and of itself, but it can also be debilitating right from the start (Herbert et al., 2005).

My conceptions of the world, my identity within it, and the baggage of these things inevitably carry over into my research and my publications. Of course, what Said saw as 'encumbering' might also be *enriching* interests, emotions, and engagements. Sharing our lives with friends and walking around with our eyes open in the field can teach us a world of things about places, and about ourselves, in an incidental and yet powerfully profound way. Clifford Geertz (1983: 57) once wrote that fieldwork demands that we 'see ourselves among others,' and that we seek balance between ourselves and others, as well as between our theories and our empiricism. In that balance, Geertz believed, we would find 'an interpretation of the way a people live which is neither imprisoned within their mental horizons, an ethnography of witchcraft as written by a witch, nor systematically deaf to the tonalities of existence, an ethnography of witchcraft as written by a geometer.' Geertz, though, was of course writing as a lone-wolf anthropologist-as-expert, as if there really was some magic button that kept him comfortably positioned halfway between witch and geometer (Keith, 1992). Most people like me start out fieldwork in other countries without this magic button. Our publications can remain in a muddle as a result.

One possible model to follow in negotiating this self/other muddle throughout the process from conceptualizing the research to writing about it is that of the anthropologists Stephen Gudeman and Alberto Rivera (1990), whose guiding principle was to see their work as a collaborative conversation, from the beginning of the fieldwork through the writing. Their notion was that ethnographic understanding 'might be nearly impossible for the single foreign researcher' who would be unable to translate 'elliptical field encounters,' but that it 'might also be impossible for the "native"' for whom too much was 'too familiar' to understand other than as 'unconnected to anything else' (Gudemann and Rivera 1989: 269). They therefore combined forces to cover one another's blind spots. A similar, and very inspirational model, appears in the conversational collaboration of Janet MacGaffey and Remy Bazenguissa-Ganga (2000) in their study of illegal transnational trading between France and the Democratic Republic of Congo. By joining together, MacGaffey and Bazenguissa-Ganga (2000: 25) overcame 'scary racial confrontations between Arabs and Congolese' and the 'running conflict between the police and the undocumented immigrants' on the fringes of Paris that became infamous around the globe five years after their book's publication. Multicultural ethnographic teamwork that focuses on the 'world-views of the marginalized' can be a means toward producing 'alternative, humane visions' of complex human geographies (Sibley, 2005: 158). Some collaborative team-based projects have had grander ambitions for 'progressive social change' (Mountz et al., 2003: 29) or 'reimagining reciprocity' (Benson and Nagar, 2006: 581) in ways that I find inspirational.

I have put a conversational collaboration approach to work on three particular occasions that resulted in publications (Myers and Muhajir 1997; Nchito and Myers 2004; Dosi et al., 2007). It certainly solves some of the issues it is supposed to solve, but it can open up others. Such partnerships can be in part *just* a solution to the angst of white Western anthropologists or cultural geographers over the fact that they 'can no longer go to the postcolonial field with quite the same ease as in former times,' as Said (1989: 209), drolly phrased it. 'Innocence is now out of the question,' and 'the customary way of doing things

both narcotizes and insulates the guild member' (Said 1989: 213). With classic texts, the questions – 'Who speaks? For what and to whom?' – are always answered by 'someone, an authoritative, explorative, elegant, learned voice,' who 'amasses evidence, theorizes, speculates about everything – except itself' (Said 1989: 212). The postcolonial critique that has foregrounded the 'difficulties … of self-other relations' makes such author-ity deeply problematic, but Robert Young (1995: 179) is right to point to how Westerners have negotiated these difficulties 'so painfully but not powerlessly.' Collaboration can easily become merely a new way to insulate the guild member.

Recent feminist scholarship on collaborative teamwork has provided means by which we can not only problematize the nature of collaborations but potentially also do better work all along the arc of it from processes through products, with accountability realigned and the character of academia quite possibly transformed somewhat toward direct activist engagement (Benson and Nagar, 2006). Clearly, much work remains in the theorization of collaboration, and in its implementation in fieldwork and publication. Pieces like Alison Mountz and colleagues (2003), Koni Benson and Richa Nagar (2006), and Katy Bennett and Pamela Shurmer-Smith (2001) provide effective and thoughtful means by which I hope to improve the collaborative projects in which I engage in the future. I can also learn from the experiences I have had, to which I now turn.

In all three of the co-authored works I discuss above, I consciously began with the idea of rejecting me being the 'learned voice' of 'someone.' I sat down with the colleagues involved the day the field projects started, and we laid out our plans together. No collaborative conversations go anywhere without each partner bringing something to the table and getting something out of it in the end. I feel, for my part, that these examples worked, in this regard. My Zambian colleague, Wilma Nchito, faced the frustration of having not been promoted for lack of a refereed publication, we set out to provide her with that, and we were able to do so. We chose to work with the South Africa-based journal, *Urban Forum*, because Wilma felt the journal and our article in it would be immediately recognized and respected by regional development specialists and most importantly her Zambian colleagues. My Zanzibari colleague, Makame Muhajir, needed a publication, too, but for less concrete reasons. For example, a scholarly publication to promote the capacity of Zanzibari planners for thinking about how to localize the United Nations Agenda 21, he reasoned, might be very helpful in persuading the UN to consider adopting Zanzibar into its Sustainable Cities Program network, and it eventually did so, with a proposition paper Muhajir then was asked to co-author.

The third paper represented a slightly different example. Here, I worked with my then newly-graduated former PhD student from Zanzibar, Mohamed Dosi, to develop a small research grant that originated in multiple conversations about and experiences with the growing Tanzanian population in Kansas. We collaborated with the two local Tanzanian associations I discussed at the beginning of the chapter to conduct the research, and to take it in directions they found useful. When Mohamed moved on to a faculty position in Tennessee, we invited a new faculty colleague at Kansas, Leonce Rushubirwa, to join in, and he was warmly embraced by the local Tanzanian organizations. The publication served both of their interests, obviously, as beginning assistant professors.

For myself, I have to say that the main gain in all three cases was in explicitly making a personal and political statement to conduct my work in that way, and to collaborate in fostering African colleagues' careers. It made me feel good about what I do, to pat myself on the back. I might even abstract from this to say I was learning from African philosophies the idea of inscribing 'the Other in the self,' but I never really thought that much about it, to be perfectly honest (Young, 2001: 172). And that is because the inequalities of

our careers will not simply go away because we publish pieces like this together or continue to collaborate on other projects (and we do). Wilma gained a promotion, and even gained entrance into the University of Zambia's doctoral program in Geography while continuing her lectureship, but the financial and professional rewards for working in Lusaka just do not remotely measure up to those in Lawrence. Muhajir helped secure the SCP affiliation for Zanzibar, and he too gained entrance into a doctoral program, at the University of Dortmund. But the horrific politics of the professional practice of urban planning in Zanzibar left him largely stymied, and the funding base for his research, let alone his family, is fitful by comparison to Wilma, to say nothing of me. Mohamed is still in a temporary visiting faculty position, unable to secure a tenure track post. Financial hardships and personal crises forced Leonce to quit academia. Yes, we are 'sharing the global history that is our element.' To paraphrase Marx, people make their own global history, to be sure, but not under conditions of their own choosing. We are just people, in a grossly unjust world. And a 'written text is merely a point amidst a continuous fabric of other texts that includes all communicative forms through which researcher, researched, and institutional frameworks are relationally defined' (Nast, 1994: 62). However much we try to make those texts 'emotionally intelligent' and balanced, they are still alive in an unbalanced world that unquestionably marginalizes them and circumscribes their impact (Bennett, 2004: 414).

(DON'T) ASK AND (DON'T) TELL

There is, then, a constant negotiation between my academic head and the practical interests of the Zambians or Tanzanians with whom I am collaborating. A key element of this negotiation concerns the question of which matters should be made public by publication, and why, and how, in comparison to matters that need not, or should not, be public property. The piece that I co-authored with Muhajir raised questions for me, in particular, about what to publish and what not to publish. We researched (in the summer of 1995) and wrote (1995–96) at a time when he served as Director of Urban Planning and Surveys for the Commission for Lands and Environment, a since-disbanded think-tank within the Revolutionary Government of Zanzibar. We had first met when he was doing fieldwork for his Masters thesis on Zanzibari urban planning, in a degree program at Curtin University of Technology in Perth, Australia, at the same time that I was doing my (similar) dissertation fieldwork. But by 1995, he was now in a major new role, and a very political one at that. The whole research process was an intellectual escape valve for him from the intense pressures of that job; stresses I can't even imagine facing. In October 1995, along with the rest of Tanzania, Zanzibar became a multi-party state, but only via a dubious election that ensured the incumbent Revolutionary Party's continuation in power by a razor-thin margin, 50.2 percent to 49.8 percent, with more spoilt votes than votes separating winner from loser. The Revolutionary Party has won two elections since then, in October 2000 and October 2005, by wider margins but with the same shadows of irregularity, and it continues to operate a government that more or less considers itself the only game in town. The government-owned television channel's logo at sign-on and sign-off time says it all: Revolution Forever.

Suffice to say, then, that many findings Muhajir and I talked out were ones I realized would put his career in jeopardy should they be published with his name on them. Even in agreeing to collaborate with me – and he did so on one other occasion as well, officially – Muhajir was putting himself in harm's way politically. The solution we emerged with was to produce a more technically-oriented, co-written piece for *Third World Planning Review* (now *International Development Planning Review*) that had a critical eye but

pulled a few punches – punches I was then able to land, if you will, in two pieces that did not have Muhajir's name on them (Myers, 1996b, 1999; Myers and Muhajir, 1997). He got fired anyway, but he lasted longer than he thought he would (until January 2001), and the ostensible reasons for his replacement had little to do with our collaboration (Zanzibar's President eliminated the whole Commission for Lands and Environment). Still, it is a humbling experience to watch helplessly as a valued collaborator and friend is steadily downsized while the government he serves dumbs itself down.

The immediacy of his displacement and underemployment for me is enhanced, for good or ill, with our very regular email and cell-phone links. I was able to bring Muhajir to Lawrence with an NSF workshop grant in 1999, our families shared the summer of 2003 in Zanzibar together thanks to a Fulbright grant that I had, and his brother has now lived in Seattle for six years, and so the sense of connection between us is very strong. He re-started his doctoral program, this time at Kansas, in January 2007. But the sense of the inter-connection of my worlds, that of Zanzibar and that of Kansas, has reached more of a collision stage as I have become increasingly drawn in to the Tanzanian community in Kansas and western Missouri. Within these new relationships, I have again faced these questions of what to ask and what to tell.

In the research of the Task Force with which I started this chapter, Mohamed Dosi and I began the project by building relationships with the leaders of these two associations, the Tanzanian Association of Wichita and the Serengeti Association of Kansas City. From the friendships and the trust that we fostered, we then worked with these leaders to write up a questionnaire survey to administer to participants in each association. Their respective associations met and chose representatives to work with us in what we came to call the Task Force, to refine the survey, and then to meet and decide on various possible courses of action. Our goal with the survey was to gain a basic understanding of who these communities were and to match what the Task Force thought it was with what ordinary members of the two associations in the different cities thought it was. We planned to use it as a starting point in focus group discussions with participants. I passed a version of the survey through the Academic Committee on Human Subjects, as the law expects of university researchers in the US, and then brought this to a dinner with our task force in a local restaurant. We made a few minor adjustments and, the following weekend, tried the thing out with a group of about 30 Tanzanians in Wichita, most of them active members of the Tanzanian Association of Wichita (known as Tawichita).

Our meeting started with an hour of waiting for others to arrive, and another hour of socializing. Each of us in the task force talked a bit about what we were up to, what might be gained from the survey, where we hoped to go afterwards in terms of community development. The Tawichita membership seemed remarkably receptive, especially considering the fact that neither I nor Mohamed had ever met any of them before. Then, there was a sort of awkward silence after people started to fill out the survey forms that we had brought and discussed with them. One of my task force colleagues sensed something amiss, and stopped the group to ask about what was going on in their heads. Finally, a young man spoke up, and I translate and paraphrase his words here:

> Well, it's the first line: the name. I filled it out, and then on the next page I saw this question about our immigration status. I know what you said about keeping these forms in a safe place, but I'm telling you, there are a lot of people here who will fill out this form quite differently about their status depending if their name is on it or not.

There was laughter, and an obvious groan of assent. Ok, we said, no names, just cross that out. A stupid mistake we'd made on a form. But as we went on, we saw that the conversations we were all having – too quickly to note, or film, or record even if we had thought we wanted to do so – were far more interesting than the silly form, told us far

more about who we were and where we wanted to go. In the months since, I have learned to mostly shut up, to hear, to rework what I might represent into what my friends want represented.

Participatory research and participatory 'counter-mapping' suggest themselves as alternatives for this negotiation – from the inputs to the outcomes of research – where 'the "researched" is no longer the quiescent object of study' (Herlihy and Knapp, 2003: 304). Such an alternative can be particularly inspiring in that it 'commonly aligns itself with the activities and needs of social movements ... [in] empowering people to make decisions and take actions' (Sletto, 2002; Herlihy and Knapp, 2003: 305). That is indeed what the whole engagement with Tawichita and Serengeti has been about for me.

Yet in these and other qualitative research models, research comes to mimic the real world of development studies. Decentralized, participatory, and community-based rhetoric 'has achieved sacrosanct status in the development universe' (Myers, 2005: 141). Like community-based development initiatives in the neoliberal developing world, collaborative and participatory research can open up room for new social networks and empowering linkages. However, the networks and links are still structured in an unequal and even authoritarian 'geopolitics of knowledge' creation and generation (Robinson, 2003: 274). And even in participatory research projects, at publication time, 'little attention is dedicated to discussing the politics of fieldwork ... [or] the geopolitical relations that create the very conditions that enable fieldwork' (Sundberg, 2003: 180). Without recognizing this, participatory research can become 'tyrannical' and incapable of 'delivering its key principles of equality, sustainability, and the empowerment of poor people' (Cooke and Kothari, 2001; Pain and Francis, 2003: 48; Benson and Nagar, 2006).

As a scholar at what is referred to in the US National Academy of Sciences classification system as a 'Research I University,' I have goals of the game that are inevitably distinct from my collaborators. Research

I schools are the major, comprehensive, PhD-granting universities in the US wherein the main focus and priority of faculty is expected to be – you guessed it – research, which this system largely understands in terms of scholarly grant-writing and publication, with some allowance here and there for performance portfolios amongst artists. Research I faculty are not simply evaluated on the quantity of their publications or total sums of their grants; they are also expected to make major contributions to the empirical and theoretical body of knowledge in their fields. But many of the 'theoretical preoccupations' in our field 'are not easily translated into direct politics' (McEwan, 2003: 414); genuine 'livelihood struggles' can all too easily become 'fodder for conceptual refinement' (Moore, 1997: 103) as I seek to produce publications. These are often 'side issues' for my Tanzanian or Zambian colleagues, collaborators, or friends (McEwan, 2003: 414) – even more for non-researchers—who are driven to more direct engagement with development processes. Fair enough, we can combine forces, perhaps, and show ways that qualitative human geography can 'start making more substantial contributions to public policy' (Burgess, 2005: 273). But if publications are to become 'a space for dialogue, a space for different meanings and interpretations,' or a space for contestation, then these gaps in motivations or intentions will still continue to loom large (Bondi, 1999: 20).

'IS HE ON OUR SIDE OR NOT?'

Self-disclosure and reflexivity have become increasingly necessary staples of qualitative human geography research publications, even in some perhaps less likely spheres like the study of Christian spirituality (Slater, 2004). To some extent, there is still more work to do to enhance reflexivity, particularly in realms beyond the personal or individual (Falconer Al-Hindi and Kawabata, 2002). There is also the danger of making ourselves and our positionality the only thing we write

about rather than a base from which we build 'partial' understandings of the world (Haraway, 1988; Butler, 2001; Kobayashi, 2001). Moreover, positionality – or situatedness – apparently involves choosing sides, and sometimes we either don't want to choose sides, have sides chosen for us, or cannot really claim consciousness of what the sides are or where *we* are in the siding. There is a need for continual recognition of the multi-faceted and multi-vocal political consciousness shifting around underneath the reflexivity – of both the near-impossibility of neutrality in (foreign) fieldwork and the uncertainty that inheres to any self-awareness or standpoint research (Abbott, 2006).

Let me illustrate this double conundrum – the nearly-impossible neutrality and the ambivalence/insecurity/not-knowingness in self-consciousness – with a story about a list-server. In the late 1990s, the Zanzibari internet listserver, Zanzinet held a debate about foreign researchers. To appreciate the debate, you need to know that Zanzinet moderates its membership to people that its leadership deems are 'Zanzibaris,' which has led to what I see as some fairly convoluted interpretations of Zanzibariness. (To wit, a middle-aged man born there but residing in Sweden since age four may be called Zanzibari, but a lifelong resident of Zanzibar whose family origins happen to be the Tanzanian mainland might not be.) A polite request to join Zanzinet made by a Euro-American researcher, Nathalie Arnold, became a subject of open debate. The applicant's request was ultimately denied on a very close vote. This led several active members to resign in protest at her exclusion, given her deep empathy with the plight of Zanzibar and her solidarity with the cause of democracy and human rights there that the, overwhelmingly anti-Revolutionary Government, membership of Zanzinet obviously shares. She is, for instance, the lead author of the Human Rights Watch study of post-election, government-sponsored violence against the opposition party's supporters in Zanzibar that occurred in January 2001 and resulted in several dozen fatalities (Arnold et al., 2002).

The debate about foreign researchers sprang to life after Nathalie's exclusion. A Zanzibari friend of mine relayed many of these messages to me, some by forwarded email and others by word of mouth, since I had never reached the point of asking to join in the discussion as Nathalie had. I consider his motivation for doing so to be his own frustration with the list's exclusivity. I eventually asked him not to forward these messages to me, but in the while that I did receive them, I saw a very lively debate about what purposes and intentions foreigners had in doing research in Zanzibar, on what side they were on.

I'll admit that I was heartened by one long and impassioned defense of me, by a member I did not know (honestly!), because the man said he had learned a great deal in my publications about aspects of city life and a history he was trained not to take seriously. He appreciated my work for opening his eyes to things he didn't think Zanzibaris themselves saw because they were too close to their lived experience but that were nonetheless important and to be valued. He focused his attention on a piece I published in *Tijdschrift voor Economische en Sociale Geographie* (or *TESG*, the Dutch Journal of Economic and Social Geography) about place names that gave him a new appreciation for creativity on the part of Zanzibaris that he had never appreciated (Myers, 1996a).

I realized from these encounters with the listserver that I had no control over who read my publications or how they read them. I would read Nathalie Arnold's work next to mine and conclude that we were both critical scholars engaged in self-reflexive analysis of Zanzibar's seemingly never-ending saga of crisis and disappointment. But others clearly can, and do, reach very different conclusions – Nathalie is anti-government, while I am the government's stooge, or Nathalie is anti-Zanzibari, while I am against the government, and so on. If I had seen the 'bullets raining' in January 2001 that the Human Rights Watch report which Nathalie co-authored documents, I would find it hard not to explicitly take sides, to say the people with the guns

(in this case, the Tanzanian army) were 'bad,' and the people having their heads beaten in (the opposition supporters), were 'good,' or at least 'not bad.' But I not only cannot fully understand everything that took place in the riots she and her co-authors researched and reported; I cannot know how what I would write would be interpreted later by the wide variety of interested parties reading it. I am glad someone on the listserver appreciated my place names piece, but I would never have any way to predict that *that* piece, and not other, more widely read or cited pieces of mine, would move a total stranger to defend my research as pro-Zanzibari.

As a further illustration of these points about neutrality and the uncertainty of knowing one's stand or how it is taken, few years after the listserver debate, in 2003, another friend in Zanzibar told me about a conversation he'd had with Zanzibar's President about my work. The President was puzzled about foreign researchers, too, he told me, and he said the President had told him he'd seen my publications here and there but wondered: 'Is he on our side or not?' My friend tried to explain that scholars didn't take sides, but the President apparently shrugged at that and ended the conversation. I went on with my research without interruption or, for once, interrogation, for two months. Others have not been so lucky. Is that because the President shrugged? Clearly, people on both sides of Zanzibar's political divide cannot imagine someone even trying to be neutral. I have still tried to do so, but I recognize that basically no one concerned sees me as such, that at various times my own allegiances or sympathies shift, and that I don't always know where they lie.

My books, *Verandahs of Power* (2003) and *Disposable Cities* (2005) are not likely to stay long on anyone's bestseller lists, and with all due respect to my Dutch colleagues, I am not all that confident of the real 'impact factor' on social change for a journal like *TESG*. But sometimes the writings, or the presidential shrugs they produce, matter far more than I may think. Obviously, in the field, it matters in terms of who I am allowed to talk to, who talks to me, who is honest with me, and so forth. American researchers in Zanzibar, specifically, have often experienced subtle – and occasionally quite menacing – surveillance. On several occasions in the last decade, Americans (and occasionally Europeans) have been deported in the middle of their research for reasons the revolutionary regime never fully articulates (Owens, 2003). If I want to keep up my research program there, I have to do my best to avoid such traumas, albeit recognizing the capricious, illogical, unpredictable nature of the expulsions that have occurred. I might, alternatively, give up and just do research in other places where this sort of thing doesn't happen quite so frequently – and I have, after all, done more than think about this alternative, since several of my recent research projects have been on the Tanzanian mainland or in Zambia. But even then, I must recognize that my publications may react back upon my ability to do research in the future. The Zanzibari diaspora is certain to pay some attention to pieces about Zanzibar, or Zambians abroad for the works on Lusaka, and my colleagues in academia that care about such matters will look, too. Students in geography or African studies courses around the world may be led or misled to conclusions by whatever side I choose to put a piece on. And obviously, my writing is a small piece of an overall puzzle of images – of representations – of Zanzibar, or Tanzania, Kenya, Zambia, or Malawi for that matter, a puzzle that gives off sparks if you get close to it. Doesn't the weight of all of these bits of knowledge impel me towards continuing to at least strive for neutrality?

Maintaining a veneer of neutrality means that I can be called upon to testify in immigration cases, for instance, and that can make an enormous difference to at least a handful of people. Thousands of Zanzibaris have sought asylum in Canada and the US over the last decade. Many have what I consider a 'well-founded fear of persecution' given those moments when bullets have been

'raining' (Arnold et al., 2002). I have been asked on a half-dozen occasions to offer testimony on their behalf. I believe that the fact that my publications cannot be easily deconstructed as favoring either the ruling party or the opposition lends weight to my testimony, but I have no way of truly knowing that. And there are bound to be times at which to much more clearly choose sides.

But to *publish* any work from this sort of *sided* research, either alone or with collaborators, there is a need to navigate the maze of reviewers. Although there are exceptions to the rule, generally speaking, the blind review processes of academic journals do not tend toward a 'dialogical approach,' and their generally 'disembodied, impartial and unlocated' character does not lead them to look favorably on research that has taken sides (Berg, 2001: 511). A livable solution might be to enmesh my own story into the research narrative. Some people are better at this than others – a gifted writer or story-teller can weave between self and story such that we know what side or sides s/he is on, know what may be warped as a result, but still know something valuable about people and places that we didn't know beforehand (see Western, 2001; Lundberg, 2003; Rose, 2003 for fine examples). Inevitably, such a workable solution leaves some details out, but this 'middle ground' approach, if it still evokes 'some of the complex, overlapping and interrelated networks, structures, constraints and possibilities,' can become almost like a new kind of novel or short story (as the groundbreaking piece by Mark Pluciennik and Quentin Drew (2000: 68) seems to me to be).

Indeed, African fiction has provided me with very real models of the negotiation of otherness, the personal, and the political, most recently and pointedly in Nuruddin Farah's *Links* (2003) and Abdulrazak Gurnah's *Desertion* (2005). *Links* will, I believe, prove to be one of the most powerful and important novels of 21st century global literature, but its importance to me here is in its main character's reminder of how little cognizance a person may have of her or his own process of choosing sides or gaining empathy. This character, Jeebleh, is a Somali who long ago chose to make a new life for himself in New York, but who is drawn to return to Mogadiscio after his mother's death just after the withdrawal of US marines in the early 1990s. Farah allows Jeebleh to disguise from himself the hidden dimensions of his reasons for returning to Somalia, and to wander blindly through the city's fiercely contested sides until he is quite clearly drawn into the internecine conflict that is destroying it. He leaves the city after a painful and traumatic series of events that shape the plot of *Links*, but many of his questions are still unresolved:

> Given the choice, Jeebleh would oppose all forms of violence. But what is one to do when there is no other way to rid society of vermin? Which would he rather be, someone who minds the opinion of others and advocates for peace, or someone who does what he can – despite the risks – to improve the lives of many others? ... Someone who kills for justice, or someone helplessly unable to do anything? (Farah, 2003: 332)

Ultimately, *Links* reminds us that as globalization expands and transnational flows or interchanges explode, otherness is no longer just for outsiders any more. Jeebleh becomes irretrievably enmeshed in the affairs of his people immediately around him in the Inferno (Farah frames the narrative with excerpts from Dante) of a post-1991 Mogadiscio that he had refused to claim as home. There is no Beatrice to pull him out of himself alive and separate from the muck. Jeebleh learns what Said suggested: the 'global history that is our element' is *our* element, and we have to think it through together, selves and others, homelands and diasporas, researchers and researched, alike. There are scars from injustice and inequality, but we are here, and our stories are *linked*.

I relate to *Links* on many levels at once. I helped to create a formal affiliation between my university and the University of Mogadiscio in 2005, through which I will – if peace allows – eventually be teaching a distance education module on, of all things,

qualitative methods. As an American, I have found myself re-reading many times his staggering account of the infamous 'Black Hawk Down' incident from the ground up, from the eyes of a Somali mother whose small child was swept up into the blades of the helicopter as it crashed in Mogadiscio that day. But it is, I guess, in how I see Zanzibar becoming Mogadiscio that I am most drawn to this book, and how I see my Zanzibari friends and collaborators – and me – in the traumatized characters helpless as their/our/my world deteriorates. 'Representation,' Said wrote (1989: 224), is 'not just an academic or theoretical quandary but ... a political choice.' But that *choice* is itself a quandary: 'Which would [I] rather be?'

Abdulrazak Gurnah's title makes baldly plain his idea of the choice that so many of those who have ruled Zanzibar over the last century, and so many of those who have struggled to transform it for the better, is: *Desertion*. The author himself starts, and then deserts, three different narratives in the book. Characters, like empires, colonies, bastard children, illicit lovers, revolutions, are deserted and desert the causes or people they've been written to stand for. It doesn't all tie together. Reviewers have critiqued Gurnah for this potentially frustrating tactic, but I got him from the foggy start, when a dazed, disillusioned, and deserted British geographer wanders out of the desert and collapses into a Swahili family that he becomes a part of, then abandons. The British deserted their empire's people, the Zanzibari revolutionaries deserted their ideals, the intellectuals that fled it deserted the cause of its liberation – just as I set out to start doing my research in Zambia and Tanganyika instead – and yet these desertions fail, because none can make a complete break. In *Desertion*, the explorer leaves a child behind; his grandchildren on either end of the encounter eventually come to know of one another's existence. There is an incompleteness to every story, Gurnah is suggesting, but colonizer and colonized, revolutionary and collaborator (and researcher and researched) are inseparable in their displacements, disorientations, ambivalences, regrets, or absences of conclusions. This is not a world of half-hour television situation comedies, but of intertwined synapses and collapses.

The ultimate lesson from these two books for me in negotiating the Other, the personal, and the political is to recognize the opportunities alongside the encumbrances that links provide and, I guess, to never lose sight of the dangers of desertion. Homi Bhabha (1992: 109) once argued that 'the place of difference and otherness ... is never entirely on the outside or implacably oppositional.' Rather than to be continually forced to choose sides, what the new and old links of contemporary times demand is to be – to rescue a word dragged through the sewers of a media war – *embedded* in the stories we tell. I don't mean this in the Iraq war reporter sense of the term, but more in terms of our recognition of how inextricable we are from the dramas of others, whether we know what side of the bed to wake up on or not. This is a world of 'overlapping territories, intertwined histories,' and constantly contested constructions of difference (Said, 1993: 3).

CONCLUSION

Representing Others is personal, it is political, and the conundrums of the negotiation are all around us. Seeing otherness as historically constituted leads to a sharing of partial understandings – both in a lack of impartiality and an incompleteness, or a lack of straightforward conclusions! – in publications that come out of qualitative fieldwork. In this chapter, I have tried to tackle three themes. These are the struggle with how to: balance self and other in publications, represent contentious findings, and manage loyalties. I have used my own research and publication experiences, and that means my assessment may inevitably not be representative. Since this is a Handbook on methods,

one might expect a guide on how to solve these struggles. I cannot really hope to succeed in that, and so instead I've tried to map out the terrain of the struggles somewhat.

In all three, intertwined struggles, the idea of choice, the recognition of a decision-making process, looms large. The choices and decisions have an ebb and flow to them that grows more dramatic in a time of collapsing distances or differences between self and other. The sharing entailed in collaborative conversations is, indeed, 'promising,' and so are the links that the contemporary world makes possible. They are encumbering, too, and fraught with highly unequal power relationships. We cannot pretend to 'see ourselves *among* others' the way Geertz wanted it. We are *with* others, *in* others, and vice-versa, and sometimes *against* others, with others against *us*, too. Being *among* implies a smug boundary and a pre-, post- and during self-awareness that just doesn't ever seem possible. Sometimes it is hard to choose sides, to see who is who, or even to balance the gaps in intentions between academic and practical worlds. Yet I would urge that we must see research relationships as ongoing, make efforts to consciously connect work and life, make room for more open, honest, or dialog-driven publications, and think critically about reflexivity and reciprocity throughout the entire research process.

REFERENCES

Abbott, D. (2006) 'Disrupting the "whiteness" of fieldwork in geography', *Singapore Journal of Tropical Geography* 27 (3): 326–41.

Arnold, N., McKim, B. and Rawlence, B. (2002) *The bullets were raining: the 2001 attack on peaceful demonstrators in Zanzibar*. New York: Human Rights Watch.

Bennett, K. (2004) 'Emotionally intelligent research', *Area* 36 (4): 414–22.

Bennett, K. and Shurmer-Smith, P. (2001) 'Writing conversation', in M. Limb and C. Dwyer (eds) *Qualitative methodologies for geographers*. London: Arnold. pp. 251–63.

Benson, K. and Nagar, R. (2006) 'Collaboration as resistance? Reconsidering the processes, products, and possibilities of feminist oral history and ethnography', *Gender, Place and Culture* 13 (5): 581–92.

Berg, L. (2001) 'Masculinism, emplacement, and positionality in peer review', *The Professional Geographer* 53 (4): 511–21.

Bhabha, H. (1992) *The location of culture*. London and New York: Routledge.

Bondi, L. (1999) 'Stages on journeys: some remarks about human geography and psychotherapeutic practice', *The Professional Geographer* 51 (1): 11–24.

Burgess, J. (2005) 'Follow the argument where it leads: some personal reflections on "policy-relevant" research', *Transactions of the Institute of British Geographers* 30 (3): 273–81.

Butler, R. (2001) 'From where I write: the place of positionality in writing', in M. Limb and C. Dwyer (eds) *Qualitative methodologies for geographers*. London: Arnold. pp. 264–76.

Cook, I. *et al.* (2005) 'Positionality/situated knowledge', in D. Atkinson, P. Jackson, D. Sibley, and N. Washbourne (eds) *Cultural geography: a critical dictionary of key concepts*. London: Tauris. pp. 16–26.

Cooke, B. and Kothari, U. (eds) (2001) *Participation: the new tyranny*? London: Zed Books.

Cupples, J. (2002) 'The field as a landscape of desire: sex and sexuality in geographical fieldwork', *Area* 34 (4): 382–90.

Dosi, M., Rushubirwa, L. and Myers, G. (2007) 'Tanzanians in the Land of Oz: diaspora and transnationality in Wichita, Kansas', *Social and Cultural Geography* 8 (5): 657–71.

Falconer Al-Hindi, K., and Kawabata, H. (2002) 'Towards a more fully reflexive feminist geography', in P. Moss (ed.) *Feminist geography in practice: research and methods*. Oxford: Blackwell. pp. 103–15.

Farah, N. (2003) *Links*. New York: Penguin.

Geertz, C. (1983) *Local knowledge*. New York: Basic Books.

Gudeman, S., and Rivera, A. (1989) Colombian conversations. *Current Anthropology* 30 (3): 267–76.

Gudeman, S. and Rivera, A. (1990) *Conversations in Colombia: the domestic economy in life and text*. Cambridge: Cambridge University Press.

Gurnah, A. (2005) *Desertion*. London: Pantheon.

Haraway, D. (1988) 'Situated knowledges: the science question in feminism and the privilege of partial perspective', *Feminist Studies* 14 (3): 575–99.

Harvey, D. (1989) *The condition of postmodernity: an enquiry into the origins of cultural change*. Oxford: Blackwell.

Herbert, S., Gallagher, J. and Myers, G. (2005) 'Fieldwork and ethnography', in N. Castree, A. Rogers, and D. Sherman (eds) *Questioning geography*. Oxford: Blackwell. pp. 226–40.

Herlihy, P. and Knapp, G. (2003) 'Participatory mapping of indigenous lands in Latin America', *Human Organization* 62 (4): 303–14.

Keith, M. (1992) 'Angry writing: (re)presenting the unethical world of the ethnographer', *Environment and Planning D: Society and Space* 10 (5): 551–68.

Kobayashi, A. (2001) 'Negotiating the personal and the political in critical qualitative research', in M. Limb and C. Dwyer (eds) *Qualitative methodologies for geographers*. London: Arnold. pp. 55–70.

Lundberg, A. (2003) 'Voyage of the ancestors', *Cultural Geographies* 10 (1): 64–83.

MacGaffey, J. and Bazenguissa-Ganga, R. (2000) *Congo-Paris: transnational traders on the margins of the law*. Oxford: James Currey.

McEwan, C. (2003) 'The West and other feminisms', in: K. Anderson, M. Domosh, S. Pile, and N. Thrift (eds) *Handbook of cultural geography*. London: Sage. pp. 405–19.

Moore, D. (1997) 'Re-mapping resistance: "ground for struggle" and the politics of place', in S. Pile and M. Keith (eds) *Geographies of resistance*. London: Routledge. pp. 87–106.

Mountz, A., Miyares, I., Wright, R. and Bailey, A. (2003) 'Methodologically becoming: power, knowledge and team research', *Gender, Place and Culture* 10 (1): 29–46.

Myers, G. (1996a) 'Naming and placing the other: power and the urban landscape in Zanzibar', *Tijdschrift voor Economische en Sociale Geografie* 87 (3): 237–46.

Myers, G. (1996b) 'Democracy and development in Zanzibar? Contradictions in land and environment planning', *Journal of Contemporary African Studies* 14 (2): 221–45.

Myers, G. (1999) 'Political ecology and urbanization: Zanzibar's construction materials industry', *Journal of Modern African Studies* 37 (1): 83–108.

Myers, G. (2003) *Verandahs of power: colonialism and space in Urban Africa*. Syracuse: Syracuse University Press.

Myers, G. (2005) *Disposable cities: garbage, governance and sustainable development in Urban Africa*. Burlington, VT: Ashgate.

Myers, G. and Muhajir, M. (1997) 'Localizing Agenda 21: environmental sustainability and Zanzibari urbanization', *Third World Planning Review* 19 (4): 367–84.

Nast, H. (1994) 'Opening remarks on "women in the field"', *The Professional Geographer* 46 (1): 54–66.

Nchito, W. and Myers, G. (2004) 'Four caveats for participatory solid waste management in Lusaka', *Urban Forum* 15 (2): 109–33.

Owens, G. (2003) 'What! Me a spy? Intrigue and reflexivity in Zanzibar', *Ethnography* 4 (1): 122–44.

Pain, R. and Francis, P. (2003) 'Reflections on participatory research', *Area* 35 (1): 46–54.

Pile, S. (1996) *The body and the city: psychoanalysis, space, and subjectivity*. London and New York: Routledge.

Pluciennik, M. and Drew, Q. (2000) '"Only connect": global and local networks, contexts and fieldwork', *Ecumene* 7 (1): 67–104.

Robinson, J. (2003) 'Postcolonializing geography: tactics and pitfalls', *Singapore Journal of Tropical Geography* 24 (3): 273–89.

Rose, G. (2003) 'Family photographs and domestic spacings: a case study', *Transactions of the Institute of British Geographers* 28 (1): 5–18.

Said, E. (1989) 'Representing the colonized: anthropology's interlocutors', *Critical Inquiry* 15: (2) 205–25.

Said, E. (1993) *Culture and imperialism*. New York: Knopf.

Schumann, J. (1993) 'The brain looks at diversity', *Journal of Multilingual and Multicultural Development* 14 (5): 321–28.

Shurmer-Smith, P. (2002) *Doing cultural geography*. London: Sage.

Sibley, D. (2005) 'Private/public', in D. Atkinson, P. Jackson, D. Sibley, and N. Washbourne (eds) *Cultural geography: a critical dictionary of key concepts*. London: Tauris. pp. 155–60.

Slater, T. (2004) 'Encountering God: personal reflections on "geographer as pilgrim"', *Area* 36 (3): 245–53.

Sletto, B. (2002) 'Producing space(s), representing landscapes: maps and resource conflicts in Trinidad', *Cultural Geographies* 9 (4): 389–420.

Söderström, O. (2005) 'Representation', in D. Atkinson, P. Jackson, D. Sibley, and N. Washbourne (eds) *Cultural geography: a critical dictionary of key concepts*. London: Tauris. pp. 11–5.

Sundberg, J. (2003) 'Masculinist epistemologies and the politics of fieldwork in Latin Americanist geography', *The Professional Geographer* 55 (2): 180–90.

Western, J. (2001) 'Africa is coming to the cape', *Geographical Review* 91 (4): 617–40.

Young, R. (1995) *Colonial desire: hybridity in theory, culture, and race*. London and New York: Routledge.

Young, R. (2001) *Postcolonialism: an historical introduction*. Oxford: Blackwell.

22

Major Disasters and General Panics: Methodologies of Activism, Affinity and Emotion in the Clandestine Insurgent Rebel Clown Army

Paul Routledge

Apply a Red Nose and Read …

We live on a planet in permanent war – a war of money against life, of profit against dignity, of progress against the future. A war that gorges itself on death and blood and shits money and toxins, deserves an obscene body of deviant soldiers – an insurgent army of rebels, which celebrates life and happiness and continuous rebellion. This army is clandestine because words, dreams, and desires are more important than biographies. Inside everyone is a lawless clown trying to escape, and nothing undermines authority like holding it up to ridicule. Run away from the circus and join the Clandestine Insurgent Rebel Clown Army (CIRCA) (www.clownarmy.org).

In this chapter I will run away (all too briefly) from the capitalist/war circus and (re)join the Clandestine Insurgent Rebel Clown Army (CIRCA). In so doing, I will discuss the methodologies of activism, affinity and emotion, and my personal reflections on what an activist geography might look like. Firstly, I will briefly discuss

what I understand activist geography to be in the context of qualitative research, before discussing the genealogy of debates within the discipline concerning 'relevance' and radicalism.

ACTIVIST GEOGRAPHY AND QUALITATIVE RESEARCH

Activist geography is concerned with action, reflection and empowerment (of oneself and others) in order to challenge oppressive power relations. More particularly, from my perspective, it is about forging mutual solidarity with resisting others[1] through critical collaboration; the creation of participatory spaces of action which are inclusive and anti-hierarchical; the nurturing of creative interaction with resisting others independent

of electoral politics; and conducting direct action (whereby we devise a plan to do something, in collaboration with others and then do it without recourse to external authorities). For an activist geography, then, 'relevance' entails making certain political commitments or commitments to certain kinds of action (Pain, 2003), where commitment is to a moral and political philosophy of social justice, and research is directed both toward conforming to that commitment and toward helping to realize the values that lie at its root.

To think about such objectives requires the adoption of a necessarily broad interpretation of activism. Ian Maxey (1999) has argued that activism is discursively produced within a range of sites, including the media, grassroots organizations and academia. Frequently, this has led to a restrictive view of activism that emphasizes dramatic, physical and 'macho' forms of action. However, Maxey argues that the social world is produced through everyday acts and thoughts that we all engage in. He understands activism to be the process of reflecting and acting upon this condition. Hence everybody is an activist, engaged in some way in producing the world, and reflexivity enables people to place themselves actively within this process: 'By actively and critically reflecting on the world and our place within it, we are more able to act in creative, constructive ways that challenge oppressive power relations rather than reinforce them' (1999: 201). Such an interpretation opens up the field of activism to everybody, and serves to entangle the worlds of academia and activism. There are no preconceptions about the forms that such an engagement might take. The importance of this inclusive definition is that it is a palliative to the privileging of certain forms of activism over others, and to the exclusivist and domineering tendencies that occur in certain activist discourses. Hence, while my activism work usually involves direct action of some kind, and is in collaboration with those involved in such action (e.g. see Routledge, 1997, 2003b), there are many

other forms of productive, creative political actions that can be, and are, taken by academics. These frequently blur the boundaries between full-time activists and academic researchers who choose, for example, to work in and with particular communities on particular issues.

All qualitative research methods share a preoccupation with systems of shared meaning and subjective understandings, their primary goal being to emphasize, communicate and help emancipate, rather than to generalize, predict and control. Given that activists share the goals of communication and emancipation, it is unsurprising that activist researchers would be drawn to qualitative research methods. Qualitative research recognizes a dynamic relationship between theory building and intensive empirical research, and that the 'real' world cannot exist independently of the relationships that are generated between the researcher and the researched. Such relationships are a prerequisite for forging the intersubjectivity which leads to an understanding of the constitution of social life, and for the appreciation, clarification and interpretation of meaning (Smith, 1994). While a range of approaches to qualitative research acknowledge the importance of such relationships, within activist geography such relationships are at their most intense, and often their most productive, because the activist academic and the community activist work together toward shared goals. Actively working alongside others enhances our understanding of how we relate to those others, which is crucial to our negotiation of the 'double hermeneutic' within qualitative research, i.e. recognizing that we as researchers construct other people's constructions of the meaning systems within which they operate.

The motivation of activist geographies is to develop practices aimed at social transformation rather than merely the 'production of knowledge' and/or the 'solving' of 'local' problems. Activist research moves beyond the acquisition, cataloguing, ordering and publishing of information toward jointly producing knowledge with resisting others to produce critical interpretations and readings of the world which are accessible and understandable to all those involved and actionable (Chatterton *et al.*, 2008).

Therefore, an activist geography stresses the inseparability of knowledge and action and is thus self-consciously interventionist in approach. For a critical geography to be fully critical one must 'walk the walk', as well as 'talk the talk' i.e. one must be critically engaged *in some way* with those others with whom one is conducting research. Such an approach grants no special privileges to the researcher and acknowledges that our understanding of the world as it is, and our actions to achieve a world as it 'ought' to be, are inseparable. By such forms of activist engagement, geographers can engage in prefigurative action, i.e. embody visions of transformation as if they are already achieved, thereby calling them into being (Graeber, 2002). There are many examples of post-capitalist ways of living already part of the present, as J.K. Gibson-Graham (2006) argued in claims about building new post-capitalist ontologies, providing a spur for activist geographies to contribute to the creation of other realities, what David Harvey (2000) terms 'spaces of hope'. Moreover, collaborations are not just about action in the research process, but how the research process can contribute to wider activism like protests, demonstrations, events, etc. Hence, activist geographies also attempt to create spaces for action: i.e. physical spaces that can be created and occupied in building commonality and connection between different groups unmediated by consumer relations or profit, those autonomous geographies discussed by Jenny Pickerill and Paul Chatterton (2006). These common places seek opportunities for transformative dialogue, mutual learning and (creative) conflict. They form participatory spaces for building modes of understanding, encounter and action which are inclusive, which nurture creative interaction with others independent of electoral politics and which can lead to critical reflection and interventions.

Through such a broad approach, and through a variety of possible engagements, activist geography can be made relevant to 'real world concerns'. While the concern with 'relevance' can be shared by both qualitative and quantitative researchers, it is the formers' preoccupation with relationships (between researcher and researched as well as between theory construction and empirical research) that make such concerns particularly pertinent.

RELEVANCE AND RADICALISM IN GEOGRAPHY

Discussions about the relevance of geography to 'real world concerns' have been a part of the modern discipline since its founding, in the second half of the nineteenth century, when early articulations of an activist geography could be found in the work of anarchist geographer Peter Kropotkin. Such concerns were to re-emerge in the late 1960s in response to the putatively 'value-free' orientation of geographical research at that time. Many geographers believed that this masked a complicity with the social forces at the root of inequality, racism, and the alienation that marked modern life (see e.g. Morrill, 1969; Peet, 1969). In reaction, many geographers turned toward more humanist approaches rooted in moral philosophy and toward radical theories and politics rooted in anarchism, Marxism, and other critical movements. As a result various efforts were undertaken to better facilitate direct involvement by geographers in the solving of social problems (see e.g. Berry, 1972; Harvey, 1972; White, 1972; Harvey, 1974).

The advent of radical geography in the late 1960s heralded the return of a 'dissenting tradition' (Blaut, 1979) in geography, originally articulated by Kropotkin, and coincided with an era of civil unrest, environment protests, the emergence of the women's movement, student riots, anti-war campaigns and anti-colonial struggles in and against the US,

France, Britain and other countries (especially in the Global South). It was the perceived disjuncture between academic geography and contemporary socio-economic problems and struggles that inspired early radical geographers like William Bunge, James Blaut and Richard Peet to call for the 'relevancy' of geographical work (Peet, 1977: 11) and the establishment of a people's geography in which research was focused on politically-charged questions and solutions and geographers actively involved themselves with the peoples and communities that they studied. Moreover, it also precipitated dramatic changes in the traditional idea of the 'field' and the geographer's relationship to those who lived there. Bunge's 'Geographical Expeditions' in Detroit between 1969 and 1970 were one of the most original and unique examples. The expedition projects were experiments at uniting both community concerns and mobilization with academic expertise and research. It was an engagement between the problems of economic, social and political marginalization in an African American community in Detroit, and engaged faculty and students at the University of Michigan. The idea was to combine academic and local expertise to create effective political tools, community empowerment, consciousness-raising, and provide educational opportunities (suited to greater or lesser degrees) for those inner-city communities (Bunge, 1977).

Radical geography could thus be seen as a 'contact zone' (Merrifield, 1995: 64) between the academy and activism, a point of 'contamination' and hybridity (see Routledge, 1996), wherein the importance of values to the practice of geography was crucial (Harvey, 1973; Buttimer, 1974). This meant asking 'big questions' about geopolitics, ecological transformation, economic restructuring, human welfare, war and peace. For David Harvey (1984: 10), such big questions implied developing historical materialist 'people's geographies' 'that open[ed] the way to the creation of new forms of society in which common people have the power to create their own geography and history in the

image of liberty and mutual respect of opposed interests' (quoted in Staeheli and Mitchell, 2005: 359). Moreover, commitment to certain values has direct implications for certain kinds of research practices, an issue that was to become of prime concern to feminist geographers.

Since the early 1990s there has been a resurgence of interest in questions of political relevance within geography. Relevance has been variously interpreted as pertinence, commitment and application (Dear, 1999); 'the degree to which geographers make a contribution to the analysis and resolution of major economic, environmental and social problems' (Pacione, 1999, quoted in Beaumont et al., 2005: 119); and 'an attitude and a set of practices intended to produce research that will be useful in some way-large or small, in public or private venues, or even in changing ways of thinking or conceptualizing issues-but that may not be manifest in any particular policy or outcome' (Staeheli and Mitchell, 2005: 357). Such concerns have frequently focused upon the contribution geographers can make to the wider policy agenda and to the politics of the pedagogic process (e.g. see Castree, 2000; Demeritt, 2000; Massey, 2000; Pollard et al., 2000; Smith, 2000).

The role of public policy in sustaining, if not enhancing, the inequalities and exploitation that are inherent to contemporary capitalism, have been raised since Harvey's (1974) question 'What kind of geography for what kind of public policy?' Thus while Ron Martin (2001) has argued that geographers have a moral duty to improve the world, not just to understand it, others have argued that geographers should more actively involve themselves in the local and national state apparatus to influence public policy, not least because policy research is legitimate and potentially creative in such realms as the environmental, unemployment and poverty reduction, devolution, financial regulation; electoral reform, and urban planning (Peck, 1999). Moreover, policy engagement may occur with multiple actors beyond the formal state apparatus, such as non-governmental organizations (NGOs) and other actors within civil society in NGOs (Beaumont *et al.*, 2005).

While the emergence of radical geography raised the issues of political relevance of the discipline and direct engagement of geographers in the lives of those beyond the academy, feminist geography developed a very powerful critique of research methodology and the voices or ideas silenced by it. Feminist geography has emphasized politically committed research (Nast, 1994), including promoting dialog between, rather than an 'objective' distancing from, activist-academics and the people they study; recognition and negotiation of the differential power relations within the research process and how these might be addressed (Farrow *et al.*, 1995); the treatment of positionality (particularly the position of the activist-academic as an ethnographer, and multiple activist-academic positionings), situated knowledge (Merrifield, 1995) and representation (Nast, 1994); and the notion that the process of research (topic selection, field work, etc.) is just as important as the finished product in terms of the dynamics and political implications of actions during each phase – issues of who the research is produced 'for' and whose needs does it meet (Nast, 1994; Farrow *et al.*, 1995). Further, feminist research methods have argued for a recognition that social theory and social policy must acknowledge that differences in identity matter seriously and need to be incorporated into research practices; for the intersubjective understanding between activist-academic and researched; and for a sensitivity to the place-specificity of research (e.g. McDowell, 1992; Staeheli and Lawson, 1994; Laurie *et al.*, 1999; Moss, 2002).

However, despite the accomplishments of radical and feminist geographers, Lynn Staeheli and Don Mitchell (2005) note that while such theoretical developments have perhaps drawn geography closer to the heart of the main debates in the social sciences and humanities, they may have also drawn it further from the social movements, political

formations, policy makers and lay people that many geographers hope to reach (e.g. see Kitchin and Hubbard, 1999; Castree, 2000). As a result some geographers have lamented anew the separation between critical sectors of the discipline and activism going on 'outside' the academy (e.g. see Blomley, 1994; Castree, 1999; Wills, 2002). Hence calls have been made for critical geographers to become politically engaged outside the academy in social movements, community groups, protests, etc. (Chouinard, 1994; Routledge, 1996; Fuller, 1999; Maxey, 1999; Cumbers and Routledge, 2004). One of the clearest articulations has been by Duncan Fuller and Rob Kitchin (2004) who have argued that academics have a social responsibility, given their training, access to information, and freedom of expression, to make a difference on the ground, through activist research. Drawing upon feminist praxis, they see the role of the academic as primarily that of an enabler or facilitator, acting in collaboration with diverse communities. Radical and critical praxis is thus committed to exposing the socio-spatial processes that (re)produce inequalities between people and places; challenging and changing those inequalities; and bridging the divide between theorization and praxis. They bemoan the fact that there is still some scholarly distance between geographers activism and their teaching, research and publishing activities, critical praxis consisting of little else beyond pedagogy and academic writing. They posit that the structural constraints of the desire to maintain the power of the academy in knowledge production, and the desire to shape the education system for the purposes of the neoliberal status quo work to delimit and limit the work of radical/critical geographers.

Such debates within geography are taking place at a time in which there is increased social mobilization and conflict around the world. Issues such as globalizing capitalism, trade agreements, failed development, neoliberalism and the war on terrorism have been met by opposition ranging from the Zapatista rebellion in Chiapas (Routledge, 1998), to grassroots globalization networks (articulated through global days of action, social forums etc. see Routledge, 2003a), to violent insurgencies (e.g. in Iraq). Responses to these dynamics and the discussions within geography have already begun to emerge. One notable effort is the People's Geography Project, organized out of Syracuse, and its effort at making research and geographical concepts relevant to social struggles, e.g. through the Syracuse hunger project (see www.peoples-geography.org). Other responses have come from critical development work, marked by efforts to construct venues for community or organizational input on development and planning work (e.g. Howitt, 1993). What follows is my personal approach to activist geography, heavily influenced, of course, by many of the debates that I have just discussed. It articulates 'not so much my position in the field, as the way the field is both within and without myself' (Riles, 2001: 20).

METHODOLOGIES OF ACTIVISM, AFFINITY AND EMOTION

Revolt, resistance, breakdown, conspiracy, alternative is everywhere. (Latour 2002, quoted in Thrift, 2004: 59)

Activist methodologies are conceptualised with an eye to both communication and emancipation, confronting, and seeking solutions to, issues of social, economic and environmental injustice. They are conceptualized and carried out in collaboration with activist (and sometimes academic) others – the precise contours of such collaboration being worked through in cooperation with those others (e.g. see Routledge, 2002). In so doing, activist researchers invariably are confronted with issues of power, ethics and personal political responsibility, some of which I will discuss below.

Such methodologies can be written about in a variety of ways in both academic and non-academic forums – the extent of autho-

rial distance from one's subject matter being a matter of personal choice rather than academic protocol. However, critical engagement with issues of justice can invest such narratives with political and emotional power because the activist researcher is *writing from within* a particular issue or struggle. Moreover, critical engagement implies an active process of attempting to bring about specific outcomes (in practices, policies, etc.) and is thus less inclusive (and more focused) than Staeheli and Mitchell's (2005) interpretation of relevance quoted above. While such involvement can raise concerns about bias, this can be ameliorated through a critical reflexivity on behalf of the researcher.

There will, of course, be many interpretations about what an activist geography could comprise. I have spent the past 15 years working with, and conducting research about, social movements, both their particular struggles and their work within broader networks of association. Here I want to sketch out a methodological manifesto based upon recent activist research and praxis. In so doing I do not want to foreclose other paths and critical engagements that geographers might choose to make. Indeed, at the International Conference of Critical Geography in Mexico City in 2005, I was struck by the diversity of politically committed engagements that geographers were involved in, both within and beyond the academy. Rather, I will discuss some of my personal experiences in the CIRCA, and in so doing provide a personal interpretation of activist geography which raises certain broader issues of concern to critical geographers: activism, affinity, emotion and their entanglements, ethics and power.

Activism: Living theory beyond words

In 2005, July 6–8 the G8 (group of eight nations) met at Gleneagles, Scotland. The G8 – consisting of the US, Canada, Japan, Britain, Germany, France, Italy and

Russia – holds annual summits where top government officials discuss issues of macro-economic management (i.e. running the neo-liberal global economy), international trade, terrorism, energy, arms control, etc. With the emergence of the global justice (anti-capitalist) mobilisations, such summits have been accompanied by protests – both at the places where the G8 meet, and elsewhere across the globe. These protests provide a critique of neoliberal capitalism, debate alternatives to it, and challenge the 'business-as-usual' performance of such summits by attempting to disrupt their operation.

In the months prior to the G8 protests, an idea spread meme-like around Britain and abroad: for there to be an army of clowns deployed during the G8 protests. This was the CIRCA. Clandestine because the spectacle of celebrity was refused – without real names, faces or noses, CIRCA wanted to show that words, dreams, and desires are more important than biographies. Hence activists took ridiculous military names: Private Joke, Corporal Punishment, Sergeant Ina, Major Disaster, Colonel Oftruth, General Panic etc. Insurgent because CIRCA had risen up from nowhere and was everywhere – having emerged from various cities in the UK, and from the US, Ireland, Belgium and France. Rebels because CIRCA celebrated life and happiness more than 'revolution' and because rebellions continue forever. Clowns because CIRCA believed that inside everyone is a lawless clown trying to escape and because nothing undermines authority like holding it up to ridicule. An army because CIRCA believed that we live on a planet in permanent war – a war of money against life, of profit against dignity, of progress against the future. An army because a war that gorges itself on death and blood and defecates money and toxins, deserves an obscene body of deviant soldiers. We were circa because we were approximate and ambivalent, neither here nor there, but in the most powerful of all places, the place in-between order and chaos (Routledge, 2005).

The call of the rebel clown also spread to various British cities – London, Bristol, Manchester, Birmingham, Sheffield, Aberdeen, Edinburgh, Newcastle, Glasgow – and to parts of Europe and the US. In early July, as people from around the world gathered in Edinburgh for a week of actions around the G8 meeting in Gleneagles, Scotland, so the clowns converged. On July 2, the day of the Make Poverty History march, I remember the glorious sight of 150 rebel clowns, spread out across the street, sandwiched between the car park and the student union building of Edinburgh University, applying clown make-up to our faces, preparing for our first collective meeting to decide what our actions would be for the day.

Activism cannot simply be bounded off from other aspects of everyday life: our lives are entwined with the lives of others – through the legacies of colonialism, through flows of capital and commodities, through modern telecommunications, etc. – which demand that academics become politically sensitive to the needs and rights of distant strangers (Corbridge, 1993, hooks, 1994). Some of my own reflections have concerned the ambiguous third space within and between academia and activism, noting that there are myriad avenues of affinity between academics and activists; and that, as critical geographers we need to be attentive to issues of representational, ethical, and political practice that attend such collaborations (Routledge, 1996, 2002).

Because the personal is political and relational, an activist geography implies a commitment to deconstruct at least some of the barriers that exist between academics and the lives of the people they professes to represent, so that scholarly work interprets and effects social change (Kobayashi, 1994). Critical collaborative engagement with resisting others must recognize that, as academics, we are entangled within broader powers of association and intellectual production – with the institutions that employ us and/or fund our research, and their location within a global hierarchy that privileges the West's economic systems, institutions and policy 'experts' at the expense of those of the rest of the world. Such associations grant us certain securities and advantages – e.g. economic, political, representational – that may not be enjoyed by those with whom we collaborate. Hence academics frequently enjoy a range of privileges that may include mobility, funding, class, ethnicity, gender and nationality (see Nast, 1994; Routledge, 2002).

However, while we cannot fully escape our institutional or locational identities, we can as activist geographers subvert them, making them work for us in political ways that attempt to effects social, environmental and political changes. This implies that the 'field' of our fieldwork becomes 'located and defined in terms of specific political objectives' which 'ideally work toward critical and liberatory ends' (Nast, 1994: 57). In his critique on the lack of political commitment amongst contemporary academics, Pierre Bourdieu (1998) called for collaboration and new forms of communication between activist-academics and activists. Such forms of collective research are seen as interdisciplinary and international, bringing together social scientists and activists.

According to Bourdieu, academics must take care not to act as symbolic figureheads for social movements, or act as experts who give activists lessons providing answers to all social movement questions, or, indeed import hierarchical methods of debate such as committees in resistance formations. Rather, what Bourdieu called 'collective intellectuals' must seek common ground and common cause with resisting others in a non-hierarchical manner, to break the appearance of unanimity which is the greater part of the symbolic force of dominant discourses within society (1998: vii–viii). This will require an ethics of struggle to be developed within academia, one that is with resisting others as well as for them, that accepts moral and political responsibility as an act of self-constitution (Bauman, 1993). As Doreen Massey (2004) notes, such responsibility is relational, embodied, and implies extension (i.e. not being restricted to the immediate or very local). It is about nurturing affinity with others.

Affinity

Practically, affinity consists of a group of people who share common ground (friends, lovers, shared beliefs and dreams, etc), and who can provide supportive, sympathetic spaces for its members to articulate, listen to one another, share concerns, emotions, fears, etc. The politics of affinity enables people to provide support and solidarity for one another. Ideally, such a politics of research should be built on consensus decision-making, which is non-hierarchical and participatory, embodying flexible, fluid modes of action. The common values and beliefs articulated within the politics of affinity constitute a 'structure of feeling' resting upon collective experiences and interpretations, which are co-operative rather than competitive, and which are predicated upon taking political action. The idea of consensus here is based upon the notion of mutual solidarity – constructing the grievances and aspirations of geographically and culturally different people as interlinked. Mutual solidarity enables connections to be drawn that extend beyond the local and particular, by recognizing and respecting differences between people while at the same time recognizing similarities (for example, in people's aspirations) (Olesen, 2005). It is about imagining global subjectivities through similarities of experience, recognizing the shared opportunities and techniques of struggle (Starr, 2005).

During the G8 protests, there were 15 different rebel clown affinity groups from different places. For example, there were groups called Glasgow Kiss, the Cloon Army, Group Sex, Backward Intelligence, etc. Affinity was nurtured in a variety of ways. First, through a series of day-long clowning workshops, and subsequent affinity group meetings, clowning techniques were practised and refined. These provided a common repertoire of clowning practices – including group play, movements, gestures, and language – that were shared by all CIRCA participants. Second, all CIRCA 'clownbatants' shared a common 'multiform'. We wore personalized clown faces and rebel clown uniforms that were deconstructed, decorated and subverted according to the individual creativity of each person and/or group. These created a sense of affinity within diversity. Third, the workshops and multiforms helped to develop group dynamics and close interpersonal relations. Despite the seriousness of the protests against the G8, clown workshops and actions involved a great deal of play and laughter which helped to forge deep bonds between people and groups. Feeling part of a rebel army, sharing aspects of uniform and language, while at the same time acting autonomously in affinity groups and having our own specific clown characters, was empowering and provided us with a deep sense of solidarity.

During the protests, we held clown councils, whereby we would all sit in a circle and have meetings based upon consensus decision-making. Each affinity group would propose a spokesperson who would sit at the front of their group and discuss matters with the other affinity group's spokespersons. Each issue raised by the 'spokes council' would be discussed by each affinity group amongst themselves and their decision communicated back to the entire council via their spokesperson. Once consensus on each issue was reached we would move on to the next issue. These councils were held every day during the protests, at first in Edinburgh, and then at the rural convergence site near Stirling. Each group also kept in contact via mobile phone. In the clown councils we might agree to differ and to allow each group to pursue its own set of actions during the protests. Or we might all agree on a specific strategy during one of the protests.

Clown actions contained an element of dissimulation, or the unexpected, what Sun Tzu, author of *The Art of War*, termed 'being unknowable as the dark'. By this he is

referring to the crucial attributes of fluidity and adaptation – the interchange of surprise unorthodox movements and orthodox direct confrontation, mixing together into a whole. Fluidity and adaptation are primary characteristics of affinity groups. The personnel and workings of such groups are fluid and decentralized. There are no real leaders (although there are temporary organizers of particular actions) which both reflect the autonomist philosophy of such groups as well as posing deep problems for surveillance and control by the authorities. We tried to remain open to the spontaneity of clowning and of the event, so as not to become too rigid in our action and play (Routledge, 2005).

Of course, any form of collaboration with resisting others takes place within shifting, context-dependent relations of ethics and power that influence the construction of the field, and the intersubjective relations between academics and activists. While difference may be negotiated, and engaged with in an enabling and potentially transformative way, it is undertaken within a fragmented space of fluid and fragile connections and fissures. In attempts to practice a critically engaged geography, activist-academics must be cognizant of moving between their various identities (e.g. as an academic, as an activist), and be aware of the effects of this movement on their research and collaboration as a whole. Ethical and power relations mean that collaboration is 'fraught with difficulties of both a professional and personal nature, with anxieties developing as the personal and professional spheres of activist-academic/activist are combined, intertwined, manipulated and recast' (Fuller, 1999: 226).

Activist geographers must be attentive to the problematic power relations that exist between (research) collaborators. Power circulates through social relations, it is ubiquitous and productive (Foucault, 1978, 1980). However, power is not an absolute. Authority is always incomplete and is part of a web of discursive interpretations, imbued with different and differing meanings (Gibson-Graham, 1994). We are, as activist academics, situated in a webbed space across gaps in understanding, saturated with power and uncertainty (Rose 1997). As such it becomes crucial to theorize and negotiate both the differences in power between collaborators and the connections forged through such collaboration. It is important to note that these differences in power are diverse and entangled (see Sharp *et al.*, 2000). Collaborations between activist geographers and others are neither relationships of difference articulated through an objectifying distance; nor relationships of sameness, since: 'situating knowledge through transparent reflexivity gives no space to understanding across difference' (Rose, 1997: 313). Rather than map distance and difference between distinctly separate agents, we need to ask how difference – for example regarding power relations – is constituted, tracing its destabilizing emergence during the research process itself (Rose, 1997).

Negotiating power relations means working *with* groups to uncover structures of power to *em*power people to take control of their own lives. However, even in the collaborative politics of affinity, power accrues to different people at different times, depending on the context (see Routledge, 2002). Attempts to equalize power relations should be made as much as possible. However, activist-academics are frequently in a position of power by virtue of their ability to name the categories, control information about the research agenda, define interventions and come and go as research scientists (Staeheli and Lawson, 1995). Because power circulates, in difference and in unity, in relations of empowerment and disempowerment (Gibson-Graham, 1994) there are many 'powers' that accrue to research subjects within the research process that might empower as well as disempower the activist-academic. Despite our best intentions, there are a powers at play in any collaborative research process. A differential power is at work, which privileges research collaborators unequally under different circumstances. Hence, while in CIRCA I felt that

decision-making powers were spread relatively evenly, the decisions concerning this representation of CIRCA have been entirely my own. This raises crucial questions concerning the extent to which, even in collaborative research, an activist-academic and her collaborators become equal co-subjects in the research process. Just as 'we need to listen, contextualize, and admit to the power we bring to bear as multiply-positioned authors in the research process' (Nast, 1994: 59), so we also need to be attentive to the power that our collaborators bring to the research process.

We are constituted through the performance of myriad, heterogeneous, and messy moments and modes of being-in-the-world and through the living fabrics of association and relation that configure that world. Communication between people (and particularly between academics and activists), eye to heart to mind, replete with intonations and gestures, are crucial to forming common ground and affinity. The ideas brainstormed, plans hatched, schemes discarded, itineraries planned, logistics worked through, arguments settled – all require, in part, interpersonal meetings – face-to-face encounters that enable the embodying of affinities. In particular, it is the conducting of action with others – in demonstrations, blockades, occupations, street theatre, etc. – that forge the bonds of association crucial to the creation of common ground. Such considerations are intimately entwined with what Laura Pulido (2003) calls the 'interior life of politics': the entanglement of the emotions, psychological development, souls, passions and minds of activist-academic collaborators.

Emotion

Emotions are personal feelings that occur in relational encounters with human and non-human others. Politically, emotions are intimately bound up with power relations and also with relations of affinity, and are a means of initiating action. We become politically active because we feel something profoundly – such as injustice or ecological destruction. This emotion triggers changes in us that motivate us to engage in politics. It is our ability to transform our feelings about the world into actions that inspire us to participate in political action. Affinity with others under such conditions creates intensive encounters (what Hakim Bey [1991: 23] termed a 'seizure of presence'), wherein practical politics – embodied, intersubjective and relational – is practised. Collaborative association with (activist) others, necessitates interaction with others, through the doing of particular actions and the experiencing of personal and collective emotions, through creativity and imagination, through embodied, relational practices that produce political effects (Anderson and Smith, 2001; Bennett, 2004; Thien, 2005).

CIRCA was not an excuse for activists to dress up as clowns and bring color and laughter to protests. Rather, the purpose was to develop a form of political activism that brought together the practices of clowning and non-violent direct action. The purpose was to develop a methodology that helped to transform and sustain the inner emotional life of the activists involved as well as being an effective technique for taking direct action. This was because CIRCA believed that a destructive tendency within many activist movements has been the forgetting of the inner work of personal transformation and healing. By working with the body – through various clowning games and maneuvers – the purpose was to acknowledge and reveal the fears and anxieties as well as joys and pleasures of being human in these times. CIRCA believed that the emotional life of activists was a site of struggle as well as the streets. CIRCA was an attempt to change the way we feel as well as the way we struggle. Innovative forms of creative street action – materialized as various clown 'operations' – were understood as being crucial for building and inspiring movements. CIRCA's aim was to bring clowning back to the street, to reclaim its disobedience and give it back the social function it once had: its ability to disrupt, critique

and heal – adding disorder to the world in order to expose its lies and speak the truth. The clown soldiers that made up CIRCA attempted to embody life's contradictions, they were both fearsome and innocent, entertainers and dissenters, healers and laughing stocks. Clowning, like carnival, attempted to suspend and mock everyday law and order (Routledge, 2005).

This form of emotional politics played out in both the interior life of the clowns and in that of other activists. At times it also seemed to affect some of the authorities. For example, the CIRCA Operation HA.HA.HAA (Helping Authorities House Arrest Half-witted Authoritarian Androids) was deployed to invert the logic and expectations of the July 6 demonstrations against the G8. Instead of trying to climb the fences and disrupt the meeting, CIRCA wanted to deploy rebel clowns to keep the world's most dangerous 'errorists' (the G8 politicians) under house arrest in perpetuity, by building the fences around their meeting place at the Gleneagles hotel higher, and never letting them out. While this entailed an element of street theatre, CIRCA was also concerned to undermine and ridicule the intimidation and provocation of security forces at demonstrations. For example, by blowing kisses to riot cops behind their shields; or by hogging the lenses of police cameras, and following the evidence gathering teams around, mocking them and preventing them from conducting their surveillance. During the Make Poverty History march in Edinburgh, a large group of black bloc brothers and sisters were surrounded and detained by police. CIRCA was mobilized to provide solidarity, encircling the cops who were encircling the black bloc. Our presence contributed in some small way to the police finally releasing them. Various protestors at the G8 protests told us that we had helped diffuse tense situations at certain times. Moreover, CIRCA clowning attempted to access the person behind the police uniform. During CIRCA operations, I witnessed police officers smiling and laughing in interaction with rebel clowns, and even mimicking the clown salute. This entailed the right thumb of the right hand being held to the nose, with the hand vertical, palm facing to the left, and the fingers wiggling. It was used when clowns met each other, and whenever clownbatants encountered authority figures such as the police (Routledge, 2005).

Of course the intensity of feeling generated in protest situations can generate powerful emotional ties between people, engaging the body and senses, in deep emotional connections with others that can generate personal and political affinities. During the G8 protests I performed a complex of identities: clown, witness, friend, activist and academic, which took precedence at different times. The self is a performed character – the performer and her/his body provide the peg onto which a 'collaborative manufacture' is hung for a period of time (Goffman, 1956: 252–3). The performed self is subject to the contingencies and complexities of space/time and is thus dynamic, changeable and multiple, and inscribed with a variety of social meanings (Parr, 1998). Performance is complex (because of the many different positionalities that we occupy at any one time – including those of gender, class, ethnicity – and their interrelations), uncertain (because our performances of our assigned identities always carry the risk of being misperformed) and incomplete (since only by repetition are these identities sustained) (Rose, 1997). We are situated (as activist-academics) not by what we know but by what we uncertainly perform.

Performed identities are dynamic, shifting and unstable, they are manipulated, promoted, resisted, negotiated and accepted through our relations with our collaborators (Madge, 1993). A recognition that self-identity (and the identity of others in relation to our identity) is unstable and ambiguous, potentially destabilizes the problematic 'powers' that are invested in the 'all-knowing' academic. As a result, spaces may be opened for the consideration of the boundaries and interfaces of power relations and knowledge that exist between collaborators establishing common ground (Madge, 1993). As activist geographers we need to negotiate the entanglement of activism and academia, being in Cindi Katz's words 'always, everywhere, in "the field"' (1994: 72). This requires practising a particularist and relational ethics of struggle (see hooks, 1994), pertinent to the place-specificity of our research and to the politics of affinity and emotion discussed above.

Relational ethics

Ethical considerations are clearly important in the practice, subject matter and research priorities of geography. Their place in the discipline raise crucial questions concerning the role played by concepts of social justice in geographical research, and the extent to which ethical conduct is desirable, definable and/or enforceable in the practice of geography (Proctor, 1998). Pulido (2003) argues that there are three benefits to cultivating a dialogue on ethics in political activism. First, we cultivate relations of honesty, truth and interpersonal acknowledgment. Hence it is important for activist academics to be open about their 'dual' positionalities of activist and academic when working with others. Second, it allows us to build a genuine moral language. Pulido argues that the left has settled for making arguments based on policy, fiscal analyses, legal precedents and history to almost the complete exclusion of ethics. Third, it contributes to us becoming more fully conscious human beings. While political consciousness is distinguished by its focus on structures, practices and social relations of societal and global power; self-consciousness refers to self-knowledge, including the understanding of one's past and present; one's motivations, desires, fears, needs and relationship to the larger world: hence an politics of affinity and relationality.

The ethics of activist geography need to be relational and contextual, a product of reciprocity between collaborators, negotiated in practice (Bailey, 2001). Relational ethical positionalities need to be for dignity, self-determination and empowerment acknowledging that any collaborative 'we' constitutes the performance of multiple lived worlds, and an entangled web of power relationships. Collaboration can enable what Gibson-Graham term a 'partial identification' (1994: 218) between ourselves and resisting others, and an articulation of a temporary common ground, wherein relations of difference and power (e.g. concerning gender, age, ethnicity, class, sexuality, etc.) are negotiated across distances of culture, space and positionality in the search for mutual understanding.

As a result, in practical terms, an activist methodology would *at least* involve: (i) researchers sending their previous work to resisting others when asking for permission to conduct research and activism with them; (ii) researchers collaborating with resisting others on the types of research to be conducted once in the field; (iii) researchers engaging in some form of collaboration with resisting others while in the field in addition to their personal research; and (iv) all research concerning the work of resisting others being shared with those others before it was submitted for publication (see Routledge, 2003c).

Having said this, in workable affinities with others, we do not necessarily experience things differently as activist-academics than we do as people/activists, and do not necessarily need to be wary of 'over-involvement' with our research subjects (Fuller, 1999). As a result, any notion of the 'all knowing' and detached activist-academic is destabilized. I was (and remain) part of CIRCA,[2] while at other times being a critical geographer who writes chapters such as this (about CIRCA, and hence, partly myself) for academic publications. The boundaries between my roles as 'activist' and 'geographer' are always in flux, always being negotiated. So too the interpersonal dynamics and intersubjectivities within the affinity group process. This 'third space' is thus a place of invention and transformational encounters, a dynamic in-between space that is imbued with traces, relays, ambivalences, ambiguities and contradictions, with the feelings and practices of both identities (see Routledge, 1996).

A relational ethics is based on the notion of difference in relation, constituted in an intersubjective manner where difference is neither denied, essentialized nor exoticized but rather engaged with in an enabling and potentially transformative way (Katz, 1992; Kitchin, 1999). A relational ethics is about decolonizing oneself, getting used to not being the expert. It is about mutual solidarity through the process of mutual discovery and knowing one another. A relational ethics is attentive to the social context of collaboration and our situatedness with respect to that context. It is enacted in a material, embodied way, for example through relations of friendship, solidarity and empathy. Hence, through my work with CIRCA I have developed deep working affinities with others. One result of such affinity has been that one Rebel Clown friend has become a graduate student of mine, herself becoming an activist-academic in the process.

It is rare that such connections are enacted in a symmetrical way, emerging as they do from the performance of multiple lived worlds, whose interactions are usually forged under unequal relations of power (Whatmore, 1997). A relational ethics thus requires that we are sensitive to the contingency of things, and that our responsibility to others and to difference is connected to the responsibility to act (Slater, 1997). Such a responsibility, within the context of political struggle, implies that activist-academics take sides, albeit in a critical way. We need to embrace a politics of recognition that identifies and defends only those differences that can be coherently combined with social and environmental justice (Fraser, 1997). This critical engagement can serve to be vigilant to those 'minor' reversals within resistance practices, such as occurs with the creation of internal hierarchies, the silencing of dissent, peer pressure and even violence; or in how various forces of hegemony are internalized, reproduced, echoed and traced within such

practices. Ideally, critical engagement would be able to confront, negotiate and enter into dialogue with the manifestations of dominating power within resistance formations from sensitivity to the 'feeling space' of one's collaborators (see Sharp *et al.*, 2000).

FOR AN ACTIVIST GEOGRAPHY

Much of the discussion above gestures to the complications of working in the 'third space' between activism and academia (Routledge, 1996), not least because the academy is traditionally suspicious of highly engaged, participatory and transparently ethico-politically 'committed' inquiry, but also sometimes because activists are (often justifiably) suspicious of the intentions of academics (i.e. whether they more interested in career boosting than social change). Therefore, activist geographers need to consider how the norms and conventions of academic practice may work in contradiction to those of activist practice, and, indeed, the practices of activist-academics. For example, there is always a tension between criticality and censorship. Collaboration raises the question of how critical an academic can be of his/her activist collaborators and still continue to support, rather than undermine, their goals. There is also the tension between collaboration and careerism. Critical engagement raises the question of how these, at times, opposing dimensions of an academic's lifeworld fit together into a meaningful assemblage when ranged against an academic's institutional responsibilities. In other words, how do academics balance their personal desires and interests with those with whom they work? (Routledge, 2002).

There are no easy 'cut out and keep' answers to these questions. Young academics, in particular, have to negotiate the time constraints that university teaching places upon them as well as the institutional constraints of the tenure process. Zygmunt Bauman (1992) argues that the interpretive strategy of academia gestates an ontology within which only language is accredited with the attribute of reality. Indeed 'reality' itself – be it the realm of culture, politics, economics – becomes 'an object of study, something to be mastered only cognitively, as a meaning, and not practically, as a task' (1992: 23). In other words, where academics are involved in political action at all, it tends to be in the representational, rather than in the material, realm. The autonomy of intellectual discourse is highly valued by academics, and according to Bauman, staunchly defended 'against the rebels from its own ranks who jeopardize the comforts of freedom, drawing the dusty skeleton of political commitment out of the old family cupboard' (1992: 16).

Pursuing activist methodologies may thus entail problems and privations on behalf of (young) academics, for example through delays in promotion, or failure to gain tenure. Moreover, these may be particularly acute within the increasingly neoliberal university system. However, being actively involved outside of the academy in order to affect some form of social change can be both a rewarding personal experience as well as bringing potential insights into one's academic work. There are many examples of geographers who have become involved, in different ways, politically. Some of the hazards and potentials of such engagement are discussed in the current work of Paul Chatterton and Jenny Pickerill on autonomous geographies (see also Pickerill, 2003; Gordon and Chatterton, 2004); the contributors to the 'Research, action and 'critical' geographies' theme issue of *Area* (1999, 31 (3)); and the recent e-volume by Duncan Fuller and Rob Kitchin (2004).

However, activist desires sit in an uneasy relationship to that academic desire to conduct research and to be published. They are identities performed on different stages and for different audiences and necessitate the negotiation of different powers at work in the collaboration process – our own power as activist-academics, the entangled relations of power between us and our collaborators, and the limitations, possibilities and deployments of this power. Within these entangled powers, the importance of reflexivity is crucial, since we miss an important dimension of self-reflexivity if we neglect to examine our own capacity to facilitate change in the lives of others in addition to merely representing them (Kesby, 1998). Although critical collaboration enables academics to potentially play a greater role in effecting social change, the entangled powers that are entailed sit uneasily together, and thus we need to acknowledge an embodied politics that is committed yet partial in perspective (Hyndman, 2003). Creating common ground with resisting others serves to highlight and 'ground' differences (in language, ethnicity, power, access to resources, etc.) in particular ways in particular places. When placed in such active proximity, difference (in ways of being, talking, acting) can be both recognized and negotiated.

Activist-geographic praxis acknowledges the importance of letting myriad flowers bloom in the academic imagination, while recognizing the importance of tempering the privilege of academics to pursue personal research agendas with an ethics of political responsibility to resisting others. Such responsibility extends beyond teaching within the academy (to relatively privileged students), in order for academic research to 'make its deliberations more consequential for the poorer eighty per cent of the population of the world' (Appadurai, 2000: 3). Activist geography is concerned with grounding our theories and imaginations in the messy unpredictability of everyday life, and embodying radicalism that situates the geographical and academic imagination within the key political debates and actions of our time – politicizing the personal. For example, actively resisting, rather than bemoaning or complying with, the neoliberal restructuring of academia (see Castree, 1999, 2002); living alternative geographical possibilities in addition to theorising about them; radicalizing geography to actively engage with the wretched of the earth (Cumbers and Routledge, 2004). In particular, an activist geography can contribute to the creation of new political spaces and potentially new forms of collaborative power. One doesn't have to become a rebel clown in order to realise this. Myriad forms of engagement are possible. For example, as activist-academics we can reclaim streets, blockade military bases and barricade corporate offices; we can occupy land, warehouses, unoccupied houses; we can use our skills in popular health and education outreach; we can participate in social centres, infoshops, guerrilla gardens and independent media initiatives; we can culture jam and decommodify corporate/private space; we can contribute to direct democracy and autonomist experiments in everyday living through practising consensus-based politics; we can engage in the long-term work of contributing to, and constructing, socially just and environmentally sustainable communities. Ultimately, an activist geography prioritizes grounded, embodied political action, the role of theory being to contribute to, be informed by, and be grounded in such action, in order to create and nurture mutual solidarity and collective action, a liberatory politics of affinity.

ACKNOWLEDGMENTS

I would like to thank Steve Herbert and my anonymous referees for their comments on an earlier draft of this chapter.

NOTES

1. By 'resisting others' I mean communities, groups, social movements, or non-government organisations (NGOs) who are challenging various practices of dominating power. Dominating power refers to that power which attempts to control or coerce others, impose its will upon others, or manipulate the consent of others. These circumstances may involve domination, exploitation and subjection at the material, symbolic or psychological levels.

This dominating power can be located within the realms of the state, the economy and civil society, and articulated within social, economic, political and cultural relations and institutions. Patriarchy, racism and homophobia are all faces of dominating power which attempt to discipline, silence, prohibit or repress difference or dissent. Dominating power engenders inequality, and asserts the interests of a particular class, caste, race, or political configuration at the expense of others, for example through particular development projects associated with neoliberal capitalism.

2. For example during the summer of 2006, I visited Oslo, Norway to conduct a Clown Army training of Norwegian activists.

REFERENCES

Anderson, K. and Smith, S.J. (2001) 'Editorial: emotional geographies,' *Transactions of the Institute of British Geographers* 26 (1): 7–10.

Appadurai, A. (2000) 'Grassroots globalization and the research imagination', *Public Culture* 12 (1): 1–19.

Bailey, C. (2001) 'Geographers doing household research: intrusive research and moral accountability,' *Area* 33 (1): 107–10.

Bauman, Z. (1992) *Intimations of postmodernity*. London: Routledge.

Beaumont, J., Loopmans, M. and Uitermark, J. (2005) 'Politicization of research and the relevance of geography: some experiences and reflections for an ongoing debate,' *Area* 37 (1): 118–26.

Bennett, K. (2004) 'Emotionally intelligent research,' *Area* 36 (4): 414–22.

Berry, B. (1972) 'More on relevance and policy analysis,' *Area* 4: 77–80.

Bey, H. (1991) *T.A.Z.* Brooklyn. Autonomedia.

Blaut, J.M. (1979) 'The dissenting tradition,' *Annals of the Association of American Geographers* 69 (1): 157–64.

Blomley, N. (1994) 'Activism and the academy,' *Environment and Planning D: Society and Space.* 12: 383–85.

Bourdieu, P. (1998) *Acts of resistance.* Cambridge: Polity Press.

Bunge, W. (1977) 'The first years of the Detroit geographical expedition: a personal report,' in R. Peet (ed.) *Radical Geography*. London: Methuen. pp. 31–9.

Buttimer, A. (1974) 'Values in geography.' Resource paper #24, Association of American Geographers Commission on College Geography.

Castree, N. (1999) '"Out there?" "In here?" Domesticating critical geography.' *Area* 31 (1): 81–6.

Castree, N. (2000) 'Professionalism, activism and the university: whither "critical geography",' *Environment and Planning A* 32 (6): 955–70.

Castree, N. (2002) 'Border geography,' *Area* 34 (1): 103–8.

Chatterton, P., Fuller, D. and Routledge, P. (2008) 'Relating action to activism: theoretical and methodological reflections,' in S. Kindon, R. Pain and M. Kesby (eds) *Participatory action research approaches and methods: connecting people, participation and place.* London: Routledge. pp. 216–22.

Chouinard, V. (1994) 'Reinventing radical geography: is all that's left right?' *Environment and planning D: society and Space* 12 (1): 2–6.

Corbridge, S. (1993) 'Marxisms, modernities and moralities: development praxis and the claims of distant strangers,' *Environment and Planning D: Society and Space* 11 (4): 449–72.

Cumbers, A. and Routledge, P. (2004) 'Alternative geographical imaginations: introduction,' *Antipode* 36 (5): 818–28.

Dear, M. (1999) 'The relevance of postmodernism,' *Scottish Geographical Magazine* 115 (2): 143–50.

Demeritt, D. (2000) 'The new social contract for science: accountability, relevance and value in US and UK science research and policy,' *Antipode* 32 (3): 308–29.

Farrow, H., Moss, P. and Shaw, B. (1995) 'Symposium on feminist participatory research,' *Antipode* 27 (1): 77–101.

Foucault, M. (1978) *The history of sexuality: an introduction.* Translated by Robert Hurley. Harmondsworth: Penguin.

Foucault, M. (1980) *Power/knowledge: selected interviews and other writings, 1972–1977.* Edited by C. Gordon and translated by C. Gordon *et al.* New York: Pantheon.

Fraser, N. (1997) *Justice interruptus: critical reflections on the 'postsocialist' condition.* London: Routledge.

Fuller, D. (1999) 'Part of the action, or "going native"? Learning to cope with the "politics of integration",' *Area* 31 (3): 221–28.

Fuller, D. and Kitchin, R. (2004) 'Radical theory/critical praxis: academic geography beyond the academy?' in D. Fuller and R. Kitchin (eds) *Critical theory/ radical praxis: making a difference beyond the academy?* Vernon and Victoria, BC, Canada: Praxis (e)Press. pp. 1–20.

Gibson-Graham, J-K. (1994) '"Stuffed if I know!" Reflections on post-modern feminist social research,' *Gender, Place and Culture* 1 (2): 205–24.

Gibson-Graham, J-K. (2006) *A postcapitalist politics.* Minneapolis: University of Minnesota Press.

Goffman, E. (1956) *The presentation of self in everyday life.* London: Penguin Books.

Gordon, N. and Chatterton, P. (2004) *Taking back control: a journey through Argentina's popular uprising.* Leeds: School of Geography, University of Leeds.

Graeber, D. (2002) 'The new anarchists,' *New Left Review* 13: 61–73.

Harvey, D. (1972) 'Revolutionary and counter-revolutionary theory in geography and the problem of ghetto formation,' *Antipode* 4 (2): 1–2.

Harvey, D. (1973) *Social justice and the city.* London: Edward Arnold.

Harvey, D. (1974) 'What kind of geography for what kind of public policy?' *Transactions of the Institute of British Geographers* 63: 18–24.

Harvey, D. (2000) *Spaces of hope.* Berkeley, CA: University of California Press.

hooks, b. (1994) *Teaching to transgress.* London: Routledge.

Howit, R. (1993) 'Social impact assessment as "applied people's geography,"' *Australian Geographical Studies* 31 (2): 127–140.

Hyndman, J. (2003) 'Beyond either/or: a feminist analysis of September 11th,' *ACME: An International E-journal for Critical Geographies* 2 (1): 1–13.

Katz, C. (1992) 'All the world is staged: intellectuals and the process of ethnography,' *Environment and Planning D: Society and Space* 10: 495–510.

Katz, C. (1994) 'Playing the field: questions of fieldwork in geography.' *The Professional Geographer* 46 (1): 67–72.

Kesby, M. (1998) 'PRA praxis, beyond the representational impasse?: struggling between theory and practice in the context of gender focused HIV research in rural Zimbabwe.' Invited seminar paper, Department of Geography Research Seminar Series, University of Glasgow, 27th November (unpublished).

Kitchin, R. and Hubbard, P. (1999) 'Editorial: research, action and "critical" geographies,' *Area* 31 (3): 195–98.

Kitchin, R.M. (1999) 'Ethics and morals in geographical studies of disability,' in J. Proctor and D. Smith (eds) *Geography and ethics: journeys through a moral terrain.* London: Routledge. pp. 223–36.

Kobayashi, A. (1994) 'Coloring the field: gender, "race" and the politics of fieldwork,' *The Professional Geographer* 46 (1): 73–80.

Kropotkin, P.A. (1908) *Mutual aid.* London: Heineman.

Kropotkin, P.A. (1974) *Fields, factories, and workshops tomorrow.* London: Allen and Unwin.

Laurie, N., Dwyer, C., Holloway, S. and Smith, F. (1999) *Geographies of new temininities.* Harlow: Longman.

McDowell, L. (1992) 'Doing gender: feminism, feminists and research methods in human geography,' *Transactions of the Institute of British Geography* NS 17 (4): 399–415.

Madge, C. (1993) 'Boundary disputes: comments on Sidaway (1992),' *Area* 25 (3): 294–9.

Martin, R. (2001) 'Geography and public policy: the case of the missing agenda,' *Progress in Human Geography* 25 (2): 189–210.

Massey, D. (1994) *Space, Place and gender.* Minneapolis: University of Minnesota Press.

Massey, D. (2000) 'Editorial: practising political relevance', *Transactions of the Institute of British Geography* NS 25 (2): 131–33.

Massey, D. (2004) 'Geographies of responsibility,' *Geografiska Annaler* 86 B (1): 5–18.

Maxey, I. (1999) 'Beyond boundaries? Activism, academia, reflexivity and research,' *Area* 31 (3): 199–208.

Merrifield, A. (1995) 'Situated knowledge through exploration: reflections on Bunge's "Geographical Expeditions",' *Antipode* 27 (1): 49–70.

Morrill, R. (1969) 'Geography and the transformation of society,' *Antipode* 1 (1): 6–9.

Moss, P. (ed.) (2002) *Feminist geography in practice: research and methods.* Oxford: Blackwell.

Nast, H. (1994) 'Opening remarks on "women in the field",' *The Professional Geographer* 46 (1): 54–66.

Olesen, T. (2005) *International Zapatismo.* London: Zed Books.

Pain, R. (2003) 'Social geography: on action-oriented research,' *Progress in Human Geography* 7 (5): 649–57.

Parr, H. (1998) 'Mental health, ethnography and the body,' *Area* 30 (1): 28–37.

Peck, J. (1999) 'Editorial: grey geography?' *Transactions of the Institute of British Geographers* NS 24 (2): 131–35.

Peet, R. (1969) 'A new left geography,' *Antipode* 1 (1): 3–5.

Peet, R. (1977) *Radical geography.* London: Methuen.

Pickerill, J. (2003) *Cyberprotest: environmental activism online.* Manchester: Manchester University Press.

Pickerill, J. and Chatterton, P. (2006) 'Notes towards autonomous geographies: creation, resistance and self-management as survival tactics,' *Progress in Human Geography* 30 (6): 730–46.

Pollard, J., Henry, N., Bryson, J. and Daniels, P. (2000) 'Shades of grey? Geographers and policy,' *Transactions of the Institute of British Geographers* NS 25 (2): 243–48.

Proctor, J.D. (1998) 'Ethics in geography: giving moral form to the geographical imagination,' *Area* 30 (1): 8–18.

Pulido, L. (2003) 'The interior life of politics,' *Ethics, Place and Environment* 6 (1): 46–52.

Riles, A. (2001) *The network inside out.* University of Michigan Press: Michigan.

Rose, G. (1997) 'Situating knowledges: positionality, reflexivities and other tactics,' *Progress in Human Geography* 21 (3): 305–20.

Routledge, P. (1996) 'The third space as critical engagement,' *Antipode* 28 (4): 397– 419.

Routledge, P. (1997) 'The imagineering of resistance: Pollok free state and the practice of postmodern politics,' *Transactions of the Institute of British Geographers* NS 22 (3): 359–76.

Routledge, P. (1998) 'Going globile: spatiality, embodiment and mediation in the Zapatista insurgency,' in S. Dalby and G. O'Tuathail (eds) *Rethinking Geopolitics.* London: Routledge. pp. 240–60.

Routledge, P. (2002) 'Travelling east as Walter Kurtz: identity, performance and collaboration in Goa, India,' *Environment and Planning D: Society and Space* 20 (4): 477–98.

Routledge, P. (2003a) 'Convergence space: process geographies of grassroots globalisation networks,' *Transactions of the Institute of British Geographers* 28 (3): 333–49.

Routledge, P. (2003b) 'Voices of the dammed: discursive resistance amidst erasure in the Narmada Valley, India,' *Political Geography* 22 (3): 243–70.

Routledge, P. (2003c) 'River of resistance: critical collaboration and the dilemmas of power and ethics,' *Ethics, Place and Environment* 6 (1): 66–73.

Routledge, P. (2005) 'Reflections on the G8: an interview with General Unrest of the Clandestine Insurgent Rebel Clown Army (CIRCA).' *ACME: An International E-Journal for Critical Geography* 3 (2): 112–20.

Sharp, J., Routledge, P., Philo, C., and Paddison, R. (eds) (2000) *Entanglements of power: geographies of domination/resistance.* London: Routledge.

Slater, D. (1997) 'Spatialities of power and postmodern ethics – rethinking geopolitical encounters,' *Environment and Planning D: Society and Space* 15 (1): 55–72.

Smith, D. (2000) 'Social justice revisited,' *Environment and Planning A* 32 (7): 1149–62.

Smith, S.J. (1994) 'Qualitative methods,' in R.J. Johnstone, D. Gregory and D.M. Smith (eds) *The dictionary of human geography.* Oxford: Blackwell. pp. 491–2.

Staeheli, L.A. and Lawson, V.A. (1994) 'A discussion of "women in the field": the politics of feminist fieldwork,' *The Professional Geographer* 46 (1): 96–102.

Staeheli, L.A. and Lawson, V.A. (1995) 'Feminism, praxis and human geography,' *Geographical Analysis* 27: 321–38.

Staeheli L.A. and Mitchell, D. (2005) 'The complex politics of relevance in geography,' *Annals of the Association of American Geographers* 95 (2): 357–72.

Starr. A. (2005) *Global revolt.* London: Zed.

Thien, D. (2005) 'After or beyond feeling? A consideration of affect and emotion in geography,' *Area* 37 (4): 450–56.

Thrift, N. (2004) 'Intensities of feeling: towards a spatial politics of affect,' *Geografiska Annaler* 86 B(1): 57–78.

Whatmore, S. (1997) 'Dissecting the autonomous self: hybrid cartographies for a relational ethics,' *Environment and Planning D: Society and Space* 15 (1): 37–53.

White, G. (1972) 'Geography and public policy,' *The Professional Geographer* 24 (2): 101–4.

Wills, J. (2002) 'Political economy III: neoliberal chickens, Seattle and geography,' *Progress in Human Geography* 26 (1): 90–100.

23

Reflections on Teaching Qualitative Methods in Geography

Deborah G. Martin

INTRODUCTION: THE STATE OF QUALITATIVE METHODS IN GEOGRAPHY

After a heyday of dominance in the 1950s and 1960s, quantitative methods have been joined by an increased use of qualitative methods in research (Eyles and Smith, 1998; Limb and Dwyer, 2001; Hay, 2005; DeLyser, 2008). Indeed, Iain Hay (2005: 10) argues that, 'In the last twenty-five years the pendulum of geographical methods within human geography has swung firmly from quantitative to qualitative methods ... Qualitative methods have been in the ascendant since the 1980s.' Further evidence of this trend is the growing membership of the Qualitative Research Specialty Group (QRSG) of the Association of American Geographers (AAG): it was established in 2000 with 91 members; now in 2006 it boasts 247 members, 58 percent of whom are students. This is a modest-size specialty group.[1] Clearly, in many ways, qualitative methods are pervasive, accepted, and important to the practice of human geography (see also DeLyser, 2008).

At the same time, however, geographers are not training the future researchers and professors of the discipline how to conduct qualitative research in any systematic or widespread manner. Of the 52 PhD-granting geography programs in the United States (US), only 13 offer a qualitative methods course for graduate students. (I have limited my discussion to graduate programs, with the idea that they are the ones primarily training future geography *researchers*.) An additional 10 departments do offer qualitative methods as part of a general research methods course. However, fully 34 of the PhD-granting departments offer quantitative methods, with only two additional departments incorporating quantitative methods into a general research methods course. Clearly, teaching qualitative research methods to geographers is a little outside of the mainstream in graduate programs in the US. At the same time, however, a glass-half-full approach to this data indicates that fully a quarter of all PhD-granting geography departments offer qualitative methods! This is surely an advance from 10 or 20 years ago, but geographers need to train future geographers in qualitative methods to ensure excellence in our discipline.

In this chapter, I consider the imperatives, rewards, and challenges in teaching qualitative geography. I focus on situating qualitative research epistemologically and in terms of specific methods, and hope to show the pleasures of such teaching practice, as well as the tensions. Despite the progress in the teaching of qualitative methods in US geography programs, I see three problems for qualitative methods in geography if they continue to be widely practiced but with little formal instruction: First, poorly-conducted qualitative research is possible. Second, poorly-conducted qualitative research hurts all of us who strive for rigor in our research, potentially painting all qualitative geography with the same broad brush of inferior quality. Third, qualitative geography might not be able to maintain its current relative level of respect if high standards are not passed on to future generations of geographers. Each of these problems can certainly be addressed in part by teaching qualitative methods, especially if such teaching is paired with greater engagement by geographers in conversations about what 'good' qualitative methods are, and how we teach them (part of the purpose of the Qualitative Research specialty group is to foster such conversations, as is the case with this book!). Excellent textbooks are now available for geographers wanting to teach qualitative methods within a disciplinary framework (for example, Eyles and Smith, 1988; Limb and Dwyer, 2001; Blunt et al., 2003; Clifford and Valentine, 2003; Flowerdew and Martin, 2005; Hay, 2005). Additionally, there is a multitude of non-discipline specific qualitative methodology books and monographs (see especially those published by Sage: Holstein and Gubrium, 1995; Morgan, 1997; Maxwell, 2001; Yin, 2003; Denzin and Lincoln, 2005; Israel and Hay, 2006; Creswell, 2007). These resources are indicators of the previously-mentioned growth in qualitative methodologies, and they provide a framework for a focus within the discipline on teaching and discussing qualitative methods.

QUALITATIVE RESEARCH, DATA, AND PEDAGOGY

We must confront the question of what, exactly, we mean by qualitative methods, before deciding the best approach to teaching them. Norman Denzin and Yvonna Lincoln (2000) argue that qualitative research form its own discipline, uniting disparate areas of study under a common methodological umbrella. From its roots in the 1920s and 1930s in both the Chicago School of Sociology and in Anthropology, the goal of qualitative research originally was to study 'the other' (Denzin and Lincoln, 2000). Now, it may be best understood as an approach to knowledge that emphasizes interpretation and understanding, particularly of daily life-experiences and meanings. A host of methods can be included in the category 'qualitative' (and may be undertaken in conjunction with quantitative methods). These include case study, participant observation, interviews, focus groups, and archival research.

Emphasizing the interpretive elements of qualitative methods does not mean that only qualitative methods (as opposed to quantitative ones) require interpretation; nor does it suggest that qualitative methods do not contribute to other aspects of knowledge production such as explanation.[2] Indeed, both quantitative and qualitative methods demand epistemological engagement and interpretation of researchers from the very start of a research design (Dixon and Jones, 1998; Singleton and Straits, 2005). Further, while qualitative researchers usually do not make claims about the generalizability of their findings to other places and people, they certainly use them to generalize theory and understanding about social life, meaning, and geographies (Hanson and Pratt, 2003; Yin, 2003). These generalizations may explain more about social worlds than (quantitative) findings that show patterns across a space or population. (Clearly, however, both types of methods help produce knowledge; together, they might explain more than either approach can in isolation; see Hanson and Pratt, 2003). Nonetheless, there are some inherent differences between the dominant underlying assumptions of quantitative data and that of qualitative data of which researchers need to be cognizant, and which should be explicit in a qualitative methods course.

Many quantitative methods rest upon an inherent assumption – dominant in much of traditional 'science' – that what can be observed or measured can be correlated with an understanding of cause and effect, leading to explanations about, and predications of, future observations (Singleton and Straits, 2005). Qualitative data is not *necessarily* incompatible with this epistemology. Certainly, combinations of qualitative and quantitative data suggest that the two can be productively combined, in part to demonstrate and explain patterns, and to generalize across, while demonstrating the complexities of, specific cases (e.g. Hanson and Pratt, 1995; 2003; Martin and Holloway, 2005). However, many, if not most of the epistemologies of knowledge that underlie qualitative research, suggest that knowledge is contextual, interpreted, and always negotiated (as are all forms of knowledge) (Haraway, 1991). Some of the knowledge that qualitative data seeks to identify is not observable; it requires in-depth discussion about peoples' understandings, and their values. Further, such constructivist/interpretivist, and poststructuralist epistemologies inherently hold that any knowledge derived from an exchange among people (such as interviews or focus groups) is knowledge that is produced itself through the exchange, not a pre-existing set of beliefs that are uncovered and exposed by the researcher (Haraway, 1991; Miller, 1993; Gibson-Graham, 1994; Holstein and Gubrium, 1995; Pratt, 1999). While such data reveal complexities and contexts, therefore, they do so in highly contingent and fluid ways. The implications of constructivist notions of knowledge for teaching a set of methods is profound, because they require some acknowledgment of the (differing) epistemological foundations of qualitative research.

The focus in much of qualitative research in geography on interpretation and understanding – or, at least, on revealing the complexities and contexts of daily lives and geographies, as Susan Hanson and Geraldine Pratt (2003) suggest – poses a challenge for pedagogy. What does it mean, exactly, to teach interpretation, or understanding? Perhaps even more fundamentally, can interpretation or understanding be taught? Or in an alternative approach, does knowledge of a set of steps or tools lead comfortably and easily to interpretation? In my own teaching of qualitative geography, I walk a fine line between trying to inculcate students with an awareness of and facility with the steps they might take to 'do' qualitative research, and communicating the implications inherent in gathering and interpreting such data. It is important for students to understand the underlying rationales for particular methods, and what sort of knowledge the methods can produce within different epistemological frameworks (Del Casino *et al.*, 2000 provide a very useful chart for seeing these different frameworks and knowledge). Courses in qualitative methods, I believe, ought to confront the different ways that particular methods can be used, so that students can make decisions about what they hope to achieve in their research, and how they will go about doing and explaining it. It is inherent to the process of doing qualitative research that researchers will be confronted with dilemmas about conflicting stories, presence of strong emotions, and challenges of how to represent their 'data' and broader knowledge gained. Having an opportunity to confront these issues *before* designing a 'real' qualitative research study might be the most important value in qualitative methods courses.

LEARNING AND TEACHING

One of my favorite graduate seminars to teach is qualitative research methods. I like it because I always learn from it, and because, somewhat unexpectedly, it's been a consistent part of my overall sense of contribution to my departmental program, because of its role in developing the 'research skills' of our students. This feeling of contribution has come largely from the respect and appreciation accorded to the course, and my teaching of it, from my students and colleagues. By and large, I have found geography faculty at the two institutions at which I have been privileged to teach to be happy to have a qualitative course for graduate students. More substantively, these colleagues have been quite supportive of the notion of qualitative methods as an acceptable 'skills' course for a graduate program. In both institutions, the faculty meetings in which we affirmed that the qualitative research course could be taken by a student to meet a 'skills' requirement were short on dissent, and quickly decided. The message I received in both instances was that, of course qualitative research methods are a legitimate method in geography, and ought to be taught as such.

In approaching the teaching of qualitative geography, however, I face the challenge of presenting a set of methods that have, at their common base, a goal of understanding, with embedded epistemologies that stress interpretation and question universal knowledge. Consequently, in my course I try to balance social theories of knowledge ('epistemology') with specific, nuts-and-bolts prescriptions for collecting and analyzing data ('methods'). My students would undoubtedly argue that I err on the theory side; they often seek more 'how-tos' than I am at times willing to give. Why my reluctance, I have wondered in the face of their feedback? To be sure, they often praise the theoretical and philosophical explorations we engage about knowledge and science and research. But, at the same time, they wonder if qualitative methods aren't more standardized than I seem to present. Perhaps they are correct. I sense a disconnect between the norms and expectations of my students and that of my own graduate experience. There is a difference, I am sure, between coming of age as a

scholar in the times when one-quarter of all PhD programs in the United States teach qualitative methods, and doing so when qualitative methods were barely taught at all (or, at least, not in my own program, or that of any of my peers in other graduate programs in the 1990s).

In discussions with my peers, from my own and other institutions, it seems that many of us followed a very individual path to learning qualitative methods: we read about them in informal directed-readings courses, took courses in other departments (such as Sociology or Anthropology), and/or generally followed a trial-and-error process in our dissertation research. Partly as a result of this somewhat haphazard process, many current faculty in geography departments who do qualitative research may not teach it, and may not have ever had a formal course in such research or its methods. Consequently, we may not really know how to teach something that we learned through a sometimes painful trial-and-error process. Indeed, we may not even view ourselves as sufficiently 'expert' to teach the broad range of approaches and methods that fall under the umbrella of 'qualitative research'. Nonetheless, our (perhaps haphazard) experiences provide a basis for thinking about, and enacting, more systematic pedagogical approaches to qualitative methods, while retaining an acknowledgment of the contingencies and particularities of any application of qualitative data and data-collection to a specific research question.

Although I love teaching qualitative research, it was a challenge the first time I did so, prompted in large part by enthusiasm and encouragement from a combination of colleagues and graduate students. It was particularly challenging to translate the experiences of my own research into a coherent examination of a set of methods and theories about knowledge. In some ways, this shift to role of 'expert' is common to all scholars who start teaching for the first time, regardless of subject matter. But there is a more pernicious problem in the teaching of qualitative research, one that rests on the notion of praxis. In short, how do we teach something that many of us learned by doing and which inherently requires doing to fully understand? Teaching access to such knowledge, therefore, is counter-intuitive and potentially misleading. Two principles help navigate this problem: First, qualitative methods ought not be taught in a vacuum. Students also need systematic exposure to epistemology in their substantive research seminars. Second, students need opportunities to 'practice' methods. Assignments that allow or require students to 'test out' certain methods, and reflect upon them, help students to gain confidence, and to see the linkages between theories of knowledge and means to gather and analyze data to contribute to the production of knowledge.

EPISTEMOLOGY, METHODOLOGY, AND METHODS

The contradiction between teaching methods that are personal and highly situational, and that of training expert researchers, is for me the crux of the challenge of teaching qualitative research in geography. What is it that we are trying to teach when we teach qualitative methods in geography? In my own course, I seek to strike a balance between teaching something about the epistemology of knowledge underlying my own approach to qualitative data – one that seems similar to a lot of qualitative research published in geography (for example, Gibson-Graham, 1994; Kobayashi and Peake, 1994; Pratt, 1999) – and a set of methods informed by a particular methodology.

Sandra Harding (1987: 2–3) distinguishes between epistemology, or 'a theory of knowledge;' methodology, or 'a theory and analysis of how research should proceed;' and method, or 'techniques for gathering evidence'. In a qualitative methods course, I think it is worthwhile to highlight these three distinct stages of knowledge, understanding, and acquisition. While certainly in practice they

blur together, students' choices of particular methodologies and methods will be more thoughtful if fully grounded in knowledge of epistemology and methodology, rather than merely a set of methods. I find that many students seek a set of methods (or techniques) that they can follow in a step-wise fashion in the field, and may not want to 'get philosophical' in a methods course by exploring epistemology. Although I am sympathetic to that desire and want them to have an understanding of specific methods, I insist that the practice of qualitative research rests upon particular epistemological and methodological foundations, and that they need to know something about those foundations in order to make reasoned judgments in their research. In the remainder of this chapter, I want to explore how I seek simultaneously to teach something about epistemology, methodology, and methods in my qualitative research course.[3]

PUTTING IT ALL TOGETHER IN ONE COURSE

Course design: Research seminar

The focus in qualitative research on interpretation and understanding has led me to create a course that approaches qualitative methods as a set of philosophies as much as a set of tools. My approach has also been shaped quite explicitly by the medium and audience: a seminar for graduate students. Like any seminar, each week is structured around a particular theme (ranging from a first week introduction on 'why qualitative methods', to a second week on 'ethics' and three subsequent weeks on 'epistemologies', then focusing on particular methods within the 'qualitative' umbrella, including interviews, focus groups, and archival data, before shifting to issues of analysis and writing – 'representing qualitative research'). Students take turns leading each class by writing questions for class discussion, and the goal of each class period is to produce some understanding of the significance of the 'theme' for the week in light of the overall goal of understanding qualitative research in geography.

As a methodology class, we focus on 'how to' as well: in addition to developing an understanding of various approaches to knowledge within qualitative research, we discuss how the readings help us learn to use a particular method. Certainly, qualitative methods *could* be presented in a classroom as a set of tools that can be applied in almost any context. One of the inevitable topics of many seminar discussions is how a particular method, such as focus groups, can look very different depending on the epistemology of the researchers using it. A methods-only approach, however, leaves students somewhat bereft in linking their own research questions to broader theoretical debates, and to making and defending their claims about knowledge production. Therefore, my course takes as a starting point that the specific methods cannot be fully used and understood without an appreciation of the underlying epistemologies and logics that make them appropriate for producing particular forms of knowledge in specific contexts.

My graduate 'qualitative research methods' seminar usually enrolls a mix of geography PhD students, and master's students in international development. These two groups of students have vastly different research time-frames, expectations, and needs. The course was originally developed to serve primarily interdisciplinary PhD students, but a change in institutional contexts brought the addition of the development master's students, and has highlighted the dilemma between teaching epistemology and methodology versus teaching methods. Most of the master's students are poised to enter a 'field' site (almost always in a non-US context) in the following semester, and eager to learn a set of tools that they can apply in the field. The geography students are generally more willing to engage a series of questions about epistemology, in part because they are

doctoral students, are they are often simultaneously enrolled in a required departmental course on 'explanation in geography' (a course on theories and epistemologies in the discipline). Nonetheless, they, too, would like to have a set of techniques about which they believe they have enough knowledge to confidently write about them in a research proposal and use them in a field setting, even if that 'field' might be a more distant prospect (one or two years away).

Structure and readings

I have traditionally started off the course with an explicit foray into theories of knowledge, following an initial week in which we seek to define the term 'qualitative methods' and have some contemporary examples (see Denzin and Lincoln, 2000; Crang, 2002).[4] While this epistemological focus conflicts explicitly with the students' desire to focus on methods, I insist that they need to know contexts in which the methods are applied, and to what ends; in terms of findings and knowledge gained. The first week aims to define and situate qualitative research. With readings from Denzin and Lincoln (2000) Vincent Del Casino and colleagues (2000); Michael Hill (1981); and Mike Crang (2002), I expose students to the idea that qualitative research might involve radically different conceptualizations of knowledge than those dominant in quantitative research.[5] My purpose is less to give a comprehensive review of epistemology, and more to provide a common language and framework for understanding different approaches to knowledge within qualitative research, and outside of it. The readings of this and subsequent early weeks offer a common reference point for course participants, one to which we return as we discuss particular methods.

Following the introduction and a foray into how geographers consider and use qualitative research, we explicitly address epistemology for two weeks (out of 15 weeks in a semester schedule). We first examine ideas of hermeneutics and interpretivism (Geertz, 1973; Dixon and Jones, 1998; Schwandt, 2000), as well as a short sampling of Foucault (1970: ix–xxiv, 1–16) to identify concepts within post-structuralism. The Foucault excerpt is always challenging yet also fun; it offers his reading of the seventeenth century painting *Las Meninas* by Diego Velázquez, in which Foucault identifies the limits of representation (for another, less dense interpretation of the representations in *Las Meninas*, see Searle, 1980). Some students agonize over understanding Foucault, but I stress that the point is to see his critique of representation, and to take the hermeneutic and interpretivist readings together with the Foucault to consider what kind of evidence our data may provide, and how we understand it. The goal of these readings is not to be comprehensive introductions of epistemological stances, but rather to hint at, and identify key aspects of various approaches to knowledge. This first week of 'epistemological' readings begins the conversation about theories of knowledge, and how they link to methods and methodologies. Following the Del Casino *et al.* (2000) reading of the week before, which explicitly contrasts different epistemological stances in connection with a single research topic, students can start to identify differences in knowledge production across epistemologies. I ask students to consider their own thoughts about the 'real' world, what it is we can know about it, and what sort of data and evidence they therefore seek.

The second – and final – of the formal readings on epistemologies provides brief introductions or *précis* of feminism (Harding, 1987; 1991; Eyles, 1993; Moss, 1993; Rose, 1993) and constructivism (Ibarra and Kitsuse, 1993; Miller, 1993). Both extend and connect explicitly to the previous week on hermeneutics, interpretivism, and post-structuralism: I aim not to be comprehensive, but to identify core approaches to knowledge that stress and draw explicitly – but not exclusively – on qualitative data. From this point,

students have an epistemological grounding and framework from which to consider, critique, learn, and evaluate various qualitative methods.

For the rest of the semester, we read examples of research using particular methods, specifically, and in the order in which I present them: case study; grounded theory; ethnography and observation;[6] participatory action research; interviews; focus groups; life histories; and archival research. For each of these, I try to provide one or more readings that illustrate the technique, discuss issues and problems in using the method, and occasionally, which describe in detail how to proceed with the method. (I have found the chapters in Hay (2005) as particularly useful for providing some of the 'how tos' for each method.)

Integrating theory and methods in discussions and assignments

Despite the apparent disjuncture in the course structure between 'theory/epistemology' and 'methods', the course discussions actually involve considerable integration of the two. The early weeks' emphasis on epistemology means that we have a common set of theories about knowledge to return to in our discussions of the specific examples of methods. Over the four (bi-annual) semesters that I have taught the course in two different departments, this connection between theory and methods has become more explicit. At the same time, the course now has more 'how to' readings than it did initially; I have discovered more readings on using particular methods, and have responded to student requests for them.[7] (For example, in spring 2007, I included several chapters from Hay (2005), as well as selections from Bruce Berg (2001), Joseph and Maxwell (2001), which offer explicit, step-by-step approaches to data collection and analysis. At the same time, some of these – especially the latter two – gloss over many of the fundamental issues of epistemology underlying the choice of particular methodological steps, such as a sampling or coding strategy.)

I also use assignments to help students practice qualitative research, and to reflect upon the process of gathering and analyzing data. In one assignment, I have students 'test out' a particular method, and write up a reflective report on what they learned about doing the method, what sort of data they were able to produce, and what claims they think they might be able to make from it (if they were doing a full-fledged research project using that method). I have also had students analyze a transcript from one of my research projects (with all names and locations changed to ensure the confidentiality of interview participants). The transcript-analysis assignment offers a simulation of an extreme grounded theory, in which the students come to the data without having read any theory on the topic, or having even developed the research or interview questions! The most interesting product from that assignment was the discussion about what each student 'found' in the data: diverse researcher interests can lead to very different coding strategies and reports of findings, as any constructivist, hermeneutic, or post-structural epistemology would suggest! Finally, I assign a short (five-page) research proposal at the end of the semester, to help students make the links between their own research interests, data collection, and knowledge production. For some students, writing a proposal is very difficult because they may not yet be at the formal proposal writing stage in their studies: The exercise in starting one helps them to link what they are learning about methods and epistemology with their substantive research interests.

Despite the philosophy-versus-practice tensions in my course, I am convinced that students gain more practical methodological tools when the course integrates methodology and epistemology into conversations about specific methods. Ultimately, I believe such an approach will carry students

through when, inevitably, they have to change procedures in the field, or when a planned methodological step does not follow the textbook or ideal examples. If students understand the underlying principles about the data they are generating, what sort of knowledge they expect it to contribute to, and why, then they will have the flexibility and understanding to make smart decisions about how to proceed with data collection and analysis. Indeed, my focus in the course aims to instill a lifelong passion and ability for qualitative methods, even as sub-disciplinary and individual philosophies of knowledge, and the research questions posed, will certainly change over time.

Ethics

One crucial aspect of instilling flexibility and understanding in methods is to explicitly embed research ethics throughout the course. Like the tension between epistemology and methods, ethics presents its own bundle of contradictory information: details and strategies for addressing institutional review boards and achieving permission to conduct research involving human subjects; and ethical dilemmas which reflect the highly personal and contingent nature of much qualitative research. It, perhaps more than any other part of teaching or considering using qualitative methods, highlights the tension between practical concerns of doing research on the one hand, and philosophies of knowledge on the other. My approach to date has been explicitly and implicitly to work ethics into class discussions, by fostering and encouraging debate about the ethics of the research we read in class. In the second week of readings, I include two readings about research ethics (Dowling, 2005; Hay, 2006), both of which address institutional review boards, but which also consider research ethics far beyond a regulatory framework. I also include a selection from a book (Duneier, 1999) about how the author achieved informed consent and full permission from participants for his use of their words and life-experiences in his book. Finally, as part of class discussion on that day, I also show students the website for our university's Institutional Review Board (IRB) Human Subjects Committee. This exposure to the bureaucracy of ethical regulation is often very intimidating to students, but I emphasize the importance of knowing about and engaging with ethical review boards, as well as practicing ongoing ethical reflection in all research projects. (Mark Israel and Iain Hay (2006) cover the issue of ethical practice and ethical regulation in great detail, while I (Martin, 2007) discuss the limitations of regulation in light of participatory philosophies.)

The readings on ethics, like those on epistemology, provide a basic framework for further discussions of research ethics throughout the course. A simple week of readings on ethics in research is not sufficient to 'cover' ethics, but it introduces the topic in a way that we can return to throughout subsequent class discussions. Despite the limitations, my explicit incorporation of ethics and the dilemmas of doing engaged qualitative work has prompted some great discussions in my qualitative methods class. For example, on one occasion we were discussing ethnography, and had read selections from Lila Abu-Lughod's (1999) account of her research in Egypt. One student asked whether the resulting book was at all ethical. I was taken aback by the suggestion that any compromise in the personal relationships that develop in a research setting ought necessarily take precedence over the research product itself. Yet such a question is fundamental to truly confronting and understanding the challenges and opportunities of qualitative research. It prompted a long discussion among class participants about researchers' relationships with their participants, and what obligations or restrictions they (ought to) pose. We came to no definitive conclusions – ethics in research is far too context-dependent, in my opinion, for generic rules (a contradiction to the operating assumptions of IRBs, to be

sure!). But the conversation made explicit the dilemmas and decisions inherent to qualitative research.[8]

CONCLUSION

My approach to teaching qualitative research methods to geography and international development graduate students has been to explicitly grapple with the tension between teaching epistemologies of how and why to do qualitative research, and students seeking more of the 'how tos' of qualitative research. Crang (2005: 225) perhaps sums up this tension best when he argues that: 'Indeed, qualitative research is often torn between a constructivist approach and a longing to convey a "real" sense of the field.' He writes of the desire of scholars to represent their research findings in ways that communicate the complexities, richness, and realities of their many research 'fields'; yet his comment applies too to the practice of qualitative research itself, especially in how to teach it to others. This tension is unlikely to diminish in the future; instead we need to find ways of embracing it, and using it to refine our approach to grounding students in the rigours of qualitative research. The fact that one quarter of all PhD-granting geography departments offer qualitative methods suggests that qualitative research is a recognized and important approach in geography. Qualitative research methods must, therefore, be taught. What is a little trickier, however, is the execution, or the pedagogy: *how* is one to teach qualitative research methods? The answer lies in acknowledgement of practice, grounded in our own 'trial-and-error' processes. Perhaps it is experience, however haphazard in retrospect, that enhances and truly enables the teaching of qualitative research methods. But it is also a matter of putting these experiences in a broader context, one focused on the purposes of research, the range of questions to pose and approaches to 'data' that foster various kinds of answers.

The pedagogy of qualitative geography is thus deeply rooted in personal experience with qualitative research, and reflection upon the connection of those experiences to (our own and others') always emerging epistemologies and methodologies. It is a hard task, but a critical one!

ACKNOWLEDGMENTS

My sincere thanks to the editors, Dydia DeLyser, Steve Herbert, Stuart Aitken, Mike Crang, and Linda McDowell, for inviting me to contribute this chapter, and especially to Dydia for our conversations about teaching qualitative methods. Special thanks also to Danielle Fontaine at Clark University for her research and editing assistance.

NOTES

1. According to the AAG main office, as of fall 2006, the GIS specialty group was the largest with almost 2,000 members, but QRSG was not the smallest.

2. Thanks to one of my anonymous reviewers for reminding me of this point!

3. This course was originally developed with Hilda Kurtz, so much of the organizational logic and content derives equally from her experiences and input.

4. Specific readings identified here and in the following paragraphs of this section are drawn from my syllabi of spring, 2005, and spring, 2007. For readings representing progress reports on the state of the subfield of qualitative geography (such as Crang, 2002), I update periodically for more recent reviews.

5. In particular, Hill (1981) defines and explains how positivism dominates – or did at one time – geographical analyses.

6. I do suggest that observation can be a method without being fully ethnographic: we discuss varying levels of researcher involvement for observation/ethnography. Generally, participant observation, for example, involves a shorter time-commitment, and less intensive involvement with the community in the study, than ethnography (e.g., a participant observer may enter and leave the 'field' site frequently, whereas an ethnographer generally stays in the field

for a substantial period of time (Stewart, 1998; Jorgensen, 1989).

7. I am sympathetic to students' desires for step-by-step methods. At the same time, I maintain the emphasis on understanding theories of knowledge production, and try to make explicit my rationale for emphasizing epistemologies and methodologies in conjunction with methods.

8. I also reminded the class that quantitative methods has its own ethical dilemmas – such as what to count, and how – even if these are not always explicitly acknowledged.

REFERENCES

Abu-Lughod, L. (1999) *Veiled sentiments: honor and poetry in a Bedouin society.* Berkeley: University of California Press.

Berg, B. (2001) *Qualitative research methods for the social sciences.* Boston: Allyn and Bacon.

Blunt, A., May, J., Pinder, D., Ogborn, M. and Gruffudd, P. (eds) (2003) *Cultural geography in practice.* London: Edward Arnold.

Clifford, N. and Valentine, G. (eds) (2006) *Key methods in geography.* Thousand Oaks, CA: Sage Publications.

Crang, M. (2002) 'Qualitative methods: the new orthodoxy?', *Progress in Human Geography* 26 (5): 647–55.

Crang, M. (2005) 'Qualitative methods: there is nothing outside the text?', *Progress in Human Geography* 29 (2): 225–33.

Creswell, J.W. (2007) *Qualitative inquiry and research design*, 2nd ed. Thousand Oaks, CA: Sage Publications.

Del Casino, V.J., Grimes, A.J., Hanna, S.P. and Jones, J.P. (2000) 'Methodological frameworks for the geography of organizations', *Geoforum* 31 (4): 523–38.

DeLyser, D. (2008) 'Teaching qualitative research', *Journal of Geography in Higher Education* 32 (2): 233–44.

Denzin, N.K. and Lincoln, Y.S. (2000) 'Introduction: the discipline and practice of qualitative research', in N.K. Norman and Y.S. Lincoln (eds) *Handbook of qualitative research*, 2nd edition. Thousand Oaks, CA: Sage Publications. pp. 1–28.

Denzin, N.K. and Lincoln, Y.S. (eds) (2005) *The Sage handbook of qualitative research*, 3rd edition. Thousand Oaks, CA: Sage Publications.

Dixon, D. and Jones, J.P. (1998) 'My dinner with Derrida', *Environment and Planning A* 30: 247–60.

Dowling, R. (2005) 'Power, subjectivity, and ethics in qualitative research', in I. Hay (ed.) *Qualitative research methods in human geography*, 2nd ed. Oxford: Oxford University Press. pp. 19–29.

Duneier, M. (1999) *Sidewalk*. New York: Farrar, Straus and Giroux.

Eyles, J. (1993) 'Feminist and interpretive method: how different?', *Canadian Geographer* 37 (1): 50–2.

Eyles, J. and Smith, D.M. (1988) *Qualitative methods in human geography*. Cambridge: Polity Press.

Flowerdew, R. and Martin, D. (eds) (2005) *Methods in human geography: a guide for students doing a research project*, 2nd edition. Prentice Hall.

Foucault, M. (1970) *The order of things*. London: Tavistock Publications.

Geertz, C. (1973) *Interpretation of cultures*. New York: Basic Books.

Gibson-Graham, J.K. (1994) '"Stuffed if I know!": reflections on postmodern feminist social research', *Gender, Place, and Culture* 1 (2):205–24.

Hanson, S. and Pratt, G. (1995) *Gender, work, and space*. New York and London: Routledge.

Hanson, S. and Pratt, G. (2003) 'Learning about labour: combining qualitative and quantitative methods', in A. Blunt, P. Gruffudd, J. May, M. Ogborn, and D. Pinder (eds) *Cultural geography in practice*. London: Edward Arnold. pp. 106–18.

Haraway, D. (1991) *Simians, cyborgs, and women: the reinvention of nature*. New York: Routledge.

Harding, S. (1987) 'Introduction: is there a feminist method?', in S. Harding (ed.) *Feminism and methodology*. Bloomington, IN and Milton Keynes, UK: Indiana University Press and Open University Press. pp. 1–14.

Harding, S. (1991) *Whose science? Whose knowledge?* New York: Cornell University Press.

Hay, I. (ed.) (2005) *Qualitative research methods in human geography*, 2nd edition. Oxford: Oxford University Press.

Hay, I. (2006) 'Ethical practice in geographical research', in N. Clifford and G. Valentine, (eds) *Key methods in geography*. Thousand Oaks, CA: Sage Publications. pp. 37–53.

Hill, M.R. (1981) 'Positivism: a "hidden" philosophy in geography', in M. Harvey and B. Hollis (eds) *Themes in geographic thought*. London: Croom Helm. pp. 38–60.

Holstein, J.A. and Gubrium, J.F. (1995) *The active interview*. Thousand Oaks, CA: Sage Publications.

Ibarra, P.R. and Kitsuse, J.I. (1993) 'Vernacular constituents of moral discourse: an interactionist proposal for the study of social problems', in J. Holstein and G. Miller (eds) *Reconsidering social constructionism: debates in social problems theory*. New York: Aldine de Gruyter. pp. 25–58.

Israel, M. and Hay, I. (2006) *Research ethics for social scientists: between ethical conduct and regulatory compliance*. London and Thousand Oaks, CA: Sage Publications.

Jorgensen, D.L. (1989) *Participant observation: a methodology for human studies*. Newbury Park, CA: Sage Publications.

Kobayashi, A. and Peake, L. (1994) 'Unnatural discourse: "race" and gender in geography', *Gender, Place, and Culture* 1 (2): 225–43.

Limb, M. and Dwyer, C. (eds) (2001) *Qualitative methodologies for geographers: issues and debates*. London and New York: Oxford University Press.

Martin, D.G. (2007) 'Bureaucratization of ethics: institutional review boards and participatory research', *ACME: An International E-Journal for Critical Geographies* 6 (3): 319–28.

Martin, D.G. and Holloway, S. (2005) 'Organizing diversity: Scales of demographic change and neighborhood organizing in St. Paul, Minnesota', *Environment and Planning A* 37 (6): 1091–112.

Maxwell, J.A. (2001) *Qualitative research design: an interactive approach*. Thousand Oaks, CA: Sage Publications.

Miller, L.J. (1993) 'Claims-making from the underside: marginalization and social problems analysis', in J. Holstein and G. Miller (eds) *Reconsidering social constructionism: Debates in social problems theory*. New York: Aldine de Gruyter. pp. 349–76.

Morgan, D. (1997) *Focus groups as qualitative research*, 2nd ed. Thousand Oaks, CA: Sage Publications.

Moss, P. (1993) 'Focus: feminism as method', *Canadian Geographer* 37 (1): 48–9.

Pratt, G. (1999) 'From registered nurse to registered nanny: discursive geographies of Filipina domestic workers in Vancouver, BC', *Economic Geography*. 75 (3): 215–37.

Rose, D. (1993) 'On feminism, method and methods in human geography: an idiosyncratic overview', *Canadian Geographer* 37 (1): 57–61.

Schwandt, T. (2000) 'Three epistemological stances for qualitative inquiry: interpretivism, hermeneutics, and constructionism', in N. Denzin and Y. Lincoln (eds) *Handbook of qualitative research*. Thousand Oaks, CA: Sage Publications. pp. 189–213.

Searle, J.R. (1980) '"Las Meninas" and the paradoxes of pictorial representation', *Critical Inquiry* 6 (3): 477–88.

Silverman, D. (1993) *Interpreting qualitative data.* Thousand Oaks, CA: Sage Publications.

Singleton, R.A. and Straits, B.C. (2005) *Approaches to social research*, 4th ed. New York and Oxford: Oxford University Press.

Stewart, A. (1998) *The ethnographer's method.* Thousand Oaks, CA: Sage Publications.

Yin, R.K. (2003) *Case study research: design and methods*, 3rd ed. Thousand Oaks, CA: Sage Publications.

Index

Supporting researchers for more than forty years

Research methods have always been at the core of SAGE's publishing. Sara Miller McCune founded SAGE in 1965 and soon after, she published SAGE's first methods book, Public Policy Evaluation. A few years later, she launched the Quantitative Applications in the Social Sciences series – affectionately known as the "little green books".

Always at the forefront of developing and supporting new approaches in methods, SAGE published early groundbreaking texts and journals in the fields of qualitative methods and evaluation.

Today, more than forty years and two million little green books later, SAGE continues to push the boundaries with a growing list of more than 1,200 research methods books, journals, and reference works across the social, behavioral, and health sciences.

From qualitative, quantitative, mixed methods to evaluation, SAGE is the essential resource for academics and practitioners looking for the latest methods by leading scholars.

www.sagepublications.com

Research Methods Books
from SAGE

Basics of
QUALITATIVE
RESEARCH
3e

Juliet Corbin
Anselm Strauss

The
Mixed
Methods
Reader

Vicki L. Plano Clark ▪ John W. Creswell

DOING
QUALITATIVE
RESEARCH
USING
YOUR COMPUTER

A PRACTICAL GUIDE

CHRIS HAHN

SECOND EDITION
INTERVIEWS
Learning the Craft of Qualitative Research Interviewing

Steinar Kvale
Svend Brinkmann

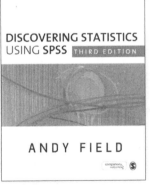

DISCOVERING STATISTICS
USING SPSS THIRD EDITION

ANDY FIELD

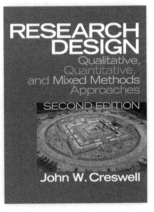

RESEARCH
DESIGN
Qualitative,
Quantitative,
and Mixed Methods
Approaches
SECOND EDITION

John W. Creswell

www.sagepub.co.uk

SAGE

The Qualitative Research Kit

Edited by Uwe Flick

Read sample chapters online now!

www.sagepub.co.uk